Lecture Notes in Computer Science   12913

Advanced Research in Computing and Software Science
Subline of Lecture Notes in Computer Science

More information about this subseries at http://www.springer.com/series/7408

Cezara Drăgoi · Suvam Mukherjee ·
Kedar Namjoshi (Eds.)

Static Analysis

28th International Symposium, SAS 2021
Chicago, IL, USA, October 17–19, 2021
Proceedings

 Springer

Editors
Cezara Drăgoi
Informal Systems, Inria, ENS,
DI - Ecole Normale Supérieure
Paris, France

Suvam Mukherjee ⓘ
Microsoft Corporation
Redmond, WA, USA

Kedar Namjoshi
Nokia Bell Labs
Murray Hill, NJ, USA

ISSN 0302-9743   ISSN 1611-3349   (electronic)
Lecture Notes in Computer Science
ISBN 978-3-030-88805-3   ISBN 978-3-030-88806-0   (eBook)
https://doi.org/10.1007/978-3-030-88806-0

LNCS Sublibrary: SL2 – Programming and Software Engineering

This Springer imprint is published by the registered company Springer Nature Switzerland AG
The registered company address is: Gewerbestrasse 11, 6330 Cham, Switzerland

Preface

This volume contains the proceedings of the 28th edition of the International Static Analysis Symposium, SAS 2021, held during October 17–19, 2021, in Chicago, USA. The conference was a co-located event of SPLASH, the ACM SIGPLAN conference on Systems, Programming, Languages, and Applications: Software for Humanity. Travel restrictions as a result of the COVID-19 pandemic forced us to organize the conference in hybrid form.

Static analysis is widely recognized as a fundamental tool for program verification, bug detection, compiler optimization, program understanding, and software maintenance. The series of Static Analysis Symposia has served as the primary venue for the presentation of theoretical, practical, and application advances in the area. Previous symposia were held in Chicago (virtual), Porto, Freiburg, New York, Edinburgh, Saint-Malo, Munich, Seattle, Deauville, Venice, Perpignan, Los Angeles, Valencia, Kongens Lyngby, Seoul, London, Verona, San Diego, Madrid, Paris, Santa Barbara, Venice, Pisa, Paris, Aachen, Glasgow, and Namur.

SAS 2021 called for papers on topics including, but not limited to, abstract domains, abstract interpretation, automated deduction, data flow analysis, debugging techniques, deductive methods, emerging applications, model checking, data science, program optimizations and transformations, program synthesis, program verification, security analysis, tool environments and architectures, theoretical frameworks, and type checking. Authors were encouraged to submit artifacts accompanying their papers to strengthen evaluations and the reproducibility of results. A new feature this year encouraged short submissions on experience with static analysis tools, industrial reports, and case studies, along with tool papers, brief announcements of work in progress, well-motivated discussions of new questions or new areas, etc.

The conference employed a double-blind reviewing process with an author response period, supported on EasyChair. The Program Committee used a two-round review process, where each submission received at least three first-round reviews, which the authors could then respond to. This year, SAS had 40 submitted papers (33 regular, 7 short). Of these, 22 papers were accepted for publication (18 regular, 4 short) and appear in this volume. The submitted papers were authored by researchers around the world: from France, the USA, Canada, Germany, the Netherlands, Japan, India, China, Australia, and several other countries. The author response period was followed by a two-week Program Committee discussion where consensus was reached on the papers to be accepted, after a thorough assessment of the relevance and the quality of the work.

We view the artifacts as being equally important for the success and development of static analysis as the written papers. It is important for researchers to be able to independently reproduce experiments, which is greatly facilitated by having the original artifacts available. Suvam Mukherjee, the artifact committee chair, set up the artifact committee and introduced three new features in the artifact review process which we expect will be carried through in future editions of SAS. The first is the ability to submit Docker images as artifacts, in addition to Virtual Machine images. Second, a public archival repository for the artifacts has been set up on Zenodo, hosted at https://zenodo.org/communities/sas-2021/. Third, artifacts have badges awarded at three levels: Validated (correct functionality), Extensible (with source code), and Available (on the Zenodo repository). The artwork for the badges is by Arpita Biswas (Harvard University) and Suvam Mukherjee. Each artifact was evaluated by three members of the artifact evaluation committee. SAS had 20 artifact submissions, of which 16 were accepted, a high percentage.

In addition to the contributed papers, SAS 2021 also featured three invited talks by distinguished researchers: Gerard Holzmann (Nimble Research, USA), Cristina Cifuentes (Oracle Labs, Australia), and Mooly Sagiv (Tel Aviv University, Israel). The Program Committee also selected the recipient of the Radhia Cousot Young Researcher Best Paper Award, given to a paper with a significant contribution from a student. This award was instituted in memory of Radhia Cousot, for her fundamental contributions to static analysis as well as one of the main promoters and organizers of the SAS series of conferences.

The SAS program would not have been possible without the efforts of many people. We thank them all. The members of the Program Committee, the artifact evaluation committee and the external reviewers worked tirelessly to select a strong program, offering constructive and helpful feedback to the authors in their reviews. The organizing committee of SPLASH 2021, chaired by Hridesh Rajan (Iowa State University, USA), and the hybridization committee, chaired by Jonathan Aldrich (CMU, USA), were tremendously helpful in navigating the conference through these difficult times. The SAS steering committee provided much needed support and advice. Finally, we thank Springer for their support of this event as well as for publishing these proceedings.

October 2021

Cezara Drăgoi
Suvam Mukherjee
Kedar Namjoshi

Organization

Program Committee Chairs

Cezara Drăgoi   Inria, ENS, and Informal Systems, France
Kedar Namjoshi   Nokia Bell Labs, USA

Steering Committee

Sandrine Blazy   University of Rennes 1, France
Bor-Yuh Evan Chang   University of Colorado Boulder and Amazon, USA
Patrick Cousot   New York Univ., USA
Thomas Jensen   Inria, France
David Pichardie   ENS, France
Andreas Podelski   University of Freiburg, Germany
Francesco Ranzato   University of Padova, Italy
Xavier Rival   Inria, France
Mihaela Sighireanu   IRIF, France

Program Committee

Gogul Balakrishnan   Google, USA
Josh Berdine   Facebook, UK
Vijay D'Silva   Google, USA
Michael Emmi   Amazon Web Services, USA
Constantin Enea   University of Paris, IRIF, and CNRS, France
Jerome Feret   Inria, France
Roberto Giacobazzi   University of Verona and IMDEA, Italy
Patrice Godefroid   Microsoft Research, USA
Arie Gurfinkel   University of Waterloo, Canada
Ranjit Jhala   University of California, San Diego, USA
Burcu Kulahcioglu Ozkan   Delft University of Technology, Netherlands
Akash Lal   Microsoft Research, India
Francesco Logozzo   Facebook, USA
Kenneth L. McMillan   University of Texas at Austin, USA
Antoine Miné   Sorbonne Université, France
Andreas Podelski   University of Freiburg, Germany
Thomas Reps   University of Wisconsin–Madison, USA
Xavier Rival   Inria, CNRS, and ENS, France
Mihaela Sighireanu   IRIF, Université Paris Diderot, France
Gagandeep Singh   VMware Research and University of Illinois Urbana-Champaign, USA
Lenore Zuck   University of Illinois at Chicago, USA

Artifact Evaluation Chair

Suvam Mukherjee   Microsoft, USA

Artifact Evaluation Committee

Rosa Abbasi Boroujeni   MPI-SWS, Germany
Suguman Bansal   University of Pennsylvania, USA
Ranadeep Biswas   IRIF, Université Paris Diderot and CNRS, France
Ajay Brahmakshatriya   Massachusetts Institute of Technology, USA
Marco Campion   University of Verona, Italy
Prantik Chatterjee   IIT Kanpur, India
Berk Cirisci   IRIF, Université Paris Diderot and CNRS, France
Samvid Dharanikota   Microsoft Research, India
Peixuan Li   Pennsylvania State University, USA
Muhammad Numair Mansur   MPI-SWS, Germany
Francesco Parolini   Sorbonne Université, France
Nisarg Patel   New York University, USA
Stanly Samuel   Indian Institute of Science, India
Anton Xue   University of Pennsylvania, USA

Additional Reviewers

Berkeley Churchill
David Delmas
Caterina Urban
Raphaël Monat
Thomas Genet
Armaël Guéneau

Invited Talks

Oracle Parfait: The Flavour of Real-World Vulnerability Detection and Intelligent Configuration

Cristina Cifuentes

Oracle Labs
cristina.cifuentes@oracle.com

Abstract. The Parfait static code analysis tool focuses on detecting vulnerabilities that matter in C, C++, Java and Python languages. Its focus has been on key items expected out of a commercial tool that lives in a commercial organisation, namely, precision of results (i.e., high true positive rate), scalability (i.e., being able to run quickly over millions of lines of code), incremental analysis (i.e., being able to run over deltas of the code quickly), and usability (i.e., ease of integration into standard build processes, reporting of traces to the vulnerable location, etc). Today, Parfait is used by thousands of developers at Oracle worldwide on a day-to-day basis.

In this presentation we'll sample a flavour of Parfait – we explore some real world challenges faced in the creation of a robust vulnerability detection tool, look into two examples of vulnerabilities that severely affected the Java platform in 2012/2013 and most machines since 2017, and conclude by recounting what matters to developers for integration into today's continuous integration and continuous delivery (CI/CD) pipelines. Key to deployment of static code analysis tools is configuration of the tool itself – we present our experiences with use of machine learning to automatically configure the tool, providing users with a better out-of-the-box experience.

Interactive Code Analysis

Gerard J. Holzmann

Nimble Research
gholzmann@acm.org

Abstract. Static code analyzers have become indispensable especially for safety critical software development. But, they do have a few drawbacks as well.

For starters, and for good reason, the commercial tools can be quite slow, and they are certainly not suitable for interactive use. I'll describe a new tool called Cobra, that I'm currently developing, which can resolve types of queries interactively, even on very large code bases. Queries can be scripted or predefined in libraries. The tool is designed to be easy to use, and is freely available.

Pointer Analysis of Bytecode Programs for Effective Formal Verification of Smart Contracts

John Toman[1], James Wilcox[1], and Mooly Sagiv[2]

[1] Certora john
james@certora.com
[2] Tel Aviv University
msagiv@acm.org

Abstract. Low-level bytecode programs are difficult to handle by formal reasoning, particularly in the case of sound and precise reasoning about memory operations. There is often no distinguished allocation operation: high-level object allocations are affected via pointer arithmetic. Type information is lost in the compilation: the abstraction of memory is simply a flat unstructured array of bytes. To recover high-level information, a sound pointer analysis is an invaluable resource. Such an analysis enables optimizations and elucidates program behavior that would otherwise be obscured in a low-level setting. This talk describes a new static analysis algorithm we have developed for sound pointer analysis for low-level bytecode. We make this broad problem tractable by first restricting our focus to bytecode programs that manage memory via a bump allocator that operates on a distinguished free pointer. In other words, we target bytecode programs where memory is divided into disjoint regions, each of which corresponds to an "object." Our analysis algorithm uses a novel technique for mapping updates of a distinguished free pointer to provably non-aliased abstract addresses, which enables standard pointer analysis techniques. Our static pointer analysis uses a "trust but verify" approach: we build our analysis on the expectation that the compiler has properly managed memory via the free pointer/bump allocator, but at each step, we verify that regions of memory allocated via the bump allocator are properly disjoint, i.e., every read/write of memory provably accesses only one, distinct region. This talk discusses our practical experience using this analysis in verifying smart contracts that run on the Ethereum Virtual Machine. In particular, we outline multiple high-profile memory management bugs uncovered by our analysis, and the downstream optimizations and precision improvements unlocked by our pointer analysis results.

Contents

Fast and Efficient Bit-Level Precision Tuning

Assalé Adjé[1], Dorra Ben Khalifa[1(✉)], and Matthieu Martel[1,2]

[1] LAMPS Laboratory, University of Perpignan, 52 Av. P. Alduy, Perpignan, France
{assale.adje,dorra.ben-khalifa,matthieu.martel}@univ-perp.fr
[2] Numalis, Cap Omega, Rond-point Benjamin Franklin, Montpellier, France

Abstract. In this article, we introduce a new technique for precision tuning. This problem consists of finding the least data types for numerical values such that the result of the computation satisfies some accuracy requirement. State of the art techniques for precision tuning use a trial-and-error approach. They change the data types of some variables of the program and evaluate the accuracy of the result. Depending on what is obtained, they change more or less data types and repeat the process. Our technique is radically different. Based on semantic equations, we generate an Integer Linear Problem (ILP) from the program source code. Basically, this is done by reasoning on the most significant bit and the number of significant bits of the values which are integer quantities. The integer solution to this problem, computed in polynomial time by a classical linear programming solver, gives the optimal data types at the bit level. A finer set of semantic equations is also proposed which does not reduce directly to an ILP problem. So we use policy iteration to find the solution. Both techniques have been implemented and we show that our results encompass the results of state-of-the-art tools.

Keywords: Static analysis · Computer arithmetic · Integer linear problems · Numerical accuracy · Policy iteration

1 Introduction

Let us consider a program P computing some numerical result R, typically but not necessarily in the IEEE754 floating-point arithmetic [1]. Precision tuning then consists of finding the smallest data types for all the variables and expressions of P such that the result R has some desired accuracy. These last years, much attention has been paid to this problem [8,11,14,16,17,24]. Indeed, precision tuning makes it possible to save memory and, by way of consequence, it has a positive impact on the footprint of programs concerning energy consumption, bandwidth usage, computation time, etc.

A common point to all the techniques cited previously is that they follow a trial-and-error approach. Roughly speaking, one chooses a subset S of the variables of P, assigns to them smaller data types (e.g. binary32 instead

© Springer Nature Switzerland AG 2021
C. Drăgoi et al. (Eds.): SAS 2021, LNCS 12913, pp. 1–24, 2021.
https://doi.org/10.1007/978-3-030-88806-0_1

of `binary64` [1]) and evaluates the accuracy of the tuned program P'. If the accuracy of the result returned by P' is satisfying then new variables are included in S or even smaller data types are assigned to certain variables already in S (e.g. `binary16`). Otherwise, if the accuracy of the result of P' is not satisfying, then some variables are removed from S. This process is applied repeatedly, until a stable state is found. Existing techniques differ in their way to evaluate the accuracy of programs, done by dynamic analysis [14,16,17,24] or by static analysis [8,11] of P and P'. They may also differ in the algorithm used to define S, delta debugging being the most widespread method [24]. A notable exception is FPTuner [8] which relies on a local optimization procedure by solving quadratic problems for a given set of candidate datatypes. A more exhaustive state-of-the-art about precision tuning techniques is given in [7].

Anyway all these techniques suffer from the same combinatorial limitation: If P has n variables and if the method tries k different data types then the search space contains k^n configurations. They scale neither in the number n of variables (even if heuristics such as delta debugging [24] or branch and bound [8] reduce the search space at the price of optimality) or in the number k of data types which can be tried. In particular, bit level precision tuning, which consists of finding the minimal number of bits needed for each variable to reach the desired accuracy, independently of a limited number k of data types, is not an option.

So the method introduced in this article for precision tuning of programs is radically different. Here, no trial-and-error method is employed. Instead, the accuracy of the arithmetic expressions assigned to variables is determined by semantic equations, in function of the accuracy of the operands. By reasoning on the number of significant bits of the variables of P and knowing the weight of their most significant bit thanks to a range analysis performed before the tuning phase (see Sect. 3), we are able to reduce the problem to an Integer Linear Problem (ILP) which can be optimally solved in one shot by a classical linear programming solver (no iteration). Concerning the number n of variables, the method scales up to the solver limitations and the solutions are naturally found at the bit level, making the parameter k irrelevant. An important point is that the optimal solution to the continuous linear programming relaxation of our ILP is a vector of integers, as demonstrated in Sect. 4.2. By consequence, we may use a linear solver among real numbers whose complexity is polynomial [25] (contrarily to the linear solvers among integers whose complexity is NP-Hard [22]). This makes our precision tuning method solvable in polynomial-time, contrarily to the existing exponential methods. Next, we go one step further by introducing a second set of semantic equations. These new equations make it possible to tune even more the precision by being less pessimistic on the propagation of carries in arithmetic operations. However the problem does not reduce any longer to an ILP problem (min and max operators are needed). Then we use policy iteration (PI) [9] to find efficiently the solution.

Both methods have been implemented inside a tool for precision tuning named POP. Formerly, POP was expressing the precision tuning problem as a set of first order logical propositions among relations between linear integer expressions [2–4,6]. An SMT solver (Z3 in practice [21]) was used repeatedly to find the existence of a solution with a certain weight expressing the number of significant bits (nsb) of variables. In the present article, we compare experimentally our new methods to the SMT based method previously used by POP and to the Precimonious tool [14,24]. These experiments on programs coming from mathematical libraries or other applicative domains such as IoT [2,3] show that the technique introduced in this article for precision tuning clearly encompasses the state of the art techniques.

The rest of this article is organized as follows. In the next section, we provide a motivating example. We then present in Sect. 3 some essential background on the functions needed for the constraint generation and also we detail the set of constraints for both ILP and PI methods. Section 4 presents the proofs of correctness. We end up in Sect. 5 by showing that our new technique exhibits very good results in practice before concluding in Sect. 6.

2 Running Example

A motivating example to better explain our method is given by the code snippet of Fig. 1. In this example, we aim at modeling the movement of a simple pendulum without damping. Let $l = 0.5$ m be the length of this pendulum, $m = 1$ kg its mass and $g = 9.81$ m $\cdot s^{-2}$ Newton's gravitational constant. We denote by θ the tilt angle in radians as shown in Fig. 1 (initially $\theta = \frac{\pi}{4}$). The Equation describing the movement of the pendulum is given in Eq. (1).

$$m \cdot l \cdot \frac{d^2\theta}{dt^2} = -m \cdot g \cdot \sin\theta \tag{1}$$

Equation (1) being a second order differential equation. We need to transform it into a system of two first order differential equations for resolution. We obtain $y_1 = \theta$ and $y_2 = \frac{d\theta}{dt}$. By applying Euler's method to these last equations, we obtain Eq. (2) implemented in Fig. 1.

$$\frac{dy_1}{dt} = y_2 \quad \text{and} \quad \frac{dy_2}{dt} = -\frac{g}{l} \cdot \sin y_1 \tag{2}$$

The key point of our technique is to generate a set of constraints for each statement of our imperative language introduced further in Sect. 3. For our example, we suppose that all variables, before POP analysis, are in double precision (source program in the top left corner of Fig. 1) and that a range determination is performed by dynamic analysis on the program variables (we plan to use a static analyzer in the future). POP assigns to each node of the program's syntactic tree a unique control point in order to determine easily the number of significant bits of the result as mentioned in the bottom corner of Fig. 1. Some notations can be highlighted about the structure of POP source code. For instance, the annotation $g^{\ell_1} = 9.81^{\ell_0}$ denotes that this instance of g has the unique control point ℓ_1. As well, we have the statement require_nsb(y2,20) which informs the tool that the user wants to get on variable y2 only 20 significant bits (we consider that a result has n significants if the relative error between the exact and approximated results is less than 2^{-n}). Finally, the minimal precision needed for the inputs

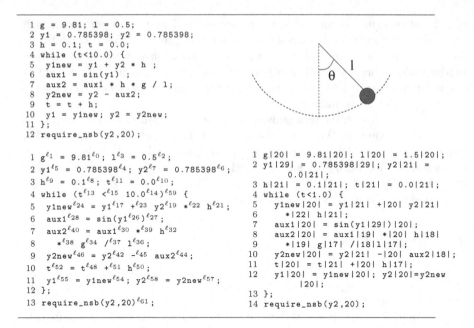

Fig. 1. Top left: source program. Top right: pendulum movement for $\theta = \frac{\pi}{4}$. Bottom left: program annotated with labels and with inferred accuracies (right).

and intermediary results satisfying the user assertion is observed on the bottom right corner of Fig. 1. In this code, if we consider for instance lines 5 and 6, then `y1new|20|` means that the variable needs 20 significant bits at this point. Similarly, `y1` and `y2` need 21 bits each and the addition requires 20 bits.

In the next section, we detail the ILP and PI formulations for precision tuning implemented in POP. Also, we show the nature of constraints generated for the pendulum example and consequently the new data types already presented in Fig. 1. Note that our tool achieves precision tuning only. The inputs are the program and the ranges over the variables of the program. We insist on the fact that POP is not able to produce those ranges or to verify the correctness of the input ranges. Those ranges are understood as intervals. This range inference is completely external to our tool and has to be performed by an invariant generator or an analyzer. To simplify the implementation, we use a dynamic analysis which produces an under-approximation under the form of intervals. Static analyzers with sophisticated abstract domains could be used such as [10]. In particular the efficiency of our techniques for loops depends on the precision of the range analysis for loops. The sensibility of our precision tuning to the estimate of the ranges depends on the following point. We use in the tuning phase the ufp of the values. So we are sensible to the order of magnitude of the ranges but not to the exact values. For example, we will obtain the same tuning with the ranges $[3.4, 6.1]$ and $[2.5, 7.8]$. But, obviously we get a worst tuning if we use $[0.0, 1000.0]$.

3 Generation of Constraints for Bit-Level Tuning

In this section, we start with providing essential definitions for understanding the rest of the article. Also, we define a simple imperative language from which we generate semantic equations in order to determine the least precision needed for the program numerical values. Then, we will focus on the two sets of constraints obtained when using the simple ILP and the more complex PI formulation which optimizes the carry bits that propagate throughout computations.

3.1 Preliminary Notations and Definitions

Our technique is independent of a particular computer arithmetic (e.g. IEEE754 [1] and POSIT [15]). In fact, we manipulate numbers for which we know the unit in the first place (ufp) and the number of significant digits (nsb). We also assume that the constants occurring in the source codes are exact and we bound the errors introduced by the finite precision computations. Then, in the following, $\mathsf{ufp}_e(x)$ and $\mathsf{nsb}_e(x)$ denote the ufp and nsb of the error on x (note that $\mathsf{nsb}_e(x)$ may be infinite in some cases). These functions are defined hereafter and a more intuitive presentation is given in Fig. 2.

Unit in the First Place. The unit in the first place of a real number x (possibly encoded up to some rounding mode by a floating-point or a fixpoint number) is given in Eq. (3). This function is independent of the representation of x.

$$\mathsf{ufp}(x) = \begin{cases} \min\{i \in \mathbb{Z} : 2^{i+1} > |x|\} = \lfloor \log_2(|x|) \rfloor & \text{if } x \neq 0, \\ 0 & \text{if } x = 0. \end{cases} \tag{3}$$

Number of Significant Bits. Intuitively, $\mathsf{nsb}(x)$ is the number of significant bits of x. Let $\hat{x}$ the approximation of x in finite precision and let $\varepsilon(x) = |x - \hat{x}|$ be the absolute error. Following Parker [23], if $\mathsf{nsb}(x) = k$, for $x \neq 0$, then

$$\varepsilon(x) \leq 2^{\mathsf{ufp}(x)-k+1} \tag{4}$$

In addition, if $x = 0$ then $\mathsf{nsb}(x) = 0$. For example, if the exact binary value 1.0101 is approximated by either $x = 1.010$ or $x = 1.011$ then $\mathsf{nsb}(x) = 3$.

Unit in the Last Place. The unit in the last place ulp of x is defined by

$$\mathsf{ulp}(x) = \mathsf{ufp}(x) - \mathsf{nsb}(x) + 1. \tag{5}$$

Computation Errors. The unit in the first place of the error on x is $\mathsf{ufp}_e(x) = \mathsf{ufp}(x) - \mathsf{nsb}(x)$. The number of significant bits of the computation error on x is denoted $\mathsf{nsb}_e(x)$. It is used to optimize the function ξ defined in Eq. (6). As mentioned earlier, we assume that there is no error on any constant c arising in programs, i.e. $\mathsf{nsb}_e(c) = 0$. Nevertheless, the nsb_e of the results of elementary operations may be greater than 0. For instance, if we add two constants c_1, c_2 in x such that $\mathsf{ufp}_e(c_1) \geq \mathsf{ufp}_e(c_2)$ then $\mathsf{nsb}_e(x) = \mathsf{ufp}_e(c_1) - (\mathsf{ufp}_e(c_2) - \mathsf{nsb}_e(c_2))$ which corresponds to the nsb of the resulting error (see Fig. 2). The unit in the last place of the computation error on x is denoted $\mathsf{ulp_e}(x)$ and we have $\mathsf{ulp_e}(x) = \mathsf{ufp_e}(x) - \mathsf{nsb_e}(x) + 1$.

Carry Bit. During an operation between two numbers c_1 and c_2, a carry bit can be propagated through the operation. We model the carry bit by a function denoted ξ computed as shown in Fig. 2:

If the ulp of one of the two operands c_1 or c_2 is greater than the ufp of the other one (or conversely) then c_1 and c_2 are not aligned and $\xi = 0$ (otherwise $\xi = 1$). Recall that, for a number x, we have $\mathsf{ufp_e}(x) = \mathsf{ufp}(x) - \mathsf{nsb}(x)$. In Sect. 3.3, we will use the ξ function to optimize the error terms. The over-approximation of ξ by supposing that it is always equal to 1 leads to the analysis of Sect. 3.2. However, when many operations are done in a program which has to compute with some tens of nsb, adding one bit is far from being negligible. Consequently, a refined analysis is presented in Sect. 3.3 where ξ is formulated by min and max operators. Let c_1 and c_2 be the operands of some operation whose result is x. The optimized ξ function of Sect. 3.3 is given by

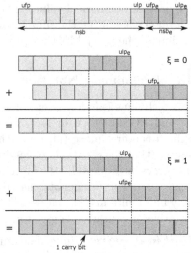

Fig. 2. Schematic representation of ufp, nsb and ulp for values and errors. Representation of the carry bit function ξ.

$$\xi(x)(c_1, c_2) = \begin{cases} 0 & \mathsf{ulp_e}(c_1) \geq \mathsf{ufp_e}(c_2), \\ 0 & \mathsf{ulp_e}(c_2) \geq \mathsf{ufp_e}(c_1), \\ 1 & \text{otherwise.} \end{cases}$$

In Fig. 5, an equivalent yet less intuitive definition of ξ is used which corresponds to Eq. (6) in Lemma 1.

Lemma 1. *Let c_1 and c_2 be the operands of some operation whose result is x.*

$$\xi(x)(c_1, c_2) = \begin{cases} 0 & \mathsf{ufp_e}(c_1) - \mathsf{nsb_e}(c_1) \geq \mathsf{ufp}(c_2) - \mathsf{nsb}(c_2) \ \ or \ \ conversely, \\ 1 & otherwise. \end{cases} \tag{6}$$

$\ell \in Lab \quad x \in Id \quad \odot \in \{+, -, \times, \div\} \quad math \in \{\sin, \cos, \tan, \arcsin, \log, \ldots\}$

Expr $\ni$ **e** : e ::= $c\#p^\ell \mid x^\ell \mid e_1^{\ell_1} \odot^\ell e_2^{\ell_2} \mid math(e^{\ell_1})^\ell \mid sqrt(e^{\ell_1})^\ell$

Cmd $\ni$ **c** : c ::= $c_1^{\ell_1}; c_2^{\ell_2} \mid x =^\ell e^{\ell_1} \mid while^\ell\ b^{\ell_0}\ do\ c_1^{\ell_1} \mid if^\ell\ b^{\ell_0}\ then\ c_1^{\ell_1}\ else\ c^{\ell_2} \mid require\_nsb(x, n)^\ell$

Fig. 3. Language of input programs.

3.2 Integer Linear Problem Formulation

First, we define in Fig. 3 the simple imperative language in which our input programs are written.

We denote by Id the set of identifiers and by Lab the set of control points of the program as a means to assign to each element $e \in Expr$ and $c \in Cmd$ a unique control point $\ell \in Lab$. First, in $c\#p$, p indicates the initial number of significant bits of the constant c in the source code. Next, the statement $\texttt{require\_nsb}(x, n)^\ell$ indicates the minimal number of significant bits n that a variable x must have at a control point ℓ. The rest of the grammar is standard.

As we have mentioned, we are able to reduce the problem of determining the lowest precision on variables and intermediary values in programs to an Integer Linear Problem (ILP) by reasoning on their unit in the first place (ufp) and the number of significant bits (nsb). In addition, we assign to each control point ℓ an integer variable $\mathsf{nsb}(\ell)$ corresponding to the nsb of the arithmetic expressions. Note that $\mathsf{nsb}(\ell)$ is determined by solving the ILP generated by the rules of Fig. 4. Let us also mention that, in order to avoid cumbersome notations, the constraints introduced hereafter assume that the programs handle scalar values instead of the intervals given by the range analysis. A generalisation to intervals is introduced in [18] for a comparable (yet not linear) set of constraints.

Let us now focus on the rules of Fig. 4 where $\varrho : Id \rightarrow Id \times Lab$ is an environment which relates each identifier x to its last assignment x^ℓ: Assuming that $x :=^\ell e^{\ell_1}$ is the last assignment of x, the environment ϱ maps x to x^ℓ. Then, $\mathcal{E}[e]\,\varrho$ generates the set of constraints for an expression $e \in Expr$ in the environment ϱ. In the sequel, we formally define these constraints for each element of our language. No constraint is generated for a constant $c\#p$ as mentioned in Rule (CONST) of Fig. 4. For Rule (ID) of a variable x^ℓ, we require that the nsb at control point ℓ is less than its nsb in the last assignment of x given in $\varrho(x)$. For a binary operator $\odot \in \{+, -, \times, \div\}$, we first generate the set of constraints $\mathcal{E}[e_1^{\ell_1}]\varrho$ and $\mathcal{E}[e_2^{\ell_2}]\varrho$ for the operands at control points ℓ_1 and ℓ_2. Considering Rule (ADD), the result of the addition of two numbers is stored in control point ℓ. Recall that a range determination is performed before the accuracy analysis, $\mathsf{ufp}(\ell)$, $\mathsf{ufp}(\ell_1)$ and $\mathsf{ufp}(\ell_2)$ are known at constraint generation time.

In the present ILP of Fig. 4, we over-approximate the function ξ by $\xi(\ell)(\ell_1, \ell_2) = 1$ for all ℓ, ℓ_1 and ℓ_2. To wrap up, for the addition (Rule (ADD)), we have the $\mathsf{nsb}(\ell) = \mathsf{ufp}(\ell) - \mathsf{ufp}_e(\ell)$. More precisely, let us consider the addition $c_1^{\ell_1} +^\ell c_2^{\ell_2}$ and let us assume that $\mathsf{prec}(\ell)$ denotes the precision of this operation. The error $\varepsilon(\ell)$ is bound by $\varepsilon(c_1^{\ell_1} +^\ell c_2^{\ell_2}) \leq \varepsilon(c_1^{\ell_1}) + \varepsilon(c_2^{\ell_2}) + 2^{\mathsf{ufp}(c_1+c_2)-\mathsf{prec}(\ell)}$ and

$$\mathsf{ufp}_e(\ell) = \max\big(\mathsf{ufp}(\ell_1) - \mathsf{nsb}(\ell_1), \mathsf{ufp}(\ell_2) - \mathsf{nsb}(\ell_2), \mathsf{ufp}(l) - \mathsf{prec}(\ell)\big) + \xi(\ell)(\ell_1, \ell_2) \tag{7}$$

Since $\mathsf{nsb}(\ell) \leq \mathsf{prec}(\ell)$, we may get rid of the last term in Eq. (7) and the two constraints generated for Rule (ADD) are derived from Eq. (8).

$$\mathsf{nsb}(\ell) \leq \mathsf{ufp}(\ell) - \max\big(\mathsf{ufp}(\ell_1) - \mathsf{nsb}(\ell_1), \mathsf{ufp}(\ell_2) - \mathsf{nsb}(\ell_2)\big) - \xi(\ell)(\ell_1, \ell_2) \tag{8}$$

$$\mathcal{E}[c\#p^\ell]\varrho = \emptyset \quad \text{(Const)} \qquad \mathcal{E}[x^\ell]\varrho = \{\mathsf{nsb}(\varrho(x)) \geq \mathsf{nsb}(\ell)\} \quad \text{(Id)}$$

$$\mathcal{E}[e_1^{\ell_1} +^\ell e_2^{\ell_2}]\varrho = \mathcal{E}[e_1^{\ell_1}]\varrho \;\cup\; \mathcal{E}[e_2^{\ell_2}]\varrho$$
$$\cup$$
$$\{\mathsf{nsb}(\ell_1) \geq \mathsf{nsb}(\ell) + \mathsf{ufp}(\ell_1) - \mathsf{ufp}(\ell) + \xi(\ell)(\ell_1, \ell_2),$$
$$\mathsf{nsb}(\ell_2) \geq \mathsf{nsb}(\ell) + \mathsf{ufp}(\ell_2) - \mathsf{ufp}(\ell) + \xi(\ell)(\ell_1, \ell_2)\} \qquad \text{(Add)}$$

$$\mathcal{E}[e_1^{\ell_1} -^\ell e_2^{\ell_2}]\varrho = \mathcal{E}[e_1^{\ell_1}]\varrho \;\cup\; \mathcal{E}[e_2^{\ell_2}]\varrho$$
$$\cup$$
$$\{\mathsf{nsb}(\ell_1) \geq \mathsf{nsb}(\ell) + \mathsf{ufp}(\ell_1) - \mathsf{ufp}(\ell) + \xi(\ell)(\ell_1, \ell_2),$$
$$\mathsf{nsb}(\ell_2) \geq \mathsf{nsb}(\ell) + \mathsf{ufp}(\ell_2) - \mathsf{ufp}(\ell) + \xi(\ell)(\ell_1, \ell_2)\} \qquad \text{(Sub)}$$

$$\mathcal{E}[e_1^{\ell_1} \times^\ell e_2^{\ell_2}]\varrho = \mathcal{E}[e_1^{\ell_1}]\varrho \;\cup\; \mathcal{E}[e_2^{\ell_2}]\varrho$$
$$\cup$$
$$\{\mathsf{nsb}(\ell_1) \geq \mathsf{nsb}(\ell) + \xi(\ell)(\ell_1, \ell_2) - 1, \quad \mathsf{nsb}(\ell_2) \geq \mathsf{nsb}(\ell) + \xi(\ell)(\ell_1, \ell_2) - 1\} \qquad \text{(Mult)}$$

$$\mathcal{E}[e_1^{\ell_1} \div^\ell e_2^{\ell_2}]\varrho = \mathcal{E}[e_1^{\ell_1}]\varrho \;\cup\; \mathcal{E}[e_2^{\ell_2}]\varrho$$
$$\cup$$
$$\{\mathsf{nsb}(\ell_1) \geq \mathsf{nsb}(\ell) + \xi(\ell)(\ell_1, \ell_2) - 1, \quad \mathsf{nsb}(\ell_2) \geq \mathsf{nsb}(\ell) + \xi(\ell)(\ell_1, \ell_2) - 1\} \qquad \text{(Div)}$$

$$\mathcal{E}\left[\sqrt{e^{\ell_1}}^\ell\right]\varrho = \mathcal{E}[e^{\ell_1}]\varrho \;\cup\; \{\mathsf{nsb}(\ell_1) \geq \mathsf{nsb}(\ell)\} \quad \text{(Sqrt)}$$

$$\mathcal{E}\left[\phi(e^{\ell_1})^\ell\right]\varrho = \mathcal{E}[e^{\ell_1}]\varrho \cup \{\mathsf{nsb}(\ell_1) \geq \mathsf{nsb}(\ell) + \varphi\} \text{ with } \phi \in \{\sin, \cos, \tan, \log, \ldots\} \quad \text{(Math)}$$

$$\mathcal{C}\left[x :=^\ell e^{\ell_1}\right]\varrho = \left(C, \varrho[x \mapsto \ell]\right) \text{ where } C = \mathcal{E}[e_1^{\ell_1}]\varrho \cup \{\mathsf{nsb}(\ell_1) \geq \mathsf{nsb}(\ell)\} \quad \text{(Assign)}$$

$$\mathcal{C}\left[c_1^{\ell_1} ; c_2^{\ell_2}\right]\varrho = \left(C_1 \cup C_2, \varrho_2\right)$$
$$\text{where } (C_1, \varrho_1) = \mathcal{C}\left[c_1^{\ell_1}\right]\varrho \text{ and } (C_2, \varrho_2) = \mathcal{C}\left[c_2^{\ell_2}\right]\varrho_1 \qquad \text{(Seq)}$$

$$\mathcal{C}[\text{if}^\ell\ e^{\ell_0} \text{ then } c^{\ell_1} \text{ else } c^{\ell_2}]\varrho = (C_1 \cup C_2 \cup C_3, \varrho')$$
$$\text{where } \left| \begin{array}{l} \forall x \in \mathrm{Id},\ \varrho'(x) = \ell,\ (C_1, \varrho_1) = \mathcal{C}[c^{\ell_1}]\varrho,\ (C_2, \varrho_2) = \mathcal{C}[c^{\ell_2}]\varrho, \\ C_3 = \bigcup_{x \in \mathrm{Id}} \{\mathsf{nsb}(\varrho_1(x)) \geq \mathsf{nsb}(\ell),\ \mathsf{nsb}(\varrho_2(x)) \geq \mathsf{nsb}(\ell)\} \end{array} \right. \quad \text{(Cond)}$$

$$\mathcal{C}[\text{while}^\ell\ e^{\ell_0} \text{ do } c^{\ell_1}]\varrho = (C_1 \cup C_2, \varrho')$$
$$\text{where } \left| \begin{array}{l} \forall x \in \mathrm{Id},\ \varrho'(x) = \ell,\ (C_1, \varrho_1) = \mathcal{C}[c^{\ell_1}]\varrho' \\ C_2 = \bigcup_{x \in \mathrm{Id}} \{\mathsf{nsb}(\varrho(x)) \geq \mathsf{nsb}(\ell),\ \mathsf{nsb}(\varrho_1(x)) \geq \mathsf{nsb}(\ell)\} \end{array} \right. \quad \text{(While)}$$

$$\mathcal{C}[\text{require\_nsb}(x, \mathsf{p})^\ell]\varrho = \{\mathsf{nsb}(\varrho(x)) \geq \mathsf{p}\} \quad \text{(Req)}$$

$$\xi(\ell)(\ell_1, \ell_2) = 1$$

Fig. 4. ILP constraints with pessimistic carry bit propagation $\xi = 1$.

Rule (Sub) for the subtraction is obtained similarly to the addition case. For Rule (Mult) of multiplication (and in the same manner Rule(Div)), the reasoning mimics the one of the addition. Let c_1 and c_2 be two numbers and c the result of their product, $c = c_1^{\ell_1} \times^\ell c_2^{\ell_2}$. We denote by $\varepsilon(c_1)$, $\varepsilon(c_2)$ and $\varepsilon(c)$ the errors on c_1, c_2 and c, respectively. The error $\varepsilon(c)$ of this multiplication is $\varepsilon(c) = c_1 \cdot \varepsilon(c_2) + c_2 \cdot \varepsilon(c_1) + \varepsilon(c_1) \cdot \varepsilon(c_2)$. These numbers are bounded by

$$
\begin{aligned}
2^{\mathsf{ufp}(c_1)} \le c_1 \le 2^{\mathsf{ufp}(c_1)+1} \quad &\text{and} \quad 2^{\mathsf{ufp}(c_1)-\mathsf{nsb}(c_1)} \le \varepsilon(c_1) \le 2^{\mathsf{ufp}(c_1)-\mathsf{nsb}(c_1)+1} \\
2^{\mathsf{ufp}(c_2)} \le c_2 \le 2^{\mathsf{ufp}(c_2)+1} \quad &\text{and} \quad 2^{\mathsf{ufp}(c_2)-\mathsf{nsb}(c_2)} \le \varepsilon(c_2) \le 2^{\mathsf{ufp}(c_2)-\mathsf{nsb}(c_2)+1} \\
2^{\mathsf{ufp}(c_1)+\mathsf{ufp}(c_2)-\mathsf{nsb}(c_2)} + 2^{\mathsf{ufp}(c_2)+\mathsf{ufp}(c_1)-\mathsf{nsb}(c_1)} &\le \varepsilon(c) \le 2^{\mathsf{ufp}(c)-\mathsf{nsb}(c)+1} \\
+ 2^{\mathsf{ufp}(c_1)+\mathsf{ufp}(c_2)-\mathsf{nsb}(c_1)-\mathsf{nsb}(c_2)}&
\end{aligned}
\tag{9}
$$

We get rid of the last term $2^{\mathsf{ufp}(c_1)+\mathsf{ufp}(c_2)-\mathsf{nsb}(c_1)-\mathsf{nsb}(c_2)}$ of the error $\varepsilon(c)$ which is strictly less than the former two ones. By assuming that $\mathsf{ufp}(c_1 + c_2) = \mathsf{ufp}(c)$ and by reasoning on the exponents, we obtain the equations of Rule (MULT).

$$
\mathsf{nsb}(\ell_1) \ge \mathsf{nsb}(\ell) + \xi(\ell)(\ell_1, \ell_2) - 1 \quad \text{and} \quad \mathsf{nsb}(\ell_2) \ge \mathsf{nsb}(\ell) + \xi(\ell)(\ell_1, \ell_2) - 1 \ .
$$

The accuracy of math functions depends on each implementation (for example this is not in the IEEE754 Standard). It is then difficult to propose something independent of the user's library. Then, for the elementary functions such as logarithm, exponential and the hyperbolic and trigonometric functions gathered in Rule (MATH), each implementation has its own nsb which we have to know to model the propagation of errors in our analyses. To cope with this limitation, we consider that each elementary function introduces a loss of precision of φ bits, where $\varphi \in \mathbb{N}$ is a parameter of the analysis and consequently of our tool, POP. In future work, we plan to reverse the question and to let the tool find the minimal accuracy needed for functions by including their accuracy in the constraint systems.

The rules of commands are rather classical, we use control points to distinguish many assignments of the same variable and also to implement joins in conditions and loops. Given a command c and an environment ϱ, $\mathcal{C}[c] \varrho$ returns a pair (C, ϱ') made of a set C of constraints and of a new environment ϱ'. The function $\mathcal{C}$ is defined by induction on the structure of commands in Figs. 4 and 5. For conditionals, we generate the constraints for the **then** and **else** branches plus additional constraints to join the results of both branches. Currently, we do not take care of the guards. As a result, we analyze both the **then** and **else** branches of the **if** statement with the whole environment. This is correct but it is a source of imprecision. Concerning loops, we relate the number of significants bits at the end of the **body** to the nsb of the same variables and the beginning of the loop as shown in Rule (WHILE).

Back to Line 5 of the pendulum program of Sect. 2, we generate seven constraints as shown in Eq. (10).

$$
C_1 = \left\{
\begin{array}{l}
\mathsf{nsb}(\ell_{17}) \ge \mathsf{nsb}(\ell_{23}) + (-1) + \xi(\ell_{23})(\ell_{17}, \ell_{22}) - (-1), \\
\mathsf{nsb}(\ell_{22} \ge \mathsf{nsb}(\ell_{23} + 0 + \xi(\ell_{23})(\ell_{17}, \ell_{22}) - (1), \\
\mathsf{nsb}(\ell_{19}) \ge \mathsf{nsb}(\ell_{22}) + \xi(\ell_{22})(\ell_{19}, \ell_{21}) - 1, \\
\mathsf{nsb}(\ell_{21}) \ge \mathsf{nsb}(\ell_{22}) + \xi(\ell_{22})(\ell_{19}, \ell_{21}) - 1, \\
\mathsf{nsb}(\ell_{23}) \ge \mathsf{nsb}(\ell_{24}), \ \xi(\ell_{23})(\ell_{17}, \ell_{22}) \ge 1, \ \xi(\ell_{22})(\ell_{19}, \ell_{21}) \ge 1
\end{array}
\right\}
\tag{10}
$$

The first two constraints are for the addition. As mentioned previously, the ufp are computed by a prior range analysis. Then, at constraint generation time, they are constants. For our example, $\mathsf{ufp}(\ell_{17}) = -1$. This quantity occurs in the first constraints. The next two constraints are for the multiplication. The fifth constraint $\mathsf{nsb}(\ell_{23}) \geq \mathsf{nsb}(\ell_{24})$ is for the assignment and the last two constraints are for the constant functions $\xi(\ell_{23})(\ell_{17}, \ell_{22})$ and $\xi(\ell_{22})(\ell_{19}, \ell_{21})$, respectively for the addition and multiplication. For a user requirement of 20 bits on the variable y2 (all variables are in double precision initially), POP succeeds in tuning the majority of variables of the pendulum program into single precision with a total number of bits at bit level equivalent to 274 (originally the program used 689 bits). The new mixed precision formats obtained are: y1new|20| = y1|21| +|20| y2|22| ×|22| h|22|.

3.3   Policy Iteration for Optimized Carry Bit Propagation

The policy iteration algorithm is used to solve nonlinear fixpoint equations when the function is written as the infimum of functions for which a fixpoint can be easily computed. The infimum formulation makes the function not being differentiable in the classical sense. The one proposed in [9] to solve smallest fixpoint equations in static analysis requires the fact that the function is order-preserving to ensure the decrease of the intermediate solutions provided by the algorithm. In this article, because of the nature of the semantics, we propose a policy iterations algorithm for a non order-preserving function.

More precisely, let F be a map from a complete lattice L to itself such that $F = \inf_{\pi \in \Pi} f^{\pi}$. Classical policy iterations solve $F(\mathbf{x}) = \mathbf{x}$ by generating a sequence $(\mathbf{x}^k)_k$ such that $f^{\pi^k}(\mathbf{x}^k) = \mathbf{x}^k$ and $\mathbf{x}^{k+1} < \mathbf{x}^k$. The set Π is called the set of policies and f^{π} a policy map (associated to π). The set of policy maps has to satisfy the selection property meaning that for all $\mathbf{x} \in L$, there exists $\pi \in \Pi$ such that $F(\mathbf{x}) = f^{\pi}(\mathbf{x})$. This is exactly the same as for each $\mathbf{x} \in L$, the minimization problem $\mathrm{Min}_{\pi \in \Pi} f^{\pi}(\mathbf{x})$ has an optimal solution. If Π is finite and F is order-preserving, policy iterations converge in finite time to a fixpoint of F. The number of iterations is bounded from above by the number of policies. Indeed, a policy cannot be selected twice in the running of the algorithm. This is implied by the fact that the smallest fixpoint of a policy map is computed. In this article, we adapt policy iterations to the problem of precision tuning. The function F here is constructed from inequalities depicted in Fig. 4 and Fig. 5. We thus have naturally constraints of the form $F(\mathbf{x}) \leq \mathbf{x}$. We will give details about the construction of F at Proposition 1. Consequently, we are interested in solving:

$$\mathrm{Min}_{\mathsf{nsb}, \mathsf{nsb}_e} \sum_{\ell} \mathsf{nsb}(\ell) \text{s.t.} F \begin{pmatrix} \mathsf{nsb} \\ \mathsf{nsb}_e \end{pmatrix} \leq \begin{pmatrix} \mathsf{nsb} \\ \mathsf{nsb}_e \end{pmatrix} \quad \mathsf{nsb} \in \mathbb{N}^{Lab}, \ \mathsf{nsb}_e \in \mathbb{N}^{Lab} \quad (11)$$

Let $\xi : Lab \to \{0, 1\}$. We write S_{ξ}^1 the system of inequalities depicted in Fig. 4 and S_{ξ}^2 the system of inequalities presented at Fig. 5. Note that the final system of inequalities is $S_{\xi} = S_{\xi}^1 \cup S_{\xi}^2$ meaning that we add new constraints to S_{ξ}^1. If the system S_{ξ}^1 is used alone, ξ is the constant function equal to 1. Otherwise, ξ is defined by the formula at the end of Fig. 5.

$$\mathcal{E}'[c\#p^\ell]\varrho = \{\mathsf{nsb}_e(\ell) = 0\} \quad (\text{Const}') \qquad \mathcal{E}'[x^\ell]\varrho = \{\mathsf{nsb}_e(\varrho(x)) \geq \mathsf{nsb}_e(\ell)\} \quad (\text{Id}')$$

$$\mathcal{E}'[e_1^{\ell_1} +^\ell e_2^{\ell_2}]\varrho = \mathcal{E}'[e_1^{\ell_1}]\varrho \;\cup\; \mathcal{E}'[e_2^{\ell_2}]\varrho \quad (\text{Add}')$$
$$\cup$$
$$\left\{ \begin{array}{c} \mathsf{nsb}_e(\ell) \geq \mathsf{nsb}_e(\ell_1),\; \mathsf{nsb}_e(\ell) \geq \mathsf{nsb}_e(\ell_2), \\ \mathsf{nsb}_e(\ell) \geq \mathsf{ufp}(\ell_1) - \mathsf{ufp}(\ell_2) + \mathsf{nsb}(\ell_2) - \mathsf{nsb}(\ell_1) + \mathsf{nsb}_e(\ell_2) + \xi(\ell)(\ell_1,\ell_2), \\ \mathsf{nsb}_e(\ell) \geq \mathsf{ufp}(\ell_2) - \mathsf{ufp}(\ell_1) + \mathsf{nsb}(\ell_1) - \mathsf{nsb}(\ell_2) + \mathsf{nsb}_e(\ell_1) + \xi(\ell)(\ell_1,\ell_2) \end{array} \right\}$$

$$\mathcal{E}'[e_1^{\ell_1} -^\ell e_2^{\ell_2}]\varrho = \mathcal{E}'[e_1^{\ell_1}]\varrho \;\cup\; \mathcal{E}'[e_2^{\ell_2}]\varrho \quad (\text{Sub}')$$
$$\cup$$
$$\left\{ \begin{array}{c} \mathsf{nsb}_e(\ell) \geq \mathsf{nsb}_e(\ell_1),\; \mathsf{nsb}_e(\ell) \geq \mathsf{nsb}_e(\ell_2), \\ \mathsf{nsb}_e(\ell) \geq \mathsf{ufp}(\ell_1) - \mathsf{ufp}(\ell_2) + \mathsf{nsb}(\ell_2) - \mathsf{nsb}(\ell_1) + \mathsf{nsb}_e(\ell_2) + \xi(\ell)(\ell_1,\ell_2), \\ \mathsf{nsb}_e(\ell) \geq \mathsf{ufp}(\ell_2) - \mathsf{ufp}(\ell_1) + \mathsf{nsb}(\ell_1) - \mathsf{nsb}(\ell_2) + \mathsf{nsb}_e(\ell_1) + \xi(\ell)(\ell_1,\ell_2) \end{array} \right\}$$

$$\mathcal{E}'[e_1^{\ell_1} \times^\ell e_2^{\ell_2}]\varrho = \mathcal{E}'[e_1^{\ell_1}]\varrho \;\cup\; \mathcal{E}'[e_2^{\ell_2}]\varrho \quad (\text{Mult}')$$
$$\cup$$
$$\left\{ \mathsf{nsb}_e(\ell) \geq \mathsf{nsb}(\ell_1) + \mathsf{nsb}_e(\ell_1) + \mathsf{nsb}_e(\ell_2) - 2,\; \mathsf{nsb}_e(\ell) \geq \mathsf{nsb}(\ell_2) + \mathsf{nsb}_e(\ell_2) + \mathsf{nsb}_e(\ell_1) - 2 \right\}$$

$$\mathcal{E}'[e_1^{\ell_1} \div^\ell e_2^{\ell_2}]\varrho = \mathcal{E}'[e_1^{\ell_1}]\varrho \;\cup\; \mathcal{E}'[e_2^{\ell_2}]\varrho \quad (\text{Div}')$$
$$\cup$$
$$\left\{ \mathsf{nsb}_e(\ell) \geq \mathsf{nsb}(\ell_1) + \mathsf{nsb}_e(\ell_1) + \mathsf{nsb}_e(\ell_2) - 2,\; \mathsf{nsb}_e(\ell) \geq \mathsf{nsb}(\ell_2) + \mathsf{nsb}_e(\ell_2) + \mathsf{nsb}_e(\ell_1) - 2 \right\}$$

$$\mathcal{E}'\left[\sqrt{e^{\ell_1}}^{\,\ell}\right]\varrho = \mathcal{E}'[e_1^{\ell_1}]\varrho \;\cup\; \left\{\mathsf{nsb}_e(\ell) \geq \mathsf{nsb}_e(\ell_1)\right\} \quad (\text{Sqrt}')$$

$$\mathcal{E}'\left[\phi(e^{\ell_1})^\ell\right]\varrho = \mathcal{E}'[e_1^{\ell_1}]\varrho \;\cup\; \left\{\mathsf{nsb}_e(\ell) \geq +\infty\right\} \text{ with } \phi \in \{\sin,\cos,\tan,\log,\ldots\} \quad (\text{Math}')$$

$$\mathcal{C}'\left[x := ^\ell e^{\ell_1}\right]\varrho = \left(C, \varrho[x \mapsto \ell]\right) \text{ where } C = \mathcal{E}'[e_1^{\ell_1}]\varrho \cup \{\mathsf{nsb}_e(\ell_1) \geq \mathsf{nsb}_e(\ell)\} \quad (\text{Assign}')$$

$$\mathcal{C}'\left[c_1^{\ell_1}; c_2^{\ell_2}\right]\varrho = \left(C_1 \cup C_2, \varrho_2\right) \text{ with } (C_1, \varrho_1) = \mathcal{C}'\left[c_1^{\ell_1}\right]\varrho \text{ and } (C_2, \varrho_2) = \mathcal{C}'\left[c_2^{\ell_2}\right]\varrho_1 \quad (\text{Seq}')$$

$$\mathcal{C}'[\text{if}^\ell \; e^{\ell_0} \text{ then } c^{\ell_1} \text{ else } c^{\ell_2}]\,\varrho = (C_1 \cup C_2 \cup C_3, \varrho')$$
$$\text{where} \left| \begin{array}{l} \forall x \in \mathrm{Id},\; \varrho'(x) = \ell,\; (C_1, \varrho_1) = \mathcal{C}'[c^{\ell_1}]\,\varrho,\; (C_2, \varrho_2) = \mathcal{C}'[c^{\ell_2}]\,\varrho, \\ C_3 = \bigcup_{x \in \mathrm{Id}} \{\mathsf{nsb}_e(\varrho_1(x)) \geq \mathsf{nsb}_e(\ell),\; \mathsf{nsb}_e(\varrho_2(x)) \geq \mathsf{nsb}_e(\ell)\} \end{array} \right. \quad (\text{Cond}')$$

$$\mathcal{C}'[\text{while}^\ell \; e^{\ell_0} \text{ do } c^{\ell_1}]\,\varrho = (C_1 \cup C_2, \varrho')$$
$$\text{where} \left| \begin{array}{l} \forall x \in \mathrm{Id},\; \varrho'(x) = \ell,\; (C_1, \varrho_1) = \mathcal{C}'[c^{\ell_1}]\,\varrho' \\ C_2 = \bigcup_{x \in \mathrm{Id}} \{\mathsf{nsb}_e(\varrho(x)) \geq \mathsf{nsb}_e(\ell),\; \mathsf{nsb}_e(\varrho_1(x)) \geq \mathsf{nsb}_e(\ell)\} \end{array} \right. \quad (\text{While}')$$

$$\mathcal{C}'[\text{require\_nsb}(x,\mathrm{p})^\ell]\varrho = \emptyset \quad (\text{Req}')$$

$$\xi(\ell)(\ell_1,\ell_2) = \min \left(\begin{array}{c} \max\left(\mathsf{ufp}(\ell_2) - \mathsf{ufp}(\ell_1) + \mathsf{nsb}(\ell_1) - \mathsf{nsb}(\ell_2) - \mathsf{nsb}_e(\ell_2), 0\right), \\ \max\left(\mathsf{ufp}(\ell_1) - \mathsf{ufp}(\ell_2) + \mathsf{nsb}(\ell_2) - \mathsf{nsb}(\ell_1) - \mathsf{nsb}_e(\ell_1), 0\right), 1 \end{array} \right)$$

Fig. 5. Constraints solved by PI with min and max carry bit formulation.

Proposition 1. *The following results hold:*

1. Let ξ the constant function equal to 1. The system S_ξ^1 can be rewritten as $\{\mathsf{nsb} \in \mathbb{N}^{Lab} \mid F(\mathsf{nsb}) \leq (\mathsf{nsb})\}$ where F maps $\mathbb{R}^{Lab}$ to itself, $F(\mathbb{N}^{Lab}) \subseteq$

($\mathbb{N}^{Lab}$) *and has coordinates which are the maximum of a finite family of affine order-preserving functions.*

2. *Let ξ the function such that $\xi(\ell)$ equals the function of Fig. 5. The system S_ξ can be rewritten as $\{(\mathsf{nsb}, \mathsf{nsb}_e) \in \mathbb{N}^{Lab} \times \mathbb{N}^{Lab} \mid F(\mathsf{nsb}, \mathsf{nsb}_e) \leq (\mathsf{nsb}, \mathsf{nsb}_e)\}$ where F maps $\mathbb{R}^{Lab} \times \mathbb{R}^{Lab}$ to itself, $F(\mathbb{N}^{Lab} \times \mathbb{N}^{Lab}) \subseteq (\mathbb{N}^{Lab} \times \mathbb{N}^{Lab})$ and all its coordinates are the min-max of a finite family of affine functions.*

Note that, in the first case, F does not map from $\mathbb{R}^{Lab} \times \mathbb{R}^{Lab}$ to itself. It is easy to extend F as a map from $\mathbb{R}^{Lab} \times \mathbb{R}^{Lab}$ to itself without affecting its intrinsic behaviour. From Proposition 1, when S_ξ is used, we can write F as $F = \min_{\pi \in \Pi} f^\pi$, where f^π is the maximum of a finite family of affine functions and thus used a modified policy iterations algorithm. The set of policies here is a map $\pi : Lab \mapsto \{0, 1\}$. A choice is thus a vector of 0 or 1. A policy map f^π is a function $\mathbb{N}^{Lab}$ to itself such that the coordinates are $f_\ell^\pi(\ell)$. If the coordinate $f_\ell^\pi(\ell)$ depends on ξ then $\xi(\ell) = \pi(\ell)$. Otherwise, the function is the maximum of affine functions and a choice is not required.

Corollary 1. *Any feasible solution of Problem (11) satisfies our ILP constraints of Fig. 4 (or Fig. 5 if ξ is not fixed to 1).*

Proposition 2 (Algorithm correctness). *The sequence $(\sum_{\ell \in Lab} \mathsf{nsb}^k(\ell))_{0 \leq k \leq K}$ generated by Algorithm 1 satisfies the following properties:*

1. *$K < +\infty$ i.e. the sequence is of finite length;*
2. *each term of the sequence furnishes a feasible solution for Problem (11);*
3. *$\sum_{\ell \in Lab} \mathsf{nsb}^{k+1}(\ell) < \sum_{\ell \in Lab} \mathsf{nsb}^k(\ell)$ if $k < K-1$ and $\sum_{\ell \in Lab} \mathsf{nsb}^K(\ell) = \sum_{\ell \in Lab} \mathsf{nsb}^{K-1}(\ell)$;*
4. *the number k is smaller than the number of policies.*

Algorithm 1: Non-monotone Policy Iterations Algorithm

Result: An over-approximation of an optimal solution of Equation 11
1 Let $k := 0$, $S := +\infty$;
2 Choose $\pi^0 \in \Pi$;
3 Select an optimal solution of $(\mathsf{nsb}^k, \mathsf{nsb}_e{}^k)$ the integer linear program:

$$\mathrm{Min}\left\{\sum_{\ell \in Lab} \mathsf{nsb}(\ell) \mid f^{\pi^k}(\mathsf{nsb}, \mathsf{nsb}_e) \leq (\mathsf{nsb}, \mathsf{nsb}_e),\ \mathsf{nsb} \in \mathbb{N}^{Lab},\ \mathsf{nsb}_e \in \mathbb{N}^{Lab}\right\};$$

    if $\sum_{\ell \in Lab} \mathsf{nsb}^k(\ell) < S$ **then**
4 | $S := \sum_{\ell \in Lab} \mathsf{nsb}^k(\ell)$;
5 | Choose $\pi^{k+1} \in \Pi$ such that $F(\mathsf{nsb}^k, \mathsf{nsb}_e{}^k) = f^{\pi^{k+1}}(\mathsf{nsb}^k, \mathsf{nsb}_e{}^k)$;
6 | $k := k + 1$ and go to 3;
7 **else**
8 | Return S and nsb^k.
9 **end**

Figure 5 displays the new rules that we add to the global system of constraints in which the only difference is to activate the optimized function ξ instead of its over-approximation in Fig. 4. As mentioned in Eq. (6), to compute the ulp of the errors on the operands, we need to estimate the number of bits of the error $\mathsf{nsb_e}$ for each operand on which all the rules of Fig. 5 are based. By applying this reasoning, the problem do not remain an ILP any longer. Let us concentrate on the rules of Fig. 5. The function $\mathcal{E}'[e]\,\varrho$ generates the new set of constraints for an expression $e \in Expr$ in the environment ϱ. For Rule (CONST$'$), the number of significant bits of the error $\mathsf{nsb_e} = 0$ whereas we impose that the $\mathsf{nsb_e}$ of a variable x at control point ℓ is less than the last assignment of $\mathsf{nsb_e}$ in $\varrho(x)$ as shown in Rule (ID$'$) of Fig. 5. Considering Rule (ADD$'$), we start by generating the new set of constraints $\mathcal{E}'[e_1^{\ell_1}]\varrho$ and $\mathcal{E}'[e_2^{\ell_2}]\varrho$ on the operands at control points ℓ_1 and ℓ_2. Then, we require that $\mathsf{nsb_e}(\ell) \geq \mathsf{nsb_e}(\ell_1)$ and $\mathsf{nsb_e}(\ell) \geq \mathsf{nsb_e}(\ell_2)$ where the result of the addition is stored at control point ℓ. Additionally, $\mathsf{nsb_e}(\ell)$ is computed as shown hereafter.

$$\mathsf{nsb_e}(\ell) \geq \max \left(\begin{array}{c} \mathsf{ufp}(\ell_1) - \mathsf{nsb}(\ell_1) \\ \mathsf{ufp}(\ell_2) - \mathsf{nsb}(\ell_2) \end{array} \right) - \min \left(\begin{array}{c} \mathsf{ufp}(\ell_1) - \mathsf{nsb}(\ell_1) - \mathsf{nsb_e}(\ell_1) \\ \mathsf{ufp}(\ell_2) - \mathsf{nsb}(\ell_2) - \mathsf{nsb_e}(\ell_2) \end{array} \right) + \xi(\ell)(\ell_1, \ell_2)$$

By breaking the min and max operators, we obtain the constraints on $\mathsf{nsb_e}(\ell)$ of Rule (ADD$'$). For the subtraction, the constraints generated are similar to the addition case. Considering now Rule (MULT$'$), as we have defined in Sect. 3.2, $\varepsilon(c) = c_1 \cdot \varepsilon(c_2) + c_2 \cdot \varepsilon(c_1) + \varepsilon(c_1) \cdot \varepsilon(c_2)$ where $c = c_1^{\ell_1} \times^{\ell} c_2^{\ell_2}$. By reasoning on $\mathsf{ulp_e}$, we bound $\varepsilon(c)$ by

$$\varepsilon(c) \leq 2^{\mathsf{ufp}(c_1)} \cdot 2^{\mathsf{ufp}(c_2) - \mathsf{nsb}(c_2) - \mathsf{nsb_e}(c_2) + 1} + 2^{\mathsf{ufp}(c_2)} \cdot 2^{\mathsf{ufp}(c_1) - \mathsf{nsb}(c_1) - \mathsf{nsb_e}(c_1) + 1}$$
$$+ 2^{\mathsf{ufp}(c_2) + \mathsf{ufp}(c_1) - \mathsf{nsb}(c_1) - \mathsf{nsb}(c_2) - \mathsf{nsb_e}(c_1) - \mathsf{nsb_e}(c_2) + 2}$$

By selecting the smallest term $\mathsf{ufp}(c_2) + \mathsf{ufp}(c_1) - \mathsf{nsb}(c_1) - \mathsf{nsb}(c_2) - \mathsf{nsb_e}(c_1) - \mathsf{nsb_e}(c_2) + 2$, we obtain that

$$\mathsf{nsb_e}(\ell) \geq \max \left(\begin{array}{c} \mathsf{ufp}(\ell_1) + \mathsf{ufp}(\ell_2) - \mathsf{nsb}(\ell_1) \\ \mathsf{ufp}(\ell_1) + \mathsf{ufp}(\ell_2) - \mathsf{nsb}(\ell_2) \end{array} \right) - \begin{array}{c} \mathsf{ufp}(\ell_1) + \mathsf{ufp}(\ell_2) - \mathsf{nsb}(\ell_1) - \\ \mathsf{nsb}(\ell_2) - \mathsf{nsb_e}(\ell_1) - \mathsf{nsb_e}(\ell_2) + 2 \end{array}$$

Finally, by simplifying the equation above we found the constraints of Rule (MULT$'$) in Fig. 5 (same for Rule (DIV$'$)). For Rule (SQRT$'$), we generate the constraints on the expression $\mathcal{E}'[e_1^{\ell_1}]\varrho$ and we require that $\mathsf{nsb_e}$ of the result stored at control point ℓ is greater than the $\mathsf{nsb_e}$ of the expression a control point ℓ_1. For Rule (MATH$'$), we assume that $\mathsf{nsb_e}(\ell)$ is unbounded. Concerning the commands, we define the set $\mathcal{C}'[c]\,\varrho$ which has the same function as $\mathcal{C}$ defined in Fig. 4. The reasoning on the commands also remains similar except that this time we reason on the number of bits of the errors $\mathsf{nsb_e}$. The only difference is in Rule (REQ$'$) where the set of constraints is empty. Let us recall that the constraints C_2 of Fig. 5 are added to the former constraints C_1 of Fig. 4 and are sent to a linear solver (GLPK in practice).

Now, let us take again the pendulum program of Fig. 1. By analyzing Line 5 of our program, we have to add the following set of constraints C_2 of Eq. (12), along with the former set C_1 of Eq. (10). In fact, policy iteration makes it possible to break the min in the $\xi(\ell_{23})(\ell_{17}, \ell_{22})$ function by choosing the max between ufp(ℓ_{22}) − ufp(ℓ_{17}) − nsb(ℓ_{17}) − nsb(ℓ_{22}) − nsb$_e$(ℓ_{17}) and 0, the max between ufp(ℓ_{17}) − ufp(ℓ_{22}) + nsb(ℓ_{22}) − nsb(ℓ_{17}) − nsb$_e$(ℓ_{22}) and 0 and the constant 1. Next, it becomes possible to solve the corresponding ILP. If no fixed point is reached, POP iterates until a solution is found. By applying this optimization, the new formats are presented in lines 5 and 6 of the bottom right corner of Fig. 1: y1new|20| = y1|21| +|20| y2|21| ×|22| h|21|. By comparing with the formats obtained with the ILP formulation, a gain of precision of 1 bit is observed on variables y2 and h (total of 272 bits at bit level for the optimized program).

$$C_2 = \begin{cases} \mathsf{nsb_e}(\ell_{23}) \geq \mathsf{nsb_e}(\ell_{17}), \mathsf{nsb_e}(\ell_{23}) \geq \mathsf{nsb_e}(\ell_{22}), \\ \mathsf{nsb}(\ell_{23}) \geq -1 - 0 + \mathsf{nsb}(\ell_{22}) - \mathsf{nsb}(\ell_{17}) + \mathsf{nsb_e}(\ell_{22}) + \xi(\ell_{23}, \ell_{17}, \ell_{22}), \\ \mathsf{nsb_e}(\ell_{23}) \geq 0 - (-1) + \mathsf{nsb}(\ell_{17}) - \mathsf{nsb}(\ell_{22}) + \mathsf{nsb_e}(\ell_{17}) + \xi(\ell_{23}, \ell_{17}, \ell_{22}), \\ \mathsf{nsb_e}(\ell_{23}) \geq \mathsf{nsb_e}(\ell_{24}), \mathsf{nsb_e}(\ell_{22}) \geq \mathsf{nsb}(\ell_{19}) + \mathsf{nsb_e}(\ell_{19}) + \mathsf{nsb_e}(\ell_{21}) - 2, \\ \mathsf{nsb_e}(\ell_{22}) \geq \mathsf{nsb}(\ell_{21}) + \mathsf{nsb_e}(\ell_{21}) + \mathsf{nsb_e}(\ell_{19}) - 2, \\ \xi(\ell_{23})(\ell_{17}, \ell_{22}) = \min \begin{pmatrix} \max \big(0 - 6 + \mathsf{nsb}(\ell_{17}) - \mathsf{nsb}(\ell_{22}) - \mathsf{nsb_e}(\ell_{17}), 0\big), \\ \max \big(6 - 0 + \mathsf{nsb}(\ell_{22}) - \mathsf{nsb}(\ell_{17}) - \mathsf{nsb_e}(\ell_{22}), 0\big), 1 \end{pmatrix} \end{cases}$$

(12)

4   Correctness

4.1   Soundness of the Constraint System

Let ≡ denote the syntactic equivalence and let $e^\ell \in Expr$ be an expression. We write Const(e^ℓ) the set of constants occurring in the expression e^ℓ. For example, Const($18.0^{\ell_1} \times^{\ell_2} x^{\ell_3} +^{\ell_4} 12.0^{\ell_5} \times^{\ell_6} y^{\ell_7} +^{\ell_8} z^{\ell_9}$) = $\{18.0^{\ell_1}, 12.0^{\ell_5}\}$. Also, we denote by τ : Lab → ℕ a function mapping the labels of an expression to a nsb. The notation $\tau \models \mathcal{E}[e^\ell]\varrho$ means that τ is the minimal solution to the ILP $\mathcal{E}[e^\ell]\varrho$. We write $\varrho_\perp$ the empty environment ($dom(\varrho_\perp) = \emptyset$). The small step operational semantics of our language is displayed in Fig. 6. It is standard, the only originality being to indicate explicitly the nsb of constants. For the result of an elementary operation, this nsb is computed in function of the nsb of the operands. Lemma 2 asses the soundness of the constraints for one step of the semantics.

$$\frac{\varrho(x) = c\#\mathsf{p}}{\langle x^\ell, \varrho \rangle \longrightarrow \langle c^\ell \#\mathsf{p}, \varrho \rangle}$$

$$\frac{c = c_1 \odot c_2, \ \mathsf{p} = \mathsf{ufp}(c) - \mathsf{ufp_e}(c^\ell \#\mathsf{p})}{\langle c_1^{\ell_1} \#p_1 \odot^\ell c_2^{\ell_2} \#p_2, \varrho \rangle \longrightarrow \langle c\#\mathsf{p}, \varrho \rangle} \quad \odot \in \{+, -, \times, \div\}$$

$$\frac{\langle e_1^{\ell_1}, \varrho \rangle \longrightarrow \langle e_1'^{\ell_1}, \varrho \rangle}{\langle e_1^{\ell_1} \odot^\ell e_2^{\ell_2}, \varrho \rangle \longrightarrow \langle e_1'^{\ell_1} \odot^\ell e_2^{\ell_2}, \varrho \rangle} \qquad \frac{\langle e_2^{\ell_2}, \varrho \rangle \longrightarrow \langle e_2'^{\ell_2}, \varrho \rangle}{\langle c_1^{\ell_1} \#\mathsf{p} \odot^\ell e_2^{\ell_2}, \varrho \rangle \longrightarrow \langle c_1^{\ell_1} \#\mathsf{p} \odot^\ell e_2'^{\ell_2}, \varrho \rangle}$$

Fig. 6. Small step operational semantics of arithmetic expressions.

Lemma 2. *Given an expression $e^\ell \in Expr$, if $e^\ell \to e'^\ell$ and $\tau \models \mathcal{E}[e^\ell]\varrho_\perp$ then for all $c^{\ell_c}\#p \in \mathsf{Const}(e'^\ell)$ we have $p = \tau(\ell_c)$.*

Proof. By case examination of the rules of Fig. 4. Hereafter, we focus on the most interesting case of addition of two constants. Recall that $\mathsf{ufp_e}(\ell) = \mathsf{ufp}(\ell) - \mathsf{nsb}(\ell)$ for any control point ℓ. Assuming that $e^\ell \equiv c_1^{\ell_1} +^\ell c_2^{\ell_2}$ then by following the reduction rule of Fig. 6, we have $e^\ell \to c^\ell\#p$ with $p = \mathsf{ufp}(c) - \mathsf{ufp_e}(c)$. On the other side, by following the set of constraints of Rule (ADD) in Fig. 4 we have $\mathcal{E}[e^\ell]\varrho = \{\mathsf{nsb}(\ell_1) \geq \mathsf{nsb}(\ell) + \mathsf{ufp}(\ell_1) - \mathsf{ufp}(\ell) + \xi(\ell)(\ell_1, \ell_2), \mathsf{nsb}(\ell_2) \geq \mathsf{nsb}(\ell) + \mathsf{ufp}(\ell_2) - \mathsf{ufp}(\ell) + \xi(\ell)(\ell_1, \ell_2)\}$. These constraints can be written as

$$\mathsf{nsb}(\ell) \leq \mathsf{ufp}(\ell) - \mathsf{ufp}(\ell_1) + \mathsf{nsb}(\ell_1) - \xi(\ell)(\ell_1, \ell_2)$$
$$\mathsf{nsb}(\ell) \leq \mathsf{ufp}(\ell) - \mathsf{ufp}(\ell_2) + \mathsf{nsb}(\ell_2) - \xi(\ell)(\ell_1, \ell_2)$$

and may themselves be rewritten as Eq. (8), i.e.

$$\mathsf{nsb}(\ell) \leq \mathsf{ufp}(\ell) - \max\big(\mathsf{ufp}(\ell_1) - \mathsf{nsb}(\ell_1), \mathsf{ufp}(\ell_2) - \mathsf{nsb}(\ell_2)\big) - \xi(\ell)(\ell_1, \ell_2) \ .$$

Since, obviously, $\mathsf{ufp}(c) = \mathsf{ufp}(\ell)$ and since the solver finds the minimal solution to the ILP, it remains to show that

$$\mathsf{ufp_e}(\ell) = \max\big(\mathsf{ufp}(\ell_1) - \mathsf{nsb}(\ell_1), \mathsf{ufp}(\ell_2) - \mathsf{nsb}(\ell_2), \mathsf{ufp}(\ell) - \mathsf{prec}(\ell)\big) + \xi(\ell)(\ell_1, \ell_2)$$

which corresponds to the assertion of Eq. (7). Consequently, $\mathsf{nsb}(\ell) = p$ as required, for this case, in Fig. 6. □

Theorem 1. *Given an expression $e^\ell \to e'^\ell$. If $e^\ell \to^* e'^\ell$ and if $\tau \models \mathcal{E}[e^\ell]\varrho_\perp$, then $\forall\ c^{\ell_c}\#p \in \mathsf{Const}(e'^\ell)$ we have $p = \tau(\ell_c)$.*

4.2 ILP Nature of the Problem

In this section, we give insights about the complexity of the problem. The computation relies on integer linear programming. Integer linear programming is known to belong to the class of NP-Hard problems. A lower bound of the optimal value in a minimization problem can be furnished by the continuous linear programming relaxation. This relaxation is obtained by removing the integrity constraint. Recall that a (classical) linear program can be solved in polynomial-time. Then, we can solve our problem in polynomial-time if we can show that the continuous linear programming relaxation of our ILP has an unique optimal solution with integral coordinates. Proposition 3 presents a situation where a linear program has a unique optimal solution which is a vector of integers.

Proposition 3. *Let $G : [0, +\infty)^d \mapsto [0, +\infty)^d$ be an order-preserving function such that $G(\mathbb{N}^d) \subseteq \mathbb{N}^d$. Suppose that the set $\{y \in \mathbb{N}^d \mid G(y) \leq y\}$ is non-empty. Let $\varphi : \mathbb{R}^d \mapsto \mathbb{R}$ a strictly monotone function such that $\varphi(\mathbb{N}^d) \subseteq \mathbb{N}$. Then, the minimization problem below has an unique optimal solution which is integral.*

$$\operatorname*{Min}_{y \in [0, +\infty)^d} \varphi(y) \ \text{ s. t. } G(y) \leq y$$

Theorem 2. *Assume that the system S of inequalities depicted in Fig. 4 has a solution. The smallest amount of memory $\sum_{\ell \in Lab} \mathsf{nsb}(\ell)$ for S can be computed in polynomial-time by linear programming.*

Proof. The function $\sum_{\ell \in Lab} \mathsf{nsb}(\ell)$ is strictly monotone and stable on integers. From the first statement of Proposition 1, the system of constraints is of the form $F(\mathsf{nsb}) \leq \mathsf{nsb}$ where F is order-preserving and stable on integers. By assumption, there exists a vector of integers nsb s.t. $F(\mathsf{nsb}) \leq \mathsf{nsb}$. We conclude from Proposition 3. □

For the second system, in practice, we get integral solutions to the continuous linear programming relaxation of our ILP of Eq. (11). However, because of the lack of monotonicity of the functions for the rules (ADD) and (SUB) of Fig. 4, we cannot exploit Proposition 4 to prove the polynomial-time solvability.

5   Experimental Results

In this section, we aim at evaluating the performance of our tool POP implementing the techniques of Sect. 3. We have evaluated POP on several numerical programs. Two of them were used as a benchmark for precision tuning in prior work [24] and are coming from the GNU scientific library (GSL): **arclength** and **simpson** program which corresponds to an implementation of the widely used Simpson's rule [19]. The next three programs were used as benchmarks for POP in its former version [2,3,6]. The **rotation** program performs a matrix-vector product to rotate a vector around the z axis by an angle of θ [6]. The **accelerometer** program measures an inclination angle [2]. The **lowPassFilter** program [3] is taken from a pedometer application [20]. These last two programs come from the IoT field. We also experiment POP on a **2-Body** problem program and the **pendulum** program already introduced in Sect. 2.

The experiments shown in Table 1 present the tuning results produced by POP for each error threshold 10^{-4}, 10^{-6}, 10^{-8} and 10^{-10}. This is for compatibility with Precimonious which uses decimal thresholds. Technically, we translate these error thresholds into nsb. In Table 1, we represent by "TH" the error threshold given by the user. "BL" is the percentage of optimization at bit level. "IEEE" denotes the percentage of optimized variables in IEEE754 formats (`binary16`, `binary32`, etc.) In IEEE mode, the nsb obtained at bit level is approximated by the upper number of bits corresponding to a IEEE754 format. "ILP-time" is the total analysis time of POP in the case of ILP formulation. We have also "PI-time" to represent the time passed by POP to find the right policy and to resolve the precision tuning problem. "H", "S", "D" and "LD" denote respectively the number of variables obtained in, half, single, double and long-double precision when using the PI formulation that clearly displays better results.

Table 1. Precision tuning results for POP for the ILP and PI methods.

Program	TH	BL	IEEE	ILP-time	BL	IEEE	PI-time	H	S	D	LD
Arclength	10^{-4}	61%	43%	0.9 s	62%	45%	1.5 s	8	88	25	0
	10^{-6}	50%	21%	0.9 s	51%	21%	1.4 s	2	45	74	0
	10^{-8}	37%	3%	0.8 s	38%	4%	1.6 s	2	6	113	0
	10^{-10}	24%	−1%	1.0 s	25%	−1%	1.7 s	2	0	116	3
	10^{-12}	12%	−17%	0.3 s	14%	−8%	1.5 s	2	0	109	10
Simpson	10^{-4}	64%	45%	0.1 s	67%	56%	0.5 s	6	42	1	0
	10^{-6}	53%	30%	0.2 s	56%	31%	0.5 s	1	27	21	0
	10^{-8}	40%	4%	0.1 s	43%	7%	0.3 s	1	5	43	0
	10^{-10}	27%	1%	0.1 s	28%	1%	0.4 s	1	0	48	0
	10^{-12}	16%	1%	0.1 s	16%	1%	0.3 s	0	1	48	0
Accelerometer	10^{-4}	73%	61%	0.2 s	76%	62%	1.0 s	53	69	0	0
	10^{-6}	62%	55%	0.2 s	65%	55%	1.0 s	2	102	0	0
	10^{-8}	49%	15%	0.2 s	52%	18%	1.0 s	2	33	69	0
	10^{-10}	36%	1%	0.2 s	39%	1%	1.0 s	2	0	102	0
	10^{-12}	25%	1%	0.2 s	28%	1%	1.0 s	2	0	102	0
Rotation	10^{-4}	78%	66%	0.08 s	79%	68%	1.3 s	46	38	0	0
	10^{-6}	67%	53%	0.08 s	68%	56%	0.5 s	12	70	2	0
	10^{-8}	53%	29%	0.07 s	54%	29%	0.4 s	0	46	38	0
	10^{-10}	40%	0%	0.1 s	41%	0%	0.5 s	0	0	84	0
	10^{-12}	29%	0%	0.09 s	30%	0%	0.5 s	0	0	48	0
LowPassFilter	10^{-4}	68%	46%	1.8 s	69%	46%	10.7 s	260	581	0	0
	10^{-6}	57%	38%	1.8 s	58%	45%	11.0 s	258	580	3	0
	10^{-8}	44%	−7%	2.0 s	45%	−7%	11.4 s	258	2	581	0
	10^{-10}	31%	−7%	1.7 s	32%	−7%	10.9 s	258	0	583	0
	10^{-12}	20%	−7%	1.8 s	21%	−7%	11.3 s	258	0	583	0
2-Body	10^{-4}	41%	51%	0.81 s	41%	51%	0.82 s	5	39	5	0
	10^{-6}	18%	49%	0.78 s	18%	49%	0.9 s	0	44	5	0
	10^{-8}	−7%	5%	0.8 s	−7%	5%	0.78 s	0	5	44	0
	10^{-10}	−34%	−2%	0.8 s	−34%	−2%	0.9	0	0	48	1
	10^{-12}	−57%	−11%	0.9 s	−57%	−11%	1.0 s	0	0	44	0
Pendulum	10^{-4}	71%	54%	0.15 s	71%	54%	0.4 s	0	13	0	0
	10^{-6}	60%	50%	0.2 s	60%	50%	0.5 s	0	12	1	0
	10^{-8}	47%	0%	0.12 s	47%	0%	0.4 s	0	0	13	0
	10^{-10}	33%	0%	0.16 s	34%	0%	0.5	0	0	13	0
	10^{-12}	22%	0%	0.11 s	22%	0%	0.4 s	0	0	13	0

Let us focus on the first "TH", "BL", "IEEE" and "ILP-time" columns of Table 1. We compute the improvements compared to the case where all variables are in double precision before tuning. For the **arclength** program, the optimization reaches 61% at bit-level while it achieves 43% in IEEE mode (100% is the percentage of all variables initially in double precision, 121 variables for the original **arclength** program that used 7744 bits). This is obtained in only 0.9 second by applying the ILP formulation. When we refine the solution by applying the policy iteration method (from the sixth column), POP attains 62% at bit-level and 43% for the IEEE mode. Although POP needs more analysis time to find and iterate

Table 2. Comparison between POP(ILP), POP(SMT) and Precimonious: number of bits saved by the tool and time in seconds for analyzing the programs.

Program	Tool	#Bits saved - Time in seconds			
		Threshold 10^{-4}	Threshold 10^{-6}	Threshold 10^{-8}	Threshold 10^{-10}
Arclength	POP(ILP) (28)	**2464b.**–1.8s	**2144b.**–1.5s	**1792b.**–1.7s	**1728b.**–1.8s
	POP(SMT) (22)	1488b.–4.7 s	1472b.–3.04 s	864b.–3.09 s	384b.–2.9 s
	Precimonious (9)	576b.–146.4 s	576b.–156.0 s	576b.–145.8 s	576b.–215.0 s
Simpson	POP(ILP) (14)	**1344b.**–0.4 s	**1152b.**–0.5 s	**896b.**–0.4 s	**896b.**–0.4 s
	POP(SMT) (11)	896b.–2.9 s	896b.–1.9 s	704b.–1.7 s	704b.–1.8 s
	Precimonious (10)	704b.–208.1 s	704b.–213.7 s	704b.–207.5 s	704b.–200.3 s
Rotation	POP(ILP) (25)	**2624b.**–0.47 s	2464b.–0.47 s	2048b.–0.54 s	1600b.–0.48 s
	POP(SMT) (22)	1584b.–1.85 s	2208b.–1.7 s	1776b.–1.6 s	1600b.–1.7 s
	Precimonious (27)	2400b.–9.53 s	**2592b.**–12.2 s	**2464b.**–10.7 s	**2464b.**–7.4 s
Accel.	POP(ILP) (18)	**1776b.**–1.05 s	**1728b.**–1.05 s	**1248b.**–1.04 s	**1152b.**–1.03 s
	POP(SMT) (15)	1488b.–2.6 s	1440b.–2.6 s	1056–2.4 s	960b.–2.4 s
	Precimonious (0)	–	–	–	–

between policies, the time of analysis remain negligible, not exceeding 1.5 seconds. For a total of 121 variables for the **arclength** original program, POP succeeds in tuning 8 variables to half precision (H), 88 variables passes to single precision (S) whereas 25 variables remain in double precision (D) for an error threshold of 10^{-4}. We remark that our second method displays better results also for the other user error thresholds. For the **simpson**, **accelerometer**, **rotation** and **lowPassFilter**, the improvement is also more important when using the PI technique than when using the ILP formulation. For instance, for an error threshold of 10^{-6} for the **simpson** program, only one variable passes to half precision, 27 variables turns to single precision while 21 remains in double precision with 56% of percentage of total number of bits at bit level using the policy iteration method. Concerning the 2-**Body** and the **pendulum** codes, the two techniques return the same percentage at bit level and IEEE mode for the majority of error thresholds except for the **pendulum** program where POP reaches 34% at bit level when using the PI method for a threshold of 10^{-10}.

Now, we stress on the negative percentages that we obtain in Table 1, especially for the **arclength** program with 10^{-10} and 10^{-12} for the columns IEEE, the **lowPassFilter** program for errors of 10^{-8}, 10^{-10} and 10^{-12} and finally for the 2-**Body** for almost all the error thresholds. In fact, POP is able to return new formats for any threshold required by the user without additional cost nor by increasing the complexity even if it fails to have a significant improvement on the program output. To be specific, taking again the **arclength** program, for an error of 10^{-12}, POP fulfills this requirement by informing the user that this precision is achievable only if 10 variables passes to the long double precision (LD) which is more than the original program whose variables are all in double precision. By doing so, the percentage of IEEE formats for both ILP and PI formulations reaches −17% and −8%, respectively. Same reasoning is adopted for the **lowPassFilter** which spends more time, nearly 12 seconds, with the policy iteration technique to find the optimized formats (total of 841 variables). For the 2-**Body** program, for an error threshold of 10^{-8}, the number of bits after optimization attains 2452 bits where the original program used only 2597 bits which corresponds to a percentage of -7% at bit level. Note that in these cases, other tools like Precimonious [24] fail to propose formats.

Table 2 shows a comparison between the new version of POP combining both ILP and PI formulations called POP(ILP), the former version of POP that uses the Z3 SMT solver coupled to binary search to find optimal solution [6], called POP(SMT) and the prior state-of the-art Precimonious [24]. The results of the mixed precision tuning are shown for the **arclength, simpson, rotation** and **accelerometer** programs. Let us mention that some examples used in Precimonious benchmarks [24] cannot be analyzed as-is by POP for implementation reasons (calls to external libraries or use of syntactic forms not yet implemented in our tool). Conversely, let us also mention that Precimonious fails to tune (with zero improvement) some examples handled by POP, e.g. **lowPassFilter**. Since POP (in its both versions) and Precimonious implement two different techniques, we have adjusted the criteria of comparison in several points. First, we mention that POP optimizes much more variables than Precimonious. While it disadvantages POP, we only consider in the experiments of Table 2 the variables optimized by Precimonious to estimate the quality of the optimization. Second, let us note that the error thresholds are expressed in base 2 in POP and in base 10 in Precimonious. For the relevance of comparisons, all the thresholds are expressed in base 10 in Tables 1 and 2. In practice, POP will use the base 2 threshold immediately lower than the required base 10 threshold. In Table 2, we indicate in bold the tool that exhibits better results for each error threshold and each program. Starting with the **arclength** program, POP(ILP) displays better results than the other tools by optimizing 28 variables. For an error threshold of 10^{-4}, 2464 bits are saved by POP(ILP) in 1.8 seconds while POP(SMT) saved only 1488 bits in more time (11 seconds). Precimonious were the slowest tool on this example, more than 2 minutes with 576 bits for only 9 variables optimized. For the **simpson** program, POP(ILP) do also better than both other tools. However, for the **rotation** program, POP(ILP) saves more bits than the other tools only for an error of 10^{-4} while Precimonious do well for this program for the rest of error thresholds. Finally, Precimonious fails to tune the **accelerometer** program (0 variables) at the time that POP(ILP) do faster (only 1 s) to save much more bits than POP(SMT) for any given error threshold.

In [4,5], we show how POP generates MPFR code [13] with the precision returned by the tuning and we run the programs. We also run a MPFR version with high precision (e.g. 300 bits) and compute the error that we compare to the threshold. The results show that the thresholds are respected.

6 Conclusion and Perspectives

In this article, we have introduced a new technique for precision tuning, clearly different from the existing ones. Instead of changing more or less randomly the data types of the numerical variables and running the programs to see what happens, we propose a semantical modelling of the propagation of the numerical errors throughout the code. This yields a system of constraints whose minimal solution gives the best tuning of the program, furthermore, in polynomial time. Two variants of this system are proposed. The first one corresponds to a pure ILP. The second one, which optimizes the propagation of carries in the elementary operations can be solved using policy iterations [9]. Proofs of correctness concerning the soundness of the analysis and the integer nature of the solutions have been presented in Sect. 4 and experimental results showing the efficiency of our method have been introduced in Sect. 5.

Compared to other approaches, the strength of our method is to find directly the minimal number of bits needed at each control point to get a certain accuracy on the results. Consequently, it is not dependant of a certain number of data types (e.g. the IEEE754 formats) and its complexity does not increase as the number of data types increases. The information provided may also be used to generate computations in the fixpoint arithmetic with an accuracy guaranty on the results. Concerning scalability, we generate a linear number of constraints and variables in the size of the analyzed program. The only limitation is the size of the problem accepted by the solver. Note that the number of variables could be reduced by assigning the same precision to a whole piece of code (for example an arithmetic expression, a line of code, a function, etc.) Code synthesis for the fixpoint arithmetic and assigning the same precision to pieces of code are perspectives we aim at explore at short term.

At longer term, other developments of the present work are planned. First we wish to adapt the techniques developed in this article to the special case of Deep Neural Networks for which it is important to save memory usage and computational resources. Second, we aim at using our precision tuning method to guide lossy compression techniques for floating-point datasets [12]. In this case, the bit-level accuracy inferred by our method would determine the compression rate of the lossy technique.

A   Appendix

We need a lemma on some algebraic operations stable on the set of functions written as the min-max of a finite family of affine functions. The functions are defined on $\mathbb{R}^d$.

Lemma 1. *The following statements hold:*

- *The sum of two min-max of a finite family of affine functions is a min-max of a finite family of affine functions.*
- *The maximum of two min-max of a finite family of affine functions is a min-max of a finite family of affine functions.*

Proof. Let g and h be two min-max of a finite family of affine functions and $f = g + h$. We have $g = \min_i \max_j g^{ij}$ and $h = \min_k \max_l h^{kl}$. Let $x \in \mathbb{R}^d$. There exist i, k such that $f(x) \geq \max_j g^{ij}(x) + \max_l h^{kl}(x) = \max_{j,l} g^{ij}(x) + h^{kl}(x)$. We have also, for all i, k, $f(x) \leq \max_j g^{ij}(x) + \max_l h^{kl}(x) = \max_{j,l} g^{ij}(x) + h^{kl}(x)$. We conclude that $f(x) = \min_{i,k} \max_{j,l} g^{ij}(x) + h^{kl}(x)$ for all x. We use the same argument for the max.   □

Proposition 2. *The following results hold:*

1. *Let ξ the constant function equal to 1. The system S_ξ^1 can be rewritten as $\{\mathsf{nsb} \in \mathbb{N}^{Lab} \mid F(\mathsf{nsb}) \leq (\mathsf{nsb})\}$ where F maps $\mathbb{R}^{Lab} \times \mathbb{R}^{Lab}$ to itself, $F(\mathbb{N}^{Lab} \times \mathbb{N}^{Lab}) \subseteq (\mathbb{N}^{Lab} \times \mathbb{N}^{Lab})$ and has coordinates which are the maximum of a finite family of affine order-preserving functions.*
2. *Let ξ the function such that $\xi(\ell)$ equals the function defined at Fig. 5. The system S_ξ can be rewritten as $\{(\mathsf{nsb}, \mathsf{nsb_e}) \in \mathbb{N}^{Lab} \times \mathbb{N}^{Lab} \mid F(\mathsf{nsb}, \mathsf{nsb_e}) \leq (\mathsf{nsb}, \mathsf{nsb_e})\}$ where F maps $\mathbb{R}^{Lab} \times \mathbb{R}^{Lab}$ to itself, $F(\mathbb{N}^{Lab} \times \mathbb{N}^{Lab}) \subseteq (\mathbb{N}^{Lab} \times \mathbb{N}^{Lab})$ and all its coordinates are the min-max of a finite family of affine functions.*

Proof. We only give details about the system S_ξ^1 (Fig. 4). By induction on the rules. We write $L = \{\ell \in Lab \mid F_\ell \text{ is constructed}\}$. This set is used in the proof to construct F inductively.

For the rule (CONST), there is nothing to do. For the rule (ID), if the label $\ell' = \rho(x) \in L$ then we define $F_{\ell'}(\mathsf{nsb}) = \max(F_{\ell'}(\mathsf{nsb}), \mathsf{nsb}(\ell))$. Otherwise $F_{\ell'}(\mathsf{nsb}) = \mathsf{nsb}(\ell)$. As $\mathsf{nsb} \mapsto \mathsf{nsb}(\ell)$ is order-preserving and the maximum of one affine function, $F_{\ell'}$ is the maximum of a finite family of order-preserving affine functions since max preserves order-preservation.

For the rules (ADD), (SUB), (MULT), (DIV), (MATH) and (ASSIGN), by induction, it suffices to focus on the new set of inequalities. If $\ell_1 \in L$, we define F_{ℓ_1} as the max with old definition and $RHS(\mathsf{nsb})$ i.e. $F_{\ell_1}(\mathsf{nsb}) = \max(RHS(\mathsf{nsb}), F_{\ell_1}(\mathsf{nsb}))$ where $RHS(\mathsf{nsb})$ is the right-hand side part of the new inequality. If $\ell_1 \notin L$, we define $F_{\ell_1}(\mathsf{nsb}) = RHS(\mathsf{nsb})$. In the latter rules, $RHS(\mathsf{nsb})$ are order-preserving affine functions. It follows that F_{ℓ_1} is the maximum of a finite family of order-preserving affine functions.

The result follows by induction for the rule (SEQ).

The rules (COND) and (WHILE) are treated as the rules (ADD), (SUB), (MULT), (DIV), (MATH) and (ASSIGN), by induction and the consideration of the new set of inequalities.

The last rule (REQ) constructs $F_{\rho(x)}$ either as the constant function equal to p at label $\rho(x)$ or the maximum of the old definition of $F_{\rho(x)}$ and p if $\rho(x) \in L$. The proof for the system S_ξ uses the same arguments and Lemma 1.   □

Proposition 3 (Algorithm correctness). *The sequence $(\sum_{\ell \in Lab} \mathsf{nsb}^k(\ell))_{0 \leq k \leq K}$ generated by Algorithm 1 satisfies the following properties:*

1. *$K < +\infty$ i.e. the sequence is of finite length;*
2. *each term of the sequence furnishes a feasible solution for Problem (11);*
3. *$\sum_{\ell \in Lab} \mathsf{nsb}^{k+1}(\ell) < \sum_{\ell \in Lab} \mathsf{nsb}^k(\ell)$ if $k < K - 1$ and $\sum_{\ell \in Lab} \mathsf{nsb}^K(\ell) = \sum_{\ell \in Lab} \mathsf{nsb}^{K-1}(\ell)$;*
4. *the number k is smaller than the number of policies.*

Proof. Let $\sum_{\ell \in Lab} \mathrm{nsb}^k(\ell)$ be a term of the sequence and $(\mathrm{nsb}^k, \mathrm{nsb_e}^k)$ be the optimal solution of $\mathrm{Min}\{\sum_{\ell \in Lab} \mathrm{nsb}(\ell) \mid f^{\pi^k}(\mathrm{nsb}, \mathrm{nsb_e}) \leq (\mathrm{nsb}, \mathrm{nsb_e}), \; \mathrm{nsb} \in \mathbb{N}^{Lab}, \; \mathrm{nsb_e} \in \mathbb{N}^{Lab}\}$. Then $F(\mathrm{nsb}^k, \mathrm{nsb_e}^k) \leq f^{\pi^k}(\mathrm{nsb}^k, \mathrm{nsb_e}^k)$ by definition of F. Moreover, $F(\mathrm{nsb}^k, \mathrm{nsb_e}^k) = f^{\pi^{k+1}}(\mathrm{nsb}^k, \mathrm{nsb_e}^k)$ and $f^{\pi^k}(\mathrm{nsb}^k, \mathrm{nsb_e}^k) \leq (\mathrm{nsb}^k, \mathrm{nsb_e}^k)$. This proves the second statement. Furthermore, it follows that $f^{\pi^{k+1}}(\mathrm{nsb}^k, \mathrm{nsb_e}^k) \leq (\mathrm{nsb}^k, \mathrm{nsb_e}^k)$ and $(\mathrm{nsb}^k, \mathrm{nsb_e}^k)$ is feasible for the minimisation problem for which $(\mathrm{nsb}^{k+1}, \mathrm{nsb_e}^{k+1})$ is an optimal solution. We conclude that $\sum_{\ell \in Lab} \mathrm{nsb}^{k+1}(\ell) \leq \sum_{\ell \in Lab} \mathrm{nsb}^k(\ell)$ and the Algorithm terminates if the equality holds or continues as the criterion strictly decreases. Finally, from the strict decrease, a policy cannot be selected twice without terminating the algorithm. In conclusion, the number of iterations is smaller than the number of policies. □

Proposition 4. *Let $G : [0, +\infty)^d \mapsto [0, +\infty)^d$ be an order-preserving function such that $G(\mathbb{N}^d) \subseteq \mathbb{N}^d$. Suppose that the set $\{y \in \mathbb{N}^d \mid G(y) \leq y\}$ is non-empty. Let $\varphi : \mathbb{R}^d \mapsto \mathbb{R}$ a strictly monotone function such that $\varphi(\mathbb{N}^d) \subseteq \mathbb{N}$. Then, the minimization problem below has an unique optimal solution which is integral.*

$$\underset{y \in [0, +\infty)^d}{\mathrm{Min}} \; \varphi(y) \; \text{ s. t. } \; G(y) \leq y$$

Proof. Let $L := \{x \in [0, +\infty)^d \mid G(x) \leq x\}$ and $u = \inf L$. It suffices to prove that $u \in \mathbb{N}^d$. Indeed, as φ is strictly monotone then $\varphi(u) < \varphi(x)$ for all $x \in [0, +\infty)^d$ s.t. $G(x) \leq x$ and $x \neq u$. The optimal solution is thus u. If $u = 0$, the result holds. Now suppose that $0 < u$, then $0 \leq G(0)$. Let $M := \{y \in \mathbb{N}^d \mid y \leq G(y), y \leq u\}$. Then $0 \in M$ and we write $v := \sup M$. As M is a complete lattice s.t. $G(M) \subseteq M$, from Tarski's theorem, v satisfies $G(v) = v$ and $v \leq u$. Moreover, $v \in \mathbb{N}^d$ and $v \leq u$. Again, from Tarski's theorem, u is the smallest fixpoint of G, it coincides with v. Then $u \in \mathbb{N}^d$. □

References

1. ANSI/IEEE: IEEE Standard for Binary Floating-point Arithmetic, std 754–2008 edn. (2008)
2. Ben Khalifa, D., Martel, M.: Precision tuning and internet of things. In: International Conference on Internet of Things, Embedded Systems and Communications, IINTEC 2019, pp. 80–85. IEEE (2019)
3. Ben Khalifa, D., Martel, M.: Precision tuning of an accelerometer-based pedometer algorithm for IoT devices. In: International Conference on Internet of Things and Intelligence System, IOTAIS 2020, pp. 113–119. IEEE (2020)
4. Ben Khalifa, D., Martel, M.: An evaluation of POP performance for tuning numerical programs in floating-point arithmetic. In: 4th International Conference on Information and Computer Technologies, ICICT 2021, Kahului, HI, USA, 11–14 March 2021, pp. 69–78. IEEE (2021)
5. Ben Khalifa, D., Martel, M.: A study of the floating-point tuning behaviour on the n-body problem. In: Gervasi, O., et al. (eds.) ICCSA 2021. LNCS, vol. 12953. Springer, Cham (2021). https://doi.org/10.1007/978-3-030-86976-2_12

6. Ben Khalifa, D., Martel, M., Adjé, A.: POP: a tuning assistant for mixed-precision floating-point computations. In: Hasan, O., Mallet, F. (eds.) FTSCS 2019. CCIS, vol. 1165, pp. 77–94. Springer, Cham (2020). https://doi.org/10.1007/978-3-030-46902-3_5

7. Cherubin, S., Agosta, G.: Tools for reduced precision computation: a survey. ACM Comput. Surv. **53**(2), 1–35 (2020)

8. Chiang, W., Baranowski, M., Briggs, I., Solovyev, A., Gopalakrishnan, G., Rakamaric, Z.: Rigorous floating-point mixed-precision tuning. In: Proceedings of the 44th ACM SIGPLAN Symposium on Principles of Programming Languages, POPL, pp. 300–315. ACM (2017)

9. Costan, A., Gaubert, S., Goubault, E., Martel, M., Putot, S.: A policy iteration algorithm for computing fixed points in static analysis of programs. In: Etessami, K., Rajamani, S.K. (eds.) CAV 2005. LNCS, vol. 3576, pp. 462–475. Springer, Heidelberg (2005). https://doi.org/10.1007/11513988_46

10. Cousot, P., et al.: The ASTREÉ analyzer. In: Sagiv, M. (ed.) ESOP 2005. LNCS, vol. 3444, pp. 21–30. Springer, Heidelberg (2005). https://doi.org/10.1007/978-3-540-31987-0_3

11. Darulova, E., Horn, E., Sharma, S.: Sound mixed-precision optimization with rewriting. In: Proceedings of the 9th ACM/IEEE International Conference on Cyber-Physical Systems, ICCPS, pp. 208–219. IEEE Computer Society/ACM (2018)

12. Diffenderfer, J., Fox, A., Hittinger, J.A.F., Sanders, G., Lindstrom, P.G.: Error analysis of ZFP compression for floating-point data. SIAM J. Sci. Comput. **41**(3), A1867–A1898 (2019)

13. Fousse, L., Hanrot, G., Lefèvre, V., Pélissier, P., Zimmermann, P.: MPFR: a multiple-precision binary floating-point library with correct rounding. ACM Trans. Math. Softw. **33**, 13-es (2007)

14. Guo, H., Rubio-González, C.: Exploiting community structure for floating-point precision tuning. In: Proceedings of the 27th ACM SIGSOFT International Symposium on Software Testing and Analysis, ISSTA 2018, pp. 333–343. ACM (2018)

15. Gustafson, Y.: Beating floating point at its own game: posit arithmetic. Supercomput. Front. Innov. Int. J. **4**(2), 71–86 (2017). https://doi.org/10.14529/jsfi170206

16. Kotipalli, P.V., Singh, R., Wood, P., Laguna, I., Bagchi, S.: AMPT-GA: automatic mixed precision floating point tuning for GPU applications. In: Proceedings of the ACM International Conference on Supercomputing, ICS, pp. 160–170. ACM (2019)

17. Lam, M.O., Hollingsworth, J.K., de Supinski, B.R., LeGendre, M.P.: Automatically adapting programs for mixed-precision floating-point computation. In: International Conference on Supercomputing, ICS 2013, pp. 369–378. ACM (2013)

18. Martel, M.: Floating-point format inference in mixed-precision. In: Barrett, C., Davies, M., Kahsai, T. (eds.) NFM 2017. LNCS, vol. 10227, pp. 230–246. Springer, Cham (2017). https://doi.org/10.1007/978-3-319-57288-8_16

19. McKeeman, W.M.: Algorithm 145: adaptive numerical integration by Simpson's rule. Commun. ACM **5**(12), 604 (1962)

20. Morris, D., Saponas, T., Guillory, A., Kelner, I.: RecoFit: using a wearable sensor to find, recognize, and count repetitive exercises. In: Conference on Human Factors in Computing Systems (2014)

21. de Moura, L., Bjørner, N.: Z3: an efficient SMT solver. In: Ramakrishnan, C.R., Rehof, J. (eds.) TACAS 2008. LNCS, vol. 4963, pp. 337–340. Springer, Heidelberg (2008). https://doi.org/10.1007/978-3-540-78800-3_24

22. Papadimitriou, C.H.: On the complexity of integer programming. J. ACM (JACM) **28**(4), 765–768 (1981)

23. Parker, D.S.: Monte Carlo arithmetic: exploiting randomness in floating-point arithmetic. Technical report CSD-970002, University of California (Los Angeles) (1997)
24. Rubio-González, C., et al.: Precimonious: tuning assistant for floating-point precision. In: International Conference for High Performance Computing, Networking, Storage and Analysis, SC 2013, pp. 27:1–27:12. ACM (2013)
25. Schrijver, A.: Theory of Linear and Integer Programming. Wiley, New York (1998)

Hash Consed Points-To Sets

Mohamad Barbar[1,2] and Yulei Sui[1(✉)]

[1] University of Technology Sydney, Ultimo, Australia
`yulei.sui@uts.edu.au`
[2] CSIRO's Data61, Sydney, Australia

Abstract. Points-to analysis is a fundamental static analysis, on which many other analyses and optimisations are built. The goal of points-to analysis is to statically approximate the set of abstract objects that a pointer can point to at runtime. Due to the nature of static analysis, points-to analysis introduces much redundancy which can result in duplicate points-to sets and duplicate set union operations, particularly when analysing large programs precisely. To improve performance, there has been extensive effort in mitigating duplication at the algorithmic level through, for example, cycle elimination and variable substitution.

Unlike previous approaches which make algorithmic changes to points-to analysis, this work aims to improve the underlying data structure, which is less studied. Inspired by hash consing from the functional programming community, this paper introduces the use of hash consed points-to sets to reduce the effects of this duplication on both space and time without any high-level algorithmic change. Hash consing can effectively handle duplicate points-to set by representing points-to sets once, and referring to such representations through references, and can speed up duplicate union operations through efficient memoisation. We have implemented and evaluated our approach using 16 real-world C/C++ programs (more than 9.5 million lines of LLVM instructions). Our results show that our approach speeds up state-of-the-art Andersen's analysis by 1.85× on average (up to 3.21×) and staged flow-sensitive analysis (SFS) by 1.69× on average (up to 2.23×). We also observe an average ≥4.93× (up to ≥15.52×) memory usage reduction for SFS.

Keywords: Points-to analysis · Hash consing · Memoisation

1 Introduction

Points-to analysis is a fundamental static analysis used to, for example, detect memory errors [32,53], detect concurrency bugs [9,37], perform typestate verification [17,51], enforce control-flow integrity [14,15], perform symbolic execution [48,49], and perform code embedding [10,45]. The aim of points-to analysis

© Springer Nature Switzerland AG 2021
C. Drăgoi et al. (Eds.): SAS 2021, LNCS 12913, pp. 25–48, 2021.
https://doi.org/10.1007/978-3-030-88806-0_2

is to compute an approximation of the set of abstract objects that a pointer can refer to. Inclusion-based analysis, as the most commonly used form of points-to analysis, formulates points-to resolution as a set constraint solving problem whereby each program statement produces one or more set constraints which are translated into union operations between two points-to sets and are solved until a fixed-point is reached.

When analysing real-world programs, many pointers may yield exactly the same points-to sets during constraint resolution. This becomes more prevalent especially as analyses become more precise. For example, unlike flow-insensitive analysis which computes a single points-to set for each pointer, flow-sensitive analysis computes and maintains points-to sets at different program points, but unfortunately introduces many duplicate points-to sets. Table 1 provides the proportions of duplicate points-to sets under two popular points-to analyses (Andersen's analysis [36] and staged flow-sensitive analysis or SFS [23]) for 16 real-world programs. Columns 2 and 5 show the number of pointers maintained in the analyses. Columns 3 and 6 list the number of those pointers which refer to the 5 most common points-to sets. Columns 4 and 7 list the proportions of the pointers in Columns 3 and 6. The empty points-to set and pointers which have an empty points-to set are excluded. Both Andersen's analysis and SFS are field-sensitive inclusion-based analyses, however, SFS maintains pointers on a per program point basis to achieve flow-sensitivity, resulting in more pointers and duplicate points-to sets. We see that, on average, the 5 most common points-to sets are referred to by around 60% and 90% of pointers for Andersen's analysis and SFS, respectively. Clearly, repeatedly representing the same points-to sets is redundant, memory-wise.

Furthermore, since the resulting points-to sets of many pointers are the same, most may have reached that result with the same union operations and it is very costly to perform duplicate unions. That is, if two pointers points-to set are the same (i.e., $pt(p) = pt(q)$) by the end of the analysis, it is possible that both points-to sets were built up through the same union operations. Thus, many union operations are in fact duplicates of operations which have been previously performed. This has strong implications on performance as conducting points-to set unions produced by the set constraints forms a bulk of analysis time.

Both the number of duplicate points-to sets tracked and the number of unions performed can be reduced but most previous solutions have been analysis-specific requiring algorithmic changes, which may not be applicable to other points-to analyses. For example, either, or, both, can be achieved by merging equivalent pointers offline [4,21–23,39] or online [20,29,34], selectively applying precision [30,41], or carefully choosing how to solve constraints [35,36]. Despite these efforts, duplication still exists and pushing the boundaries through algorithmic changes to the points-to analysis may lead to increasingly diminishing returns on performance.

In this paper, we aim to explore solutions at the data structure level – which is easily applicable to a range of points-to analyses – to reduce the influence of these duplicate operations and points-to sets on time and space. We leverage the idea of hash consing [7,16,19,24], which aims to quickly identify structurally equivalent values, from the functional programming community, to help solve

Table 1. The number of pointers tracked, the number of those pointers which refer to one of the 5 most common points-to sets, and that proportion for Andersen's analysis and SFS.

Program	Andersen's			SFS		
	Pointers	Top 5	Prop.	Pointers	Top 5	Prop.
dhcpcd	21572	13651	63.28%	851784	839518	98.56%
nsd	38328	28022	73.11%	2423193	2399449	99.02%
tmux	49080	36999	75.39%	4331232	2483020	57.33%
gawk	47673	30631	64.25%	8467667	8353204	98.65%
bash	36924	27118	73.44%	6067608	5470244	90.15%
mutt	65756	44886	68.26%	8261029	7897442	95.60%
lynx	260220	181359	69.69%	17451804	16362946	93.76%
xpdf	105743	55651	52.63%	32507885	32387655	99.63%
python3	184189	119043	64.63%	114439707	94946890	82.97%
svn	213125	167042	78.38%	91817728	88324837	96.20%
emacs	250739	163956	65.39%	252728727	248665346	98.39%
git	243388	132674	54.51%	182364152	155306147	85.16%
kakoune	182631	55491	30.38%	37689778	37157978	98.59%
ruby	114277	66634	58.31%	71941456	69333326	96.37%
squid	725067	389949	53.78%	189749146	159336073	83.97%
wireshark	326974	147939	45.24%	23789094	22960321	96.52%
Geo. Mean			60.48%			91.19%

the problem of duplicate points-to sets and unions operations. Hash consing is the process of maintaining single immutable representations of data structures which can then be shared elsewhere referentially [38, 42]. In our context, this means that each unique points-to set is maintained only once such that points-to sets becomes persistent.

Originally, hash consing was used to memoise construction to avoid creating the same object twice, transforming construction into a hash table lookup of the elements of the object. If we view our union operation as a constructor, taking two points-to sets to create a new one, we can transform many union operations into hash table lookups (of a pair of references), which would be much cheaper than standard set unions as points-to sets become larger. Thus hash consing is a means for efficient memoisation allowing us to perform faster set unions. During points-to set resolution, we build up hash tables of previously performed operations, and use those results if the same operation occurs again.

Moreover, with points-to sets being represented as references we can perform fast comparisons between such sets in constant, instead of linear, time. Thus, we also explore the possibility of practically skipping some set operations completely by exploiting mathematical set properties. For example, since each points-to set, e.g., x and y, is represented as a reference, the operands of a union like $x \cup y$ can be compared cheaply for equality, in which case the result is x/y, since the union operation is idempotent.

Our approach is efficient yet simple to implement, independent to the points-to analysis used, maintains precision, and works alongside the many algorithmic advances listed earlier. Moreover, our approach does not mandate a specific representation of points-to sets as long as each pointer would otherwise be assigned discrete points-to sets. As far as we know, this paper is the first to describe general hash consing and its effects to the base aspects of inclusion-based points-to analysis. We have implemented our approach on top of points-to analysis framework SVF [47] and evaluated our approach using 16 real-world open-source programs (more than 9.5 million lines of LLVM instructions). For these programs, we find an average improvement in time taken of 1.85× for Andersen's analysis and 1.69× for SFS, and we observe improvements of up to 3.21× and 2.23× for the two analyses, respectively. Along with improved time, we see roughly the same memory usage for Andersen's analysis and an average reduction of ≥4.93× (up to ≥15.52×) for SFS.

To summarise, our contributions are:

- Persistent points-to data structure using hash consed points-to sets with less memory for precise whole program points-to analyses.
- The use of hash consing to more efficiently perform points-to set union operations through cheap memoisation and exploitation of set properties.
- An evaluation of the impact of hash consing on field-sensitive Andersen's analysis and SFS using 16 real world open source C/C++ programs, as well as a discussion on the amount of duplication found in these analyses.

2 Background and Motivation

This section first introduces a program representation for points-to analysis to be built upon. We then provide a brief summary of whole-program flow-insensitive and flow-sensitive inclusion-based points-to analysis. Finally, we give two short examples to illustrate the presence of duplicate points-to sets and union operations produced by these two analyses to motivate how hash consing can help.

2.1 Background

Like many other C/C++ analyses [2,4,23,30,47], we perform points-to analysis on top of the LLVM-IR of a program. In LLVM's partial SSA form [28], the set of all program variables $\mathcal{V} = \mathcal{O} \cup \mathcal{P}$ is split into two subsets: (1) $\mathcal{O}$, or the set of *address-taken variables*, which represents all possible abstract memory objects and their fields, and (2) $\mathcal{P}$, or the set of *top-level variables*, which represents all stack virtual registers (symbols starting with %) and global pointers (symbols starting with @). Top-level variables, $\mathcal{P}$, are explicit in that they are accessed directly whereas address-taken objects, $\mathcal{O}$, are implicit and can only be accessed indirectly at LOAD and STORE instructions through top-level variables.

Given $p, q \in \mathcal{P}$ and $o \in \mathcal{O}$, after the SSA conversion, we represent a C/C++ program using the following five types of instructions:

- ALLOC instructions, $p = alloc_o$, representing allocation of abstract object o.
- COPY instructions, $p = q$, representing assignment between two top-level pointers.
- FIELD instructions, $p = \&q \rightarrow f_i$, representing assignment of the i-th field (f_i) of the object which q points to.
- LOAD instructions, $p = *q$, representing assignment from a dereferenced top-level pointer.
- STORE instructions, $*p = q$, representing assignment to an abstract memory object through a dereferenced top-level pointer.

With the above instructions, Fig. 1 presents a flow-insensitive inclusion-based analysis commonly referred to as Andersen's analysis [1] augmented with field-sensitivity [35]. Each pointer p is assigned a points-to set $pt(p)$ representing an approximation of the set of abstract memory objects that p may point to. Andersen's analysis is performed by generating constraints between points-to sets according to the five inference rules. The COPY, LOAD, and STORE rules produce inclusion or union constraints like $pt(q) \subseteq pt(p)$ which means the points-to set of p is the union of its old value and the points-to set of q, i.e., $pt(p) = pt(p) \cup pt(q)$. The produced constraints are iteratively solved with points-to sets growing monotonically until a fixed-point is reached.

$$[\text{ALLOC}] \; \frac{p = alloc_o}{\{o\} \subseteq pt(p)} \qquad [\text{COPY}] \; \frac{p = q}{pt(q) \subseteq pt(p)} \qquad [\text{FIELD}] \; \frac{p = \&q \rightarrow f_i \quad o \in pt(q)}{\{o.f_i\} \subseteq pt(p)}$$

$$[\text{LOAD}] \; \frac{p = *q \quad o \in pt(q)}{pt(o) \subseteq pt(p)} \qquad [\text{STORE}] \; \frac{*p = q \quad o \in pt(p)}{pt(q) \subseteq pt(o)}$$

Fig. 1. Inference rules for a flow-insensitive inclusion-based points-to analysis.

More precise analyses typically need to compute and maintain more points-to relations. For example, in a flow-sensitive analysis, an object accessed at different program points can have different points-to sets, thus requiring more points-to sets and constraints. Figure 2 gives a simple inclusion-based flow-sensitive analysis [30] augmented with field-sensitivity. Since the analysis is flow-sensitive, the order of instructions now matters and so each instruction is prefixed by a label like ℓ to represent the points-to information at a particular program point.

Unlike flow-insensitive analysis which computes a single points-to set for each variable, flow-sensitive analysis maintains separate points-to sets at different program points for each memory object. To represent points-to information flow-sensitively, points-to sets of memory objects are maintained before $(pt[\overline{\ell}](o))$ and after $(pt[\underline{\ell}](o))$ instructions. Thus, points-to sets need to be propagated within program points through the   [SU/WU]   rule and, if there exists control flow between two instructions ($\ell \rightarrow \ell'$), across program points through the   [CFLOW]

$$[\text{ALLOC}] \; \frac{\ell : p = alloc_o}{\{o\} \subseteq pt(p)} \quad [\text{COPY}] \; \frac{\ell : p = q}{pt(q) \subseteq pt(p)} \quad [\text{FIELD}] \; \frac{p = \&q \rightarrow f_i \quad o \in pt(q)}{\{o.f_i\} \subseteq pt(p)}$$

$$[\text{LOAD}] \; \frac{\ell : p = *q \quad o \in pt(q)}{pt[\bar{\ell}](o) \subseteq pt(p)} \quad\quad\quad [\text{STORE}] \; \frac{\ell : *p = q \quad o \in pt(p)}{pt(q) \subseteq pt[\ell](o)}$$

$$[\text{SU/WU}] \; \frac{\ell : *p = \_ \quad o \in \mathcal{O} \setminus kill(\ell)}{pt[\bar{\ell}](o) \subseteq pt[\ell](o)} \quad\quad [\text{CFLOW}] \; \frac{\ell \rightarrow \ell'}{\forall o \in \mathcal{O}. \; pt[\ell](o) \subseteq pt[\bar{\ell'}](o)}$$

$$kill(\ell : *p = \_) \triangleq \begin{cases} \{o\} & \text{if } pt(p) \equiv \{o\} \wedge o \text{ is singleton} \\ \mathcal{O} & \text{if } pt(p) \equiv \varnothing \\ \varnothing & \text{otherwise} \end{cases}$$

Fig. 2. Inference rules for a field-sensitive and flow-sensitive inclusion-based points-to analysis.

rule. This all results in extra set unions between points-to sets being performed. With the *kill* function, the [SU/WU] rule can perform strong updates for singletons [30], another way flow-sensitivity produces more precise results.

To reduce some of these redundancies, state-of-the-art flow-sensitive analyses like staged flow-sensitive analysis (SFS) [23] perform points-to propagation on a sparse def-use graph rather than a control-flow graph of a program. Despite this, redundancies still exist, and duplication is high, as will be shown in Sect. 4.

2.2 Motivating Examples

In this section, we show the duplication of points-to sets and operations that occurs in flow-insensitive and flow-sensitive analyses. First, let us consider flow-insensitive analysis of a small program fragment in Fig. 3a where $p, q, r, x, y \in \mathcal{P}$ and $o_1, o_2, o_3, o_4 \in \mathcal{O}$ and Fig. 3b shows the constraints produced to analyse this program fragment following the rules in Fig. 1. Since the analysis is flow-insensitive, we solve for a points-to set per variable. We use $pt(p)$ to denote the points-to set of pointer p and use $\{o_1\}_p$ to denote the value of $pt(p)$ when it, for example, contains the points-to target o_1. In analysing the program fragment, we assume $pt(p) = \{o_1\}$, $pt(q) = \{o_2\}$, and $pt(r) = \{o_3, o_4\}$.

In practice, these constraints are handed to a constraint solver [13,20,35,36] which will perform unions like those in Fig. 3c until a fixed-point is reached, i.e., when points-to sets no longer change. In Fig. 3c, operations are numbered with the constraints they correspond to and duplicate initial operations are highlighted in grey. For brevity, we have only shown the first operation which would result from a constraint. Ultimately, each constraint actually results in the same union being performed so 3 of the operations are duplicates of the first. In real-world programs, such points-to sets may be large, containing hundreds or thousands of objects, meaning repeatedly performing these unions can be expensive. The resulting points-to sets of the analysis are shown in Fig. 3d, with duplicates

$1 : *p = r;$ $1 : \forall o \in pt(p). \ pt(r) \subseteq pt(o)$ $1 : \{o_3, o_4\}_r \subseteq \{ \ \}_{o_1}$

$2 : *q = r;$ $2 : \forall o \in pt(q). \ pt(r) \subseteq pt(o)$ $2 : \boxed{\{o_3, o_4\}_r} \subseteq \{ \ \}_{o_2}$

$3 : x = *p;$ $3 : \forall o \in pt(p). \ pt(o) \subseteq pt(x)$ $3 : \{o_3, o_4\}_{o_1} \subseteq \{ \ \}_x$

$4 : y = *q;$ $4 : \forall o \in pt(q). \ pt(o) \subseteq pt(y)$ $4 : \{o_3, o_4\}_{o_2} \subseteq \{ \ \}_y$

(a) Program fragment.   (b) Constraints.

(c) Initial operations.

$pt(p) = \{o_1\}$ $pt(q) = \{o_2\}$ $pt(r) = \{o_3, o_4\}$ $pt(x) = \boxed{\{o_3, o_4\}}$ $pt(y) = \boxed{\{o_3, o_4\}}$

$pt(o_1) = \boxed{\{o_3, o_4\}}$ $pt(o_2) = \boxed{\{o_3, o_4\}}$ $pt(o_3) = \{ \ \}$ $pt(o_4) = \boxed{\{ \ \}}$

(d) Result.

Fig. 3. Example program fragment in (a), the constraints generated for Andersen's analysis in (b), the initial operations performed to fulfil the constraints in (c), and the final results in (d). We assume $pt(p) = \{o_1\}$, $pt(q) = \{o_2\}$, and $pt(r) = \{o_3, o_4\}$. Duplicate points-to sets and operations are highlighted in grey.

also highlighted in grey. We see that 5 of the 9 points-to sets have occurred before, pointing to much duplication. This can be problematic as points-to sets grow, with statically sized representations, or as analyses introduce more variables.

We shorten the program fragment above in Fig. 4a[1] to illustrate the same issues in flow-sensitive points-to analysis. Figure 4b lists the constraints generated according to the rules in Fig. 2 followed by the initial operations performed to fulfil those constraints and the final result of the analysis in Figs. 4c and 4d. As before, we highlight duplicate operations and points-to sets in grey.

Since the analysis is flow-sensitive, we need to maintain points-to sets of objects at program points for precise results, thus resulting in more pointers being kept track of. By maintaining points-to sets at program points, we also require more operations to handle the flow of control. This can all be seen by the increase in number of operations and points-to sets in Figs. 4c and d despite the smaller program fragment. The improved precision can be seen through the differing points-to sets of some objects at different program points, for example, $pt[\overline{1}](o_1) \neq pt[\underline{1}](o_1)$. However, this increased precision comes at a cost of increased redundancy as some points-to sets do not differ between program points, like those of o_3 and o_4. Thus, we see that there are only 4 unique points-to sets out of 19, and 3 unique operations out of 14, meaning that the analysis is maintaining duplicate points-to sets and performing duplicate operations.

We note that SFS, one of the analyses we evaluate our approach on, can remove some of this duplication and redundancy through complex algorithmic changes to the analysis in Fig. 2, but much duplication still exists, as will be seen in Sect. 4. We also note that although many points-to sets in these exam-

---

[1] Due to the large number of points-to sets and unions flow-sensitive analysis produces.

$$1 : \forall o \in pt(p). \ pt(r) \subseteq pt(o)$$
$$1 : \forall o \in \mathcal{O}. \ pt[\overline{1}](o) \subseteq pt[\underline{1}](o)$$
$$1/2 : \forall o \in \mathcal{O}. \ pt[\underline{1}](o) \subseteq pt[\overline{2}](o)$$
$$2 : \forall o \in pt(q). \ pt(r) \subseteq pt(o)$$
$$2 : \forall o \in \mathcal{O}. \ pt[\overline{2}](o) \subseteq pt[\underline{2}](o)$$

$$1 : *p = r;$$
$$2 : *q = r;$$

(a) Program fragment.   (b) Constraints.

$1 : \{o_3, o_4\}_r \subseteq \{\ \}_{[\underline{1}]o_1}$ $2 : \{o_3, o_4\}_r \subseteq \{\ \}_{o_2}$

$1 : \{\ \}_{[\overline{1}]o_1} \subseteq \{o_3, o_4\}_{[\underline{1}]o_1}$ $1/2 : \{o_3, o_4\}_{[\underline{1}]o_1} \subseteq \{\ \}_{[\overline{2}]o_1}$ $2 : \{o_3, o_4\}_{[\overline{2}]o_1} \subseteq \{\ \}_{[\overline{2}]o_1}$

$1 : \{\ \}_{[\overline{1}]o_2} \subseteq \{\ \}_{[\underline{1}]o_2}$ $1/2 : \{\ \}_{[\underline{1}]o_2} \subseteq \{\ \}_{[\overline{2}]o_2}$ $2 : \{\ \}_{[\overline{2}]o_2} \subseteq \{o_3, o_4\}_{[\overline{2}]o_2}$

$1 : \{\ \}_{[\overline{1}]o_3} \subseteq \{\ \}_{[\underline{1}]o_3}$ $1/2 : \{\ \}_{[\underline{1}]o_3} \subseteq \{\ \}_{[\overline{2}]o_3}$ $2 : \{\ \}_{[\overline{2}]o_3} \subseteq \{\ \}_{[\overline{2}]o_3}$

$1 : \{\ \}_{[\overline{1}]o_4} \subseteq \{\ \}_{[\underline{1}]o_4}$ $1/2 : \{\ \}_{[\underline{1}]o_4} \subseteq \{\ \}_{[\overline{2}]o_4}$ $2 : \{\ \}_{[\overline{2}]o_4} \subseteq \{\ \}_{[\overline{2}]o_4}$

(c) Initial operations.

$$pt(p) = \{o_1\} \quad pt(q) = \{o_2\} \quad pt(r) = \{o_3, o_4\}$$

$$pt[\overline{1}](o_1) = \{\ \} \quad pt[\overline{1}](o_2) = \{\ \} \quad pt[\overline{1}](o_3) = \{\ \} \quad pt[\overline{1}](o_4) = \{\ \}$$

$$pt[\underline{1}](o_1) = \{o_3, o_4\} \quad pt[\underline{1}](o_2) = \{\ \} \quad pt[\underline{1}](o_3) = \{\ \} \quad pt[\underline{1}](o_4) = \{\ \}$$

$$pt[\overline{2}](o_1) = \{o_3, o_4\} \quad pt[\overline{2}](o_2) = \{\ \} \quad pt[\overline{2}](o_3) = \{\ \} \quad pt[\overline{2}](o_4) = \{\ \}$$

$$pt[\underline{2}](o_1) = \{o_3, o_4\} \quad pt[\underline{2}](o_2) = \{o_3, o_4\} \quad pt[\underline{2}](o_3) = \{\ \} \quad pt[\underline{2}](o_4) = \{\ \}$$

(d) Result.

Fig. 4. Example program fragment in (a), the constraints generated for a flow-sensitive analysis in (b), the initial operations performed to fulfil the constraints in (c), and the final results in (d). We assume $pt(p) = \{o_1\}$, $pt(q) = \{o_2\}$, and $pt(r) = \{o_3, o_4\}$. Duplicate points-to sets and operations are highlighted in grey.

ples were empty sets which can be easily represented, real-world programs show duplication of larger points-to sets and more complex union operations.

3   Approach

This section introduces hash consed points-to sets and its application to points-to analysis. We then describe optimisations that can use hash consing to efficiently exploit set properties for further performance improvement.

3.1   Hash Consed Points-To Sets

Hash consing is used to create immutable data structures which can be shared (referentially) to avoid duplication. A common example of hash consing is string interning [18, §3.10.5] whereby a compiler or runtime stores strings in a global pool and assigns pointers to strings in that global pool rather than private copies. In our context, we want points-to sets to be stored once in a global pool, so that we deal with references to points-to sets rather than concrete points-to sets.

To do this, whenever a points-to set is created, we perform an interning routine. We check if that points-to set exists in our global pool, and

- If it exists, return a reference to the equivalent set in the global pool.
- Otherwise, add the points-to set to the global pool and return a reference to the newly added points-to set.

This process can be achieved by a single hash table mapping each points-to sets to a single canonical reference. Now, instead of using $pt(p)$ during the analysis, we use $pt_r(p)$ which is a reference to the points-to set of p in the global pool. Dereferencing a points-to set reference as $dr(pt_r(p))$ would be equivalent to $pt(p)$ and can be used to iterate over the points-to set, for example. Given that $pt_r(p) = pt_r(q)$, $dr(pt_r(p))$ and $dr(pt_r(q))$ would also be equivalent and actually be accessing the same singly stored points-to set in the global pool. This can save significant memory if duplicate points-to sets are common.

On its own, this process does not save time, and may cost more time to perform the interning routine, especially as we perform many unions creating points-to sets which need to be interned. Since each unique points-to set exists once in the program, we can efficiently memoise operations, including the union operation. This can be achieved by a hash table, which we call an operations table, mapping two points-to set references to the points-to set reference which refers to the result of the actual operation. The union between two points-to set references $pt_r(p) \cup pt_r(q)$ can be performed by looking up the union operations table with the $\langle pt_r(p), pt_r(q) \rangle$ pair as the key (i.e., operation), and

- If the key exists, returning the associated value, i.e., the reference to the result of the operation.
- Otherwise, performing a concrete union between $dr(pt_r(p))$ and $dr(pt_r(q))$, interning the result, associating the operation with the result in the operations table, and returning it.

With many union operations being duplicates, those would be performed as constant time hash table lookups, rather than linear time set unions[2] which can be expensive depending on sizes of points-to sets. The intersection and difference operations can also be memoised the same way, if necessary.

Without hash consing, memoising operations would not be efficient as we would need to hash entire points-to sets, i.e., we would map $\langle pt(p), pt(q) \rangle$ to another concrete points-to set rather than mapping a reference pair to a reference. Collisions would also be expensive to resolve as determining equality would then be linear in the size of the colliding points-to set pairs. With references, equality can be determined in constant time.

---

[2] For our SVF-based implementation we use sparse bit-vectors (Sect. 4.1).

$$\boxed{\begin{array}{l} \{o_1\} \mapsto r_1 \\ \{o_2\} \mapsto r_2 \\ \{o_3, o_4\} \mapsto r_3 \\ \{\ \} \mapsto r_4 \end{array}}$$

(a) Global pool mapping points-to sets to references.

$$\boxed{\langle r_3, r_4 \rangle \mapsto r_3}$$

(b) Union operations table.

$$pt_r(p) = r_1 \quad pt_r(q) = r_2 \quad pt_r(r) = r_3 \quad pt_r(x) = r_3 \quad pt_r(y) = r_3$$
$$pt_r(o_1) = r_3 \quad pt_r(o_2) = r_3 \quad pt_r(o_3) = r_4 \quad pt_r(o_4) = r_4$$

(c) Result.

Fig. 5. Global pool of points-to sets in (a), the union operations table in (b), and the result in (c) using references instead of concrete points-to sets for the analysis in Fig. 3.

$$\boxed{\begin{array}{l} \{o_1\} \mapsto r_1 \\ \{o_2\} \mapsto r_2 \\ \{o_3, o_4\} \mapsto r_3 \\ \{\ \} \mapsto r_4 \end{array}}$$

(a) Global pool mapping points-to sets to references.

$$\boxed{\begin{array}{l} \langle r_3, r_4 \rangle \mapsto r_3 \\ \langle r_4, r_4 \rangle \mapsto r_4 \\ \langle r_4, r_3 \rangle \mapsto r_3 \end{array}}$$

(b) Union operations table.

$$pt(p) = r_1 \quad pt(q) = r_2 \quad pt(r) = r_3$$
$$pt[\overline{1}](o_1) = r_4 \quad pt[\overline{1}](o_2) = r_4 \quad pt[\overline{1}](o_3) = r_4 \quad pt[\overline{1}](o_4) = r_4$$
$$pt[\underline{1}](o_1) = r_3 \quad pt[\underline{1}](o_2) = r_4 \quad pt[\underline{1}](o_3) = r_4 \quad pt[\underline{1}](o_4) = r_4$$
$$pt[\overline{2}](o_1) = r_3 \quad pt[\overline{2}](o_2) = r_4 \quad pt[\overline{2}](o_3) = r_4 \quad pt[\overline{2}](o_4) = r_4$$
$$pt[\underline{2}](o_1) = r_3 \quad pt[\underline{2}](o_2) = r_3 \quad pt[\underline{2}](o_3) = r_4 \quad pt[\underline{2}](o_4) = r_4$$

(c) Result.

Fig. 6. Global pool of points-to sets in (a), the union operations table in (b), and the result in (c) using references instead of concrete points-to sets for the analysis in Fig. 4.

Figures 5 and 6 show how our analysis would look for the examples in Figs. 3 and 4 respectively. Three of the four union operations between points-to sets $\{o_3, o_4\}$ and $\{\ \}$ are performed as cheap lookups in the operations table in Fig. 5b. This is because the first time we perform a concrete operation, we cache it in the operations table, and perform a fast lookup on subsequent operations. As in Fig. 5c, we store references to points-to sets in the global pool (Fig. 5a) rather than concrete points-to sets, and so we only store 4 concrete points-to sets. Figure 6 illustrates that all the initial points-to unions in the flow-sensitive example are translated into 3 unique reference operations. Furthermore, for the flow-sensitive example, the effect of using references into the global pool for points-to sets is more drastic since there are so many pointers tracked, saving significant memory.

3.2   Exploiting Set Properties

In this section, we describe some optimisations which exploit the properties of sets to further improve efficiency of union operations on hash consed points-to sets. We note that even though our rules in Figs. 1 and 2 only perform unions, practical implementations may perform intersection and difference operations. Furthermore, clients may perform some of these operations too, like alias analysis which performs intersection tests. These operations can be memoised in the same way as unions above, and we exploit their properties in this section too.

Commutative Operations. For commutative operations like unions and intersections, performing an operation twice with the operands flipped is duplication though this would not be detected in the operations tables. For example, assuming $pt_r(p) = x$ and $pt_r(q) = y$, if we perform $x \cup y = z$ for the first time, we would store a mapping from the pair $\langle x, y \rangle$ to the result z in the union operations table. If the analysis was to perform $y \cup x$, it would not find the operation memoised, despite the result also being z, as $\langle y, x \rangle$ would not be cached in the union operations table.

To resolve this, operations should always be ordered deterministically. This is easy to achieve with hash consing because points-to sets are references and can be compared in constant time. Now, to perform $x \cup y$ or $y \cup x$, we would perform the operation in the same order depending on whether x is "less than" y, and so only a single instance would be stored in the union operations table. In Fig. 6b, the first and third operation are actually equivalent, and under this scheme would be stored once as $\langle r_3, r_4 \rangle \mapsto r_3$.

Property Operations. In some cases, the result of an operation can be determined instantly with only trivial comparisons without any concrete operation or hash table lookup. We refer to these cases as *property operations*, and we describe these cases for unions, intersections, and differences below. We set e to refer to the empty points-to set, and for commutative operations (i.e., unions and intersections), we assume the operands have already been ordered and that the reference e is the least reference (so it is always the first operand in the commutative operations it appears in).

Unions. Given the ordered union operation between references x and y, $x \cup y$, and that the result would be r,

$$x = e \Rightarrow r = y, \text{ and}$$
$$x = y \Rightarrow r = x.$$

All operations in Figs. 5b and 6b are actually property operations and caching is unnecessary.

Intersections. Given the ordered intersection operation between references x and y, $x \cap y$, and that the result would be r,

$$x = e \Rightarrow r = e, \text{ and}$$
$$x = y \Rightarrow r = x.$$

Difference. Given the difference operation between references x and y, $x - y$, and that the result would be r,

$$x = e \Rightarrow r = e,$$
$$y = e \Rightarrow r = x, \text{ and}$$
$$x = y \Rightarrow r = e.$$

Preemptive Memoisation. After performing an actual operation and caching that operation in the operation table, we can preemptively cache other operations too by exploiting standard set properties. This would avoid performing an actual operation later if the analysis needed that result. An implementation can choose which operations are worth preemptively memoising and which are not.

Unions. Assume the ordered operation $x \cup y = r$ is not a property operation. If $x \neq r$, we can instantly determine and cache

$$x \cup r = r, \text{ and}$$
$$x \cap r = x,$$

and similarly if $y \neq r$,

$$y \cup r = r, \text{ and}$$
$$y \cap r = y.$$

We guard with the conditions $x \neq r$ and $y \neq r$ because in each of these cases the preemptively cached unions would be property unions.

Intersections. Assume the ordered operation $x \cap y = r$ is not a property operation. If $r \neq e \wedge x \neq r$, we can instantly determine and cache

$$x \cap r = r, \text{ and}$$
$$x \cup r = x,$$

and similarly if $r \neq e \wedge y \neq r$,

$$y \cap r = r, \text{ and}$$
$$y \cup r = y.$$

We are not interested in preemptively memoising when $r = e$ because these intersections and unions would otherwise be property operations.

Difference. Assume the difference operation $x - y = r$ is not a property operation. If $r \neq e \wedge x \neq r$ we can instantly determine and cache

$$x \cup r = x, \text{ and}$$
$$x \cap r = r,$$

and similarly if $r \neq e$,

$$y - r = y,$$
$$r - y = r, \text{ and}$$
$$r \cap y = e.$$

4   Evaluation

This section describes our implementation, programs used to evaluate our approach, and then discusses results obtained when applying our hash consed points-to sets to state-of-the-art inclusion-based flow-insensitive analysis (Andersen's analysis [1,36]) and inclusion-based flow-sensitive analysis (staged flow-sensitive analysis [23]).

4.1   Implementation and Experimental Setup

We have implemented our approach using open source points-to analysis framework SVF [47] built on LLVM 10.0.0. We have not modified any algorithms, rather just how points-to sets are represented, that is, when an analysis attempts to perform a union or access a points-to set, our code is called. For concrete points-to sets, we use LLVM's sparse bit-vector. SVF's flow-insensitive points-to analysis or Andersen's analysis uses a state-of-the-art constraint resolution algorithm, *wave propagation* [36], and performs cycle detection. Indirect calls (function pointers and virtual calls) are resolved on-the-fly during points-to resolution. SVF's flow-sensitive analysis is staged flow-sensitive analysis (SFS) as described in Section V of the original work [23]. Unlike Fig. 2, SFS performs points-to analysis on a pre-computed def-use graph, not a control-flow graph, vastly reducing the number of constraints. Both analyses are field-sensitive and assume analysed programs do not perform pointer arithmetic to access fields. Fields of struct objects are distinguished by their unique indices [35].

Table 2. Program versions, bitcode sizes, lines of LLVM instructions, and descriptions.

Program	Version	Size	LOI	Description
dhcpcd	9.3.4	1.19 MB	82 939	DHCP client
nsd	4.3.4	1.72 MB	117 191	Name server
tmux	3.1c	2.41 MB	156 872	Terminal multiplexer
gawk	5.1.0	2.48 MB	179 805	GNU AWK interpreter
bash	5.0.18	2.68 MB	196 168	Bourne Again Shell (Unix shell)
mutt	2.0.3	3.28 MB	224 500	Text-based email client
lynx	2.8.9	5.31 MB	287 159	Text-based web browser
xpdf	4.03	7.90 MB	494 764	PDF viewer
python3	3.7.9	9.80 MB	635 361	Python 3 interpreter
svn	1.14.0	11.40 MB	673 144	Version control system
emacs	27.2	11.85 MB	804 291	extensible text editor
git	2.29.2	12.29 MB	739 968	Distributed version control system
kakoune	2020.08.04	12.39 MB	733 327	Modal text editor
ruby	2.7.2	13.05 MB	864 114	Ruby interpreter
squid	4.13	20.36 MB	1 252 756	Web proxy cache
wireshark	3.4.0	32.59 MB	2 145 391	Network packet analyser

For our hash consed points-to sets, we map concrete points-to sets to unique integer identifiers (which act as our references), and a second map, implemented as an array for performance, mapping those identifiers back to the concrete points-to set. This allows us to use 32-bit identifiers, rather than 64-bit addresses as would be required if our references were pointers. Our operations tables are implemented as maps mapping two such identifiers to another. Our hash function is simply the concatenation of the two 32-bit identifier operands which is another benefit of using integral identifiers as references.

We have run Andersen's analysis and SFS with and without hash consed points-to sets on 16 real-world open source programs from various domains. Table 2 lists these programs along with their version, bitcode size, number of lines of LLVM instructions, and a short description. xpdf, kakoune, squid, and wireshark are written in C++ and the remainder are C programs. We ran the analyses on a machine running 64-bit Ubuntu 18.04.2 LTS with an Intel Xeon 6132 processor and we limited analyses to 100 GB of memory. To measure time, we use C's clock function and to measure memory we refer to the maximum resident set size of the entire SVF execution reported by GNU's time.

Table 3. Time taken (seconds) and memory usage (GB) for Andersen's analysis with and without hash consing, followed by the time and memory difference of the two approaches.

Program	Baseline		Hash consed		Time diff.	Memory diff.
	Time	Memory	Time	Memory		
dhcpcd	4.52	0.30	3.58	0.28	1.26×	1.07×
nsd	9.32	0.55	7.23	0.51	1.29×	1.07×
tmux	18.86	0.59	14.11	0.56	1.34×	1.05×
gawk	19.92	0.64	14.15	0.58	1.41×	1.10×
bash	10.93	0.64	7.29	0.58	1.50×	1.11×
mutt	41.79	1.01	20.09	0.95	2.08×	1.06×
lynx	61.09	1.11	44.51	1.03	1.37×	1.08×
xpdf	179.52	1.94	111.80	1.88	1.61×	1.03×
python3	5509.52	4.13	1779.64	3.51	3.10×	1.18×
svn	5869.05	4.24	1829.20	2.82	3.21×	1.50×
emacs	5082.81	13.63	2651.32	13.05	1.92×	1.05×
git	5905.84	6.73	2499.55	6.79	2.36×	0.99×
kakoune	673.88	3.07	263.08	3.26	2.56×	0.94×
ruby	67.32	2.74	32.08	2.58	2.10×	1.06×
squid	2752.84	6.30	949.33	5.03	2.90×	1.25×
wireshark	271.60	6.42	211.42	6.21	1.28×	1.03×
Geo. Mean					1.85×	1.09 ×

4.2 Results and Discussion

In this section, we discuss the effects of hash consing on points-to analysis. We first look at Andersen's analysis then SFS, and conclude with a brief discussion on preemptive memoisation.

Andersen's Analysis. Table 3 shows the time and memory of Andersen's analysis with and without hash consing, and comparisons are shown in the **Time diff.** and **Memory diff.** columns. We see a positive trend in time, showing that using hash consing speeds up the analysis by a geometric mean of 1.85× for our programs. At most, the analysis is 3.21× faster, and at worst 1.26× faster. Generally, slower to analyse programs saw the greatest improvement in speed, with all programs which originally took over 5000 s to analyse seeing an improvement of over 2× with the exception of emacs which saw a slightly lower improvement.

For memory, we see around the same usage generally with the hash consed analysis using slightly more or slightly less. We have not implemented garbage collection for the global pool of points-to sets. When there exists no references to a certain points-to set in the global pool, that points-to set can be destroyed, or

Table 4. Number of union operations which are concrete operations, property operations (and their proportion), lookups into the union operations table (and their proportion), and the total for Andersen's analysis using our approach.

Program	Concrete	Property	Lookup	Total
dhcpcd	3766 (3.10%)	58 424 (48.14%)	59 185 (48.76%)	121 375
nsd	2900 (1.76%)	98 068 (59.45%)	64 001 (38.80%)	164 969
tmux	5651 (1.58%)	102 511 (28.58%)	250 552 (69.85%)	358 714
gawk	6378 (2.26%)	155 251 (55.09%)	120 172 (42.64%)	281 801
bash	1358 (0.93%)	126 307 (86.61%)	18 167 (12.46%)	145 832
mutt	8135 (3.07%)	145 604 (55.02%)	110 881 (41.90%)	264 620
lynx	10 750 (3.19%)	188 602 (56.04%)	137 205 (40.77%)	336 557
xpdf	29 622 (4.32%)	249 768 (36.41%)	406 582 (59.27%)	685 972
python3	33 274 (3.16%)	560 048 (53.25%)	458 319 (43.58%)	1 051 641
svn	22 879 (1.45%)	808 308 (51.13%)	749 564 (47.42%)	1 580 751
emacs	92 677 (4.61%)	809 938 (40.27%)	1 108 850 (55.13%)	2 011 465
git	124 333 (9.03%)	684 809 (49.73%)	567 897 (41.24%)	1 377 039
kakoune	86 364 (8.72%)	394 225 (39.81%)	509 693 (51.47%)	990 282
ruby	11 090 (3.15%)	195 495 (55.47%)	145 827 (41.38%)	352 412
squid	55 792 (3.23%)	796 024 (46.09%)	875 241 (50.68%)	1 727 057
wireshark	47 856 (3.02%)	592 647 (37.34%)	946 580 (59.64%)	1 587 083
Geo. Mean	– (2.98%)	– (48.40%)	– (44.24%)	

garbage collected. This would save memory, as intermediate points-to sets which are no longer in use litter the global pool. We strongly suspect that garbage collection of the global pool can further save memory and eliminate memory usage regressions, which we would like to explore in the future.

Table 4 lists the union operations performed by the Andersen's analysis and categorises them as concrete (unique) unions, property unions, or lookups. When we preemptively memoise, we count such an operation as a property operation. We see that in every program, less than 10% of unions are concrete unions, meaning the remainder are either property unions, and thus trivial, or duplicates of a non-property union. In fact, we only see more than 5% for two programs, git and kakoune. In most programs, the number of property unions and lookups are roughly even. It is interesting to note that despite the small number of unions (compared to more precise analyses, as will be seen in the next section), hash consing has produced a noticeable speedup.

SFS. Table 5 shows the time taken and memory used by SFS with and without hash consing. For time, we see a very similar to trend to that of Andersen's analysis. Unexpectedly, considering how many more constraints flow-sensitive analysis

Table 5. Time taken (seconds) and memory usage (GB) for SFS with and without hash consing, followed by the time and memory difference of the two approaches. OOM means the analysis exhausted the allocated 100 GB of memory.

Program	Baseline		Hash consed		Time diff.	Memory diff.
	Time	Memory	Time	Memory		
dhcpcd	77.27	1.08	73.04	0.66	1.06×	1.65×
nsd	113.39	2.97	75.76	0.74	1.50×	4.02×
tmux	280.09	3.33	212.25	1.14	1.32×	2.93×
gawk	1526.61	12.13	685.78	2.42	2.23×	5.02×
bash	337.01	8.55	165.28	1.51	2.04×	5.65×
mutt	797.92	13.95	400.08	2.15	1.99×	6.49×
lynx	3256.47	26.71	1594.90	3.65	2.04×	7.32×
xpdf	OOM	OOM	7210.36	6.44	–	≥15.52×
python3	OOM	OOM	23534.00	16.72	–	≥5.98×
svn	OOM	OOM	14000.10	22.61	–	≥4.42×
emacs	OOM	OOM	51367.00	44.50	–	≥2.25×
git	OOM	OOM	49264.50	39.59	–	≥2.53×
kakoune	OOM	OOM	12845.40	9.49	–	≥10.53×
ruby	OOM	OOM	4250.19	9.77	–	≥10.24×
squid	OOM	OOM	72733.50	37.53	–	≥2.66×
wireshark	OOM	OOM	24820.20	14.50	–	≥6.90×
Geo. Mean					1.69×	≥4.93×

can produce, we see a lower geometric mean of 1.69×. This can be explained by the lack of analysis timing data for 9 programs without hash consing, i.e., the baseline, because those analyses exceeded the allocated 100 GB of memory, and thus we cannot draw a time comparison. If sufficient memory resources were available, we would expect to see a much larger average improvement as these 9 benchmarks are the largest and would be likely improve most. This can be gleaned from the data in Table 6 which shows the union type breakdown for SFS. We see that the number of unions is very high giving much room for our approach to improve time. Concrete unions never exceed 1% when using hash consing, thus hash consing and memoisation have improved over 99% of unions for our programs. We also see that, compared to Andersen's analysis, a larger proportion of unions have become property unions rather than lookups.

As for memory usage in Table 5, we see a significant improvement with a geometric mean reduction of over 4.93×, and at most over 15.52× (xpdf). Hash consing brings memory requirements to a level acceptable for commodity hardware: of the 9 programs which exceeded the allocated 100 GB in the baseline analysis, 6 now require less than 32 GB, and all suffice with less than 64 GB.

Table 6. Number of union operations which are concrete operations, property operations (and their proportion), lookups into the union operations table (and their proportion), and the total number of unions for SFS using hash consing.

Program	Concrete	Property	Lookup	Total
dhcpcd	858 019 (0.95%)	60 000 495 (66.20%)	29 772 284 (32.85%)	90 630 798
nsd	106 236 (0.06%)	131 385 659 (70.44%)	55 032 002 (29.50%)	186 523 897
tmux	265 726 (0.05%)	515 202 000 (89.33%)	61 282 554 (10.63%)	576 750 280
gawk	2 568 240 (0.11%)	1 674 478 472 (72.11%)	645 178 369 (27.78%)	2 322 225 081
bash	27 701 (0.01%)	435 565 965 (84.61%)	79 195 559 (15.38%)	514 789 225
mutt	319 829 (0.02%)	1 033 079 848 (78.53%)	282 194 806 (21.45%)	1 315 594 483
lynx	788 833 (0.02%)	3 836 871 871 (79.72%)	975 346 188 (20.26%)	4 813 006 892
xpdf	2 375 069 (0.02%)	9 475 061 599 (76.93%)	2 838 361 665 (23.05%)	12 315 798 333
python3	1 125 561 (0.00%)	27 494 110 299 (83.29%)	5 516 560 498 (16.71%)	33 011 796 358
svn	9 536 154 (0.04%)	15 950 564 702 (73.53%)	5 731 542 295 (26.42%)	21 691 643 151
emacs	40 525 287 (0.04%)	62 746 471 959 (67.68%)	29 925 669 621 (32.28%)	92 712 666 867
git	15 868 477 (0.03%)	36 002 062 086 (75.28%)	11 805 253 473 (24.69%)	47 823 184 036
kakoune	833 730 (0.00%)	21 708 874 709 (81.56%)	4 907 142 103 (18.44%)	26 616 850 542
ruby	1 219 328 (0.01%)	11 142 763 302 (83.49%)	2 202 254 328 (16.50%)	13 346 236 958
squid	3 080 598 (0.00%)	117 192 828 125 (85.99%)	19 097 056 263 (14.01%)	136 292 964 986
wireshark	9 219 867 (0.06%)	7 534 330 653 (50.97%)	7 237 949 555 (48.97%)	14 781 500 075
Geo. Mean	– (0.02%)	– (75.61%)	– (22.10%)	

Even though our implementation does not include garbage collection of unnecessary intermediate points-to sets in the global pool, our approach still shows significant memory reduction for more precise analyses like SFS. With garbage collection we expect to see an even greater improvement in memory usage.

Effect of Preemptive Memoisation. For our programs, preemptive memoisation generally does not have a discernible effect on time. This is because preemptive memoisation reduces the number of concrete unions *after* the application of our techniques (i.e., after our other techniques have made the most expensive operations cheaper, like transforming N occurrences of a particularly expensive union into one concrete union followed by $N-1$ lookups). That is, it reduces the number of the already reduced concrete unions (second column of Tables 4 and 6). Regardless, we notice that the number of concrete unions does meaningfully shrink. For example, for Andersen's and SFS respectively, we see about 2500 and 1 million fewer for svn, about 10000 and 500000 fewer for squid, and about 1000 and 7 million fewer for emacs. This indicates that as input programs grow and the difference in concrete unions starts to have a noticeable effect on time (e.g., when points-to sets become unreasonably large), the role preemptive memoisation plays can become more significant. As expected, we see a slight increase in memory usage due to storing more operations in the operations table (each entry taking 12 bytes, modulo any table overhead).

5   Related Work

Inclusion-Based Points-To Analysis. The study of inclusion-based points-to analysis has a long history [1,6,13,20,26,29,35,36,39,44,46]. Resolving points-to relations in inclusion-based analysis is formalised as a set-constraint problem often solved by using a constraint graph of a program. To boost the performance of points-to analysis, most existing efforts focus on improving the analysis at the algorithmic level (e.g., via developing more efficient constraint solvers [35,36, 44]) or simplifying the constraint graph (e.g., cycle elimination [13,20], variable substitution [21,39], or selective precision [30,41]).

Despite these efforts, redundant and duplicate points-to sets and operations still exist and can not be completely tamed by existing techniques. Pushing the boundaries through algorithmic changes to the points-to analysis may produce increasingly diminishing returns on performance. Unlike previous approaches which simplify constraints or make algorithmic changes to points-to analysis, the goal of this work is to improve underlying data structures.

Data Structures for Points-To Analysis. There has been a handful of work on using and developing data structures, particularly through better representing points-to sets, for efficient points-to analysis. For computing and representing points-to sets, several data structures have been used including binary decision diagrams (BDDs) [5,52], bit-vectors [22,23,31] and explicit representations such as B-trees [8] and hash-based sets [31]. BDD-based points-to analysis often requires expensive variable reordering to be efficient. Thus the benefits may not outweigh using explicit representations [8]. Moreover, they often require algorithmic changes to the points-to analysis [5,54], introducing extra implementation complexity. Bit-vectors as arguably the most popular data structure to represent points-to sets having been used in mainstream frameworks such as Soot [31], WALA [50], and LLVM-based static analysis tools [23,40,47]. Bit-vectors have been shown more efficient than hash-based sets and sorted arrays [31], and BDDs [22]. In this paper, we demonstrate that our hash consed points-to sets work well on top of LLVM's sparse bit-vectors to boost the performance of state-of-the-art flow-insensitive and flow-sensitive points-to analyses.

Hash Consing for Static Analysis. In unpublished work [25], Heintze described splitting points-to sets into two parts: a unique part (called an overflow list) and a shared part. The shared part can be described as hash consing and thus implements a finer-grained hash consing since it does this on subsets rather than entire sets. However, no memoisation is performed, and doing so would be less effective due to the overflow list where, for example, two sets may be equivalent but not share any parts (i.e. the unique parts are different and the shared parts are different). The data structure is also much more difficult to implement whereas what we have presented can be retrofitted onto most set-like data structures exposing necessary operations (largely the set union operation). An implementation is available in Soot [43] as the `SharedHybridSet`.

Hash consing has also more generally been explored for static analysis to represent, for example, memory maps and program states [12,33], invocation graphs [11], subtrees [3], and constants [27], with success. Static analyses are ripe for hash consing and memoisation because they are by nature approximations designed to capture a *class* of runtime data and so contain many duplicate data structures, operations, or both. We believe this work is the first to apply hash consing to the base aspects of points-to analysis, i.e. points-to sets and their unions, describe extra optimisations, and show why points-to analysis is perfectly suited for hash consing.

6   Conclusion

This paper uses hash consed points-to sets to produce a persistent data structure to reduce duplicate points-to sets, saving space, and memoise union operations, saving time, without any high-level algorithmic changes. Hash consing can effectively handle duplication during points-to resolution by representing points-to sets once and referring to such representations through references. Our approach can speed up duplicate union operations through efficient memoisation and operand comparisons. We have evaluated our approach using 16 real-world C/C++ programs (>9.5 million lines of LLVM instructions). We observe an average memory reduction of $\geq 4.93\times$ (up to $\geq 15.52\times$) in staged flow-sensitive analysis (SFS) and an average speed up of $1.69\times$ (up to $2.23\times$). We also observe a speed up in state-of-the-art Andersen's analysis of $1.85\times$ on average (up to $3.21\times$) while using roughly the same amount of memory.

Acknowledgements. We thank the reviewers for their suggestions on improving this work. The first author is supported by a PhD scholarship funded by CSIRO's Data61. This research is supported by Australian Research Grants DP200101328 and DP210101348.

References

1. Andersen, L.O.: Program analysis and specialization for the C programming language. Ph.D. thesis, University of Copenhagen, Denmark (1994)
2. Balatsouras, G., Smaragdakis, Y.: Structure-sensitive points-to analysis for C and C++. In: Rival, X. (ed.) SAS 2016. LNCS, vol. 9837, pp. 84–104. Springer, Heidelberg (2016). https://doi.org/10.1007/978-3-662-53413-7_5
3. Ball, T., Rajamani, S.K.: Bebop: a path-sensitive interprocedural dataflow engine. In: Proceedings of the 2001 ACM SIGPLAN-SIGSOFT Workshop on Program Analysis for Software Tools and Engineering, PASTE 2001, pp. 97–103. ACM, USA (2001). https://doi.org/10.1145/379605.379690
4. Barbar, M., Sui, Y., Chen, S.: Object versioning for flow-sensitive pointer analysis. In: 2021 IEEE/ACM International Symposium on Code Generation and Optimization, CGO 2021, pp. 222–235. IEEE Computer Society, USA (2021). https://doi.org/10.1109/CGO51591.2021.9370334

5. Berndl, M., Lhoták, O., Qian, F., Hendren, L., Umanee, N.: Points-to analysis using BDDs. In: Proceedings of the ACM SIGPLAN 2003 Conference on Programming Language Design and Implementation, PLDI 2003, pp. 103–114. ACM, USA (2003). https://doi.org/10.1145/781131.781144
6. Blackshear, S., Chang, B.-Y.E., Sankaranarayanan, S., Sridharan, M.: The flow-insensitive precision of Andersen's analysis in practice. In: Yahav, E. (ed.) SAS 2011. LNCS, vol. 6887, pp. 60–76. Springer, Heidelberg (2011). https://doi.org/10.1007/978-3-642-23702-7_9
7. Braibant, T., Jourdan, J.H., Monniaux, D.: Implementing and reasoning about hash-consed data structures in Coq. J. Autom. Reason. **53**(3), 271–304 (2014). https://doi.org/10.1007/s10817-014-9306-0
8. Bravenboer, M., Smaragdakis, Y.: Strictly declarative specification of sophisticated points-to analyses. In: Proceedings of the 24th ACM SIGPLAN Conference on Object Oriented Programming Systems Languages and Applications, OOPSLA 2009, pp. 243–262. ACM, USA (2009). https://doi.org/10.1145/1640089.1640108
9. Chen, H., et al.: MUZZ: thread-aware grey-box fuzzing for effective bug hunting in multithreaded programs. In: 29th USENIX Security Symposium, USENIX Security 2020, pp. 2325–2342 (2020)
10. Cheng, X., Wang, H., Hua, J., Xu, G., Sui, Y.: DeepWukong: statically detecting software vulnerabilities using deep graph neural network. ACM Trans. Softw. Eng. Methodol. (TOSEM) **30**(3), 1–33 (2021). https://doi.org/10.1145/3436877
11. Choi, W., Choe, K.M.: Cycle elimination for invocation graph-based context-sensitive pointer analysis. Inf. Softw. Technol. **53**(8), 818–833 (2011). https://doi.org/10.1016/j.infsof.2011.03.003
12. Cuoq, P., Kirchner, F., Kosmatov, N., Prevosto, V., Signoles, J., Yakobowski, B.: Frama-C. In: Eleftherakis, G., Hinchey, M., Holcombe, M. (eds.) SEFM 2012. LNCS, vol. 7504, pp. 233–247. Springer, Heidelberg (2012). https://doi.org/10.1007/978-3-642-33826-7_16
13. Fähndrich, M., Foster, J.S., Su, Z., Aiken, A.: Partial online cycle elimination in inclusion constraint graphs. In: Proceedings of the ACM SIGPLAN 1998 Conference on Programming Language Design and Implementation, PLDI 1998, pp. 85–96. ACM, USA (1998). https://doi.org/10.1145/277650.277667
14. Fan, X., Sui, Y., Liao, X., Xue, J.: Boosting the precision of virtual call integrity protection with partial pointer analysis for C++. In: Proceedings of the 26th ACM SIGSOFT International Symposium on Software Testing and Analysis, ISSTA 2017, pp. 329–340. ACM, USA (2017). https://doi.org/10.1145/3092703.3092729
15. Farkhani, R.M., Jafari, S., Arshad, S., Robertson, W., Kirda, E., Okhravi, H.: On the effectiveness of type-based control flow integrity. In: Proceedings of the 34th Annual Computer Security Applications Conference, ACSAC 2018, pp. 28–39. ACM, USA (2018). https://doi.org/10.1145/3274694.3274739
16. Filliâtre, J.C., Conchon, S.: Type-safe modular hash-consing. In: Proceedings of the 2006 Workshop on ML, ML 2006, pp. 12–19. ACM, USA (2006). https://doi.org/10.1145/1159876.1159880
17. Fink, S.J., Yahav, E., Dor, N., Ramalingam, G., Geay, E.: Effective typestate verification in the presence of aliasing. ACM Trans. Softw. Eng. Methodol. **17**(2) (2008). https://doi.org/10.1145/1348250.1348255
18. Gosling, J., Joy, B., Steele, G.L., Bracha, G., Buckley, A.: The Java Language Specification, Java SE 8 Edition, 1st edn. Addison-Wesley Professional (2014)
19. Goubault, J.: Implementing functional languages with fast equality, sets and maps: an exercise in hash consing. Journées Francophones des Langages Applicatifs, 222–238 (1994)

20. Hardekopf, B., Lin, C.: The ant and the grasshopper: fast and accurate pointer analysis for millions of lines of code. In: Proceedings of the 28th ACM SIGPLAN Conference on Programming Language Design and Implementation, PLDI 2007, pp. 290–299. ACM, USA (2007). https://doi.org/10.1145/1250734.1250767

21. Hardekopf, B., Lin, C.: Exploiting pointer and location equivalence to optimize pointer analysis. In: Nielson, H.R., Filé, G. (eds.) SAS 2007. LNCS, vol. 4634, pp. 265–280. Springer, Heidelberg (2007). https://doi.org/10.1007/978-3-540-74061-2_17

22. Hardekopf, B., Lin, C.: Semi-sparse flow-sensitive pointer analysis. In: Proceedings of the 36th Annual ACM SIGPLAN-SIGACT Symposium on Principles of Programming Languages, POPL 2009, pp. 226–238. ACM, USA (2009). https://doi.org/10.1145/1480881.1480911

23. Hardekopf, B., Lin, C.: Flow-sensitive pointer analysis for millions of lines of code. In: Proceedings of the 9th Annual IEEE/ACM International Symposium on Code Generation and Optimization, CGO 2011, pp. 289–298. IEEE Computer Society, USA (2011). https://doi.org/10.1109/CGO.2011.5764696

24. Hash consing (2020). https://en.wikipedia.org/wiki/Hash_consing

25. Heintze, N.: Analysis of large code bases: the compile-link-analyze model (1999, unpublished). http://web.archive.org/web/20050513012825/cm.bell-labs.com/cm/cs/who/nch/cla.ps

26. Heintze, N., Tardieu, O.: Ultra-fast aliasing analysis using CLA: a million lines of C code in a second. In: Proceedings of the ACM SIGPLAN 2001 Conference on Programming Language Design and Implementation, PLDI 2001, pp. 254–263. ACM, USA (2001). https://doi.org/10.1145/378795.378855

27. Hubert, L., et al.: Sawja: static analysis workshop for Java. In: Beckert, B., Marché, C. (eds.) FoVeOOS 2010. LNCS, vol. 6528, pp. 92–106. Springer, Heidelberg (2011). https://doi.org/10.1007/978-3-642-18070-5_7

28. Lattner, C., Adve, V.: LLVM: a compilation framework for lifelong program analysis & transformation. In: Proceedings of the International Symposium on Code Generation and Optimization: Feedback-Directed and Runtime Optimization, CGO 2004, p. 75. IEEE Computer Society, USA (2004). https://doi.org/10.1109/CGO.2004.1281665

29. Lei, Y., Sui, Y.: Fast and precise handling of positive weight cycles for field-sensitive pointer analysis. In: Chang, B.-Y.E. (ed.) SAS 2019. LNCS, vol. 11822, pp. 27–47. Springer, Cham (2019). https://doi.org/10.1007/978-3-030-32304-2_3

30. Lhoták, O., Chung, K.C.A.: Points-to analysis with efficient strong updates. In: Proceedings of the 38th Annual ACM SIGPLAN-SIGACT Symposium on Principles of Programming Languages, POPL 2011, pp. 3–16. ACM, USA (2011). https://doi.org/10.1145/1926385.1926389

31. Lhoták, O., Hendren, L.: Scaling Java points-to analysis using SPARK. In: Hedin, G. (ed.) CC 2003. LNCS, vol. 2622, pp. 153–169. Springer, Heidelberg (2003). https://doi.org/10.1007/3-540-36579-6_12

32. Livshits, V.B., Lam, M.S.: Tracking pointers with path and context sensitivity for bug detection in C programs. In: Proceedings of the 9th European Software Engineering Conference Held Jointly with 11th ACM SIGSOFT International Symposium on Foundations of Software Engineering, ESEC/FSE 2011, pp. 317–326. ACM, USA (2003). https://doi.org/10.1145/940071.940114

33. Manevich, R., Ramalingam, G., Field, J., Goyal, D., Sagiv, M.: Compactly representing first-order structures for static analysis. In: Hermenegildo, M.V., Puebla, G. (eds.) SAS 2002. LNCS, vol. 2477, pp. 196–212. Springer, Heidelberg (2002). https://doi.org/10.1007/3-540-45789-5_16

34. Pearce, D.J., Kelly, P.H., Hankin, C.: Online cycle detection and difference propagation for pointer analysis. In: Proceedings of the Third IEEE International Workshop on Source Code Analysis and Manipulation, SCAM 2003, pp. 3–12. IEEE Computer Society, USA (2003). https://doi.org/10.1109/SCAM.2003.1238026

35. Pearce, D.J., Kelly, P.H., Hankin, C.: Efficient field-sensitive pointer analysis of C. ACM Trans. Program. Lang. Syst. **30**(1), 4:1–4:42 (2007). https://doi.org/10.1145/1290520.1290524

36. Pereira, F.M.Q., Berlin, D.: Wave propagation and deep propagation for pointer analysis. In: Proceedings of the 7th Annual IEEE/ACM International Symposium on Code Generation and Optimization, CGO 2009, pp. 126–135. IEEE Computer Society, USA (2009). https://doi.org/10.1109/CGO.2009.9

37. Pratikakis, P., Foster, J.S., Hicks, M.: LOCKSMITH: context-sensitive correlation analysis for race detection. In: Proceedings of the 27th ACM SIGPLAN Conference on Programming Language Design and Implementation, PLDI 2006, pp. 320–331. ACM, USA (2006). https://doi.org/10.1145/1133981.1134019

38. What is Referential Transparency? (2017). https://www.sitepoint.com/what-is-referential-transparency

39. Rountev, A., Chandra, S.: Off-line variable substitution for scaling points-to analysis. In: Proceedings of the ACM SIGPLAN 2000 Conference on Programming Language Design and Implementation, PLDI 2000, pp. 47–56. ACM, USA (2000). https://doi.org/10.1145/349299.349310

40. Schubert, P.D., Hermann, B., Bodden, E.: PhASAR: an inter-procedural static analysis framework for C/C++. In: Vojnar, T., Zhang, L. (eds.) TACAS 2019. LNCS, vol. 11428, pp. 393–410. Springer, Cham (2019). https://doi.org/10.1007/978-3-030-17465-1_22

41. Smaragdakis, Y., Bravenboer, M., Lhoták, O.: Pick your contexts well: understanding object-sensitivity. In: Proceedings of the 38th Annual ACM SIGPLAN-SIGACT Symposium on Principles of Programming Languages, POPL 2011, pp. 17–30. ACM, USA (2011)

42. Sondergaard, H., Sestoft, P.: Referential transparency, definiteness and unfoldability. Acta Informatica **27**(6), 505–517 (1990)

43. Soot (2021). https://github.com/soot-oss/soot

44. Sridharan, M., Fink, S.J.: The complexity of Andersen's analysis in practice. In: Palsberg, J., Su, Z. (eds.) SAS 2009. LNCS, vol. 5673, pp. 205–221. Springer, Heidelberg (2009). https://doi.org/10.1007/978-3-642-03237-0_15

45. Sui, Y., Cheng, X., Zhang, G., Wang, H.: Flow2Vec: value-flow-based precise code embedding. Proc. ACM Program. Lang. **4**(OOPSLA), 1–27 (2020). https://doi.org/10.1145/3428301

46. Sui, Y., Xue, J.: On-demand strong update analysis via value-flow refinement. In: Proceedings of the 2016 24th ACM SIGSOFT International Symposium on Foundations of Software Engineering, FSE 2016, pp. 460–473. ACM, USA (2016). https://doi.org/10.1145/2950290.2950296

47. Sui, Y., Xue, J.: SVF: Interprocedural static value-flow analysis in LLVM. In: Proceedings of the 25th International Conference on Compiler Construction, CC 2016, pp. 265–266. ACM, USA (2016). https://doi.org/10.1145/2892208.2892235

48. Trabish, D., Kapus, T., Rinetzky, N., Cadar, C.: Past-sensitive pointer analysis for symbolic execution. In: Proceedings of the 28th ACM Joint Meeting on European Software Engineering Conference and Symposium on the Foundations of Software Engineering, ESEC/FSE 2020, pp. 197–208. ACM, USA (2020). https://doi.org/10.1145/3368089.3409698

49. Trabish, D., Mattavelli, A., Rinetzky, N., Cadar, C.: Chopped symbolic execution. In: Proceedings of the 40th International Conference on Software Engineering, ICSE 2018, pp. 350–360. ACM, USA (2018). https://doi.org/10.1145/3180155.3180251

50. The T. J. Watson libraries for analysis (WALA) (2021). http://wala.sf.net/

51. Wang, H., et al.: Typestate-guided fuzzer for discovering use-after-free vulnerabilities. In: Proceedings of the ACM/IEEE 42nd International Conference on Software Engineering, ICSE 2020, pp. 999–1010. ACM, USA (2020). https://doi.org/10.1145/3377811.3380386

52. Whaley, J.: Context-sensitive pointer analysis using binary decision diagrams. Ph.D. thesis, Stanford University, USA (2007)

53. Yan, H., Sui, Y., Chen, S., Xue, J.: Spatio-temporal context reduction: a pointer-analysis-based static approach for detecting use-after-free vulnerabilities. In: Proceedings of the 40th International Conference on Software Engineering, ICSE 2018, pp. 327–337. ACM, USA (2018). https://doi.org/10.1145/3180155.3180178

54. Zhu, J., Calman, S.: Symbolic pointer analysis revisited. In: Proceedings of the ACM SIGPLAN 2004 Conference on Programming Language Design and Implementation, PLDI 2004, pp. 145–157. ACM, USA (2004). https://doi.org/10.1145/996841.996860

Backward Symbolic Execution
with Loop Folding

Marek Chalupa[✉][iD] and Jan Strejček[iD]

Masaryk University, Brno, Czech Republic
{chalupa,strejcek}@fi.muni.cz

Abstract. *Symbolic execution* is an established program analysis technique that aims to search all possible execution paths of the given program. Due to the so-called path explosion problem, symbolic execution is usually unable to analyze all execution paths and thus it is not convenient for program verification as a standalone method. This paper focuses on *backward symbolic execution (BSE)*, which searches program paths backwards from the error location whose reachability should be proven or refuted. We show that this technique is equivalent to performing *k-induction* on control-flow paths. While standard BSE simply unwinds all program loops, we present an extension called *loop folding* that aims to derive loop invariants during BSE that are sufficient to prove the unreachability of the error location. The resulting technique is called *backward symbolic execution with loop folding (BSELF)*. Our experiments show that BSELF performs better than BSE and other tools based on *k*-induction when non-trivial benchmarks are considered. Moreover, a sequential combination of symbolic execution and BSELF achieved very competitive results compared to state-of-the-art verification tools.

1 Introduction

Symbolic execution (SE) [55] is a widely used technique for static program analysis. In principle, SE runs the program on symbols that represent arbitrary input values with the aim to explore all execution paths. This approach is inherently doomed to suffer from the *path explosion* problem. In other words, it typically runs out of available resources before finishing the analysis as the number of all execution paths is often very large or even infinite. Moreover, some execution paths may be infinite, which is another obstacle that makes SE fail to completely analyze the program.

Many techniques modifying or extending SE have been introduced to mitigate the path explosion problem. Some of them try to reduce the set of considered execution paths [19,72,79,81] or process multiple execution paths at once [45,57,74].

© Springer Nature Switzerland AG 2021
C. Drăgoi et al. (Eds.): SAS 2021, LNCS 12913, pp. 49–76, 2021.
https://doi.org/10.1007/978-3-030-88806-0_3

Others focus on the efficient processing of program loops [38,73,78], computation of reusable function summaries [3,37,68], or they do not symbolically execute nested [62] or library [60] functions as these are assumed to be correct. There are also approaches combining SE with other established techniques like predicate abstraction [39], counterexample-guided abstraction refinement (CEGAR) [15], or interpolation [46,63]. We refer to a recent survey [6] for more information about symbolic execution and its applications.

Our original research goal was to study possible combinations of SE and k-induction [77] for program verification, in particular for the *error location reachability* problem, i.e., the problem to decide whether there exists an execution of the program that reaches an error location. k-induction has been introduced as a technique for checking safety properties of symbolic transition systems by induction with respect to the length of paths in the system. It has been also adapted to model checking software [12,29,35,69], where the induction is typically led with respect to the number of loop iterations. We show that in the context of error location reachability problem, k-induction applied to control-flow paths of a given program corresponds to *backward symbolic execution* with the breadth-first search strategy. This is the first result of the paper.

Backward symbolic execution (BSE) [22,28,42] is the backward version of SE: it starts at the program location whose reachability is to be determined and symbolically executes the program backwards until it either reaches the initial location or all analyzed paths become infeasible. Similarly, as in the case of SE, this process may never terminate.

Let us illustrate the difference between SE and BSE on a very simple example. Assume that we want to verify the validity of the assertion in the program in Fig. 1 (top left). In other words, we need to decide the error location reachability problem for the location *err* in the corresponding control-flow automaton (top right). SE assigns to each variable v the symbol $\underline{v}$ representing its input value. Further, SE gradually builds the *SE tree* (bottom left) of paths starting in *init*. Each node in the SE tree is labelled with a triple $l \mid m \mid \phi$ of the current program location l, the memory content m, and the *path condition* ϕ, which is the weakest precondition on input values that makes the program follow the path leading from the tree root to the node. Whenever a path becomes infeasible, i.e., its path condition becomes unsatisfiable, SE stops executing this path (we draw such nodes dotted). Clearly, the assertion is valid iff the tree does not contain any node that is labelled with *err* and a satisfiable path condition. The assertion in Fig. 1 is valid, but SE cannot prove it as the SE tree is infinite.

BSE works similarly, but it proceeds from the error location backward to *init*. In other words, instead of computing the weakest precondition of paths that start in *init*, it computes the weakest precondition of paths that end in *err*. Note also that because BSE directly computes the precondition, it does not need to keep the contents of memory. For the program in Fig. 1, the BSE tree (bottom right) is finite and because there is no feasible path from *init* to *err*, it proves that the assertion is valid.

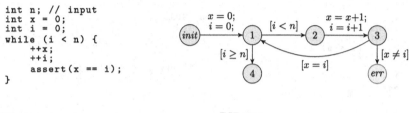

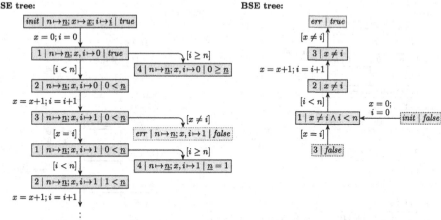

Fig. 1. Top part presents a simple program (left) and the corresponding control-flow automaton (right) with *err* location representing the assertion violation. The bottom part shows the infinite SE tree (left) starting in the initial location *init*, and the BSE tree (right) starting in the error location *err*.

Now consider a similar program given in Fig. 2. This time, the results of SE and BSE are switched: the SE tree (bottom left) is finite and implies the validity of the assertion, but the BSE tree (bottom right) is infinite and thus inconclusive.

The main difference between examples in Figs. 1 and 2 from the BSE perspective is the position of the assertion. In both cases, BSE first processes the negation of the assertion. But only in the example with the assertion inside the loop, it is processed again and this time in the positive form, which makes the path infeasible. This illustrates that a valid assertion inside a program loop may be a loop invariant that is able to prove its own validity (it is inductive).

A standard solution to checking assertions that are not strong enough to prove their own validity is to use externally generated invariants [11,18,20,43]. In this work, we address this issue by extending BSE with *loop folding* that attempts to infer inductive invariants during BSE. *Backward symbolic execution with loop folding (BSELF)* is the second result presented in this paper.

We have implemented both BSE and BSELF. Our experimental evaluation shows that BSELF is significantly more efficient than BSE and other tools implementing k-induction on non-trivial benchmarks. Further, our experiments indicate that a sequential combination of SE and BSELF forms a powerful tool fully comparable with state-of-the-art verification tools.

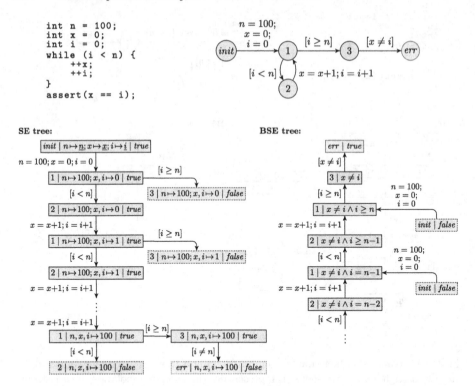

Fig. 2. Top part presents a simple program (left) and the corresponding control-flow automaton (right) with *err* location representing the assertion violation. The bottom part shows the infinite SE tree (left) starting in the initial location *init*, and the BSE tree (right) starting in the error location *err*.

The paper is organized as follows. The next section provides necessary definitions. Section 3 studies BSE, k-induction, and the relation between them. The algorithm BSELF is described in Sect. 4 and the experimental evaluation is presented in Sect. 5. Finally, Sect. 6 discusses related work.

2   Preliminaries

In this paper, we consider programs represented as *control-flow automata (CFAs)* [13]. A CFA $A = (L, init, err, E)$ consists of a finite set L of *program locations*, an *initial location* $init \in L$, an *error location* $err \in L \smallsetminus \{init\}$, and a finite set $E \subseteq (L \smallsetminus \{err\}) \times Ops \times L$ of edges between program locations which are labeled with operations. An operation is either an *assumption* (denoted in figures with blue text in square brackets, e.g., $[x > 5]$) or a sequence of assignments (e.g., $x = y + 10; y = 5$). If a location has two or more outgoing edges, then all these edges have to be labeled with assumptions such that any valuation satisfies at most one of these assumptions. The error location has no outgoing edges.

A *control-flow path* or simply a *path* π in a CFA is a nonempty finite sequence of succeeding edges $\pi = (l_0, o_0, l_1)(l_1, o_1, l_2) \ldots (l_{n-1}, o_{n-1}, l_n) \in E^+$. Locations l_0 and l_n are *start* and *target locations* of the path and we refer to them with $sl(\pi)$ and $tl(\pi)$, respectively. By $Locs(\pi)$ we denote the set of locations on π, i.e., $Locs(\pi) = \{l_i \mid 0 \le i \le n\}$. A path with start location *init* is called *initial*. A path is called *error path* if its target location is err and it is called a *safe path* otherwise. The *length* of the path π is denoted by $|\pi|$ and is equal to the number of edges on π, i.e. $|\pi| = n$.

We assume that our CFAs are *reducible* [47], i.e., every loop has a single entry location. The entry location of a program loop is called the *loop header*. We further assume that there are no nested loops in CFAs. Given a loop header h, by $LoopPaths(h)$ we denote the set of paths corresponding to a single iteration of the loop. Formally, $LoopPaths(h)$ is the set of all paths π such that $sl(\pi) = tl(\pi) = h$ and h does not appear inside π (i.e., $\pi = (h, o_0, l_1)(l_1, o_1, l_2) \ldots (l_{n-1}, o_{n-1}, h)$ where $l_1, l_2, \ldots, l_{n-1} \ne h$). We extend the $Locs$ notation to loops identified by their headers such that $Locs(h) = \cup_{\pi \in LoopPaths(h)} Locs(\pi)$.

To simplify the presentation, we assume that programs manipulate only variables of a fixed bit-width integer type. A *program state* (or simply a *state*) is fully specified by a pair (l, v) of the current program location l and the current valuation v of program variables. An *initial state* consists of the initial location *init* and an arbitrary valuation. Given an edge $(l, [\psi], l') \in E$ labelled with an assumption ψ, we write $(l, v) \xrightarrow{(l, [\psi], l')} (l', v)$ for each valuation v satisfying ψ. Given an edge $(l, soa, l') \in E$ labelled with a sequence of assignments soa, we write $(l, v) \xrightarrow{(l, soa, l')} (l', v')$ for all valuations v and v' such that v' arises from v by performing the sequence of assignments. We generalize the notation to paths: given a program path $\pi = (l_0, o_0, l_1) \ldots (l_{n-1}, o_{n-1}, l_n)$, we write $(l_0, v_0) \xrightarrow{\pi} (l_n, v_n)$ whenever there exist valuations $v_1, v_2, \ldots, v_{n-1}$ satisfying $(l_i, v_i) \xrightarrow{(l_i, o_i, l_{i+1})} (l_{i+1}, v_{i+1})$ for each $0 \le i < n$. A path π is *feasible from a state* (l, v) if $(l, v) \xrightarrow{\pi} (l', v')$ holds for some state (l', v'). A path is called *feasible* if it is feasible from some program state. Note that if two paths are feasible from the same program state, then one of these paths has to be a prefix of the other.

In this paper, we study the *error location reachability* problem, i.e., the problem to decide whether a given CFA contains a feasible initial error path. The CFA is called *correct* if there is no such path. If the CFA is not correct, then any feasible initial error path is called an *error witness*.

In the following, we often work with a set of states that have the same program location and their valuations are models of some formula ϕ over program variables. Such a set is denoted as (l, ϕ) and it is formally defined as

$$(l, \phi) = \{(l, v) \mid v \text{ satisfies } \phi\}.$$

A state (l', v') is *reachable from* (l, ϕ) if there exist $(l, v) \in (l, \phi)$ and a path π such that $(l, v) \xrightarrow{\pi} (l', v')$. A set (l, ϕ) is called *inductive* if each state reachable from (l, ϕ) with the location l is again in (l, ϕ). A set (l, ϕ) is an *invariant* if it contains all states with the location l that are reachable from $(init, true)$.

Given a formula ϕ and a path π, let $\pi^{-1}(\phi)$ denote the weakest precondition of ϕ for the sequence of the operations along π. Formally, $\pi^{-1}(\phi)$ is a formula that is satisfied by a valuation v if and only if $(sl(\pi), v) \xrightarrow{\pi} (tl(\pi), v')$ for some v' satisfying ϕ. The formula $\pi^{-1}(\phi)$ can be computed from π and ϕ for example by symbolic execution of the path. Clearly, a path π is feasible if and only if $\pi^{-1}(true)$ is satisfiable.

In general, we work with quantifier-free first-order formulas over a decidable theory. Each such a formula can be transformed into *conjunctive normal form (CNF)*, which is a conjunction of *clauses*, where each clause is a disjunction of *literals* and a literal is an atomic formula or its negation. We assume that there exists a decision procedure $sat(\phi)$ which returns *true* if ϕ is satisfiable and *false* otherwise. We say that two formulas are *disjoint* if their conjunction is unsatisfiable.

3 Backward Symbolic Execution and k-Induction

This section recalls backward symbolic execution and k-induction [77]. Moreover, it shows that the two techniques provide equivalent results when applied to the error location reachability problem.

3.1 Backward Symbolic Execution (BSE)

Backward symbolic execution (BSE) [22], sometimes also called *symbolic backward execution* [6], computes the weakest preconditions [26] of control-flow paths by a slightly different process than SE. In particular, paths are explored in the opposite direction: from the error location towards the initial location. BSE either shows that all error paths are infeasible, or it finds a feasible initial error path, or it runs forever. We assume that paths are explored in the shortest-first order. A high-level formulation of BSE is provided in Algorithm 1.

Input: CFA $A = (L, init, err, E)$
Output: *correct* if A is correct, an error witness π otherwise

$workbag \leftarrow E \cap (L \times Ops \times \{err\})$
while $workbag \neq \emptyset$ **do**
    $\pi \leftarrow$ pick a path of the minimal length from $workbag$
    $workbag \leftarrow workbag \setminus \{\pi\}$
    if π is feasible **then**
        if π is initial **then return** error witness π
        $workbag \leftarrow workbag \cup \{e\pi \mid e \in E \wedge tl(e) = sl(\pi)\}$
return *correct*

Algorithm 1: The backward symbolic execution (BSE) algorithm.

In the beginning, *workbag* is set to contain all paths of length 1 leading to the error location. Until *workbag* is empty, it takes a path from *workbag* and checks its feasibility. If the path is infeasible, it is discarded. In the opposite case, we check whether the path is also initial and report it as an error witness if the answer is positive. Otherwise, we prolong the path by each edge leading to its start location (i.e., we prolong it in the *backward* direction) and put all these prolonged paths to *workbag*. If *workbag* gets empty, it means that all initial error paths have an infeasible suffix and thus they are infeasible. Because each iteration picks a path of the minimal length from *workbag*, BSE invoked on an incorrect CFA eventually reports an error witness even if the number of feasible error paths is infinite. Unfortunately, there are correct programs for which BSE does not terminate as illustrated in Fig. 2. More specifically, BSE does not terminate on correct CFAs with infinitely many feasible error paths.

Theorem 1. *Let P be the set of all feasible error paths of a CFA A. BSE executed on A*

- *returns an error witness if P contains an initial path;*
- *returns* correct *if P is finite and contains no initial path;*
- *does not terminate if P is infinite and contains no initial path.*

Proof. We start with a simple observation. Let $\pi \in P$ be a path of length n and, for each $0 < i \leq n$, let π_i be the suffix of π of length i. As π is a feasible error path, each suffix π_i is also a feasible error path and thus $\pi_i \in P$. Path π_1 of length 1 is inserted to *workbag* during its initialization. For each $0 < i < n$, when π_i is processed by BSE, either it is initial and reported as an error witness, or π_{i+1} is inserted to *workbag*.

Assume that A is incorrect, i.e., P contains an initial path. Let $\pi \in P$ be a feasible initial error path of the minimal length. Hence, no proper suffix of π is initial. The observation implies that for all $0 < i < n$, processing of π_i inserts π_{i+1} to *workbag*. When $\pi = \pi_n$ is processed, it is returned as an error witness unless other error witness is found sooner.

Now assume that A is correct, i.e., P contains no initial path. Note that *workbag* can contain only error paths of length one, paths in P, and paths of the form $e\pi$ such that $\pi \in P$. Hence if P is finite, there are only finitely many paths that can appear in *workbag*. Moreover, every path can be inserted to *workbag* at most once. Altogether, we get that finiteness of P implies that *workbag* gets empty after a finite number of iterations and BSE returns *correct*.

If P is infinite and contains no initial path, the observation implies that every $\pi \in P$ eventually gets to *workbag*. Since every iteration of BSE removes only one path from *workbag* and P is infinite, BSE does not terminate.   □

Note that usual implementations of BSE do not check the feasibility of each path in *workbag* from scratch [22,23] as Algorithm 1 does. Instead, they gradually build the BSE tree of all feasible error paths as shown in Figs. 1 and 2 by computing the weakest preconditions incrementally: for a path of the form $e\pi$, the value of $(e\pi)^{-1}(true)$ is computed from the previously computed $\pi^{-1}(true)$

Input: CFA $A = (L, \mathit{init}, \mathit{err}, E)$
Output: *correct* if A is correct, an error witness π otherwise

$k \leftarrow 1$
while *true* **do**
    foreach initial path π of length k **do**   // base case
        if π is feasible and $tl(\pi) = \mathit{err}$ **then return** error witness π

    inductionstepfail $\leftarrow$ *false*   // induction step
    foreach safe path π of length k **do**
        if π is feasible **then**
            foreach $e = (tl(\pi), o, \mathit{err}) \in E$ **do**
                if πe is feasible **then**
                    inductionstepfail $\leftarrow$ *true*

    if $\neg$*inductionstepfail* **then return** *correct*
    $k \leftarrow k + 1$

Algorithm 2: The algorithm for k-induction on control-flow paths.

using the relation $(e\pi)^{-1}(\mathit{true}) = e^{-1}(\pi^{-1}(\mathit{true}))$. We employ this incremental approach in Sect. 4 where we extend BSE with loop folding.

3.2 k-Induction

The *k-induction* [77] technique uses induction to prove the correctness of transition systems. Adapted to CFAs, it is sufficient to prove these two statements for some $k > 0$ to show that the CFA is correct:

(Base case). All feasible initial paths of length at most k are safe.
(Induction step). Each feasible path of length $k + 1$ that has a safe prefix of
    length k is also safe.

If the base case does not hold, then there exists a feasible initial error path and the CFA is not correct. To prove the induction step, we consider each feasible safe path π of length k and check that all paths that arise by prolonging π with an edge leading to the error location are infeasible. If this check fails, we cannot make any conclusion. Thus we try to prove both statements again for $k + 1$. If we check the statements for $k = 1, 2, \ldots$, the base case can be simplified to checking only paths of length (exactly) k. The whole process is formalized in Algorithm 2.

The k-induction algorithm applied to an incorrect CFA eventually returns an error witness of the minimal length. When applied to a correct CFA, it either returns *correct* or it does not terminate.

Theorem 2. *Let P be the set of all feasible error paths of a CFA A. k-induction executed on A*

– *returns an error witness if P contains an initial path;*
– *returns* correct *if P is finite and contains no initial path;*
– *does not terminate if P is infinite and contains no initial path.*

Proof. Assume that A is incorrect, i.e., P contains an initial path. Let $\pi \in P$ be a feasible initial error path of the minimal length and let $n = |\pi|$. For each $0 < k < n$, the base case holds as all feasible initial paths of the length k are safe (due to the minimality of $|\pi|$) and the induction step cannot be proven as the suffix of π of length $k + 1$ is a feasible error path with a safe prefix of length k. Hence, k-induction reaches the iteration for $k = n$ where the base case identifies π or another feasible initial error path of length n as an error witness.

Now assume that A is correct, i.e., P contains no initial path. The base case clearly holds for each k. The induction step holds for k if and only if all paths in P have length at most k. If P contains a path π of length at least $k + 1$, then it also contains the suffix of π of length $k + 1$. This suffix is a feasible error path with a safe feasible prefix of length k. Hence, the induction step fails for k. If all paths in P have length at most k, then all feasible paths of length $k + 1$ are safe and the induction step holds. To sum up, if P is finite, the k-induction returns *correct* in the iteration where $k = \max\{|\pi| \mid \pi \in P\}$. If P is infinite, the induction step always fails as for any k there exists a path in P longer than k and thus k-induction does not terminate. $\square$

Note that when k-induction is applied to finite transition systems instead of CFAs, the incompleteness can be fixed by restricting the induction step only to acyclic paths [77].

3.3   Equivalence of BSE and k-Induction

Theorems 1 and 2 imply that BSE and k-induction return an error witness or the value *correct* in identical cases. On an incorrect CFA, both algorithms detect an error witness of the minimal length. On a correct CFA with a finite set P of all feasible error paths, the k-induction terminates for $k = \max\{|\pi| \mid \pi \in P\}$ and the longest path processed by BSE has length at most $k + 1$ (as k-induction in fact checks paths of length $k + 1$ for the given k).

If we look once again at Algorithm 2, we can see that the induction step can be simplified. Instead of analysing each feasible path π of length k and checking whether it can be prolonged into a feasible error path of the form πe, we can directly look for all error paths of length $k + 1$ and check their feasibility. This form of the k-induction algorithm gets closer to BSE. The main difference is that BSE checks only the feasibility of error paths of length $k + 1$ that have a feasible suffix of length k. Hence, we can see BSE as an optimized version of the k-induction algorithm.

4   BSE with Loop Folding (BSELF)

This section introduces our extension of BSE called *backward symbolic execution with loop folding (BSELF)*. Loop folding targets the incompleteness of BSE. Similar to other verification techniques, we approach this problem by using invariants that constraint the state space analyzed by BSE. Instead of relying on external invariant generators, we compute the invariants directly in BSELF. That allows us to compute disjunctive invariants which can be hard to discover for invariant-generation algorithms [43, 67, 71, 80].

Before describing BSELF in detail, we give a brief description of its functioning. BSELF is searching the program backwards from err as regular BSE. The difference comes when it runs into a loop, i.e., when it finds a feasible error path π with $tl(\pi) = err$ and $sl(\pi) = l$ where l is a loop header. Normal BSE would continue the backward search, unwinding the loop. BSELF, instead, attempts to fold the loop – infer an inductive invariant from which is the path π infeasible. The loop folding successively generates *invariant candidates*. An invariant candidate is a formula ξ such that the set of states (l, ξ) is inductive and π is infeasible from (l, ξ), i.e., $\xi \wedge \pi^{-1}(true)$ is unsatisfiable. The generation continues until either some invariant candidate is shown to be an actual invariant or a pre-set bound is reached, in which case we give up the current loop folding attempt. If an inductive invariant from which π is infeasible have been found, the search on π is terminated. Otherwise, BSELF continues BSE as if no loop folding took place. Irrespective of the result of the folding, we remember all the generated invariant candidates (if any) in an auxiliary set O_l so that we can recycle work if we hit l again on some path. The check of whether an invariant candidate is an invariant is performed by a nested call of BSELF. This way, we automatically handle sequentially chained loops.

The idea behind loop folding is the following. We start with an *initial invariant candidate* ξ_0 that we derive from π and/or previously computed invariant candidates stored in O_l. The set of states (l, ξ_0) is inductive and the program contains no nested loops, so ξ_0 must describe a set of states in which the program may be during some *last* iterations of the loop (this, in fact, holds for any invariant candidate). So if (l, ξ_0) is not an invariant, there is a possibility that adding states from previous iterations will make it an invariant. Thus, we compute the set of states in which the program may be one iteration before entering (l, ξ_0) and try to overapproximate these states to cover more than just one previous iteration of the loop. This step provides us with a new invariant candidate. If it gives rise to an invariant, we are done. Otherwise, we repeat the process to obtain a new invariant candidate and so on.

Precisely speaking, loop folding does not extend one invariant candidate all over again. Every invariant candidate can be extended to several new invariant candidates. Given an invariant candidate ξ, we first compute the pre-image of (l, ξ) along every path of the loop (thus we get $|LoopPaths(l)|$ pre-images). Every non-empty pre-image (l, ψ) from which is π infeasible is then overapproximated to one or more sets (l, ψ') such that $\psi' \vee \xi$ is a new invariant candidate (i.e., $\psi \implies \psi'$, $(l, \psi' \vee \xi)$ is inductive, and $(\psi' \vee \xi) \wedge \pi^{-1}(true)$ is unsatisfiable). Therefore, loop folding generates a tree of invariant candidates instead of a single sequence of invariant candidates.

Procedure $BSELF(loc, \phi_0, infoldloop)$
   Input: location $loc \in L$, formula ϕ_0 over program variables, a boolean $infoldloop$
   Output: *correct* meaning that no state of (loc, ϕ_0) is reachable from $(init, true)$, or
       incorrect meaning that a state of (loc, ϕ_0) is reachable from $(init, true)$, or
       unknown meaning that the procedure finished without decision

  initialize *queue* with $(loc, \phi_0, \emptyset)$
  while *queue* is not empty **do**
     $(l, \phi, visited) \leftarrow$ pop item from *queue*

     if $\neg sat(\phi)$ **then continue**
     if $l = init$ **then return** *incorrect*

     if l is a loop header **then**   // start of the loop folding extension
        if $FoldLoop(l, \phi, visited)$ **then return** *correct*
        if $infoldloop$ **then return** *unknown*
        $visited \leftarrow visited \cup \{l\}$ // end of the loop folding extension

     foreach $e = (l', o, l) \in E$ **do**
        push $(l', e^{-1}(\phi), visited)$ to *queue*
  return *correct*

Algorithm 3: The main procedure of the BSELF algorithm.

We note that giving up loop folding is an important part of the design of BSELF. It has several effects: first, it constraints the time spent in computations that could stall the algorithm for a long time, e.g., nested calls of BSELF that check the invariance of invariant candidates. Second, remember that we store all invariant candidates generated for a loop l in O_l. After we give up a folding of the loop l on π, the next trial of folding l on a path derived from π will use also invariant candidates generated on other paths than π. Symmetrically, attempts to fold the loop l on other paths than π will use the invariant candidates computed during the loop folding of l on π. Finally, during loop folding, we never merge a newly generated invariant candidate into a previously generated candidate, i.e., we preserve the tree structure of candidates during loop folding. This tree structure is forgotten by storing candidates to O_l and thus further attempts to fold the loop l can merge these candidates generated for different paths through the loop and thus find invariants that need such a merging (see the last example of Subsect. 4.5).

4.1 The BSELF Algorithm

The pseudocode of BSELF is shown in Algorithm 3. To shorten the notation, we assume that an input CFA $(L, init, err, E)$ is fixed. Further, for each loop header l, the algorithm uses

– a global variable O_l initially set to $\emptyset$, which stores constructed *invariant candidates* at l, and
– a parameter $\kappa_l \geq 0$ which bounds the effort to infer an invariant at l in a single visit of l.

These global variables and parameters appear only in procedure *FoldLoop*. To decide the error location reachability problem, one should call *BSELF*(*err*, *true*, *false*).

If we ignore the loop folding extension, Algorithm 3 is just an efficient version of Algorithm 1. The difference is that preconditions are now computed incrementally along individual edges of CFA instead of executing whole error paths. Since we lost the information about the length of paths, we use a first-in first-out *queue* instead of a workbag to achieve the shortest-path search order. The parameter *infoldloop* and sets *visited* have an effect only inside *FoldLoop* procedure. Indeed, Algorithm 3 executed with *infoldloop* = *false* never returns *unknown*.

Before discussing the central procedure *FoldLoop* presented in Algorithm 4, we describe how it is used in the main BSELF loop. Whenever BSELF hits a loop header l with the states (l, ϕ) (further called the *error states*), we call the procedure *FoldLoop* which attempts to find an invariant (l, ρ) that proves the unreachability of the current error states, i.e., such that $\rho \wedge \phi$ is unsatisfiable. If the procedure succeeds, we return *correct*. If it fails, we check whether *infoldloop* = *true*. If it is the case, then BSELF was called from inside *FoldLoop* and we return *unknown*. This is to ensure progress and avoid stalling in nested calls of *FoldLoop*. Finally, if *infoldloop* = *false*, we update *visited* with l to remember that we have visited this loop on the current path and continue searching paths like in regular BSE.

Now we turn our attention to the procedure *FoldLoop* (Algorithm 4). In the following, by an *invariant candidate at location* l we mean a formula ξ such that (l, ξ) is disjoint with (l, ϕ) and inductive, i.e., each state with location l reachable from (l, ξ) is also in (l, ξ). We talk just about an invariant candidate if l is clear from the context. The procedure *FoldLoop* maintains a *workbag* of triples (ψ, ξ, k), where ξ is an invariant candidate at l, ψ is the latest extension of ξ (i.e., the last set of states added to ξ), and k is the remaining number of extensions of this candidate that we allow to try. Initially, we set k to κ_l, so every candidate is extended maximally κ_l times.

First, we ask the procedure *InitialInvariantCandidate* for an initial invariant candidate ψ at l. Then we call the procedure *Overapproximate* that returns a set of overapproximated candidates. That is, each ψ' returned from *Overapproximate* is again an invariant candidate and (l, ψ') is a superset of (l, ψ). Then we put the triples (ψ', ψ', κ_l) to *workbag* and remember ψ' also in O_l for possible future attempts of folding this loop.

In every iteration of the main cycle, a triple (ψ, ξ, k) is picked from *workbag*. Then we check whether the corresponding candidate ξ is an invariant. As the candidate is inductive, it is sufficient to check that ξ holds whenever we enter the loop header l from outside of the loop. Hence, we consider all edges $e = (l', o, l)$ that enter the loop from outside and call *BSELF*(l', $e^{-1}(\neg\xi)$, *true*) to detect if

Procedure *FoldLoop(l, φ, visited)*
 Input: location $l \in L$, formula ϕ over program variables, and set *visited* $\subseteq L$
 Output: *true* if an invariant disjoint with (l, ϕ) is found; *false* otherwise

$\psi \leftarrow InitialInvariantCandidate(l, \phi, visited)$
if $\neg sat(\psi)$ **then return** *false*
$workbag \leftarrow \emptyset$
for $\psi' \in Overapproximate(l, \psi, false, \psi, \phi)$ **do**
   $workbag \leftarrow workbag \cup \{(\psi', \psi', \kappa_l)\}$
   $O_l \leftarrow O_l \cup \{\psi'\}$ // update known invariant candidates

while $workbag \neq \emptyset$ **do**
   $(\psi, \xi, k) \leftarrow$ pick item from $workbag$
   $workbag \leftarrow workbag \smallsetminus \{(\psi, \xi, k)\}$
   $fail \leftarrow false$ // check if (l, ξ) is an invariant
   foreach $e = (l', o, l) \in E$ outside any loop **do**
      if $BSELF(l', e^{-1}(\neg\xi), true) \neq correct$ **then**
         $fail \leftarrow true$
         break
   if $fail = false$ **then return** *true*
   if $k > 0$ **then**   // extend the candidate
      foreach $\pi \in LoopPaths(l)$ **do**
         $\psi' \leftarrow \pi^{-1}(\psi)$
         if $\neg sat(\psi' \wedge \phi)$ **then**
            for $\psi'' \in Overapproximate(l, \psi', \psi, \xi, \phi)$ **do**
               $workbag \leftarrow workbag \cup \{(\psi'', \psi'' \vee \xi, k - 1)\}$
               $O_l \leftarrow O_l \cup \{\psi'' \vee \xi\}$ // update known candidates
 return *false*

Algorithm 4: The procedure *FoldLoop(l, φ)* looking for invariants disjoint with (l, ϕ).

ξ always holds when entering l. If the answer is *correct* for all considered edges, then no state in $(l, \neg\xi)$ is reachable from $(init, true)$ and we found an invariant (l, ξ) disjoint with (l, ϕ).

Otherwise, if $k > 0$ then we try to extend the candidate by new states. Specifically, we take every loop path $\pi \in LoopPaths(l)$ and compute the precondition $\psi' = \pi^{-1}(\psi)$ with respect to ψ (the previous extension of the candidate). Note that the set $(l, \psi' \vee \psi)$ is again inductive as (l, ψ) is inductive and all executions of the program from (l, ψ') must end up in $(l, \psi) \subseteq (l, \psi \vee \psi')$. If ψ' is disjoint with ϕ, then ψ' is also an invariant candidate. We put the triples corresponding to overapproximations of this candidate to *workbag* and update the known candidates in the O_l set. Intuitively, the described process of extending a candidate corresponds to computing the set of states in which the program is one iteration before getting into ψ along $\pi \in LoopPaths(l)$ and overapproximating this set to cover not just one, but possibly multiple previous iterations of the loop (along any path).

The main cycle is repeated until either an invariant is found or *workbag* gets empty. Even if we fail to find an invariant in a particular call to *FoldLoop*, it is possible that we find one when BSELF reaches l again. This is because the procedure *InitialInvariantCandidate* (which is described later in detail) not only reuses candidates stored in O_l to recycle the work, but it can even merge several candidates originally computed for different paths through the loop and from different attempts of folding the loop with the header l.

To make the description of loop folding complete, it remains to describe the procedures *InitialInvariantCandidate* and *Overapproximate*.

4.2   The Computation of the Initial Invariant Candidate

The procedure *InitialInvariantCandidate* computes the initial invariant candidate during loop folding. It gets the current error states (l, ϕ) and the set *visited* of loop headers where the loop folding failed during the exploration of the current path, and produces a formula ψ such that the set (l, ψ) is disjoint with (l, ϕ) and inductive.

Let Π_e be the set of safe paths starting in l that exit the loop without finishing a single iteration. Formally, Π_e contains the paths $\pi_e = (l_0, o_0, l_1)(l_1, o_1, l_2) \ldots (l_{n-1}, o_{n-1}, l_n)$ such that $l_0 = l$, $l_1, \ldots, l_{n-1} \in Locs(l) \setminus \{l\}$, and $l_n \notin Locs(l) \cup \{err\}$. Further, we set

$$\psi_e = \neg\phi \wedge \bigvee_{\pi_e \in \Pi_e} \pi_e^{-1}(true).$$

Note that ψ_e is an invariant candidate as it is disjoint with ϕ and inductive because it enforces that the loop is left without finishing any other iteration (and we cannot reach the loop again as the program has no nested loops).

The procedure *InitialInvariantCandidate* works as follows. If $l \notin visited$, then BSELF tries to fold this loop for the first time during exploration of the current path. In this case, ψ_e seems to be a reasonable invariant candidate. However, we would like to recycle the work from previous loop foldings on l (executed on different paths), so we extend ψ_e with all possible candidates stored in O_l that are disjoint with ϕ and subsume ψ_e. Hence, the procedure returns the formula

$$\psi_1 = \psi_e \vee \bigvee_{\substack{\xi \in O_l \\ \psi_e \implies \xi \\ \neg sat(\xi \wedge \phi)}} \xi.$$

If $l \in visited$, then BSELF previously failed to fold this loop during exploration of the current path. In this case, we combine the candidates stored in O_l. More precisely, we define formulas

$$\psi_2 = \bigvee_{\substack{\xi \in O_l \\ \psi_e \implies \xi \\ \neg sat(\xi \wedge \phi)}} \xi \qquad \text{and} \qquad \psi_3 = \bigvee_{\substack{\xi \in O_l \\ \neg sat(\xi \wedge \phi)}} \xi$$

where ψ_2 is a formula that joins all candidates stored in O_l that are disjoint with ϕ and subsume ψ_e. If $sat(\psi_2) = true$ (i.e., we found some suitable candidates in O_l) we return it. Otherwise, we return ψ_3 which gives up on subsumption and just gathers all the candidates stored in O_l that are disjoint with ψ. Note that there may be no such candidates and therefore ψ_3 can be just *false*.

4.3   Overapproximation of an Inductive Set

The procedure $Overapproximate(l, \psi', \psi, \xi, \phi)$ gets the current error states (l, ϕ), an invariant candidate ξ together with its last extension ψ, and the newly suggested extension ψ'. The procedure produces a set of extensions ψ'' that are overapproximations of ψ' (i.e., $\psi' \implies \psi''$) and they are valid extensions of ξ. Formula ψ'' is a *valid extension* of ξ if the following two conditions hold.

1. $(l, \psi'' \vee \xi)$ is disjoint with (l, ϕ). As (l, ξ) and (l, ϕ) are always disjoint, the condition holds if and only if $\psi'' \wedge \phi$ is unsatisfiable.
2. $(l, \psi'' \vee \xi)$ is inductive. As (l, ξ) is inductive, it is sufficient to check that after one loop iteration starting from (l, ψ'') we end up in $(l, \psi'' \vee \xi)$. This condition holds if and only if

$$\bigvee_{\pi \in LoopPaths(l)} \left(\psi'' \wedge \pi^{-1}(\neg(\psi'' \vee \xi)) \right)$$

is unsatisfiable.

Note that Algorithm 4 ensures that the value of ψ' is always a valid extension of ξ.

Our overapproximation procedure works in several steps. In the first step, we collect relations that are implied by ψ' (sometimes together with ψ). Specifically, we derive these kinds of relations:

Type 1. Equalities of the form $x = c$, where x is a program variable and c is a constant.

Type 2. Linear equalities of the form $x \pm y = a$ or $x \pm y = a \cdot z$, where x, y, z are program variables and a is a constant.

Type 3. Relations $a \leq x \leq b \wedge x \equiv 0 \,(\text{mod } b - a)$ for a program variable x and constants $a < b$ such that either $\psi' \implies x = a$ and $\psi \implies x = b$, or $\psi \implies x = a$ and $\psi' \implies x = b$.

Type 4. A formula μ' created from a sub-formula μ of ψ' by the substitution of x with y (or vice versa), where x, y are program variables or constants such that $\psi' \implies x = y$ and $\mu \neq \mu'$.

To collect these relations, we use satisfiability queries. For example, to check whether ψ' implies the relation $x - y = a \cdot z$ for some a, we first check the satisfiability of $\psi' \wedge (x - y = A \cdot z)$ where A is an uninterpreted constant. If the answer is positive, we get a model that assigns some value a to A. Now we check the satisfiability of $\psi' \wedge (x - y = A \cdot z) \wedge A \neq a$. If it is unsatisfiable, then ψ' implies $x - y = a \cdot z$.

In the second step, we create a formula ρ by conjoining the relations of type 1 to ψ' and transforming this new formula to CNF. Note that ρ is equivalent to ψ'. The rest of the overapproximation procedure tries to overapproximate $\rho \wedge R$ for every relation R of type 2–4, yielding potentially many valid extensions of ψ'. To reduce the number of considered relations, we use only those that are not implied by any other relation. Additionally, we try also $R = true$ which leads to overapproximating plain ρ.

Given a relation R, we try to drop clauses of ρ while keeping $\rho \wedge R$ a valid extension. Note that at the beginning, $\rho \wedge R$ is again equivalent to ρ. Let us choose a clause c in ρ and let $\delta = \rho_{-c} \wedge R$, where ρ_{-c} denotes the formula ρ without the clause c. Note that δ is an overapproximation of ρ. If δ is also a valid extension of ξ, we replace ρ with ρ_{-c}. Otherwise, we keep clause c in ρ. We repeat this process until no clause can be dropped. Finally, let ρ' be the formula $\rho \wedge R$.

The fourth step tries to relax the inequalities in ρ'. It tries to replace each inequality $e_1 \leq e_2$ (resp. $e_1 < e_2$) in ρ' with $e_1 \leq e_2 + r$ (resp. $e_1 < e_2 + r$) where r is a constant as large as possible such that the modified ρ' is a valid extension. We search this constant r using the bisection method. If we find such an $r \neq 0$, we must also check that the modified formula is an overapproximation of ψ'. Note that it does not have to be the case, for example, due to integer overflows. If the modified ρ' is an overapproximation, we keep it and continue with the next inequality. A crucial point is to apply this step also to equalities by taking each equality clause $e_1 = e_2$ as $(e_1 \leq e_2) \wedge (e_1 \geq e_2)$.

The last step is similar to the third one: we drop clauses from the current ρ' as long as the formula is a valid extension of ξ. In contrast to the third step, now we try to drop also clauses that were originally in R and thus were not dropped in the third step. The resulting formula has to be a valid extension of ξ and an overapproximation of ψ' by construction.

Similarly, as with filtering relations, we now filter the computed extensions and return only those that are not implied by any other extension.

Note that the result of overapproximating steps are sensitive to the order in which the clauses are processed and to the order in which inequalities are relaxed.

4.4   Optimizations

In our implementation, we use also two optimizations of BSELF. The first optimization is that when we try to fold a loop for the first time, we continue BSE until we unwind the whole loop once along every loop path before we start the actual folding. If the current error becomes infeasible during unwinding, we directly return *true*. This way we avoid loop folding of loops that are easily verifiable by pure BSE.

The second optimization is that we annotate loop headers with generated loop invariants which are then used in BSE. This has no effect on the algorithm as the invariants are always stored also in O_l sets – should the invariant make a path infeasible during BSE, it will get to the initial inductive candidate during loop folding and is discovered again. However, there is the overhead of overapproximating and checking the invariance again.

```
1  int x; // input          1  int n = 1000000;      1  int x; // input
2  int i = 0;               2  int x = 0;            2  int y; // input
3  assume(x == 1);          3  int i = 0;            3  int n; // input
4  while (i < 1000000) {    4  while (i < n) {       4  assume(x >= 0 &&
5      if (i == 5)          5      ++i;              5          x <= y && y < n);
6          --x;             6  }                     6  while (x < n) {
7      ++x;                 7  while (x < n) {        7      ++x;
8      ++i;                 8      ++x;              8      if (x > y)
9  }                        9  }                     9          ++y;
10                          10                        10  }
11  assert(x == i);         11  assert(x == i);       11  assert(y == n);
```

Fig. 3. Three programs verifiable with BSELF.

4.5   Examples

In this subsection, we give examples of running BSELF on the program from Fig. 2 and three programs in Fig. 3 that all trigger a different behavior of BSELF.

Program in Fig. 2. In this program, BSELF first hits the loop with the error states $(1, \phi) = (1, x \neq i \wedge i \geq n)$. There are no stored invariant candidates, so the initial invariant candidate is inferred as $\psi_e = ((x = i \vee i < n) \wedge i \geq n)$. It is simplified and overapproximated to $x = i$, which is directly identified as an invariant.

Figure 3 (Left). In this program, BSELF computes the initial invariant candidate and overapproximates it to $\xi_0 = (1000000 \leq i \wedge x = i)$. It is not an invariant, so BSELF tries to extend it. Although the loop has two paths, the only possible pre-image of ξ_0 is $x = i \wedge i = 999999$. The later equality is relaxed to $999999 \leq 999993 + i$ which simplifies to $6 \leq i$ and ξ_0 is extended with $\psi_1'' = (6 \leq i \wedge x = i)$ to $\xi_1 = ((1000000 \leq i \wedge x = i) \vee (6 \leq i \wedge x = i))$. This is still not an invariant, but the extension of ξ_1, which is computed as an overapproximation of the pre-image of ψ_1'', is $(i = x - 1 \wedge i \leq 5)$ which together with ξ_1 forms an invariant.

Figure 3 (Middle). This program shows that BSELF is not constrained to one loop only. Let us call the first loop $L4$ and the other loop $L7$ and set $\kappa_{L4} = \kappa_{L7} = 1$. The loop folding at $L7$ starts with the candidate $i = x \wedge x \geq n$. The nested call of BSELF to check whether this candidate is invariant leads to folding the loop $L4$ with the initial inductive candidate $i \geq n \wedge i = x$. This folding fails after one extension (because the limit on the number of extensions $\kappa_{L4} = 1$ is hit), the nested instance of BSELF terminates and the top-level instance of BSELF continues extending the candidate at $L7$ to $(i = x \wedge x \geq n) \vee (n = i \wedge x < n)$. This set of states is again checked for invariance, leading to folding the loop $L4$ which succeeds after 1 extension with the invariant $(i \geq n \wedge (x = i \vee n = i) \wedge (n =$

$i \vee x \geq n) \wedge (x < n \vee x = i)) \vee (i < n \wedge (x < n \vee x = 1 + i))$ that in turn proves that $(i = x \wedge x \geq n) \vee (n = i \wedge x < n)$ is invariant at $L7$.

Figure 3 (Right). Assume that $\kappa_{L6} = 1$. BSELF starts folding $L6$ with the error set $y \neq n \wedge x < n$ from which it derives the initial candidate $\xi_0 = (y = n)$. Two extended candidates are generated, namely $\xi_1 = (y = n \vee (n > x \wedge n - 1 \leq y \wedge y \leq n))$ and $\xi_2 = (y = n \vee (y = x \wedge y \leq n))$. Neither of these candidates is an invariant and we hit the limit on the number of extensions, therefore the folding fails. However, ξ_1 and ξ_2 were stored into O_{L6}. BSELF continues unwinding the loop, hitting its header two more times on different paths. In both cases, the initial invariant candidate is drawn from O_{L6} and it is $\psi = \xi_1 \vee \xi_2$ as both these sets are disjunctive with the new error states. In one case ψ is overapproximated to $y = n \vee n \leq y$ and in the other it is overapproximated to $n - 1 \leq y \vee y = x \vee 1 + x \leq y \vee y = n$. The overapproximations are different because they were done with respect to different error states. However, both are identified as invariants and BSELF terminates.

5   Experimental Evaluation

We have implemented BSE and BSELF[1] in the symbolic executor SLOWBEAST [1]. SLOWBEAST is written in Python and uses Z3 [64] as the SMT solver. It takes LLVM [58] bitcode as input.

As BSELF aims to improve BSE on programs with loops, our evaluation uses the benchmarks of the category *ReachSafety-Loops* from the *Competition on Software Verification (SV-COMP)* 2021 [9][2]. Every benchmark is a sequential C program with explicitly marked error locations. The category contains 770 benchmarks out of which 536 are safe and 234 are unsafe.

In experiments with BSELF, BSE, and SE, we compile each benchmark with CLANG to LLVM, inline procedure calls, and flatten nested loops. Even after this preprocessing, some of the benchmarks do not meet the assumptions of BSELF, which is designed primarily for integer programs and does not support the reading of input inside loops. In such cases, loop folding may fail and BSELF falls back to performing BSE. In experiments with BSELF, we set the parameter κ_l to $2 \cdot |LoopPaths(l)| - 1$ for each loop header l.

We first compare BSELF against BSE and then we compare both these techniques to state-of-the-art verification tools. All experiments were conducted on machines with *AMD EPYC* CPU with the frequency 3.1 GHz. For each tool, the run on a benchmark was constrained to 1 core and 8 GB of RAM and 900 s of CPU time. We used the utility BENCHEXEC [16] to enforce resources isolation and to measure their usage.

---

[1] The artifact with implementation and experiments infrastructure can be found at https://doi.org/10.5281/zenodo.5220293.

[2] https://github.com/sosy-lab/sv-benchmarks, commit 3d1593c.

5.1 Comparison of BSELF and BSE

First, we turn our attention to the comparison of BSELF and BSE. The scatter plot in Fig. 4 (left) shows the running time of BSE and BSELF on all benchmarks that were decided by at least one of the algorithms. We can see that BSELF can decide many benchmarks that are out of the scope of BSE (green crosses on the top). Not surprisingly, there are also benchmarks where BSE beats BSELF as computing invariants has non-negligible overhead (red crosses and black crosses under the diagonal line). The quantile plot on the right shows that BSELF performs better on the considered benchmark set than BSE.

The observation from the plots is confirmed by the total numbers of decided benchmarks in Table 1. BSELF was able to solve 65 more safe benchmarks. On unsafe instances, BSE performs better which is expected as BSELF focuses on proving the correctness rather than on finding bugs.

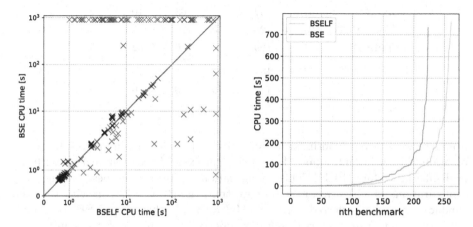

Fig. 4. The left plot provides comparison of running times of BSELF and BSE on benchmarks solved by at least one of them. Green crosses represent benchmarks decided only by BSELF, red crosses are benchmarks decided only by BSE, and black crosses are benchmarks decided by both algorithms. The right plot shows how many benchmarks each algorithm decides with the timeout set to the value on y-axis. (Color figure online)

5.2 Comparison of BSELF to State-of-the-Art Tools

Now we compare BSELF to state-of-the-art tools that can use k-induction and to tools that performed well in the *ReachSafety-Loops* category in SV-COMP 2021. The first set of tools is formed by CPACHECKER [14] and ESBMC [34,36]. These tools combine *bounded model checking (BMC)* with k-induction, where the induction parameter is the number of iterations of loops instead of the length of paths. To solve the incompleteness problem of k-induction, both tools use invariants [11,36]. We used the configuration -kInduction-kipdrdfInvariants of CPACHECKER (referred to as CPA-KIND) that employs external invariants

Table 1. The total number of benchmarks and non-trivial benchmarks solved by the tools. The tools are divided into three groups: tools that use k-induction, other unbounded tools, and bounded tools. The column *safe* (*unsafe*) reports the number of solved benchmarks with an unreachable (reachable, respectively) error location. The column *wrong* shows the number of wrong decisions by the tool.

	All (770)			Non-trivial (299)		
	Safe	Unsafe	Wrong	Safe	Unsafe	Wrong
BSE	144	80	0	64	1	0
BSELF	209	53	0	104	0	0
CPA-KIPDR	245	125	2	58	0	2
ESBMC-KIND	284	161	3	42	9	3
SE+BSELF	373	161	0	102	0	0
CPA-SEQ	318	151	2	72	4	2
DIVINE	316	152	2	63	10	2
UAUTOMIZER	255	126	0	126	5	0
VERIABS	412	199	0	136	32	0
CPA-BMC	255	142	2	0	0	2
SE	273	142	0	0	0	0

from interval analysis (continuously generated in parallel to k-induction) in combination with invariants inferred from counter-examples to k-induction with a PDR-like procedure [10,11]. This configuration performed the best among the configurations of CPACHECKER that we tried. ESBMC was run with the -s kinduction option (referred to as ESBMC-KIND). In this setup, ESBMC computes invariants using interval analysis, injects them as annotations into the program, and then runs BMC with k-induction [36].

Tools that performed well in SV-COMP 2021 are DIVINE [7], UAUTOMIZER [48], VERIABS [2], and another configuration of CPACHECKER called CPA-SEQ. We call these tools collectively as *sv-comp tools*. DIVINE is a control-explicit data-symbolic model-checker. UAUTOMIZER models programs as automata and reduces the verification problem to deciding a language emptiness (internally implemented using interpolation-based predicate analysis with CEGAR). VERIABS is a software verifier that uses a portfolio of techniques selected heuristically according to a given program. One of the techniques is also BMC with k-induction. CPA-SEQ combines several approaches including value analysis and predicate abstraction. All these tools were run in their settings for SV-COMP 2021. We also created a configuration SE+BSELF where we run SE for 450 s and for the remaining 450 s we run BSELF (if SE did not decide the result).

Finally, we ran BMC and SE on all benchmarks with the purpose to tell apart benchmarks that are easy to handle by simple state space enumeration. Benchmarks that can be easily decided neither with BMC (we used BMC implementation from the tool CPACHECKER) nor with SE (we used SE from SLOWBEAST) are further dubbed as *non-trivial*. Out of the 770 benchmarks, 299 benchmarks were non-trivial.

Table 1 shows that all approaches but BSE outperform BSELF when compared on all benchmarks. However, this superiority is mostly caused by the ability to decide easy tasks by entirely unwinding loops. The configuration SE+BSELF that runs SE before BSELF shows that it is the case. If we compare the tools on non-trivial benchmarks, BSELF is able to solve more benchmarks than the other k-induction-based tools and is surpassed only by UAUTOMIZER and VERIABS in the comparison of all tools. SE+BSELF is highly competitive with sv-comp tools. Indeed, the only tool that performs better is VERIABS, which is not that surprising as it selects a suitable verification technique (including BMC with k-induction) for each program.

Table 2 provides the cross-comparison of individual tools on non-trivial benchmarks by any of the approaches. Among k-induction-based tools, BSELF dominates CPA-KIND and ESBMC-KIND in these numbers, which suggests that loop folding is a stronger invariant generation technique than those used by these tools.

Table 2. Cross-comparison on non-trivial benchmarks. Numbers in rows show how many benchmarks the tool in the row decided and the tool in the column did not.

	BSE	BSELF	CPA-KIPDR	ESBMC-KIND	SE+BSELF	CPA-SEQ	DIVINE	UAUTOMIZER	VERIABS
BSE	–	3	28	50	4	27	49	15	31
BSELF	42	–	56	88	2	56	63	38	34
CPA-KIPDR	21	10	–	46	11	8	34	4	15
ESBMC-KIND	36	35	39	–	36	27	34	18	18
SE+BSELF	41	0	55	87	–	55	62	37	33
CPA-SEQ	38	28	26	52	29	–	41	5	20
DIVINE	57	32	49	56	33	38	–	28	7
UAUTOMIZER	81	65	77	98	66	60	86	–	50
VERIABS	134	98	125	135	99	112	102	87	–

6   Related Work

Related work on symbolic execution was discussed in Sect. 1. *Backward symbolic execution* [22], or *symbolic backward execution* [6] has been paid less attention in the area of automatic code verification than its forward counterpart. Its roots can be tracked to backward symbolic analysis of protocols by Danthine and Bremer [25], and Holzmann et al. [50]. Chandra et al. [22] use interprocedural BSE with function summaries [75] and path pruning to find bugs in Java programs. Chen and Kim use BSE in the tool STAR [23], basically following the approach of Chandra et al., to compute the precondition of a program crash – BSE is guided by the given crash report to reproduce a bug. Arzt et al. [4] use BSE in a very similar manner. None of these works consider loop invariants.

Although BSE on its own is not very popular in automatic software verification, its principal foundation – the weakest precondition – is cherished in deductive verification [8,26,31,59].

Our work was motivated by finding a synergy of symbolic execution with k-induction. The first use of k-induction is attributed to Sheeran et al. [77] who used it to model check hardware designs. Many other model checking approaches follow up on this work [17,44,53,56,65,70]. The k-induction scheme has been transferred also to software model checking, where it is usually applied only to loops [11,21,29,35].

Our technique infers loop invariants. There are plenty of works on this topic [5,18,20,24,27,30,40–43,51,54,66,76], but a relatively few of the works target disjunctive invariants [27,40–42,66,76,80] that arise naturally in loop folding in BSELF.

Loop acceleration computes the reflexive and transitive closure of loop iterations [49] or its supersets or subsets [33,61]. It can be used to infer or help to infer inductive invariants [49,51,61] or, in general, for the verification of safety properties with model checking or abstract interpretation. BSELF could benefit from accelerators to speed up BSE and loop folding.

Similar to loop acceleration is *loop summarization* [80] which deals with inferring *loop summaries* [38]. A loop summary is a relation that associates a set of output states (a post-condition) of the loop to a given set of input states (a pre-condition) of the loop [37,38]. With loop summaries, one is able to skip the execution of loops and directly apply the loops' effect instead of unwinding them [78]. Such an application would directly help BSE(LF) in scaling on programs with loops as it removes the need to unwind/fold loops.

Inferring relations when overapproximating inductive sets in BSELF is similar to the use of predicates in *predicate abstraction* [32,52].

7   Conclusion

In this work, we showed that performing k-induction on control-flow paths is equivalent to running backward symbolic execution (BSE) with the breadth-first search strategy. Then we introduced *loop folding*, a technique to infer disjunctive invariants during BSE that can help to solve a new class of benchmarks that were previously out of the scope of BSE. We compared BSE with loop folding (BSELF) with pure BSE, several k-induction-based tools, and also with the state-of-the art tools that performed well on the *ReachSafety-Loops* category in SV-COMP 2021. Compared to each of these tools, BSELF is able to solve benchmarks that the other tool is not, which makes it a valuable addition to the portfolio of program verification approaches.

In the future, we want to explore the possibilities of using the information from failed induction checks and try different overapproximation methods, e.g., some PDR-like procedure.

References

1. SlowBeast. https://gitlab.fi.muni.cz/xchalup4/slowbeast. Accessed 15 Aug 2021
2. Afzal, M., et al.: VeriAbs: verification by abstraction and test generation. In: 34th IEEE/ACM International Conference on Automated Software Engineering, ASE 2019, pp. 1138–1141. IEEE (2019). https://doi.org/10.1109/ASE.2019.00121
3. Anand, S., Godefroid, P., Tillmann, N.: Demand-driven compositional symbolic execution. In: Ramakrishnan, C.R., Rehof, J. (eds.) TACAS 2008. LNCS, vol. 4963, pp. 367–381. Springer, Heidelberg (2008). https://doi.org/10.1007/978-3-540-78800-3_28
4. Arzt, S., Rasthofer, S., Hahn, R., Bodden, E.: Using targeted symbolic execution for reducing false-positives in dataflow analysis. In: Proceedings of the 4th ACM SIGPLAN International Workshop on State of the Art in Program Analysis, SOAP@PLDI 2015, pp. 1–6. ACM (2015). https://doi.org/10.1145/2771284.2771285
5. Awedh, M., Somenzi, F.: Automatic invariant strengthening to prove properties in bounded model checking. In: Proceedings of the 43rd Design Automation Conference, DAC 2006, pp. 1073–1076. ACM (2006). https://doi.org/10.1145/1146909.1147180
6. Baldoni, R., Coppa, E., D'Elia, D.C., Demetrescu, C., Finocchi, I.: A survey of symbolic execution techniques. ACM Comput. Surv. **51**(3), 50:1–50:39 (2018). https://doi.org/10.1145/3182657
7. Baranová, Z., et al.: Model checking of C and C++ with DIVINE 4. In: D'Souza, D., Narayan Kumar, K. (eds.) ATVA 2017. LNCS, vol. 10482, pp. 201–207. Springer, Cham (2017). https://doi.org/10.1007/978-3-319-68167-2_14
8. Barnett, M., Leino, K.R.M.: Weakest-precondition of unstructured programs. In: Proceedings of the 2005 ACM SIGPLAN-SIGSOFT Workshop on Program Analysis for Software Tools and Engineering, PASTE 2005, pp. 82–87. ACM (2005). https://doi.org/10.1145/1108792.1108813
9. Beyer, D.: Software verification: 10th comparative evaluation (SV-COMP 2021). In: TACAS 2021. LNCS, vol. 12652, pp. 401–422. Springer, Cham (2021). https://doi.org/10.1007/978-3-030-72013-1_24
10. Beyer, D., Dangl, M.: Software verification with PDR: an implementation of the state of the art. In: TACAS 2020. LNCS, vol. 12078, pp. 3–21. Springer, Cham (2020). https://doi.org/10.1007/978-3-030-45190-5_1
11. Beyer, D., Dangl, M., Wendler, P.: Boosting k-induction with continuously-refined invariants. In: Kroening, D., Păsăreanu, C.S. (eds.) CAV 2015. LNCS, vol. 9206, pp. 622–640. Springer, Cham (2015). https://doi.org/10.1007/978-3-319-21690-4_42
12. Beyer, D., Dangl, M., Wendler, P.: Combining k-induction with continuously-refined invariants. CoRR abs/1502.00096 (2015). http://arxiv.org/abs/1502.00096
13. Beyer, D., Henzinger, T.A., Jhala, R., Majumdar, R.: The software model checker Blast. Int. J. Softw. Tools Technol. Transf. **9**(5–6), 505–525 (2007). https://doi.org/10.1007/s10009-007-0044-z

14. Beyer, D., Keremoglu, M.E.: CPACHECKER: a tool for configurable software verification. In: Gopalakrishnan, G., Qadeer, S. (eds.) CAV 2011. LNCS, vol. 6806, pp. 184–190. Springer, Heidelberg (2011). https://doi.org/10.1007/978-3-642-22110-1_16

15. Beyer, D., Lemberger, T.: Symbolic execution with CEGAR. In: Margaria, T., Steffen, B. (eds.) ISoLA 2016. LNCS, vol. 9952, pp. 195–211. Springer, Cham (2016). https://doi.org/10.1007/978-3-319-47166-2_14

16. Beyer, D., Löwe, S., Wendler, P.: Reliable benchmarking: requirements and solutions. STTT **21**(1), 1–29 (2019). https://doi.org/10.1007/s10009-017-0469-y

17. Bjesse, P., Claessen, K.: SAT-based verification without state space traversal. In: Hunt, W.A., Johnson, S.D. (eds.) FMCAD 2000. LNCS, vol. 1954, pp. 409–426. Springer, Heidelberg (2000). https://doi.org/10.1007/3-540-40922-X_23

18. Bjørner, N., Browne, A., Manna, Z.: Automatic generation of invariants and intermediate assertions. Theor. Comput. Sci. **173**(1), 49–87 (1997). https://doi.org/10.1016/S0304-3975(96)00191-0

19. Boonstoppel, P., Cadar, C., Engler, D.: RWset: attacking path explosion in constraint-based test generation. In: Ramakrishnan, C.R., Rehof, J. (eds.) TACAS 2008. LNCS, vol. 4963, pp. 351–366. Springer, Heidelberg (2008). https://doi.org/10.1007/978-3-540-78800-3_27

20. Bradley, A.R., Manna, Z.: Property-directed incremental invariant generation. Formal Aspects Comput. **20**(4–5), 379–405 (2008). https://doi.org/10.1007/s00165-008-0080-9

21. Brain, M., Joshi, S., Kroening, D., Schrammel, P.: Safety verification and refutation by k-invariants and k-induction. In: Blazy, S., Jensen, T. (eds.) SAS 2015. LNCS, vol. 9291, pp. 145–161. Springer, Heidelberg (2015). https://doi.org/10.1007/978-3-662-48288-9_9

22. Chandra, S., Fink, S.J., Sridharan, M.: Snugglebug: a powerful approach to weakest preconditions. In: Proceedings of the 2009 ACM SIGPLAN Conference on Programming Language Design and Implementation, PLDI 2009, pp. 363–374. ACM (2009). https://doi.org/10.1145/1542476.1542517

23. Chen, N., Kim, S.: STAR: stack trace based automatic crash reproduction via symbolic execution. IEEE Trans. Softw. Eng. **41**(2), 198–220 (2015). https://doi.org/10.1109/TSE.2014.2363469

24. Cousot, P., Halbwachs, N.: Automatic discovery of linear restraints among variables of a program. In: Conference Record of the Fifth Annual ACM Symposium on Principles of Programming Languages, POPL 1978, pp. 84–96. ACM Press (1978). https://doi.org/10.1145/512760.512770

25. Danthine, A., Bremer, J.: Modelling and verification of end-to-end transport protocols. Comput. Netw. (1976) **2**(4), 381–395 (1978). https://www.sciencedirect.com/science/article/pii/037650757890017X

26. Dijkstra, E.W.: A Discipline of Programming. Prentice-Hall (1976). https://www.worldcat.org/oclc/01958445

27. Dillig, I., Dillig, T., Li, B., McMillan, K.L.: Inductive invariant generation via abductive inference. In: Proceedings of the 2013 ACM SIGPLAN International Conference on Object Oriented Programming Systems Languages & Applications, OOPSLA 2013, pp. 443–456. ACM (2013). https://doi.org/10.1145/2509136.2509511

28. Dinges, P., Agha, G.A.: Targeted test input generation using symbolic-concrete backward execution. In: ACM/IEEE International Conference on Automated Software Engineering, ASE 2014, pp. 31–36. ACM (2014). https://doi.org/10.1145/2642937.2642951

29. Donaldson, A.F., Kroening, D., Rümmer, P.: Automatic analysis of DMA races using model checking and k-induction. Formal Methods Syst. Des. **39**(1), 83–113 (2011). https://doi.org/10.1007/s10703-011-0124-2

30. Fedyukovich, G., Bodík, R.: Accelerating syntax-guided invariant synthesis. In: Beyer, D., Huisman, M. (eds.) TACAS 2018. LNCS, vol. 10805, pp. 251–269. Springer, Cham (2018). https://doi.org/10.1007/978-3-319-89960-2_14

31. Filliâtre, J.: Deductive software verification. Int. J. Softw. Tools Technol. Transf. **13**(5), 397–403 (2011). https://doi.org/10.1007/s10009-011-0211-0

32. Flanagan, C., Qadeer, S.: Predicate abstraction for software verification. In: Conference Record of POPL 2002: The 29th SIGPLAN-SIGACT Symposium on Principles of Programming Languages, POPL 2002, pp. 191–202. ACM (2002). https://doi.org/10.1145/503272.503291

33. Frohn, F.: A calculus for modular loop acceleration. In: TACAS 2020. LNCS, vol. 12078, pp. 58–76. Springer, Cham (2020). https://doi.org/10.1007/978-3-030-45190-5_4

34. Gadelha, M.R., Monteiro, F.R., Morse, J., Cordeiro, L.C., Fischer, B., Nicole, D.A.: ESBMC 5.0: an industrial-strength C model checker. In: 33rd ACM/IEEE International Conference on Automated Software Engineering (ASE 2018), pp. 888–891. ACM, New York (2018)

35. Gadelha, M.Y.R., Ismail, H.I., Cordeiro, L.C.: Handling loops in bounded model checking of C programs via k-induction. STTT **19**(1), 97–114 (2017). https://doi.org/10.1007/s10009-015-0407-9

36. Gadelha, M.R., Monteiro, F., Cordeiro, L., Nicole, D.: ESBMC v6.0: verifying C programs using k-induction and invariant inference. In: Beyer, D., Huisman, M., Kordon, F., Steffen, B. (eds.) TACAS 2019. LNCS, vol. 11429, pp. 209–213. Springer, Cham (2019). https://doi.org/10.1007/978-3-030-17502-3_15

37. Godefroid, P.: Compositional dynamic test generation. In: Proceedings of the 34th ACM SIGPLAN-SIGACT Symposium on Principles of Programming Languages, POPL 2007, pp. 47–54. ACM (2007). https://doi.org/10.1145/1190216.1190226

38. Godefroid, P., Luchaup, D.: Automatic partial loop summarization in dynamic test generation. In: Proceedings of the 20th International Symposium on Software Testing and Analysis, ISSTA 2011, pp. 23–33. ACM (2011). https://doi.org/10.1145/2001420.2001424

39. Godefroid, P., Nori, A.V., Rajamani, S.K., Tetali, S.: Compositional may-must program analysis: unleashing the power of alternation. In: Proceedings of the 37th ACM SIGPLAN-SIGACT Symposium on Principles of Programming Languages, POPL 2010, pp. 43–56. ACM (2010). https://doi.org/10.1145/1706299.1706307

40. Gopan, D., Reps, T.: Lookahead widening. In: Ball, T., Jones, R.B. (eds.) CAV 2006. LNCS, vol. 4144, pp. 452–466. Springer, Heidelberg (2006). https://doi.org/10.1007/11817963_41

41. Gopan, D., Reps, T.: Guided static analysis. In: Nielson, H.R., Filé, G. (eds.) SAS 2007. LNCS, vol. 4634, pp. 349–365. Springer, Heidelberg (2007). https://doi.org/10.1007/978-3-540-74061-2_22

42. Gulwani, S., Juvekar, S.: Bound analysis using backward symbolic execution. Technical report MSR-TR-2009-156, Microsoft Research (2009)

43. Gupta, A., Rybalchenko, A.: InvGen: an efficient invariant generator. In: Bouajjani, A., Maler, O. (eds.) CAV 2009. LNCS, vol. 5643, pp. 634–640. Springer, Heidelberg (2009). https://doi.org/10.1007/978-3-642-02658-4_48

44. Gurfinkel, A., Ivrii, A.: K-induction without unrolling. In: 2017 Formal Methods in Computer Aided Design, FMCAD 2017, pp. 148–155. IEEE (2017). https://doi.org/10.23919/FMCAD.2017.8102253

45. Hansen, T., Schachte, P., Søndergaard, H.: State joining and splitting for the symbolic execution of binaries. In: Bensalem, S., Peled, D.A. (eds.) RV 2009. LNCS, vol. 5779, pp. 76–92. Springer, Heidelberg (2009). https://doi.org/10.1007/978-3-642-04694-0_6

46. Harris, W.R., Sankaranarayanan, S., Ivancic, F., Gupta, A.: Program analysis via satisfiability modulo path programs. In: Proceedings of the 37th ACM SIGPLAN-SIGACT Symposium on Principles of Programming Languages, POPL 2010, pp. 71–82. ACM (2010). https://doi.org/10.1145/1706299.1706309

47. Hecht, M.S., Ullman, J.D.: Characterizations of reducible flow graphs. J. ACM 21(3), 367–375 (1974). https://doi.org/10.1145/321832.321835

48. Heizmann, M., Hoenicke, J., Podelski, A.: Software model checking for people who love automata. In: Sharygina, N., Veith, H. (eds.) CAV 2013. LNCS, vol. 8044, pp. 36–52. Springer, Heidelberg (2013). https://doi.org/10.1007/978-3-642-39799-8_2

49. Hojjat, H., Iosif, R., Konečný, F., Kuncak, V., Rümmer, P.: Accelerating interpolants. In: Chakraborty, S., Mukund, M. (eds.) ATVA 2012. LNCS, pp. 187–202. Springer, Heidelberg (2012). https://doi.org/10.1007/978-3-642-33386-6_16

50. Holzmann, G.J.: Backward symbolic execution of protocols. In: Protocol Specification, Testing and Verification IV, Proceedings of the IFIP WG6.1 Fourth International Workshop on Protocol Specification, Testing and Verification, pp. 19–30. North-Holland (1984)

51. Jeannet, B., Schrammel, P., Sankaranarayanan, S.: Abstract acceleration of general linear loops. In: The 41st Annual ACM SIGPLAN-SIGACT Symposium on Principles of Programming Languages, POPL 2014, pp. 529–540. ACM (2014). https://doi.org/10.1145/2535838.2535843

52. Jhala, R., Podelski, A., Rybalchenko, A.: Predicate abstraction for program verification. In: Handbook of Model Checking, pp. 447–491. Springer, Cham (2018). https://doi.org/10.1007/978-3-319-10575-8_15

53. Jovanovic, D., Dutertre, B.: Property-directed k-induction. In: 2016 Formal Methods in Computer-Aided Design, FMCAD 2016, pp. 85–92. IEEE (2016). https://doi.org/10.1109/FMCAD.2016.7886665

54. Karr, M.: Affine relationships among variables of a program. Acta Inform. 6, 133–151 (1976). https://doi.org/10.1007/BF00268497

55. King, J.C.: Symbolic execution and program testing. Commun. ACM 19(7), 385–394 (1976). https://doi.org/10.1145/360248.360252

56. Vediramana Krishnan, H.G., Vizel, Y., Ganesh, V., Gurfinkel, A.: Interpolating strong induction. In: Dillig, I., Tasiran, S. (eds.) CAV 2019. LNCS, vol. 11562, pp. 367–385. Springer, Cham (2019). https://doi.org/10.1007/978-3-030-25543-5_21

57. Kuznetsov, V., Kinder, J., Bucur, S., Candea, G.: Efficient state merging in symbolic execution. In: ACM SIGPLAN Conference on Programming Language Design and Implementation, PLDI 2012, pp. 193–204. ACM (2012). https://doi.org/10.1145/2254064.2254088

58. Lattner, C., Adve, V.S.: LLVM: a compilation framework for lifelong program analysis & transformation. In: CGO 2004, pp. 75–88. IEEE Computer Society (2004). https://doi.org/10.1109/CGO.2004.1281665

59. Leino, K.R.M.: Efficient weakest preconditions. Inf. Process. Lett. 93(6), 281–288 (2005). https://doi.org/10.1016/j.ipl.2004.10.015

60. Li, G., Ghosh, I.: Lazy symbolic execution through abstraction and sub-space search. In: Bertacco, V., Legay, A. (eds.) HVC 2013. LNCS, vol. 8244, pp. 295–310. Springer, Cham (2013). https://doi.org/10.1007/978-3-319-03077-7_20

61. Madhukar, K., Wachter, B., Kroening, D., Lewis, M., Srivas, M.K.: Accelerating invariant generation. In: Formal Methods in Computer-Aided Design, FMCAD 2015, pp. 105–111. IEEE (2015)
62. Majumdar, R., Sen, K.: Latest: lazy dynamic test input generation. Technical report UCB/EECS-2007-36, EECS Department, University of California, Berkeley (2007)
63. McMillan, K.L.: Lazy annotation for program testing and verification. In: Touili, T., Cook, B., Jackson, P. (eds.) CAV 2010. LNCS, vol. 6174, pp. 104–118. Springer, Heidelberg (2010). https://doi.org/10.1007/978-3-642-14295-6_10
64. de Moura, L., Bjørner, N.: Z3: an efficient SMT solver. In: Ramakrishnan, C.R., Rehof, J. (eds.) TACAS 2008. LNCS, vol. 4963, pp. 337–340. Springer, Heidelberg (2008). https://doi.org/10.1007/978-3-540-78800-3_24
65. de Moura, L., Rueß, H., Sorea, M.: Bounded model checking and induction: from refutation to verification. In: Hunt, W.A., Somenzi, F. (eds.) CAV 2003. LNCS, vol. 2725, pp. 14–26. Springer, Heidelberg (2003). https://doi.org/10.1007/978-3-540-45069-6_2
66. Nguyen, T., Kapur, D., Weimer, W., Forrest, S.: Using dynamic analysis to generate disjunctive invariants. In: 36th International Conference on Software Engineering, ICSE 2014, pp. 608–619. ACM (2014). https://doi.org/10.1145/2568225.2568275
67. Popeea, C., Chin, W.-N.: Inferring disjunctive postconditions. In: Okada, M., Satoh, I. (eds.) ASIAN 2006. LNCS, vol. 4435, pp. 331–345. Springer, Heidelberg (2007). https://doi.org/10.1007/978-3-540-77505-8_26
68. Qiu, R., Yang, G., Pasareanu, C.S., Khurshid, S.: Compositional symbolic execution with memoized replay. In: 37th IEEE/ACM International Conference on Software Engineering, ICSE 2015, pp. 632–642. IEEE Computer Society (2015). https://doi.org/10.1109/ICSE.2015.79
69. Rocha, W., Rocha, H., Ismail, H., Cordeiro, L., Fischer, B.: DepthK: a k-induction verifier based on invariant inference for C programs. In: Legay, A., Margaria, T. (eds.) TACAS 2017. LNCS, vol. 10206, pp. 360–364. Springer, Heidelberg (2017). https://doi.org/10.1007/978-3-662-54580-5_23
70. Roux, P., Delmas, R., Garoche, P.: SMT-AI: an abstract interpreter as oracle for k-induction. Electron. Notes Theor. Comput. Sci. **267**(2), 55–68 (2010). https://doi.org/10.1016/j.entcs.2010.09.018
71. Sankaranarayanan, S., Ivančić, F., Shlyakhter, I., Gupta, A.: Static analysis in disjunctive numerical domains. In: Yi, K. (ed.) SAS 2006. LNCS, vol. 4134, pp. 3–17. Springer, Heidelberg (2006). https://doi.org/10.1007/11823230_2
72. Santelices, R.A., Harrold, M.J.: Exploiting program dependencies for scalable multiple-path symbolic execution. In: Proceedings of the Nineteenth International Symposium on Software Testing and Analysis, ISSTA 2010, pp. 195–206. ACM (2010). https://doi.org/10.1145/1831708.1831733
73. Saxena, P., Poosankam, P., McCamant, S., Song, D.: Loop-extended symbolic execution on binary programs. In: Proceedings of the Eighteenth International Symposium on Software Testing and Analysis, ISSTA 2009, pp. 225–236. ACM (2009). https://doi.org/10.1145/1572272.1572299
74. Sen, K., Necula, G.C., Gong, L., Choi, W.: MultiSE: multi-path symbolic execution using value summaries. In: Proceedings of the 2015 10th Joint Meeting on Foundations of Software Engineering, ESEC/FSE 2015, pp. 842–853. ACM (2015). https://doi.org/10.1145/2786805.2786830
75. Sharir, M., Pnueli, A., et al.: Two approaches to interprocedural data flow analysis. New York University, Courant Institute of Mathematical Sciences (1978)

76. Sharma, R., Dillig, I., Dillig, T., Aiken, A.: Simplifying loop invariant generation using splitter predicates. In: Gopalakrishnan, G., Qadeer, S. (eds.) CAV 2011. LNCS, vol. 6806, pp. 703–719. Springer, Heidelberg (2011). https://doi.org/10.1007/978-3-642-22110-1_57

77. Sheeran, M., Singh, S., Stålmarck, G.: Checking safety properties using induction and a SAT-solver. In: Hunt, W.A., Johnson, S.D. (eds.) FMCAD 2000. LNCS, vol. 1954, pp. 127–144. Springer, Heidelberg (2000). https://doi.org/10.1007/3-540-40922-X_8

78. Slaby, J., Strejček, J., Trtík, M.: Compact symbolic execution. In: Van Hung, D., Ogawa, M. (eds.) ATVA 2013. LNCS, vol. 8172, pp. 193–207. Springer, Cham (2013). https://doi.org/10.1007/978-3-319-02444-8_15

79. Wang, H., Liu, T., Guan, X., Shen, C., Zheng, Q., Yang, Z.: Dependence guided symbolic execution. IEEE Trans. Softw. Eng. **43**(3), 252–271 (2017). https://doi.org/10.1109/TSE.2016.2584063

80. Xie, X., Chen, B., Zou, L., Liu, Y., Le, W., Li, X.: Automatic loop summarization via path dependency analysis. IEEE Trans. Softw. Eng. **45**(6), 537–557 (2019). https://doi.org/10.1109/TSE.2017.2788018

81. Yi, Q., Yang, Z., Guo, S., Wang, C., Liu, J., Zhao, C.: Eliminating path redundancy via postconditioned symbolic execution. IEEE Trans. Softw. Eng. **44**(1), 25–43 (2018). https://doi.org/10.1109/TSE.2017.2659751

Accelerating Program Analyses in Datalog by Merging Library Facts

Yifan Chen[1], Chenyang Yang[1], Xin Zhang[1]([✉]), Yingfei Xiong[1], Hao Tang[2],
Xiaoyin Wang[3], and Lu Zhang[1]

[1] Key Laboratory of High Confidence Software Technologies, MoE,
Department of Computer Science and Technology, EECS, Peking University,
Beijing, China
{yf_chen,chenyangy,xin,xiongyf,zhanglucs}@pku.edu.cn
[2] Alibaba Group, Hangzhou, China
albert.th@alibaba-inc.com
[3] Department of Computer Science, University of Texas at San Antonio,
San Antonio, TX, USA
xiaoyin.wang@utsa.edu

Abstract. Static program analysis uses sensitivity to balance between precision and scalability. However, finer sensitivity does not necessarily lead to more precise results but may reduce scalability. Recently, a number of approaches have been proposed to finely tune the sensitivity of different program parts. However, these approaches are usually designed for specific program analyses, and their abstraction adjustments are coarse-grained as they directly drop sensitivity elements.

In this paper, we propose a new technique, 4DM, to tune abstractions for program analyses in Datalog. 4DM merges values in a domain, allowing fine-grained sensitivity tuning. 4DM uses a data-driven algorithm for automatically learning a merging strategy for a library from a training set of programs. Unlike existing approaches that rely on the properties of a certain analysis, our learning algorithm works for a wide range of Datalog analyses. We have evaluated our approach on a points-to analysis and a liveness analysis, on the DaCapo benchmark suite. Our evaluation results suggest that our technique achieves a significant speedup and negligible precision loss, reaching a good balance.

Keywords: Static analysis · Datalog · Data-driven analysis · Domain-wise merging

1 Introduction

One key problem in program analysis is to choose what information to keep in the program abstraction in order to balance its precision and scalability. It is often controlled through a domain of sensitivity elements. For example, call-site sensitivity [17,19] distinguishes information under different calling contexts using the string of most recent call sites, and it is parameterized by the length

© Springer Nature Switzerland AG 2021
C. Drăgoi et al. (Eds.): SAS 2021, LNCS 12913, pp. 77–101, 2021.
https://doi.org/10.1007/978-3-030-88806-0_4

of this string. In general, the finer the sensitivity is, the higher the precision is, yet the lower the scalability is. However, it is not always the case. Under some circumstances, coarse-grained sensitivity is enough and making it finer does not lead to higher precision. Using fine-grained sensitivity in such cases would lead to unnecessary time cost.

In order to reduce the time spent by such "inefficient" sensitivity, many existing approaches focus on using sensitivity selectively. A common practice is to drop sensitivity elements at specific program points. Take tuning call-site sensitivity as an example: Smaragdakis et al. [20] used a crafted rule to decide whether to keep the contexts for specific call sites; Jeong et al. [11] tried to cut the context length for each call site using a data-driven method; and Zhang et al. [27] proposed an approach which started by dropping all contexts and then selectively added them back by identifying call sites where adding contexts helps. However, a binary choice of whether to drop a sensitivity attribute can be too coarse-grained to achieve the best precision and efficiency. Imagine, in a 1-object-sensitive points-to analysis, a method is invoked by 10 different objects at a call site, 9 of them leading to the same analysis result while the other one leading to a different result. Dropping all of the contexts would lead to imprecise analysis, but keeping the contexts leads to 8 rounds of unproductive analysis.

Recently, Tan et al. [21] proposed a different idea of tuning abstraction which is more fine-grained. Their method, MAHJONG, merges heap objects into different equivalent classes according to type and field-points-to information. In the previous example, if certain conditions are met, MAHJONG could merge the 9 objects that lead to the same analysis result, therefore achieving the same precision as a 1-object-sensitive analysis but with better efficiency. However, this approach is limited to tuning heap abstraction for type-related queries in points-to analysis. Specifically, it only allows merging heap objects and relies on a pre-analysis to identify which objects to merge. If the query is not about types, e.g., querying aliases of a variable, it is not applicable.

We propose a new merging-based method, named **4DM** (Data-Driven Datalog Domain-wise Merging), to resolve the weakness of the above two approaches. For given domains, 4DM's **domain-wise merging** merges concrete values that contribute to similar results into the same abstract value. It makes finer adjustment on domains of sensitivity elements by merging into multiple abstract values than simply dropping as in context reduction. Furthermore, it generalizes context reduction. For example, reducing the contexts for a particular call site c from 2-objective-sensitive to 1-object-sensitive can be seen as transforming all triples (o_i^1, o_i^2, c) to $(*, o_i^2, c)$, where o_i^1 and o_i^2 are the calling contexts and $*$ is an abstract value. 4DM merges values in various domains as opposed to only heap objects, e.g. call sites, program points, variables, and can be applied to tune various sensitivities in a wide range of analyses.

In order to apply merging to various domains in different analyses, 4DM employs a general framework for **Datalog**-based analyses. It transforms Datalog rules to embed merging in them, and guarantees soundness.

```
 1 package library;              package client1;                              1
 2                               import library;                               2
 3 public class Lib {            public class Clt1 {                            3
 4   public static A id(A x){       public static void main(String[] args){     4
 5     return x;                      A p1 = new A(); // o_1                     5
 6   }                               A p2 = new A(); // o_2                      6
 7   public static A foo(A u){       x1 = library.Lib.id(p1); // cs_1           7
 8     v = id(u); // cs_5            x2 = library.Lib.id(p1); // cs_2           8
 9     return v;                      x3 = library.Lib.foo(p2); // cs_3         9
10   }                               x4 = library.Lib.bar(p2); // cs_4         10
11   public static A bar(A s){       assert(x1==x2); // Q1: safe?              11
12     t = id(s); // cs_6            assert(x3==x4); // Q2: safe?              12
13     return t;                      assert(x1==x3); // Q3: safe?             13
14   }                             }                                          14
15 }                             }                                            15
```

Listing 1.1. Example code that higher sensitivity leads unnecessary computation

Now the challenge is to find an effective merging strategy under 4DM's representation that accelerates analysis while keeping precision. Our insight to address this challenge is that library code occupies a large part in analysis and the merging strategy on shared library code would be similar for different programs. Under this insight, we propose a **data-driven** method to learn a good merging for programs that share a common library.

We have implemented 4DM, and evaluated it on two different Datalog-based analyses, a points-to analysis and a liveness analysis. The results suggest 4DM could achieve significant speedup on both analyses with minimal precision loss.

This paper makes the following contributions:

- A general framework for accelerating analyses in Datalog by merging sensitivity elements.
- A learning algorithm to discover an effective strategy for merging sensitivity elements in library code.
- Empirical evaluation that demonstrates the effectiveness our approach.

The rest of this paper is organized as follows. Section 2 uses a motivating example to give a comprehensive overview of 4DM. Section 3 prepares some knowledge of Datalog. Section 4 describes how to apply 4DM's merging to Datalog rules in detail and proves some of its important properties. Section 5 explains 4DM's algorithm to learns a merging strategy from input programs that share a common library. Section 6 describes the implementation and evaluation of 4DM.

2 Overview

In this section, we informally describe 4DM using a motivating example.

Listing-1.1 demonstrates an example where finer-grained sensitivity leads to unnecessary computation. The code snippet contains two packages, i.e. `library` and `client1`. Package `library` declares method `foo`, `bar` and `id`. Package `client1` declares method `main`. In the comments, $cs_1 \ldots cs_6$ represent the six call sites in the program, while o_1, o_2 represent abstract objects allocated by `new` statements in the corresponding lines. At the end of the `main` method, the developer queries whether three assertions may be violated, denoted as **Q1**, **Q2**, and **Q3** respectively. It is easy to see that while **Q1** and **Q2** hold, **Q3** does not.

We can derive the correct results by applying a 1-call-site-sensitive (*1cs*) points-to analysis. In particular, it is sufficient to distinguish calls to `id` in `main` and calls to `id` in `foo` and `bar`. When applying a 1cs analysis, there are 4 different contexts for variable x in line 5 of `library`, and x points to different objects in these contexts, as follows.

$$x \mapsto \{o_1\} \text{ in two contexts } [cs_1], [cs_2]$$
$$x \mapsto \{o_2\} \text{ in two contexts } [cs_5], [cs_6]$$

While 1cs analysis successfully resolves all three queries, there is redundancy in the computation. In particular, distinguishing the call sites cs_1 and cs_2 does not increase the precision. Similar for cs_5 and cs_6. Ideally we want to remove such redundancy.

2.1 Accelerating by Domain-Wise Merging

Before introducing our idea, let us first see whether we can remove this redundancy using existing methods. A dominating approach for tuning analysis abstractions is to select different sensitivities for different program points [10, 11, 14–16, 26]. In this case, it allows dropping the contexts for certain call sites to `id`. However, to preserve the precision, we can only drop the contexts either for both $\{cs_1, cs_2\}$ or for both $\{cs_5, cs_6\}$. However, there is still redundancy in the call sites where the context is not dropped. On the other hand, a previous merging-based approach, Mahjong [21], only allows merging heap objects.

4DM uses a novel method for abstraction-tuning, which we refer to as "domain-wise merging". In the running example, our approach would conclude that the call sites cs_1 and cs_2 have the same effect on the queries (**Q1**, **Q2** and **Q3**) and thus can be merged. Therefore, our approach would treat them as an equivalent class and use symbol $*_1$ to represent the equivalent class. Similarly, our approach would identify cs_5 and cs_6 as equivalent and use $*_2$ to represent the class. As a result, the original four contexts for variable x in line 5 become 2 contexts:

$$[*_1] = \{[cs_1], [cs_2]\} \text{ and } [*_2] = \{[cs_5], [cs_6]\}$$

This merged abstraction of calling contexts removes the redundancy in the original analysis while keeping the precision.

In order to apply the idea of domain-wise merging to different sensitivities in a wide range of analysis, we propose a general framework that allows rich ways to merge facts in Datalog-based analyses (Sect. 4). Further, we prove that under this framework, any merging strategy would yield a sound analysis if the original analysis is sound.

```
 1 package client2;
 2 import library;
 3 public class Clt2 {
 4   public static void main(String[] args) {
 5     A q1 = new A(); // o3
 6     y1 = library.Lib.foo(p1); // cs7
 7     y2 = library.Lib.bar(p1); // cs8
 8     assert(y1==y2); // Q4: safe?
 9   }
10 }
```

Listing 1.2. Another example client that uses the `library` package

2.2   Learning a Merging over Library Code

While the above framework defines the space of sound merging strategies, the next question is how to find a merging that accelerates the analysis while keeping the precision as much as possible.

We propose a data-driven method focusing on library code. Many modern program analyses spend a large portion of its time in analyzing large library code (e.g., JDK for Java programs). Based on the assumption that different programs use libraries in similar ways, we can obtain a heuristic that merges facts in a library by observing analysis runs on a training set of programs that share this library. Then we can use this heuristic to accelerate analyzing a new program that also uses this library.

For example, suppose there is another client package `client2` in Listing-1.2 that also invokes `foo` and `bar` in the `library` package. Similar to the `client1`, it passes the same object to these two functions. At the end, there is an aliasing assertion **Q4**. In a 1cs analysis, it still takes a large portion of runtime on package `library`, while the merging strategy on `library` is the same as `client1`, as merging call sites cs_5 and cs_6 in function `foo` and `bar` can accelerate the analysis without losing precision for **Q4**. Inspired by this observation, we can discover this merging strategy by trying out various merging strategies on `client1`, and then use this strategy to accelerate analyzing `client2`.

We describe a general method for obtaining such merging strategies in Sect. 5. In particular, our approach allows training on multiple programs. When the training set is large enough, we are confident that the learnt merging can be applied to programs outside the training set. Furthermore, our framework is general to allow specifically-designed training algorithms for certain analyses, and our evaluation shall demonstrate such an algorithm for liveness analysis.

3   Preliminary

Before we describe 4DM, we first briefly introduce Datalog. Datalog is a declarative logic programming language, which started for querying deductive database. Recently, it has been widely used for specifying program analyses.

		(relations)	$r \in \mathbb{R} = \{R^0, R^1, \ldots\}$
(program)	$C ::= \bar{c};\ o$	(variables)	$v \in \mathbb{V} = \{X, Y, \ldots\}$
(rule)	$c ::= l \leftarrow \bar{l}$	(constants)	$d \in \mathbb{D} = \{0, 1, \ldots\}$
(literal)	$l ::= r(\bar{a})$	(domains)	$D \in \mathbb{M} = \{D_1, D_2, \ldots\} \subseteq \mathcal{P}(\mathbb{D})$
(argument)	$a ::= v \mid d$		$dom(r) = \overline{D}$
(output)	$o ::= \,'output'\ \bar{r}$	(tuples)	$t \in \mathbb{T} \subseteq \mathbb{R} \times \mathbb{D}^*$
		(substitutions)	$\sigma \in \Sigma \subseteq \mathbb{V} \to \mathbb{D}$

Fig. 1. Syntax of Datalog and auxiliary definitions

$$[\![C]\!] \in \mathcal{P}(\mathbb{T}) \qquad F_C, f_c \in \mathcal{P}(\mathbb{T}) \to \mathcal{P}(\mathbb{T})$$
$$[\![C]\!] = lfp(F_C) \quad F_C(T) = T \cup \bigcup\{f_c(T) \mid c \in C\}$$
$$f_{l_0 \leftarrow l_1, \ldots, l_n}(T) = \{\sigma(l_0) \mid \sigma(l_k) \in T \ for \ 1 \le k \le n$$
$$\wedge \sigma(l_0)[i] \in dom(l_0)[i] \ for \ 1 \le i \le |l_0|\}$$

Fig. 2. Semantics of Datalog

The syntax of Datalog is listed in Fig. 1. A Datalog program is constructed from a list of rules and an output instruction. (Here, overbar like $\bar{c}$ represents a list of zero, one or more elements.) Each rule has a head and a body. A head is one literal, and a body is a list of literals. Each literal consists of a relation name and several arguments. Each argument is either a variable or a constant. We call literals containing no variables as **ground literals** or **tuples**, and call constants in tuples as values. A rule should be well-formed, in the sense that all variables occurring in the head should also appear in the body. In addition, we use an output instruction to mark some relations as the analysis results.

All relations are assigned with domains for each of its dimensions. The domain constrains possible constants that a variable at this dimension can be substituted with, and constants should also conform the constraints. We define a relation **super-domain** among domains: – when a variable appears both in the head and body in rule, the corresponding domain D_H in the head is a (direct) super-domain of the corresponding domain D_B in the body, – and transitively, super-domains of D_H are also super-domains of D_B.

Each Datalog program C denotes a set of tuples derived using its rules, as detailed in Fig. 2. Each rule $l_0 \leftarrow l_1, \ldots, l_n$ is interpreted as deriving a tuple from known tuples: if there exists a substitution σ such that $\sigma(l_1), \ldots, \sigma(l_n)$ are all known tuples, and every constant in $\sigma(l_0)$ satisfies the domain constraint, $\sigma(l_0)$ is derived. The program denotes the least fixed-point (lfp) of repeated applications of the rules in C. We use a subscript $[\![C]\!]_o$ to denote the derived tuples of output relations o.

Usually, we want to keep all derived tuples, so we require that if domain D_H in the head is a super-domain of D_B in the body, D_H's valueset should also be a superset of D_B's. Thus, the domain constraints are always satisfied during derivation.

4 Constructing Domain-Wise Merging in Datalog

In this subsection we introduce our definition of domain-wise merging and how we transform the Datalog rules to implement domain-wise merging.

4.1 1-Domain-Wise Merging

We first give our definition of 1-domain-wise merging, which specifies what elements in a domain should be merged into an abstract element. Then we discuss how to transform the Datalog rules to support this kind of merging. Finally, we prove our transformation is sound: any facts that can be produced by the original rule set can still be produced by the transformed rule set.

Defining Merging. Usually, for a Datalog program, we only cares about derived tuples of output relations. Our goal is to keep derived tuples in output relations unchanged, so we hope not to merge any values in domains of output relations. We also need to avoid merging values in the domains where output tuples are derived from. Therefore, we first give the definition of sensitivity domains, in which the values can be merged.

Definition 1 (Sensitivity Domain). *For a Datalog program C and a set of output relations o, a domain $D \in \mathbb{M}$ is a sensitivity domain iff no domain of output relations is D's super-domain.*

Then, a 1-domain-wise merging is defined as a function mapping concrete values in a domain to abstract values. When multiple concrete values are mapped to the same abstract values, these values are merged. As a result, the domain itself is also changed.

Definition 2 (1-Domain-Wise Merging). *A (1-domain-wise) merging in the sensitivity domain D_α is a function that maps some of its values $\Delta = \{d_1, d_2, \ldots\}$ to abstract values $\widehat{\Delta} = \{\alpha_1, \alpha_2, \ldots\}$ while keeping other values unchanged.*

$$\pi : D_\alpha \to \widehat{D_\alpha}, \text{ where } \widehat{D_\alpha} = (D_\alpha \backslash \Delta) \cup \widehat{\Delta}$$

In Sect. 5 we shall discuss how to obtain mergings through learning over a set of client programs.

Transforming Datalog Programs. When we have a merging π on domain D_α, we would like to perform the Datalog analysis over the merged abstract values rather than the original concrete values to accelerate the analysis. Therefore, we propose a transformation of Datalog rules to apply this merging.

We start from replacing all occurrences of the concrete values to merge in D_α with abstract values, changing D_α to $\widehat{D_\alpha}$:

– If there is a constant d in the corresponding dimension of D_α, it is changed to $\pi(d)$.

– If D_α is derived from other domains, or say, there is a variable X of D_α in a
rule head,

$$R^0(\dots, X : D_\alpha, \dots) \leftarrow \dots, R^k(\dots, X, \dots), \dots.$$

we add a relation $Abstract(X, \widehat{X})$ $(dom(Abstract) = D_\alpha \times \widehat{D_\alpha})$ in the rule
body and change X in the head to $\widehat{X}$,

$$R^0(\dots, \widehat{X} : \widehat{D_\alpha}, \dots) \leftarrow \dots, R^k(\dots, X, \dots), \dots, Abstract(X, \widehat{X}).$$

Thus, every time a constant in D_α is derived by this rule, it is merged into
$\widehat{D_\alpha}$.

– If D_α derives to its super-domain, or say, there is a variable X of D_α in a
rule body and the same variable of D_β in the rule head, the concrete values
to merge in D_β should also be replaced with abstract values by derivation.
It involves no syntactical change, but D_β should be changed to $(\widehat{D_\beta} \backslash \Delta) \cup \widehat{\Delta}$.
Transitively, all super-domains of D_α are changed. The previously described
transformations are applied to all these super-domains. In the following paragraphs, we refer to D_α and all its super-domains as *merging domains*.

However, the change in domains will break some original derivation, when
two domains in the body of a rule joins with each other, i.e.,

$$R^0(\dots) \leftarrow \dots, R^i(\dots, X, \dots), \dots, R^j(\dots, X, \dots), \dots.$$

If D_i and D_j, domains of X in the two relations, are both non-merging domains
or both merging domains, the equivalence of values between the two domains are
unchanged, so original derivation still holds. However, if D_i is a merging domain
but D_j is not (the order does not matter here), the derivation would break after
replacing concrete values in D_i with abstract values, because the abstract values
cannot match the unchanged concrete values in D_j. To restore the derivation,
the rule should be transformed as:

$$R^0(\dots) \leftarrow \dots, R^k(\dots, X, \dots), \dots, R^l(\dots, \widehat{X}, \dots), \dots, Abstract(X, \widehat{X}).$$

When X is substituted with the original concrete constant d and $\widehat{X}$ is substituted
with abstract value $\pi(d)$, the derivation still holds.

We use an example to demonstrate the effect of the rule transformation.
Figure 3(a) shows a proof tree that is used to derive a points-to instance of
the example in Sect. 2. Each node is a tuple derived from other tuples by a
rule. Node (3) is derived from (1)(2) by rule I and Node (7) is derived from
(3)(4)(5)(6) by rule II. Note that the second domain of $CallGraph(CG)$ is the
call-site of a function call, and the third domain of CG is context of called
function, represented by its most recent call-site. In (3), it means call-site cs_1
under initial context $\#$ calls method id with context cs_1, and we would like to
replace cs_1 in the context of called functions with abstract value $*_1$, while keep
the cs_1 in call-site domain unchanged.

Figure 3(b) shows a proof tree after our transformation. When the call-site
cs_1 in *Invoke* derives into the context domain of CG in (3), the transformed

rule for CG replace it with abstract value $*_1$; meanwhile, the call-site domain in CG is not super-set of the context domain, so the cs_1 in the second dimension of CG is not replaced. Furthermore, though rule II is not transformed, its first domain - context of variable - is a super-domain of context of called function in CG according to rule II, so cs_1 in (7) is also changed accordingly.

Soundness. Finally, we show that our transformation is sound: any relation that can be produced by the original rules is still produced by the transformed rules.

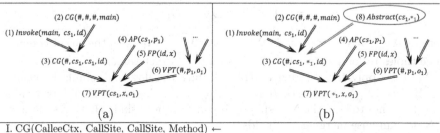

I. CG(CalleeCtx, CallSite, CallSite, Method) ←
    Invoke(Callee, CallSite, Method), CG(CallerCtx, Caller, CalleeCtx, Callee).
II. VPT(CalleeCtx, FormalVar, Obj) ←
    CallGraph(CallerCtx, CallSite, CalleeCtx, Method), ActualParam(CallSite, ActualVar),
    FormalParam(Method, FormalVar), VarPointsTo(CallerCtx, ActualVar, Obj).

Fig. 3. An example of embedding merging rules within proof trees

Theorem 1 (Soundness). *For a Datalog program C, given a domain-wise merging of sensitivity elements π on domain D_π, the derived tuples of output relations after applying π, denoted as $[\![C|\pi]\!]_o$, contains all of the original derived tuples $[\![C]\!]_o$, i.e. $[\![C]\!]_o \subseteq [\![C|\pi]\!]_o$.*

Proof. For any derived tuple of relations in the original Datalog analysis, C, $R(d_1, d_2, \ldots) \in [\![C]\!]$, there is a derivation for it. According to the process of transforming Datalog rules, the derivation still holds after transforming the rules and replacing merged concrete values with abstract values. So by induction, $\Pi[R(d_1, d_2, \ldots)] = R(\Pi(d_1), \Pi(d_2), \ldots) \in [\![C|\pi]\!]$ ($\Pi(d) = \pi(d)$ if d is in merging domains, otherwise $\Pi(d) = d$). Since an output relation R_o has no super-domain of D_π, its tuples are unchanged, so $R_o(d_1, d_2, \ldots) \in [\![C|\pi]\!]$. Thus, $[\![C]\!]_o \subseteq [\![C|\pi]\!]_o$ is proved.

The above theorem concerns only the standard Datalog. In practice, negation operator $\neg$ is frequently used, which supports the negation operation over relations. Unfortunately, the above soundness property does not hold if negations is made on the domain to be merged. In such a case, we may still merge the domains where no negation is applied, or merge the values that are in a negated domain but would never be involved in a negation calculation during an execution.

4.2 N-Domain-Wise Merging

Under some circumstances, there are several sensitivity domains in a Datalog program to which we can apply mergings. We can find mergings in these domains and apply these mergings one by one, but this approach cannot capture the correlation among these sensitivity domains. For example, in a context-sensitive points-to analysis, heap objects and their contexts are usually combined to derive some relations, such as field points-to relations. So we attempt to extend our merging function on the Cartesian product of multiple sensitivity domains:

$$\pi : D_1 \times \cdots \times D_N \to \widehat{D_{1...N}}$$

Here $\widehat{D_{1 \times \cdots \times N}} = (D_1 \times \cdots \times D_N \backslash \Delta_{1...N}) \cup \widehat{\Delta_{1...N}}$, $\Delta_{1...N}$ is the set of concrete value tuples to merge and $\widehat{\Delta_{1...N}}$ is the set of abstract values.

We can apply the merging by transforming Datalog rules similarly, changing $Abstract(X, \widehat{X})$ to $Abstract(X_1, \ldots, X_N, \widehat{X}, \ldots, \widehat{X})$ ($\widehat{X}$ is the abstract value copied N times to keep the N-D shape). It can be proved similarly that soundness of N-domain-wise merging still holds.

However, there is a challenge in defining such an N-dimension-wise merging function. Here we take the 2-dimension case of heap objects (D_H) and heap contexts (D_C), for illustration. Basically we can define arbitrary merging function in the form: $\pi_{H,C}(d_H, d_C) = (\widehat{d}, \widehat{d})$. However, in an object-sensitive setting, values of heap contexts are derived from values of heap objects, i.e. D_C is D_H's super-domain. Replacing values of D_H would change the values in D_C as well. How can we define a merging function on the values that depends on the results of this function? To resolve this recursive dependency, we propose **Incremental Merging**. Instead of defining π directly, we define a series of mergings, the first one merging a single domain and the others each merging a larger set of domains.

Here we introduce the 2-dimension case. Suppose we want to define a merging π on two domains D_1 and D_2, and D_2 is a super-domain of D_1.

We first merge in the D_1 independently by defining $\pi_1 : D_1 \to \widehat{D_1}$.

Since D_2 is a super-set of D_1, it is also changed according to transformation of rules. But we can know the changes in D_2 through the output of π_1. Then we make a second merging in changed domain $\widehat{D_2}$, but dependent on the merged values in $\widehat{D_1}$, by a function $\pi_2 : \widehat{D_1} \times \widehat{D_2} \to \widehat{D_{1,2}}$.

Thus, (d_1, d_2) in $D_1 \times D_2$ is merged to $(\widehat{d}, \widehat{d})$, where $\widehat{d} = \pi_2(\pi_1(d_1), \pi_1(d_2))$. The added argument $\widehat{D_1}$ in π_2 allows us to make different mergings on D_2 dependently on D_1, thus still capturing the correlation between the two domains.

Incremental Merging can be extended to general N-dimensional cases as well. We present it in Appendix A.

4.3 Properties of Mergings

We have introduced how to transform Datalog rules to apply merging, and proved its soundness. Then we need to choose a good merging.

The number of different mergings over a given domain is equivalent to the number of different partitions of its value set $Bell(n)$ (where n is the size of the set), which is prohibitively large[1]. In general, when more values are merged, the datalog program may run faster, but meanwhile it is more likely to lose the original precision. We can formalize that the precision of results is monotone to the mergings.

First we need to define a partial order over mergings.

Definition 3 (Partial Order of Mergings). *Given a set of N sensitivity domains $D_1 \ldots D_N$, a merging π_a of $D_1 \times \cdots \times D_N$ is finer than another merging π_b (and π_b is coarser than π_a) iff any tuple of elements merged into one tuple of abstract values in π_a are also merged into one tuple of abstract values in π_b.*

$$\pi_a \succeq \pi_b \iff \forall x_1, y_1 \in D_1, \ldots, x_N, y_N \in D_N,$$
$$\pi_a(x_1, \ldots, x_N) = \pi_a(y_1, \ldots, y_N) \to \pi_b(x_1, \ldots, x_N) = \pi_b(y_1, \ldots, y_N).$$

We can also define the **Meet** and **Join** since merging values in a domain is equivalent to partitioning over its value set.

Thus, mergings of sensitive elements form a lattice. And the (transformed) Datalog program is a function on this lattice. Then we can prove the monotonicity of analysis results on this lattice (we present the proof in Appendix B).

Theorem 2 (Monotonicity). *Given a Datalog program C. If the merging π_b of the domains $D_1, \ldots, D_N$ is a finer merging than π_a, then applying π_b to C will deduce no fewer results than π_a. It means*

$$\pi_a \succeq \pi_b \to [\![C|\pi_a]\!]_o \subseteq [\![C|\pi_b]\!]_o$$

As is shown in the example in Sect. 2, the monotonicity is not strict and there are some mergings that generate just the same results as origin.

Definition 4 (Precision-preserving merging). *Given a Datalog program C. A merging π is a precision-preserving merging on iff $[\![C|\pi]\!]_o = [\![C]\!]_o$.*

All the precision preserving merging can keep the precision of the original result. Among these mergings, in order to improve efficiency, we want to find one that reduces the domain size as much as possible. So we define maximal merging as our target of finding mergings.

Definition 5 (Maximal Merging). *A precision-preserving merging π_a is a maximal merging iff there is no other precision preserving merging is coarser than π_a.*

5 Algorithm

We have proved soundness of domain-wise merging and defined maximal merging as a good merging. Our current goal is approximating the target merging.

---

[1] Bell number can be recursively calculated as $B(n+1) = \Sigma_{k=0}^{n} C_n^k B(n)$.

5.1   Learn Merging Heuristics of Library Facts from Input Programs

The first challenge is that our defined maximal merging is specific to one given input program. It would be time-consuming if we use a pre-analysis to generate a maximal merging every time before analyzing a new program. So a general merging that can apply to different programs is preferable.

While it is impossible to find a universal merging that suits all kinds of input programs, the good news is that we can take advantage of the fact that large part of modern software is shared library code. Library code is usually large and analyzing it occupies a large portion of the analysis time. Among library functions, some functions are internal methods that are always called by other library functions; some are called in a fixed pattern due to code paradigms: therefore, library codes share similar behaviour across different client codes.

Based on this observation, we can assume that if a merging can reduce running time with precision kept for analysis on a rather large number of input programs that share a library, it can also accelerate the analysis on other input programs using the same library. Thus, we can generate a merging heuristic for this library by learning from these input programs as a training set. Though there is no guarantee that precision is kept on new programs because they are not the same as the training programs, we can introduce fewer false positives by enlarging the training set.

When the user specifies a sensitivity domain to merge, 4DM first finds out all the values of the specified domain for each input program in the training set. It can be done either by collecting from input instances or running an original analysis to dump the sensitivity domain. Then it selects ones that are only related to the library from the union set of these values, and explores a merging on this set that reduces execution time and keeps precision for all input programs in the training set. We take the found merging as a merging heuristic for the library.

With a library heuristic, we can apply a merging to another program using this library, where only values specified by the heuristic are merged while other values stay unchanged.

5.2   Finding a Maximal Merging

How can we find a good merging on the set of library-related values? That is the remaining problem we need to solve in this part.

If we have some insight about the rules and domains we want to merge, we can use a specifically-designed rule to find a good merging. For example, we can use the heap equivalent automata from Tan et al. [21] as a guide to generate merging heuristics of *Heap* domain in analysis.

And what if we do not have enough insight? We propose a highly general method GenMax. We use a greedy algorithm to partition these values iteratively. In each iteration, we find a maximal set of concrete values that can be replaced by one assigned abstract value while preserving the original precision. In this situation, no more values in this domain can be added into this set without losing

---

Algorithm 5.1: Enumeration

Input : Set of all concrete values $\mathbb{E}$
Output: Current merging set N
Data: Set of concrete values outside merging set C
Data: Set of unchecked concrete values M

1 **begin**
2      $N \leftarrow \emptyset$;
3      $C \leftarrow \emptyset$;
4      $M \leftarrow \mathbb{E}$;
5   **for** $v \in \mathbb{E}$ **do**
6          $M \leftarrow M - \{v\}$;
7   **if** *merge* $N \cup \{v\}$ *preserves precision* **then**
8              $N \leftarrow N \cup \{v\}$
9   **end**
10         $C \leftarrow C \cup \{v\}$;
11   **end**
12 **end**

---

precision, so they are excluded from the rest of values in following iterations. When all values are tested, the algorithm terminates.

This resulting merging is maximal, i.e. any two abstract values cannot be merged without losing precision. According to definition, there can be more than one maximal merging for the given set of concrete values, but evaluation in Sect. 6 shows the maximal merging found by our greedy algorithm is adequate.

To find a maximal merging set in every iteration, we explore two different approaches, an enumerative one and a randomized one.

Enumeration for Maximal Merging Set. In order to find the maximal number of mergeable concrete values, a direct method is to enumerate over every concrete value. As is shown in Algorithm-5.1, given the set of all concrete values $\mathbb{E}$, each time we randomly choose one unchecked value from $\mathbb{E}$, check whether it can be added into current merging set, until all values are checked. Note that the analysis is embedded with rules of merging through Sect. 4. In this method, number of calls to logic analysis is linear to the size of the set of abstract values. But the time complexity is worse than $O(|\mathbb{E}|)$ because runtime of each attempt of analysis also gets longer when input program grows larger. This method would be too time-consuming especially for large programs.

Active Learning for Maximal Merging Set. It would be better if we can try to add more than one concrete values into current merging set at once. Liang et al. [16] proposes an active learning algorithm, ActiveCoarsen, to find a minimal binary abstraction which is estimated to be more efficient. The algorithm is transformed in our setting and described in Algorithm-5.2.

Each time, ActiveCoarsen picks multiple concrete values by the ratio α, and tries to add them into current merging set. If failed, put the concrete values back

---

Algorithm 5.2: ActiveCoarsen

    Input   : Set of all concrete values $\mathbb{E}$
    Input   : Probability of random selection α
    Output: Set of concrete values outside merging set N
    Data: Set of undetermined concrete values M
    Data: Set of random-selected concrete values T

1 **begin**
2    $N \leftarrow \emptyset$;
3    $M \leftarrow \mathbb{E}$;
4   **while** M *is not empty* **do**
5       $T \leftarrow select(M, \alpha)$;
6   **if** *merge* $N \cup T$ *preserves precision* **then**
7          $N \leftarrow N \cup T$;
8          $M \leftarrow M - T$;
9   **end**
10   update α;
11   **end**
12 **end**

---

and re-pick again. If we set $\alpha = e^{-\frac{1}{s}}$, where s is the size of the maximal merging set of concrete values, the expected number of calls to the analysis is $O(s \log n)$. However, we have no knowledge of the size s. Liang et al. [16] also introduce a mechanism for setting and updating α without knowledge of s, which is detailed in their article.

Optimization. Though `ActiveCoarsen` tries more concrete values at a time, when the size of remaining concrete values in M is small, randomly selecting more than one value to merge at each trial would be less effective than plain enumeration. We approximately calculate that when the remaining size n is smaller than about $(1 + \sqrt{5})/2$ times the size s of minimal critical set, it would be better to switch to enumeration for minimal critical set.

Another optimization is that since each iteration we expand a merging set to max, the generated merging sets would get smaller since remaining concrete values get fewer. The benefit-cost ratio would decrease a lot. So after finding several large merging sets, we cut the exploration of merging early.

6 Implementation and Evaluation

To evaluate the effectiveness and generality of our approach 4DM, we implemented 4DM in Python and compared it with existing approaches over two different Datalog-based analyses: points-to analysis and liveness analysis.

6.1   Points-to Analysis

We first carried out an experiment on a context-sensitive points-to analysis over Java programs. The analysis is from the Doop framework [3]. We use 2-object-sensitive+heap (2o1h) as the sensitivity configuration in our evaluation because it is the most precise configuration on which most benchmark projects can be analysed with reasonable amount of time. We transformed the Soufflé implementation of Datalog rules as input of 4DM's merging.

In this experiment, we trained abstractions for all libraries in JDK. The abstraction is the Cartesian product of domains *Heap* and *HeapContext*. Since in the setting of object-sensitivity, heap context is a super-domain of heap objects, we used incremental abstraction on them as described in Sect. 4.

We selected 15 Java projects as subjects from Dacapo benchmark [2] and pjbench [18]. We excluded some projects (*bloat*, *batik* and *jython*) from our subject set because it takes too long time to run 2o1h analysis on them.

To check whether 4DM is stable when using different training sets, we performed a 5-fold cross-validation over the selected projects. In particular, we randomly partitioned these projects into 5 groups, each containing 3 projects. In each fold of cross-validation, every 4 groups form a training set and the remaining one group forms a testing set. We apply the learned merging heuristics from the 12 programs to the rest 3 programs. Each column in Fig. 4 and each segment in Table 1 show the results on one group by training on the other 4 groups (e.g., tradebeans, chart, and fop are a group). Though it takes 2 to 3 days to find a merging heuristic from a training set, the learnt heuristic can be reused across different programs in the testing set, and thus, the training process is offline. The execution time and precision measures in the following paragraphs are the results on the testing set.

In our evaluation, we compare the execution time and precision of 4DM with 3 existing approaches:

- Standard 2o1h analysis (denoted as *2o1h*). This is the baseline.
- The 2o1h analysis with Mahjong [21] (denoted as *Mahjong*). Its execution consists of two parts: the pre-analysis is a light-weight analysis to learn merging rules and the post-analysis is the 2o1h analysis based on the merging rules learned from the pre-analysis.
- The 2o1h analysis with a variant of Mahjong (denoted as *Mahjong(lib)*). The process is similar to *Mahjong*, but the difference is that all values outside JDK are excluded from the merging sets generated by pre-analysis.

In our evaluation, we try to answer the following three research questions:

RQ1: How effective our technique is on the acceleration of points-to analysis? To answer this question, we present the execution time of compared approaches in Fig. 4. All the execution time is measured on a machine with 2 Intel Xeon Gold 6230 CPUs and 512 GB RAM, equipped with Ubuntu 18.04 and JDK 1.7.0-80. All analyses are executed single-threaded. In the Figure, the execution time of each project is presented as a cluster of four columns. From left to right,

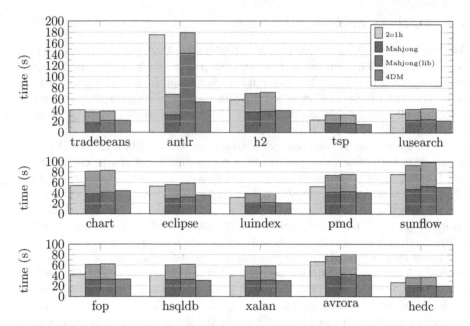

Fig. 4. Comparison of execution time (in sec)

the columns represent the execution time of *2o1h*, *Mahjong*, *Mahjong(lib)*, and *4DM* respectively. For *Mahjong* and *Mahjong(lib)*, the lighter-color part of the column represents the pre-analysis time, and the darker-color part of the column represents the post-analysis time.

From this figure, we can observe that our technique can significantly accelerate the points-to analysis compared with the standard implementation *2o1h* on all the experimented projects (with an average speedup of 1.6×).

Comparing with the post-analysis of *Mahjong*, *4DM* is faster in 6 of the 15 projects, and slower in 9. The difference in time is modest in most of the projects. But if we take *Mahjong*'s pre-analysis for each project into account, *4DM* is significantly faster than *Mahjong* on all projects. While merging learnt by *4DM* can be applied to different programs sharing the common library once it is obtained, the pre-analysis in *Mahjong* must be executed whenever analyzing a new project.

Since *4DM* only merges library elements, we also compare it with a variant of *Mahjong* which merges only heap objects in the library, and *4DM* is faster than *Mahjong(lib)*'s post-analysis in 10 of 15 projects. It implies that *4DM*'s data-driven method learnt a comparably good merging as the specifically-designed strategy in *Mahjong*.

RQ2: How much precision loss 4DM causes? To answer this question, we use two commonly used metrics for the precision of points-to analysis - polymorphic virtual call-sites (abbreviated as *poly*) and may-failing typecasts (abbreviated as *cast*), and compare experimented approaches on the two metrics. The more call-sites the analysis identified as polymorphic and the more typecasts the analysis identified as may-failing, the analysis is more imprecise.

The details are in Table 1. Columns *poly* and *cast* present the number of polymorphic virtual call-sites and may-failing typecasts detected by baseline *2o1h*, and Columns *Δpoly* and *Δcast* refers to the number of additional false positives detected by other approaches compared with the baseline *2o1h*.

According to analysis results, the precision loss of our technique is minimal. Compared with standard *2o1h*, *4DM* causes no precision loss in 10 out of 15 projects. In the remaining projects, the highest precision loss happens in the *eclipse* project, with 3.0% extra polymorphic virtual call-sites reported. Comparing with *Mahjong*, though the maximal precision loss of *Mahjong* (2.0% in *cast* of *eclipse*) is smaller than *4DM*, it loses precision in *cast* in more projects than *4DM*. Thus, we can conclude that our approach is also comparable to *Mahjong* in precision loss.

RQ3: Is our approach stable when using different training sets? We need to check that if the training set changes, 4DM's learnt merging heuristic still reach a significant acceleration with minimal precision loss. From evaluation results in **RQ1** and **RQ2**, we can see that all the five sets of heuristics generated with five different training sets achieve significant acceleration and minimal

Table 1. Comparison of precision loss.

Analysis	2o1h		Mahjong		Mahjong (lib)		4DM	
Program	poly	cast	Δpoly	Δcast	Δpoly	Δcast	Δpoly	Δcast
tradebeans	850	567	0	1	0	0	0	0
chart	1446	1279	0	1	0	0	3	3
fop	838	519	0	1	0	0	0	0
antlr	1643	640	0	1	0	0	0	0
eclipse	1318	1020	14	20	0	0	40	10
hsqldb	802	515	0	1	0	0	0	0
h2	942	559	0	2	0	0	0	0
luindex	929	549	0	1	0	0	0	0
xalan	808	514	0	1	0	0	0	0
tsp	784	441	0	1	0	0	0	0
pmd	886	911	0	1	0	0	0	0
avrora	936	715	0	1	0	0	2	0
lusearch	1136	596	0	1	0	0	0	0
sunflow	2000	1528	0	1	0	0	25	8
hedc	871	458	0	1	0	0	25	10

precision loss. Thus, we can conclude that our technique is stable across different training sets.

RQ4: What is the performance of our approach in large applications? We excluded 3 large projects (*bloat, batik* and *jython*) previously, as it takes a long time to run the training algorithm in Sect. 5 on them. But we can apply the learnt heuristics from smaller projects to accelerate the points-to analysis on large approaches. We apply the 5 heuristics learnt above to the 3 projects, and find that both *bloat* and *batik* are accelerated with a minimal precision loss (*bloat* speeds up by 1.0% with 0 precision loss, *batik* speeds up by 11.0% with precision loss less than 1%). However, *jython* still exceeds a 3-h time limit. The details are in Appendix C.

Evaluation Summary on Points-to Analysis. From the answers of the above research questions, we can see that (1) 4DM can significantly accelerate baseline *2o1h* with minimal precision loss; (2) compared with *Mahjong*, 4DM can achieve comparable efficiency and precision loss without performing pre-analysis for each new project; and (3) 4DM's efficiency and precision are stable when using different training sets.

6.2   Liveness Analysis

In this subsection, we evaluate our method on an inter-procedure liveness analysis over Java programs to validate the generality of our approach.

To further challenge our approach on generality, we use a different domain, program points, as the sensitivity domain for liveness analysis. The observation is that for many program points, their live variable sets are exactly the same, i.e. there exists much redundant propagation in the analysis. If we view program points as sensitivity elements, and apply domain-wise merging, we could speed up the analysis by reducing redundant computation from tuning flow-sensitivity.

In particular, in order to find appropriate merging for sensitivity elements, we use the following heuristic: if two program points are adjacent in the control flow graph, and the kill sets of them are empty, then the two program points are mergeable. By considering all adjacent pairs in the control flow graph, we could obtain our desired abstraction for the program.

Experiment Setting. We evaluated our approach on 9 projects from Dacapo benchmark. They are divided into 3 groups and each group contains 3 projects. For each group, we learn a unique abstraction of the library code by applying 4DM, and test the library abstraction on the other two groups.

Results. Our approach accelerates the liveness analysis on all of the benchmarks. The average speed-up is 19.8%, and the average precision loss is 4.9%. The detailed performance is listed in Appendix D.

We stress that we only use a simple heuristic in a new domain, and the results show that our method still works remarkably well. It indicates that by carefully choosing domains, and applying various learning techniques, our method could speed up many other analyses in a way orthogonal to existing works.

7   Related Work

There have been many approaches proposed to accelerate program analysis. Among these approaches, three types are relevant to our paper.

Context Reduction. Lhoták and Hendren [13] conducts an empirical study that demonstrates there are very few contexts related to the precision of the analysis results. Liang et al. [16] propose to finding the minimal set of call sites that preserve the precision. The result shows that most call sites does not affect the precision. Both Lhoták and Hendren [13] and Liang et al. [16] do not directly accelerate context-sensitive analysis, instead they see opportunities to reduce contexts for acceleration. Actually, the algorithm for finding minimal partitions in our paper are inspired by Liang et al. [16]

Based on the above observation, researchers [10,11,14,15,26,27] propose to adjust context sensitivities at different program points to accelerate context-sensitive points-to analysis. There are two main directions. One is refinement, that is, iteratively increasing sensitivity on some program points on demand to improve precision. For example, Zhang et al. [27] starts from the most coarse abstraction and finds suitable program points to increase context length using an online SAT-solver-based algorithm, to reduce false positives. The other is coarsening, which analyzes the code beforehand, and performs the full analysis with coarser sensitivity at specific program points. For example, Li et al. [14] neglects context sensitivity in some methods which are calculated during pre-processing phase.

As is already mentioned in the overview, our domain-wise merging could merge redundant contexts in a fine-grained way that cannot be implemented by these approaches. On the other hand, our method considers more in a coarsening direction as it merges concrete values. As a result, in the future potentially our approach could develop in another direction, combined with refinement-based methods. Furthermore, our work deals with not only context-sensitive points-to analysis but also more general cases.

Equivalence Classes. The idea of equivalence classes has already been used to accelerate analysis. Cycle detection [8,9,16] is a common way to detect variable and object equivalence, which can reduce the number of variables or objects in points-to analysis. Tan et al. [21] uses an idea of equivalent automata to merging type-consistent heap objects. In addition, Xu and Rountev [25] and Xiao and Zhang [24] exploit context equivalence and use custom encoding to merge contexts, and are also considered as ways for context reduction. Our definition of domain-wise merging could be viewed as a generalization of the previous abstractions. Our approach can automatically learn the merging from a training set, in contrast to existing approaches relying on properties of certain analyses.

Library Summarization. Library summarization techniques keep only necessary library facts in library summaries so as to accelerate client analysis. Client analysis can use summaries for reasoning, without inner reasoning for the library. Tang et al. [22,23] propose conditional reachability to summarize all potential reachability between library boundaries. Polymer [12] learns library behavior from training clients to create conditional summaries for a library. However, a full summarization of the library is usually too large to store and load. For example, the summary produced by Tang et al. [22] needs tens of Gigabytes for some of the JDK classes over a simple data-dependence analysis. In contrast to these approaches that try to fully summarize the library, our work tries to learn a merging that is suitable for analyzing the library. The learnt merging heuristic of heap objects with heap contexts for the whole JDK library in our evaluation in Sect. 6.1 consist of only around 1000 lines of Datalog facts, respective for different training sets. Such a merging heuristic is easy to store and load.

Abstract Interpretation of Logic Programs. There is classic literature on extending abstract interpretation to logic programs [1,4–7]. Previous research on this topic mainly aims to analyze properties of logic programs themselves, such as variable binding and predicate type; while in 4DM, the analysis is expressed in a logic program but it analyzes properties of other programs. But the way 4DM transforms Datalog programs and merges analysis values can be viewed as abstracting the Datalog program expressing the analysis. It lifts the "concrete domain" of the original analysis values to the abstract domain of merged values. This is a special case of abstract interpretation of logic programs.

8   Conclusion

In this paper we have introduced 4DM, a new framework for tuning abstractions in a program analysis using domain-wise merging. In particular, it uses a data-driven method to automatically learn an effective merging heuristic for library code from a training set of programs. 4DM can be applied to merging different kinds of sensitivity elements in various analyses that are expressed in Datalog. Our evaluation results show that our approach significantly accelerates a context-sensitive pointer analysis and a flow-sensitive liveness analysis with minimal precision loss.

Acknowledgements. This work is supported in part by the National Key Research and Development Program of China No. 2019YFE0198100, National Natural Science Foundation of China under Grant Nos. 61922003, and a grant from ZTE-PKU Joint Laboratory for Foundation Software.

A   Incremental Merging in N-Domain-Wise Cases

Here we describe how to define an incremental merging function for general cases of N-domain-wise merging.

Suppose we want to define a merging function on N domains $D_1, D_2, \ldots, D_N$. Without loss of generality, we suppose D_i can only be a super-domain of D_j when $i > j$. We define π_i $(1 \leq i \leq N)$ by induction:

- When $i = 1$, we can define an arbitrary 1-domain-wise merging function on D_1.
- Suppose we have defined a function $\pi_i : D_1 \times \cdots \times D_i \to \widehat{D_{1\ldots i}}$, we can define $\pi_{i+1} : D_1 \times \cdots \times D_i \times D_{i+1} \to \widehat{D_{1\ldots i+1}}$ with a helper function π'_{i+1}:

$$\pi'_{i+1} : \widehat{D_{1\ldots i}} \times \widehat{D_{i+1}} \to \widehat{D_{1\ldots i+1}}$$

Here $\widehat{D_{i+1}}$ represents the changed domain of original D_{i+1} after applying the merging π_i, and $\pi_{i+1}(d_1, \ldots, d_i, d_{i+1}) = \pi'_{i+1}(\pi_i(d_1, \ldots, d_i), \pi_i(d_{i+1}))$. Note that $\pi_i(d_{i+1})$, which d_{i+1} would become under π_i, is determined after applying π_i to the Datalog program.

With $\pi = \pi_N$, we get an N-domain-wise merging function on $D_1 \times \cdots \times D_N$.

B   Proof: The Monotonicity of Mergings

Theorem 3 (Monotonicity). *Given a Datalog program C. If the merging π_b of the domains $D_1, \ldots, D_N$ is a finer merging than π_a, then applying π_b to C will deduce no fewer results than π_a. It means*

$$\pi_a \succeq \pi_b \to [\![C|\pi_a]\!]_o \subseteq [\![C|\pi_b]\!]_o$$

Proof. Given a Datalog program C, any derivation on the proof tree in $[\![C|\pi_a]\!]$ has the form

$$R^0(\Pi_a(d_1^0), \Pi_a(d_2^0), \ldots) ::= \ldots, R^j(\Pi_a(d_1^j), \Pi_a(d_2^j), \ldots), \ldots.$$

(note that the concrete values $\{d_i^j\}$ may not originally match with each other, but get matched after applying Π_a).

As is defined, for any domain D, $\forall x, y \in D, \Pi_a(x) = \Pi_a(y) \to \Pi_b(x) = \Pi_b(y)$, so in $[\![C|\pi_b]\!]$'s proof tree,

$$R^0(\Pi_b(d_1^0), \Pi_b(d_2^0), \ldots) ::= \ldots, R^j(\Pi_b(d_1^j), \Pi_b(d_2^j), \ldots), \ldots.$$

also holds as a renaming of the previous instantiation.

Therefore, $[\![C|\pi_a]\!]_o \subseteq [\![C|\pi_b]\!]_o$.

C   Detailed Performance of 4DM in Points-to Analysis on Large Projects

Table 2 presents the performance of 4DM by applying learnt heuristics from small projects to large projects. Each column of 4DM shows the result of applying a heuristic learnt from a training set of 12 projects. The partition of training set is the same as in Sect. 6.1.

Table 2. Performance of applying heuristics learnt by 4DM from small projects to large projects.

Project	Analysis	2o1h	4DM				
			1	2	3	4	5
bloat	time (s)	3122.32	3083.92	3093.46	3082.87	3097.3	3100.15
	poly	1577	1577	1577	1577	1577	1577
	cast	1526	1526	1526	1526	1526	1526
batik	time (s)	1001.57	908.73	894.49	882.18	886.73	879.52
	poly	4798	4836	4831	4846	4812	4828
	cast	2445	2473	2467	2476	2453	2459

D   Detailed Performance of 4DM in Liveness Analysis

Table 3 shows the detailed results of applying 4DM to liveness analysis.

One practical concern in evaluation is that liveness analysis is usually very fast, hence random events in the processor could have a big influence on the measured run time of compiled executable. We tackle this problem by using Soufflé interpreter to run the analysis and obtain a more reliable record of analysis time.

We use a T-test to check whether the distribution of analysis time changes significantly after merging. The smaller the p-value, the stronger the evidence that two distributions are different. We perform 50 independent runs for each benchmark and analysis. The analysis time is the average of the 50 runs, and the p-value is calculated base on these data.

We measure the precision by the size of calculated live-variable set at all call sites. Note that since our approach is sound, this property is non-decreasing; and the less the size increases, the more precise the analysis is.

Table 3. Performance for liveness analysis. lib1 = {luindex, sunflow, hsqldb}, lib2 = {avrora, batik, bloat}, lib3 = {chart, lusearch, pmd}.

		avrora	batik	bloat	chart	lusearch	pmd	hsqldb	luindex	sunflow
Original	Analysis time (s)	5.09	13.37	5.14	7.81	3.36	4.95	6.71	3.33	6.33
	#call-sites live-var	43735	126230	73215	64332	43493	71099	68129	38380	50085
lib1	Analysis time (s)	4.4	11.84	4.45	6.41	2.34	3.5	—	—	—
	Speed up (%)	13.6	11.4	13.4	17.9	30.4	29.3	—	—	—
	p-value	2.58E−74	3.32E−69	1.81E−82	2.40E−91	7.31E−117	3.54E−114	—	—	—
	#call-sites live-var	45401	128879	75067	69117	45388	73587	—	—	—
	Precision loss (%)	3.8	2.1	2.5	7.4	4.4	3.5	—	—	—
lib2	Analysis time (s)	—	—	—	6.47	2.35	3.46	5.52	2.34	5.57
	Speed up (%)	—	—	—	17.2	30.1	30.1	17.7	29.7	12.0
	p-value	—	—	—	4.16E−83	1.12E−114	4.48E−117	1.73E−82	7.08E−110	1.95E−72
	#call-sites live-var	—	—	—	66783	45790	73518	71003	40590	52675
	Precision loss (%)	—	—	—	3.9	5.3	3.4	4.2	5.8	5.2
lib3	Analysis time (s)	4.39	11.77	4.44	—	—	—	5.48	2.32	5.34
	Speed up (%)	13.7	11.9	13.6	—	—	—	18.3	30.3	15.6
	p-value	1.70E−85	6.31E−72	6.78E−85	—	—	—	8.49E−93	5.12E−115	2.22E−84
	#call-sites live-var	45880	129707	75644	—	—	—	71334	40695	57910
	Precision loss (%)	4.9	2.8	3.3	—	—	—	4.7	6.0	15.6

References

1. Barbuti, R., Giacobazzi, R., Levi, G.: A general framework for semantics-based bottom-up abstract interpretation of logic programs. ACM Trans. Program. Lang. Syst. (TOPLAS) **15**(1), 133–181 (1993)
2. Blackburn, S.M., et al.: The DaCapo benchmarks: Java benchmarking development and analysis. In: Proceedings of the 21st Annual ACM SIGPLAN Conference on Object-Oriented Programming Systems, Languages, and Applications, OOPSLA 2006, pp. 169–190. ACM, New York (2006)
3. Bravenboer, M., Smaragdakis, Y.: Strictly declarative specification of sophisticated points-to analyses. In: Proceedings of the 24th ACM SIGPLAN Conference on Object Oriented Programming Systems Languages and Applications, pp. 243–262 (2009)
4. Cortesi, A., Filé, G.: Abstract interpretation of logic programs: an abstract domain for groundness, sharing, freeness and compoundness analysis. ACM SIGPLAN Not. **26**(9), 52–61 (1991). PEPM 1991
5. Cousot, P., Cousot, R.: Abstract interpretation and application to logic programs. J. Log. Program. **13**(2), 103–179 (1992)
6. Debray, S.K.: Global optimization of logic programs (analysis, transformation, compilation) (1987)
7. Delzanno, G., Giacobazzi, R., Ranzato, F.: Static analysis, abstract interpretation and verification in (constraint logic) programming. In: Dovier, A., Pontelli, E. (eds.) A 25-Year Perspective on Logic Programming. LNCS, vol. 6125, pp. 136–158. Springer, Heidelberg (2010). https://doi.org/10.1007/978-3-642-14309-0_7
8. Fähndrich, M., Foster, J.S., Su, Z., Aiken, A.: Partial online cycle elimination in inclusion constraint graphs. In: Proceedings of the ACM SIGPLAN 1998 Conference on Programming Language Design and Implementation (PLDI), Montreal, Canada, 17–19 June 1998, pp. 85–96 (1998)
9. Hardekopf, B., Lin, C.: The ant and the grasshopper: fast and accurate pointer analysis for millions of lines of code. In: Proceedings of the ACM SIGPLAN 2007 Conference on Programming Language Design and Implementation, San Diego, California, USA, 10–13 June 2007, pp. 290–299 (2007)
10. Jeon, M., Jeong, S., Oh, H.: Precise and scalable points-to analysis via data-driven context tunneling. PACMPL **2**(OOPSLA), 140:1–140:29 (2018)
11. Jeong, S., Jeon, M., Cha, S.D., Oh, H.: Data-driven context-sensitivity for points-to analysis. PACMPL **1**(OOPSLA), 100:1–100:28 (2017)
12. Kulkarni, S., Mangal, R., Zhang, X., Naik, M.: Accelerating program analyses by cross-program training. In: Proceedings of the 2016 ACM SIGPLAN International Conference on Object-Oriented Programming, Systems, Languages, and Applications, OOPSLA 2016, Part of SPLASH 2016, Amsterdam, The Netherlands, 30 October–4 November 2016, pp. 359–377 (2016)
13. Lhoták, O., Hendren, L.J.: Context-sensitive points-to analysis: is it worth it? In: Compiler Construction, Proceedings of the 15th International Conference, CC 2006, Held as Part of the Joint European Conferences on Theory and Practice of Software, ETAPS 2006, Vienna, Austria, 30–31 March 2006, pp. 47–64 (2006)
14. Li, Y., Tan, T., Møller, A., Smaragdakis, Y.: Precision-guided context sensitivity for pointer analysis. PACMPL **2**(OOPSLA), 141:1–141:29 (2018)

15. Li, Y., Tan, T., Møller, A., Smaragdakis, Y.: Scalability-first pointer analysis with self-tuning context-sensitivity. In: Proceedings of the 2018 ACM Joint Meeting on European Software Engineering Conference and Symposium on the Foundations of Software Engineering, ESEC/SIGSOFT FSE 2018, Lake Buena Vista, FL, USA, 04–09 November 2018, pp. 129–140 (2018)

16. Liang, P., Tripp, O., Naik, M.: Learning minimal abstractions. In: Proceedings of the 38th ACM SIGPLAN-SIGACT Symposium on Principles of Programming Languages, POPL 2011, Austin, TX, USA, 26–28 January 2011, pp. 31–42 (2011)

17. Nielson, F., Nielson, H.R., Hankin, C.: Principles of Program Analysis. Springer, Heidelberg (1999). https://doi.org/10.1007/978-3-662-03811-6

18. pjBench: parallel Java benchmarks (2014)

19. Shivers, O.: Control-flow analysis of higher-order languages (1991)

20. Smaragdakis, Y., Kastrinis, G., Balatsouras, G.: Introspective analysis: context-sensitivity, across the board. In: Proceedings of the 35th ACM SIGPLAN Conference on Programming Language Design and Implementation, PLDI 2014, pp. 485–495. ACM, New York (2014)

21. Tan, T., Li, Y., Xue, J.: Efficient and precise points-to analysis: modeling the heap by merging equivalent automata. In: Proceedings of the 38th ACM SIGPLAN Conference on Programming Language Design and Implementation, PLDI 2017, pp. 278–291. ACM, New York (2017)

22. Tang, H., Wang, D., Xiong, Y., Zhang, L., Wang, X., Zhang, L.: Conditional Dyck-CFL reachability analysis for complete and efficient library summarization. In: Yang, H. (ed.) ESOP 2017. LNCS, vol. 10201, pp. 880–908. Springer, Heidelberg (2017). https://doi.org/10.1007/978-3-662-54434-1_33

23. Tang, H., Wang, X., Zhang, L., Xie, B., Zhang, L., Mei, H.: Summary-based context-sensitive data-dependence analysis in presence of callbacks. In: Proceedings of the 42nd Annual ACM SIGPLAN-SIGACT Symposium on Principles of Programming Languages, POPL 2015, Mumbai, India, 15–17 January 2015, pp. 83–95 (2015)

24. Xiao, X., Zhang, C.: Geometric encoding: forging the high performance context sensitive points-to analysis for Java. In: Proceedings of the 20th International Symposium on Software Testing and Analysis, ISSTA 2011, Toronto, ON, Canada, 17–21 July 2011, pp. 188–198 (2011)

25. Xu, G., Rountev, A.: Merging equivalent contexts for scalable heap-cloning-based context-sensitive points-to analysis. In: Proceedings of the 2008 International Symposium on Software Testing and Analysis, ISSTA 2008, pp. 225–236. ACM, New York (2008)

26. Yan, H., Sui, Y., Chen, S., Xue, J.: Spatio-temporal context reduction: a pointer-analysis-based static approach for detecting use-after-free vulnerabilities. In: Proceedings of the 40th International Conference on Software Engineering, ICSE 2018, Gothenburg, Sweden, 27 May–03 June 2018, pp. 327–337. ACM (2018)

27. Zhang, X., Mangal, R., Grigore, R., Naik, M., Yang, H.: On abstraction refinement for program analyses in datalog. In: ACM SIGPLAN Conference on Programming Language Design and Implementation, PLDI 2014, Edinburgh, United Kingdom, 09–11 June 2014, pp. 239–248. ACM (2014)

Static Analysis of Endian Portability by Abstract Interpretation

David Delmas[1,2](✉) [ID], Abdelraouf Ouadjaout[2] [ID], and Antoine Miné[2,3] [ID]

[1] Airbus Operations S.A.S., 316 route de Bayonne, 31060 Toulouse Cedex 9, France
david.delmas@airbus.com
[2] Sorbonne Université, CNRS, LIP6, 75005 Paris, France
{abdelraouf.ouadjaout,antoine.mine}@lip6.fr
[3] Institut Universitaire de France, 1 rue Descartes, 75231 Paris Cedex 5, France

Abstract. We present a static analysis of endian portability for C programs. Our analysis can infer that a given program, or two syntactically close versions thereof, compute the same outputs when run with the same inputs on platforms with different byte-orders, *a.k.a.* endiannesses. We target low-level C programs that abuse C pointers and unions, hence rely on implementation-specific behaviors undefined in the C standard.

Our method is based on abstract interpretation, and parametric in the choice of a numerical abstract domain. We first present a novel concrete collecting semantics, relating the behaviors of two versions of a program, running on platforms with different endiannesses. We propose a joint memory abstraction, able to infer equivalence relations between little- and big-endian memories. We introduce a novel symbolic predicate domain to infer relations between individual bytes of the variables in the two programs, which has near-linear cost, and the right amount of relationality to express (bitwise) arithmetic properties relevant to endian portability. We implemented a prototype static analyzer, able to scale to large real-world industrial software, with zero false alarms.

Keywords: Formal methods · Abstract interpretation · Abstract domains · Static analysis · C programming language · Portability · Endianness · Industrial application

This work is performed as part of a collaborative partnership between Sorbonnne Université/CNRS (LIP6) and Airbus. This work is partially supported by the European Research Council under the Consolidator Grant Agreement 681393 – MOPSA.

C. Drăgoi et al. (Eds.): SAS 2021, LNCS 12913, pp. 102–123, 2021.
https://doi.org/10.1007/978-3-030-88806-0_5

1   Introduction

There is no consensus on the representation of a multi-byte scalar value in computer memory [9]. Some systems store the least-significant byte at the lowest address, while others do the opposite. The former are called little-endian, the latter big-endian. Such systems include processor architectures, network protocols and data storage formats. For instance, Intel processors are little-endian, while internet protocols and some legacy processors, such as SPARC, are bigendian. As a consequence, programs relying on assumptions on the encoding of scalar types may exhibit different behaviors when run on platforms with different byte-orders, *a.k.a.* endiannesses. The case occurs typically with low-level C software, such as device drivers or embedded software. Indeed, the C standard [19] leaves the encoding of scalar types partly unspecified. The precise representation of types is standardized in implementation-specific *Application Binary Interfaces* (ABI), such as [2], to ensure the interoperability of compiled programs, libraries, and operating systems. Although it is possible to write fully portable, ABIneutral C code, the vast majority of C programs rely on assumptions on the ABI of the platform, such as endianness. Therefore, the typical approach used, when porting a low-level C program to a new platform with opposite endianness, is to eliminate most of the byte-order-dependent code, and to wrap the remainder, if any, in conditional inclusion directives, which results in two syntactically close endian-specific variants of the same program. A desirable property, which we call endian portability, is that a program computes the same outputs when run with the same inputs on the little- and big-endian platforms. By extension, we also say that a program is endian portable if two endian-specific variants thereof compute the same outputs when run with the same inputs on their respective platforms. In this paper, we describe a static analysis which aims at inferring the endian portability of large real-world low-level C programs.

Motivating Example. For instance, Example 1 features a snippet of code for reading network input. The sequence of bytes read from the network is first stored into integer variable x. Assume variable y has the same type. x is then either copied, or byte-swapped into y, depending on the endianness of the platform. Our analysis is able to infer that Example 1 is endian portable, *i.e.* both endianspecific variants compute the same value for y, whatever the values of the bytes read from the network. This property is expressed by the assertion at line 8.

Example 1. Reading input in network byte-order.

```
1    read_from_network((uint8_t *)&x, sizeof(x));
2  # if __BYTE_ORDER == __LITTLE_ENDIAN
3      uint8_t *px = (uint8_t *)&x, *py = (uint8_t *)&y;
4      for (int i=0; i<sizeof(x); i++) py[i] = px[sizeof(x)-i-1];
5  # else
6      y = x;
7  # endif
8    assert_sync(y);
```

Example 1 abuses pointers to bypass the C type system, a common practice in low-level programming known as *type punning*. Alternatively, some implementations rely on bitwise arithmetics. E.g., if x and y have type `uint32_t`, the little-endian case may be rewritten as `((x & 0xff000000) >> 24) | ((x & 0xff0000) >> 8) | ((x & 0xff00) << 8) | ((x & 0xff) << 24)`. Other implementations rely on compiler built-in functions, or assembly code, possibly using dedicated processor instructions. Examples can be seen in the Linux implementations of the POSIX `htons` and `htonl` functions, converting values between host and network byte-order. Our analysis is able to analyze all the above C implementations successfully, as well as alternative implementations (with stubs for assembly code). In the following of the paper, unless otherwise stated, we will implicitly refer to a version of Example 1 where variables have type `uint16_t`.

Approach. Low-level programs exhibit different semantics when run on platforms with different endiannesses. We thus model them as so-called double programs. The little-endian program is called the first (or left, or little-endian) version of the double program, while the big-endian program is called the second (or right, or big-endian) version. Both versions may share the same source code, or present syntactic differences (if conditional inclusion is used). Our approach to endian portability is to devise a joint, whole-program static analysis of a double program able to infer equivalences between the input-output relations of its versions. To this aim, we define a memory model able to represent a joint abstraction of their memories. We first parameterize a standard memory domain for low-level C programs with an explicit endianness parameter. Then, we lift it to double programs, and tailor it to infer, and represent symbolically, relevant equalities between little- and big-endian memories. We rely on a dedicated numerical domain based on symbolic predicates, to infer complementarity relations between individual bytes of program variables, such as those established by bitwise arithmetic operations. We validate our approach by analyzing large industrial low-level embedded C programs designed to be endian portable.

Related Work. Several approaches to endian portability are developed in the literature. [30] relies on a source-to-source translation, which is only sound with respect to annotations provided by the programmer, whereas we require no annotations. [5] extends a compiler to generate code that executes with the opposite byte order semantics as the underlying architecture, at the cost of a performance penalty. Annotations are also required for soundness in some cases. [21] relies on dynamic analysis, which can find portability errors, but cannot prove endian portability formally, unlike our method. The SPARSE [6] static analysis tool used by Linux kernel developers relies on pervasive type annotations to detect endiannesses issues, but comes with no formal guarantee.

To our knowledge, no prior work uses sound static analysis to infer endian portability. Yet, our approach leverages prior work. We build on a memory abstract domain [24], [27, Sect. 5.2] developed for run-time error analysis of low-level C programs able to expose endian-dependent behaviors, and on double program semantics developed for patch analysis [14,15]. Our symbolic predicate domain is based on previous work on predicate domains [26], and symbolic constant propagation [25]. Our domain is also reminiscent of the Slice domain introduced in [7,8] for another purpose, and implemented differently.

Contributions. The main contributions of this work are:

- We present a novel concrete collecting semantics, relating the behaviors of two versions of a program, running on platforms with different endiannesses.
- We propose a joint memory abstraction able to infer equivalence relations between little- and big-endian memories.
- We introduce a novel symbolic predicate domain to infer relations between individual bytes of the variables in the two programs, which has near-linear cost, and the right amount of relationality to express (bitwise) arithmetic properties relevant to endian portability.
- We implemented our analysis on the MOPSA [20,29] platform. Our prototype is able to scale to large real-world industrial software, with zero false alarms.

The paper is organised as follows. Section 2 formalizes the concrete collecting semantics, Sect. 3 describes the memory abstraction, Sect. 4 describes the numerical abstraction and introduces a novel numeric domain, Sect. 5 presents experimental results with a prototype implementation. Section 6 concludes.

2   Syntax and Concrete Semantics

Following the standard approach to abstract interpretation [10], we develop a concrete collecting semantics for a C-like language for double programs. The $\parallel$ operator may occur anywhere in the parse tree to denote syntactic differences between the left (little-endian) and right (big-endian) versions of a double program. However, $\parallel$ operators cannot be nested: a double program only describes a pair of programs. Given double program P with variables in $\mathcal{V}$, we call its left (resp. right) version $P_1 = \pi_1(P)$ (resp. $P_2 = \pi_2(P)$), where π_1 (resp. π_2) is a version extraction operator, defined by induction on the syntax, keeping only the left (resp. right) side of $\parallel$ symbols. For instance, $\pi_1(x \leftarrow 1 \parallel y \leftarrow 0) = x \leftarrow 1$, and $\pi_2(x \leftarrow 1 \parallel y \leftarrow 0) = y \leftarrow 0$, while $\pi_1(z \leftarrow 0) = z \leftarrow 0 = \pi_2(z \leftarrow 0)$. Recall that syntactic differences between P_1 and P_2 may be distinct from semantic differences. Syntactically different statements may exhibit the same semantics in P_1 and P_2, like in Example 1, while syntactically equal statements may exhibit different semantics, like with the C statement $*((\textbf{char}*)\&x)=1$, when integer variable x is such that $sizeof(x) > 1$.

2.1   Syntax

Simple programs P_1 and P_2 enjoy a standard, C-like syntax presented in Fig. 1. Statements *stat* are built on top of expressions *expr* and Boolean conditions *cond*. The syntax of double statements *dstat* includes specific **assume_sync** and

$$
\begin{array}{ll}
\textit{scalar-type} ::= \textit{int-sign int-type} \mid \mathbf{ptr} & \textit{int-sign} ::= \mathbf{signed} \mid \mathbf{unsigned} \\
\textit{type} \quad ::= \textit{scalar-type} \mid \dots & \textit{int-type} ::= \mathbf{char} \mid \mathbf{short} \mid \mathbf{int} \mid \mathbf{long} \mid \mathbf{long\ long}
\end{array}
$$

$$
\begin{array}{ll}
\circ \quad ::= - \mid \sim \mid (\textit{scalar-type}) \\
\diamond \quad ::= + \mid - \mid * \mid / \mid \% \mid \& \mid \mid \mid \char`^ \mid \gg \mid \ll
\end{array}
\qquad
\begin{array}{ll}
\textit{expr} ::= *_{\textit{scalar-type}}\ \textit{expr} \\
\quad \mid \& V \\
\quad \mid [c_1, c_2] & c_1, c_2 \in \mathbb{Z}
\end{array}
$$

$$
\begin{array}{ll}
\textit{stat} ::= *_{\textit{scalar-type}}\ \textit{expr} \leftarrow \textit{expr} \\
\quad \mid \mathbf{if}\ \textit{cond}\ \mathbf{then}\ \textit{stat}\ \mathbf{else}\ \textit{stat} \\
\quad \mid \dots
\end{array}
\qquad
\begin{array}{ll}
\quad \mid \circ\ \textit{expr} \\
\quad \mid \textit{expr} \diamond \textit{expr}
\end{array}
$$

$$
\begin{array}{ll}
\textit{dstat} ::= \textit{stat} \\
\quad \mid \textit{stat} \parallel \textit{stat} \\
\quad \mid \textit{spec} \\
\quad \mid \mathbf{if}\ \textit{dcond}\ \mathbf{then}\ \textit{dstat}\ \mathbf{else}\ \textit{dstat} \\
\quad \mid \dots
\end{array}
\qquad
\begin{array}{ll}
\textit{cond} \quad ::= \textit{expr} \bowtie 0 \quad \bowtie \in \{\le, \ge, =, \ne, <, >\} \\
\textit{spec} \quad ::= \mathbf{assume\_sync}(\textit{expr}) \\
\quad \mid \mathbf{assert\_sync}(\textit{expr}) \\
\textit{dcond} ::= \textit{cond} \\
\quad \mid \textit{cond} \parallel \textit{cond}
\end{array}
$$

Fig. 1. Syntax of simple and double programs.

assert_sync statements, used for specifications. The former is used to express assumptions on program inputs, while the latter is used to express assertions on program outputs: **assume_sync**(e) introduces the assumption that expression e evaluates to the same value in double program versions P_1 and P_2, while **assert_sync**(e) checks that the value of e is identical in both versions, and fails otherwise. Expression $[c_1, c_2]$ chooses a value non-deterministically between constants c_1 and c_2. The double statement $x \leftarrow [c_1, c_2]$ may assign different values to variable x in the two program versions. In contrast, the sequence $x \leftarrow [c_1, c_2]$; **assume_sync**(x) ensures that x holds the same non-deterministic value in both versions.

Expressions rely on a C-like type-system. Integer and pointer types are collectively referred to as scalar types. Expressions support pointer arithmetic, expressed as byte-level offset arithmetic. All left-values are assumed to be preprocessed to dereferences $*_\tau e$ (*i.e.* $*((\tau*)e)$ in C) where τ is a scalar type, and e is a pointer expression. Note that dereferences are limited to scalar types, and the dereferenced type is explicit in the syntax.

2.2   Semantics of Low-Level Simple C Programs

The semantics of simple programs is parameterized by an ABI. In this paper, we assume program versions have the same ABIs, but for endianness. Let $\mathcal{A} \triangleq \{\mathcal{L}, \mathcal{B}\}$ denote the possible endiannesses (little- and big-endian). The sizes of types, in contrast, are the same for both program versions. We thus assume a unique function $\textit{sizeof} \in \textit{type} \to \mathbb{N}$ given, which provides these sizes (in bytes).

Pointer values are modeled as (semi-)symbolic addresses of the form $\langle V, i \rangle \in \mathcal{A}ddr \triangleq \mathcal{V} \times \mathbb{Z}$, which indicate an offset of i bytes from the first byte of V. Special pointer values are defined for C's NULL and dangling pointers: $\mathcal{P}tr \triangleq \mathcal{A}ddr \cup \{\mathbf{NULL}, \mathbf{invalid}\}$.

Let $\mathbb{B} \triangleq [0, 255] \cup (\mathcal{P}tr \times \mathbb{N})$ describe the possible numeric byte values and symbolic pointer bytes. We keep pointer values symbolic as their precise numeric values depend on memory allocation strategies outside the scope of the analysis. $\langle p, i \rangle \in \mathbb{B}$ denotes the i−th byte in the memory representation of the pointer

$$\mathbb{E}[\![*_\tau e]\!]_\alpha \rho \triangleq \{ v \mid \langle V, o \rangle \in \mathbb{E}[\![e]\!]_\alpha \rho \wedge 0 \le o \le sizeof(V) - sizeof(\tau)$$
$$\wedge \, v \in bdec_{\tau,\alpha}(\rho\langle V, o \rangle, \dots, \rho\langle V, o + sizeof(\tau) - 1\rangle)) \}$$
$$\mathbb{S}[\![*_\tau e_1 \leftarrow e_2]\!]_\alpha R \triangleq$$
$$\bigcup_{\rho \in R}\{ \rho[\forall i < sizeof(\tau) : \langle V, o + i \rangle \mapsto b_i] \mid \langle V, o \rangle \in \mathbb{E}[\![e_1]\!]_\alpha \rho$$
$$\wedge \, 0 \le o \le sizeof(V) - sizeof(\tau) \wedge (b_0, \dots, b_{sizeof(\tau)-1}) \in benc_{\tau,\alpha}(\mathbb{E}[\![e_2]\!]_\alpha \rho) \}$$

Fig. 2. Concrete semantics of memory reads and writes.

value p. Expressions manipulate scalar values, which may be numeric (machine integers) or pointer values. We denote the set of values as $\mathbb{V} \triangleq \mathbb{Z} \cup \mathcal{P}tr$. The definition of the most concrete semantics requires a family of representation functions $benc_{\tau,\alpha} \in \mathbb{V} \to \mathcal{P}(\mathbb{B}^*)$, that convert a scalar value of given type $\tau \in scalar\text{-}type$ and endianness $\alpha \in \mathcal{A}$ into a sequence of $sizeof(t)$ byte values. We denote as $bdec_{\tau,\alpha} \in \mathbb{B}^* \to \mathcal{P}(\mathbb{V})$ the converse operation. For instance, on a 32-bit platform, $benc_{\text{unsigned int},\mathcal{L}}(1) = \{ (1, 0, 0, 0) \}$, $bdec_{\text{unsigned short},\mathcal{B}}(0, 1) = \{ 1 \}$, and $benc_{\text{ptr},\mathcal{L}}(p) = \{ (\langle p, 0 \rangle, \langle p, 1 \rangle, \langle p, 2 \rangle, \langle p, 3 \rangle) \}$. This seemingly trivial encoding allows modeling copying pointer values byte per byte, as done e.g. by `memcpy`. Note that the $benc_{\tau,\alpha}$ and $bdec_{\tau,\alpha}$ functions return a set of possible values. For instance, reinterpreting a pointer value as an integer, as in $bdec_{\text{int},\mathcal{L}} \circ benc_{\text{ptr},\mathcal{L}}(p)$, returns the full range of type **int**. We do not detail the definitions of these functions here, for the sake of conciseness. An example may be found in [27, Sec. 5.2].

Environments are elements of $\mathcal{E} \triangleq Addr \rightharpoonup \mathbb{B}$. The semantics $\mathbb{E}[\![expr]\!] \in \mathcal{A} \to \mathcal{E} \to \mathcal{P}(\mathbb{V})$ and $\mathbb{S}[\![stat]\!] \in \mathcal{A} \to \mathcal{P}(\mathcal{E}) \to \mathcal{P}(\mathcal{E})$ for simple expressions and statements is defined by standard induction on the syntax. We therefore only show, on Fig. 2, the semantics $\mathbb{E}[\![*_\tau e]\!]_\alpha$ and $\mathbb{S}[\![*_\tau e_1 \leftarrow e_2]\!]_\alpha$ for memory reads and writes, given endianness $\alpha \in \mathcal{A}$. Bytes are fetched and decoded with $bdec_{\tau,\alpha}$ when reading from memory in expression $*_\tau e$, while values computed by expression e_2 are encoded into bytes with $benc_{\tau,\alpha}$ when writing to memory in assignment $*_\tau e_1 \leftarrow e_2$. Note that illegal memory accesses are silently omitted to simplify the presentation.

2.3 Semantics of Double Programs

We now lift simple program semantics $\mathbb{S}$ to double program semantics $\mathbb{D}$. As both simple program versions $P_k = \pi_k(P)$ have concrete states in $\mathcal{E}$, the double program P has concrete states in $\mathcal{D} \triangleq \mathcal{E} \times \mathcal{E}$. The semantics of P_k is parameterized by its endianness $\alpha_k \in \mathcal{A}$. We assume, without loss of generality, that P_1 is the little-endian version, and P_2 the big-endian one.

$\mathbb{D}[\![s]\!] \in \mathcal{P}(\mathcal{D}) \to \mathcal{P}(\mathcal{D})$ describes the relation between input and output states of s, which are pairs of states of simple programs. The definition for $\mathbb{D}[\![s]\!]$ is shown on Fig. 3. $\mathbb{D}$ leverages previous work on patch analysis [14,15]. It is defined by induction on the syntax, so as to allow for a modular definition and joint analyses of double programs. Note that $\mathbb{D}$ is parametric in $\mathbb{S}$.

The semantics for the empty program is the identity function. The semantics $\mathbb{D}[\![s_1 \| s_2]\!]$ for the composition of two syntactically different statements reverts

$$\mathbb{D}[\![\, dstat \,]\!] \in \mathcal{P}(\mathcal{D}) \to \mathcal{P}(\mathcal{D})$$

$$
\begin{aligned}
\mathbb{D}[\![\, \mathbf{skip} \,]\!] &\triangleq \lambda X.\, X \\
\mathbb{D}[\![\, s_1 \parallel s_2 \,]\!] X &\triangleq \bigcup_{(\rho_1,\rho_2)\in X} \prod_{k\in\{1,2\}} \mathbb{S}[\![\, s_k \,]\!]_{\alpha_k} \{\rho_k\} \\
\mathbb{D}[\![\, l \leftarrow e \,]\!] &\triangleq \mathbb{D}[\![\, l \leftarrow e \parallel l \leftarrow e \,]\!] \\
\mathbb{D}[\![\, \mathbf{assume\_sync}(e) \,]\!] X &\triangleq \{\, (\rho_1,\rho_2) \in X \mid \exists v \in \mathbb{V} : \forall k \in \{1,2\} : \mathbb{E}[\![\, e \,]\!]_{\alpha_k}\rho_k = \{v\} \,\} \\
\mathbb{D}[\![\, s\,;\, t \,]\!] &\triangleq \mathbb{D}[\![\, t \,]\!] \circ \mathbb{D}[\![\, s \,]\!] \\
\mathbb{D}[\![\, \mathbf{if}\ e_1 \bowtie 0 \parallel e_2 \bowtie 0\ \mathbf{then}\ s\ \mathbf{else}\ t \,]\!] &\triangleq \mathbb{D}[\![\, s \,]\!] \circ \mathbb{F}[\![\, e_1 \bowtie 0 \parallel e_2 \bowtie 0 \,]\!] \\
&\mathrel{\dot{\cup}} \mathbb{D}[\![\, \pi_1(s) \parallel \pi_2(t) \,]\!] \circ \mathbb{F}[\![\, e_1 \bowtie 0 \parallel e_2 \not\bowtie 0 \,]\!] \\
&\mathrel{\dot{\cup}} \mathbb{D}[\![\, \pi_1(t) \parallel \pi_2(s) \,]\!] \circ \mathbb{F}[\![\, e_1 \not\bowtie 0 \parallel e_2 \bowtie 0 \,]\!] \\
&\mathrel{\dot{\cup}} \mathbb{D}[\![\, t \,]\!] \circ \mathbb{F}[\![\, e_1 \not\bowtie 0 \parallel e_2 \not\bowtie 0 \,]\!] \\
\mathbb{D}[\![\, \mathbf{if}\ c\ \mathbf{then}\ s\ \mathbf{else}\ t \,]\!] &\triangleq \mathbb{D}[\![\, \mathbf{if}\ c \parallel c\ \mathbf{then}\ s\ \mathbf{else}\ t \,]\!] \\
\mathbb{D}[\![\, \mathbf{while}\ e_1 \bowtie 0 \parallel e_2 \bowtie 0\ \mathbf{do}\ s \,]\!] X &\triangleq \mathbb{F}[\![\, e_1 \not\bowtie 0 \parallel e_2 \not\bowtie 0 \,]\!](\mathrm{lfp}\ H) \\
\mathbb{D}[\![\, \mathbf{while}\ c\ \mathbf{do}\ s \,]\!] &\triangleq \mathbb{D}[\![\, \mathbf{while}\ c \parallel c\ \mathbf{do}\ s \,]\!]
\end{aligned}
$$

$$\text{where}\quad \mathbb{F}[\![\, e_1 \bowtie 0 \parallel e_2 \bowtie 0 \,]\!] X \triangleq \{\, (\rho_1,\rho_2) \in X \mid \forall k \in \{1,2\} : \exists v_k \in \mathbb{E}[\![\, e_k \,]\!]_{\alpha_k}\rho_k : v_k \bowtie 0 \,\}$$

$$
\begin{aligned}
\text{and}\quad H(I) &\triangleq X \\
&\mathrel{\dot{\cup}} \mathbb{D}[\![\, s \,]\!] \circ \mathbb{F}[\![\, e_1 \bowtie 0 \parallel e_2 \bowtie 0 \,]\!] I \\
&\mathrel{\dot{\cup}} \mathbb{D}[\![\, \pi_1(s) \parallel \mathbf{skip} \,]\!] \circ \mathbb{F}[\![\, e_1 \bowtie 0 \parallel e_2 \not\bowtie 0 \,]\!] I \\
&\mathrel{\dot{\cup}} \mathbb{D}[\![\, \mathbf{skip} \parallel \pi_2(s) \,]\!] \circ \mathbb{F}[\![\, e_1 \not\bowtie 0 \parallel e_2 \bowtie 0 \,]\!] I
\end{aligned}
$$

Fig. 3. Denotational concrete semantics of double programs.

to the pairing of the simple program semantics of individual simple statements s_1 and s_2. The semantics for assignments is defined with this construct. The semantics of **assume_sync** and **assert_sync** statements filters away environments where the left and right versions of a double program may disagree on the value of expression e. In addition, **assert_sync** raises an alarm if e may evaluate to different values in P_1 and P_2. We omit alarms from the semantics for conciseness. The semantics for the sequential composition of statements boils down to the composition of the semantics of individual statements. The semantics for selection statements relies on the filter $\mathbb{F}[\![\, e_1 \bowtie 0 \parallel e_2 \bowtie 0 \,]\!]$ to distinguish between cases where both versions agree on the value of the controlling expression, and cases where they do not (*a.k.a.* unstable tests). There are two stable and two unstable test cases, according to the evaluations of the two conditions. The semantics for stable test cases is standard. The semantics for unstable test cases is defined by the composition of left version of the **then** branch, filtered by the condition, and of the right version of the **else** branch, filtered by the negation of the condition (and the dual case). The semantics for (possibly unbounded) iteration statements is defined using the least fixpoint of a function defined similarly.

2.4   Properties of Interest

We wish to prove the functional equivalence between the left and right versions of a given double program $P \in dstat$, restricted to a set of distinguished outputs, specified with the **assert_sync** primitive. Let $x_0 \in \mathcal{D}$ be an initial double-program state. The set of states reachable by P is $\mathbb{D}[\![\, P \,]\!]\{x_0\}$. Let Ω be a set of output left-values of program P. The property of interest is that $\pi_1(P)$

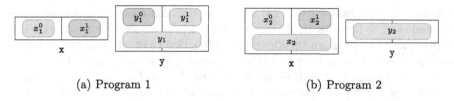

(a) Program 1   (b) Program 2

Fig. 4. Memory cells of Example 1: $\square = b_0$, $\square = b_1$, $\square = b_0 \times 2^8 + b_1$.

and $\pi_2(P)$ compute equal values for all outputs:

$$\forall l \in \Omega : \forall \langle \rho_1, \rho_2 \rangle \in \mathbb{D}[\![P]\!] \{ x_0 \} : \exists v \in V : \forall k \in \{1, 2\} : \mathbb{E}[\![l]\!]_{\alpha_k} \rho_k = \{ v \}.$$

For instance, let S denote the set of reachable states of Example 1, before line 8:
$S = \{ \langle [x_1^o \mapsto b_o, y_1^o \mapsto b_{1-o}], [x_2^o \mapsto b_o, y_2^o \mapsto b_o] \rangle \mid o \in \{0, 1\}, (b_0, b_1) \in [0, 255]^2 \}$,
where b_0 and b_1 denote the values of bytes read from the network, and we write
x_i^o and y_i^o for $\langle x, o \rangle$ and $\langle y, o \rangle$ in program version i. The portability property
expressed at line 8 is $y_1^0 + 2^8 y_1^1 = 2^8 y_2^0 + y_2^1$, which can be proved from S.

Our concrete collecting semantics $\mathbb{D}$ is not computable in general. We will
thus rely on computable abstractions, to infer this property by static analysis.
Note that the use of **assume_sync** and **assert_sync** in specifications allows for
both whole-program analysis, and separate analyses of program parts.

3   Memory Abstraction

Though we aim at designing a computable abstract semantics in Sect. 4, we
first tailor a (non computable) abstraction of our memory model. We rely on
the Cells memory abstraction of simple programs [24], [27, Sect. 5.2]. In order to
handle C programs computing with machine integers of multiple sizes, with byte-
level access to their encoding through type-punning, this domain represents the
memory as a dynamic collection of scalar variables, termed cells, holding values
for the scalar memory dereferences discovered during the analysis. It maintains
a consistent abstract state despite the introduction of overlapping cells by type-
punning. We lift this memory abstraction to double programs, and we extend it
for representing equalities between cells symbolically.

3.1   Cells

We first consider the finite universe $Cell \triangleq V \times \mathbb{N} \times scalar\text{-}type \times \mathcal{A}$ of cells of
one program. A cell $\langle V, o, \tau, \alpha \rangle \in Cell$ is denoted as a variable V, an offset o, and
information specifying the encoding of values: a scalar type τ and endianness α.
To account for both programs, we introduce *projected cells* as $\widetilde{Cell} \triangleq Cell \times \{1, 2\}$,
where 1 (resp. 2) denotes a cell in the memory of P_1 (resp. P_2).

For instance, consider the program in Example 1. We show in Fig. 4 the cells
synthesized at the end of the program. Let $x_k \triangleq \langle x, 0, \mathbf{u16}, \alpha_k, k \rangle$ denote 2-byte

cells for x in Program $k \in \{1,2\}$, where $\alpha_1 = \mathcal{L}$ and $\alpha_2 = \mathcal{B}$. 1-byte cells are denoted as $x_k^o \triangleq \langle x, o, \mathbf{u8}, \alpha_k, k \rangle$ where $o \in \{0, 1\}$. The cells for y are defined in a similar way. Both program versions first call function `read_from_network`, which reads a stream of bytes from an external source, and writes it into a buffer. The same stream is read by both program versions. A stub for `read_from_network` is shown in Fig. 5. After completion of the call, we have $x_1^0 = b_0 = x_2^0$ and

```
void read_from_network(u8 buf[], u32 size) {
    for (int i=0; i<size; i++) {
        buf[i] = [0,255];
        assume_sync( buf[i] );
    }
}
```

Fig. 5. Stub for `read_from_network` function.

$x_1^1 = b_1 = x_2^1$, where b_0 and b_1 are the first and second bytes read from the network, respectively. Then, Program 1 swaps the bytes of x into those of y: $x_1^0 = y_1^1$ and $x_1^1 = y_1^0$. Program 2, in contrast, assigns x to y. x is thus read as a 2-byte cell, while only 1-byte cells are present. Therefore, the Cells domain synthesizes x_2 by adding the constraint $x_2 = 2^8 x_2^0 + x_2^1$, following big-endian byte-order, before performing the assignment $y_2 \leftarrow x_2$. To sum up, we obtain the following constraints:

$$x_1^0 = x_2^0 = y_1^1 \qquad x_1^1 = x_2^1 = y_1^0 \qquad y_2 = x_2$$

In addition to the cell constraints on x and y:

$$x_1 = x_1^0 + 2^8 x_1^1 \qquad y_1 = y_1^0 + 2^8 y_1^1 \qquad x_2 = 2^8 x_2^0 + x_2^1 \qquad y_2 = 2^8 y_2^0 + y_2^1$$

Our goal is to prove that $y_1 = y_2$ given such constraints. To do so, we want to leverage numerical domains to abstract the values of cells. However, such constraints require an expressive domain, such as polyhedra or linear equalities, that can hamper the scalability of the analysis. In addition, we note that we need to infer many equalities, most of them between the left and right versions of the same cells. This is no surprise as we expect most variables to hold equal values in the little- and big-endian memories most of the time, with only local differences. Rather than relying completely on the expressiveness of the underlying numeric domain, we first optimize our memory model for this common case, introducing the concept of shared bi-cells, which act as a symbolic representation of cells equality.

3.2   Shared Bi-Cells

We denote as $\mathcal{B}icell \triangleq \widetilde{\mathcal{C}ell} \cup (\widetilde{\mathcal{C}ell} \times \widetilde{\mathcal{C}ell})$ the set of bi-cells. A bi-cell is either a projected cell in $\widetilde{\mathcal{C}ell}$, or a pair of such cells in $\widetilde{\mathcal{C}ell} \times \widetilde{\mathcal{C}ell}$ assumed to hold equal value, called a *shared bi-cell*. Bi-cell sharing allows a single representation, in the memory environment, for two projected cells from different program versions at the same memory location and holding equal values. Abstract memory states of double programs are modeled as a choice of a set of bi-cells $C \subseteq \mathcal{B}icell$, and a set of scalar environments on C. Let $\mathcal{D}^{\flat} \triangleq \bigcup_{C \subseteq \mathcal{B}icell} \{ \langle C, R \rangle \mid R \in \mathcal{P}(C \to \mathbb{V}) \}$ be the associated abstract domain. An abstract state represents a set of concrete byte-level memories in $\mathcal{D} = \mathcal{E} \times \mathcal{E}$. The values of the bytes of these memories must satisfy all the numeric constraints on bi-cells implied by the environments:

$$\gamma_{\mathcal{B}icell}\langle C, R \rangle \triangleq \{ (\mu_1, \mu_2) \in \mathcal{D} \mid \exists \rho \in R : \forall c_k = \langle V, o, \tau, \alpha, k \rangle \in \widetilde{\mathcal{C}ell} :$$
$$\forall c \in occ(c_k, C) : \exists (b_0, \dots, b_{sizeof(\tau)-1}) \in benc_{\tau, \alpha}(\rho(c)) :$$
$$\forall 0 \leq i < sizeof(\tau) : \mu_k \langle V, o + i \rangle = b_i \}$$

where $occ \in \widetilde{\mathcal{C}ell} \times \mathcal{P}(\mathcal{B}icell) \to \mathcal{P}(\mathcal{B}icell)$ records occurrences of a projected cell among bi-cells: $occ(c, C) \triangleq \{ c' \in C \mid c' = c \vee \exists c'' : c' = \langle c, c'' \rangle \vee c' = \langle c'', c \rangle \}$.

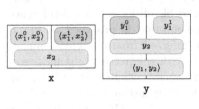

Fig. 6. Shared bi-cells of Example 1.

In Fig. 6, we depict the bi-cells obtained after analyzing the program shown in Example 1. For variable x, since `read_from_network` writes the same value to x_1^0 and x_2^0, we can synthesize the shared bi-cell $\langle x_1^0, x_2^0 \rangle$ to represent the equality $x_1^0 = x_2^0$. In a similar way, we synthesize the shared bi-cell $\langle x_1^1, x_2^1 \rangle$. Therefore, as opposed to the separate representation of the memories of Programs 1 and 2 in Fig. 4, the joint representation induced by bi-cell sharing allows reducing the burden on numeric domains. In the following, we describe more involved cell synthesis operations that allow us to realize $\langle y_1, y_2 \rangle$, and thus to infer that $y_1 = y_2$.

3.3   Cell Synthesis

A cornerstone of our memory model is bi-cell synthesis. In order to read or write a scalar value to a given location of memory, we must create a suitable bi-cell, or retrieve an existing one from the environment. To guarantee the soundness of the analysis when adding a new bi-cell, it is necessary to ensure that values assigned to it are consistent with those of existing overlapping bi-cells. Our memory domain first attempts to synthesize shared bi-cells if an equality can be inferred from the environment, by pattern-matching. In case of failure, it safely defaults to a pair of projected bi-cells, the values of which are set according to those of existing overlapping bi-cells.

We have already used shared bi-cell synthesis implicitly on Fig. 6. When reading variable y at the end of Example 1, the memory domain attempts to synthesize $\langle y_1, y_2 \rangle$, as a proof of $y_1 = y_2$. To this aim, it searches, among possible patterns, for an existing cell, equal to both y_1 and y_2. x_2 is a candidate, assuming equality $x_2 = y_2$ is recorded in (an abstraction of) the environment. Then the domain looks for 1-byte bi-cells for y_1 and x_2, and finds the four blue and red cells from Fig. 6. As y_1 and x_2 have opposite endian encodings, it queries the

$$\phi^\flat \langle V, o, \tau \rangle \langle C, R \rangle \triangleq$$

$$\begin{cases} \langle c_1, c_2 \rangle & \text{if } equal(c_1, c_2, \alpha_1, \alpha_2) \langle C, R \rangle & \text{where } c_i = \langle V, o, \tau, \alpha_i, i \rangle, \\ \langle c_1^*, c_2 \rangle & \text{else if } equal(c_1, c_2, \alpha_2, \alpha_2) \langle C, R \rangle & c_i^* = \langle V, o, \tau, \alpha_{3-i}, i \rangle, \\ \langle c_1, c_2^* \rangle & \text{else if } equal(c_1, c_2, \alpha_1, \alpha_1) \langle C, R \rangle & \alpha_1 = \mathcal{L}, \text{ and} \\ \top & \text{otherwise} & \alpha_2 = \mathcal{B}. \end{cases}$$

Fig. 7. Shared bi-cell synthesize function.

environment for equalities $y_1^0 = {}^\bullet\langle x_1^1, x_2^1 \rangle$ and $y_1^1 = \langle x_1^0, x_2^0 \rangle$. The success of the synthesis relies on pattern-matching, and three equalities which may be inferred by a numerical domain implementing simple symbolic propagation.

Shared Bi-Cell Synthesis. More generally, function $\phi^\flat$ formalizes the patterns matched attempting to synthesize a shared bi-cell for a given dereference $c \in Cell_0 \triangleq \mathcal{V} \times \mathbb{N} \times scalar\text{-}type$. An implementation is proposed in Fig. 7. Firstly, it returns $\langle c_1, c_2 \rangle$ if $c_1 = c_2$ may be inferred from the environment, where $c_i = \langle c, \alpha_i, i \rangle$ are projected versions of c, with the native endiannesses of their respective platforms. Otherwise, it returns $\langle c_1^*, c_2 \rangle$, where c_1^* is a big-endian projected bi-cell of Program 1, if $c_1^* = c_2$ holds. For instance, $\langle x_1^*, x_2 \rangle$ will be synthesized if variable x is read after the end of Example 1. Otherwise, it returns $\langle c_1, c_2^* \rangle$, where c_2^* is a little-endian projected bi-cell of Program 2, if $c_1 = c_2^*$ holds. Finally, if all fails, it returns an error $\top$. $\phi^\flat \in Cell_0 \to \mathcal{D}^\flat \to \widetilde{Cell}^2 \cup \{\top\}$ relies on predicate $equal$ to compare two projected bi-cells of the same type, with specified endianness encodings. An implementation is shown on Fig. 8. $equal$ returns $true$ when compared cells are part of a shared bi-cell, or when equality is ensured by the environment. Otherwise, it compares individual 1-byte bi-cells of the same weights 2^{8w}, at endianness-dependent offsets: $offset(w, s, \alpha) \triangleq w$ if $\alpha = \mathcal{L}$, and $s - w - 1$ otherwise. Otherwise, $equal$ searches for candidate projected bi-cells in the environment, equal to both c and c'. In the formula, we denote the set of projected bi-cells in the environment as $flatten(C) \triangleq \{ c \in \widetilde{Cell} \mid c \in C \vee \exists c' \in C : \langle c, c' \rangle \in C \vee \langle c', c \rangle \in C \}$. $equal$ returns $true$ in case of success, $false$ otherwise.

Projected Bi-Cell Synthesis. If all attempts to synthesize a shared bi-cell $\langle c_1, c_2 \rangle$, $\langle c_1^*, c_2 \rangle$, or $\langle c_1, c_2^* \rangle$ fail, our memory domain creates the pair of projected bi-cells c_1 and c_2 instead. To set their values soundly, it calls $\phi_1(c_1)(C)$ and $\phi_2(c_2)(C)$, where $\phi_i(c_i)(C)$ returns a syntactic expression denoting (an abstraction of) the value of c_i as a function of cells existing in C. For instance, $\phi_1(\langle y, 0, \mathbf{u16}, \mathcal{B}, 1 \rangle)(C) = 2^8 y_1^0 + y_1^1$ at the end of Example 1 (see Fig. 6).

To define the synthesize functions ϕ_1 and $\phi_2 \in \widetilde{Cell} \to \mathcal{P}(Bicell) \to expr$ for projected bi-cells, we first need to define a generic cell synthesize function $\phi \in Cell \to \mathcal{P}(Cell) \to expr$, such that $\phi(c)(C)$ returns a syntactic expression denoting (an abstraction of) the value of the cell c as a function of cells in C. ϕ is designed as an extension to multiple endianness encodings of the cell synthesize function originally proposed in [27, sec. 5.2].

$equal(\langle V, o, \tau, -, k\rangle, \langle V', o', \tau, -, k'\rangle, \alpha, \alpha')\langle C, R\rangle \triangleq$
  let $c = \langle V, o, \tau, \alpha, k\rangle$ and $c' = \langle V', o', \tau, \alpha', k'\rangle$ and $s = sizeof(\tau)$ in
  $\langle c, c'\rangle \in C \vee \langle c', c\rangle \in C \vee$
  $(\exists(x, x') \in occ(c, C) \times occ(c', C) : \forall \rho \in R : \rho(x) = \rho(x')) \vee$
  $\left(\forall 0 \le w < s : equal(c^{offset(w,s,\alpha)}, c'^{\,offset(w,s,\alpha')}, \alpha, \alpha')\langle C, R\rangle\right) \vee$
  $(\exists x \in flatten(C) \setminus \{c, c'\} : equal(c, x, \alpha, \alpha_x)\langle C, R\rangle \wedge equal(c', x, \alpha', \alpha_x)\langle C, R\rangle)$

where c^p denotes the 1-byte bi-cell $\langle V, o + p, \mathbf{u8}, \alpha, k\rangle$ (and respectively for c'^p),
and α_x denotes the endianness encoding of x.

Fig. 8. Equality test between projected bi-cells.

$\phi\langle V, o, t, e\rangle(C) \triangleq$
$\begin{cases} \langle V, o, t, e\rangle & \text{if } \langle V, o, t, e\rangle \in C \\ wrap(\langle V, o, t', e\rangle, range(t)) & \text{else if } \langle V, o, t', e\rangle \in C \wedge t, t' \in int\text{-}type \wedge sizeof(t) = sizeof(t') \\ byte(\langle V, o - b, t', e'\rangle, w(e', b, sizeof(t'))) \\ \qquad \text{else if } \langle V, o - b, t', e'\rangle \in C \wedge t = \mathbf{u8} \wedge t' \in int\text{-}type \wedge b < sizeof(t') \\ wrap(\sum_{i=0}^{sizeof(t)-1} 2^{8 \times w(e,i,sizeof(t))} \times \langle V, o + i, \mathbf{u8}, e_i\rangle, range(t)) \\ \qquad \text{else if } \forall 0 \le i < sizeof(t) : \langle V, o + i, \mathbf{u8}, e_i\rangle \in C \wedge t \in int\text{-}type \\ range(t) & \text{else if } t \in scalar\text{-}type \\ \mathbf{invalid} & \text{else if } t = \mathbf{ptr} \end{cases}$

Fig. 9. Generic cell synthesize function.

An example implementation is proposed in Fig. 9. Firstly, if the cell already exists ($c \in C$), it is directly returned by ϕ. Otherwise, ϕ looks for integer cells of the same size and different signedness, and converts them using function $wrap$ to model wrap-around, and function $range$ for the range of the type: $wrap(v, [l, h]) \triangleq \min\{v' \mid v' \ge l \wedge \exists k \in \mathbb{Z} : v = v' + k(h - l + 1)\}$, and $range(t) \triangleq [0, 2^{8s} - 1]$ if t is unsigned, and $[-2^{8s-1}, 2^{8s-1} - 1]$ if t is signed, where $s = sizeof(t)$. Thirdly, ϕ extracts unsigned bytes from integers. Fourthly, ϕ aggregates unsigned bytes into integers. Function $w \in \mathcal{A} \times \mathbb{N}^2 \to \mathbb{N}$ is used to model the endianness-dependent weight of bytes in integers: $w(\mathcal{L}, b, s) \triangleq b$ and $w(\mathcal{B}, b, s) \triangleq s - b - 1$. The value of the byte of weight 2^{8w} in integer x is: $byte(x, w) = \lfloor x/2^{8w} \rfloor \mod 2^8$. When all fails, ϕ returns the full range of the type (or $\mathbf{invalid}$, for a pointer). Many definitions are possible for ϕ, e.g. adding cases to support floats, or to synthesize integer cells from cells of opposite endianness.

To define ϕ_1 and ϕ_2, we project bi-cells of the appropriate side onto cells, apply ϕ, and lift the resulting cell expression back to a bi-cell expression. More precisely, to compute $\phi_1\langle c, 1\rangle(C)$, we first project the bi-cell set C to the cells of program version 1: $C_1 \triangleq \{x \mid \langle x, 1\rangle \in C \vee \exists y : \langle\langle x, 1\rangle, \langle y, 2\rangle\rangle \in C\}$. Then, we retrieve the constraints on cell c by applying the generic cell synthesize function: $e_1 \triangleq \phi(c)(C_1)$. Finally, $\phi_1\langle c, 1\rangle(C)$ is obtained by substituting every cell x occurring in e_1 with an element of $occ(\langle x, 1\rangle, C)$. Note that e_1 is a syntactic expression over cells in C_1, and $occ(\langle x, 1\rangle, C) \ne \emptyset$ for all $x \in C_1$. The definition of $\phi_2\langle c, 2\rangle(C)$ is analogue.

Cell Addition. Cell addition, $add\text{-}cell^\flat \in Cell_0 \to \mathcal{D}^\flat \to \mathcal{D}^\flat$, then simply adds the cell(s) and initializes their value(s).

$$add\text{-}cell^\flat(c)\langle C, R \rangle \triangleq$$

    if $\phi^\flat(c)\langle C, R \rangle = \langle x_1, x_2 \rangle$ **then**

        $\langle C \cup \{ \langle x_1, x_2 \rangle \}, \{ \rho[\langle x_1, x_2 \rangle \mapsto v] \mid \rho \in R, \, v \in \mathbb{E}[\![\, \phi_1(x_1)(C) \,]\!]_{\alpha_1}\rho \} \rangle$

    else

        $\langle C \cup \{c_1, c_2\}, \{ \rho[\forall i : c_i \mapsto v_i] \mid \rho \in R, \, \forall i : v_i \in \mathbb{E}[\![\, \phi_i(c_i)(C) \,]\!]_{\alpha_i}\rho \} \rangle$

where $c_1 = \langle c, \mathcal{L}, 1 \rangle$ and $c_2 = \langle c, \mathcal{B}, 2 \rangle$.

3.4   Abstract Join

The abstract join must merge environment sets defined on heterogeneous bi-cell sets. We therefore define a unification function $unify \in (\mathcal{D}^\flat)^2 \to (\mathcal{D}^\flat)^2$. $unify(\langle C_1, R_1 \rangle, \langle C_2, R_2 \rangle)$ adds, with $add\text{-}cell^\flat$, any missing cells to $\langle C_1, R_1 \rangle$ and $\langle C_2, R_2 \rangle$: respectively $C_2 \setminus C_1$ and $C_1 \setminus C_2$. Let $\langle C_1', R_1' \rangle$ and $\langle C_2', R_2' \rangle$ be the resulting abstract states. C_1' and C_2' may include both projected and shared bi-cells. A shared bi-cell that does not occur in both C_1' and C_2' cannot be soundly included in the unified state, as it conveys equality information that holds for one abstract state only. All such cells are thus removed before unification. Formally, $unify(\langle C_1, R_1 \rangle, \langle C_2, R_2 \rangle) = (\langle C_{12}, R_1'' \rangle, \langle C_{12}, R_2'' \rangle)$, where $C_{12} = (C_1' \cup C_2') \setminus (((C_1' \cup C_2') \setminus \widetilde{Cell}) \setminus (C_1' \cap C_2'))$, and $R_k'' = \{ \rho_{|C_{12}} \mid \rho \in R_k' \}$. The abstract join may now be defined as: $\langle C_1, R_1 \rangle \sqcup \langle C_2, R_2 \rangle \triangleq \langle C_{12}, R_1'' \cup R_2'' \rangle$.

3.5   Semantics of Simple Statements

Before defining the semantics for double statements in this domain, we first define the semantics $\mathbb{E}_k^\flat[\![\, *_t e \,]\!] \in \mathcal{D}^\flat \to \mathcal{P}(\mathbb{V})$ and $\mathbb{S}_k^\flat[\![\, *_t e_1 \leftarrow e_2 \,]\!] \in \mathcal{P}(\mathcal{D}^\flat) \to \mathcal{P}(\mathcal{D}^\flat)$ for simple memory reads and writes, in program version $k \in \{1, 2\}$.

Evaluations. To compute $\mathbb{E}_k^\flat[\![\, *_t e \,]\!]\langle C, R \rangle$, we first resolve $*_t e$ into a set L of projected bi-cells on side k, by evaluating e into a set of pointer values, and gathering projected bi-cells corresponding to valid pointers:

$$L \triangleq \{ \langle V, o, t, \alpha_k, k \rangle \mid \langle V, o \rangle \in \mathbb{E}[\![\, e \,]\!]_{\alpha_k}\rho, \, \rho \in R, \, 0 \le o \le sizeof(V) - sizeof(t) \}$$

Then, we call $add\text{-}cell^\flat$ to ensure that all the target cells in L are in the abstract environment, which updates $\langle C, R \rangle$ to $\langle C_0, R_0 \rangle$. Finally: $\mathbb{E}_k^\flat[\![\, *_t e \,]\!]\langle C, R \rangle = \{ \rho(c) \mid \rho \in R_0, \, c \in L \}$.

Assignments. The semantics of assignments $\mathbb{S}_k^\flat[\![\, *_t e_1 \leftarrow e_2 \,]\!]\langle C, R \rangle$ involves more steps. Like for evaluations, we start with resolving $*_t e_1$ into a set L of projected bi-cells on side k. Then, we realize the cells in L using $add\text{-}cell^\flat$: let $\langle C_0, R_0 \rangle$ be the updated environment. Some of the projected bi-cells in L may have been realized into shared bi-cells. Let $S \triangleq (C_0 \setminus C) \cap \widetilde{Cell}^2$ be the set of such shared bi-cells. Elements of S represent equalities between bi-cells projected on side k, and on side opposite to k. Such equalities may no longer hold, after assignment on side k. Therefore, we split shared bi-cells of S into their left and right projections, in a copy-on-write strategy. The updated environment is:

$$\langle C_0', R_0' \rangle = \langle C_0 \cup \bigcup_{\langle c, c' \rangle \in S} \{ c, c' \}, \{ c \mapsto \begin{cases} \rho(x) \text{ if } \exists x \in occ(c, S) \neq \emptyset \\ \rho(c) \text{ otherwise} \end{cases} \mid \rho \in R_0 \} \rangle$$

Finally, we update the environment for the projected bi-cells written (elements of L), with the possible values of e_2. However, this is not sufficient: it is also necessary to update the environment for any overlapping bi-cells, including shared bi-cells that have been split into pairs of projected cells. A sound and efficient (though possibly coarse) solution is to simply remove them. Indeed, removing any bi-cell is always sound in our memory model: it amounts to losing information, as we loose constraints on the byte-representation of the memory. Let $\Omega \subseteq C_0' \setminus L$ be the set of such bi-cells: elements of Ω are shared bi-cells and projected bi-cells on side k, with offsets and sizes such that they overlap some element of L. The updated environment is:

$$\mathbb{S}_k^\flat [\![*_t e_1 \leftarrow e_2]\!] \langle C, R \rangle = \langle C_0' \setminus \Omega,$$
$$\{ \rho_{|C_0' \setminus \Omega} [\forall c \in L : c \mapsto v] \mid \rho \in R_0', v \in \mathbb{E}_k^\flat [\![e_2]\!] \langle C_0', R_0' \rangle \} \rangle$$

3.6 Semantics of Double Statements

We are now ready to define the semantics $\mathbb{D}^\flat [\![dstat]\!] \in \mathcal{D}^\flat \to \mathcal{D}^\flat$ of double statements in this domain. Like $\mathbb{D}$, $\mathbb{D}^\flat$ is defined by induction on the syntax. We focus on base cases, as inductive cases are unchanged.

The semantics $\mathbb{D}^\flat [\![s_1 \parallel s_2]\!]$ for two syntactically different statements composes simple programs semantics: $\mathbb{D}^\flat [\![s_1 \parallel s_2]\!] \triangleq \mathbb{S}_2^\flat [\![s_2]\!] \circ \mathbb{S}_1^\flat [\![s_1]\!]$. The semantics for **assume_sync**, **assert_sync**, and $\mathbb{F}^\flat [\![e_1 \bowtie 0 \parallel e_2 \bowtie 0]\!]$ are mostly unchanged, but for symbolic simplifications taking advantage of symbolic representations of equalities in our domain, for improved efficiency and precision. In particular, when e is a deterministic expression containing a single dereference, then $\mathbb{D}^\flat [\![\textbf{assume\_sync}(e)]\!]$ adds a shared bi-cell for this dereference to the abstract environment. Consistently, $\mathbb{D}^\flat [\![\textbf{assert\_sync}(e)]\!]$ first tests whether e is deterministic, and its dereferences evaluate to shared bi-cells. In this case, $\mathbb{D}^\flat [\![\textbf{assert\_sync}(e)]\!]$ raises no alarm. Otherwise, the semantics uses environment functions ρ to test equalities of bi-cell values, like for $\mathbb{D}$. A similar symbolic simplification is used for the $\mathbb{F}^\flat [\![\cdot]\!]$ filter: $\mathbb{F}^\flat [\![e \bowtie 0 \parallel e \not\bowtie 0]\!] \langle C, R \rangle = \emptyset$ (hence the test is stable) when e is deterministic and all dereferences evaluate to shared bi-cells, which is the common case. For instance, when evaluating $\mathbb{D} [\![\textbf{if} \, (x < y) \, \textbf{then} \, s \, \textbf{else} \, t]\!]$, if the dereferences for variable x and y evaluate to shared bi-cells, the two unstable tests cases are $\bot$.

Assignments. In an assignment $\mathbb{D}^\flat [\![*_t e_1 \leftarrow e_2]\!] \langle C, R \rangle$, although both programs execute the same syntactic assignment, their semantics are different, as are their endiannesses. In addition, available bi-cells may be different. By default, double assignments are straightforward extensions of simple assignments: $\mathbb{D}^\flat[\![\,*_t\, e_1 \leftarrow e_2\,]\!] = \mathbb{S}_2^\flat[\![\,*_t\, e_1 \leftarrow e_2\,]\!] \circ \mathbb{S}_1^\flat[\![\,*_t\, e_1 \leftarrow e_2\,]\!]$. We introduce two precision optimizations, taking advantage of implicit equalities represented by shared bi-cells. We first transform $*_t\, e_1$ and the dereferences in e_2 into sets of bi-cells L and R, respectively. R may be empty, as e_2 may be a constant expression. Then, we realize the cells in L and R, using $add\text{-}cell^\flat$. Let $\langle C_0, R_0 \rangle$ be the updated environment. Two optimizations are possible, depending on e_1, e_2, L, and R.

Optimization 1: Assignment of Shared Bi-Cells. If e_1 and e_2 are deterministic expressions, and if they evaluate to bi-cells that are all shared ($L \cup R \subseteq \widetilde{Cell}^2$), then Programs 1 and 2 write the same value to the same destination. We thus update shared destination bi-cells (in L), and remove any overlapping bi-cells. Formally:

$$\mathbb{D}^\flat[\![\,*_t\, e_1 \leftarrow e_2\,]\!]\,\langle C, R \rangle = \langle C_0 \setminus \Omega,$$
$$\{\, \rho_{|C_0 \setminus \Omega}[\forall c \in L : c \mapsto v] \mid \rho \in R_0,\ v \in \mathbb{E}_1^\flat[\![\,e_2\,]\!]\,\langle C_0, R_0 \rangle \,\} \rangle,$$

where $\Omega \subseteq C_0 \setminus L$ is the set of (shared or projected) bi-cells overlapping elements of L. The choice of evaluating $\mathbb{E}_1^\flat[\![\,e_2\,]\!]$ (rather than $\mathbb{E}_2^\flat[\![\,e_2\,]\!]$) is arbitrary, as they are equal. Indeed, endianness $\alpha_1 = \mathcal{L}$ is not used by $\mathbb{E}_1^\flat[\![\,e_2\,]\!]$, as all the necessary cells are materialized before evaluating expression e_2.

Optimization 2: Copy Assignment. If the conditions for optimization *1* are satisfied, and if, in addition, $e_2 = *_t\, e_2'$, and both $*_t\, e_1$ and $*_t\, e_2'$ evaluate to single bi-cells ($|L| = |R| = 1$), then we are dealing with a copy assignment. We may thus soundly copy a memory information from the source $\{l\} = L$ to the destination $\{r\} = R$, so as to further improve precision. We therefore create a copy of r, and any smaller bi-cell for the same bytes, to a corresponding bi-cell for the bytes of l. Newly created destination bi-cells have the sides and endiannesses of their sources. The environment is updated accordingly, to reflect equalities between sources and destinations.

4 Value Abstraction

Connecting to Numerical Domains. We now rely on numeric abstractions to abstract further $\mathbb{D}^\flat$ into a computable abstract semantics $\mathbb{D}^\sharp$, resulting in an effective static analysis. Like [27, Sec. 5.2], our memory domain translates memory reads and writes into purely numerical operations on synthetic bi-cells, that are oblivious to the double semantics of double programs: each bi-cell is viewed as an independent numeric variable, and each numeric operation is carried out on a single bi-cell store, as if emanated from a single program. In particular, we notice that the transfer function for simple assignments $\mathbb{S}_k^\flat[\![\,*_t\, e_1 \leftarrow e_2\,]\!]$ described in Sect. 3.5 has the form of that of an assignment in a purely numeric language, where bi-cells play the roles of the numeric variables. This property is a key motivation for the Cell domain and the extension presented in this paper. Bi-cells may thus be fed, as variables, to a numerical abstract domain for environment abstraction. Any standard numerical domain, such as polyhedra [11], may be used. Yet, as we aim at scaling to large programs, we restrict ourselves to combinations of efficient non-relational domains, intervals and congruences [17], together with a dedicated symbolic predicate domain.

We thus assume an abstract domain $\mathcal{D}_C^\sharp$ given, with concretization γ_C, for each bi-cell set $C \subseteq \mathit{Bicell}$. It abstracts $\mathcal{P}(C \rightarrow \mathbb{Z}) \simeq \mathcal{P}(\mathbb{Z}^{|C|})$, i.e., sets of points in a $|C|$−dimensional vector space. A cell of integer type naturally corresponds to a dimension in an abstract element. We also associate a distinct dimension to each cell with pointer type; it corresponds to the offset o of a symbolic pointer $\langle V, o \rangle \in \mathcal{P}tr$. In order to abstract fully pointer values, we enrich the abstract numeric environment with a map P associating to each pointer cell the set of variables it may point to. Hence, the abstract domain becomes:
$$\mathcal{D}^\sharp \triangleq \{ \langle C, R^\sharp, P \rangle \,|\, C \subseteq \mathit{Cell}, \, R^\sharp \in \mathcal{D}_C^\sharp, \, P \in P_C \rightarrow \mathcal{P}(\mathcal{V} \cup \{ \mathbf{NULL}, \mathbf{invalid} \}) \},$$
where $P_C \subseteq C$ is the subset of bi-cells of pointer type. We refer to [27, Sec. 5.2] for a formal presentation of the concretization and the abstract operators.

Introducing a Dedicated Symbolic Predicate Domain. Recall Example 1 from Sect. 1. Various implementations are possible for the byte-swaps enforcing endian portability of software. Though Example 1 shows an implementation relying on type-punning, implementations relying on bitwise arithmetics are also commonplace. In addition, system-level software, such as [31], often rely on combinations of type-punning and bitwise arithmetics. Example 2 is a simplified instance of such programming idioms: as y has type **unsigned char**, y|0xff00 and (y<<8)|0xff represent the same 16-bit word in different endiannesses.

Example 2. Byte-wise equal memories in different endiannesses.

```
1    u16 x; u8 y = rand_u8(), *p = &x;
2    assume_sync(y);
3  # if __BYTE_ORDER == __LITTLE_ENDIAN
4      x = y | 0xff00;
5  # else
6      x = (y << 8) | 0xff;
7  # endif
8    assert_sync(p[0]); assert_sync(p[1]);
```

For a successful analysis of Example 2, the numerical domain must interpret bitwise arithmetic expressions precisely, and infer relations such as: the low-order (respectively high-order) byte of the little-endian (respectively big-endian) version of integer x is equal to y. Then, the interpretation of dereferences of p by the memory domain introduces similar relations between cells, thanks to the bi-cell synthesize function. In this example, it infers that the little-endian version of the low-address (respectively high-address) byte cell in x is equal to the low-order (respectively high-order) byte of x – and the converse for big-endian.

Predicate Abstract Domain. We use a domain based on pattern matching of expressions to detect arithmetic manipulations of byte values commonly implemented as bitwise arithmetics. It is not sufficient to match each expression independently, as computations are generally spread across sequences of statements. We need, in addition, to maintain some state that retains and propagates information between statements. We maintain this state in a predicate domain $Pred^{\sharp} \triangleq C \rightarrow Bits$, which maps each bi-cell $c \in C \subseteq Bicell$ to a syntactic expression e in a language $Bits$, as a symbolic representation of predicate $c = e$.

$$Bits ::= \top \mid Slice$$

$$Slice ::= n \mid c \mid \overrightarrow{c[i,j)}^{k} \mid (Slice \mid Slice) \qquad (n \in \mathbb{Z}, c \in C, i,j,k \in \mathbb{N})$$

$\top$ denotes the absence of information. Otherwise, a syntactic predicate expression may be either a bit-slice, or a bitwise OR of bit-slices. A bit-slice may be an integer constant n, a bi-cell c, or a slice expression $\overrightarrow{c[i,j)}^{k}$ denoting the value obtained by shifting the bits of c between i and $j-1$ to position k: $\overrightarrow{c[i,j)}^{k} \triangleq \lfloor (c \bmod 2^{j})/2^{i} \rfloor \times 2^{k}$. Each term of a bitwise OR of bit-slices represents a interval of bits, e.g. $[k, k+j-i)$ for a term $\overrightarrow{c[i,j)}^{k}$. We assume that bit-intervals do not overlap: each bit from the result comes from a single cell or constant. The ordering is flat, based on syntactic predicate equality:

$$X^{\sharp} \sqsubseteq^{\sharp} Y^{\sharp} \overset{\triangle}{\iff} \forall c \in C : X^{\sharp}(c) = Y^{\sharp}(c) \vee Y^{\sharp}(c) = \top$$

An abstract element $X^{\sharp} \in Pred^{\sharp}$ denotes the set of environments that satisfy all the predicates in $X^{\sharp}$, where predicates are evaluated as expressions:

$$\gamma_{Pred}(X^{\sharp}) \triangleq \{\, \rho \in C \rightarrow \mathbb{V} \mid \forall c \in C : X^{\sharp}(c) = \top \vee \rho(c) = \mathbb{E}[\![X^{\sharp}(c)]\!]\rho \,\}$$

We do not present the abstract operators in this paper. Like that of the related symbolic constant domain [25], they are based on symbolic propagation, and implement simple algebraic simplifications. They exhibit similar, near-linear time cost in our experiments.

Analysis of Example 2. Before line 8, three cells are synthesized by the memory domain: $C_8 = \{\, x_1, x_2, y_{12} \,\}$, where $x_1 = \langle x, 0, \mathbf{u16}, \mathcal{L}, 1 \rangle$ is the little-endian projected bi-cell of variable x, $x_2 = \langle x, 0, \mathbf{u16}, \mathcal{B}, 2 \rangle$ is the big-endian one, and $y_{12} = \langle \langle y, 0, \mathbf{u8}, \mathcal{L}, 1 \rangle, \langle y, 0, \mathbf{u8}, \mathcal{B}, 2 \rangle \rangle$ is a shared bi-cell.

- y_{12} is created at line 2, and represents the fact that variable y has the same value in the little- and big-endian versions.
- The transfer function for assignment of the symbolic predicate domain infers invariants $x_1 = y_{12} \mid 65280$ from line 4, and $x_2 = 255 \mid \overrightarrow{y_{12}[0,8)}^{8}$ from line 6.
- Then, the dereferences of pointer p at line 8 are interpreted by the memory domain. Four more cells $\{\, x_k^o \mid (k,o) \in \{1,2\} \times \{0,1\} \,\}$ are added to the abstract environment, to denote the bytes of variable x in the little- and big-endian programs. More precisely, $x_1^o = \langle x, o, \mathbf{u8}, \mathcal{L}, 1 \rangle$, and $x_2^o = \langle x, o, \mathbf{u8}, \mathcal{B}, 2 \rangle$, at offsets $o \in \{0,1\}$. Following the bi-cell synthesize functions ϕ_1 and ϕ_2, these new bi-cells are added together with assumptions on their values. In practice, these assumptions are four tests, used by the memory domain to filter the abstract environment. These tests are $x_1^o = byte(x_1, o)$, and $x_2^o = byte(x_1, 1-o)$, for offsets $o \in \{0,1\}$, with $byte(n,k) = \lfloor n/2^{8k} \rfloor \bmod 2^8$. These tests are then interpreted by the numerical domain, and the symbolic

predicate domain in particular, as $x_1^0 = byte'(x_1, o)$, and $x_2^0 = byte'(x_2, 1-o)$, with $byte'(n, k) = \overrightarrow{n[8k, 8k+8)}^0$.

- Finally, the assertion line 8 is interpreted as tests $x_1^0 = x_2^0$ and $x_1^1 = x_2^1$ by the memory domain. The transfer function for tests in the symbolic predicate domain replaces all bi-cells with the symbolic expressions bound to them, if any. The tests are thus $\overrightarrow{(y_{12} \mid 65280)[0, 8)}^0 = \left(255 \mid \overrightarrow{y_{12}[0, 8)}^8\right)^{\overrightarrow{}^0}[8, 16)$ and

$\overrightarrow{(y_{12} \mid 65280)[8, 16)}^0 = \left(255 \mid \overrightarrow{y_{12}[0, 8)}^8\right)^{\overrightarrow{}^0}[0, 8)$. Both tests evaluate to true, using symbolic simplifications (and integer arithmetic computations) supported by the transfer function.

Hence, the assertions line 8 are proved correct: at the end of the program, the memories for variable x are byte-wise equal in the little and big-endian versions.

5 Evaluation

We implemented our analysis into the MOPSA platform [20,29] designed to support modular developments of precise static analyses for multiple languages and multiple properties. Our prototype is composed of 3,000 lines of OCaml: 45% for the memory abstraction, 36% for the symbolic predicate domain, and 19% for double program management and iterators. It leverages 31,000 lines (excluding parsers) of elementary functions of MOPSA: framework and utilities (64%), generic iterators and numeric domains for analyses of all languages (11%), specific iterators and memory domains for the C language (25%). We have experimented our prototype on small idiomatic examples, open source software, and large industrial software. The analyses were run on a 3.4 GHz Intel® Xeon® CPU.

5.1 Idiomatic Examples

We first check the precision and robustness of our analysis against a collection of small double C programs (between 20 and 100 LOC), inspired by various implementations of byte-swaps in Linux drivers, POSIX htonl functions, and industrial software.

A set of 9 programs illustrate network data processing. These programs are similar to Example 1 of Sect. 1. They receive an integer from the network, increment it, and send over the result. Necessary byte-swaps are implemented for little-endian versions of these programs. Each example program implements a different byte-swapping technique on a 2, 4, or 8-byte integer: type-punning with pointer casts (like in Example 1), unions, or bitwise arithmetics. Refer to Examples 4, 5, and 6 in artifact [16] for the source codes. We also analyze Example 2 from Sect. 4 to demonstrate the efficiency of our symbolic predicate domain.

Our prototype also handles floating-point data, which was omitted in the paper for the sake of conciseness. We developed small floating-point examples representative of industrial use-cases of Sect. 5.3. They include byte-swappings of simple or double precision floating-point numbers sent to or received from the network, on architectures where integers and floats are guaranteed to have the same byte-order. Type-punning is used to reinterpret floats as integers of the same size, which are byte-swapped using bitwise arithmetics. Also, a combination of type-punning and byte-swapping is used to extract exponents from double precision floats. The source codes of these Examples 8 and 9 is available in artifact [16]. All analyses run in less than 200 ms and report no false alarm.

5.2 Open Source Benchmarks

We then check the soundness, precision, and modularity of our analysis on three benchmarks based on open source software available on GitHub, with multiple commits for bug-fixes related to endianness portability. Refer to Examples 10, 11, and 12 in artifact [16] for relevant source codes excerpts. We analyze slices between 100 and 250 LOC, using primitives **assume_sync** and **assert_sync** for modular specifications of program parts.

Our first benchmark is an implementation of a tunneling driver [31] based on the Geneve [18] encapsulation network protocol, which uses big-endian integers as tunnel identifiers. The driver was introduced in the Linux kernel, and patched several times for endianness-related issues detected by SPARSE [6]. Then, a performance optimization introduced a new endianness portability bug, which SPARSE failed to detect. It was fixed a year later. Our analysis soundly reports this bug, as well as previous issues detected by SPARSE. It reports no alarm on the fixed code. Our second benchmark is a core library of the mlx5 Linux driver [23] for ethernet and RDMA net devices [22]. We analyze a slice related to a patch, committed to fix an endianness bug introduced 3 years earlier, and undetected by SPARSE despite the use of relevant annotations. The fix turned out to be incomplete, and was updated 6 months later. Our analysis soundly reports bugs on the two first versions, and no alarm on the third. Our third benchmark is extracted from a version of Squashfs [35], a compressed read-only filesystem for Linux, included in the LineageOS [34] alternative Android distribution. We analyze a slice related to a patch, committed to fix an endianness bug undetected by SPARSE due to a lack of type annotations. Our analysis soundly reports the bug, and no alarm on the fixed version. All the analyses run within 1 s.

5.3 Industrial Case Study

We analyzed two components of a prototype avionics application, developed at Airbus for a civil aircraft. This application is written in C, and primarily targets an embedded big-endian processor. Nonetheless, it must be portable to little-endian commodity hardware, as its source code is reused as part of a simulator used for functional verification of SCADE [3] models. The supplement to the applicable aeronautical standard [32] related to model-based development [1] mandates, in this case, that *"an analysis should provide compelling evidence that the simulation approach provides equivalent defect detection and removal as testing of the Executable Object Code"*. Airbus, known to rely on formal methods for other verification objectives [4,12,13,28,33], is currently considering the use of static analysis to verify this portability property.

Endianness is the main difference between the ABIs of the embedded computer and the simulator. We thus experimented our prototype analyzer on the modules of the application integrated to the simulator, to which we refer as A and S. Modules A and S are data-intensive reactive software, processing thousands of global variables, with very flat call graphs. Module A is in charge of acquiring and emitting data through aircraft buses. It is composed of about 1 million LOC, most of which generated automatically from a description of the avionics network. It handles integers, Booleans, single and double precision floats. The code features bounded loops, memcpys, pointer arithmetics, and type-punning with unions and pointer casts. It also uses bitwise arithmetics, among which several thousand byte-swaps related to endianness portability. Module S is in charge of the main applicative functions. It is composed of about 300,000 LOC, most of which generated automatically from SCADE models. It handles mostly Booleans and double precision floats. It features bounded loops and bitwise arithmetics, but no type-punning. The target application is required to meet its specifications for long missions. Analysis entry points contain loops with several million iterations to emulate this execution context.

Both analyses run in 5 abstract iterations. The analysis of A runs in 20.4 h and uses 5.5 GB RAM. The analysis of S runs in 9.7 h and uses 2.7 GB RAM. We worked with the development and simulation teams to analyze early prototypes, and incorporate findings into the development cycle. On current versions of both modules, both analyses report zero alarm related to endianness.

6   Conclusion

We presented a sound static analysis of endian portability for low-level C programs. Our method is based on abstract interpretation, and parametric in the choice of a numerical abstract domain. We first presented a novel concrete collecting semantics, relating the behaviors of two versions of a program, running on platforms with different endiannesses. Then we proposed a joint memory abstraction, able to infer equivalence relations between little- and big-endian memories. We introduced a novel symbolic predicate domain to infer relations between individual bytes of the variables in the two programs, which has near-linear cost. We implemented a prototype static analyzer, able to scale to large real-world industrial software, with zero false alarms.

In future work, we aim at extending our analysis to further ABI-related properties, such as portability between different layouts of C types, or sizes of machine integers. We also anticipate that our bi-cell sharing approach will benefit the analysis of patches [14,15] modifying C data-types, even if the two versions run under the same ABI. Finally, we are considering an industrial deployment

of our endian portability analysis, as a means to address avionics certification
objectives related to simulation fidelity, as mentioned in Sect. 5.3.

References

1. DO-331: Model-based development and verification supplement to DO-178C and
   DO-278A (2011)
2. AT & T, The Santa Cruz Operation Inc.: System V application binary interface
   (1997)
3. Berry, G.: SCADE: synchronous design and validation of embedded control software. In: Ramesh, S., Sampath, P. (eds.) Next Generation Design and Verification
   Methodologies for Distributed Embedded Control Systems, pp. 19–33. Springer,
   Dordrecht (2007). https://doi.org/10.1007/978-1-4020-6254-4_2
4. Brahmi, A., Delmas, D., Essoussi, M.H., Randimbivololona, F., Atki, A., Marie, T.:
   Formalise to automate: deployment of a safe and cost-efficient process for avionics
   software. In: 9th European Congress on Embedded Real Time Software and Systems (ERTS 2018), Toulouse, France, January 2018. https://hal.archives-ouvertes.
   fr/hal-01708332
5. Brevnov, E., Domeika, M., Loenko, M., Ozhdikhin, P., Tang, X., Willkinson, H.:
   BEC: bi-endian compiler technology for porting byte order sensitive applications
   16(1), 42–61 (2012)
6. Brown, N.: Sparse: a look under the hood (2016). https://lwn.net/Articles/689907/
7. Chevalier, M.: Proving the security of software-intensive embedded systems by
   abstract interpretation. Ph.D. thesis, Université PSL, November 2020
8. Chevalier, M., Feret, J.: Sharing ghost variables in a collection of abstract domains.
   In: Beyer, D., Zufferey, D. (eds.) VMCAI 2020. LNCS, vol. 11990, pp. 158–179.
   Springer, Cham (2020). https://doi.org/10.1007/978-3-030-39322-9_8
9. Cohen, D.: On holy wars and a plea for peace. Computer **14**(10), 48–54 (1981).
   https://doi.org/10.1109/C-M.1981.220208
10. Cousot, P., Cousot, R.: Abstract interpretation: a unified lattice model for static
    analysis of programs by construction or approximation of fixpoints. In: POPL 1977,
    pp. 238–252. ACM, January 1977
11. Cousot, P., Halbwachs, N.: Automatic discovery of linear restraints among variables
    of a program. In: POPL 1978, pp. 84–97. ACM (1978)
12. Delmas, D., Souyris, J.: Astrée: from research to industry. In: Nielson, H.R., Filé,
    G. (eds.) SAS 2007. LNCS, vol. 4634, pp. 437–451. Springer, Heidelberg (2007).
    https://doi.org/10.1007/978-3-540-74061-2_27
13. Delmas, D., Goubault, E., Putot, S., Souyris, J., Tekkal, K., Védrine, F.: Towards
    an industrial use of FLUCTUAT on safety-critical avionics software. In: Alpuente,
    M., Cook, B., Joubert, C. (eds.) FMICS 2009. LNCS, vol. 5825, pp. 53–69. Springer,
    Heidelberg (2009). https://doi.org/10.1007/978-3-642-04570-7_6
14. Delmas, D., Miné, A.: Analysis of program differences with numerical abstract
    interpretation. In: PERR 2019, Prague, Czech Republic, April 2019
15. Delmas, D., Miné, A.: Analysis of software patches using numerical abstract inter-
    pretation. In: Chang, B.-Y.E. (ed.) SAS 2019. LNCS, vol. 11822, pp. 225–246.
    Springer, Cham (2019). https://doi.org/10.1007/978-3-030-32304-2_12
16. Delmas, D., Ouadjaout, A., Miné, A.: Artifact for static analysis of endian porta-
    bility by abstract. Interpretation (2021). https://doi.org/10.5281/zenodo.5206794

17. Granger, P.: Static analysis of arithmetic congruences. Int. J. Comput. Math. **30**, 165–199 (1989)
18. Gross, J., Ganga, I., Sridhar, T.: Geneve: generic network virtualization encapsulation. RFC 8926, RFC Editor, November 2020
19. ISO/IEC JTC1/SC22/WG14 working group: C standard. Technical report 1124, ISO & IEC (2007)
20. Journault, M., Miné, A., Monat, R., Ouadjaout, A.: Combinations of reusable abstract domains for a multilingual static analyzer. In: Chakraborty, S., Navas, J.A. (eds.) VSTTE 2019. LNCS, vol. 12031, pp. 1–18. Springer, Cham (2020). https://doi.org/10.1007/978-3-030-41600-3_1
21. Kápl, R., Parízek, P.: Endicheck: dynamic analysis for detecting endianness bugs. In: TACAS 2020. LNCS, vol. 12079, pp. 254–270. Springer, Cham (2020). https://doi.org/10.1007/978-3-030-45237-7_15
22. Mahameed, S.: Mellanox, mlx5 RDMA net device support (2017). https://lwn.net/Articles/720074/
23. Mellanox Technologies: mlx5 core library (2020). https://github.com/torvalds/linux/tree/master/drivers/net/ethernet/mellanox/mlx5/core
24. Miné, A.: Field-sensitive value analysis of embedded C programs with union types and pointer arithmetics. In: Proceedings of the ACM SIGPLAN/SIGBED Conference on Languages, Compilers, and Tools for Embedded Systems (LCTES 2006), pp. 54–63. ACM, June 2006
25. Miné, A.: Symbolic methods to enhance the precision of numerical abstract domains. In: Emerson, E.A., Namjoshi, K.S. (eds.) VMCAI 2006. LNCS, vol. 3855, pp. 348–363. Springer, Heidelberg (2005). https://doi.org/10.1007/11609773_23
26. Miné, A.: Abstract domains for bit-level machine integer and floating-point operations. In: Proceedings of the 4th International Workshop on Invariant Generation (WING 2012), p. 16. No. HW-MACS-TR-0097, Computer Science, School of Mathematical and Computer Science, Heriot-Watt University, UK, June 2012
27. Miné, A.: Static analysis by abstract interpretation of concurrent programs. Technical report, École normale supérieure, May 2013
28. Miné, A., Delmas, D.: Towards an industrial use of sound static analysis for the verification of concurrent embedded avionics software. In: Proceedings of the 15th International Conference on Embedded Software (EMSOFT 2015), pp. 65–74. IEEE CS Press, October 2015
29. Miné, A., Ouadjaout, A., Journault, M.: Design of a modular platform for static analysis. In: The Ninth Workshop on Tools for Automatic Program Analysis (TAPAS 2018), Fribourg-en-Brisgau, Germany, August 2018. https://hal.sorbonne-universite.fr/hal-01870001
30. Nita, M., Grossman, D.: Automatic transformation of bit-level C code to support multiple equivalent data layouts. In: Hendren, L. (ed.) CC 2008. LNCS, vol. 4959, pp. 85–99. Springer, Heidelberg (2008). https://doi.org/10.1007/978-3-540-78791-4_6
31. Red Hat Inc: Generic network virtualization encapsulation (2017). https://github.com/torvalds/linux/blob/master/drivers/net/geneve.c
32. S.C of RTCA: DO-178C: Software considerations in airborne systems and equipment certification (2011)
33. Souyris, J., Wiels, V., Delmas, D., Delseny, H.: Formal verification of avionics software products, pp. 532–546 (2009)
34. The LineageOS Project: Lineageos (2020). https://github.com/LineageOS/
35. The Squashfs Project: Squashfs (2020). https://github.com/LineageOS/android_kernel_sony_msm8960t/tree/lineage-18.1/fs/squashfs

Verified Functional Programming of an Abstract Interpreter

Lucas Franceschino[1]([✉]) [iD], David Pichardie[2] [iD], and Jean-Pierre Talpin[1] [iD]

[1] Inria-Irisa Rennes, Rennes, France
lucas.franceschino@inria.fr
[2] ENS Rennes, Rennes, France

Abstract. Abstract interpreters are complex pieces of software: even if the abstract interpretation theory and companion algorithms are well understood, their implementations are subject to bugs, that might question the soundness of their computations.

While some formally verified abstract interpreters have been written in the past, writing and understanding them requires expertise in the use of proof assistants, and requires a non-trivial amount of interactive proofs. This paper presents a formally verified abstract interpreter fully programmed and proved correct in the F* verified programming environment. Thanks to F* refinement types and SMT prover capabilities we demonstrate a substantial saving in proof effort compared to previous works based on interactive proof assistants. Almost all the code of our implementation, proofs included, written in a functional style, are presented directly in the paper.

1 Introduction

Abstract interpretation is a theory of sound approximation. However, most of available abstract interpreters do not formally establish a relation between their algorithmic theory and implementations. Several abstract interpreters have been proven correct. The most notable one is Verasco [11], a static analyser of C programs that has been entirely written, specified and proved in the proof assistant Coq. However, understanding the implementation and proof of Verasco requires an expertise with Coq and proof assistants.

Proofs in Coq are achieved thanks to extensive use of proof scripts, that are very difficult for non expert to read. By contrast with a handwritten proof, a Coq proof can be very verbose, and often does not convey a good intuition for the idea behind a proof. Thus, writing and proving sound a static analyzer is

© Springer Nature Switzerland AG 2021
C. Drăgoi et al. (Eds.): SAS 2021, LNCS 12913, pp. 124–143, 2021.
https://doi.org/10.1007/978-3-030-88806-0_6

a complex and time-consuming task: for example, Verasco requires about 17k lines [11] of manual Coq proofs. Such an effort, however, yields the strongest guarantees and provides complete trust in the static analyser.

This paper showcases the implementation of a sound static analyser using the general-purpose functional programming language $F^\star$. Equipped with dependent types and built-in SMT solver facilities, $F^\star$ provides both an OCaml-like experience and proof assistant capacities. It recently shined with the Project Everest [1], which delivered a series of formally verified, high-performance, cryptographic libraries: HACL* [16], ValeCrypt [4] and EverCrypt [15]; that are for instance used and deployed in Mozilla Firefox. While $F^\star$ can always resort to proof scripts similar to Coq's ones, most proof obligations in $F^\star$ are automatically discharged by the SMT solver Z3 [9].

We present an abstract interpreter equipped with the numerical abstract domain of intervals, forward and backward analyses of expressions, widening, and syntax-directed loop iteration. This paper makes the following contributions.

- It demonstrates the ease of use of $F^\star$ for verified static analysis: we implement a verified abstract interpreter, and show about 95% of its 527 lines of code (proof included) directly in the paper.
- As far as we know, it is the first time SMT techniques are used for verifying an abstract interpreter.
- We gain an order of magnitude in the number of proof lines in comparison with similar works implemented in Coq.

Related Work. Efforts in verified abstract interpretation are numerous [3,5,8,14], and go up to Verasco [11], a modular, real-world abstract interpreter verified in Coq. Blazy et al. [3] and Verasco follow closely the modular design of Astrée [6]; we exhibit a similar modularity on a smaller scale. However, such analysers require a non-trivial amount of mechanized proofs: in constrast, this paper shows that implementing a formally verified abstract interpreter with very little manual proofs is possible. So far, verified abstract interpreters have been focused on concretization-based formalizations. The work of Darais et al. [7] is the only one to really consider the use of Galois connections. They provide a minimalist abstract inteperter for imperative language but this interpreter seems very limited compared to ours. They use the Agda proof assistant which is comparable to Coq in terms of proof verbosity.

Overview. Section 2 defines IMP, the language our abstract interpreter deals with, to which is given an operational semantics in Sect. 3. Then Sect. 4 formalizes lattices and abstract domains, while Sect. 5 instantiates them with the abstract domain of intervals. Section 6 derives more specific abstract domains, for numeric expressions and for memories. The latter is instantiated by Sect. 7, that implements an abstract weakly-relational memory. Finally, Sect. 8 presents the abstract interpretation of IMP statements.

The F* development is available on GitHub[1] or as supplementary material [2]. The resulting analyser is available online as a web application at https://w95psp.github.io/verified-abstract-interpreter.

2 IMP: A Small Imperative Language

To present our abstract intrepreter, we first show the language on which it operates: IMP. It is a simple imperative language, equipped with memories represented as functions from variable names `varname` to signed integers, int_m. This presentation lets the reader unfamiliar with F* get used to its syntax: IMP's F* definition looks like OCaml; the main difference is the explicit type signatures for constructors in algebraic data types. IMP has numeric expressions, encoded by the type `expr`, and statements `stmt`. Booleans are represented numerically: 0 represents `false`, and any other value stands for true. The enumeration `binop` equips IMP with various binary operations. The constructor `Unknown` encodes an arbitrary number. Statements in IMP are the assignment, the non-deterministic choice, the sequence and the loop.

```
type varname = | VA | VB | VC | VD    type mem τ = varname → τ
type binop = | Plus | Minus | Mult | Eq | Lt | And | Or
type expr = | Const:  int_m → expr    | Var: varname → expr
            | BinOp: binop → expr → expr → expr | Unknown
type stmt = | Assign: varname → expr → stmt | Assume: expr → stmt
            | Seq:        stmt → stmt → stmt | Loop:   stmt → stmt
            | Choice: stmt → stmt → stmt
```

The type int_m is a *refinement* of the built-in F* type $\mathbb{Z}$: while every integer lives in the type $\mathbb{Z}$, only those that respect certain bounds live in int_m. Numerical operations (+, - and ×) on machine integers wrap on overflow, i.e. adding one to the maximal machine integer results in the minimum machine integer. We do not give the detail of their implementation.

3 Operational Semantics

This section defines an operational semantics for IMP. It is also a good way of introducing more F* features.

We choose to formulate our semantics in terms of sets. Sets are encoded as maps from values to propositions `prop`. Those are logical statements and shouln't be confused with booleans. Below, ⊆ quantifies over every *inhabitant* of a type: stating whether such a statement is true or false is clearly not computable. Arbitrarily complex properties can be expressed as propositions of type `prop`.

In the listing below, notice the greek letters: we use them throughout the paper. They denote implicit type arguments: for instance, below, ∈ works for any set `set` τ, with any type τ. F* provides the propositional operators ∧, ∨

---

[1] https://github.com/W95Psp/verified-abstract-interpreter.

and ==, in addition to boolean ones (&&, || and =). We use them below to define the union, intersection and differences of sets.

```
type set τ = τ → prop              let (∈) (x: τ) (s: set τ) = s x
let (∩) s₀ s₁ = λx→x∈s₀ ∧ x∈s₁    let (\) s₀ s₁ = λv→s₀ v ∧ ˜(s₁ v)
let (∪) (s₀ s₁: set τ): set τ = λx → x ∈ s₀ ∨ x ∈ s₁
let (⊆) (s₀ s₁: set τ): prop = ∀ (x: τ). x ∈ s₀ ⟹ x ∈ s₁
let set_inverse (s: set intₘ): set intₘ = λ(i: intₘ) → s (-i)
```

To be able to work conveniently with binary operations on integers in our semantics, we define lift_binop, that lifts them as set operations. For example, the set lift_binop (+) a b (a and b being two sets of integers) corresponds to $\{va + vb \mid va \in a \land vb \in b\}$.

```
let lift_binop (op: τ → τ → τ) (a b: set τ): set τ
  = λr → ∃ (va:τ). ∃ (vb:τ). va ∈ a ∧ vb ∈ b ∧ r == op va vb
unfold let lift op = lift_binop (concrete_binop op)
```

The binary operations we consider are enumerated by binop. The function concrete_binop associates these syntactic operations to integer operations. For convenience, lift maps a binop to a set operation, using lift_binop. This function is inlined by F* directly when used because of the keyword unfold; intuitively lift behaves as a macro.

```
unfold let concrete_binop (op: binop): intₘ → intₘ → intₘ
  = match op with | Plus → n_add | Lt → ltₘ | ... | Or → oriₘ
```

The operational semantics for expressions is given as a map from memories and expressions to sets of integers. Notice the use of both the syntax val and let for the function osem_expr. The val syntax gives osem_expr the type mem→expr→set intₘ, while the let declaration gives its definition. The semantics itself is uncomplicated: Unknown returns the set of every intₘ, a constant or a Var returns a singleton set. For binary operations, we lift them as set operations, and make use of recursion.

```
val osem_expr: mem → expr → set intₘ
let rec osem_expr m e = λ(i: intₘ)
  → match e with | Const x → i==x | Var v → i==m v | Unknown → ⊤
  | BinOp op x y → lift op (osem_expr m x) (osem_expr m y) i
```

The operational semantics for statements maps a statement and an initial memory to a set of admissible final memories. Given a statement s, an initial memory m_i and a final one m_f, osem_stmt s m_i m_f (defined below) is a proposition stating whether the transition is possible.

```
val osem_stmt (s: stmt): mem → set mem
let rec osem_stmt (s: stmt) (mᵢ m_f: mem)
  = match s with
  | Assign v e → ∀w. if v = w then m_f v ∈ osem_expr mᵢ e
```

$$\text{else } m_f \ w \ == \ m_i \ w$$

| Seq a b $\rightarrow \exists$ (m_1: mem). $m_1 \in$ osem$_{stmt}$ a m_i $\land$ $m_f \in$ osem$_{stmt}$ b m_1
| Choice a b $\rightarrow$ $m_f \in$ (osem$_{stmt}$ a m_i $\cup$ osem$_{stmt}$ b m_i)
| Assume e $\rightarrow$ m_i == m_f $\land$ ($\exists$ (x: int$_m$). x $\neq$ 0 $\land$ x $\in$ osem$_{expr}$ m_i e)
| Loop a $\rightarrow$ closure (osem$_{stmt}$ a) m_i m_f

The simplest operation is the assignment of a variable v to an expression e: the transition is allowed if every variable but v in m_i and m_f is equal and the final value of v matches with the semantics of e. Assuming that an expression is true amounts to require the initial memory to be such that at least a non-zero integer (that is, the encoding of true) belongs to osem$_{expr}$ m_i e. The statement Seq a b starting from the initial memory m_i admits m_f as a final memory when there exists (i) a transition from m_i to an intermediate memory m_1 with statement a and (ii) a transition from m_1 to m_f with statement b. The operational semantics for a loop is defined as the reflexive transitive closure of the semantics of its body. The closure function computes such a closure, and is provided by F*'s standard library.

4   Abstract Domains

Our abstract interpreter is parametrized over relational domains. We instantiate it later with a weakly-relational [6] memory. This section defines lattices and abstract domains. Such structures are a natural fit for typeclasses [13], which allow for ad hoc polymorphism. In our case, it means that we can have one abstraction for lattices for instance, and then instantiate this abstraction with implementations for, say, sets of integers, then intervals, etc. Typeclasses can be seen as record types with dedicated dependency inference. Below, we define the typeclass lattice: defining an instance for a given type equips this type with a lattice srtucture.

Refinement Types. Below, the syntax x:τ{p x} denotes the type whose inhabitants both belong to τ and satisfy the predicate p. For example, the inhabitant of the type bot:$\mathbb{N}${$\forall$(n:$\mathbb{N}$). bot$\leq$n} is 0: it is the (only) smallest natural number. To typecheck x:τ, F* collects the *proof obligations* implied by "x has the type τ", and tries to discharge them with the help of the SMT solver. If the SMT solver is able to deal with the proof obligations, then x:τ typechecks. In the case of "0 is of type bot:$\mathbb{N}${$\forall$(n:$\mathbb{N}$). bot$\leq$n}", the proof obligation is $\forall$(n:$\mathbb{N}$). 0$\leq$n.

Below, most of the types of the fields from the record type lattice are refined. Typechecking i against the type lattice τ yields a proof obligation asking (among other things) for i.join to go up in the lattice and for bottom to be a lower bound. Thus, if "i has type lattice τ" typechecks, it means there exists a proof that the properties written as refinements in lattice's definition hold on i. We found convenient to let bottom represent unreachable states. Note lattice is under-specified, i.e. it doesn't require join to be provably a least upper bound, since such a property plays no role in our proof of soundness. This choice follows Blazy and et al. [3].

```
class lattice τ = { corder: order τ
  ; join: x:τ → y:τ → r:τ {corder x r ∧ corder y r}
  ; meet: x:τ → y:τ → r:τ {corder r x ∧ corder r y}
  ; bottom: bot:τ {∀x. corder bot x}; top: top:τ {∀x. corder x top}}
```

For our purpose, we need to define what an abstract domain is. In our setting, we consider concrete domains with powerset structure. The typeclass adom encodes them: it is parametrized by a type τ of abstract values. For instance, consider itv the type for intervals: adom itv would be the type inhabited by correct abstract domains for intervals.

Implementing an abstract domain amounts to implementing the following fields: (i) c, that represents the type to which abstract values τ concretizes; (ii) adom$_{lat}$, a lattice for τ; (iii) widen, a widening operator; (iv) γ, a monotonic concretization function from τ to set c; (v) order_measure, a measure ensuring the abstract domain doesn't admit infinite increasing chains, so that termination is provable for fixpoint iterations; (vi) meet$_{law}$, that requires meet to be a correct approximation of set intersection; (vii) top$_{law}$ and bot$_{law}$, that ensure the lattice's bottom concretization matches with the empty set, and similarly for top.

```
class adom τ = { c: Type; adom_lat: lattice τ                    ·
  ; γ: (γ: (τ → set c) {∀ (x y: τ). corder x y ⟹ (γ x ⊆ γ y)})
  ; widen: x:τ → y:τ → r:τ {corder x r ∧ corder y r}
  ; order_measure: measure adom_lat.corder
  ; meet_law: x:τ → y:τ → Lemma ((γ x ∩ γ y) ⊆ γ (meet x y))
  ; bot_law: unit → Lemma (∀ (x:c). ~(x ∈ γ bottom))
  ; top_law: unit → Lemma (∀ (x:c). x ∈ γ top)}
```

Notice the refinement types: we require for instance the monotony of γ. Every single instance for adom will be checked against these specifications. No instance of adom where γ is not monotonic can exist. With a proposition p, the Lemma p syntax signals a function whose outcome is computationally irrelevant, since it simply produces (), the inhabitant of the type unit. However, it does not produces an arbitrary unit: it produces an inhabitant of _:unit {p}, that is, the type unit refined with the goal p of the lemma itself.

For praticity, we define some infix operators for adom$_{lat}$ functions. The syntax {|...|} lets one formulate typeclass constraints: for example, (⊑) below ask F* to resolve an instance of the typeclass adom for the type τ, and name it l. Below, (⊓) instantiates the lemma meet$_{law}$ explicitly: meet$_{law}$ x y is a unit value that carries a proof in the type system.

```
let (⊑) {|l:adom τ|} = l.adom_lat.corder
let (⊔) {|l:adom τ|} (x y:τ): r:τ { corder x r ∧ corder y r
                        ∧ (γ x ∪ γ y) ⊆ γ r } = join x y
let (⊓) {|l:adom τ|} (x y:τ): r:τ { corder r x ∧ corder r y
```

$$\wedge \ (\gamma \ \mathtt{x} \cap \gamma \ \mathtt{y}) \subseteq \gamma \ \mathtt{r} \ \}$$

```
= let _ = meetₗₐw x y in meet x y
```

Lemmas are functions that produce refined **unit** values carrying proofs. Below, given an abstract domain i, and two abstract values x and y, `join_lemma i x y` is a proof concerning i, x and y. Such an instantiation can be manual (i.e. below, i.top_law () in top_lemma), or automatic. The automatic instantiation of a lemma is decided by the SMT solver. Below, we make use of the `SMTPat` syntax, that allows us to give the SMT solver a list of patterns. Whenever the SMT solver matches a pattern from the list, it instantiates the lemma in stake. The lemma `join_lemma` below states that the union of the concretization of two abstract values x and y is below the concretization of the abstract join of x and y. This is true because of γ's monotony: we help a bit the SMT solver by giving a hint with **assert**. This lemma is instantiated each time a proof goal contains $\mathtt{x} \sqsubseteq \mathtt{y}$.

Because of a technical limitation, we cannot write SMT patterns directly in the meetₗₐw, botₗₐw and topₗₐw fields of the class adom: thus, below we reformulate them.

```
let top_lemma (i: adom τ)        (let bot_lemma, meet_lemma = ...)
  : Lemma (∀ (x: i.c). x ∈ i.γ i.adomₗₐₜ.top)
          [SMTPat (i.γ i.adomₗₐₜ.top)] = i.top_law ()
let join_lemma (i: adom τ) (x y: τ)
  : Lemma ((i.γ x ∪ i.γ y) ⊆ i.γ (i.adomₗₐₜ.join x y))
          [SMTPat (i.adomₗₐₜ.join x y)]
  = let r = i.adomₗₐₜ.join x y in assert (γ x ⊆ γ r ∧ γ y ⊆ γ r)
```

5   An Example of Abstract Domain: Intervals

Until now, the F* code we presented was mostly specificational. This section presents the abstract domain of intervals, and thus shows how proof obligations are dealt with in F*. Below, the type itv' is a dependent tuple: the refinement type on its right-hand side component up depends on low. If a pair (x,y) is of type itv', we have a proof that $\mathtt{x} \leq \mathtt{y}$.

```
type itv' = low:intₘ & up:intₘ {low≤up}      type itv = withbot itv'
```

The machine integers being finite, itv' naturally has a top element. However, itv' cannot represent the empty set of integers, whence itv, that adds an explicit bottom element using withbot. The syntax Val? returns true when a value is not Bot. For convenience, mk makes an interval out of two numbers, and itv_card computes the cardinality of an interval. We use it later to define a measure for intervals. inbounds x holds when $\mathtt{x}:\mathbb{Z}$ fits machine integer bounds.

```
type withbot (a: Type) = | Val: v:a → withbot a | Bot
let mk (x y: ℤ): itv = if inbounds x && inbounds y && x ≤ y
                       then Val ⟨x,y⟩ else Bot
let itv_card (i:itv):ℕ = match i with | Bot→0 | Val i→dsnd i - dfst i + 1
```

Below, lat_{itv} is an instance of the typeclass lattice for intervals: intervals are ordered by inclusion, the meet and join operations consist in unwrapping withbot, then playing with bounds. lat_{itv} is of type lattice itv: it means for instance that we have the proof that the join and meet operators respect the order $\text{lat}_{\text{itv}}.\text{corder}$, as stated in the definition of lattice. Note that here, not a single line of proof is required: F* transparently builds up proof obligations, and asks the SMT to discharge them, that does so automatically.

```
instance lat_itv: lattice itv =
  { corder = withbot_ord #itv' (λ⟨a,b⟩ ⟨c,d⟩ → a≥c && b≤d)
  ; join = (λ(i j: itv) → match i, j with
       | Bot, k | k, Bot → k
       | Val ⟨a,b⟩, Val ⟨c,d⟩ → Val ⟨min a c, max b d⟩)
  ; meet = (λ(x y: itv) → match x, y with
       | Val ⟨a,b⟩, Val ⟨c,d⟩ → mk (max a c) (min b d)
       | _ → Bot); bottom = Bot; top = mk min_int_m max_int_m }
```

Such automation is possible even with more complicated definitions: for instance, below we define the classical widening with thresholds. Without a single line of proof, widen is shown as respecting the order corder.

```
let thresholds: list int_m = [min_int_m;-64;-32;-16;-8;-4;4;8;16;32...]
let widen_bound_r (b: int_m): (r:int_m {r>b ∨ b=max_int_m}) =
  if b=max_int_m then b else find' (λ(u:int_m) → u>b) thresholds
let widen_bound_l (b: int_m): (r:int_m {r<b ∨ b=min_int_m}) =
  if b=min_int_m then b else find' (λ(u:int_m) → u<b) (rev thresholds)
let widen (i j: itv): r:itv {corder i r ∧ corder j r}
  = match i, j with | Bot, x | x, Bot → x
  | Val⟨a,b⟩,Val⟨c,d⟩ →Val ⟨ (if a≤c then a else widen_bound_l c)
                          , (if b≥d then b else widen_bound_r d)⟩
```

Similarly, turning itv into an abstract domain requires no proof effort. Below itv_{adom} explains that intervals concretize to machine integers ($c = \text{int}_m$), how it does so (with $\gamma = \text{itv}_\gamma$), and which lattice is associated with the abstract domain ($\text{adom}_{\text{lat}} = \text{lat}_{\text{itv}}$). As explained previously, the proof of a proposition p in F* can be encoded as an inhabitant of a refinement of unit, whence the "empty" lambdas: we let the SMT solver figure out the proof on its own.

```
let itv_γ: itv→set int_m = withbot_γ (λ(i:itv') x→dfst i≤x ∧ x≤dsnd i)
instance itv_adom: adom itv = { c = int_m    ; adom_lat = lat_itv; γ = itv_γ
  ; meet_law = (λ_ _→()); bot_law = (λ_→()); top_law = (λ_→())
  ; widen = widen    ; order_measure={f=itv_card;max=size_int_m}}
```

5.1   Forward Binary Operations on Intervals

Most of the binary operations on intervals can be written and shown correct without any proof. Our operators handle machine integer overflowing: for instance, add_overflows returns a boolean indicating whether the addition of two integers overflows, solely by performing machine integer operations. The refinement of add_overflows states that the returned boolean r should be true if and only if the addition in $\mathbb{Z}$ differs from the one in int_m. The correctness of itv_{add} is specified as a refinement: the set of the additions between the concretized values from the input intervals is to be included in the concretization of the abstract addition. Its implementation is very simple, and its correctness proved automatically.

```
let add_overflows (a b: int_m)
  : (r: bool {r ⟺ int_arith.n_add a b ≠ int_m_arith.n_add a b})
  = ((b<0) = (a<0)) && abs a > max_int_m - abs b
let itv_add (x y: itv): (r: itv {(γ x + γ y) ⊆ γ r})
  = match x, y with | Val ⦇a, b⦈, Val ⦇c, d⦈
                      → if add_overflows a c || add_overflows b d
                        then top else Val ⦇a + c, b + d⦈ | _→Bot
```

However the SMT solver sometimes misses some necessary lemmas. In such cases, we can either guide the SMT solver by discriminating cases and inserting hints, or go fully manual with a tactic system à la Coq. Below, the assert uses tactics: everything within the parenthesis following the by keyword is a computation that manipulates proof goals. Our aim is to prove that subtracting two numerical sets a and b is equivalent to adding a with the inverse of b.

Unfortunately, due to the nature of lift_binop, this yields existential quantifications which are difficult for the SMT solver to deal with. After normalizing our goal (with compute ()), and dealing with quantifiers and implications (forall_intro, implies_intro and elim_exists), we are left with $\exists y.\ b\ (-y) \wedge r{=}x{+}y$ knowing $b\ z \wedge r{=}x{-}z$ given some z as an hypothesis. Eliminating $\exists y$ with $-z$ is enough to complete the proof.

We sadly had to prove that (not too complicated) fact by hand. This however shows the power of $F^\star$. Its type system is very expressive: one can state arbitrarily mathematically hard propositions (for which automation is hopeless). In such cases, one can always resort to Coq-like manual proving to handle hard proofs.

```
let set_inverse (s: set int_m): set int_m = λ(i: int_m) → s (-i)
let lemma_inv (a b: set int_m)
  : Lemma ((a-b) ⊆ (a+set_inverse b)) [SMTPat (a+set_inverse b)]
  = assert ((a-b) ⊆ (a+set_inverse b)) by (  compute ();
      let _= forall_intro () in let p_0 = implies_intro () in
      let witX,p_1 = elim_exists (binder_to_term p_0) in
      let witY,p_1 = elim_exists (binder_to_term p_1) in
      let z: ℤ = unquote (binder_to_term witY) in
      witness witX; witness (quote (-z)))
```

Notice the SMT pattern: the lemma lemma$_{inv}$ will be instantiated each time the SMT deals with an addition involving an inverse. Defining the subtraction itv$_{sub}$ is a breeze: it simply performs an interval addition and an interval inversion. Here, no need for a single line of proof for its correctness (expressed as a refinement).

```
let itvinv (i: itv): (r: itv {set_inverse (γ i) ⊆ γ r})
  = match i with | Val(lower, upper) → Val(-upper, -lower) | _ → i
let itvsub (x y:itv): (r: itv {(γ x - γ y) ⊆ γ r}) = itvadd x (itvinv y)
```

Proving multiplication sound on intervals requires a lemma which is not inferred automatically:

$$\forall x \in [a,b], y \in [b,c].\,[\min(ac,ad,bc,bd),\max(ac,ad,bc,bd)]$$

In that case, decomposing that latter lemma into sublemmas lemma$_{min}$ and lemma$_{mul}$ is enough. Apart from this lemma, itv$_{mul}$ is free of any proof term.

```
let lemmamin (a b c d: ℤ) (x: ℤ{a≤x ∧ x≤b}) (y: ℤ{c≤y ∧ y≤d})
  : Lemma (x×y≥a×c ∨ x×y≥a×d ∨ x×y≥b×c ∨ x×y≥b×d) = ()
unfold let inbtw (x: ℤ) (l u: ℤ) = l≤u ∧ x≥1 ∧ x≤u
let lemmamul (a b c d x y: ℤ)
  : Lemma (requires inbtw x a b ∧ inbtw y c d)
    (ensures x×y ≥ (a×c) `min` (a×d) `min` (b×c) `min` (b×d)
           ∧ x×y ≤ (a×c) `max` (a×d) `max` (b×c) `max` (b×d))
    [SMTPat (x×y); SMTPat (a×c); SMTPat (b × d)]
  = lemmamin a b c d x y; lemmamin (-b) (-a) c d (-x) y


let mul_overflows (a b:intm):(r:bool{r≠inbounds (int_arith.nmul a b)})
  = a ≠ 0 && abs b > maxintm `divm` (abs a)
let itvmul (x y: itv): r:itv {(γ x × γ y) ⊆ γ r}
  = match x, y with
    | Val (a, b), Val (c, d) →
        let l = (a×c) `min` (a×d) `min` (b×c) `min` (b×d) in
        let r = (a×c) `max` (a×d) `max` (b×c) `max` (b×d) in
        if mul_overflows a c || mul_overflows a d
        || mul_overflows b c || mul_overflows b d
        then top else Val (l, r)
    | _ → Bot
```

The forward boolean operators for intervals require no proof at all; here we only give their type signatures. A function of interest is itv_as_bool: it returns TT when an interval does not contain 0, FF when it is the singleton 0, Unk otherwise.

```
let β (x: intm): itv = mk x x
let itveq (x y:itv): r:itv {(γ x `neq` γ y) ⊆ γ r} =... let itvlt =...
```

```
let itv_cγ (i: itv) (x:int_m): r:bool {r ⟺ itv_γ i x} =...
let itv_as_bool (x:itv): ubool   // with type ubool = |Unk|TT|FF
  = if β 0=x || Bot?x then FF else if itv_cγ x 0 then Unk else TT
let itv_andi (x y: itv): (r: itv {(γ x `n_and` γ y) ⊆ γ r})
  = match itv_as_bool x, itv_as_bool y with
  | TT, TT → β 1 | FF, _ | _, FF → β 0 | _, _ → mk 0 1
let itv_ori (x y: itv): (r: itv {(γ x `n_or` γ y) ⊆ γ r}) =...
```

5.2   Backward Operators

While a forward analysis for expressions is essential, another powerful analysis
can be made thanks to backward operators. Typically, it aims at extracting
information from a test, and at refining the abstract values involved in this test,
so that we gain in precision on those abstract values. Given a concrete binary
operator $\oplus$, we define $\overleftarrow{\oplus}$ its abstract backward counterpart. Let three intervals
$x^\#$, $y^\#$, and $r^\#$. $\overleftarrow{\oplus}$ $x^\#$ $y^\#$ $r^\#$ tries to find the most precise intervals $x^{\#\#}$ and
$y^{\#\#}$ supposing $\gamma\ x^\# \oplus \gamma\ y^\# \subseteq \gamma\ r^\#$. The soundness of $\overleftarrow{\oplus}$ $x^\#$ $y^\#$ $r^\#$ can be
formulated as below. We later generalize this notion of soundness with the type
$\text{sound}_{\overleftarrow{op}}$, which is indexed by an abstract domain and a binary operation.

$$\text{let } x^{\#\#},\ y^{\#\#} = (\overleftarrow{\oplus})\ x^\#\ y^\#\ r^\#\ \text{in}$$
$$\forall\ x\ y.\ (x \in \gamma\ x^\# \wedge y \in \gamma\ y^\# \wedge op\ x\ y \in \gamma\ r^\#)$$
$$\implies (x \in \gamma\ x^{\#\#} \wedge y \in \gamma\ y^{\#\#})$$

As the reader will discover in the rest of this section, this statement of soundness
is proved entirely automatically against each and every backward operator for
the interval domain. For op a concrete operator, $\text{sound}_{\overleftarrow{op}}$ itv op is inhabited
by sound backward operators for op in the domain of intervals. If one shows that
$\overleftarrow{\oplus}$ is of type $\text{sound}_{\overleftarrow{op}}$ itv (+), it means exactly that $\overleftarrow{\oplus}$ is a sound backward
binary interval operator for (+). The rest of the listing shows how light in proof
and OCaml-looking the backward operations are. Below, we explain how $\overleftarrow{\text{it}}$
works: it is a bit complicated because it hides a "$\overleftarrow{\text{ge}}$" operator.

```
let ādd: sound_op̄ itv n_add = λx y r → x ⊓ (r-y), y ⊓ (r-x)
let s̄ub: sound_op̄ itv n_sub = λx y r → x ⊓ (r+y), y ⊓ (x-r)
let m̄ul: sound_op̄ itv n_mul = λx y r →
  let h (i j:itv) = (if j=β1 then i⊓r else i) in h x y, h y x
let ēq: sound_op̄ itv n_eq
  = λx y r → match itv_as_bool r with | TT → x⊓y,x⊓y | _ → x,y
let (\) (x y: itv): (r: itv {(γ x \ γ y) ⊆ γ r}) =...
let ānd: sound_op̄ itv n_and
  = λx y r → match itv_as_bool r,itv_as_bool x,itv_as_bool y with
  | FF, TT, _ → x, y ⊓ β 0       | FF, _, TT → x ⊓ β 0, y
  | TT, _, _ → x \ β 0, y \ β 0  | _ → x, y
```

```
let o̅r̅: sound_ōp̅ itv n_or
  = λx y r → match itv_as_bool r,itv_as_bool x,itv_as_bool y with
    | TT,FF,Unk | TT,FF,FF → x, y \ β 0 | TT,Unk,FF → x \ β 0, y
    | FF, _, TT | FF, TT, _ → x ⊓ β 0, y ⊓ β 0 | _ → x, y
```

Let us look at $\overleftarrow{lt}$. Knowing whether $x < y$ holds, $\overleftarrow{lt}$ helps us refining x and y to more precise intervals. Let x be the interval $[0; \max_{int_m}]$, y be $[5; 15]$ and r be $[0; 0]$. Since the singleton $[0; 0]$ represents `false`, $\overleftarrow{lt}$ x y r aims at refining x and y knowing that $x < y$ doesn't hold, that is, knowing $x \geq y$. In this case, $\overleftarrow{lt}$ finds x' = $[5; \max_{int_m}]$ and y' = $[5; 15]$. Indeed, when r is $[0; 0]$, itv_as_bool r equals to FF. Then we rewrite $\neg(x < y)$ either as $y < x + 1$ (when x is `incrementable`) or as $y - 1 < x$. In our case, x's upper bound is $\max_{int_m}$ (the biggest int_m): x is not incrementable. Thus we rewrite $\neg([0; \max_{int_m}] < [5; 15])$ as $[6; 16] < [0; \max_{int_m}]$.

Despite of these different case handling, the implementation of $\overleftarrow{lt}$ required no proof: the SMT solver takes care of everything automatically.

```
let l̅t̅_true (x y: itv)
  = match x, y with | Bot, _ | _, Bot → x,y
    | Val⦇a,b⦈, Val⦇c,d⦈ → mk a (min b (d-1)), mk (max (a+1) c) d
let decrementable i=Val?i&&dfst(Val?.v i)>min_int_m  let incr.=...
let l̅t̅: sound_ōp̅ itv n_lt
  = λx y r → match itv_as_bool r with | TT → l̅t̅_true x y
    | FF → if incrementable x // x < y ⟺ y > x+1
          then let ry, rx = l̅t̅_true y (itv_add x (β 1)) in
               itv_sub rx (β 1), ry
          else if decrementable y // x < y ⟺ y-1 > x
               then let ry, rx = l̅t̅_true (itv_sub y (β 1)) x in
                    rx, itv_add ry (β 1)
               else x,y | _ → x, y
```

6   Specialized Abstract Domains

Abstract domains are defined in Sect. 4 as lattices equipped with a sound concretization operation. Our abstract interpreter analyses IMP programs: its expressions are numerical, and IMP is equipped with a memory. Thus, this section defines two specialized abstract domains: one for numerical abstractions, and another one for memory abstractions.

6.1   Numerical Abstract Domains

In the Sect. 5.2, we explain what a sound backward operator is in the case of the abstract domain of intervals. There, we mention a more generic type $sound_{\overline{op}}$ that states soundness for such operators in the context of any abstract domain. We present its definition below:

```
type sound_op⃖ (a:Type) {|l:adom a|} (op:l.c→l.c→l.c)
  = op⃖: (a → a → a → (a & a)) {
      ∀ (x# y# r#: a). let x##, y## = op⃖ x# y# r# in
        (∀ (x y: l.c). (x ∈ γ x# ∧ y ∈ γ y# ∧ op x y ∈ γ r#)
            ⟹ (x ∈ γ x## ∧ y ∈ γ y##))}
```

We define the specialized typeclass num_{adom} for abstract domains that concretize to machine integers. A type that implements an instance of num_{adom} should also have an instance of adom, with int_m as concrete type. Whence the fields na_{adom}, and $adom_{num}$. Moreover, we require a computable concretization function cgamma, that is, a function that maps abstract values to computable sets of machine integers: int_m → bool. The β operator lifts a concrete value in the abstract world. We also require the abstract domain to provide both sound forward and backward operator for every syntactic operator of type binop presented in Sect. 2. The function abstract_binop maps an operator op of type binop to a sound forward abstract operator. Its soundness is encoded as a refinement. Similarly, abstract⃖_binop maps a binop to a corresponding sound backward operator. To ease backward analysis, gt_0 and lt_0 are abstractions for non-null positive and negative integers.

```
class num_adom (a: Type) =
{ na_adom: adom a; adom_num: squash (na_adom.c == int_m)
; cgamma: x#:a → x:int_m → b:bool {b ⟺ x ∈ γ x#}
; abstract⃖_binop: op:_→ i:a → j:a → r:a {lift op (γ i) (γ j) ⊆ γ r}
; abstract_binop: (op: binop) → sound_op⃖ a (concrete_binop op)
; gt_0: x#:a {∀(x:int_m). x>0 ⟹ x ∈ γ x#}
; lt_0: x#:a {∀(x:int_m). x<0 ⟹ x ∈ γ x#}; β: x:int_m→r:a{x ∈ γ r} }
```

For a proposition p, the $F^\star$ standard library defines squash p as the type _:unit{p}, that is, a refinement of the unit type. This can be seen as a lemma with no parameter.

Instance for Intervals. The Sect. 5 defines everything required by num_{adom}, thus below we give an instance of the typeclass num_{adom} for intervals.

```
instance itv_num_adom: num_adom itv = {
  na_adom = solve; adom_num = (); cgamma = itv_cγ; β = (λ x → β x);
  abstract⃖_binop = (function | Plus → itv_add ... | Or → itv_ori);
  abstract_binop = (function | Plus → add⃖ ... | Or → or⃖ );
  lt_0 = (mk min_{int_m} (-1)); gt_0 = (mk ( 1) max_{int_m}) }
```

6.2   Memory Abstract Domains

From the perspective of IMP statements, an abstract domain for abstract memories is fairly simple. An abstract memory should be equipped with two operations: assignment and assumption. Those are directly related to their syntactic counterpart `Assume` and `Assign`. Thus, mem_{adom} has a field `assume_` and a field `assign`. The correctness of these operations are elegantly encoded as refinement types.

Let us explain the refinement of `assume_`: let $m_0^\#$ an abstract memory, and e an expression. For every concrete memory m_0 abstracted by $m_0^\#$, the set of acceptable final memories $\text{osem}_{\text{stmt}}$ (`Assume e`) m_0 should be abstracted by `assume_` $m_0^\#$ e.

```
class memadom μ = { maadom: adom μ; mamem: squash (maadom . c == mem);
    assume_: m0#:μ → e:expr → m1#:μ
      {∀ (m0: mem{m0 ∈ γ m0#}). osemstmt (Assume    e) m0 ⊆ γ m1#};
    assign: m0#:μ → v:varname → e:expr → m1#:μ
      {∀ (m0: mem{m0 ∈ γ m0#}). osemstmt (Assign v e) m0 ⊆ γ m1#}}
```

7 A Weakly-Relational Abstract Memory

In this section, we define a weakly-relational abstract memory. This abstraction is said weakly-relational because the entrance of an empty abstract value in the map systematically launches a reduction of the whole map to `Bot`. Below we define an abstract memory (`amem`) as either an unreachable state (`Bot`), or a mapping (`map` τ) from `varname` to abstract values τ. The mappings `map` τ are equipped with the utility functions `mapi`, `map1`, `map2` and `fold`.

```
type map τ =...                     type amem τ = withbot (map τ)
let get': map τ→varname→τ =...    let fold: (τ→τ→τ) →map τ→τ =...
let mapi: (varname → τ → β) → map τ → map β =...
let map1: (τ→β)  → map τ → map β = λf → mapi (λ_ → f)
let map2: (τ→β→γ) → map τ → map β → map γ =...
```

A Lattice Structure. The listing below presents `amem` instances for the type-classes `order`, `lattice` and mem_{adom}. Once again, the various constraints imposed by these different typeclasses are discharged automatically by the SMT solver.

```
let amem_update (k: varname) (v: τ) (m: amem τ): amem τ
  = match m with | Bot → Bot
    | Val m → Val (mapi (λk' v' → if k'=k then v else v') m)
instance amemlat {| l: adom τ |}: lattice (amem τ) =
  { corder = withbotord (λm0 m1 → fold (&&) (map2 corder m0 m1))
  ; join = (λx y → match x, y with
      | Val x, Val y → Val (map2 join x y) | m,Bot | _,m → m)
  ; meet = (λx y → match x, y with
      | Val x, Val y →
          let m = map2 (⊓) x y in
          if fold (||) (mapi (λ_ v → l.adomlat.corder v bottom) m)
```

```
          then Bot else Val m
      | _ → Bot); bottom = Bot; top = ...}
instance amem_adom {|l:adom τ|}: adom (amem τ) = { c = mem' l.c
  ; adom_lat=solve; meet_law=(λ_ _→()); top_law=(λ_→()); bot_law=(λ_→())
  ; γ = withbot_γ (λm# m → fold (∧) (mapi (λv x → m v ∈ γ x) m#))
  ; widen = (λx y → match x, y with
      | Val x, Val y → Val (map₂ widen x y) | m,Bot | _,m → m)
  ; order_measure = let {max; f} = l.order_measure in
      { f = (function | Bot → 0 | Val m# → 1 + fold (+) (map₁ f m#))
      ; max = 1 + max × 4 }}
```

The rest of this section defines a mem$_{adom}$ instance for our memories amem. The typeclass mem$_{adom}$ is an essential piece in our abstract interpreter: it provides the abstract operations for handling assumes and assignments.

Forward Expression Analysis. We define asem$_{expr}$, mapping expressions to abstract values of type τ. It is defined for any abstract domain, whence the typeclass argument {|num$_{adom}$ τ|}. The abstract interpretation of an expression e given m$_0^{\#}$ an initial memory is defined below as asem$_{expr}$ m$_0^{\#}$ e. It is specified via a refinement type to be a sound abstraction of e's operational semantics osem$_{expr}$ m$_0$ e. This function leverages the operators from the different typeclasses for which we defined instances just above. β:int$_m$→τ and abstract_binop:binop→... come from num$_{adom}$, while top:τ comes from lattice.

```
val get: m:amem τ {Val? m}→varname→τ      let get (Val m) = get' m
let rec asem_expr {|num_adom τ|} (m_0^#: amem τ) (e: expr)
  : (r: τ { ∀ (m_0: mem). m_0 ∈ γ m_0^# ⟹ osem_expr m_0 e ⊆ γ r })
  = if m_0^# ⊑ bottom then bottom else
      match e with | Const x → β x | Unknown → top | Var v → get m_0^# v
      | BinOp op x y → abstract_binop op (asem_expr m_0^# x) (asem_expr m_0^# y)
```

Backward Analysis. Our aim is to have an instance for our memory of mem$_{adom}$: it expects an assume_ operator. Thus, below a backward analysis is defined for expressions. Given an expression e, an abstract value r$^{\#}$ and a memory m$_0^{\#}$, $\overleftarrow{asem}$ e r$^{\#}$ m$^{\#}$ computes a new abstract memory. That abstract memory refines the abstract values held in m$_0^{\#}$ as much as possible under the hypothesis that e lives in r$^{\#}$. The soundness of this analysis is encoded as a refinement on the output memory. Given any concrete memory m$_0$ and integer v approximated by r$^{\#}$, if the operational semantics of e at memory m$_0$ contains v, then m$_0$ should also be approximated by the output memory.

When e is a constant which is not contained in the concretization of the target abstract value r$^{\#}$, the hypothesis "e lives in r$^{\#}$" is false, thus we translate that fact by outputting the unreachable memory bottom. In opposition, when e is Unknown, the hypothesis brings no new knowledge, thus we return the initial memory $m_0^\#$. In the case of a variable lookup (i.e. e = Var v for some v), we consider $x^\#$, the abstract value living at v. Since our goal is to craft the most precise memory such that Var v is approximated by $r^\#$, we alter $m_0^\#$ by assigning $x^\# \sqcap r^\#$ at the variable v. Finally, in the case of binary operations, we make use of the backward operators and of recursion. Note that it is the only place where we need to insert a hint for the SMT solver: we assert an equality by asking $F^\star$ to normalize the terms. We state explicitly that the operational semantics of a binary operation reduces to two existentials: we manually unfold the definition of $osem_{expr}$ and lift_binop. The decreases clause explains to $F^\star$ why and how the recursion terminates.

```
let rec a͞s͞e͞m {|l:num_adom τ|} (e: expr) (r#: τ) (m0#: amem τ)
 : Tot (m1#: amem τ { (* decreases: *) m1# ⊑ m0# ∧ (* soundness: *)
      (∀(m0 :mem) (v:int_m) . (v∈γ r# ∧ m0 ∈γ m0# ∧ v ∈ osem_expr m0 e)
                        ⟹ m0 ∈ γ m1#)}) (decreases e)
  = if m0# ⊑ bottom then bottom else match e with
  | Const x → if cgamma r# x then m0# else bottom | Unknown → m0#
  | Var v→let x#: τ = r# ⊓ get m0# v in
          if x# ⊑ bottom then Bot else amem_update v x# m0#
  | BinOp op ex ey → let o͞p = abstract_binop op in
        let x#, y# = o͞p (asem_expr m0# ex) (asem_expr m0# ey) r# in
        let r#: amem τ = a͞s͞e͞m ex x# m0# ⊓ a͞s͞e͞m ey y# m0# in
        assert_norm (∀ (m: mem) (v: int_m). v ∈ osem_expr m e
            ⟺ (∃ (x y:int_m). x ∈ osem_expr m ex ∧ y ∈ osem_expr m ey
                    ∧ v == concrete_binop op x y));
        r#
```

Iterating the Backward Analysis. While a concrete test is idempotent, it is not the case for abstract ones. Our goal is to refine an abstract memory under a hypothesis as much as possible. Since a͞s͞e͞m is proven sound and decreasing, we can repeat the analysis as much as we want. We introduce prefixpoint that computes a pre-fixpoint. However, even if the function from which we want to get a prefixpoint is decreasing, this is not a guarantee for termination. The type measure below associates an order to a measure that ensures termination. Such a measure cannot be implemented for a lattice that has infinite decreasing or increasing chains. We also require a maximum for this measure, so that we can reverse the measure easily in the context of postfixpoints iteration.

```
type measure #a (ord: a → a → bool)
  = { f: f: (a → ℕ) {∀ x y. x `ord` y ⟹ x ≠ y ⟹ f x < f y}
    ; max: (max: ℕ {∀ x. f x < max}) }
```

Let us focus on prefixpoint: given an order ⊑ with its measure m, it iterates a decreasing function f, starting from a value x. The argument r is a binary relation which is required to hold for every couple $(x, f\ x)$. r is also required to be transitive, so that morally $r\ x\ (f^n\ x)$ holds. $\texttt{prefixpoint}$ is specified to return a prefixpoint y, that is, with $r\ x\ y$ holding.

```
let rec prefixpoint ((⊑): order τ) (m: measure (⊑))
   (r: τ→τ→prop {trans r}) (f: τ→τ {∀e. f e ⊑ e ∧ r e (f e)}) (x:τ)
   : Tot (y: τ{r x y ∧ f y == y ∧ y ⊑ x}) (decreases (m.f x))
   = let x' = f x in if x ⊑ x' then x else prefixpoint (⊑) m r f x'
```

Below is defined $\overleftarrow{\texttt{asem}}\texttt{\_fp}$ the iterated version of $\overleftarrow{\texttt{asem}}$. Besides using $\texttt{prefixpoint}$, the only thing required here is to spell out $\texttt{t}$, the relation we want to ensure.

```
let asem_fp {|numadom τ|} (e:expr) (r:τ) (m0#:amem τ)
   : Tot (m1#: amem τ {(∀ (m0:mem) (v:intm). m1#⊑m0# ∧
                      (v∈γ r ∧ m0∈γm0# ∧ v∈osemexpr m0 e) ⟹ m0∈γm1#)})
   = let t (m0# m1#: amem τ) = ∀ (m: mem) (v: intm).
        (v ∈ γ r ∧ m ∈ γ m0# ∧ v ∈ osemexpr m e) ⟹ m ∈ γ m1# in
     prefixpoint corder order_measure t (asem e r) m0#
```

A $\texttt{mem}_{\texttt{adom}}$ instance We defined both a forward and backward analysis for expressions. Implementing an $\texttt{mem}_{\texttt{adom}}$ instance for $\texttt{amem}$ is thus easy, as shown below. For any numerical abstract domain τ, $\texttt{amemory\_mem\_adom}$ provides an $\texttt{mem}_{\texttt{adom}}$, that is, an abstract domain for memories, providing nontrivial proofs of correctness. Still, this is proven automatically.

```
instance amemory_mem_adom {| nd: numadom τ |}: memadom (amem τ) =
   let adom: adom (amem τ) = amemadom in { maadom = adom; mamem = ()
   ; assume_ = (λm# e → asem_fp e gt0 m# ⊔ asem_fp e lt0 m#)
   ; assign = (λm# v e → let v#: τ = asemexpr m# e in
                    if v# ⊑ bottom then Bot else amem_update v v# m#)}
```

8   Statement Abstract Interpretation

Wrapping up the implementation of our abstract interpreter, this section presents the abstract interpretation of IMP statements. For every memory type μ that instantiates the typeclass of abstract memories $\texttt{mem}_{\texttt{adom}}$, the abstract semantics $\texttt{asem}_{\texttt{stmt}}$ maps statements and initial abstract memories to final memories. $\texttt{mem}_{\texttt{adom}}$ is defined and proven correct below.

Given a statement $\texttt{s}$, and an initial abstract memory $m_0^\#$, $\texttt{mem}_{\texttt{adom}}$ $\texttt{s}$ $m_0^\#$ is a final abstract memory so that for any initial concrete memory $\texttt{m}$ approximated by $m_0^\#$ and for any acceptable final concrete memory $\texttt{m}'$ considering the operational semantics, $\texttt{m}'$ is approximated by $\texttt{mem}_{\texttt{adom}}$ $\texttt{s}$ $m_0^\#$. Here, we give two hints to the SMT solver: by normalization ($\texttt{assert\_norm}$), we unfold the operational semantics in the case of choices or sequences. The analysis of an assignment or an assume is very easy since we already have operators defined for these cases. In the case of the sequence of two statements, we simply recurse. Similarly, when the statement is a choice, we recurse on its two possibilities. Then the two resulting abstract memories are merged back together. The last case to be handled is the loop, that is some statement of the shape Loop body. We compute a fixpoint $m_1^{\#}$ for body, by widening: it therefore approximates correctly the operational semantics of Loop body, since it is defined as a transitive closure. F*'s standard library provides the lemma stable_on_closure; of which we give a simplified signature below. The concretization $\gamma \, m_1^{\#}$ is a set, that is a predicate: we use this lemma with $\gamma \, m_1^{\#}$ as predicate p and with the operational semantics as relation r.

```
val simplified_stable_on_closure: r:(τ → τ → prop) → p:(τ → prop)
  → Lemma (requires ∀ x y. p x ∧ r x y ⟹ p y)
          (ensures ∀ x y. p x ∧ closure r x y ⟹ p y)
```

```
let rec asem_stmt {| md: mem_adom μ |} (s: stmt) (m_0^#: μ)
  : (m_1^#:μ {∀(m m':mem). (m∈γ m_0^# ∧ m'∈osem_stmt s m) ⟹ m'∈γ m_1^#})
  = assert_norm(∀s_0 s_1 (m_0 mf:mem). osem_stmt (Seq s_0 s_1) m_0 mf
      == (∃(m_1:mem). m_1 ∈ osem_stmt s_0 m_0 ∧ mf ∈ osem_stmt s_1 m_1));
    assert_norm(∀a b (m_0 mf:mem). osem_stmt (Choice a b) m_0 mf
      == (mf ∈ (osem_stmt a m_0 ∪ osem_stmt b m_0)));
    if m_0^# ⊑ bottom then bottom
    else match s with          | Assign v e → assign m_0^# v e
    | Assume e → assume_ m_0^# e | Seq s t → asem_stmt t (asem_stmt s m_0^#)
    | Choice a b → asem_stmt a m_0^# ⊔ asem_stmt b m_0^#
    | Loop body→let m_1^#: μ = postfixpoint corder order_measure
                  (λ(m^#:μ) → widen m^# (asem_stmt body m^# <: μ))
              in stable_on_closure (osem_stmt body) (γ m_1^#) (); m_1^#
```

Below we show the definition of postfixpoint, which is similar to prefixpoint. However, it is simpler because it only ensures its outcome is a postfixpoint.

```
let rec postfixpoint ((⊑): order τ) (m: measure (⊑))
  (f: τ → τ {∀ x. x ⊑ f x}) (x: τ)
  : Tot (y: τ{f y == y ∧ (⊑) x y}) (decreases (m.max - m.f x))
  = let x' = f x in if x' ⊑ x then x else postfixpoint (⊑) m f x'
```

9   Conclusion and Further Works

We presented almost the entire code of our abstract interpreter for IMP. Our approach to abstract interpretation is concretization-based, and follows the methodology of [3,11]. While using F*, we did not encountered any issue regarding expressiveness, and additionally gained a lot in proof automatization, to finally implement a fairly modular abstract interpreter. The table below compares the line-of-proof vs. line-of-code ratio of our implementation compared to some of the available verified abstract interpreters. Ours is up to 17 times more proof efficient. It is very compact, and requires a negligible amount of manual proofs. This comparison has its limits, since the different formalizations do not target the same programming languages: [11] and [3] handles the full C language, while [5] and the curent paper deal with more simple imperative languages. Also, proof effort usually does not scale linearly.

	Code	Proof	Ratio	Feature set
This paper	487	39	0.08	Simple imperative language
Pichardie et al. [5]	3 725	5 020	1.35	Simple imperative language
Verasco [11]	16 847	17 040	1.01	CompCert C langage
Blazy et al. [3]	4 000	3 500	0.87	CompCert C langage

The sources of our abstract interpreter sources are available along with a set of example programs; building it natively or as a web application is easy, reproducible[2] and automated.

This work is very far from the scope of Verasco which required about four years of human time [10,12], but our results, which required 3 months of work with F* expertise, are very encouraging.

Further Work. We aim at following the path of Verasco by adding real-world features to our abstract interpreter and consider a more realistic target language such as one of the CompCert C-like input languages. One of the weakenesses of Verasco is its efficiency. Using Low*, a C DSL for F*, it is possible to write (with a nontrivial additionnal effort related to Low*) a very efficient C and formally verified abstract interpreter. This development also opens the path for enriching F* automation via verified abstract interpretation.

Acknowledgements. This work is supported by a European Research Council (ERC) Consolidator Grant for the project VESTA, funded under the European Union's Horizon 2020 Framework Programme (grant agreement 772568).

References

1. Provably secure communication software. https://project-everest.github.io/
2. Supplementary materials. https://zenodo.org/record/5168401
3. Blazy, S., Laporte, V., Maroneze, A., Pichardie, D.: Formal verification of a C value analysis based on abstract interpretation. In: Logozzo, F., Fähndrich, M. (eds.) SAS 2013. LNCS, vol. 7935, pp. 324–344. Springer, Heidelberg (2013). https://doi.org/10.1007/978-3-642-38856-9_18 https://arxiv.org/abs/1304.3596

---

[2] Our build process relies on the purely functional Nix package manager.

4. Bond, B., et al.: Vale: verifying high-performance cryptographic assembly code. In: Proceedings of the USENIX Security Symposium. USENIX, August 2017. Distinguished Paper Award. https://www.microsoft.com/en-us/research/publication/vale-verifying-high-performance-cryptographic-assembly-code/

5. Cachera, D., Pichardie, D.: A certified denotational abstract interpreter. In: Kaufmann, M., Paulson, L.C. (eds.) ITP 2010. LNCS, vol. 6172, pp. 9–24. Springer, Heidelberg (2010). https://doi.org/10.1007/978-3-642-14052-5_3 https://hal.inria.fr/inria-00537810/document

6. Cousot, P., et al.: The ASTREÉ analyzer. In: Sagiv, M. (ed.) ESOP 2005. LNCS, vol. 3444, pp. 21–30. Springer, Heidelberg (2005). https://doi.org/10.1007/978-3-540-31987-0_3

7. Darais, D., Might, M., Van Horn, D.: Galois transformers and modular abstract interpreters: reusable metatheory for program analysis. In: Proceedings of the 2015 ACM SIGPLAN International Conference on Object-Oriented Programming, Systems, Languages, and Applications, OOPSLA 2015, pp. 552–571 (2015). https://doi.org/10.1145/2814270.2814308

8. David, P.: Interprétation abstraite en logique intuitionniste: extraction d'analyseurs Java certifiés. Ph.D. thesis, Université Rennes 1 (2005). in French

9. De Moura, L., Bjørner, N.: Z3: an efficient SMT solver. In: International Conference on Tools and Algorithms for the Construction and Analysis of Systems, pp. 337–340 (2008). http://www.audentia-gestion.fr/MICROSOFT/z3.pdf

10. Jourdan, J.H.: Verasco: a formally verified C static analyzer. Theses, Universite Paris Diderot-Paris VII, May 2016

11. Jourdan, J.H., Laporte, V., Blazy, S., Leroy, X., Pichardie, D.: A formally-verified C static analyzer. In: 42nd Symposium Principles of Programming Languages, pp. 247–259. ACM Press (2015). https://hal.archives-ouvertes.fr/tel-01327023/document

12. Laporte, V.: Verified static analyzes for low-level languages. Theses, Université Rennes 1, November 2015

13. Martínez, G., et al.: Meta-F*: proof automation with SMT, tactics, and metaprograms. In: 28th European Symposium on Programming (ESOP), pp. 30–59 (2019). https://fstar-lang.org/papers/metafstar

14. Nipkow, T.: Abstract interpretation of annotated commands. In: Beringer, L., Felty, A. (eds.) ITP 2012. LNCS, vol. 7406, pp. 116–132. Springer, Heidelberg (2012). https://doi.org/10.1007/978-3-642-32347-8_9

15. Protzenko, J., et al.: Evercrypt: a fast, verified, cross-platform cryptographic provider. In: IEEE Symposium on Security and Privacy. IEEE, May 2020. https://www.microsoft.com/en-us/research/publication/evercrypt-a-fast-veri%ef%ac%81ed-cross-platform-cryptographic-provider/

16. Zinzindohoué, J.K., Bhargavan, K., Protzenko, J., Beurdouche, B.: HACL: a verified modern cryptographic library. In: Proceedings of the 2017 ACM SIGSAC Conference on Computer and Communications Security, CCS 2017, pp. 1789-1806. Association for Computing Machinery (2017). https://doi.org/10.1145/3133956.3134043

Disjunctive Interval Analysis

Graeme Gange[1] , Jorge A. Navas[2] , Peter Schachte[3] ,
Harald Søndergaard[3]([✉]) , and Peter J. Stuckey[1]

[1] Faculty of Information Technology, Monash University, Melbourne, Australia
[2] SRI International, Menlo Park, CA, USA
[3] School of Computing and Information Systems, The University of Melbourne,
Melbourne, Australia
harald@unimelb.edu.au

Abstract. We revisit disjunctive interval analysis based on the Boxes abstract domain. We propose the use of what we call range decision diagrams (RDDs) to implement Boxes, and we provide algorithms for the necessary RDD operations. RDDs tend to be more compact than the linear decision diagrams (LDDs) that have traditionally been used for Boxes. Representing information more directly, RDDs also allow for the implementation of more accurate abstract operations. This comes at no cost in terms of analysis efficiency, whether LDDs utilise dynamic variable ordering or not. RDD and LDD implementations are available in the Crab analyzer, and our experiments confirm that RDDs are well suited for disjunctive interval analysis.

Keywords: Abstract interpretation · Boxes · Decision diagrams · Integer abstract domains

1 Introduction

The perennial challenge in the design of program analyses is to find an appropriate balance between precision and efficiency. A natural way to improve precision of analysis is to design an abstract domain that supports path-sensitive analysis, that is, allows for a degree of *disjunctive* information to be expressed. However, abstract domains are rarely closed under disjunction, as the cost of disjunctive closure usually leads to prohibitively expensive analysis.

In this paper we are concerned with the analysis of integer manipulating procedural programs. The abstract domain studied here is the Boxes domain [11], applied to $\mathbb{Z}$, the set of integers.[1] Assume we are given n integer variables $v_1, \ldots, v_n$. A *bounds constraint* takes one of the forms $v_i \leq k$ or $v_i \geq k$, where k is an integer constant. An *integer box* is any set $B \subseteq \mathbb{Z}^n$ that can be expressed as a (possibly empty) conjunction of bounds constraints. The Boxes domain consists of any set $S \subseteq \mathbb{Z}^n$ which can be written as a finite union $\bigcup_{i=1}^{j} B_i$, such that $B_1, \ldots, B_j$ are integer boxes. Some examples are given in Fig. 1: (a) shows

---

[1] With a little additional effort, the approach extends to rationals and floating point numbers.

© Springer Nature Switzerland AG 2021
C. Drăgoi et al. (Eds.): SAS 2021, LNCS 12913, pp. 144–165, 2021.
https://doi.org/10.1007/978-3-030-88806-0_7

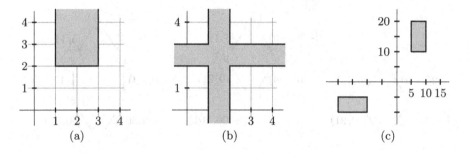

Fig. 1. Examples of Boxes elements.

an integer box, namely $x \in [1,4) \wedge y \in [2,\infty)$; (b) shows the Boxes element $x \in [1,3) \vee y \in [2,4)$; and (c) shows the element

$$(x \in [-20,-9) \wedge y \in [-10,-4)) \vee (x \in [5,11) \wedge y \in [10,21))$$

Elements of Boxes are generally non-convex sets. The domain is closed under both (finite) intersection and union, as well as under complement. This clearly sets Boxes apart from more commonly studied *relational* abstract domains, such as zones [20], octagons [21], and convex polyhedra [7]. Note that, while it is a non-relational abstract domain, Boxes can still express conditional constraints, such as $x \geq 2 \Rightarrow (y \geq 0 \wedge y \leq 4)$.

To implement Boxes, Gurfinkel and Chaki [11] proposed the use of linear decision diagrams (LDDs) [3]. The inspiration for LDDs came from the better known binary decision diagrams (BDDs) [2]. But in an LDD, a decision node (a non-terminal node) no longer corresponds to a Boolean variable; instead it holds a primitive constraint in some theory. As with BDDs, non-terminal nodes in LDDs always have fan-out 2. LDDs can express any Boolean combination of primitive constraints, and in the Boxes case, "primitive constraint" means "bounds constraint" (only), such as $x \leq 42$. LDDs can utilise *sharing* of sub-structures, which reduces memory requirements and allows for a canonical representation.

However, LDDs (with primitive constraints taken from some theory T) come with a disadvantage: inability to precisely analyse expressions that fall outside the theory. This happens since many operations rely on a T-solver. With LDD-boxes, much precision is lost in the context of non-linear[2] expressions, as Example 1 will show. Moreover, with LDDs, many abstract operations are expensive, because of the need to preserve a node order that depends not only on variable ordering, but also on logical consequence. Gurfinkel and Chaki [11] define abstract operations in terms of constraint substitution, a relatively heavyweight approach which, again, limits transformers to the supported arithmetic fragment.

---

[2] Gurfinkel and Chaki [11] consider a restricted programming language with only linear expressions and guards.

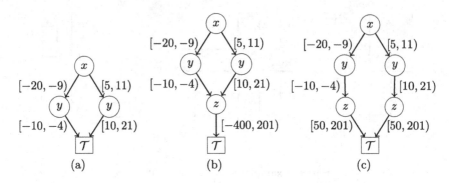

Fig. 2. (a) A Boxes state with disjunctive information, and after applying z := x * y (b) using interval approximation, and (c) using a precise transformer.

Our aim is to improve Boxes analysis through the use of a dedicated data structure that can support precise analysis, including analysis of programs involving non-linear operations. As it turns out, our proposed representation of disjunctive intervals also tends to speed up the analysis of *linear* programs, mainly because it allows *bounds-propagation* to take the place of calls to a theory solver. We use what we call "range decision diagrams" (RDDs), a variant of multi-valued decision diagrams (MDDs) [24]. Non-terminal nodes in these structures can have varying fan-out, each with each edge corresponding to a range of values for some variable. RDDs also generalize BDDs, but in a different manner to LDDs.

In this paper, we use RDDs in the context of integer predicates. We note that LDDs have a wider scope: they can support more complex theories. But for the Boxes application, in which LDDs use monadic predicates only, RDDs have exactly the same expressiveness as LDDs.

We define RDDs formally in the next section. Until then, we ask the reader to rely on intuition and the diagrams shown in Fig. 2.

Example 1. To appreciate the limitations flowing from reliance on a theory solver, consider the Boxes set from Fig. 1(c). Its RDD[3] is shown in Fig. 2(a). Given the statement z := x * y, the LDD approach must collapse the information to its non-disjunctive interval form $-20 \leq x < 11 \wedge -10 \leq y < 21$. Since the theory solver used does not understand multiplication, the analysis engine must collapse the representation, in order to calculate bounds on the multiplication. The result is the Boxes element shown in RDD form in Fig. 2(b). A precise transformer, on the other hand, computes the possible values of z on each branch in the diagram, resulting in the much more precise Fig. 2(c) with a better lower bound for z.   □

In summary, the benefit of using RDDs for Boxes analysis is improved expressiveness *and* efficiency. We introduce RDDs in Sect. 2, and Sect. 3 provides

---

[3] It is straightforward to translate an RDD to an LDD over bounds constraints, and vice versa.

algorithms for the abstract operations. We report on an experimental evaluation in Sect. 4. Related work is discussed in Sect. 5, and Sect. 6 concludes.

2   Range Decision Diagrams

By *range* we mean an integer interval of form $[i, j)$ (that is, $\{k \in \mathbb{Z} \mid i \le k < j\}$), $[i, \infty)$, or $(-\infty, i)$. A set S of ranges is *fitting* iff every pair $I_1, I_2 \in S$ is disjoint ($I_1 \cap I_2 = \emptyset$) and $\bigcup S = \mathbb{Z}$. We assume a given finite set *Var* of variables. The set of *range decision diagrams*, or RDDs, is defined recursively, as follows.

- $\mathcal{F}$ and $\mathcal{T}$ are RDDs.
- Let $M = \{(I_1, r_1), (I_2, r_2), \ldots (I_n, r_n)\}, n > 1$ be a set of pairs whose first components are ranges and whose second components are RDDs. If the set $\{I \mid (I, r) \in M\}$ is fitting, and $v \in Var$, then $\langle v, M \rangle$ is an RDD.

We may sometimes relax the fitting requirement to allow $\bigcup S \subseteq \mathbb{Z}$, in which case each missing range is understood to be paired with $\mathcal{F}$.

The meaning of an RDD r is a predicate $[\![r]\!]$, defined as follows:

$$\begin{aligned}
[\![\mathcal{F}]\!] &= \textit{false} \\
[\![\mathcal{T}]\!] &= \textit{true} \\
[\![\langle v, M \rangle]\!] &= \bigvee \{[\![r]\!] \wedge v \in I \mid (I, r) \in M\}
\end{aligned}$$

We can view the RDD as a directed acyclic graph in the obvious manner: $\mathcal{T}$ and $\mathcal{F}$ are sinks. An RDD $\langle v, M \rangle$ has a node labelled v as its root, and for each $(I, r) \in M$, an edge (with label I) from v to the root of r. We draw graphs so that arrows point downwards. We will assume a (total) precedence order $\prec$ on *Var* and construct RDDs where the path variables earlier in the ordering always appear above variables later in the ordering (this condition may be temporarily violated in algorithms).

In algorithms, it is sometimes useful to utilize a different view of a fitting RDD. We may write a non-sink RDD r as $\langle v, [r_0, k_1, r_1, \ldots, k_n, r_n] \rangle$. Here $r_0, \ldots, r_n$ are RDDs and $k_1, \ldots, k_n$ are the *split points*, with $k_1 < k_2 < \cdots < k_n$. The intention is that r_i is the co-factor of r with respect to v, over the interval $[k_i, k_{i+1})$, implicitly taking $k_0 = -\infty$ and $k_{n+1} = \infty$.[4] For a fixed variable ordering this representation is canonical, provided we ensure $r_i \ne r_{i+1}$ for all i.

The two views are for presentation only; each is faithful to the data structure used in implementation. To translate between them, we use two functions **ser** and **des** (for "serialize" and "deserialize"). **des** takes an RDD representation $\langle v, [r_0, k_1, r_1, \ldots, k_n, r_n] \rangle$ in split-point form and turns it into the deserialised $\langle v, \{((-\infty, k_1), r'_0), ([k_1, k_2), r'_1), \ldots, ([k_n, \infty), r'_n)\} \rangle$, where r'_i is the deserialised form of r_i (base cases $\mathcal{F}$ and $\mathcal{T}$ are left unchanged).

The function **ser** is its inverse, defined only for fitting RDDs; **ser**, in particular, adds edges from v to $\mathcal{F}$ for any "missing" intervals.

---

[4] This view explains our tendency to use notation like $[3, 4)$ for what is obviously a (closed) singleton integer interval.

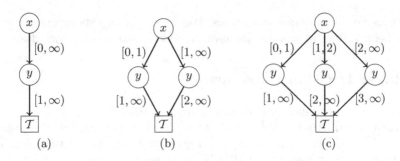

Fig. 3. A sequence of better approximations of $p(x, y) \equiv 0 \leq x \wedge x < y$.

In diagrams we omit the node $\mathcal{F}$ and its incident edges. The (serial form) RDD $\langle x, [\mathcal{F}, 0, \langle y, [\mathcal{F}, 1, \mathcal{T}]\rangle, 1, \langle y, [\mathcal{F}, 2, \mathcal{T}]\rangle]\rangle$ is shown in Fig. 3(b). Deserializing the RDD representation yields

$$
\left\langle x, \begin{cases} ((-\infty, 0), \mathcal{F}), \\ ((0, 1), \langle y, \{((-\infty, 1), \mathcal{F}), ([1, \infty), \mathcal{T})\}\rangle), \\ ([1, \infty), \langle y, \{((-\infty, 2), \mathcal{F}), ([2, \infty), \mathcal{T})\}\rangle) \end{cases} \right\rangle
$$

Applying a Boolean operator to RDDs is similar to how that is done for binary or (classical) multi-valued decision diagrams: we apply the operator pointwise on the co-factors of the nodes, and collect the result into a new node. However, unlike usual BDD or MDD operations, the intervals for the children of each node may not coincide. Thus we must first introduce additional separators that *refine* the generated intervals, enabling pointwise application of operators (we exemplify this in Sect. 3.2).

3   Implementing Boxes with RDDs

We now describe how to implement the Boxes domain with RDDs. Note again that Boxes forms a Boolean lattice, but not a complete one: there are necessarily predicates for which there can be no *best* RDD representation, instead admitting infinite chains of better and better RDD approximations. Consider the predicate $p(x, y) \equiv 0 \leq x \wedge x < y$. Figure 3(a) shows an over-approximation, $x \geq 0 \wedge y \geq 1$. We can separate the case $x = 0$ from $x \geq 1$ and obtain a marginally more precise over-approximation which excludes the infeasible valuation $\{x \mapsto 1, y \mapsto 1\}$, see Fig. 3(b). Indeed, we can split the domain of x arbitrarily often, in each step obtaining a slightly more precise RDD. Similarly there are infinite ascending chains of ever closer under-approximations.

Hence, for some arithmetic operations, we cannot hope to define optimal abstract transformers. In the context of RDDs there is, however, a natural criterion for precision, akin to the concept of interval consistency [1,4] from the constraint programming literature. Consider a constraint c over set X of variables. A *domain* D maps each variable $x \in X$ to a set of possible values for x.

Here we assume that $D(x)$ must be an interval and we say that D is *interval consistent* for c, iff, for each variable $x \in X$ with $D(x) = [\ell, u]$, each of the valuations $\{x \mapsto \ell\}$ and $\{x \mapsto u\}$ can be extended to a valuation (over all of X) satisfying $D \wedge c$. In this context, the role of *bounds-propagation* is to narrow variable domains as far as possible without breaking interval consistency.

For RDDs we need to refine the concept of consistency slightly. Note that each path ρ through the RDD induces a domain D_ρ.

Definition 1. *All-paths interval consistency.* *RDD r is all-paths interval consistent for constraint c iff, for each path ρ in r, the induced domain D_ρ is interval consistent.*

Our abstract operations strive to maintain all-paths interval consistency. Loosely this means we produce the strongest information that can possibly be inferred without resorting to speculative introduction of new disjunctive splits. Only our algorithm for inequality fails to maintain all-paths interval consistency— Example 5 will show a case of this.

3.1 Lattice Operations

The standard lattice operations are fairly straightforward. $\sqsubseteq, \sqcap, \sqcup$ coincide with the standard Boolean operators $\rightarrow, \wedge, \vee$, and can all be implemented *pointwise*: for $u \bowtie v$, we scan the children of u and v in order, applying $\bowtie$ recursively to children with overlapping intervals, and rebuild the results into a new node. As with the corresponding BDD/MDDs operations, these can be performed in $O(|u||v|)$ time. All lattice operations are optimally precise.

3.2 Variable Hoisting

An operation which will be useful for operators defined below is *hoisting* (or *interchanging*) variables. This is necessary when we would like to construct a function representing $\langle x, [r_0, k_1, \ldots, k_n, r_n] \rangle$, but where the root of r_i is earlier than x in the precedence order (so just building the node would be malformed).

For this definition, we restrict ourselves to the case where, for all r_i, every variable except (possibly) the root y are before x, so we merely need to interchange the decisions for x and y. For RDDs, this is straightforward and detailed in Fig. 4. We sort all the split points at the second level of the tree, removing duplicates and create a set $\mathcal{I}$ of covering intervals for the variable y. We fill in the matrix *Cofac* of cofactors, based on the intervals for y and x. We then construct a new node for each x interval using *Cofac*. Finally we construct a new root linked appropriately to these nodes.

Example 2. Figure 5 shows an almost-ordered RDD, where top levels x_2 and x_1 must be transposed. Figure 6 shows the matrix of cofactors $Cofac[I, I']$ generated by the algorithm. Figure 7 shows the RDD that results from hoisting.   □

function HOIST-VAR$(y, \langle x, M \rangle)$
$\quad E = \text{SORT\_NODUP}(\bigcup \{\{l, u\} \mid (\_, \langle x, M' \rangle) \in M, ([l, u), \_) \in M'\})$
$\quad \mathcal{I} = [(E[i], E[i+1]) \mid i \in 1 \ .. \ |E| - 1]$
$\quad$ **for** $(I, \langle x, M' \rangle) \in M$ **do**
$\quad\quad$ **for** $I' \in \mathcal{I}$ **do**
$\quad\quad\quad$ **let** (I^s, r') be the element in M' where $I^s \supseteq I'$
$\quad\quad\quad$ $Cofac[I, I'] \leftarrow r'$
$\quad$ **for** $I' \in \mathcal{I}$ **do**
$\quad\quad$ $r_{I'} \leftarrow \langle y, \{(I, Cofac[I, I']) \mid (I, r) \in M\} \rangle$
$\quad$ **return** $\langle x, \{(I', r_{I'}) \mid I' \in \mathcal{I}\} \rangle$

Fig. 4. Variable hoisting: How to construct a node rooted at y, representing the decision structure $\langle x, M \rangle$.

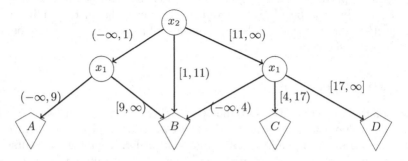

Fig. 5. A mis-ordered RDD r.

3.3   Arithmetic Operators

Gurfinkel and Chaki [11] implemented the arithmetic operators for Boxes using constraint substitution over LDDs. This has some drawbacks, relying as it does on having a theory solver for a sufficiently expressive theory of arithmetic. Instead, we construct arithmetic abstract transformers that operate directly on the RDD representations. Each transformer is formulated as a recursive traversal of the RDD, carrying with it the projection of the operation along the path to the current node. This makes implementing operators more involved, but it avoids the need for a (frequently expensive) theory solver and offers more flexibility in terms of expressiveness and the level of precision we can support. As with conventional BDD operations, we save previously computed results in a cache to avoid repeated work; nevertheless worst-case complexity of the arithmetic operators is exponential in the size of the RDD, as each path through the RDD may yield a different projected arithmetic expression.

Interval Computation. A basic step for many algorithms will be computing the interval of possible values for an expression E, given RDD r. The pseudo-code in Fig. 8 shows how to do this. We walk the RDD, substituting each variable as reached, by its possible intervals, collecting their union. Once all variables in E

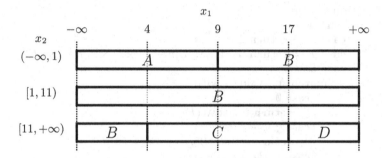

Fig. 6. Matrix of cofactors used to interchange x_1 and x_2

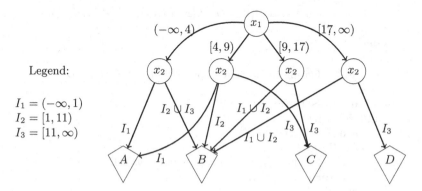

Fig. 7. The correctly ordered RDD r' after hoisting r from Fig. 5.

have been replaced by intervals, we use the function INTERVAL(E) to return the smallest interval containing the possible values of E. In the figure we use $\perp$ to denote the empty interval. MIN-VAR(E) produces the variable (from E) with the earliest precedence ($\emptyset$ if E is variable-free).

Example 3. Consider computing eval(x*y, r), the possible interval values of the expression x*y given the RDD r from Fig. 2(a). The initial call generates a call eval($[-20, -9]$*y, r') where r' is the left child of the root. This in turn generates a call eval($[-20, -9]$*$[-10, -4]$, $\mathcal{T}$) which returns $[50, 201]$. The initial call generates a second call eval($[5, 11]$*y, r'') where r'' is the right child of the root. This in turn generates a call eval($[5, 11]$*$[10, 21]$, $\mathcal{T}$) which returns $[50, 201]$. The initial call thus returns the union which is again $[50, 201]$. □

Assignments. The abstract transformers for assignments all operate in a similar manner. Let $E[y \mapsto I]$ denote the (interval-valued) expression obtained by partially evaluating E assuming $y = I$. To apply z := E to $r = \langle y, E \rangle$, we iterate over each non-$\mathcal{F}$ child (I, r') of r, recursively applying z := $E[y \mapsto I]$, and then rebuild the resulting node.

function EVAL(r, E)
  match r **with**
    case $\mathcal{F} \Rightarrow$ **return** $\perp$
    case $\mathcal{T} \Rightarrow$ **return** INTERVAL$(E[v \mapsto (-\infty, +\infty) \mid v \in \mathsf{vars}(E)])$
    case $\langle x, M \rangle \Rightarrow$
      match MIN-VAR(E) **with**
        case $\emptyset \Rightarrow$
          return INTERVAL(E)
        case y *where* $y \prec x \Rightarrow$
          return EVAL$(r, E[y \mapsto (-\infty, +\infty)])$
        case y *where* $y \succ x \Rightarrow$
          return $\bigcup\{$EVAL$(r', E) \mid (I, r') \in M, r' \neq \mathcal{F}\}$
        case $x \Rightarrow$
          return $\bigcup\{$EVAL$(r', E[x \mapsto I]) \mid (I, r') \in M, r' \neq \mathcal{F}\}$
      end
  end

Fig. 8. Evaluating the interval approximation of E on RDD r.

function EVAL-SPLIT(r, E)
  match r **with**
    case $\mathcal{F} \Rightarrow$ **return** $\mathcal{F}$
    case $\mathcal{T} \Rightarrow$
      $I \leftarrow$ INTERVAL$(E[v \mapsto (-\infty, +\infty) \mid v \in \mathsf{vars}(E))\})$
      return $\langle \epsilon, \{(I, \mathcal{T})\} \rangle$
    case $\langle x, M \rangle \Rightarrow$
      match MIN-VAR(E) **with**
        case $\emptyset \Rightarrow$
          return $(\epsilon, \{($INTERVAL$(E), r)\}))$
        case y *where* $y \prec x \Rightarrow$
          return EVAL-SPLIT$(r, E[y \mapsto (-\infty, +\infty)])$
        case y *where* $y \succeq x \Rightarrow$
          let $M' = \{(I, $ EVAL-SPLIT$(r', E[y \mapsto I])) \mid (I, r') \in M\}$
          return HOIST-VAR$(\epsilon, \langle x, M' \rangle)$
      end
  end

Fig. 9. Constructing a node, rooted at variable ϵ, encoding the possible valuations of E on RDD r. We use HOIST-VAR to percolate the valuations of E up to the root.

Once we reach (or skip) variable $\mathbf{z}$, we have two options. We can compute the interval I containing the possible values of the residual E, and apply $\mathbf{z} := I$ at the current node. Alternatively, we can construct the resulting RDD *as if* $\mathbf{z}$ were below all variables in E, then percolate $\mathbf{z}$ back up to the correct location. The latter is the analogue of the substitution-based approach used by Chaki, Gurfinkel and Strichman [3]; the former is less precise, but reduces the growth of the RDD. In practice the less precise version loses too much precision. Pseudo-code for the latter approach is shown in Fig. 9.

function APPLY(r, **z** := E)
  match r **with**
    case $\mathcal{F} \Rightarrow$ **return** $\mathcal{F}$
    case $\mathcal{T} \Rightarrow$
      $I \leftarrow$ INTERVAL($E[v \mapsto (-\infty, +\infty) \mid v \in \mathsf{vars}(E))]$)
      return $\langle \epsilon, \{(I, \mathcal{T})\} \rangle$
    case $\langle x, C \rangle \Rightarrow$
      if $x \preceq z$ **then**
        $r \leftarrow$ EVAL-SPLIT(r, E)   ▷ Constructs a node rooted at ϵ
        if $x = z$ **then**
          $r \leftarrow$ FORGET(r, x)
        return $r[\epsilon \mapsto z]$
      else
        match MIN-VAR(E) **with**
          case $\emptyset \Rightarrow$ ▷ E fully evaluated
            return $\langle z, \{(\text{INTERVAL}(E), r)\} \rangle$
          case y *where* $y \prec x \Rightarrow$ ▷ y unconstrained in r
            $E' \leftarrow E[y \mapsto (-\infty, +\infty)]$
            $C' \leftarrow \{(I, \text{APPLY}(r', z := E')) \mid (I, r') \in C\}$
          case y *where* $y \succ x \Rightarrow$ ▷ E independent of x
            $C' \leftarrow \{(I, \text{APPLY}(r', z := E)) \mid (I, r') \in C\}$
          case $x \Rightarrow$
            $C' \leftarrow \{(I, \text{APPLY}(r', z := E[y \mapsto I])) \mid (I, r') \in C\}$
        end
        return $\langle x, C' \rangle$
  end

Fig. 10. Abstract version of **z** := E given RDD r, for some arithmetic expression E.

The algorithm in Fig. 10 is instantiated for the cases where E is a linear expression ($\sum_i c_i x_i + I$), n-ary product ($\prod_i x_i \times I$) or (binary) division (x/y). In each case, we specialize the generic algorithm slightly:

- For linear expressions, we terminate if some variable in E is skipped (in which case E, and therefore **z**, is unconstrained).
- For products, we handle negative, zero, and positive ranges separately, and apply early termination when some variable is zero or unbounded.
- For division, we again perform case-splits on sign, and terminate early on zero and unbounded inputs.

Example 4. Consider the RDD in Fig. 11(a). APPLY(r, **z** := **E**) constructs the RDD shown in Fig. 11(b). For x_2 the split points are the extreme values of $3x_1 + 8x_3 + 10$, along the possible paths, that is, 77, 93, 113, and 241; hence the x_2 fan-out of three. In general, for each path ρ of r, APPLY(r, **z** := **E**) constructs an all-paths interval consistent RDD, introducing an edge for **z** that is tight with respect to the projection of E along ρ. For linear expressions, APPLY constructs the smallest such RDD (though not for multiplication and division, owing to our speculative splits on sign).   □

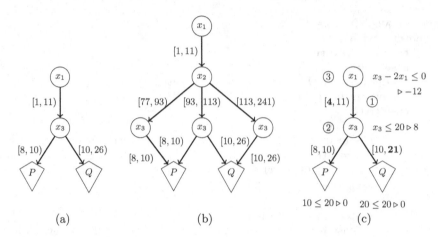

Fig. 11. With full splitting, evaluating $x_2 := 3x_1 + 8x_3 + 10$ on (a) yields (b). Applying $x_3 - 2x_1 \leq 0$ on (a) yields (c), with tightened bounds shown in bold: ① the downwards phase finds upper bound 20 for x_3; ② the upwards phase notes the lower bound 8 and ③ uses this information ($2x_1 \geq 8$) to improve the lower bound on x_1.

Arithmetic Constraints. The abstract transformer for an arithmetic constraint apply$(r, E \leq k)$ is very similar to that for assignment. Again we traverse the RDD depth-first, passing the projection of our constraint onto the current valuation, then reconstruct the result on the way back up. But during reconstruction, we also return the projection of E onto the variable *beneath* the current node which we use to perform bounds-propagation on edge ranges. The pseudo-code is given in Fig. 12. Each call returns the resulting RDD, together with an upper bound to be applied to the RDD above. At each node involved in the expression (lines 33–36), we recursively apply the projected constraint along each outgoing edge, and use the returned upper bound to prune the bounds of the edge.

Example 5. Figure 11(c) shows the effect of applying $x_3 - 2x_1 \leq 0$ to the RDD from Fig. 11(a). Each node is annotated with $C \rhd \ell$, where C is the projected constraint we constructed in the downward phase, and ℓ the lower-bound which was returned upwards.   □

Unlike assignment, APPLY$(r, E \leq k)$ does not in general yield an all-paths interval consistent RDD—it (implicitly) introduces splits on the way down, but TRIM-LEQ only uses the returned lower bound on E for pruning, rather than introducing new splits. A slightly more precise RDD for the case considered in Example 5 would have an additional split point for x_1, namely 5. That would bar some spurious solutions, such as $Q \wedge x_1 = 4 \wedge x_3 = 13$. An algorithm that maintains all-paths interval consistency also in the case of inequalities is perfectly possible, but in practice we find the cost of doing so outweighs any advantage.

Bounds Extraction/Box Hull. The *box hull* operation takes boxes $\mathcal{B}$ and produces a *stick* mapping each variable to the smallest interval covering its feasible

```
 1: function TRIM-LEQ(cx + E ≤ k, I, r)
 2:     u_r, r' ← APPLY(r, E ≤ k − c min(I))
 3:     I_r ← I ∩ (−∞, u_r/c)
 4:     if I_r = ∅ then
 5:         return ∞, (∅, F)
 6:     else
 7:         return l_r − c min(I), (I_r, r')
 8: function APPLY(r, E ≤ k)
 9:     match r, E with
10:         case F, _ ⇒ return ∞, F
11:         case _, 0 ⇒                          ▷ E fully evaluated
12:             if k < 0 then
13:                 return ∞, F
14:             else
15:                 return 0, r
16:         case T, ax ⇒              ▷ One unconstrained variable, can be bounded
17:             return −∞, ⟨x, {((−∞, k/a), r)}⟩
18:         case T, ax + E ⇒     ▷ At least two unconstrained, cannot infer anything
19:             return −∞, T
20:         case ⟨x, M⟩, ay + E' where y ≺ x ⇒      ▷ y currently unconstrained in r,
21:                                                  ▷ check if E' is bounded
22:             I_{E'} ← EVAL(r, E')
23:             y_{ub} ← ⌈(k − min I_{E'})/a⌉
24:             if y_{ub} is finite then
25:                 return −∞, ⟨y, {((−∞, y_{ub}), r)}⟩
26:             else
27:                 return −∞, r
28:         case ⟨x, M⟩, ay + E' where y ≻ x ⇒              ▷ E independent of x
29:             R ← {l_c, (I, c') | (I, c) ∈ M and l_c, c' = APPLY(c, E ≤ k)}
30:             l_r ← min{l_c | _, (l_c, _) ∈ R}
31:             r' ← ⟨x, {(I, c') | _, (I, c') ∈ R}⟩
32:             return l_r, r'
33:         case ⟨x, M⟩, ax + E' ⇒
34:             R ← {TRIM-LEQ(ax + E ≤ k, I, r') | (I, r') ∈ M}
35:             l_c ← min{l_c | l_c, _ ∈ R}
36:             return l_c, ⟨x, {(I_c, c') | _, (I_c, c') ∈ R}⟩
37: end
```

Fig. 12. Applying a constraint $\sum_i c_i x_i \leq k$ on RDD r. For simplicity, we restrict consideration to positive c_i.

valuations. The box hull algorithm of Gurfinkel and Chaki [11] proceeds by merging all feasible children of the root node (using $\sqcup$), then recursively building the hull of the single remaining child. However, while the final result is compact, the successive joins may cause an exponential growth in the intermediate results. Instead, we construct the box hull in two stages: we first traverse the RDD to collect lower and upper bounds of each variable, then construct the hull RDD directly.

function LOWER-BOUNDS($\langle x, M \rangle$)
  let $[d_0, k_1, \ldots, k_n, d_n] = \mathbf{ser}(M)$
  $i_0 \leftarrow$ **if** $(d_0 = \mathcal{F})$ **then** 1 **else** 0
  $B \leftarrow$ LOWER-BOUNDS(d_{i_0})
  for $i \in i_0 + 1 \ldots n$ **do**
    if $d_i \neq \mathcal{F}$ **then**
      $B \leftarrow$ LOWER-BOUNDS-R(d_i, B)
  $seen(\langle x, M \rangle) \leftarrow true$
  if $d_0 = \mathcal{F}$ **then**
    return $[(x, k_1)|B]$
  else
    return B

function LOWER-BOUNDS-R($\langle r, M \rangle, B$)
  let $[d_0, k_1, \ldots, k_n, d_n] = \mathbf{ser}(M)$
  match B **with**
    case $[] \Rightarrow$
      return $[]$
    case $[(x', k')|B']$ *where* $x \succ x' \Rightarrow$
      return LOWER-BOUNDS-R($\langle x, M \rangle, B'$)
    case $[(x', k')|B'] \Rightarrow$
      if $seen(\langle x, M \rangle)$ **then**
        return $[(x', k')|B']$
      $seen(\langle x, M \rangle) \leftarrow true$
      for $i \in 0 \ldots n$ **do**
        if $d_i \neq \mathcal{F}$ **then**
          $B' \leftarrow$ LOWER-BOUNDS-R(d_i, B')
      if $x = x' \wedge d_0 = \mathcal{F}$ **then**
        return $[(x', \min(k', k_1))|B']$
      else
        return B'
  end

Fig. 13. Extracting lower bounds of all variables from RDD $\langle x, M \rangle$. Upper bound extraction is similar. The *seen* markers are used to avoid re-processing a previously explored node.

The algorithm for extracting bounds is given in Fig. 13. On the leftmost feasible path in r, it constructs an ordered list of variables having finite lower bounds. On the remaining paths, it updates the current set of bounds, removing any variables that are skipped or are unbounded. This operation takes time linear in the size of the input RDD. Unfortunately, the operation is not cached across calls (as we update bounds information in-place, rather than merge bounds from subgraphs).

3.4 Widening

The last operator we need is a widening, ∇, to ensure convergence. A standard approach to constructing a sound widening is based on the notion of *stability*: we decompose the domain into a finite set of individual properties, and any *unstable* properties—those which are not preserved (under entailment) from the previous iteration—are weakened (usually discarded) to eliminate infinite ascending chains.

If we were working with pure BDDs or classical MDDs (with finite domains), the join would be sufficient, as there are only finitely many cofactors, and each cofactor can increase at most once. But with RDDs, a difficulty arises when the *position* of a split changes.

Example 6. Consider the following sequence of iterates:

$$r_0 \equiv \langle x, \{((-\infty, 0), \mathcal{T}), \ ([0, +\infty), \mathcal{F})\}\rangle$$
$$r_1 \equiv \langle x, \{((-\infty, 1), \mathcal{T}), \ ([1, +\infty), \mathcal{F})\}\rangle$$
$$r_i \equiv \langle x, \{((-\infty, i), \mathcal{T}), \ ([i, +\infty), \mathcal{F})\}\rangle$$

If we apply a 'widening' pointwise, we get the chain:

$$w_0 = r_0 \equiv \langle x, \{((-\infty, 0), \mathcal{T}), \ ([0, +\infty), \mathcal{F})\}\rangle$$
$$w_1 = w_0 \triangledown r_1 \equiv \langle x, \{((-\infty, 0), \mathcal{T}), \ ([0, 1), \mathcal{T}\triangledown\mathcal{F}), \ ([1, +\infty), \mathcal{F})\}\rangle = r_1$$
$$w_2 = w_1 \triangledown r_2 \equiv \langle x, \{((-\infty, 1), \mathcal{T}), \ ([1, 2), \mathcal{T}\triangledown\mathcal{F}), \ ([2, +\infty), \mathcal{F})\}\rangle = r_2$$
$$w_i = w_{i-1} \triangledown r_i \equiv \langle x, \{((-\infty, i-1), \mathcal{T}), \ ([i-1, i), \mathcal{T}\triangledown\mathcal{F}), \ ([i, +\infty), \mathcal{F})\}\rangle = r_i$$

Looking at the result for any one fixed value of x, there are no infinite chains. But the overall widening sequence is nevertheless an infinite ascending chain. □

The problem just exemplified arises when the *target* of a child remains stable, but its *range* shrinks. The widening of Gurfinkel and Chaki [11] handles the situation by detecting when this has occurred, and instead taking the value of (one of) its unstable siblings. For Example 6, we notice that the transition to $\mathcal{F}$ was unchanged but its range decreased, so we take the neighbouring $\mathcal{T}$ value instead.

We can adapt the same widening strategy for the RDD representation. Figure 14 gives the detailed widening algorithm; WIDEN(u, v) is the function that calculates $u \triangledown v$. As with other lattice operations, we walk over both operands in lock-step. But as $\triangledown$ is asymmetric, the main case of WIDEN(u, v) (lines 34–39) iterates over the edges of u, and, for each edge, calls WIDEN-EDGE to compute the (possibly refined) widening of the corresponding ranges of v. WIDEN-EDGE walks over the edges of v applying widening pointwise (lines 12–19), substituting stable children with their left unstable sibling (line 16). The *first* edge of course has no such sibling, so the algorithm starts (lines 5–8) by finding the first unstable successor if one exists (if not, the entire edge was stable, so it can be returned)[5].

The argument for termination of the widening algorithm is the following.

1. The operator is increasing by construction.
2. Note that (a) it is not possible to have an infinite ascending chain of refined split positions and (b) for any one (fixed) split position there is no infinite ascending chain. Namely, each co-factor leads to a finite ascending chain: whenever a new split location is introduced, the co-factors on both sides increase strictly.

---

[5] As presented, this differs slightly from [11] in that we select the *left* sibling as replacement in WIDEN-EDGE, where [11] selects the right. We also implemented a right-biased variant, and differences are minimal.

```
 1: function WIDEN-EDGE(x, M_x, [y_0, k_1, ..., k_m, y_m])
 2:     d_y ← y_0
 3:     i ← 1
 4:     d ← x∇d_y
 5:     while d = x ∧ i ≤ m ∧ k_i < M_x do                    ▷ Find first unstable child d
 6:         d_y ← y_i
 7:         i ← i + 1
 8:         d ← x∇d_y
 9:     if i > m ∨ k_m ≥ M_x then                             ▷ Only one child, no subdivision
10:         return [d], [d_y, k_i, y_i, ..., k_m, y_m]
11:     E_out ← [d]              ▷ Replace any stable children with d to ensure convergence
12:     while i ≤ m ∧ k_m < M_x do
13:         d_y ← y_i
14:         d' ← x∇d_y
15:         if d' = x then
16:             d' ← d
17:         E_out ← E_out ++ [k_i, d']
18:         d ← d'
19:         i ← i + 1
20:     return (E_out, [d_y, k_i, y_i, ..., k_m, y_m])
21: function WIDEN(u, v)
22:     match (u, v) with
23:         case (T, _) ⇒ return T
24:         case (F, v) ⇒ return v
25:         case (⟨x, M⟩, v) ⇒
26:             let [r_0, k_1, r_1, ..., k_n, r_n] = ser(M)
27:             let ⟨x', E_v⟩ = v
28:             if x ≺ x' then
29:                 return ⟨x, [r_0∇v, k_1, r_1∇v, ..., k_n, r_n∇v]⟩
30:             else if x' ≺ x then
31:                 (E_out, _) ← WIDEN-EDGE(u, +∞, ser(E_v))
32:                 return ⟨x', des(E_out)⟩
33:             else
34:                 E_out ← []
35:                 for i ∈ 1 ... n do
36:                     (E'_i, E_v) ← WIDEN-EDGE(r_{i-1}, k_i, ser(E_v))
37:                     E_out ← E_out ++ E'_i
38:                 (E_n, _) ← WIDEN-EDGE(r_n, +∞, ser(E_v))
39:                 return ⟨x, des(E_out ++ E_n)⟩
40:     end
```

Fig. 14. Widening on Boxes, adapted to the RDD representation.

4   Experimental Evaluation

We have implemented all the RDD operations required by the Boxes domain, following the algorithms described in this paper. Apart from the node representation, the architecture of the underlying RDD package is relatively standard: a unique table mapping node structures to canonical representations, and a cache to record the results of recent computations. The implementation is available at https://bitbucket.org/gkgange/mdd-boxes.

The evaluation that we now report on has had two aims: First, to compare scalability of rdd-boxes with the existing ldd-boxes implementation. Second, to compare precision of the two implementations in order to assess the impact of the more precise abstract transformers provided by rdd-boxes.

4.1   Experimental Setup

For the evaluation, we integrated our RDD-based implementation of Boxes into the Crab[6] abstract interpreter, which already provides LDD-based Boxes. We evaluated both implementations on a collection of C programs using Clam[7], an LLVM frontend for Crab.

The programs used for testing were taken from the 2019 Software Verification Competition. We chose 190 programs from the ControlFlow and Loops categories. These programs are already annotated with assertions. ControlFlow is a challenging set of programs for abstract interpretation because the instances generally require path-sensitive reasoning. However, they do not require a deep memory analysis. They constitute a good test suite for Boxes because this abstract domain is expressive enough to prove the majority of assertions. Nevertheless, both rdd-boxes and ldd-boxes needed to use a widening delay of 15 to produce precise results. The second selected category, Loops, is quite different from ControlFlow: the programs are much smaller and neither memory analysis nor path sensitivity is required. However, the majority of programs have many nested loops or require complex (although typically linear) loop invariants. We used Loops to evaluate the effect of the widening operations in both implementations.

All experiments have been carried out on a 2.1 GHz AMD Opteron processor 6172 with 32 cores and 64 GB on a Ubuntu 18.04 Linux machine. From those 32 cores, we used 16 cores to run multiple instances of Crab in parallel, but each instance was executed sequentially.

For rdd-boxes, we statically order variables according to the order in which they first appear in the program. For ldd-boxes, we used two orderings: the same static ordering used by rdd-boxes, and the dynamic ordering used by Gurfinkel and Chaki [11], based on the Cudd library's CUDD_REORDER_GROUP_SIFT option.

It is important to note that the ldd-boxes library[8] does not provide support for arbitrary linear or tree expressions as other libraries such as Apron [14] do. ldd-boxes only supports assignments of the form $x \leftarrow (k_1 \times y) + [k_2, k_3]$ and linear constraints of the form $(k_1 \times x)$ relop k_2 where k_1, k_2, k_3 are integers, relop are the standard relational operators $\{\leq, \geq, <, >, =, \neq\}$, and x and y are variables.

---

[6] Available at https://github.com/seahorn/crab.

[7] Available at https://github.com/seahorn/clam.

[8] Available at https://github.com/seahorn/ldd.

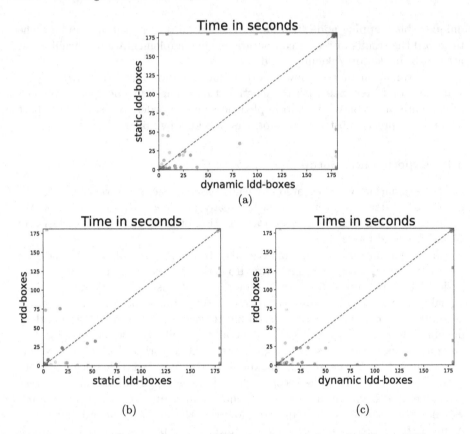

Fig. 15. Three graphs to compare analysis time in seconds on 190 Control Flow and Loops programs with timeout of 180 s and memory limit of 8 GB. The marker ● represents domains finished before exhausting resources, ✖ represents timeout, and ◆ memory-out. The size of a marker reflects the number of scatter points at that location.

For all other cases, the abstract interpreter Crab simplifies arbitrary expressions by extracting interval constraints until the simplified expression can be supported by the ldd-boxes library. The current Crab implementation safely ignores arithmetic operations with non-unit coefficients. For our benchmarks, LLVM did not generate any instruction with non-unit coefficients.

4.2 Performance

Figure 15 compares efficiency of the three implementations on the set of SV-COMP benchmarks. The top part (a) shows the result of static ordering plotted against that of dynamic ordering for ldd-boxes. Different orderings can have a significant impact on performance, and there is no clear winner. In the bottom part, we compare rdd-boxes with ldd-boxes using static (b) and dynamic (c)

Table 1. Comparing the precision of LDD-boxes with static ordering, LDD-boxes with dynamic reordering, and two variants of RDD-boxes on SV-COMP programs for which all the domains terminated with timeout of 180 s and memory limit of 8 GB.

Implementation	Programs	Total assertions	Proven assertions
static `ldd-boxes`	168	628	497
dynamic `ldd-boxes`	168	628	494
linear `rdd-boxes`	168	628	504
`rdd-boxes`	168	628	510

ordering. Independently of variable ordering, the `rdd-boxes` analysis tends to be faster. With a time limit of 180 s, `rdd-boxes` timed out for 7 programs, while static and dynamic `ldd-boxes` timed out for 13 and 12 programs, respectively.

To understand the causes of the performance differences, we manually inspected several programs. We hypothesize that the main reason why `ldd-boxes` and `rdd-boxes` differ significantly in performance is the above-mentioned process of interval extraction that takes place in the Crab analyzer. This interval extraction for `ldd-boxes` is quite expensive, which sometimes makes `rdd-boxes` significantly faster. On the other hand, it may equally make `rdd-boxes` slower since `rdd-boxes` performs optimal transfer functions (which may introduce more disjunctive splits), while `ldd-boxes` does not, owing to its limited API.

4.3 Precision

Table 1 compares the precision of the two `ldd-boxes` implementations, together with two variants of `rdd-boxes` for the SV-COMP test suite: the version used for our performance evaluation which precisely supports both linear and non-linear operations, and a variant that only supports linear operations (linear `rdd-boxes`) and relies on the Crab analyzer to *linearize* [22] non-linear expressions.

Column Programs is the total number of programs for which all three implementations finished without exhausting resources. Total Assertions is the total number of assertions checked by the analysis, and Proven Assertions is the total number of proven assertions.

The variable ordering can affect the precision of widening. We believe this can explain the differences between the `ldd-boxes` implementations and linear `rdd-boxes`. Note that linear `rdd-boxes` is more precise than the `ldd-boxes` implementations, because of a more precise modelling of linear operations. The precise modelling of non-linear operations in `rdd-boxes` further improves the number of proven assertions (510 vs 504)—a relatively small, but, to an end user potentially significant, gain.

As a baseline comparison, using a traditional convex interval analysis, we were able to prove 392 of the 628 assertions, that is, 62%. Disjunctive information is, as expected, critical in the context of program verification.

5   Related Work

Early examples of disjunctive analysis were primarily found in work on abstract interpretation of *declarative* programming languages [15,17] (the "Pos" domain for groundness dependency analysis of logic programs [17] is a rare example of an abstract domain for *relational* analysis that is closed under conjunction *and* disjunction). The abstract domain refinement known as "disjunctive completion" was introduced by Cousot and Cousot [5]. Giacobazzi and Ranzato [9] explored the fact that different domain "bases" may induce identical disjunctive completions, leading to the concept of a least (or most abstract) disjunctive basis [9].

Decision diagrams for disjunctive domains are of interest also in symbolic model checking, for example for analysis of timed automata. In that context, Strehl and Thiele [25] have made use of "function graphs" which, in their "reduced" form, correspond to RDDs. Strehl and Thiele capture transition relations through an additional concept of "interval mapping functions". Implementation details are somewhat sparse, but it appears that only simple (linear) transformations are considered. Join and widening are not of relevance in model checking applications.

Clock decision diagrams (CDDs) [16] generalise Strehl and Thiele's function graphs, by allowing nodes that represent either single (clock) variables X or *differences* $X - Y$. That way, not only bounds can be expressed; it is possible to use CDDs to express difference constraints such as $X = Y$ and $X - Z \in [0, 3]$, so that CDDs support a limited form of *relational* analysis. CDDs are not canonical, and the abstract operations that would be required for program analysis (as opposed to the clock operations considered in [16]) would seem quite difficult to implement. For a program analysis tool to achieve the added expressiveness that is offered by CDDs, it would probably make better sense to use a product domain that incorporates a standard implementation of Zones [20]. Other BDD variants have been proposed that have constraints as nodes, such as difference decision diagrams (DDDs) [23] and EQ-BDDs [10].

Dominant sources of imprecision in classical abstract interpretation are *join points*—program points that represent a confluence of flow from several points. If an analysis is able to distinguish program states based on different execution traces that lead to a given program point, then imprecise joins can be avoided or delayed, resulting in greater precision of analysis. Approaches to introduction of such (limited) disjunctive information include loop unrolling and (flow- or value-based) trace partitioning [12,19]. The idea that decision tree structures can represent control flow is reflected in various abstract domains or functors, based on decision diagrams. Examples include the "segmented decision trees" [6] designed to support analysis of array processing programs, and the decision structures used in the FuncTion analyzer [26] for proving termination based on synthesised ranking functions. Jeannet's BDDAPRON library [13] provides a broad framework for the implementation of "logico-numeric" abstract domains, supporting analysis of programs with a mixture of finite-type and numeric variables.

Regarding interval analysis, the DisInterval abstract domain used in the Clousot analysis tool [8] allows for a limited amount of disjunctive information; while it can express monadic constraints such as $|x| > 5$, it cannot express a set such as the one depicted in Fig. 1(b). For fully disjunctive interval analysis, the most important data structure so far has been the linear decision diagram (LDD), introduced by Chaki, Gurfinkel and Strichman [3]. The Crab implementation of Boxes that we use as a baseline corresponds to the proposal by Gurfinkel and Chaki [11], that is, it uses a restricted form of LDDs, in which nodes can only be bounds constraints.

For program analysis, Typed Decisions Graphs [18] give an alternate, more concise representation of BDDs. They might be usable as a direct replacement for LDDs, but how to extend them to handle RDDs is far from obvious since they rely on representing a Boolean function to get good compression (by negating arcs).

6   Conclusion

We have demonstrated the importance of well-chosen data structures for disjunctive interval analysis. Our focus has been on the case of variables with integer types, but an extension to rationals or floating point numbers is not difficult (the main added complication is the need to identify split points as left- or right-included, that is, to distinguish whether a range bound is included or not).

For simplicity, we have also assumed the use of integers of unlimited precision. It would not be difficult to adapt the algorithms to the case of fixed-width integers, as the RDD representation is agnostic about the underlying representation of intervals.

The use of a dedicated data structure (RDDs) for interval sets has led us to a disjunctive interval analysis that is more efficient than the current LDD-based alternative. The use of RDDs offers a more precise analysis of non-linear arithmetic expressions, and it frees us from any dependence on a theory solver. These advantages explain why we see gains in both precision and speed.

A next natural step is to explore the combination of Boxes with weakly relational abstract domains. We hypothesize that, in practice, this provides an avenue to obtain considerably greater expressiveness while still keeping analysis tractable. For example, a product that includes the Zones abstract domain should produce an efficient program analysis with the expressiveness of clock decision diagrams [16].

Acknowledgements. We thank the three anonymous reviewers for their careful reading of an earlier version of the paper, and their constructive suggestions for how to improve it. Jorge Navas has been supported by the National Science Foundation under grant number 1816936.

References

1. Apt, K.: Principles of Constraint Programming, Cambridge University Press, Cambridge (2003). https://doi.org/10.1017/CBO9780511615320

2. Bryant, R.: Symbolic Boolean manipulation with ordered binary-decision diagrams. ACM Comput. Surv. **24**(3), 293–318 (1992). https://doi.org/10.1145/136035.136043

3. Chaki, S., Gurfinkel, A., Strichman, O.: Decision diagrams for linear arithmetic. In: Proceedings of the 9th Conference on Formal Methods in Computer-Aided Design (FMCAD 2009), pp. 53–60. IEEE Comp. Soc. (2009). https://doi.org/10.1109/FMCAD.2009.5351143

4. Choi, C.W., Harvey, W., Lee, J.H.M., Stuckey, P.J.: Finite domain bounds consistency revisited. In: Proceedings of the Australian Conference on Artificial Intelligence 2006. LNCS, vol. 4304, pp. 49–58. Springer (2006). https://doi.org/10.1007/11941439_9

5. Cousot, P., Cousot, R.: Systematic design of program analysis frameworks. In: Proceedings of the Sixth ACM Symposium on Principles of Programming Languages, pp. 269–282. ACM Press (1979). https://doi.org/10.1145/567752.567778

6. Cousot, P., Cousot, R., Mauborgne, L.: A scalable segmented decision tree abstract domain. In: Manna, Z., Peled, D.A. (eds.) Time for Verification: Essays in Memory of Amir Pnueli, LNCS, vol. 6200, pp. 72–95. Springer (2010). https://doi.org/10.1007/978-3-642-13754-9_5

7. Cousot, P., Halbwachs, N.: Automatic discovery of linear restraints among variables of a program. In: Proceedings of the Fifth ACM Symposium on Principles of Programming Languages, pp. 84–97. ACM Press (1978). https://doi.org/10.1145/512760.512770

8. Fähndrich, M., Logozzo, F.: Static contract checking with abstract interpretation. In: Beckert, B., Marché, C. (eds.) Formal Verification of Object-Oriented Software. LNCS, vol. 6528, pp. 10–30. Springer (2011). https://doi.org/10.1007/978-3-642-18070-5_2

9. Giacobazzi, R., Ranzato, F.: Optimal domains for disjunctive abstract interpretation. Sci. Comput. Prog. **32**, 177–210 (1998). https://doi.org/10.1016/S0167-6423(97)00034-8

10. Groote, J.F., van de Pol, J.: Equational binary decision diagrams. In: Parigot, M., Voronkov, A. (eds.) Logic for Programming and Automated Reasoning, LNCS, vol. 1955, pp. 161–178. Springer (2000). https://doi.org/10.1007/3-540-44404-1_11

11. Gurfinkel, A., Chaki, S.: Boxes: A symbolic abstract domain of boxes. In: Cousot, R., Martel, M. (eds.) Static Analysis: Proceedings of the 17th International Symposium, LNCS, vol. 6337, pp. 287–303. Springer (2010). https://doi.org/10.1007/978-3-642-15769-1_18

12. Handjieva, M., Tzolovski, S.: Refining static analyses by trace-based partitioning using control flow. In: Levi, G. (ed.) Static Analysis, LNCS, vol. 1503, pp. 200–214. Springer (1998). https://doi.org/10.1007/3-540-49727-7_12

13. Jeannet, B.: The BddApron logico-numerical abstract domains library (2009). http://www.inrialpes.fr/pop-art/people/bjeannet/bjeannet-forge/bddapron/

14. Jeannet, B., Miné, A.: A library of numerical abstract domains for static analysis. In: Bouajjani, A., Maler, O. (eds.) Computer Aided Verification, LNCS, vol. 5643, pp. 661–667. Springer (2009). https://doi.org/10.1007/978-3-642-02658-4_52

15. Jensen, T.P.: Disjunctive strictness analysis. In: Proceedings of the 7th Annual IEEE Symposium of Logic in Computer Science, pp. 174–185. IEEE Computer Society (1992). https://doi.org/10.1109/LICS.1992.185531

16. Larsen, K.G., Pearson, J., Weise, C., Yi, W.: Clock difference diagrams. Nordic J. Comput. **6**(3), 271–298 (1999)

17. Marriott, K., Søndergaard, H.: Precise and efficient groundless analysis for logic programs. ACM Lett. Prog. Lang. Syst. **2**(1–4), 181–196 (1993). https://doi.org/10.1145/176454.176519

18. Mauborgne, L.: Abstract interpretation using typed decision graphs. Sci. Comput. Prog. **31**(1), 91–112 (1998). https://doi.org/10.1016/s0167-6423(96)00042-1

19. Mauborgne, L., Rival, X.: Trace partitioning in abstract interpretation based static analyzers. In: Sagiv, M. (ed.) Programming Languages and Systems: Proceedings of the 14th European Symposium, LNCS, vol. 3444, pp. 5–20. Springer (2005). https://doi.org/10.1007/978-3-540-31987-0_2

20. Miné, A.: A new numerical abstract domain based on difference-bound matrices. In: Danvy, O., Filinski, A. (eds.) Programs as Data Objects, LNCS, vol. 2053, pp. 155–172. Springer (2001). https://doi.org/10.1007/3-540-44978-7_10

21. Miné, A.: The Octagon abstract domain. In: Burd, E., Aiken, P., Koschke, R. (eds.) Proceedings of the Eighth Working Conference on Reverse Engineering, pp. 310–319. IEEE Computer Society (2001). https://doi.org/10.1109/WCRE.2001.957836

22. Miné, A.: Symbolic methods to enhance the precision of numerical abstract domains. In: Emerson, E.A., Namjoshi, K.S. (eds.) Verification, Model Checking, and Abstract Interpretation, LNCS, vol. 3855, pp. 348–363. Springer (2006). https://doi.org/10.1007/11609773_23

23. Møller, J., Lichtenberg, J., Andersen, H.R., Hulgaard, H.: Difference decision diagrams. In: Flum, J., Rodriguez-Artalejo, M. (eds.) Computer Science Logic, LNCS, vol. 1683, pp. 111–125. Springer (1999). https://doi.org/10.1007/3-540-48168-0_9

24. Srinivasan, A., Kam, T., Malik, S., Brayton, R.K.: Algorithms for discrete function manipulation. In: Computer-Aided Design: Proceedings of the IEEE International Conference, pp. 92–95. IEEE Computer Society (1990). https://doi.org/10.1109/ICCAD.1990.129849

25. Strehl, K., Thiele, L.: Symbolic model checking of process networks using interval diagram techniques. In: International Conference on Computer-Aided Design, pp. 686–692. ACM Press (1998). https://doi.org/10.1145/288548.289117

26. Urban, C., Miné, A.: A decision tree abstract domain for proving conditional termination. In: Müller-Olm, M., Seidl, H. (eds.) Static Analysis, LNCS, vol. 8723, pp. 302–318. Springer (2014). https://doi.org/10.1007/978-3-319-10936-7_19

Static Analysis of ReLU Neural Networks with Tropical Polyhedra

Eric Goubault[1], Sébastien Palumby[1], Sylvie Putot[1], Louis Rustenholz[1],
and Sriram Sankaranarayanan[2(✉)]

[1] LIX, Ecole Polytechnique, CNRS and Institut Polytechnique de Paris,
91128 Palaiseau, France
{eric.goubault,sebastien.palumby,sylvie.putot,
louis.rustenholz}@polytechnique.edu
[2] Engineering Center Computer Science, University of Colorado at Boulder,
Boulder, USA
sriram.sankaranarayanan@colorado.edu

Abstract. This paper studies the problem of range analysis for feedforward neural networks, which is a basic primitive for applications such as robustness of neural networks, compliance to specifications and reachability analysis of neural-network feedback systems. Our approach focuses on ReLU (rectified linear unit) feedforward neural nets that present specific difficulties: approaches that exploit derivatives do not apply in general, the number of patterns of neuron activations can be quite large even for small networks, and convex approximations are generally too coarse. In this paper, we employ set-based methods and abstract interpretation that have been very successful in coping with similar difficulties in classical program verification. We present an approach that abstracts ReLU feedforward neural networks using tropical polyhedra. We show that tropical polyhedra can efficiently abstract ReLU activation function, while being able to control the loss of precision due to linear computations. We show how the connection between ReLU networks and tropical rational functions can provide approaches for range analysis of ReLU neural networks. We report on a preliminary evaluation of our approach using a prototype implementation.

1 Introduction and Related Work

Neural networks are now widely used in numerous applications including speech recognition, natural language processing, image segmentation, control and planning for autonomous systems. A central question is how to verify that they

E. Goubault—Supported in part by the academic Chair "Engineering of Complex Systems", Thalès-Dassault Aviation-Naval Group-DGA-Ecole Polytechnique-ENSTA Paris-Télécom Paris, and AID project "Drone validation and swarms of drones".
S. Sankaranarayanan—Supported by US National Science Foundation (NSF) award # 1932189. All opinions expressed are those of the authors and not necessarily of the sponsors.

© Springer Nature Switzerland AG 2021
C. Drăgoi et al. (Eds.): SAS 2021, LNCS 12913, pp. 166–190, 2021.
https://doi.org/10.1007/978-3-030-88806-0_8

are correct with respect to some specification. Beyond correctness, we are also interested in questions such as explainability and fairness, that can in turn be specified as formal verification problems. Recently, the problem of verifying properties of neural networks has been investigated extensively under a variety of contexts. A natural neural network analysis problem is that of *range estimation*, i.e. bounding the values of neurons on the output layer, or some function of the output neurons, given the range of neurons on the input layer. A prototypical application of range estimation is the verification of the ACAS Xu - the next generation collision avoidance system for autonomous aircrafts, which is implemented by a set of neural networks [23]. Such a verification problem is translated into a range estimation problem over these neural network wherein the input ranges concern a set of possible scenarios and the outputs indicate the possible set of advisories provided by the network [24].

Another prototypical application concerns the robustness of image classification wherein we wish to analyze whether a classification label remains constant for images in a neighborhood of a given image that is often specified using ranges over a set of pixels. Robustness is akin to numerical stability analysis, and for neural nets used as decision procedures (e.g. control of a physical apparatus), this is a form of decision consistency. It is also linked to the existence or non-existence of adversarial inputs, i.e. those inputs close to a well classified input data, that dramatically change the classification [38], and may have dire consequences in the real world [16].

Many formal methods approaches that have been successfully used in the context of program verification seem to be successfully leveraged to the case of neural net verification: proof-theoretic approaches, SMT techniques, constraint based analyzers and abstract interpretation. In this paper, we are interested in developing abstract interpretation [10] techniques for feedforward networks with ReLU activation functions. ReLU feedforward networks can be seen as loop-free programs with affine assignments and conditionals with affine guards, deciding whether the corresponding neuron is activated or not. For researchers in program analysis by abstract interpretation, this is a well known situation. The solutions range from designing a scalable but imprecise analyses by convexifications of the set of possible values of each neurons throughout all layers to designing a potentially exponentially complex analysis by performing a fully disjunctive analysis. In between, some heuristics have been successfully used in program analysis, that may alleviate the burden of disjunctive analysis, see e.g. [9,28]. Among classical convex abstractions, the zones [29] are a nice and scalable abstraction, successfully used in fully-fledged abstract interpretation based static analyzers [7]. In terms of disjunctive analysis, a compact way to represent a large class of disjunctions of zones are the tropical polyhedra, used for disjunctive program analysis in e.g. [3,4]. Tropical polyhedra are, similarly to classical convex polyhedra, defined by sets of affine inequalities but where the sum is replaced by max operator and the multiplication is replaced by the addition.

Zones are interesting for synthesizing properties such as robustness of neural networks used for classifying data. Indeed, classification relies on determining which output neuron has the greatest score, translating immediately into zone-like constraints. ReLU functions $x \mapsto max(0, x)$ are tropically linear, hence an abstraction using tropical polyhedra will be exact. A direct verification of classification specifications can be done from a tropical polyhedron by computing the enclosing zone, see [4] and Sect. 2.1. In Fig. 1, we pictured the graph of the ReLU function $y = max(x, 0)$ for $x \in [-1, 1]$ (Fig. 1a), and its abstraction by 1-ReLU in DeepPoly [36] (Fig. 1b), by a zone (Fig. 1c), and by a tropical polyhedron (Fig. 1d), which is exactly the graph of the function.

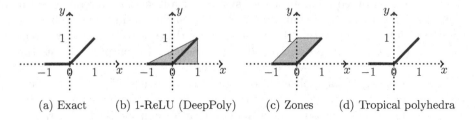

(a) Exact   (b) 1-ReLU (DeepPoly)   (c) Zones   (d) Tropical polyhedra

Fig. 1. Abstractions of the ReLU graph on $[-1, 1]$

Unfortunately, (classical) linear functions are tropically non-linear. But contrarily to program analysis where we generally discover the function to abstract inductively on the syntax, we are here given the weights and biases for the full network, allowing us to design much better abstractions than if directly using the ones available from the program verification literature.

It was recently proved [42] that the class of functions computed by a feed-forward neural network with ReLU activation functions is exactly the class of rational tropical maps, at least when dealing with rational weights and biases. It is thus natural to look for guaranteed approximants of these rational tropical maps as abstractions.

Example 1 (Running example). Consider a neural network with 2 inputs x_1 and x_2 given in $[-1, 1]$ and 2 outputs. The linear layer is defined by $h_1 = x_1 - x_2 - 1$, $h_2 = x_1 + x_2 + 1$ and followed by a ReLU layer with neurons y_1 and y_2 such that $y_1 = max(0, x_1 - x_2 - 1)$ and $y_2 = max(0, x_1 + x_2 + 1)$.

The exact range for nodes (h_1, h_2) is depicted in Fig. 2a in magenta (an octagon here), and the exact range for the output layer is shown in Fig. 2b in cyan: (y_1, y_2) take the positive values of of (h_1, h_2). In Fig. 2c, the set of values the linear node h_1 can take as a function of x_1, is represented in magenta. The set of values of the output neuron y_1 in function of x_1 is depicted in Fig. 2d, in cyan: when x_1 is negative, h_1 is negative as well, so $y_1 = 0$ (this is the horizontal cyan line on the left). When x_1 is positive, the set of values y_1 can take is the positive part of the set of values h_1 can take (pictured as the right cyan triangle). The line plus triangle is a tropical polyhedron, as we will see in Sect. 2.2.

We want to check two properties on this simple neural network:

(P_1): the input is always classified as belonging to the class identified by neuron y_2, i.e. we always have $y_2 \geq y_1$

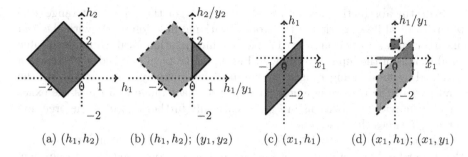

(a) (h_1, h_2) (b) (h_1, h_2); (y_1, y_2) (c) (x_1, h_1) (d) (x_1, h_1); (x_1, y_1)

Fig. 2. Exact ranges for the neural net of Example 1 on $[-1, 1] \times [-1, 1]$. (P_2) is the complement of the red square in Fig. 2d.

(P_2): in the neighborhood $[-0.25, 0.25]$ of 0 for x_1, whatever x_2 in $[-1, 1]$, the output y_1 is never above threshold 0.5 (unsafe zone materialized in red in Fig. 2d)

(P_2) is a robustness property. We see on the blue part of Fig. 2b (resp. 2d) that the first (resp. second) property is true.

As we will see in Sect. 3, our tropical polyhedron abstraction is going to give the exact graph of y_1 as a function of x_1, in cyan again, Fig. 3b.

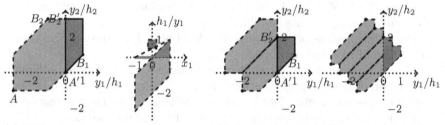

(a) With zone, trop-   (b) (x_1, h_1); (x_1, y_1) (c) Once subdivided   (d) twice subdivided
ical polyhedra   tropical polyhedra   tropical polyhedra.

Fig. 3. Abstractions of a simple neural net on $[-1, 1] \times [-1, 1]$. Dashed lines in (b) enclose the classical convexification.

Therefore we will be able to prove robustness, i.e. (P_2): the exact range for y_1 in cyan does not intersect the non complying states, in red. Note that all classically convex abstractions, whatever their intricacies, will need to extend the cyan zone up to the dashed line pictured in Fig. 3b, to get the full triangle, at the very least. This triangle is intersecting the red region making classically convex abstractions unable to prove (P_2).

Our tropical abstraction projected on the y_2, y_1 coordinates is not exact: compare the exact range in cyan in Fig. 2b with the abstraction in cyan in Fig. 3a. However, the cyan region in Fig. 3a is above the diagonal, which is enough for proving (P_1).

Still, the abstraction has an area 2.5 times larger than the exact range, due to the tropical linearization of the tropical rational function y_1. As with classical linearizations, a workaround is to make this linearization local, through suitable subdivisions of the input. We show in Fig. 3c the tropical polyhedric abstraction obtained by subdividing x_1 into two sub-intervals (namely $[-1, 0]$ and $[0, 1]$): the cyan part of the picture is much closer to the exact range (1.5 times the exact area). Subdividing further as in Fig. 3d naturally further improves the precision (area 1.25 times the exact one).

As we will see in Sect. 2.2, tropical polyhedra are particular unions of zones: the tropical polyhedra in cyan of Figs. 3a and 3c are composed of just one zone, but the tropical polyhedron in cyan in Fig. 3d and the tropical polyhedron in magenta in Fig. 3c are the union of two zones. Finally, the tropical polyhedron in magenta in Fig. 3d is the union of four zones (generated by 9 extreme points, or 5 constraints, obtained by joining results from the subdivisions of the inputs).

Contributions. Section 2 introduces the necessary background notions, in particular tropical polyhedra. We then describe the following contributions:

- Sect. 3 introduces our abstraction of (classical) affine functions from $\mathbb{R}^m$ to $\mathbb{R}^n$ with tropical polyhedra. We fully describe internal and external representations, extending the classical abstractions of assignments in the zone abstract domain [29] or in the tropical polyhedra domain [4]. We prove correctness and equivalence of internal and external representations, allowing the use of the double description method [2].
- Based on the analysis of one layer networks of Sect. 3, we show in Sect. 4 how to get to multi-layered networks.
- Finally, Sect. 5 describes our implementations in C++ and using polymake [18] and presents some promising experiments. We discuss the cost and advantages of using the double description or of relying for further abstraction on either internal or external representations of tropical polyhedra.

Related Work. There exist many approaches to neural networks verification. We concentrate here on methods and tools designed for at least range over-approximation of ReLU feedforward networks.

It is natural to consider constraint based methods for encoding the ReLU function and the combinatorics of activations in a ReLU feedforward neural net.

Determining the range of a ReLU feedforward neural net amounts to solving min and max problems under sets of linear and ReLU constraints. This can be solved either by global optimisation techniques and branch and bound mechanisms, see e.g. DeepGo [32]. The encoding of the activation combinatorics can also be seen as mixed integer linear constraints, and MILP solver used for solving the range outer-approximation problem, see e.g. [6,39], or both branch and bound and MILP techniques, like Venus [8]. Similarly, Sherlock [13,14] performs range analysis using optimization methods (MILP and a combination of local search and global branch-and-bound approach), and considers also neural nets as controllers within a feedback loop. Finally, some of these constraint-based analyzer improve the solution search by exploiting the geometry of the activation regions, [26].

A second category of such approaches is based on SMT methods, more specifically satisfiability modulo extensions of linear real arithmetic (encoding also RELU). The network is encoded in this logics and solvers provide answers to queries, in particular range over-approximation and robustness, see e.g. Marabou [25], extending Reluplex [24], and [15,22].

Range estimation for ReLU activated feedforward neural nets can also be performed using some of the abstract domains [11] that have been designed for program analysis, and in particular convex domains for numerical program verification. These include zonotopes [19,34], especially considering that feedforward neural nets with one hidden layer and ReLU activation functions are known to be characterizable by zonotopes, see e.g. [42], polyhedra [36], and other sub-polyhedric or convex abstractions like symbolic intervals [20] used in Neurify [33] extending Reluval [40] or CROWN-IBP [41].

These abstractions allow to perform range estimation, i.e. to estimate outer approximations of the values of the output neurons given a set of values for the input neurons. They also allow to deal with robustness properties around training data, by proving that the range of the neural net on a small set around a training point gives the same class of outputs.

The main difficulty with these convex abstract domains is that they tend to lose too much precision on (non-convex) ReLU functions. Several methods have been proposed to cope with this phenomenon. The first one is to improve on the abstraction of ReLU, in particular by combining the abstraction of several ReLU functions on the same layer [35]. Another solution that has been proposed in the literature is to combine abstraction and some level of combinatorial exploration of the possible neuron activations, in the line of disjunctive program analysis [9,28]. RefineZono [37] implements methods combining polyhedric abstract domains with MILP solvers for encoding ReLU activation and refining the abstractions, NNENUM [5] uses combinations of zonotopes, stars sets with case splitting methods, and Verinet [21] uses abstractions similar to the polyhedric relaxations of DeepPoly, based on symbolic-interval propagation, with adaptive refinement strategies.

2   Preliminaries and Notations

2.1   Zones

The *zone* [29] abstraction represents restricted forms of affine invariants over variables, bounds on variable differences. Let a n-dimensional variable $x = (x_1, \ldots, x_n) \in \mathbb{R}^n$. The zone domain represents invariants of the form $(\bigwedge_{1 \leq i,j \leq n} x_i - x_j \leq c_{i,j}) \wedge (\bigwedge_{1 \leq i \leq n} a_i \leq x_i \leq b_i)$. A convenient representation is using *difference bound matrices*, or DBM. In order to encode interval constraints seamlessly in this matrix, a special variable x_0, which is assumed to be a constant set to zero, is added to $x \in \mathbb{R}^n$. A DBM is then a $(n+1) \times (n+1)$

square matrix $C = (c_{ij})$, with elements in $\mathbb{R} \cup \{+\infty\}$, representing (concretisation operator) the following set of points in $\mathbb{R}^n$: $\gamma(C) = \{(x_1, \ldots, x_n) \in \mathbb{R}^n \mid \forall i, j \in [0, n], x_i - x_j \leq c_{i,j} \wedge x_0 = 0\}$.

For a matrix C that has non-empty concretization, the closure denoted C^* will be the smallest DBM for the partial order on matrices which represents $\gamma(C)$. Formally, a closed zone $C = (c_{ij})$ is such that: $\forall k \in \mathbb{N}, \forall (i_0, \ldots, i_k) \in [0, n]^{k+1}$, $c_{i_0, i_k} \leq c_{i_0, i_1} + \cdots + c_{i_{k-1}, i_k}$, $\forall i \in [0, j]$, $c_{i,i} = 0$. Every constraint in a closed zone saturates the set $\gamma(C)$.

The best abstraction in the sense of abstract interpretation [11] of a non-empty set $S \subset \mathbb{R}^n$ is the zone defined by the closed DBM: $(c)_{ij} = sup\{x_i - x_j \mid (x_1, \ldots, x_n) \in S \wedge x_0 = 0\}$.

Example 2. Consider the region defined as the union of the magenta and cyan parts of Fig. 3a in Example 1. It is a zone given by the inequalities: $(-3 \leq h_1 \leq 1) \wedge (-1 \leq h_2 \leq 3) \wedge (-4 \leq h_1 - h_2 \leq 0)$, i.e. given by the following DBM:

$$\begin{pmatrix} 0 & 3 & 1 \\ 1 & 0 & 0 \\ 3 & 4 & 0 \end{pmatrix}$$

The *octagon* [30] abstraction is an extension of the zone abstraction, which represents constraints of the form

$$\left(\bigwedge_{1 \leq i,j \leq n} \pm x_i \pm x_j \leq c_{i,j} \right) \wedge \left(\bigwedge_{1 \leq i \leq n} a_i \leq x_i \leq b_i \right)$$

A set of octagonal constraints can be encoded as a difference bound matrix, similarly to the case of zones, but using a variable change to map octagonal constraints on zone constraints. For each variable x_i, two variables are considered in the DBM encoding, that correspond respectively to $+x_i$ and $-x_i$. Note that unary (interval) constraints, such as $x_i \leq b_i$, can be encoded directly as $x_i + x_i \leq 2b_i$, so that no additional variable x_0 is needed.

Example 3. The figure below right shows the exact range (the rotated square) of h_1, h_2 of Example 1.

It is depicted in gray, as the intersection of two zones, one in cyan, Z_2, and one in olive, Z_1. Z_1 is the zone defined in Example 2 and Z_2 is the zone defined on variables $(h_1, -h_2)$ as follows:

$$(-3 \leq h_1 \leq 1) \wedge (-1 \leq h_2 \leq 3) \wedge (-2 \leq h_1 + h_2 \leq 2)$$

2.2 Tropical Polyhedra

Tropical polyhedra are similar to ordinary convex polyhedra. Both can be defined either using affine constraints, known as the external description, or as convex hulls of extremal points and rays, known as the internal description. The major difference is the underlying algebra. Instead of using the classical ring $\mathbb{R}$ of coefficients, with ordinary sum and multiplications, we use the so-called max-plus semiring $\mathbb{R}_{max}$. This semiring is based on the set $\mathbb{R}_{max} = \mathbb{R} \cup \{-\infty\}$, equipped with the addition $x \oplus y := max(x, y)$ and the multiplication $x \otimes y = x + y$. This is almost a ring: we have neutral elements $\mathbb{1} := 0$ for $\otimes$, and $\mathbb{0} = -\infty$ for $\oplus$, and an inverse for $\otimes$ on $\mathbb{R}_{max} \backslash \{\mathbb{0}\}$ but not for $\oplus$. The algebra also fits in with the usual order $\leq$ on $\mathbb{R}$, extended to $\mathbb{R}_{max}$: $x \leq y$ if and only if $x \oplus y = y$.

Tropical hyperplanes are similar to classical hyperplanes, and defined as the set of points satisfying $\bigoplus_{1 \leq i \leq k} a_i \otimes x_i \oplus c \leq \bigoplus_{1 \leq i \leq k} b_i \otimes x_i \oplus d$.

Now, as in the classical case, tropical polyhedra will be given (externally) as an intersection of n tropical hyperplanes, i.e. will be given as the location of points in $\mathbb{R}_{max}^k$ satisfying n inequalities of the form of above. This can be summarized using matrices $A = (a_{ij})$ and $B = (b_{ij})$, two $n \times k$ matrices with entries in $\mathbb{R}_{max}$, and vectors of size k C and D as $Ax \oplus C \leq Bx \oplus D$.

Still similarly to the case of ordinary convex polyhedra, tropical polyhedra can also be described internally, as generated by extremal generators (points, rays). A tropical polyhedron can then be defined as the set of vectors $x \in \mathbb{R}_{max}^k$ which can be written as a tropical affine combination of generators v^i (the extreme points) and r^j (the extreme rays) as $x = \bigoplus_{i \in I} \lambda_i v^i \oplus \bigoplus_{j \in J} \mu_j r^j$ with $\bigoplus_{i \in I} \lambda_i = \mathbb{1}$.

Example 4 (Running example). Consider again the zone consisting of the union of the magenta and cyan parts in Fig. 3a. This is a tropical polyhedron, defined externally by: $max(h_1, -3, h_2, -1, h_2, h_1) \leq max(1, h_1, 3, h_2, h_1 + 4, h_2)$.

It can also be defined internally by the extremal point A, B_1 and B_2 of respective coordinates $(-3, -1)$, $(1, 1)$ and $(-1, 3)$, depicted as dots in Fig. 3a. This means that the points z in this tropical polyhedron have coordinates (h_1, h_2) with $(h_1, h_2) = max(\lambda_0 + A, \lambda_1 + B_1, \lambda_2 + B_2)$ with $max(\lambda_0, \lambda_1, \lambda_2) = \mathbb{1} = 0$, i.e. all λ_is are negative or null, and one at least among the λ_is is zero.

For instance, when $\lambda_2 = -\infty$, z is on the tropical line linking A to B_1:

$$\left(h_1, h_2 \right) = \left(max(\lambda_0 - 3, \lambda_1 - 1), max(\lambda_0 - 1, \lambda_1 + 3) \right) \tag{1}$$

with $\lambda_0, \lambda_1 \neq 0$ and either $\lambda_0 = 0$ or $\lambda_1 = 0$. Suppose $\lambda_0 = 0$, and suppose first that $\lambda_1 \leq -4$: $(h_1, h_2) = (-3, -1)$ which is point A. Suppose now $-4 \leq \lambda_1 \leq -2$, then $(h_1, h_2) = (-3, \lambda_1 + 3)$, which is the vertical line going from A to point $(-3, 1)$. Finally, suppose $-2 \leq \lambda_1 \leq 0$, $(h_1, h_2) = (\lambda_1 - 1, \lambda_1 + 3)$ which is the diagonal going from $(-3, 1)$ to B_1. Similarly, one can show that the tropical line going from B_1 to B_2 is given by fixing $\lambda_0 = -\infty$ and making vary λ_1 and λ_2. If $\lambda_0 < 0$ then $\lambda_1 = 0$ and z is point B_1.

Now, applying the ReLU operator, which is linear in the tropical algebra, defines a tropical polyhedron with internal description given by ReLU (in each coordinate) of extreme points A, B_1 and B_2, i.e. $A' = (0, 0)$, $B_1' = B_1 = (1, 1)$ and $B_2' = (0, 3)$, see Fig. 3a. Similarly, the zone which gives h_1' as a function of x_1, see Fig. 3b, can be seen as a tropical polyhedron with extreme points $(-1, -3)$, $(1, 1)$ and $(1, -1)$. Applying ReLU to the second coordinate of these three extreme points gives three points $(-1, 0)$, $(1, 1)$ and $(1, 0)$ which generate the tropical polyhedron in cyan of Fig. 3b.

It is also easy to see that after one subdivision, Fig. 3c, the set of values for (y_1, y_2) in cyan is a tropical polyhedron with three extreme points A', B_1' and B_2. After two subdivisions, Fig. 3d, the values of y_1 as a function of h_1 is a tropical polyhedron with 4 generators (depicted as dots in Fig. 3d). Note that the tropical polyhedron of Fig. 3d is the encoding of the union of two zones, one zone being the classical convex hull of points $(0, 0)$, $(0, 1)$, $(0.5, 1.5)$, $(1, 1.5)$ and $(1, 1)$, and the other being the classical convex hull of points $(0, 1)$, $(0, 2)$, $(0.5, 2)$ and $(0.5, 1.5)$.

All tropical polyhedra can thus be described both internally and externally, and algorithms, although costly, can be used to translate an external description into an internal description and vice-versa. This is at the basis of the double description method for classical polyhedra [12] and for tropical polyhedra [2]. Double description is indeed useful when interpreting set-theoretic unions and intersections, as in validation by abstract interpretation, see [12] again for the classical case, and e.g. [4] for the tropical case: unions are easier to compute using the extreme generator representation (the union of the convex hulls of sets of points is the convex hull of the union of these sets of points) while intersections are easier to compute using the external representation (the intersection of two polyhedra given by sets of constraints is given by the concatenation of these sets of constraints).

In the sequel, we will be using explicitly the max and (ordinary) + operators in place of $\oplus$ and $\otimes$ for readability purposes.

2.3   From Zone to Tropical Polyhedra and Vice-Versa

The following proposition characterizes the construction of tropical polyhedric abstractions from zones. We show that a zone defined on n variables can be expressed as the tropical convex hull of $n + 1$ points.

Proposition 1 (Internal tropical representation of closed zones)
Let $H_{ext} \subset \mathbb{R}^n$ be the n-dimensional zone defined by the conjunction of the $(n+1)^2$ inequalities $\bigwedge_{0 \leq i, j \leq n}(x_i - x_j \leq c_{i,j})$, where $\forall i, j \in [0, n]$, $c_{i,j} \in \mathbb{R} \cup \{+\infty\}$. Assume that this representation is closed, then H_{ext} is equal to the tropical polyhedron H_{int} defined, with internal representation, as the tropical convex hull of the following extreme points (and no extreme ray):

$$A = (a_i)_{1 \leq i \leq n} := (-c_{0,1}, \ldots, -c_{0,n}),$$
$$B_k = (b_{ki})_{1 \leq i \leq n} := (c_{k,0} - c_{k,1}, \ldots, c_{k,0} - c_{k,n}), k = 1, \ldots, n,$$

Example 5. The zone of Example 2 is the tropical polyedron with the three extreme generators A, B_1 and B_2 pictured in Fig. 3a, as deduced from Proposition 1 above.

Moreover, we can easily find the best zone (and also, hypercube) that outer approximates a given tropical polyhedron, as follows [4]. Suppose we have p extreme generators and rays for a tropical polyhedron $\mathcal{H}$, $A_1, \ldots, A_p$, that we put in homogeneous coordinates in $\mathbb{R}^{n+1}$ by adding as last component 0 to the coordinates of the extreme generators, and $-\infty$ to the last component, for extreme rays, as customary for identifying polyhedra with cones, see e.g. [17].

Proposition 2 [4]. *Let A be the matrix of generators for tropical polyhedron $\mathcal{H}$ stripped out of rows consisting only of $-\infty$ entries, and A/A the residuated matrix which entries are $(A/A)_{i,j} = \min\limits_{1 \le k \le p} a_{i,k} - a_{j,k}$. Then the smallest zone containing $\mathcal{H}$ is given by the inequalities:*

$$x_i - x_j \ge (A/A)_{i,j} \qquad\qquad \text{for all } i,j = 1,\ldots,n$$
$$(A/A)_{i,n+1} \le x_i \le -(A/A)_{n+1,i} \qquad\qquad \text{for all } i = 1,\ldots,n$$

Example 6. Consider the graph of the ReLU function on $[-1, 1]$, pictured in Fig. 1d. It has as generators the two extreme points $A_1 = (-1, 0)$ and $A_2 = (1, 1)$ (the graph is the tropical segment from A_1 to A_2). Homogenizing the coordinates and putting them in a matrix A (columns correspond to generators), we have

$$A = \begin{pmatrix} -1 & 1 \\ 0 & 1 \\ 0 & 0 \end{pmatrix} \text{ and } (A/A) = \begin{pmatrix} 0 & -1 & -1 \\ 0 & 0 & 0 \\ -1 & -1 & 0 \end{pmatrix}$$

meaning that the enclosing zone is given by $-1 \le x - y \le 0$, $-1 \le x \le 1$, $0 \le y \le 1$, which is the zone depicted in Fig. 1c.

2.4 Feedforward ReLU Networks

Feedforward ReLU networks that we are considering in this paper are a succession of layers of neurons, input layer first, a given number of hidden layers and then an output layer, each computing a certain affine transform followed by the application of the ReLU activation function:

Definition 1. *A n-neurons ReLU network layer L with m inputs is a function $\mathbb{R}^m \to \mathbb{R}^n$ defined by, a weight matrix $W \in \mathcal{M}_{n,m}(\mathbb{R})$, a bias vector $b \in \mathbb{R}^n$, and an activation function $ReLU : \mathbb{R}^n \to \mathbb{R}^n$ given by $ReLU(x_1, \ldots, x_n) = (max(x_1, 0), \ldots, max(x_n, 0))$ so that for a given input $x \in \mathbb{R}^n$, its output is $L(x) = ReLU(Wx + b)$.*

Definition 2. *A multi-layer perceptron F_N is given by a list of network layers $L_0, \ldots, L_N$, where layers L_i ($i = 0, \ldots, N-1$) are n_{i+1}-neurons layers with n_i inputs. the action of F_N on inputs is defined by composing the action of successive layers: $F_N = L_N \circ \ldots \circ L_0$.*

3 Abstraction of Linear Maps

3.1 Zone-Based Abstraction

We consider in this section the problem of abstracting the graph $\mathcal{G}_f = \{(x,y) \mid y = f(x)\}$ of a linear map $f(x) = Wx + b$ with $x \in [\underline{x}_1, \overline{x}_1] \times \ldots [\underline{x}_m, \overline{x}_m]$ where $W = (w_{i,j})$ is a $n \times m$ matrix and b a n-dimensional vector, by a tropical polyhedron $\mathcal{H}_f$. We will treat the case of multilayered networks in Sect. 4.

The difficulty is that linear maps in the classical sense are not linear maps in the tropical sense, but are rather (generalized) tropical polynomials, hence the exact image of a tropical polyhedron by a (classical) linear map is not in general a tropical polyhedron. We begin by computing the best zone abstracting $\mathcal{G}_f$ and then represent it by a tropical polyhedron, using the results of Sect. 2.3. We then show in Sect. 3.2 that we can improve results using an octagon abstraction.

The tightest zone containing the image of a cube going through a linear layer can be computed as follows:

Proposition 3 (Optimal approximation of a linear layer by a zone)
Let $n, m \in \mathbb{N}$ and $f : \mathbb{R}^m \to \mathbb{R}^n$ an affine transformation defined, for all $x \in \mathbb{R}^m$ and $i \in [1, n]$, by $\big(f(x)\big)_i = \sum_{j=1}^m w_{i,j} x_j + b_i$. Let $K \subset \mathbb{R}^m$ be an hypercube defined as $K = \prod_{1 \le j \le m} [\underline{x}_j, \overline{x}_j]$, with $\underline{x}_j, \overline{x}_j \in \mathbb{R}$. Then, the tightest zone $\mathcal{H}_f$ of $\mathbb{R}^m \times \mathbb{R}^n$ containing $S := \big\{(x, f(x)) \,\big|\, x \in K\big\}$ is the set of all $(x, y) \in \mathbb{R}^m \times \mathbb{R}^n$ satisfying

$$\Big(\bigwedge_{1 \le j \le m} \underline{x}_j \le x_j \le \overline{x}_j \Big) \wedge \Big(\bigwedge_{1 \le i \le n} m_i \le y_i \le M_i \Big) \wedge \Big(\bigwedge_{1 \le i_1, i_2 \le n} y_{i_1} - y_{i_2} \le \Delta_{i_1, i_2} \Big)$$

$$\wedge \Big(\bigwedge_{1 \le i \le n, 1 \le j \le m} m_i - \overline{x}_j + \delta_{i,j} \le y_i - x_j \le M_i - \underline{x}_j - \delta_{i,j} \Big),$$

where, for all $i, i_1, i_2 \in [1, n]$ and $j \in [1, m]$:

$$m_i = \sum_{w_{i,j} < 0} w_{i,j} \overline{x}_j + \sum_{w_{i,j} > 0} w_{i,j} \underline{x}_j + b_i,$$

$$M_i = \sum_{w_{i,j} < 0} w_{i,j} \underline{x}_j + \sum_{w_{i,j} > 0} w_{i,j} \overline{x}_j + b_i,$$

$$\Delta_{i_1, i_2} = \sum_{w_{i_1,j} < w_{i_2,j}} (w_{i_1,j} - w_{i_2,j}) \underline{x}_j + \sum_{w_{i_1,j} > w_{i_2,j}} (w_{i_1,j} - w_{i_2,j}) \overline{x}_j + (b_{i_1} - b_{i_2}),$$

$$\delta_{i,j} = \begin{cases} 0, & \text{if } w_{i,j} \le 0 \\ w_{i,j}(\overline{x}_j - \underline{x}_j), & \text{if } 0 \le w_{i,j} \le 1 \\ (\overline{x}_j - \underline{x}_j), & \text{if } 1 \le w_{i,j} \end{cases}$$

The tightest zone is obtained as the conjunction of the bounds $\underline{x}_j \le x_j \le \overline{x}_j$ on input x, given as hypercube K, the bounds on the y_i and $y_{i_1} - y_{i_2}$ obtained by a direct computation of bounds of the affine transform of the input hypercube K, and finally the bounds on the differences $y_i - x_j$ given by a direct calculation.

Figure 4 shows the three different types of zones that over-approximate the range of a scalar function f, with $f(x) = \lambda x + b$, on an interval. When $\lambda < 0$, the best that can be done is to abstract the graph of f by a square, we cannot encode any dependency between $f(x)$ and x: this corresponds to the case $\delta_{i,j} = 0$ in Proposition 3. The two other cases for the definition of $\delta_{i,j}$ are the two remaining cases of Fig. 4: when λ is between 0 and 1, this is the picture in the middle, and when λ is greater than 1, this is the picture at the right hand side. As we have seen in Proposition 1 and as we will see more in detail below in Theorem 1, these zones can be encoded as tropical polyhedra. Only the points A, B and C are extreme points: D is not an extreme point of the polyhedron as it is on the tropical segment $[AC]$ (the blue, green and red dashed lines each represent a tropical segment).

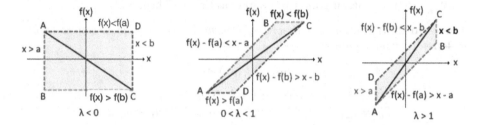

Fig. 4. The 3 cases for approximating the graph of an affine scalar function by a tropical polyhedron, on domain $[a, b]$.

For $f : \mathbb{R}^2 \to \mathbb{R}$, there are 6 cases, depending on the values of λ_1 and λ_2. In all cases, these zones can be represented as tropical polyhedra using only 4 extreme points and 4 inequalities (instead of 8 and 6 in the classical case), as we will see in Theorem 1. Figure 5 represents the resulting polyhedron for different values of λ_1 and λ_2. Each figure shows the extreme points A, B_1, B_2 and C, the faces of the polyhedron (in green), the tropical segments inside the polyhedron (in red), and the actual graph of $f(x)$ (in blue). We have the corresponding external description in Theorem 1 below:

Theorem 1. *The best zone abstraction $\mathcal{H}_f$ of of the graph $\mathcal{G}_f = \{(x_1, \ldots, x_m, y_1, \ldots, y_n) \mid \underline{x}_j \leq x_j \leq \overline{x}_j, \ y_i = f_i(x_1, \ldots, x_m)\} \subseteq \mathbb{R}^{+n}$ of the linear function $f : \mathbb{R}^m \to \mathbb{R}^n$ defined in Proposition 3 can be seen as the tropical polyhedron defined externally with $m + n + 1$ inequalities, for all $i \in [1, n]$ and $j \in [1, m]$:*

$$\max(x_1 - \overline{x}_1, \ldots, x_m - \overline{x}_m, y_1 - M_1, \ldots, y_n - M_n) \leq 0 \qquad (2)$$
$$\max(0, y_1 - M_1 + \delta_{1,j}, \ldots, y_n - M_n + \delta_{n,j}) \leq x_j - \underline{x}_j \qquad (3)$$
$$\max(0, x_1 - \overline{x}_1 + \delta_{i,1}, \ldots, x_n - \overline{x}_n + \delta_{i,n}, y_1 - d_{i,1}, \ldots, y_n - d_{i,n}) \leq y_i - m_i \qquad (4)$$

where d_{j_1,j_2} denotes the quantity $\Delta_{j_1,j_2} + m_{j_2}$ for i_1 and i_2 in $[1, n]$.

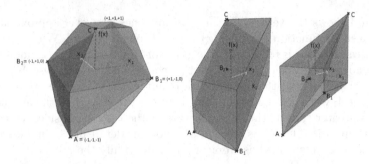

Fig. 5. Over-approximation for $\lambda_1 = \lambda_2 = 0.5$ (left), $\lambda_1 = -0.5$ and $\lambda_2 = 1.5$ (middle), and $\lambda_1 = \lambda_2 = 1.2$ (right).

We have the matching internal representation in Theorem 2:

Theorem 2. $\mathcal{H}_f$ *can also be described, internally, as the tropical convex hull of* $m + n + 1$ *extreme points:*

$$A = (\underline{x}_1, \ldots, \underline{x}_m, m_1, \ldots, m_n)$$
$$B_1 = (\overline{x}_1, \underline{x}_2, \ldots, \underline{x}_m, m_1 + \delta_{1,1}, \ldots, m_n + \delta_{n,1}) \cdots$$
$$B_m = (\underline{x}_1, \ldots, \underline{x}_{m-1}, \overline{x}_m, m_1 + \delta_{1,m}, \ldots, m_n + \delta_{n,m})$$
$$C_1 = (\underline{x}_1 + \delta_{1,1}, \ldots, \underline{x}_m + \delta_{1,m}, M_1, c_{1,2}, \ldots, c_{1,n}) \cdots$$
$$C_n = (\underline{x}_1 + \delta_{n,1}, \ldots, \underline{x}_m + \delta_{n,m}, c_{n,1}, \ldots, c_{n,n-1}, M_n)$$

where $c_{i_1,i_2} = M_{i_1} - \Delta_{i_1,i_2}$ *for* i_1 *and* i_2 *in* $[1, n]$.

Example 7 (Running example). Let us detail the computations for Example 1: $h_1 = x_1 - x_2 - 1$, $h_2 = x_1 + x_2 + 1$. We have respectively, $\delta_{1,1} = 2$, $\delta_{1,2} = 0$, $\delta_{2,1} = 2$, $\delta_{2,2} = 2$, $\Delta_{1,1} = 0$, $\Delta_{1,2} = 0$, $\Delta_{2,1} = 4$, $\Delta_{2,2} = 0$, $d_{1,1} = -3$, $d_{1,2} = -1$, $d_{2,1} = 1$, $d_{2,2} = -1$, $m_1 = -3$, $m_2 = -1$, $M_1 = 1$ and $M_2 = 3$. Hence the external description for the tropical polyhedron relating values of x_1, x_2, h_1 and h_2 are: $\max(x_1 - 1, x_2 - 1, h_1 - 1, h_2 - 3) \leq 0$, $\max(0, h_1 + 1, h_2 - 1) \leq x_1 + 1$, $\max(0, h_1 - 1, h_2 - 1) \leq x_2 + 1$, $\max(0, x_1 + 1, x_2 - 1, h_1 + 3, h_2 - 1) \leq h_1 + 3$, $\max(0, x_1 + 1, x_2 + 1, h_1 + 1, h_2 + 1) \leq h_2 + 1$ which encode all zones inequalities: $-1 \leq x_1 \leq 1$, $-1 \leq x_2 \leq 1$, $-3 \leq h_1 \leq 1$, $-1 \leq h_2 \leq 3$, $-2 \leq h_1 - x_1 \leq 0$, $-4 \leq h_1 - x_2 \leq 2$, $0 \leq h_2 - x_1 \leq 2$, $0 \leq h_2 - x_2 \leq 2$, $-4 \leq h_1 - h_2 \leq 0$. Note that the zone abstraction of [29] would be equivalent to an interval abstraction and would not infer the relations between h_1, h_2, x_1 and x_2. Now the internal representation of the corresponding zone is $A = (-1, -1, -3, -1)$, $B_1 = (1, -1, -1, 1)$, $B_2 = (-1, 1, -3, 1)$, $C_1 = (-1, -1, 1, 1)$, $C_2 = (-1, 1, -1, 3)$. The projections of these 5 extreme points on (h_1, h_2) give the points $(-3, -1)$, $(-1, 1)$, $(-3, 1)$, $(1, 1)$, $(-1, 3)$, among which $(-3, 1)$ and $(-1, 1)$ are in the tropical convex hull of $A = (-3, -1)$, $B_1 = (1, 1)$ and $B_2 = (-1, 3)$ represented in Fig. 3a. Indeed $(-3, 1)$ is on the tropical line (AB_2) and $(-1, 1)$ whereas $(-1, 1)$ is on the tropical line (AB_1) as a tropical linear combination of $-2 + B_1$ and $-2 + B_2$: $(-1, 1) = max(-2 + (1, 1), -2 + (-1, 3))$.

Example 8. Consider now function $f : \mathbb{R}^2 \to \mathbb{R}^2$ with $f(x_1, x_2) = (0.9x_1 + 1.1x_2, y_2 = 1.1x_1 - 0.9x_2)$ on $(x_1, x_2) \in [-1, 1]$. We have in particular $M_1 = 2$, $M_2 = 2$, $m_1 = -2$ and $m_2 = -2$. We compute $\delta_{1,1} = 1.8$, $\delta_{1,2} = 2$, $\delta_{2,1} = 2$ and $\delta_{2,2} = 0$ and we have indeed $y_1 + 2 \geq x_1 - 1 + \delta_{1,1} = x_1 + 0.8$, $y_2 + 2 \geq x_1 - 1 + 2 = x_1 + 1$, $y_1 + 2 \geq x_2 - 1 + \delta_{2,1} = x_1 + 1$, $y_2 + 2 \geq x_2 - 1$ and $y_1 - 2 \leq x_1 + 1 - 1.8 = x_1 - 0.8$, $y_2 - 2 \leq x_1 + 1 - 2 = x_1 - 1$, $y_1 - 2 \leq x_2 + 1 - 2 = x_2 - 1$, $y_2 - 2 \leq x_2 + 1$. Overall:

$$x_1 - 1.2 \leq y_1 \leq x_1 + 1.2$$
$$x_2 - 1 \leq y_1 \leq x_2 + 1$$
$$x_1 - 1 \leq y_2 \leq x_1 + 1$$
$$x_2 - 3 \leq y_2 \leq x_2 + 3$$

We also find $d_{1,1} = -2$, $d_{1,2} = 0.2$, $d_{2,1} = 0.2$ and $d_{2,2} = -2$. Hence $y_1 - d_{1,2} \leq y_2 - m_2$, i.e. $y_1 - 0.2 \leq y_2 + 2$ that is $y_1 - y_2 \leq 2.2$. Similarly, we find $y_2 - y_1 \leq 2 + 0.2$ hence $-2.2 \leq y_1 - y_2 \leq 2.2$.

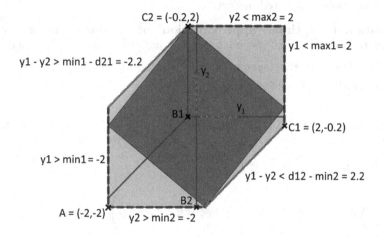

Fig. 6. Over-approximation for $f(x_1, x_2) = (0.9x_1 + 1.1x_2, y_2 = 1.1x_1 - 0.9x_2)$.

These equations can be written as linear tropical constraints as in Theorem 1:

$$max \begin{pmatrix} x_1 - 1 \\ x_2 - 1 \\ y_1 - 2 \\ y_2 - 2 \end{pmatrix} \leq 0, \; max \begin{pmatrix} 0 \\ y_1 - 0.2 \\ y_2 \end{pmatrix} \leq x_1 + 1, \; max \begin{pmatrix} 0 \\ y_1 \\ y_2 - 2 \end{pmatrix} \leq x_2 + 1$$

$$max \begin{pmatrix} 0 \\ x_1 + 0.8 \\ x_2 + 1 \\ y_1 + 2 \\ y_2 - 0.2 \end{pmatrix} \leq y_1 + 2, \; max \begin{pmatrix} 0 \\ x_1 + 1 \\ x_2 - 1 \\ y_1 - 0.2 \\ y_2 + 2 \end{pmatrix} \leq y_2 + 2$$

We now depict in Fig. 6 both the image of f as a blue rotated central square, and its over-approximation by the convex tropical polyhedron calculated as in Theorem 1 in green, in the plane (y_1, y_2). As $c_{1,1} = 2$, $c_{1,2} = -0.2$, $c_{2,1} = -0.2$ and $c_{2,2} = 2$, the extremal points are, in the (x_1, x_2, y_1, y_2) coordinates:

$$A = \begin{pmatrix} -1 \\ -1 \\ -2 \\ -2 \end{pmatrix} \quad B_1 = \begin{pmatrix} 1 \\ -1 \\ -0.2 \\ 0 \end{pmatrix} \quad B_2 = \begin{pmatrix} -1 \\ 1 \\ 0 \\ -2 \end{pmatrix} \quad C_1 = \begin{pmatrix} 0.8 \\ 1 \\ 2 \\ -0.2 \end{pmatrix} \quad C_2 = \begin{pmatrix} 1 \\ -1 \\ -0.2 \\ 2 \end{pmatrix}$$

3.2 Octagon Abstractions and $(\max, +, -)$ Algebra

As in Sect. 3.1, we consider the abstraction of the image of an hypercube K of $\mathbb{R}^m$ by an affine transformation $f : \mathbb{R}^m \to \mathbb{R}^n$ defined, for all $x \in \mathbb{R}^m$ and $i \in [1, n]$, by $\big(f(x)\big)_i = \sum_{j=1}^m w_{i,j} x_j + b_i$. But we consider here the abstraction of this image by an octagon, we will thus add some constraints on sums of variables to the abstraction computed in Sect. 3.1.

Proposition 4 (Optimal approximation of a linear layer by an octagon). *Let $K \subset \mathbb{R}^m$ be an hypercube defined as $K = \prod_j [\underline{x}_j, \overline{x}_j]$, with $\underline{x}_j, \overline{x}_j \in \mathbb{R}$. The tightest octagon of $\mathbb{R}^m \times \mathbb{R}^n$ containing $S := \Big\{ (x, f(x)) \,\Big|\, x \in K \Big\}$ is the set of all $(x, y) \in \mathbb{R}^m \times \mathbb{R}^n$ satisfying*

$$\left(\bigwedge_{1 \le j \le m} \underline{x}_j \le x_j \le \overline{x}_j \right) \wedge \left(\bigwedge_{1 \le i \le n} m_i \le y_i \le M_i \right) \wedge \left(\bigwedge_{1 \le i_1, i_2 \le m} y_{i_1} - y_{i_2} \le \Delta_{i_1, i_2} \right)$$

$$\wedge \left(\bigwedge_{1 \le i_1, i_2 \le n} L_{i_1, i_2} \le y_{i_1} + y_{i_2} \le \Gamma_{i_1, i_2} \right)$$

$$\wedge \left(\bigwedge_{1 \le i \le n, 1 \le j \le m} m_i - \overline{x}_j + \delta_{i,j} \le y_i - x_j \le M_i - \underline{x}_j - \delta_{i,j} \right)$$

$$\wedge \left(\bigwedge_{i,j} m_i + \underline{x}_j + \gamma_{i,j} \le y_i + x_j \le M_i + \overline{x}_j - \gamma_{i,j} \right)$$

where $m_i, M_i, \delta_{i,j}, \Delta_{i_1, i_2}$ are defined as in Proposition 3, and

$$\Gamma_{i_1, i_2} := \sum_{w_{i_1,j} + w_{i_2,j} < 0} \underline{x}_j(w_{i_1,j} + w_{i_2,j}) + \sum_{w_{i_1,j} + w_{i_2,j} > 0} \overline{x}_j(w_{i_1,j} + w_{i_2,j})$$

$$L_{i_1, i_2} := \sum_{w_{i_1,j} + w_{i_2,j} < 0} \overline{x}_j(w_{i_1,j} + w_{i_2,j}) + \sum_{w_{i_1,j} + w_{i_2,j} > 0} \underline{x}_j(w_{i_1,j} + w_{i_2,j})$$

$$\gamma_{i,j} := \begin{cases} 0, & \text{if } 0 \le w_{i,j} \\ -w_{i,j}(\overline{x}_j - \underline{x}_j), & \text{if } -1 \le w_{i,j} \le 0 \\ (\overline{x}_j - \underline{x}_j), & \text{if } w_{i,j} \le -1 \end{cases}$$

With the notations of Proposition 4, we have

Proposition 5. *Let M be the (classically) linear manifold in $\mathbb{R}^m \times \mathbb{R}^n \times \mathbb{R}^m \times \mathbb{R}^n$ defined by $(x^+, y^+, x^-, y^-) \in M$ if and only if $x^+ + x^- = 0$ and $y^+ + y^- = 0$. The octagon S defined in Proposition 4 is equal to the intersection of M with the tropical convex polyhedron generated by the $1 + 2n + 2m$ points $A, B_1^+, \ldots, B_m^+, B_1^-, \ldots, B_m^-, C_1^+, \ldots, C_n^+, C_1^-, \ldots, C_n^-$, where*

$$A = (\underline{x}_1, \ldots, \underline{x}_m, m_1, \ldots, m_n, -\overline{x}_1, \ldots, -\overline{x}_m, -M_1, \ldots, -M_n)$$

$$B_k^+ = (0, x^+, y^+, x^-, y^-) \text{ with } \begin{array}{lll} x_k^+ = \overline{x}_k, & x_{j\neq k}^+ = \underline{x}_j, & y_i^+ = m_i + \delta_{i,k} \\ x_k^- = -\overline{x}_k, & x_{j\neq k}^- = -\overline{x}_j, & y_i^- = -M_i + \gamma_{i,k} \end{array}$$

$$B_k^- = (0, x^+, y^+, x^-, y^-) \text{ with } \begin{array}{lll} x_k^- = -\underline{x}_k, & x_{j\neq k}^- = -\overline{x}_j, & y_i^- = -M_i + \delta_{i,k} \\ x_k^+ = \underline{x}_k, & x_{j\neq k}^+ = \underline{x}_j, & y_i^+ = m_i + \gamma_{i,k} \end{array}$$

$$C_l^+ = (0, x^+, y^+, x^-, y^-) \text{ with } \begin{array}{lll} y_l^+ = M_l, & y_{i\neq l}^+ = M_l - \Delta_{l,i}, & x_j^+ = \underline{x}_j + \delta_{l,j} \\ y_l^- = -M_l, & y_{i\neq l}^- = M_l - \Gamma_{l,i}, & x_j^- = -\overline{x}_j + \gamma_{l,j} \end{array}$$

$$C_l^- = (0, x^+, y^+, x^-, y^-) \text{ with } \begin{array}{lll} y_l^- = -m_l, & y_{i\neq l}^- = -m_l - \Delta_{i,l}, & x_j^- = -\overline{x}_j + \delta_{l,j} \\ y_l^+ = m_l, & y_{i\neq l}^+ = -m_l + L_{l,i}, & x_j^+ = \underline{x}_j + \gamma_{l,j} \end{array}$$

Example 9 (Running example). For the example network of Example 1, the formulas of Proposition 4 give the constraints:

$$
\begin{array}{lll}
-1 \leq x_1 \leq 1 & -1 \leq x_2 \leq 1 & \\
0 \leq x_1 - h_1 \leq 2 & -2 \leq x_2 - h_1 \leq 4 & -3 \leq h_1 \leq 1 \\
-4 \leq x_1 + h_1 \leq 2 & -2 \leq x_2 + h_1 \leq 0 & 0 \leq h_2 - h_1 \leq 4 \\
-2 \leq x_1 - h_2 \leq 0 & -2 \leq x_2 - h_2 \leq 0 & -2 \leq h_2 + h_1 \leq 2 \\
-2 \leq x_1 + h_2 \leq 4 & -2 \leq x_2 + h_2 \leq 4 & -1 \leq h_2 \leq 3
\end{array}
$$

And the internal description is given by Proposition 5, with the following extreme points, where coordinates are ordered as $(x_1^+, x_2^+, h_1^+, h_2^+, x_1^-, x_2^-, h_1^-, h_2^-)$:

$$(-1, -1, -3, -1, -1, -1, -1, -3)$$
$$(1, -1, -1, 1, -1, -1, -1, -3)$$
$$(-1, 1, -3, 1, -1, -1, 1, -3)$$
$$(-1, -1, -3, -1, -1, -1, -1, -3)$$
$$(1, -1, 1, 1, -1, 1, -1, -1)$$
$$(1, 1, -1, 3, -1, -1, 1, -3)$$
$$(-1, -1, -3, -1, 1, -1, 1, -1)$$
$$(-1, -1, -1, -1, -1, 1, -1, -1)$$
$$(-1, -1, -3, -1, -1, -1, -1, -3)$$
$$(-1, 1, -3, 1, 1, -1, 3, -1)$$
$$(-1, -1, -1, -1, 1, 1, 1, 1)$$

From the extremal points of the octagon abstraction above, we get the extremal points for (h_1^+, h_2^+), discarding the non extremal ones: $(-3, -1)$, $(1, 1)$ and $(-1, 3)$, and for (h_1^+, h_2^-): $(-3, -3)$, $(1, -1)$ and $(-1, 1)$ (for this last pair of variables, this gives the zone in cyan of Example 3).

4   Validation of Multi-layered Neural Networks

General Algorithm. The method developed in Sect. 3 is the cornerstone of our algorithm for analysing neural networks. A ReLU neural net consists of a chain of two kinds of computations, one which applies a classical linear transformation to their inputs, and another one one which applies a ReLU. function We have seen that the affine map transformation can be over-approximated using tropical polyhedra. ReLU being a tropical affine function, the ReLU transform is exact in tropical polyhedra. It is thus possible to use tropical polyhedra to represent reachable states for every node in the network, at least for one layer ReLU networks.

Example 10. We carry on with Example 1 and complete the final computations of Example 7. The external representation is given by the tropical linear inequalities of Example 7 together with inequalities $max(0, h_1) \leq y_1 \leq max(0, h_1)$ and $max(0, h_2) \leq y_2 \leq max(0, h_2)$. Now the corresponding tropical polyhedron is generated by the linear tropical operator ReLU on each of the extremal points A, B_1, B_2, C_1 and C_2 and gives the two extra (last) coordinates in the axes $(x_1, x_2, h_1, h_2, y_1, y_2)$, $A' = (-1, -1, -3, -1, 0, 0)$, $B_1' = (1, -1, -1, 1, 0, 1)$, $B_2' = (-1, 1, -3, 1, 0, 1)$, $C_1' = (-1, -1, 1, 1, 1, 1)$, $C_2' = (-1, 1, -3, 3, 0, 3)$. The projections of theses 5 extreme points on (h_1, y_2) give the points $(0, 0)$, $(0, 1)$, $(1, 1)$, $(0, 3)$ among which $(0, 1)$ is in the convex hull of $A' = (0, 0)$, $B_2' = B_2 = (1, 1)$ and $B_1' = (0, 3)$ represented in Fig. 3a.

The polyhedron given by the method of Sect. 3 only gives relations between 2 layers (the input and the first hidden layer). In order to get a polyhedron that represents the whole network when combining with e.g. another layer, we need to embed the first polyhedron from a space that represents only 2 layers to a higher space that represents the complete network, with one dimension per node. We will then need to intersect the polyhedra generated by each pair of layers to get the final result. Finally, as we are only interested in the input-output abstraction of the whole network, we can reduce computing costs by removing the dimensions corresponding to middle layers once those are calculated.

To this end, we use the following notations. Let $\mathcal{L} \subset \{L_0, \ldots, L_N\}$ be a set of layers, layer i containing n_{i+1} neurons as in Definition 2. Let n be the sum of all n_{i+1}, with i such that $L_i \in \mathcal{L}$ and $\mathcal{S}_{\mathcal{L}} \equiv \mathbb{R}_{max}^n$ be the tropical space in which we are going to interpret the values of the neurons on layers in $\mathcal{L}$, with each dimension of $\mathcal{S}_{\mathcal{L}}$ corresponding to a node of a layer of $\mathcal{L}$.

For $\mathcal{L}_1, \mathcal{L}_2 \subset \{L_0, \ldots, L_N\}$, for $\mathcal{H} \subset \mathcal{S}_{\mathcal{L}_1}$ a tropical polyhedron, we denote by $Proj(\mathcal{H}, \mathcal{L}_2) \subset \mathcal{S}_{\mathcal{L}_2}$ the projection of $\mathcal{H}$ onto $\mathcal{S}_{\mathcal{L}_2}$ when $\mathcal{S}_{\mathcal{L}_2} \subseteq \mathcal{S}_{\mathcal{L}_1}$ and let $Emb(\mathcal{H}, \mathcal{L}_2) \subset \mathcal{S}_{\mathcal{L}_2}$ be the embedding of $\mathcal{H}$ into $\mathcal{S}_{\mathcal{L}_2}$ when $\mathcal{S}_{\mathcal{L}_1} \subseteq \mathcal{S}_{\mathcal{L}_2}$.

The main steps of our algorithm for over-approximating the values of neurons in a multi-layer ReLU network are the following:

- We start with an initial tropical polyhedron $\mathcal{H}_0 \subset \mathcal{S}_{\{L_0\}}$ that represents the interval ranges of the input layer L_0.
- For each additional layer L_{i+1}:
  - Calculate an enclosing hypercube C_i for the nodes of layer L_i, given the current abstraction $\mathcal{H}_i \subset \mathcal{S}_{\mathcal{L}_i}$ (Sect. 2.3).
  - Calculate the polyhedron $\mathcal{P}_{i+1}$ representing relationships between layer L_i and the new layer L_{i+1}, for nodes of layer L_i taking values in C_i, as described in Sect. 3: Theorem 1 for the external description, and Theorem 2 for the internal description
  - Let $\mathcal{L}'_{i+1} = \mathcal{L}_i \cup \{L_{i+1}\}$. Calculate $\mathcal{P}'_{i+1} = Emb(\mathcal{P}_{i+1}, \mathcal{L}'_{i+1})$ (see below)
  - Intersect $\mathcal{P}'_{i+1}$ with the projection (using the internal description, see below) of the previous abstraction $\mathcal{H}_i$ to get $\mathcal{H}'_{i+1} = Emb(\mathcal{H}_i, \mathcal{L}'_{i+1}) \cap \mathcal{P}'_{i+1}$ (using the external description).
  - Choose $\mathcal{L}_{i+1} \supset \{L_{i+1}\}$, and calculate $\mathcal{H}_{i+1} = Proj(\mathcal{H}'_{i+1}, \mathcal{L}_{i+1})$. Usually, we would use $\mathcal{L}_{i+1} = \{L_0, L_{i+1}\}$ if we only want relations between the input and output layers, or $\mathcal{L}_{i+1} = \{L_0, \ldots, L_{i+1}\}$ if we want relations between every layer.

We need now to describe the projection and embedding functions $Proj$ and Emb. Let $\mathcal{L}_2 \subset \mathcal{L}_1 \subset \{L_0, \ldots, L_N\}$ be two sets of layers. Let $\mathcal{H}$ be a polyhedron on $\mathcal{S}_{\mathcal{L}_1}$. We have $\mathcal{H}' = Proj(\mathcal{H}, \mathcal{L}_2) = \{(x_i)_{L_i \in \mathcal{L}_2}, (x_i)_{L_i \in \mathcal{L}_1} \in \mathcal{H}\}$, i.e. for each point in $\mathcal{H}$, we only keep the dimensions corresponding to layers in $\mathcal{L}_2$, and discard the other dimensions. Projecting is easy with the internal description of polyhedron, as we can project the extreme points of $\mathcal{H}$ to get generators of $\mathcal{H}'$. However, we do not have a simple algorithm to project the external description of a polyhedron.

Let $\mathcal{L}_1 \subset \mathcal{L}_2 \subset \{L_0, \ldots, L_N\}$ be two sets of layers, and Δ be the sum of n_{i+1}, the number of neurons of layer L_i, for i such that $L_i \in \mathcal{L}_2 \setminus \mathcal{L}_1$. Let $\mathcal{H}$ be a polyhedron on $\mathcal{S}_{\mathcal{L}_1}$. We note that $\mathcal{S}_2 \equiv \mathcal{S}_1 \times \mathbb{R}_{max}^{\Delta}$, and thus $\mathcal{H}' = Emb(\mathcal{H}, \mathcal{L}_2) \equiv \mathcal{H} \times \mathbb{R}_{max}^{\Delta}$, i.e. we add dimensions corresponding to each node in $\mathcal{L}_2$ which are not in $\mathcal{L}_1$, and let points in $\mathcal{H}'$ take any value of $\mathbb{R}_{max}$ on these dimensions. Embedding is based on simple matrices concatenations in the external description, for more details. Embedding using the internal description is more involved and is explained after exemplifying things on a simple example.

Example 11. We consider the 1-layer neural net of Example 1, and add a second layer. The new linear layer is defined by $u_1 = y_2 - y_1 - 1$, $u_2 = y_1 - y_2 + 1$ and the output neurons are $z_1 = max(0, u_1) = max(0, y_2 - y_1 - 1)$ and $z_2 = max(0, u_2) = max(0, y_1 - y_2 + 1)$.

The enclosing cube for the tropical polyhedron $\mathcal{H}$ containing the values of neurons of the first layer L_1: y_1, y_2 of Example 1 is $[0, 1] \times [0, 3]$. The analysis of the second layer L_2, supposing its input belongs to $[0, 1] \times [0, 3]$ gives the constraint (an extract of the external representation of the resulting tropical polyhedron $\mathcal{H}'$) $-3 \leq u_1 - y_1 \leq 2$, $-2 \leq u_1 - y_2 \leq -1$, $-2 \leq$

$u_2 - y_1 \leq 1$, $-5 \leq u_2 - y_2 \leq 2$, $z_1 = max(0, u_1)$, $z_2 = max(0, u_2)$. The intersection of the embedding $Emb(\mathcal{H}', \{L_0, L_1, L_2\})$ with the embedding $Emb(\mathcal{H}, \{L_0, L_1, L_2\})$ consists, as we saw above, in concatenating the tropical constraints, in the common space of variables. This implies in particular that we add the constraint $-3 \leq y_1 - y_2 \leq 0$ to the above equations. The intersection is actually a zone intersection, where we have to normalize the corresponding DBM. A manual calculation shows that this will make use of the equalities $u_2 - y_2 = (u_2 - y_1) + (y_1 - y_2)$, $u_1 - y_1 = (u_1 - y_2) + (y_2 - y_1)$. By combining equations, we get the refined bounds (refined lower bound for the first equation, refined upper bound for the second equation) $-2 \leq u_1 - y_1 \leq 2$, $-5 \leq u_2 - y_2 \leq 1$.

Embedding a Tropical Polyhedron: Internal Description. In this paragraph, we embed a polyhedron into a higher dimensional space, using the internal description.

Suppose $\mathcal{H}$ is a tropical polyhedron in $\mathbb{R}^n$ (such as $\mathcal{P}_i$ in the previous section) that we want to embed $\mathcal{H}$ into a larger space, with an extra coordinate, which we consider bounded here within $[a, b]$. So we need to determine a presentation of the tropical polyhedron $\mathcal{H}' = \mathcal{H} \times [a, b]$.

Supposing we have m extreme points p_i for representing $\mathcal{H}$, a naive method consists in noticing that the family $(p_i, a), (p_i, b)$ is a generator of $\mathcal{H}'$ and removing non-extreme points from that list. But that would exhibit poor performance, as we get $m \times 2^k$ extreme points for $\mathcal{H}''$. We can in fact do better:

Theorem 3. *The extreme points of $\mathcal{H}'$ are $\{(p_i, a), 1 \leq i \leq m\} \cup \{(p_i, b), i \in I\}$, where I is a subset of indexes of generators of $\mathcal{H}$, $I \subset [1, m]$, such that:*

$$\forall i \in I, \forall j \in [1, m] \setminus \{i\}, p_i \oplus p_j \neq p_i \tag{5}$$
$$\forall i \in [1, m] \setminus I, \exists j \in [1, m] \setminus \{i\} \text{ s.t. } p_i \oplus p_j = p_i \tag{6}$$

Passing to the limit, this shows that the extreme points of $\mathcal{H} \times \mathbb{R}$ are $(p_i, -\infty)$, $i = 1, \ldots, m$ and the extreme rays are $(p_i, 0)$, $i \in I$ for the smallest I verifying Eq. (5) and (6). In the current implementation, we do not use extreme rays and embed $\mathcal{H}$ into larger state spaces by using large enough values for a and b.

Checking Properties on ReLU Neural Nets. Given an affine guard

$$h(x, y) = \sum_{i=1}^{m} h_i x_i + \sum_{j=1}^{n} h'_j y_j + c$$

where x_i, resp. y_j are the input, resp. output neurons, we want to determine whether, for all input values in $[-1, 1]$, we have $h(x) \geq 0$ (this can encode properties (P_1) and (P_2) of Example 1).

There are two ways to check such properties. The first one, that we have implemented, is as follows. We abstract the input output relation that the network under analysis encodes, using a tropical polyhedron $\mathcal{H}$ as described in Sect. 4. From this, we derive the smallest zone Z containing $\mathcal{H}$ as in Sect. 2.3.

Finally, we solve the linear programming problem $m = \min_{x,y \in Z} h(x,y)$ using any classical algorithm (we used glpk in our prototype). This is enough for checking (P_1) in Example 1 since $m \geq 0$ proves our property true, but not (P_2). The second way can be useful to check (P_2): here we have no choice but try to solve $m = \min_{x,y \in \mathcal{H}} h(x,y)$ which is not a convex optimization problem, in any sense (tropical nor classical). This could be encoded as MILP problem instead.

5   Implementation, Experiments and Benchmarks

Internal, External and Double Description Methods. Overall, we have developed methods for propagating an outer-approximation of the values that the different layers of neurons can take, within a MLP with ReLU activation. Let us discuss the pros and cons of using the internal description, external description and double description methods:

- The double description method allows for possibly using subdivisions, propagating values in multiple layers and projecting them onto a subset of interesting neurons (e.g. input and output layers), as well as computing an enclosing zone, for synthesizing classification properties. We have implemented this in a prototype using Polymake [18], whose results we briefly discuss below.
- The internal description allows for analyzing one layer networks, using subdivisions, project onto an interesting subset of neurons, as well as computing an enclosing zone (Sect. 2.3). We have implemented this method in C++ in a standalone prototype, nntrop, that takes as input a Sherlock file [14] describing the one hidden layer neural net to analyze plus a linear formula to be checked, and returns the tropical abstraction of the values that neurons can take, its over-approximation by a zone, and whether the linear specification is satisfied or not.
- The external description allows for analyzing multiple layer networks (see Sect. 4).

The double description method is much more expensive since the translation between the internal and external representations may be quite complex.

Experiments and Benchmarks. We briefly compare the computation times between internal description only and double description in Table 1. For each example, we indicate in the columns # inp. the number of input neurons, # out. the number of output neurons, # hid. the number of hidden layers, # neur. is the total number of neurons (input, output and hidden), t. intern is the time spent for computing the internal representation and t. double for the double description of the tropical polyhedron abstracting the corresponding neural net. Experiments are performed on a simple computer with ArchLinux and a Intel(R) Core(TM) i5-7200U CPU @ 2.50 GHz.

We of course see the influence of a potential exponential complexity for going back and forth between internal and external descriptions, but also the fact that we relied on a perl (interpreted) implementation of tropical polyhedra (the one of polymake [18], with exact rational arithmetics), which is much slower than the C++ implementation we wrote for the internal description method (although the internal description method does work in a twice as big space because it considers the octagon instead of just zone abstraction).

Table 1. Execution times (internal and double description) on sample networks.

Example	# inp.	# out.	# hid.	# neur.	t. intern. (s)	t. double (s)
running	2	2	0	4	0.006	1.83
running2	2	2	1	6	0.011	4.34
multi	2	8	1	13	0.005	3.9
krelu	2	2	0	4	0.011	1.94
tora_modified_controller	4	1	1	6	0.005	14.57
tora_modified_controller_1	4	1	1	105	0.75	815.12
quadcopter_trial_controller_3	18	1	1	49	0.009	102.54
quadcopter_trial_controller_1	18	1	1	69	0.2	469.77
quad_modified_controller	18	1	1	20	0.005	14
car_nn_controller_2	4	2	1	506	104.75	–
car_nn_controller_1	4	2	1	506	88.8	–
ex	2	1	5	59	0.195	1682.28

In Table 1, running is the network of Example 1, and running2 is the extension with an extra layer of Example 11, discussed in great length in these examples. Example krelu is the running example from [35] that we discuss at the end of this section, and tora_modified_controller, tora_modified_controller_1, quadcopter_trial_controller_3, quadcopter_trial_controller_1, quad_modified_controller, car_nn_controller_2, car_nn_controller_1 and ex are examples from the distribution of Sherlock [14]. ex is a multi-layer example for which the algorithm using only the internal representation does not compute the intersection of tropical polyhedra between layers (involving the external representation), contrarily to the double description prototype. We now discuss some of these examples below.

Network multi is a simple 2-layer, 13 neurons example with inputs x_1, x_2, outputs $y_1, y_2, \ldots, y_8$ and

$$
\begin{bmatrix} h_1 \\ h_2 \\ h_3 \end{bmatrix} = ReLU \left(\begin{bmatrix} 1 & 1 \\ 1 & -1 \\ -1 & -1 \end{bmatrix} \begin{bmatrix} x_1 \\ x_2 \end{bmatrix} \right) \quad \begin{bmatrix} y_1 \\ y_2 \\ y_3 \\ y_4 \\ y_5 \\ y_6 \\ y_7 \\ y_8 \end{bmatrix} = max \left(\left(\begin{bmatrix} 1 & 1 & 1 \\ 1 & 1 & -1 \\ 1 & -1 & 1 \\ 1 & -1 & -1 \\ -1 & 1 & 1 \\ -1 & 1 & -1 \\ -1 & -1 & 1 \\ -1 & -1 & -1 \end{bmatrix} \begin{bmatrix} h_1 \\ h_2 \\ h_3 \end{bmatrix} \right), 0 \right).
$$

Our zone based abstraction returns the following ranges: $y_1 \in [0,6]$, $y_2 \in [0,4]$, $y_3 \in [0,4]$, $y_4 \in [0,2]$, $y_5 \in [0,4]$, $y_6 \in [0,2]$, $y_5 \in [0,2]$ and $y_8 = 0$, whereas the exact ranges for y_1 to y_7 is $[0,2]$. Our algorithm is thus exact for y_4, y_6, y_7 and y_8 but not y_1, y_2, y_3 nor y_5. This is due to the fact that the zone-based tropical abstraction does represent faithfully the differences of neuron values, but not sums in particular. For instance, $y_2 = max(0, 2x_1)$ which cannot be represented exactly by our method.

Network `krelu` is a 2 layer 4 neurons example from [35]. We get the correct bounds on the outputs: $0 \leq z_1, z_2 \leq 2$, as well as relations between the inputs and the outputs: $z_j \leq x_i + 1$. However, we do not have significant relations between z_1 and z_2, as those are not tropically linear. We refer to the results obtained with 1-ReLU and 2-ReLU in [35]: they both get better relations between z_1 and z_2, in particular $z_1 + z_2 \leq 2$ which is not representable in a tropical manner (except by using an octagon based abstraction, which is outside the scope of this paper). However 1-ReLU does not keep track of relations between the inputs and the outputs, and has sub-optimal relations between the outputs, as it cannot represent the non linear ReLU function exactly. 2-ReLU, on the other hand gets both the relation between the output variables, and between the inputs and outputs correct, but is more computationally expensive.

In order to assess the efficiency of the internal description methods, we have run a number of experiments, with various number of inputs and ouputs for neural nets with one hidden layer only. The linear layers are generated randomly, with weights between -2 and 2. Timings are shown in the figure on the right (demonstrating the expected complexity, cubical in the number of neurons), where the x-axis is number of input neurons, y-axis is the number of output neurons, and z-axis is time. For 100 inputs and 100 neurons in the hidden layer, the full pipeline (checking the linear specification in particular) took about 35 s, among which the tropical polyhedron analysis took 6 s.

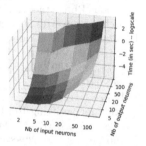

6 Conclusion and Future Work

We have explored the use of tropical polyhedra as a way to circumvent the combinatorial complexity of neural networks with ReLU activation function. The first experiments we made show that our approximations are tractable when we are able to use either the internal or the external representations for tropical polyhedra, and not both at the same time. This is akin to the results obtained in the classical polyhedron approach, where most of the time, only a sub polyhedral domain is implemented, needing only one of the two kinds of representations. It is interesting to notice that a recent paper explores the use of octohedral constraints, a three-dimensional counterpart of our octagonal representations, in the search of more tractable yet efficient abstraction for ReLU neural nets

[31]. This work is a first step towards a hierarchy of approximations for ReLU MLPs. We have been approximating the tropical rational functions that these neural nets compute by tropical affine functions, and the natural continuation of this work is to go for higher-order approximants, in the tropical world. We also believe that the tropical approach to abstracting ReLU neural networks would be particularly well suited to verification of ternary nets [27]. These ternary nets have gained importance, in particular in embedded systems: simpler weights mean smaller memory needs and faster evaluation, and it has been observed [1] that they can provide similar performance to general networks.

References

1. Alemdar, H., Caldwell, N., Leroy, V., Prost-Boucle, A., Pétrot, F.: Ternary neural networks for resource-efficient AI applications. CoRR abs/1609.00222 (2016)
2. Allamigeon, X., Gaubert, S., Goubault, E.: The tropical double description method. In: 27th International Symposium on Theoretical Aspects of Computer Science, STACS 2010 (2010)
3. Allamigeon, X.: Static analysis of memory manipulations by abstract interpretation - Algorithmics of tropical polyhedra, and application to abstract interpretation. Ph.D. thesis, École Polytechnique, Palaiseau, France (2009). https://tel. archives-ouvertes.fr/pastel-00005850
4. Allamigeon, X., Gaubert, S., Goubault, É.: Inferring min and max invariants using max-plus polyhedra. In: Alpuente, M., Vidal, G. (eds.) SAS 2008. LNCS, vol. 5079, pp. 189–204. Springer, Heidelberg (2008). https://doi.org/10.1007/978-3-540-69166-2_13
5. Bak, S., Tran, H.-D., Hobbs, K., Johnson, T.T.: Improved geometric path enumeration for verifying ReLU neural networks. In: Lahiri, S.K., Wang, C. (eds.) CAV 2020. LNCS, vol. 12224, pp. 66–96. Springer, Cham (2020). https://doi.org/10. 1007/978-3-030-53288-8_4
6. Bastani, O., Ioannou, Y., Lampropoulos, L., Vytiniotis, D., Nori, A., Criminisi, A.: Measuring neural net robustness with constraints. In: Advances in Neural Information Processing Systems (NIPS) (2016)
7. Blanchet, B., et al.: A static analyzer for large safety-critical software. In: PLDI, pp. 196–207. ACM Press, June 2003
8. Botoeva, E., Kouvaros, P., Kronqvist, J., Lomuscio, A., Misener, R.: Efficient verification of relu-based neural networks via dependency analysis. In: Proceedings of the AAAI Conference on Artificial Intelligence, vol. 34, no. 04, pp. 3291–3299 (2020). https://vas.doc.ic.ac.uk/software/neural/
9. Bourdoncle, F.: Abstract interpretation by dynamic partitioning. J. Func. Program. 2(4), 407–435 (1992)
10. Cousot, P., Cousot, R.: Abstract interpretation: a unified lattice model for static analysis of programs by construction or approximation of fixpoints. In: Conference Record of the Fourth ACM Symposium on Principles of Programming Languages, Los Angeles, California, USA, pp. 238–252, January 1977
11. Cousot, P., Cousot, R.: Abstract interpretation: a unified lattice model for static analysis of programs by construction or approximation of fixpoints. In: POPL. ACM (1977)

12. Cousot, P., Halbwachs, N.: Automatic discovery of linear restraints among variables of a program. In: Proceedings of the 5th ACM SIGACT-SIGPLAN Symposium on Principles of Programming Languages, pp. 84–96. POPL 1978, Association for Computing Machinery, New York, NY, USA (1978). https://doi.org/10.1145/512760.512770
13. Dutta, S., Chen, X., Sankaranarayanan, S.: Reachability analysis for neural feedback systems using regressive polynomial rule inference. In: HSCC (2019)
14. Dutta, S., Chen, X., Jha, S., Sankaranarayanan, S., Tiwari, A.: Sherlock - A tool for verification of neural network feedback systems: demo abstract. In: HSCC (2019)
15. Ehlers, R.: Formal verification of piece-wise linear feed-forward neural networks. In: ATVA (2017)
16. Evtimov, I., et al..: Robust physical-world attacks on machine learning models. CoRR abs/1707.08945 (2017). http://arxiv.org/abs/1707.08945
17. Gaubert, S., Katz, R.: The Minkowski theorem for max-plus convex sets. Linear Algebra Appl. **421**, 356–369 (2006)
18. Gawrilow, E., Joswig, M.: polymake: a Framework for Analyzing Convex Polytopes, pp. 43–73. Birkhäuser Basel (2000)
19. Gehr, T., Mirman, M., Drachsler-Cohen, D., Tsankov, P., Chaudhuri, S., Vechev, M.: AI2: safety and robustness certification of neural networks with abstract interpretation. In: Conférence IEEE S&P 2018 (2018)
20. Gowal, S., et al.: On the effectiveness of interval bound propagation for training verifiably robust models. CoRR abs/1810.12715 (2018). http://arxiv.org/abs/1810.12715
21. Henriksen, P., Lomuscio, A.R.: Efficient neural network verification via adaptive refinement and adversarial search. In: ECAI. Frontiers in Artificial Intelligence and Applications, vol. 325 (2020)
22. Huang, X., Kwiatkowska, M., Wang, S., Wu, M.: Safety verification of deep neural networks. In: Majumdar, R., Kunčak, V. (eds.) CAV 2017. LNCS, vol. 10426, pp. 3–29. Springer, Cham (2017). https://doi.org/10.1007/978-3-319-63387-9_1
23. Julian, K., Kochenderfer, M.J., Owen, M.P.: Deep neural network compression for aircraft collision avoidance systems. AIAA J. Guidance Control Dyn. (2018). https://arxiv.org/pdf/1810.04240.pdf
24. Katz, G., Barrett, C., Dill, D.L., Julian, K., Kochenderfer, M.J.: Reluplex: An efficient SMT solver for verifying deep neural networks. In: CAV 2017 (2017)
25. Katz, G., et al.: The Marabou framework for verification and analysis of deep neural networks. In: Dillig, I., Tasiran, S. (eds.) CAV 2019. LNCS, vol. 11561, pp. 443–452. Springer, Cham (2019). https://doi.org/10.1007/978-3-030-25540-4_26
26. Khedr, H., Ferlez, J., Shoukry, Y.: Effective formal verification of neural networks using the geometry of linear regions (2020)
27. Li, F., Liu, B.: Ternary weight networks. CoRR abs/1605.04711 (2016)
28. Mauborgne, L., Rival, X.: Trace partitioning in abstract interpretation based static analyzers. In: Programming Languages and Systems (2005)
29. Miné, A.: A new numerical abstract domain based on difference-bound matrices. In: Danvy, O., Filinski, A. (eds.) PADO 2001. LNCS, vol. 2053, pp. 155–172. Springer, Heidelberg (2001). https://doi.org/10.1007/3-540-44978-7_10
30. Miné, A.: The octagon abstract domain. High. Order Symb. Comput. **19**(1), 31–100 (2006)
31. Müller, M.N., Makarchuk, G., Singh, G., Püschel, M., Vechev, M.: Precise multi-neuron abstractions for neural network certification (2021)
32. Ruan, W., Huang, X., Kwiatkowska, M.: Reachability analysis of deep neural networks with provable guarantees. In: IJCAI (2018)

33. Shiqi, W., Pei, K., Justin, W., Yang, J., Jana, S.: Efficient formal safety analysis of neural networks. In: NIPS (2018)
34. Singh, G., Gehr, T., Mirman, M., Püschel, M., Vechev, M.: Fast and effective robustness certification
35. Singh, G., Ganvir, R., Püschel, M., Vechev, M.: Beyond the single neuron convex barrier for neural network certification. In: Advances in Neural Information Processing Systems (NeurIPS) (2019)
36. Singh, G., Gehr, T., Püschel, M., Vechev, M.: An abstract domain for certifying neural networks. In: Proceedings ACM Programming Language 3(POPL), January 2019
37. Singh, G., Gehr, T., Püschel, M., Vechev, M.: Boosting robustness certification of neural networks. In: ICLR (2019)
38. Szegedy, C., et al.: Intriguing properties of neural networks (2013). https://arxiv.org/abs/1312.6199
39. Tjeng, V., Xiao, K., Tedrake, R.: Evaluating robustness of neural networks with mixed integer programming. https://arxiv.org/abs/1711.07356
40. Wang, S., Pei, K., Whitehouse, J., Yang, J., Jana, S.: Formal security analysis of neural networks using symbolic intervals. USENIX Security (2018)
41. Zhang, H., et al.: Towards stable and efficient training of verifiably robust neural networks. In: ICLR (2020)
42. Zhang, L., G.Naitzat, Lim, L.H.: Tropical geometry of deep neural networks. In: Proceedings of the 35th International Conference on Machine Learning, vol. 80, pp. 5824–5832. PMLR (2018)

Exploiting Verified Neural Networks via Floating Point Numerical Error

Kai Jia[✉] and Martin Rinard

MIT CSAIL, Cambridge, MA 02139, USA
{jiakai,rinard}@mit.edu

Abstract. Researchers have developed neural network verification algorithms motivated by the need to characterize the robustness of deep neural networks. The verifiers aspire to answer whether a neural network guarantees certain properties with respect to all inputs in a space. However, many verifiers inaccurately model floating point arithmetic but do not thoroughly discuss the consequences.

We show that the negligence of floating point error leads to unsound verification that can be systematically exploited in practice. For a pre-trained neural network, we present a method that efficiently searches inputs as witnesses for the incorrectness of robustness claims made by a complete verifier. We also present a method to construct neural network architectures and weights that induce wrong results of an incomplete verifier. Our results highlight that, to achieve practically reliable verification of neural networks, any verification system must accurately (or conservatively) model the effects of any floating point computations in the network inference or verification system.

Keywords: Verification of neural networks · Floating point soundness · Tradeoffs in verifiers

1 Introduction

Deep neural networks (DNNs) have been successful at various tasks, including image processing, language understanding, and robotic control [30]. However, they are vulnerable to adversarial inputs [40], which are input pairs indistinguishable to human perception that cause a DNN to give substantially different predictions. This situation has motivated the development of network verification algorithms that claim to prove the robustness of a network [3,33,42], specifically that the network produces identical classifications for all inputs in a perturbation space around a given input.

Verification algorithms typically reason about the behavior of the network assuming real-valued arithmetic. In practice, however, the computation of both the verifier and the neural network is performed on physical computers that use floating point numbers and floating point arithmetic to approximate the underlying real-valued computations. This use of floating point introduces numerical

© Springer Nature Switzerland AG 2021
C. Drăgoi et al. (Eds.): SAS 2021, LNCS 12913, pp. 191–205, 2021.
https://doi.org/10.1007/978-3-030-88806-0_9

error that can potentially invalidate the guarantees that the verifiers claim to provide. Moreover, the existence of multiple software and hardware systems for DNN inference further complicates the situation because different implementations exhibit different numerical error characteristics. Unfortunately, prior neural network verification research rarely discusses floating point (un)soundness issues (Sect. 2).

This work considers two scenarios for a decision-making system relying on verified properties of certain neural networks: (i) The adversary can present arbitrary network inputs to the system while the network has been pretrained and fixed (ii) The adversary can present arbitrary inputs and also network weights and architectures to the system. We present an efficient search technique to find witnesses of the unsoundness of complete verifiers under the first scenario. The second scenario enables inducing wrong results more easily, as will be shown in Sect. 5. Note that even though allowing arbitrary network architectures and weights is a stronger adversary, it is still practical. For example, one may deploy a verifier to decide whether to accept an untrusted network based on its verified robustness, and an attacker might manipulate the network so that its nonrobust behavior does not get noticed by the verifier.

Specifically, we train robust networks on the MNIST and CIFAR10 datasets. We work with the `MIPVerify` complete verifier [42] and several inference implementations included in the PyTorch framework [29]. For each implementation, we construct image pairs (x_0, x_{adv}) where x_0 is a brightness-modified natural image, such that the implementation classifies x_{adv} differently from x_0, x_{adv} falls in a ℓ_∞-bounded perturbation space around x_0, and the verifier incorrectly claims that no such adversarial image x_{adv} exists for x_0 within the perturbation space. Moreover, we show that if modifying network architecture or weights is allowed, floating point error of an incomplete verifier `CROWN` [49] can also be exploited to induce wrong results. Our method of constructing adversarial images is not limited to our setting but is applicable to other verifiers that do not soundly model floating point arithmetic.

We emphasize that any verifier that does not correctly or conservatively model floating point arithmetic fails to provide any safety guarantee against malicious network inputs and/or network architectures and weights. Ad hoc patches or parameter tuning can not fix this problem. Instead, verification techniques should strive to provide soundness guarantees by correctly incorporating floating point details in both the verifier and the deployed neural network inference implementation. Another solution is to work with quantized neural networks that eliminate floating point issues [20].

2   Background and Related Work

Training Robust Networks: Researchers have developed various techniques to train robust networks [24,26,43,47]. Madry et al. [24] formulates the robust training problem as minimizing the worst loss within the input perturbation and proposes training on data generated by the Projected Gradient Descent

(PGD) adversary. In this work, we consider robust networks trained with the PGD adversary.

Complete Verification: Complete verification (a.k.a. exact verification) methods either prove the property being verified or provide a counterexample to disprove it. Complete verifiers have formulated the verification problem as a Satisfiability Modulo Theories (SMT) problem [3,12,17,21,34] or a Mixed Integer Linear Programming (MILP) problem [6,10,13,23,42]. In principle, SMT solvers are able to model exact floating point arithmetic [32] or exact real arithmetic [8]. However, for efficiency reasons, deployed SMT solvers for verifying neural networks all use inexact floating point arithmetic to reason about the neural network inference. MILP solvers typically work directly with floating point, do not attempt to model real arithmetic exactly, and therefore suffer from numerical error. There have also been efforts on extending MILP solvers to produce exact or conservative results [28,39], but they exhibit limited performance and have not been applied to neural network verification.

Incomplete Verification: On the spectrum of the tradeoff between completeness and scalability, incomplete methods (a.k.a. certification methods) aspire to deliver more scalable verification by adopting over-approximation while admitting the inability to either prove or disprove the properties in certain cases. There is a large body of related research [11,14,26,31,37,45,46,49]. Salman et al. [33] unifies most of the relaxation methods under a common convex relaxation framework and suggests that there is an inherent barrier to tight verification via layer-wise convex relaxation captured by such a framework. We highlight that floating point error of implementations that use a direct dot product formulation has been accounted for in some certification frameworks [36,37] by maintaining upper and lower rounding bounds for sound floating point arithmetic [25]. Such frameworks should be extensible to model numerical error in more sophisticated implementations like the Winograd convolution [22], but the effectiveness of this extension remains to be studied. However, most of the certification algorithms have not considered floating point error and may be vulnerable to attacks that exploit this deficiency.

Floating Point Arithmetic: Floating point is widely adopted as an approximate representation of real numbers in digital computers. After each calculation, the result is rounded to the nearest representable value, which induces roundoff error. A large corpus of methods have been developed for floating point analysis [2,9,38,41], but they have yet not been applied to problems at the scale of neural network inference or verification involving millions of operations. Concerns for floating point error in neural network verifiers are well grounded. For example, the verifiers `Reluplex` [21] and `MIPVerify` [42] have been observed to occasionally produce incorrect results on large scale benchmarks [15,44]. However, no prior work tries to systematically invalidate neural network verification results via exploiting floating point error.

3   Problem Definition

We consider 2D image classification problems. Let $y = \mathrm{NN}\,(x;\,W)$ denote the classification confidence given by a neural network with weight parameters W for an input x, where $x \in \mathbb{R}_{[0,1]}^{m \times n \times c}$ is an image with m rows and n columns of pixels each containing c color channels represented by floating point values in the range $[0, 1]$, and $y \in \mathbb{R}^k$ is a logits vector containing the classification scores for each of the k classes. The class with the highest score is the classification result of the neural network.

For a logits vector y and a target class number t, we define the Carlini-Wagner (CW) loss [5] as the score of the target class subtracted by the maximal score of the other classes:

$$L_{\mathrm{CW}}\,(y,\,t) = y_t - \max_{i \neq t} y_i \qquad (1)$$

Note that x is classified as an instance of class t if and only if $L_{\mathrm{CW}}\,(\mathrm{NN}\,(x;\,W)\,,\,t) > 0$, assuming no equal scores of two classes.

Adversarial robustness of a neural network is defined for an input x_0 and a perturbation bound ϵ, such that the classification result is stable within allowed perturbations:

$$\begin{aligned}
\forall x \in \mathrm{Adv}_\epsilon\,(x_0) &: L(x) > 0 \\
\text{where } L(x) &= L_{\mathrm{CW}}\,(\mathrm{NN}\,(x;\,W)\,,\,t_0) \\
t_0 &= \mathrm{argmax}\,\mathrm{NN}\,(x_0;\,W)
\end{aligned} \qquad (2)$$

In this work we consider ℓ_∞-norm bounded perturbations:

$$\mathrm{Adv}_\epsilon\,(x_0) = \{x \mid \|x - x_0\|_\infty \leq \epsilon \wedge \min x \geq 0 \wedge \max x \leq 1\} \qquad (3)$$

We use the `MIPVerify` [42] complete verifier to demonstrate our attack method. `MIPVerify` formulates (2) as an MILP instance $L^* = \min_{x \in \mathrm{Adv}_\epsilon(x_0)} L(x)$ that is solved by the commercial solver Gurobi [16]. The network is robust if $L^* > 0$. Otherwise, the minimizer x^* encodes an adversarial image.

Due to the inevitable presence of numerical error in both the network inference system and the verifier, the exact specification of $\mathrm{NN}\,(\cdot;\,W)$ (i.e., a bit-level accurate description of the underlying computation) is not clearly defined in (2). We consider the following implementations included in the PyTorch framework to serve as our candidate definitions of the convolutional layers in $\mathrm{NN}\,(\cdot;\,W)$, while nonconvolutional layers use the default PyTorch implementation:

- $\mathrm{NN}_{\mathrm{C,M}}\,(\cdot;\,W)$: A matrix-multiplication-based implementation on x86/64 CPUs. The convolution kernel is copied into a matrix that describes the dot product to be applied on the flattened input for each output value.
- $\mathrm{NN}_{\mathrm{C,C}}\,(\cdot;\,W)$: The default convolution implementation on x86/64 CPUs.
- $\mathrm{NN}_{\mathrm{G,M}}\,(\cdot;\,W)$: A matrix-multiplication-based implementation on NVIDIA GPUs.
- $\mathrm{NN}_{\mathrm{G,C}}\,(\cdot;\,W)$: A convolution implementation using the `IMPLICIT_GEMM` algorithm from the cuDNN library [7] on NVIDIA GPUs.

- $\text{NN}_{\text{G,CWG}}(\cdot; \boldsymbol{W})$: A convolution implementation using the WINOGRAD_NONFUSED algorithm from the cuDNN library [7] on NVIDIA GPUs. It is based on the Winograd convolution algorithm [22], which runs faster but has higher numerical error compared to others.

For a given implementation $\text{NN}_{\text{impl}}(\cdot; \boldsymbol{W})$, our method finds pairs of $(\boldsymbol{x}_0, \boldsymbol{x}_{\text{adv}})$ represented as single precision floating point numbers such that

1. $\boldsymbol{x}_0$ and $\boldsymbol{x}_{\text{adv}}$ are in the dynamic range of images:
$$\min \boldsymbol{x}_0 \geq 0, \ \min \boldsymbol{x}_{\text{adv}} \geq 0, \ \max \boldsymbol{x}_0 \leq 1, \ \text{and} \ \max \boldsymbol{x}_{\text{adv}} \leq 1$$
2. $\boldsymbol{x}_{\text{adv}}$ falls in the perturbation space of $\boldsymbol{x}_0$: $\|\boldsymbol{x}_{\text{adv}} - \boldsymbol{x}_0\|_\infty \leq \epsilon$
3. The verifier claims that the robustness specification (2) holds for $\boldsymbol{x}_0$
4. The implementation falsifies the claim of the verifier:
$$L_{\text{CW}}(\text{NN}_{\text{impl}}(\boldsymbol{x}_{\text{adv}}; \boldsymbol{W}), t_0) < 0$$

Note that the first two conditions are accurately defined for any implementation compliant with the IEEE-754 standard [19], because the computation only involves element-wise subtraction and max-reduction that incur no accumulated error. The Gurobi solver used by MIPVerify operates with double precision internally. Therefore, to ensure that our adversarial examples satisfy the constraints considered by the solver, we also require that the first two conditions hold for $\boldsymbol{x}'_{\text{adv}} = \text{float64}(\boldsymbol{x}_{\text{adv}})$ and $\boldsymbol{x}'_0 = \text{float64}(\boldsymbol{x}_0)$ that are double precision representations of $\boldsymbol{x}_{\text{adv}}$ and $\boldsymbol{x}_0$.

4   Exploiting a Complete Verifier

We present two observations crucial to the exploitation to be described later.

Observation 1: Tiny perturbations on the network input result in random output perturbations. We select an image $\boldsymbol{x}$ for which the verifier claims that the network makes robust predictions. We plot $\|\text{NN}(\boldsymbol{x} + \delta; \boldsymbol{W}) - \text{NN}(\boldsymbol{x}; \boldsymbol{W})\|_\infty$ against $-10^{-6} \leq \delta \leq 10^{-6}$, where the addition of $\boldsymbol{x} + \delta$ is only applied on the single input element that has the largest gradient magnitude. As shown in Fig. 1, the change of the output is highly nonlinear with respect to the change of the input, and a small perturbation could result in a large fluctuation. Note that the output fluctuation is caused by accumulated floating point error instead of nonlinearities in the network because pre-activation values of all the ReLU units have the same signs for both $\boldsymbol{x}$ and $\boldsymbol{x} + \delta$.

Observation 2: Different neural network implementations exhibit different floating point error characteristics. We evaluate the implementations on the whole MNIST test set and compare the outputs of the first layer (i.e., with only one linear transformation applied to the input) against that of $\text{NN}_{\text{C,M}}$. Figure 2 presents the histogram which shows that different implementations usually manifest different error behavior.

Method Overview: Given a network and weights $\text{NN}(\cdot; \boldsymbol{W})$, we search for image pairs $(\boldsymbol{x}_0, \boldsymbol{x}_1)$ such that the network is verifiably robust with respect to

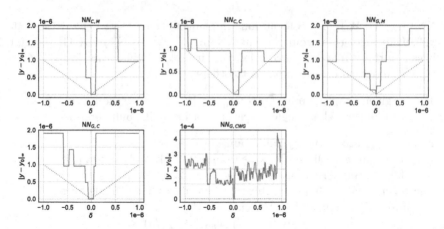

Fig. 1. Change of logits vector due to small single-element input perturbations for different implementations. The dashed lines are $y = |\delta|$.

x_0, while $x_1 \in \mathrm{Adv}_\epsilon(x_0)$ and $L_{\mathrm{CW}}(\mathrm{NN}(x_1; W), t_0)$ is less than the numerical fluctuation introduced by tiny input perturbations. We call x_0 a *quasi-safe image* and x_1 the corresponding *quasi-adversarial image*. Observation 1 suggests that an adversarial image might be obtained by randomly disturbing the quasi-adversarial image in the perturbation space. Observation 2 suggests that each implementation has its own adversarial images and needs to be handled separately. We search for the quasi-safe image by modifying the brightness of a natural image while querying a complete verifier whether it is near the boundary of robust predictions. Figure 3 illustrates this process.

Before explaining the details of our method, we first present the following proposition that formally establishes the existence of quasi-safe and quasi-adversarial images for continuous neural networks:

Proposition 1. *Let $E > 0$ be an arbitrarily small positive number. If a continuous neural network $\mathrm{NN}(\cdot; W)$ can produce a robust classification for some input belonging to class t, and it does not constantly classify all inputs as class t, then there exists an input x_0 such that*

$$0 < \min_{x \in \mathrm{Adv}_\epsilon(x_0)} L_{\mathrm{CW}}(\mathrm{NN}(x; W), t) < E$$

Let $x_1 = \mathrm{argmin}_{x \in \mathrm{Adv}_\epsilon(x_0)} L_{\mathrm{CW}}(\mathrm{NN}(x; W), t)$ be the minimizer of the above function. We call x_0 a quasi-safe image and x_1 a quasi-adversarial image.

Proof. Let $f(x) := \min_{x' \in \mathrm{Adv}_\epsilon(x)} L_{\mathrm{CW}}(\mathrm{NN}(x'; W), t)$. Since $f(\cdot)$ is composed of continuous functions, $f(\cdot)$ is continuous. Suppose $\mathrm{NN}(\cdot; W)$ is robust with respect to x_+ that belongs to class t. Let x_- be be any input such that $L_{\mathrm{CW}}(\mathrm{NN}(x_-; W), t) < 0$, which exists because $\mathrm{NN}(\cdot; W)$ does not constantly classify all inputs as class t. We have $f(x_+) > 0$ and $f(x_-) < 0$. The Poincaré-Miranda theorem asserts the existence of x_0 such that $0 < f(x_0) < E$.

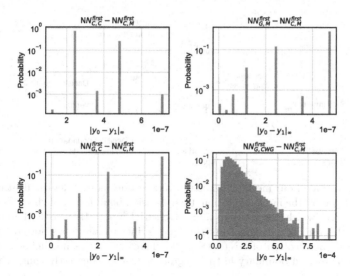

Fig. 2. Distribution of difference relative to $\mathrm{NN_{C,M}}$ of first layer evaluated on MNIST test images.

Given a particular implementation $\mathrm{NN_{impl}}(\cdot;\boldsymbol{W})$ and a natural image $\boldsymbol{x}_{\mathbf{seed}}$ which the network robustly classifies as class t_0 according to the verifier, we construct an adversarial input pair $(\boldsymbol{x_0},\boldsymbol{x_{adv}})$ that meets the constraints described in Sect. 3 in three steps:

Step 1: We search for a coefficient $\alpha \in [0,1]$ such that $\boldsymbol{x_0} = \alpha\boldsymbol{x_{seed}}$ serves as the quasi-safe image. Specifically, we require the verifier to claim that the network is robust for $\alpha\boldsymbol{x_{seed}}$ but not so for $\alpha'\boldsymbol{x_{seed}}$ with $0 < (\delta = \alpha - \alpha') < \epsilon_r$, where ϵ_r should be small enough to allow quasi-adversarial images sufficiently close to the boundary. We set $\epsilon_r = 10^{-7}$. We use binary search to minimize δ starting from $\alpha' \leftarrow 0$, $\alpha \leftarrow 1$. We found that the MILP solver often becomes extremely slow when δ is small, so we start with binary search and switch to grid search by dividing the best known δ to 16 intervals if the solver exceeds a time limit.

Step 2: We search for the quasi-adversarial image $\boldsymbol{x_1}$ corresponding to $\boldsymbol{x_0}$. We define a loss function with a tolerance of τ as $L(\boldsymbol{x},\tau) := L_{\mathrm{CW}}(\mathrm{NN}(\boldsymbol{x};\boldsymbol{W}),t_0) - \tau$, which can be incorporated in any verifier by modifying the bias of the Softmax layer. We aim to find τ_0 and τ_1, where τ_0 is the minimal confidence of all images in the perturbation space of $\boldsymbol{x_0}$, and τ_1 is slightly larger than τ_0 with $\boldsymbol{x_1}$ being the corresponding adversarial image. Formally:

$$\begin{cases} \forall \boldsymbol{x} \in \mathrm{Adv}_\epsilon(\boldsymbol{x_0}) : L(\boldsymbol{x},\tau_0) > 0 \\ \boldsymbol{x_1} \in \mathrm{Adv}_\epsilon(\boldsymbol{x_0}) \\ L(\boldsymbol{x_1},\tau_1) < 0 \\ \tau_1 - \tau_0 < 10^{-7} \end{cases}$$

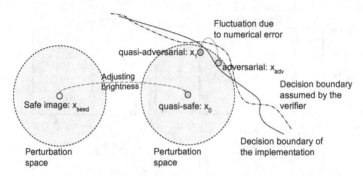

Fig. 3. Illustration of our method. Since the verifier does not model the floating point arithmetic details of the implementation, their decision boundaries for the classification problem diverge, which allows us to find adversarial inputs that cross the boundary via numerical error fluctuations. Note that the verifier usually does not comply with a well defined specification of NN $(\cdot; \boldsymbol{W})$, and therefore it does not define a decision boundary. The dashed boundary in the diagram is just for illustrative purposes.

Note that $\boldsymbol{x_1}$ is produced by the complete verifier as proof of nonrobustness given the tolerance τ_1. The above values are found via binary search with initialization $\tau_0 \leftarrow 0$ and $\tau_1 \leftarrow L_{\text{CW}}(\text{NN}(\boldsymbol{x_0}; \boldsymbol{W}), t_0)$. In addition, we accelerate the binary search if the verifier can compute the *worst* objective defined as:

$$\tau_w = \min_{\boldsymbol{x} \in \text{Adv}_\epsilon(\boldsymbol{x_0})} L_{\text{CW}}(\text{NN}(\boldsymbol{x}; \boldsymbol{W}), t_0) \tag{4}$$

In this case, we initialize $\tau_0 \leftarrow \tau_w - \delta_s$ and $\tau_1 \leftarrow \tau_w + \delta_s$. We empirically set $\delta_s = 3 \times 10^{-6}$ to incorporate the numerical error in the verifier so that $L(\boldsymbol{x_0}, \tau_w - \delta_s) > 0$ and $L(\boldsymbol{x_0}, \tau_w + \delta_s) < 0$. The binary search is aborted if the solver times out.

Step 3: We minimize $L_{\text{CW}}(\text{NN}(\boldsymbol{x_1}; \boldsymbol{W}), t_0)$ with hill climbing via applying small random perturbations on the quasi-adversarial image $\boldsymbol{x_1}$ while projecting back to $\text{Adv}_\epsilon(\boldsymbol{x_0})$ to find an adversarial example. The perturbations are applied on patches of $\boldsymbol{x_1}$ as described in Algorithm 1.

Algorithm 1. Searching adversarial examples via hill climbing

---

Input: quasi-safe image $\boldsymbol{x_0}$
Input: target class number t
Input: quasi-adversarial image $\boldsymbol{x_1}$
Input: input perturbation bound ϵ
Input: a neural network inference implementation $\text{NN}_{\text{impl}}(\cdot; \boldsymbol{W})$
Input: number of iterations N (default value 1000)
Input: perturbation scale u (default value 2e−7)
Output: an adversarial image $\boldsymbol{x_{\text{adv}}}$ or FAILED

for Index i of $\boldsymbol{x_0}$ **do**   ▷ Find the bounds $\boldsymbol{x_l}$ and $\boldsymbol{x_u}$ for allowed perturbations
    $x_l[i] \leftarrow \max(\text{nextafter}(x_0[i] - \epsilon, 0), 0)$

$x_u[i] \leftarrow \min(\text{nextafter}(x_0[i] + \epsilon, 1), 1)$
while $x_0[i] - x_l[i] > \epsilon$ **or** $\text{float64}(x_0[i]) - \text{float64}(x_l[i]) > \epsilon$ **do**
    $x_l[i] \leftarrow \text{nextafter}(x_l[i], 1)$
end while
while $x_u[i] - x_0[i] > \epsilon$ **or** $\text{float64}(x_u[i]) - \text{float64}(x_0[i]) > \epsilon$ **do**
    $x_u[i] \leftarrow \text{nextafter}(x_u[i], 0)$
end while
end for

▷ We select the offset and stride based on the implementation to ensure that perturbed tiles contribute independently to the output. The Winograd algorithm in cuDNN produces 9×9 output tiles for 13×13 input tiles and 5×5 kernels.
if $\text{NN}_{\text{impl}}(\cdot; W)$ is $\text{NN}_{\text{G,CWG}}(\cdot; W)$ **then** (offset, stride) $\leftarrow (4, 9)$
else   (offset, stride) $\leftarrow (0, 4)$
end if

for $i \leftarrow 1$ **to** N **do**
    for $(h, w) \leftarrow (0, 0)$ **to** $(\text{height}(x_1), \text{width}(x_1))$ **step** (stride, stride) **do**
        $\delta \leftarrow \text{uniform}(-u, u, (\text{stride} - \text{offset}, \text{stride} - \text{offset}))$
        $x_1' \leftarrow x_1[:]$
        $x_1'[h + \text{offset} : h + \text{stride}, w + \text{offset} : w + \text{stride}] \mathrel{+}= \delta$
        $x_1' \leftarrow \max(\min(x_1', x_u), x_l)$
        if $L_{\text{CW}}(\text{NN}_{\text{impl}}(x_1'; W), t) < L_{\text{CW}}(\text{NN}_{\text{impl}}(x_1; W), t)$ **then**
            $x_1 \leftarrow x_1'$
        end if
    end for
end for
if $L_{\text{CW}}(\text{NN}_{\text{impl}}(x_1; W), t) < 0$ **then return** $x_{\text{adv}} \leftarrow x_1$
else   **return** FAILED
end if

Experiments: We conduct our experiments on a workstation with an NVIDIA Titan RTX GPU and an AMD Ryzen Threadripper 2970WX CPU. We train the small architecture from Xiao et al. [48] with the PGD adversary and the RS Loss on MNIST and CIFAR10 datasets. The network has two convolutional layers with 4×4 filters, 2×2 stride, and 16 and 32 output channels, respectively, and two fully connected layers with 100 and 10 output neurons. The trained networks achieve 94.63% and 44.73% provable robustness with perturbations of ℓ_∞ bounded by 0.1 and 2/255 on the two datasets, respectively, similar to the results reported in Xiao et al. [48]. Our code is available at https://github.com/jia-kai/realadv.

Although our method only needs $O(-\log \epsilon)$ invocations of the verifier where ϵ is the threshold in the binary search, the verifier still takes most of the time and is too slow for a large benchmark. Therefore, for each dataset, we test our method on 32 images randomly sampled from the verifiably robustly classified test images. All the implementations that we have considered are successfully exploited. Specifically, our benchmark contains $32 \times 2 \times 5 = 320$ cases, while adversarial examples are found for 82 of them. The failed cases

Table 1. Number of adversarial examples successfully found for different neural network inference implementations

	$NN_{C,M}$	$NN_{C,C}$	$NN_{G,M}$	$NN_{G,C}$	$NN_{G,CWG}$
MNIST	2	3	1	3	7
CIFAR10	16	12	7	6	25

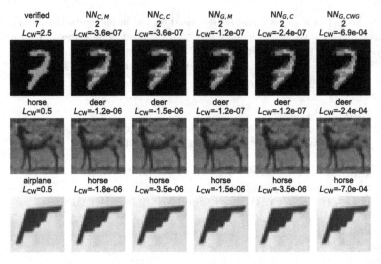

Fig. 4. The quasi-safe images with respect to which all implementations are successfully exploited, and the corresponding adversarial images.

correspond to large τ_1 values in Step 2 due to verifier timeouts or the discrepancy of floating point arithmetic between the verifier and the implementations. Let $\tau_{\text{impl}} := L_{\text{CW}} (NN_{\text{impl}} (x_1; W), t)$ denote the loss of an quasi-adversarial input on a particular implementation. Algorithm 1 succeeds on all cases with $\tau_{\text{impl}} < 8.3 \times 10^{-7}$ (35 such cases in total), while 18 among them have $\tau_{\text{impl}} < 0$ due to floating point discrepancy (i.e., the quasi-adversarial input is already an adversarial input for this implementation). The most challenging case (i.e., with largest τ_{impl}) on which Algorithm 1 succeeds has $\tau_{\text{impl}} = 3.2 \times 10^{-4}$. The largest value of τ_{impl} is 3.7. Table 1 presents the detailed numbers for each implementation. Figure 4 shows the quasi-safe images on which our exploitation method succeeds for all implementations and the corresponding adversarial images.

5   Exploiting an Incomplete Verifier

The relaxation adopted in certification methods renders them incomplete but also makes their verification claims more robust to floating point error compared to complete verifiers. In particular, we evaluate the CROWN framework [49] on our randomly selected MNIST test images and the corresponding quasi-safe images from Sect. 4. CROWN is able to verify the robustness of the network on 29 out of the 32 original test images, but it is unable to prove the robustness for any of the quasi-safe images. Note that MIPVerify claims that the network is robust with respect to all the original test images and the corresponding quasi-safe images.

Incomplete verifiers are still vulnerable if we allow arbitrary network architectures and weights. Our exploitation builds on the observation that verifiers typically need to merge always-active ReLU units with their subsequent layers to reduce the number of nonlinearities and achieve a reasonable speed. The merge of layers involves computing merged "equivalent" weights, which is different from the floating point computation adopted by an inference implementation.

We build a neural network that takes a 13×13 single-channel input image, followed by a 5×5 convolutional layer with a single output channel, two fully connected layers with 16 output neurons each, a fully connected layer with one output neuron denoted as $u = \max(\boldsymbol{W_u h_u} + b_u, 0)$, and a final linear layer that computes $\boldsymbol{y} = [u; 10^{-7}]$ as the logits vector. All the hidden layers have ReLU activation. The input $\boldsymbol{x_0}$ is taken from a Gaussian distribution. The hidden layers have random Gaussian coefficients, and the biases are chosen so that (i) the ReLU neurons before u are always activated for inputs in the perturbation space of $\boldsymbol{x_0}$ (ii) the neuron u is never activated while b_u is the maximum possible value (i.e., $b_u = -\max_{\boldsymbol{x} \in \mathrm{Adv}_\epsilon(\boldsymbol{x_0})} \boldsymbol{W_u h_u}(\boldsymbol{x})$). CROWN is able to prove that all ReLU neurons before u are always activated but u is never activated, and therefore it claims that the network is robust with respect to perturbations around $\boldsymbol{x_0}$. However, by initializing the quasi-adversarial input $\boldsymbol{x_1} \leftarrow \boldsymbol{x_0} + \epsilon \, \mathrm{sign}(\boldsymbol{W_{equiv}})$ where $\boldsymbol{W_{equiv}}$ is the product of all the coefficient matrices of the layers up to u, we successfully find adversarial inputs for all the five implementations considered in this work by randomly perturbing $\boldsymbol{x_1}$ using Algorithm 1 with a larger number of iterations ($N = 10000$) due to the smaller input size.

Note that the output scores can be manipulated to appear less suspicious. For instance, we can set $\boldsymbol{z} = \mathrm{clip}(10^7 \cdot \boldsymbol{y}, -2, 2)$ as the final output in the above example so that $\boldsymbol{z}$ becomes a more "naturally looking" classification score in the range $[-2, 2]$ and its perturbation due to floating point error is also enlarged to the unit scale. The extreme constants 10^{-7} and 10^7 can also be obfuscated by using multiple consecutive scaling layers with each one having small scaling factors such as 0.1 and 10.

6   Discussion

We have shown that some neural network verifiers are systematically exploitable. One appealing remedy is to introduce relaxations into complete verifiers, such as by verifying for a larger ϵ or setting a threshold for accepted confidence score. For example, it might be tempting to claim the robustness of a network for $\epsilon = 0.09999$ if it is verified for $\epsilon = 0.1$. We emphasize that there are no guarantees provided by any floating point complete verifier currently extant. Moreover, the difference between the true robust perturbation bound and the bound claimed by an unsound verifier might be much larger if the network has certain properties.

For example, `MIPVerify` has been observed to give NaN results when verifying pruned neural networks [15]. The adversary might also be able to manipulate the network to scale the scores arbitrarily, as discussed in Sect. 5. The correct solution requires obtaining a tight relaxation bound that is sound for both the verifier and the inference implementation, which is extremely challenging.

A possible fix for complete verification is to adopt exact MILP solvers with rational inputs [39]. There are three challenges: (i) The efficiency of exactly solving the large amounts of computation in neural network inference has not been studied and is unlikely to be satisfactory (ii) The computation that derives the MILP formulation from a verification specification, such as the neuron bound analysis in Tjeng et al. [42], must also be exact, but existing neural network verifiers have not attempted to define and implement exact arithmetic with the floating point weights (iii) The results of exact MILP solvers are only valid for an exact neural network inference implementation, but such exact implementations are not widely available (not provided by any deep learning libraries that we are aware of), and their efficiency remains to be studied.

Alternatively, one may obtain sound and nearly complete verification by adopting a conservative MILP solver based on techniques such as directed rounding [28]. We also need to ensure all arithmetic in the verifier to derive the MILP formulation soundly over-approximates floating point error. This is more computationally feasible than exact verification discussed above. It is similar to the approach used in some sound incomplete verifiers that incorporate floating point error by maintaining upper and lower rounding bounds of internal computations [36,37]. However, this approach relies on the specific implementation details of the inference algorithm—optimizations such as Winograd [22] or FFT [1], or deployment in hardware accelerators with lower floating point precision such as Bfloat16 [4], would either invalidate the robustness guarantees or require changes to the analysis algorithm. Therefore, we suggest that these sound verifiers explicitly state the requirements on the inference implementations for which their results are sound. A possible future research direction is to devise a universal sound verification framework that can incorporate different inference implementations.

Another approach for sound and complete neural network verification is to quantize the computation to align the inference implementation with the verifier. For example, if we require all activations to be multiples of s_0 and all weights to be multiples of s_1, where $s_0 s_1 > 2E$ and E is a very loose bound of possible implementation error, then the output can be rounded to multiples of $s_0 s_1$ to completely eliminate numerical error. Binarized neural networks [18] are a family of extremely quantized networks, and their verification [20,27,35] is sound and complete. However, the problem of robust training and verification of quantized neural networks [20] is relatively under-examined compared to that of real-valued neural networks [24,26,42,48].

7 Conclusion

Floating point error should not be overlooked in the verification of real-valued neural networks, as we have presented techniques that efficiently find witnesses for the unsoundness of two verifiers. Unfortunately, floating point soundness issues have not received sufficient attention in neural network verification research. A user has few choices if they want to obtain sound verification results for a neural network, especially if they deploy accelerated neural network inference implementations. We hope our results will help to guide future neural network verification research by providing another perspective on the tradeoff between soundness, completeness, and scalability.

Acknowledgments. We would like to thank Gagandeep Singh and Kai Xiao for providing invaluable suggestions on an early manuscript.

References

1. Abtahi, T., Shea, C., Kulkarni, A., Mohsenin, T.: Accelerating convolutional neural network with FFT on embedded hardware. IEEE Trans. Very Large Scale Integr. (VLSI) Syst. **26**(9), 1737–1749 (2018)
2. Boldo, S., Melquiond, G.: Computer Arithmetic and Formal Proofs: Verifying Floating-point Algorithms with the Coq System. Elsevier, Kidlington (2017)
3. Bunel, R., Lu, J., Turkaslan, I., Kohli, P., Torr, P., Mudigonda, P.: Branch and bound for piecewise linear neural network verification. J. Mach. Learn. Res. **21**(2020) (2020)
4. Burgess, N., Milanovic, J., Stephens, N., Monachopoulos, K., Mansell, D.: Bfloat16 processing for neural networks. In: 2019 IEEE 26th Symposium on Computer Arithmetic (ARITH), pp. 88–91. IEEE (2019)
5. Carlini, N., Wagner, D.: Towards evaluating the robustness of neural networks. In: 2017 IEEE Symposium on Security and Privacy (SP), pp. 39–57. IEEE (2017)
6. Cheng, C.-H., Nührenberg, G., Ruess, H.: Maximum resilience of artificial neural networks. In: D'Souza, D., Narayan Kumar, K. (eds.) ATVA 2017. LNCS, vol. 10482, pp. 251–268. Springer, Cham (2017). https://doi.org/10.1007/978-3-319-68167-2_18
7. Chetlur, S., et al.: CUDNN: efficient primitives for deep learning. arXiv preprint arXiv:1410.0759 (2014)
8. Corzilius, F., Loup, U., Junges, S., Ábrahám, E.: SMT-RAT: an SMT-compliant nonlinear real arithmetic toolbox. In: Cimatti, A., Sebastiani, R. (eds.) SAT 2012. LNCS, vol. 7317, pp. 442–448. Springer, Heidelberg (2012). https://doi.org/10.1007/978-3-642-31612-8_35
9. Das, A., Briggs, I., Gopalakrishnan, G., Krishnamoorthy, S., Panchekha, P.: Scalable yet rigorous floating-point error analysis. In: SC20, pp. 1–14. IEEE (2020)
10. Dutta, S., Jha, S., Sankaranarayanan, S., Tiwari, A.: Output range analysis for deep feedforward neural networks. In: Dutle, A., Muñoz, C., Narkawicz, A. (eds.) NFM 2018. LNCS, vol. 10811, pp. 121–138. Springer, Cham (2018). https://doi.org/10.1007/978-3-319-77935-5_9
11. Dvijotham, K., et al.: Training verified learners with learned verifiers. arXiv preprint arXiv:1805.10265 (2018)

12. Ehlers, R.: Formal verification of piece-wise linear feed-forward neural networks. In: D'Souza, D., Narayan Kumar, K. (eds.) ATVA 2017. LNCS, vol. 10482, pp. 269–286. Springer, Cham (2017). https://doi.org/10.1007/978-3-319-68167-2_19

13. Fischetti, M., Jo, J.: Deep neural networks and mixed integer linear optimization. Constraints **23**(3), 296–309 (2018). https://doi.org/10.1007/s10601-018-9285-6

14. Gehr, T., Mirman, M., Drachsler-Cohen, D., Tsankov, P., Chaudhuri, S., Vechev, M.: Ai2: safety and robustness certification of neural networks with abstract interpretation. In: 2018 IEEE Symposium on Security and Privacy (SP), pp. 3–18. IEEE (2018)

15. Guidotti, D., Leofante, F., Pulina, L., Tacchella, A.: Verification of neural networks: enhancing scalability through pruning. arXiv preprint arXiv:2003.07636 (2020)

16. Gurobi, O.: Gurobi optimizer reference manual (2020). http://www.gurobi.com

17. Huang, X., Kwiatkowska, M., Wang, S., Wu, M.: Safety verification of deep neural networks. In: Majumdar, R., Kunčak, V. (eds.) CAV 2017. LNCS, vol. 10426, pp. 3–29. Springer, Cham (2017). https://doi.org/10.1007/978-3-319-63387-9_1

18. Hubara, I., Courbariaux, M., Soudry, D., El-Yaniv, R., Bengio, Y.: Binarized neural networks. In: NeurIPS, pp. 4107–4115. Curran Associates Inc. (2016)

19. IEEE: IEEE standard for floating-point arithmetic. In: IEEE Std 754–2008, pp. 1–70 (2008)

20. Jia, K., Rinard, M.: Efficient exact verification of binarized neural networks. In: NeurIPS, vol. 33, pp. 1782–1795. Curran Associates Inc. (2020)

21. Katz, G., Barrett, C., Dill, D.L., Julian, K., Kochenderfer, M.J.: Reluplex: an efficient SMT solver for verifying deep neural networks. In: Majumdar, R., Kunčak, V. (eds.) CAV 2017. LNCS, vol. 10426, pp. 97–117. Springer, Cham (2017). https://doi.org/10.1007/978-3-319-63387-9_5

22. Lavin, A., Gray, S.: Fast algorithms for convolutional neural networks. In: Proceedings of the IEEE Conference on Computer Vision and Pattern Recognition, pp. 4013–4021 (2016)

23. Lomuscio, A., Maganti, L.: An approach to reachability analysis for feed-forward relu neural networks. arXiv preprint arXiv:1706.07351 (2017)

24. Madry, A., Makelov, A., Schmidt, L., Tsipras, D., Vladu, A.: Towards deep learning models resistant to adversarial attacks. In: ICLR (2018)

25. Miné, A.: Relational abstract domains for the detection of floating-point run-time errors. In: Schmidt, D. (ed.) ESOP 2004. LNCS, vol. 2986, pp. 3–17. Springer, Heidelberg (2004). https://doi.org/10.1007/978-3-540-24725-8_2

26. Mirman, M., Gehr, T., Vechev, M.: Differentiable abstract interpretation for provably robust neural networks. In: Dy, J., Krause, A. (eds.) Proceedings of the 35th International Conference on Machine Learning, Proceedings of Machine Learning Research, 10–15 July, vol. 80, pp. 3578–3586. PMLR, Stockholm (2018)

27. Narodytska, N., Kasiviswanathan, S., Ryzhyk, L., Sagiv, M., Walsh, T.: Verifying properties of binarized deep neural networks. In: Thirty-Second AAAI Conference on Artificial Intelligence (2018)

28. Neumaier, A., Shcherbina, O.: Safe bounds in linear and mixed-integer linear programming. Math. Prog. **99**(2), 283–296 (2004)

29. Paszke, A., et al.: PyTorch: an imperative style, high-performance deep learning library. In: NeurIPS, pp. 8024–8035. Curran Associates Inc. (2019)

30. Raghu, M., Schmidt, E.: A survey of deep learning for scientific discovery. arXiv:2003.11755 (2020)

31. Raghunathan, A., Steinhardt, J., Liang, P.S.: Semidefinite relaxations for certifying robustness to adversarial examples. In: NeurIPS, pp. 10877–10887. Curran Associates Inc. (2018)

32. Rümmer, P., Wahl, T.: An SMT-LIB theory of binary floating-point arithmetic. In: International Workshop on Satisfiability Modulo Theories (SMT), p. 151 (2010)
33. Salman, H., Yang, G., Zhang, H., Hsieh, C.J., Zhang, P.: A convex relaxation barrier to tight robustness verification of neural networks. In: NeurIPS, pp. 9832–9842 (2019)
34. Scheibler, K., Winterer, L., Wimmer, R., Becker, B.: Towards verification of artificial neural networks. In: MBMV, pp. 30–40 (2015)
35. Shih, A., Darwiche, A., Choi, A.: Verifying binarized neural networks by angluin-style learning. In: Janota, M., Lynce, I. (eds.) SAT 2019. LNCS, vol. 11628, pp. 354–370. Springer, Cham (2019). https://doi.org/10.1007/978-3-030-24258-9_25
36. Singh, G., Gehr, T., Mirman, M., Püschel, M., Vechev, M.: Fast and effective robustness certification. In: NeurIPS, pp. 10802–10813, Curran Associates, Inc. (2018)
37. Singh, G., Gehr, T., Püschel, M., Vechev, M.T.: An abstract domain for certifying neural networks. Proc. ACM Prog. Lang. **3**, 1–30 (2019)
38. Solovyev, A., Baranowski, M.S., Briggs, I., Jacobsen, C., Rakamarić, Z., Gopalakrishnan, G.: Rigorous estimation of floating-point round-off errors with symbolic taylor expansions. TOPLAS **41**(1), 1–39 (2018)
39. Steffy, D.E., Wolter, K.: Valid linear programming bounds for exact mixed-integer programming. INFORMS J. Comput. **25**(2), 271–284 (2013)
40. Szegedy, C., et al.: Intriguing properties of neural networks. In: ICLR (2014)
41. Titolo, L., Feliú, M.A., Moscato, M.M., Muñoz, C.A.: An abstract interpretation framework for the round-off error analysis of floating-point programs. In: VMCAI, pp. 516–537 (2018)
42. Tjeng, V., Xiao, K.Y., Tedrake, R.: Evaluating robustness of neural networks with mixed integer programming. In: ICLR (2019)
43. Tramer, F., Boneh, D.: Adversarial training and robustness for multiple perturbations. In: NeurIPS, pp. 5866–5876, Curran Associates Inc. (2019)
44. Wang, S., Pei, K., Whitehouse, J., Yang, J., Jana, S.: Formal security analysis of neural networks using symbolic intervals. In: 27th USENIX Security Symposium (USENIX Security 18), pp. 1599–1614 (2018)
45. Weng, L., et al.: Towards fast computation of certified robustness for relu networks. In: International Conference on Machine Learning, pp. 5276–5285 (2018)
46. Wong, E., Kolter, J.Z.: Provable defenses against adversarial examples via the convex outer adversarial polytope. arXiv preprint arXiv:1711.00851 (2017)
47. Wong, E., Rice, L., Kolter, J.Z.: Fast is better than free: revisiting adversarial training. In: ICLR (2020)
48. Xiao, K.Y., Tjeng, V., Shafiullah, N.M.M., Madry, A.: Training for faster adversarial robustness verification via inducing relu stability. In: ICLR (2019)
49. Zhang, H., Weng, T.W., Chen, P.Y., Hsieh, C.J., Daniel, L.: Efficient neural network robustness certification with general activation functions. In: NeurIPS, pp. 4939–4948. Curran Associates Inc. (2018)

Verifying Low-Dimensional Input Neural Networks via Input Quantization

Kai Jia[(✉)] and Martin Rinard

MIT CSAIL, Cambridge, MA 02139, USA
{jiakai,rinard}@mit.edu

Abstract. Deep neural networks are an attractive tool for compressing the control policy lookup tables in systems such as the Airborne Collision Avoidance System (ACAS). It is vital to ensure the safety of such neural controllers via verification techniques. The problem of analyzing ACAS Xu networks has motivated many successful neural network verifiers. These verifiers typically analyze the internal computation of neural networks to decide whether a property regarding the input/output holds. The intrinsic complexity of neural network computation renders such verifiers slow to run and vulnerable to floating-point error.

This paper revisits the original problem of verifying ACAS Xu networks. The networks take low-dimensional sensory inputs with training data provided by a precomputed lookup table. We propose to prepend an input quantization layer to the network. Quantization allows efficient verification via input state enumeration, whose complexity is bounded by the size of the quantization space. Quantization is equivalent to nearest-neighbor interpolation at run time, which has been shown to provide acceptable accuracy for ACAS in simulation. Moreover, our technique can deliver exact verification results immune to floating-point error if we directly enumerate the network outputs on the target inference implementation or on an accurate simulation of the target implementation.

Keywords: Neural network verification · Verification by enumeration · ACAS Xu network verification

1 Introduction

The Airborne Collision Avoidance System (ACAS) is crucial for aircraft safety [11]. This system aims to avoid collision with intruding aircraft via automatically controlling the aircraft or advising a human operator to take action. The ACAS typically takes low-dimensional sensory inputs, including distance, direction, and speed for the intruder and ownship aircraft, and provides a control policy which is a valuation for a set of candidate actions such as "weak left" or "strong right". Recent work has formulated aircraft dynamics under uncertainties such as advisory response delay as a partially observable Markov decision process for which dynamic programming can be used to compute values for different actions [10]. The value function computed via dynamic programming is

© Springer Nature Switzerland AG 2021
C. Drăgoi et al. (Eds.): SAS 2021, LNCS 12913, pp. 206–214, 2021.
https://doi.org/10.1007/978-3-030-88806-0_10

often stored in a lookup table with millions of entries [12] that require giga-bytes of storage. While this table could, in principle, be used to implement the ACAS, the high storage demand makes it too costly to be embedded in practi-cal flight control systems. This situation has motivated the development of table compression techniques, including block compression with reduced floating-point precision [13] and decision trees [7].

Recently, neural networks have emerged as an efficient alternative for com-pressing the lookup tables in ACAS Xu (ACAS X for unmanned aircraft) by approximating the value function with small neural networks. Specifically, Julian et al. [7] compresses the two-gigabyte lookup table into 45 neural networks with 2.4MB of storage, where each network handles a partition of the input space.

Katz et al. [9] proposes a set of safety properties for the ACAS Xu net-works, such as that a "strong right" advisory should be given when a nearby intruder is approaching from the left. These safety properties have served as a valuable benchmark to motivate and evaluate multiple verification algorithms [1,9,15,17,19]. Such verifiers typically need to perform exact or conservative analysis of the internal neural network computation [14,18]. Unfortunately, neu-ral network verification is an NP-Complete problem [9], and therefore the ver-ifiers need exponential running time in the worst case and can be very slow in practice. In particular, Bak et al. [1] recently presented the first verifier that is able to analyze the properties ϕ_1 to ϕ_4 in the ACAS Xu benchmarks with a time limit of 10 min for each case, but their verifier still needs 1.7 h to analyze the property ϕ_7.

In summary, previous techniques perform the following steps to obtain and verify their neural network controllers for ACAS:

1. Compute a lookup table containing the scores of different actions given sen-sory states via dynamic programming.
2. Train neural networks to approximate the lookup table.
3. In deployed systems, use the neural networks to provide control advisories.
   - At run time, the networks give interpolated scores for states not present in the original lookup table.
   - Neural network verifiers that analyze the internal computing of neural networks are adopted to check if the networks meet certain safety speci-fications.

We propose instead to verify neural networks with low-dimensional inputs, such as the ACAS Xu networks, via input quantization and state enumeration. Specifically, we prepend a quantization layer to the network so that all the internal computation is performed on the discretized input space. Our proposed technique performs the following steps to obtain and verify a quantized neural network:

1. We take a pretrained network and prepend an input quantization layer to the network. The input quantization should be compatible with the original lookup table, i.e., preserving the grid points in the lookup table.

2. In deployed systems, sensory inputs are first quantized by the input quantization layer. The original network then computes the scores for the quantized input.
   - At run time, the quantization process is equivalent to nearest-neighbor interpolation.
   - To verify the network for any specification, we enumerate all quantized states within the constraint of the specification and check if the network outputs meet the specification.

Our method provides the following desirable features:

1. Our method provides acceptable runtime accuracy for ACAS Xu. Our input quantization is equivalent to nearest-neighbor interpolation and gives identical results on the table grid points as the original continuous network. Julian et al. [7] has shown that nearest-neighbor interpolation on the lookup table for runtime sensory inputs provides effective collision avoidance advisories in simulation.

2. Our method enables efficient verification. Verifying the input-quantized networks for any safety specification takes nearly constant time bounded by evaluating the network on all the grid points in the quantized space. Multiple specifications can be verified simultaneously by evaluating the network on the grid once and checking the input and output conditions for each property. Our method provides a verification speedup of tens of thousands of times compared to the ReluVal [19] verifier.

3. Many existing verifiers do not accurately model floating-point arithmetic due to efficiency considerations, thus giving potentially incorrect verification results [5]. For example, Wang et al. [19] reports that Reluplex [9] occasionally produces false adversarial examples due to floating-point error. By contrast, our verification result is exact (i.e., complete and sound) and does not suffer from floating-point error because we combine input quantization and complete enumeration of the effective input space. Moreover, input quantization allows directly verifying on the target implementation or an accurate simulation of the implementation, and therefore provides trustworthy safety guarantees for given neural network inference implementations.

4. Our technique allows easily verifying more complicated network architectures, such as continuous-depth models [2]. Our verification only needs an efficient inference implementation for the networks. By contrast, extending other neural network verifiers to new network architectures requires significant effort.

We recommend input quantization for neural networks with low-dimensional inputs as long as the quantization provides sufficient accuracy for the target application and the quantization space is small enough to allow efficient enumeration. This technique enables efficient, exact, and robust verification and provides reliable performance on the deployed platform.

2 Method

We formally describe our input-quantization method. This paper uses bold symbols to represent vectors and regular symbols to represent scalars. The superscript represents derived mathematical objects or exponentiation depending on the context.

Let $\boldsymbol{f} : \mathbb{R}^n \mapsto \mathbb{R}^m$ denote the computation of a neural network on n-dimensional input space with n being a small number. We propose to use a quantized version of the network for both training and inference, defined as

$$\boldsymbol{f}^q(\boldsymbol{x}) := \boldsymbol{f}(\boldsymbol{q}(\boldsymbol{x})) \tag{1}$$

where $\boldsymbol{q}(\boldsymbol{x})$ is the quantization function such that $\boldsymbol{q}(\boldsymbol{x}) \in S$ with S being a finite-sized set. For a specification $\phi : \forall_{\boldsymbol{x}} P(\boldsymbol{x}) \implies R(\boldsymbol{f}(\boldsymbol{x}))$ where $P(\cdot)$ and $R(\cdot)$ are predicates, we verify ϕ regarding $\boldsymbol{f}^q$ by checking:

$$\phi^q : \quad \forall \boldsymbol{x}^q \in S_p \implies R(\boldsymbol{f}(\boldsymbol{x}^q)) \tag{2}$$
$$\text{where } S_p := \{\boldsymbol{q}(\boldsymbol{x}) : P(\boldsymbol{x})\}$$

Since $S_p \subseteq S$, the complexity of verifying ϕ^q is bounded by $|S|$.

We quantize each dimension of $\boldsymbol{x}$ independently via $\boldsymbol{q}(\boldsymbol{x}) = [q_1(x_1) \dots q_n(x_n)]$. Note that if some of the dimensions are highly correlated in some application, we can quantize them together to avoid a complete Cartesian product and thus reduce the size of the quantized space.

In many cases, the input space is uniformly quantized. Previous work has utilized uniform input quantization for neural network verification [4,20] and uniform computation quantization for efficient neural network inference [3]. Given a quantization step s_i and a bias value b_i, we define a uniform quantization function $q_i(\cdot)$ as:

$$q_i(x_i) = \left\lfloor \frac{x_i - b_i}{s_i} \right\rceil s_i + b_i \tag{3}$$

where $\lfloor \cdot \rceil$ denotes rounding to the nearest integer.

The values of $q_i(\cdot)$ are essentially determined according to prior knowledge about the target application and may thus be nonuniform. Let $Q_i = \{v_i^1, \cdots, v_i^k\}$ denote the range of $q_i(\cdot)$. We use nearest neighbor for nonuniform quantization:

$$q_i(x_i) = \operatorname{argmin}_{v_i^j} |v_i^j - x_i| \tag{4}$$

The ACAS Xu networks are trained on a lookup table $\boldsymbol{L} : G \mapsto \mathbb{R}^m$, where the domain $G \subset \mathbb{R}^n$ is a finite set. We choose the quantization scheme so that the quantization preserves grid points, formally $\forall \boldsymbol{x} \in G : \boldsymbol{q}(\boldsymbol{x}) = \boldsymbol{x}$. In this way, the training processes of $\boldsymbol{f}(\cdot)$ and $\boldsymbol{f}^q(\cdot)$ are identical. In fact, we directly prepend $\boldsymbol{q}(\cdot)$ as an input quantization layer to a pretrained network $\boldsymbol{f}(\cdot)$ to obtain $\boldsymbol{f}^q(\cdot)$. Note that we can use a denser quantization than the grid points in G so that prediction accuracy might get improved by using the neural network as an interpolator.

Table 1. Description of horizontal CAS inputs. The last column describes the values used to generate the lookup table, which are taken from the open-source implementation of HorizontalCAS [6] and the Appendix VI of Katz et al. [9].

Symbol	Description	Values in the lookup table
ρ (m)	Distance from ownship to intruder	32 values between 0 and 56000 [1]
θ (rad)	Angle to intruder [2]	41 evenly spaced values between $-\pi$ and π
ψ (rad)	Heading angle of intruder [2]	41 evenly spaced values between $-\pi$ and π
v_{own} (m/s)	Speed of ownship	$\{50, 100, 150, 200\}$
v_{int} (m/s)	Speed of intruder	$\{50, 100, 150, 200\}$
τ (sec)	Time until loss of vertical separation	$\{0, 1, 5, 10, 20, 40, 60\}$
α_{prev}	Previous advisory	$\{COC, WL, WR, SL, SR\}$

[1] Distance values are nonuniformly distributed. They are given in the source code of Julian and Kochenderfer [6]: https://github.com/sisl/HorizontalCAS/blob/cd72ffc073240bcd4f0eb9164f441d3ad3fdc074/GenerateTable/mdp/constants.jl#L19.
[2] Angle is measured relative to ownship heading direction.

3   Experiments

We evaluate our method on checking the safety properties for the ACAS Xu networks [9]. Note that accuracy of input-quantized networks in deployed systems is acceptable since the quantization is equivalent to nearest-neighbor interpolation that has been shown to provide effective collision avoidance advisories in simulation [7].

Experiments in this section focus on evaluating the runtime overhead of input quantization and the actual speed of verification by enumerating quantized states. We train two networks of different sizes to evaluate the scalability of the proposed method.

3.1   Experimental Setup

The horizontal CAS problem takes seven inputs as described in Table 1, and generates one of the five possible advisories: COC (clear of conflict), WL (weak left), WR (weak right), SL (strong left), and SR (strong right).

Julian et al. [8] proposes to train a collection of neural networks where each network works with a pair of specific (τ, α_{prev}) values, takes the remaining five values as network inputs, and approximates the corresponding scores in the lookup table. Although ACAS only needs to suggest the action with the maximal score, the network is still trained to approximate the original scores in the table instead of directly giving the best action because the numerical scores are used in a Kalman filter to improve system robustness in the face of state measurement uncertainty [8]. In order to maintain the action recommendation of the original table while reducing score approximation error, Julian et al. [8] adopts an asymmetric loss function that imposes a higher penalty if the network and the lookup table give different action advisories.

Katz et al. [9] proposes a few ACAS Xu safety properties as a sanity check for the networks trained by Julian et al. [8]. These properties have also served as a useful benchmark for many neural network verifiers. Although the pretrained networks of Julian et al. [8] are publicly accessible, the authors told us that they could not provide the training data or the source code due to regulatory reasons. They suggested that we use their open-source HorizontalCAS system [6] to generate the lookup tables to train our own networks. However, HorizontalCAS networks differ from the original ACAS Xu networks in that they only have three inputs by fixing $v_{own} = 200$ and $v_{int} = 185$. We modified the source code of HorizontalCAS to match the input description in Table 1 so that we can directly use the ReluVal [19] verifier.

We evaluate our method by analyzing the property ϕ_9 proposed in Katz et al. [9], which usually takes the longest time to verify among all the properties for many verifiers [9,16,19]. Other properties share a similar form but have different input constraints and output requirements. Note that property ϕ_9 is the most compatible with the open-source HorizontalCAS because the input constraints of other properties are beyond the ranges in Table 1. For example, property ϕ_1 has $v_{own} \geq 1145$ but the quantization scheme of v_{own} for the original ACAS Xu networks is not publicly available.

The specification of ϕ_9 is:

- **Description:** Even if the previous advisory was "weak right", the presence of a nearby intruder will cause the network to output a "strong left" advisory instead.
- **Tested on:** the network trained on $\tau = 5$ and $\alpha_{prev} = WR$
- **Input constraints:** $2000 \leq \rho \leq 7000$, $-0.4 \leq \theta \leq -0.14$, $-3.141592 \leq \psi \leq -3.141592 + 0.01$, $100 \leq v_{own} \leq 150$, $0 \leq v_{int} \leq 150$.

We conduct the experiments on a workstation equipped with two GPUs (NVIDIA Titan RTX and NVIDIA GeForce RTX 2070 SUPER), 128 GiB of RAM, and an AMD Ryzen Threadripper 2970WX processor. We train two neural networks for property ϕ_9 (i.e., with $\tau = 5$ and $\alpha_{prev} = WR$) with PyTorch.

Our small network has five hidden layers with 50 neurons in each layer, and our large network has seven hidden layers with 100 neurons in each layer. We use the ReLU activation.

We implement the nearest-neighbor quantization for ρ via directly indexing a lookup table. The greatest common divisor of differences between adjacent quantized ρ values is 5. Therefore, we precompute a lookup table U such that $U_{\lfloor \rho/5 \rceil}$ is the nearest neighbor of ρ in the set of quantized values. We use the `torch.index_select` operator provided by PyTorch to take elements in the lookup table in a batched manner. Other network inputs use uniform quantization as described in Table 1. We implement uniform quantization according to the Eq. (3).

3.2   Experimental Results

Let $y_i \in \mathbb{R}^5$ (resp. $\hat{y}_i \in \mathbb{R}^5$) denote the scores given by the network (resp. the original lookup table) for the five candidate actions on the ith lookup table entry.

Table 2. Accuracies achieved by the networks evaluated on the lookup table. For comparison, Julian and Kochenderfer [6] reports an accuracy of 97.9% for networks trained only with three out of the five inputs (they fixed $v_{own} = 200$ and $v_{int} = 185$). This table shows that our network achieves sufficient accuracy for practical use.

Metric	Small network	Large network
Policy accuracy	96.87%	98.54%
Score ℓ_1 error	0.052	0.026
Score ℓ_2 error	1.3×10^{-3}	3.3×10^{-4}

Table 3. Comparing verification time (in seconds) for the property ϕ_9 on two methods: the ReluVal verifier [19] that runs on multiple cores, and exhaustive enumeration in the quantized input space on a single CPU core. This table shows that verification by enumerating quantized input states is significantly faster in our case and also more scalable regarding different network sizes.

Verification method	Small network	Large network
ReluVal [19]	0.622	171.239
Input quantization - specific [1]	0.002	0.002
Input quantization - all [2]	0.384	0.866

[1] Network is evaluated on the 60 input states that fall within the input constraint of ϕ_9.
[2] Network is evaluated on all the 860,672 input states in a batched manner. This time is the upper bound for verifying any first-order specification in the form of $\forall_x P(x) \implies R(f(x))$ by ignoring the time on evaluating predicates $P(\cdot)$ and $R(\cdot)$.

We consider three accuracy measurements, assuming a uniform distribution of the table index i:

- *Policy accuracy* is the probability that the network recommends the same action as the original lookup table. Formally, it is $P(\text{argmax } y_i = \text{argmax } \hat{y}_i)$.
- *Score ℓ_1 error* measures the ℓ_1 error of approximated scores, defined as $E(\|y_i - \hat{y}_i\|_1)$, where $\|x\|_1 := \sum_i |x_i|$.
- *Score ℓ_2 error* measures the ℓ_2 error of approximated scores, defined as $E(\|y_i - \hat{y}_i\|_2)$, where $\|x\|_2 := \sqrt{\sum_i x_i^2}$.

Table 2 presents the accuracies achieved by our networks, which shows that our training achieves comparable results as the HorizontalCAS system [6].

To verify the networks, we prepend them with an input quantization layer that implements the quantization scheme given in Table 1. To verify any specification or a set of specifications, we evaluate the network on all the 860, 672 points in the quantized space and check if each input/output pair meets the specification(s). Evaluating the network on the grid points takes 0.384 s for the small network and 0.866 s for the large one. We evaluate the network on multiple inputs in a batched manner to benefit from optimized numerical computing routines included in PyTorch. Adding the quantization layer incurs about 2% runtime overhead. We do not do any performance engineering and use the off-the-shelf implementation provided by PyTorch. Our verification speed can be further improved by using multiple CPU cores or using the GPU.

We also compare our method with ReluVal [19] on verifying the property ϕ_9. The input constraint of ϕ_9 consists of only 60 states in the quantized space. Therefore, we only need to check if the network constantly gives the "weak right" advisory for all the 60 states to verify ϕ_9. As shown in Table 3, input quantization significantly reduces the verification time compared to the ReluVal solver.

4 Conclusion

This paper advocates input quantization for the verification of neural networks with low-dimensional inputs. Our experiments show that this technique is significantly faster and more scalable than verifiers that analyze the internal computations of the neural networks on verifying ACAS Xu networks. Moreover, our method does not suffer from the floating-point discrepancy between the verifier and the network inference implementation. In general, our method applies to deterministic floating-point programs that take low-dimensional inputs as long as the target application tolerates input quantization such that enumerating all the quantized values takes acceptable time.

References

1. Bak, S., Tran, H.D., Hobbs, K., Johnson, T.T.: Improved geometric path enumeration for verifying relu neural networks. In: International Conference on Computer Aided Verification, pp. 66–96, Springer (2020)
2. Chen, R.T.Q., Rubanova, Y., Bettencourt, J., Duvenaud, D.K.: Neural ordinary differential equations. In: Bengio, S., Wallach, H., Larochelle, H., Grauman, K., Cesa-Bianchi, N., Garnett, R. (eds.) Advances in Neural Information Processing Systems, vol. 31, Curran Associates, Inc. (2018). https://proceedings.neurips.cc/paper/2018/file/69386f6bb1dfed68692a24c8686939b9-Paper.pdf
3. Gholami, A., Kim, S., Dong, Z., Yao, Z., Mahoney, M.W., Keutzer, K.: A survey of quantization methods for efficient neural network inference. arXiv preprint arXiv:2103.13630 (2021)
4. Jia, K., Rinard, M.: Efficient exact verification of binarized neural networks. In: Larochelle, H., Ranzato, M., Hadsell, R., Balcan, M.F., Lin, H. (eds.) Advances in Neural Information Processing Systems, vol. 33, pp. 1782–1795, Curran Associates, Inc. (2020). https://proceedings.neurips.cc/paper/2020/file/1385974ed5904a438616ff7bdb3f7439-Paper.pdf
5. Jia, K., Rinard, M.: Exploiting verified neural networks via floating point numerical error. arXiv preprint arXiv:2003.03021 (2020)
6. Julian, K.D., Kochenderfer, M.J.: Guaranteeing safety for neural network-based aircraft collision avoidance systems. In: 2019 IEEE/AIAA 38th Digital Avionics Systems Conference (DASC), pp. 1–10, IEEE (2019)
7. Julian, K.D., Kochenderfer, M.J., Owen, M.P.: Deep neural network compression for aircraft collision avoidance systems. J. Guid. Cont. Dyn. 42(3), 598–608 (2019)

8. Julian, K.D., Lopez, J., Brush, J.S., Owen, M.P., Kochenderfer, M.J.: Policy compression for aircraft collision avoidance systems. In: 2016 IEEE/AIAA 35th Digital Avionics Systems Conference (DASC), pp. 1–10 (2016). https://doi.org/10.1109/DASC.2016.7778091

9. Katz, G., Barrett, C., Dill, D.L., Julian, K., Kochenderfer, M.J.: Reluplex: an efficient smt solver for verifying deep neural networks. In: Majumdar, R., Kunčak, V. (eds.) CAV 2017. LNCS, vol. 10426, pp. 97–117. Springer, Cham (2017). https://doi.org/10.1007/978-3-319-63387-9_5

10. Kochenderfer, M.J., et al.: Optimized Airborne Collision Avoidance, pp. 249–276. MIT Press, Boston (2015)

11. Kochenderfer, M.J., Chryssanthacopoulos, J.: Robust airborne collision avoidance through dynamic programming. Massachusetts Institute of Technology, Lincoln Laboratory, Project Report ATC-371 130 (2011)

12. Kochenderfer, M.J., Chryssanthacopoulos, J.P.: A decision-theoretic approach to developing robust collision avoidance logic. In: 13th International IEEE Conference on Intelligent Transportation Systems, pp. 1837–1842 (2010). https://doi.org/10.1109/ITSC.2010.5625063

13. Kochenderfer, M.J., Monath, N.: Compression of optimal value functions for markov decision processes. In: 2013 Data Compression Conference, pp. 501–501 (2013). https://doi.org/10.1109/DCC.2013.81

14. Liu, C., Arnon, T., Lazarus, C., Strong, C., Barrett, C., Kochenderfer, M.J.: Algorithms for verifying deep neural networks. arXiv preprint arXiv:1903.06758 (2019)

15. Singh, G., Gehr, T., Püschel, M., Vechev, M.T.: Boosting robustness certification of neural networks. In: ICLR (Poster) (2019)

16. Singh, G., Gehr, T., Püschel, M., Vechev, M.: Boosting robustness certification of neural networks. In: International Conference on Learning Representations (2019)

17. Tran, H.D., et al.: NNV: the neural network verification tool for deep neural networks and learning-enabled cyber-physical systems. In: Lahiri, S.K., Wang, C. (eds.) Computer Aided Verification, pp. 3–17, Springer International Publishing, Cham (2020). ISBN 978-3-030-53288-8

18. Urban, C., Miné, A.: A review of formal methods applied to machine learning. arXiv preprint arXiv:2104.02466 (2021)

19. Wang, S., Pei, K., Whitehouse, J., Yang, J., Jana, S.: Formal security analysis of neural networks using symbolic intervals. In: 27th USENIX Security Symposium (USENIX Security 18), pp. 1599–1614 (2018)

20. Wu, M., Kwiatkowska, M.: Robustness guarantees for deep neural networks on videos. In: IEEE/CVF Conference on Computer Vision and Pattern Recognition (CVPR), pp. 308–317 (2020)

Data Abstraction: A General Framework to Handle Program Verification of Data Structures

Julien Braine[1,3](✉), Laure Gonnord[2,3], and David Monniaux[4]

[1] ENS de Lyon, Lyon, France
Julien.Braine@ens-lyon.fr
[2] Université Claude Bernard Lyon 1, Villeurbanne, France
Laure.Gonnord@ens-lyon.fr
[3] LIP (CNRS, ENS de Lyon, Inria, Univ. Lyon), Lyon, France
[4] Univ. Grenoble Alpes, CNRS, Grenoble INP (Institute of Engineering Univ. Grenoble Alpes), VERIMAG, Grenoble, France
David.Monniaux@univ-grenoble-alpes.fr

Abstract. Proving properties on programs accessing data structures such as arrays often requires universally quantified invariants, e.g., "all elements below index i are nonzero". In this article, we propose a general data abstraction scheme operating on Horn formulas, into which we recast previously published abstractions. We show that our instantiation scheme is relatively complete: the generated purely scalar Horn clauses have a solution (inductive invariants) if and only if the original problem has one expressible by the abstraction.

Keywords: Static analysis · Horn clauses · Abstraction

1 Introduction

Static analysis of programs containing unbounded data structures is challenging, as most interesting properties require quantifiers. Even stating that all elements of an array are equal to 0 requires them ($\forall i\ a[i] = 0$), let alone more complex cases such as Example 1. In general, the satisfiability of arbitrary quantified properties on unbounded data structures is undecidable [3], thus there is no algorithm for checking that such properties are inductive, nor inferring them.

Laure Gonnord–This work was partially funded by the French National Agency of Research in the CODAS Project (ANR-17-CE23-0004-01).

C. Drăgoi et al. (Eds.): SAS 2021, LNCS 12913, pp. 215–235, 2021.
https://doi.org/10.1007/978-3-030-88806-0_11

The first step is to select an abstract domain to search for invariants, e.g., properties of the form $\forall i, P(a[i])$ for some predicate P and array a. In this paper, we describe a transformation from and to Horn clauses such that these properties may be expressed in the transformed Horn clauses without using quantifiers. For the array data structure, our scheme can optionally completely remove arrays from the transformed Horn clauses. This transformation is *sound* and *relatively complete*: the resulting problem, to be fed to a solver for Horn clauses, such as Eldarica or Z3, has a solution if and only if the original one has one within the chosen abstract domain. In short, we reduce problems involving quantifiers and arrays to problems that do not, with no loss of precision with respect to the abstract domain.

Example 1 (Running example). The following program initializes an array to even values, then increases all values by one and checks that all values are odd. We wish to prove that the assertion is verified.

```
for(k=0; k<N; k++) /*Program point For1*/ a[k] = rand()*2;
for(k=0; k<N; k++) /*Program point For2*/ a[k] = a[k]+1;
for(k=0; k<N; k++) /*Program point For3*/ assert(a[k] % 2 == 1);
```

Contributions. (i) an abstraction framework for Horn clauses using unbounded data structures, that we call *data abstraction*; (ii) the analysis of a property we call *relative completeness* in this framework (iii) and the use of that framework to handle programs with arrays and its experimental evaluation.

Contents. Section 2 introduces Horn Clauses' concepts and notations. Sections 3 and 4 expose our data abstraction framework and its *relative completeness analysis*. Section 5 considers a data abstraction for arrays. Finally, Sect. 6 proposes a full algorithm to analyze programs with arrays and its experimental evaluation.

2   Preliminaries: Horn Clauses

2.1   Solving Programs with Assertions Using Horn Clauses

Programs with assertions can be transformed into Horn clauses using tools such as SeaHorn [9] or JayHorn [14]. The syntax of Horn clauses is recalled in Definition 2. A basic transformation consists in associating a predicate to each point of the control flow graph; control edges are inductive relations (clauses), and assertions A are clauses $\neg A \rightarrow false$[1].

Example 2 (Example 1 transformed into Horn clauses). All predicates For_i have arity 3 (1 array and 2 integer parameters) and Clause (4) in bold, will be used throughout the paper.

---

[1] Tools such as SeaHorn [9] handle richer languages such as LLVM bytecode, but the generated clauses are more complex and further removed from their initial semantics. Such clauses fall within our data abstraction framework, but not within the scope of the experimental evaluation of this paper.

$$For1(a, N, 0) \tag{1}$$

$$For1(a, N, k) \wedge k < N \to For1(a[k \leftarrow r * 2], N, k + 1) \tag{2}$$

$$For1(a, N, k) \wedge k \geq N \to For2(a, N, 0) \tag{3}$$

$$\boldsymbol{For2(a, N, k) \wedge k < N \to For2(a[k \leftarrow a[k] + 1], N, k + 1)} \tag{4}$$

$$For2(a, N, k) \wedge k \geq N \to For3(a, N, 0) \tag{5}$$

$$For3(a, N, k) \wedge k < N \wedge a[k]\%2 \neq 1 \to false \tag{6}$$

$$For3(a, N, k) \wedge k < N \to For3(a, N, k + 1) \tag{7}$$

Variables are local: the a of Clause 1 is not formally related to the a of Clause 4.

A solution to such a system of Horn clauses is a set of inductive invariants suitable for proving the desired properties. Horn clause systems can be solved by tools such as Z3, Eldarica, ... A "Sat" answer means that the inductive invariants exist and thus the program is correct[2]. "Unsat" means that a counterexample was found, leading to an assertion violation. "Unknown" means the tool fails to converge on a possible invariant. Finally, the tool may also timeout.

2.2 Horn Clauses and Horn Problems

In our setting, a Horn clause is a boolean expression over free variables and predicates with at most one positive predicate.

Definition 1 (Expressions *expr*, **positive and negative predicates** P, **models** $\mathcal{M}$ **and semantics** $expr(vars)$, $[\![expr]\!]_{\mathcal{M}}$**).** *In this paper we do not constrain the theory on which expressions are written, the only constraint being that the backend solver must handle it. An expression may contain quantifiers, free variables and predicates. A predicate is a typed name which will be a set when interpreted in a model.*
Expression evaluation: There are two evaluation contexts for expressions:

1. *Models, written $\mathcal{M}$: map each predicate to a set of the corresponding domain*
2. *Environments, written vars, that to each free variable of the expression associates a value of the corresponding type's domain $[\![expr]\!]_{\mathcal{M}}$ denotes the evaluation of an expression expr in a model $\mathcal{M}$, $expr(vars)$ denotes its the evaluation in the environment vars, $[\![expr(vars)]\!]_{\mathcal{M}}$ denotes joint evaluation. Furthermore, if an expression value is independent of the model or environment, we may use it directly as its evaluation.*

---

[2] Z3 is both a SMT solver and a tool for solving Horn clauses. In SMT, a "Sat" answer often means a counterexample trace invalidating a safety property. In contrast, in Horn solving, "Sat" means a safety property is proved.

Positive and negative predicates: *A predicate instance in a boolean expression expr is deemed* negative *(resp.* positive*) if and only if there is a negation (resp. no negation) in front of it when expr is in negative normal form.*

Definition 2 (Horn Clauses, extended, normalized, satisfiability). *A* Horn clause *is simply any expression without quantifiers (but with free variables) containing at most one positive predicate.*

Extended Horn clause: *a Horn clause which may use quantifiers.*

Normalized Horn clause: *Normalized Horn clauses are in the form* $P_1(e_1) \wedge \ldots \wedge P_n(e_n) \wedge \phi \to P'(e')$ *where:*

- $e_1, \ldots, e_n, \phi, e'$ *are expressions without predicates but with free variables.*
- $P_1, \ldots, P_n$ *are the "negative" predicates*
- P' *is the positive predicate or some expression*

Satisfiability: *A set of Horn clauses* $\mathfrak{C}$ *is said to be* satisfiable *if and only if* $\exists \mathcal{M}, \forall C \in \mathfrak{C}, [\![\forall vars, C(vars)]\!]_{\mathcal{M}}$.
In this paper, we will denote clauses in capital letters: C, sets of clauses in Fraktur: $\mathfrak{C}$*, and models in calligraphic:* $\mathcal{M}$.

Definition 3 (Notations $ite, f[a \leftarrow b]$**).**
For a boolean expression b and expressions e_1, e_2*, we define the expression "if-then-else", written* $ite(b, e_1, e_2)$*, evaluating to* e_1 *when b and to* e_2 *when* $\neg b$.

For a function f (i.e. an environment) or an array, we define $f[a \leftarrow b]$ *as* $f[a \leftarrow b](x) = ite(x = a, b, f(x))$

Example 3 (Satisfiability of Example 2). The following model satisfies Example 2 with $(a, N, k) \in \mathbb{N}^3$.

1. $\mathcal{M}(For1) = \{(a, N, k) | k < N \wedge \forall i < k, a[i]\%2 = 0\}$
2. $\mathcal{M}(For2) = \{(a, N, k) | k < N \wedge \forall i < k, a[i]\%2 = 1 \wedge \forall k \leq i < N, a[i]\%2 = 0\}$
3. $\mathcal{M}(For3) = \{(a, N, k) | k < N \wedge \forall i < N, a[i]\%2 = 1\}$

Horn clauses constrain models in two ways: those with a positive predicate force the model to be a post-fixpoint of an induction relation; those without are assertions that force the model to not contain elements violating the assertion.

Horn clauses are the syntactic objects we use to write *Horn problems*. Theorem 2 formalizes the link between Horn problems and Horn clauses.

Definition 4 (Horn Problem H**, defines** $f_H, \mathcal{U}_H$**).** *A Horn problem H is a pair* $(f_H, \mathcal{U}_H)$ *where (i)* f_H *is a monotone function over models with order* $\mathcal{M}_1 \leq \mathcal{M}_2 \equiv \forall P, \mathcal{M}_1(P) \subseteq \mathcal{M}_2(P)$*. (ii)* $\mathcal{U}_H$ *is a model. It is said to be* satisfiable *if and only if* $\mathrm{lfp} f_H \leq \mathcal{U}_H$ *(where* lfp *is the least fixpoint operator).*

Theorem 1 (Horn problems as a condition on models, defines $H(\mathcal{M})$**).**
A Horn problem H is satisfiable if and only if $\exists \mathcal{M}, f_H(\mathcal{M}) \leq \mathcal{M} \wedge \mathcal{M} \leq \mathcal{U}_H$*, also written* $\exists \mathcal{M}, H(\mathcal{M})$ *with* $H(\mathcal{M}) =_{def} f_H(\mathcal{M}) \leq \mathcal{M} \wedge \mathcal{M} \leq \mathcal{U}_H$.

Remark 1. The proof of this theorem, as well as all other ones of this paper, can be found in the associated research report [4].

Theorem 2 (Horn clauses as Horn problems, defines $H_{\mathfrak{C}}$).
Let $\mathfrak{C}$ be a set of Horn clauses. There exists a Horn problem $H_{\mathfrak{C}}$, such that for any model $\mathcal{M}$, $H_{\mathfrak{C}}(\mathcal{M}) = \forall C \in \mathfrak{C}, [\![\forall vars, C(vars)]\!]_{\mathcal{M}}$. Thus, $satisfiable(\mathfrak{C}) \equiv satisfiable(H_{\mathfrak{C}})$.

2.3   Horn Problem Induced by an Abstraction

Static analysis by abstract interpretation amounts to searching for invariants (*i.e.*, models of Horn clauses in our setting) within a subset of all possible invariants called an *abstract domain*; elements of that subset are said to be *expressible by the abstraction*. We formalize abstraction as a Galois connection [5], that is, a pair (α, γ) where α denotes abstraction (*i.e.* simplification) and γ denotes the semantics (*i.e.* what the abstraction corresponds to) of abstract elements.

Definition 5 (Models expressible by the abstraction $\mathcal{G}$). *We say that a model $\mathcal{M}$ is expressible by an abstraction $\mathcal{G}$ if and only if $\mathcal{M} = \gamma_{\mathcal{G}} \circ \alpha_{\mathcal{G}}(\mathcal{M})$ or equivalently $\exists \mathcal{M}^{\#}, \mathcal{M} = \gamma_{\mathcal{G}}(\mathcal{M}^{\#})$.*

Example 4 (Models expressible by an abstraction). Consider the model $\mathcal{M}$ from Example 3. This model is expressible by the abstraction $\mathcal{G}$ such that $\forall P \in \{For1, For2, For3\}$:

1. $\alpha_{\mathcal{G}}(\mathcal{M})(P) = \{(i, a[i], N, k) | (a, N, k) \in \mathcal{M}(P)\}$
2. $\gamma_{\mathcal{G}}(\mathcal{M}^{\#})(P) = \{(a, N, k) | \forall i, (i, a[i], N, k) \in \mathcal{M}^{\#}(P)\}$

but not by the abstraction $\mathcal{G}'$ such that $\forall P \in \{For1, For2, For3\}$:

1. $\alpha_{\mathcal{G}'}(\mathcal{M})(P) = \{(a[i], N, k) | (a, N, k) \in \mathcal{M}(P)\}$
2. $\gamma_{\mathcal{G}'}(\mathcal{M}^{\#})(P) = \{(a, N, k) | \forall i, (a[i], N, k) \in \mathcal{M}^{\#}(P)\}$

The idea is that the abstraction $\mathcal{G}$ keeps the relationships between indices and values $(i, a[i])$, which is all that is needed for our invariants, whereas $\mathcal{G}'$ forgets the indices and only keeps information about the values, which is insufficient. Section 5 details what each abstraction expresses on arrays.

Definition 6 (Abstraction of a Horn problem $abs(\mathcal{G}, H)$). *The abstraction of Horn problem H by a Galois connection $\mathcal{G}$ noted $abs(\mathcal{G}, H)$, is defined by (i) $f_{abs(\mathcal{G},H)} = \alpha_{\mathcal{G}} \circ f_H \circ \gamma_{\mathcal{G}}$ (ii) $\mathcal{U}_{abs(\mathcal{G},H)} = \alpha_{\mathcal{G}}(\mathcal{U}_H)$.*

Theorem 3 (Definition $abs(\mathcal{G}, H)$ is correct). *For all $\mathcal{M}^{\#}$, the following statements are equivalent (with the notation $H(\mathcal{M})$, where H is a Horn problem and $\mathcal{M}$ a possible model, from Theorem 1): (i) $abs(\mathcal{G}, H)(\mathcal{M}^{\#})$ (ii) $H(\gamma_{\mathcal{G}}(\mathcal{M}^{\#}))$ (iii) $abs(\mathcal{G}, H)(\alpha_{\mathcal{G}} \circ \gamma_{\mathcal{G}}(\mathcal{M}^{\#}))$.*

Remark 2. From this theorem, it follows that:

1. $abs(\mathcal{G}, H)$ corresponds to the desired abstraction as: H is satisfiable by a model expressible by the abstraction $(\gamma_{\mathcal{G}}(\mathcal{M}^{\#}))$ iff $abs(\mathcal{G}, H)$ is satisfiable.
2. $abs(\mathcal{G}, H)(\mathcal{M}^{\#})$ is constructable from H and $\gamma_{\mathcal{G}}$. This will be used in Theorem 5.

2.4   Horn Clauses Transformations

A transformation is *sound* if it never transforms unsatisfiable Horn clauses (incorrect programs) into satisfiable ones (correct programs), *complete* if it never transforms satisfiable Horn clauses into unsatisfiable ones. A transformation is *complete relative to* an abstraction if it never transforms Horn clauses satisfiable in the abstract domain into unsatisfiable ones. **Together, soundness and relative completeness state that the transformation implements exactly the abstraction.**

Definition 7 (Soundness, Completeness, Relative completeness). *A transformation alg from Horn clauses to Horn clauses is said to be:*

- sound *if and only if* $\forall \mathfrak{C}, H_{alg(\mathfrak{C})}$ *satisfiable* $\Rightarrow H_{\mathfrak{C}}$ *satisfiable.*
- complete *if and only if* $\forall \mathfrak{C}, H_{\mathfrak{C}}$ *satisfiable* $\Rightarrow H_{alg(\mathfrak{C})}$ *satisfiable .*
- complete relative to $\mathcal{G}$ *iff* $\forall \mathfrak{C}, abs(\mathcal{G}, H_{\mathfrak{C}})$ *satisfiable* $\Rightarrow H_{alg(\mathfrak{C})}$ *satisfiable .*

Theorem 4 (Soundness with relative completeness is *abs***).** *If a transformation alg is sound and complete relative to* $\mathcal{G}$, *then* $\forall \mathfrak{C}, H_{alg(\mathfrak{C})}$ *satisfiable* $\equiv abs(\mathcal{G}, H_{\mathfrak{C}})$ *satisfiable.*

Relative completeness is rarely ensured in abstract interpretation; examples include some forms of policy iteration, which compute the least inductive invariant in the abstract domain. Widening operators, very widely used, break relative completeness. Previous works on arrays do not analyze relative completeness.

In this paper, we present a framework to define abstractions on data such that the relative completeness of transformations is analyzed, and proved when possible. To do so, our abstraction scheme is divided into two algorithms: (i) one that computes $abs(\mathcal{G}, H_{\mathfrak{C}})$ and thus is sound and complete relative to $\mathcal{G}$ but uses extended Horn clauses (*i.e.* Horn clauses with additional quantifiers); (ii) another which transforms these extended Horn clauses back into Horn clauses and ensures soundness and strives to ensure completeness—and is shown to ensure it in the setting of our tool. When the second algorithm ensures completeness, the framework provides an abstraction algorithm from Horn clauses to Horn clauses which is both sound and complete relative to the abstraction.

3   Data Abstraction: Abstracting Horn Clauses

3.1   Implementing Horn Clauses Abstraction

The abstraction on the syntax of Horn clauses is done by choosing a predicate to abstract. This approach can then be successively used on several predicates.

In this paper, we consider a subset of abstractions we call *data abstractions*. The semantics of a predicate is a set of unknown values and an abstraction is simply a relation in the form of a Galois connection between that set of unknown values to a "simpler" set of unknown values. The key particularity of data abstractions is that the abstraction of this set of unknown values is defined by the abstraction of its individual elements, the "data". This allows us to take advantage of the syntax of Horn clauses because the "data" is simply the expressions passed as parameters to a predicate. Furthermore, as our goal is to syntactically modify the Horn clauses, we require that the abstraction can be encoded by an explicit formula that will be used syntactically during the transformation.

Definition 8 (Data abstraction σ, defines $F_\sigma, \alpha_\sigma, \gamma_\sigma, \mathcal{G}_\sigma^P$).
Let $\mathscr{C}$ and $\mathcal{A}$ be sets. A data abstraction σ is a function from $\mathscr{C}$ to $\mathcal{P}(\mathcal{A})$ and we write F_σ the formula encoding its inclusion relation: $F_\sigma(a^\#, a) \equiv a^\# \in \sigma(a)$.[3]
It defines a Galois connection from $\mathcal{P}(\mathscr{C})$ to $\mathcal{P}(\mathcal{A})$ as follows: for $S \subseteq \mathscr{C}$, $S^\# \subseteq \mathcal{A}$, $\alpha_\sigma(S) = \bigcup_{a \in S} \sigma(a)$ and $\gamma_\sigma(S^\#) = \{a \in \mathscr{C} | \sigma(a) \subseteq S^\#\}$.
This Galois connection can be applied to a predicate P, thus yielding the Galois connection $\mathcal{G}_\sigma^P$ defined by $\alpha_{\mathcal{G}_\sigma^P}(\mathcal{M})(P') = ite(P' = P, \alpha_\sigma(\mathcal{M}(P)), \mathcal{M}(P'))$ and $\gamma_{\mathcal{G}_\sigma^P}(\mathcal{M}^\#)(P') = ite(P' = P, \gamma_\sigma(\mathcal{M}^\#(P)), \mathcal{M}^\#(P'))$.

Example 5 (Cell$_1$ abstraction of an array).
Cell$_1$ abstracts an array by the set of its cells (i.e. pairs of index and value).
$$\sigma_{Cell_1}(a) = \{(i, a[i])\} \qquad\qquad F_{\sigma_{Cell_1}}((i, v), a) \equiv v = a[i]$$

Remark 3. This data abstraction σ_{Cell_1} essentially abstracts a function a from an arbitrary index type I to an arbitrary value type by its graph $\{(i, a(i)) \mid i \in I\}$. As such, it does not lose information on individual arrays: two functions are identical if and only if they have the same graph (functional extensionality).

However, the associated $\alpha_{\sigma_{Cell_1}}$ is not injective and loses information. This is essentially because when one takes the superposition of the graphs of two or more functions, there is no way to recover which part of the graph corresponds to which function. Consider for example $a_0 : 0 \mapsto 0, 1 \mapsto 1$ and $a_1 : 0 \mapsto 1, 1 \mapsto 0$. Then, $\alpha_{\sigma_{Cell_1}}(\{a_0, a_1\}) = \{0, 1\} \times \{0, 1\}$; and thus $\alpha_{\sigma_{Cell_1}}(\{a_0, a_1\})$ contains not only a_0 and a_1, but also the constant arrays 0 and 1.

We now give the syntactic transformation on Horn clauses, so that the Horn problem induced by the transformed clauses corresponds to the abstraction of the desired predicate by the given data abstraction. We rely on Theorem 3, which states how the abstract Horn problem must be constructed and find its syntactical counterpart. Thus, if P is the predicate to be abstracted by σ, $\mathcal{M}(P)$ must be replaced by $(\gamma_\sigma(\mathcal{M}(P^\#)))(expr)$, where $\mathcal{M}(P^\#)$ is the abstracted set and $P^\#$ the "abstract predicate". Syntactically, this amounts to replacing any instance of $P(expr)$ by $\forall a^\#, F_\sigma(a^\#, expr) \to P^\#(a^\#)$.

Algorithm 1 (*dataabs($\mathfrak{C}, P, P^\#, F_\sigma$)*).
Input : $\mathfrak{C}$: *Horn clauses*; P: *predicate to abstract*; $P^\#$: *unused predicate*; F_σ.
Computation: *for each clause $C \in \mathfrak{C}$, for each $P(expr)$ in C, replace $P(expr)$ by $\forall a^\#, F_\sigma(a^\#, expr) \to P^\#(a^\#)$, where $a^\#$ is a new unused variable.*

---

[3] Classically, we denote abstract elements ($\in \mathcal{A}$) with sharps (#).

Example 6 (Using Algorithm 1 (to abstract array a (of Example 2 (with $Cell_1$).
Let us define the data abstraction $F_{\sigma_{Cell_1} \cdot \sigma_{id}^2}$ (discussed in Sect. 3.2) by:

$F_{\sigma_{Cell_1} \cdot \sigma_{id}^2}((i, v, N^\#, k^\#), (a, N, k)) \equiv v = a[i] \wedge N^\# = N \wedge k^\# = k$. And
let us execute **dataabs**(Clauses of Example 2, **For2**, **For2**$^\#$, $F_{\sigma_{Cell_1} \cdot \sigma_{id}^2}$). The
result for Clause 4: $For2(a, N, k) \wedge k < N \rightarrow For2(a[k \leftarrow a[k] + 1], N, k + 1)$ is

$$(\forall(i^\#, v^\#, N^\#, k^\#), v^\# = a[i^\#] \wedge N^\# = N \wedge k^\# = k \rightarrow For2^\#(i^\#, v^\#, N^\#, k^\#)) \wedge k < N$$
$$\rightarrow (\forall(i'^\#, v'^\#, N'^\#, k'^\#), v'^\# = a[k \leftarrow a[k] + 1][i'^\#] \wedge N'^\# = N \wedge k'^\# = k + 1$$
$$\rightarrow For2^\#(i'^\#, v'^\#, N'^\#, k'^\#)) \qquad (8)$$

where $a^\#$ from Algorithm 1 is named $(i^\#, v^\#, N^\#, k^\#)$ in the first replacement
and $(i'^\#, v'^\#, N'^\#, k'^\#)$ in the second.

Theorem 5 (Algorithm *1* is correct). *If $P^\#$ unused in $\mathfrak{C}$,*
$\forall \mathcal{M}^\#, H_{dataabs(\mathfrak{C}, P, P^\#, F_\sigma)}(\mathcal{M}^\#[P^\# \leftarrow P]) = abs(\mathcal{G}_\sigma^P, H_{\mathfrak{C}})(\mathcal{M}^\#)$*. Thus, the*
dataabs algorithm is complete relative to $\mathcal{G}_\sigma^P$.

When given a set of Horn clauses, one can abstract several predicates (*i.e.*
several program points), perhaps all of them, by applying the abstraction algorithm to them, not necessarily with the same abstraction.

3.2   Combining Data Abstractions

In Example 6, we had to manually adapt the abstraction $Cell_1$ to the predicate
$For2$ which contained three variables. We define combinators for abstractions
such that those adapted abstractions can be easily defined, and later, analyzed.

Definition 9 ($\sigma_{id}, \sigma_\perp, \sigma_1 \cdot \sigma_2, \sigma_1 \circ \sigma_2$). *These abstractions and combinators*
are defined by

1. $\sigma_{id}(x) = \{x\}$; $F_{\sigma_{id}}(x^\#, x) \equiv x^\# = x$.
2. $\sigma_\perp(x) = \{\perp\}$; $F_{\sigma_\perp}(x^\#, x) \equiv x^\# = \perp$
3. $\sigma_1 \cdot \sigma_2(x_1, x_2) = \sigma_1(x_1) \times \sigma_2(x_2)$; $F_{\sigma_1 \cdot \sigma_2}((x_1^\#, x_2^\#), (x_1, x_2)) \equiv F_{\sigma_1}(x_1^\#, x_1) \wedge$
   $F_{\sigma_2}(x_2^\#, x_2)$
4. $\sigma_1 \circ \sigma_2(x) = \bigcup\limits_{x_2^\# \in \sigma_2(x_2)} \sigma_1(x_2^\#)$; $F_{\sigma_1 \circ \sigma_2}(x^\#, x) \equiv \exists x_2^\# : F_{\sigma_1}(x^\#, x_2^\#) \wedge$
   $F_{\sigma_2}(x_2^\#, x)$

where σ_{id} is the "no abstraction" abstraction, $\sigma_\perp$ abstracts into the unit type
(singleton $\perp$) and is used with the $\cdot$ combinator to project a variable out, $\sigma_1 \cdot \sigma_2$
abstracts pairs by the cartesian product of their abstractions, and $\sigma_1 \circ \sigma_2$ emulates
applying σ_1 after σ_2.

We have given in this section a general scheme for abstracting Horn clauses
using *data abstraction* and shown its correctness. This scheme transforms Horn
clauses into extended Horn clauses: new quantifiers ($\forall a^\#$) are introduced which
makes current solvers [12, 18] struggle. We shall now see how to get rid of these
quantifiers while retaining relative completeness.

4   Data Abstraction: Quantifier Removal

4.1   A Quantifier Elimination Technique Parametrized by *insts*

Contrarily to other approaches that use general-purpose heuristics [2], we design our quantifier elimination from the abstraction itself, which allows us to analyze the completeness property of the quantifier elimination algorithm.

The quantifiers introduced by the abstraction scheme are created either by: 1. The $\forall a^{\#}$ of Algorithm 1, which is handled in this paper. 2. Quantifiers within F_σ (*i.e.* when abstraction composition is used). In this paper, we only handle existential quantifiers in prenex position of F_σ which is sufficient for the abstractions of this paper[4].

Quantifiers are generated for each instance of the abstracted predicate, and to remove the quantifiers, we separate these instances into two classes: 1. The case when the predicate instance is positive. This case is handled by replacing the quantified variables by free variables, possibly renaming them to avoid name clashes. This is correct as these quantifiers would be universal quantifiers when moved to prenex position and thus have same semantics as free variables when considering the satisfiability of the clauses. 2. The case when the predicate instance is negative. In this case, when moved to prenex position, the quantifiers would be existential and thus can not be easily simplified. We use a technique called *quantifier instantiation* [2], which replaces a quantifier by that quantifier restricted to some finite set of expressions I called *instantiation set* (*i.e.* $\forall a^{\#}, expr$ is replaced by $\forall a^{\#} \in I, expr$), which, as I is finite, can be unrolled to remove that quantifier.

Therefore, our quantifier elimination algorithm takes a parameter *insts* which returns the instantiation set for each abstracted negative predicate instance; and eliminates quantifiers according to their types (negative or positive).

Definition 10 (Instantiation set heuristic $insts(F_\sigma, a, ctx)$). *insts is said to be an instantiation set heuristic if and only if: 1. insts takes three parameters: F_σ, the abstraction; a, the variable that was abstracted; ctx, the context in which the quantifiers are removed. 2. $insts(F_\sigma, a, ctx)$ returns an instantiation set for the pair of quantifiers $a^{\#}$ (the quantified variable corresponding to the abstraction of a) and q (the prenex existential quantifiers of F_σ). Thus its type is a set of pairs of expressions where the first expression is for $a^{\#}$ and the second for the prenex existential quantifiers of F_σ.*

To ease the writing of the algorithm, we assume that the input clauses to the quantifier elimination algorithm have been created using the abstraction scheme at most once for each predicate (one may use abstraction composition to emulate applying it twice) on Horn clauses that where initially normalized. Furthermore, as we will be manipulating existential quantifiers within F_σ, we will define $F_\sigma[q]$ such that $F_\sigma(a^{\#}, a) = \exists q, F_\sigma[q]a^{\#}, a)$. In order words, $F_\sigma[q]$ is F_σ where the

---

[4] In practice this can be expanded by analyzing what the quantifiers within F_σ would give when moved to prenex position.

prenex existential quantifiers have been replaced by the value q. We will use ()
as value for q when F_σ has no prenex existential quantifiers.

Algorithm 2 (Quantifier elimination algorithm *eliminate*).
Input:

- *C, an (extended) clause of the form $e_1 \wedge \ldots \wedge e_n \rightarrow e'$*
- *insts an instantiation heuristic as in Definition 10*

Computation:

1. *//We transform quantifiers from the positive instance e' into free variables*
   $e'_{res} := free\_var\_of\_positive\_quantifiers(e')$
2. *For i from 1 to n*
   (a) *//We look if e_i is the abstraction of a predicate, if it is not, $e_{res_i} = e_i$*
       Let $(F_{\sigma_i}, a_i, P_i^\#)$ such that $e_i = \forall a^\#, F_{\sigma_i}(a^\#, a_i) \rightarrow P_i^\#(a^\#)$
       If impossible, $e_{res_i} = e_i$ and go to next loop iteration.
   (b) *//We compute the context for that instance*
       Let $ctx_i = e_{res_1} \wedge \ldots \wedge e_{res_{i-1}} \wedge e_{i+1} \wedge \ldots \wedge e_n \rightarrow e'_{res}$
   (c) *//We compute the instantiation set for that abstraction.*
       Let $I_i = insts(F_{\sigma_i}, a_i, ctx_i)$
   (d) *//We finally compute e_i after instantiation*
       Let $e_{res_i} = \bigwedge_{(a^\#, q) \in I_i} F_{\sigma_i}[q](a^\#, a_i) \rightarrow P_i^\#(a^\#)$
3. *Return $e_{res_1} \wedge \ldots \wedge e_{res_n} \rightarrow e'_{res}$*

Example 7 (Eliminating quantifiers of Clause 8 of Example 6). Let us apply
eliminate on:
$$\forall i^\#, v^\#, N^\#, k^\#, v^\# = a[i^\#] \wedge N^\# = N \wedge k^\# = k \rightarrow For2^\#(i^\#, v^\#, N^\#, k^\#) \wedge k < N$$
$$\rightarrow \forall i'^\#, v'^\#, N'^\#, k'^\#, v'^\# = a[k \leftarrow a[k]+1][i'^\#] \wedge N'^\# = N \wedge k'^\# = k+1$$
$$\rightarrow For2^\#(i'^\#, v'^\#, N'^\#, k'^\#)$$
In this extended clause, $n = 2$ an can be decomposed into e_1, e_2 and e'.
The instantiation algorithm then follows the following steps:

1. Step 1, computes e'_{res} as given in Clause 9
2. We enter Step 2 with $i = 1$ and it matches the pattern.
3. We compute the context and call *insts* (call of Eq. 11). Let us assume it
   returns $\{(k, a[k], N, k), (i^\#, a[i^\#], N, k)\}$ (which is the value returned by the
   instantiation set heuristic we construct later in this paper).
4. We get e_{res_1} as given in Clause 9
5. We enter Step 2 with $i = 2$ and it does not match the pattern. Thus, $e_{res_2} = e_2$

The final clause is thus

$$(a[k] = a[k] \wedge N = N \wedge k = k \rightarrow For2^\#(k, a[k], N, k) \wedge$$
$$a[i'^\#] = a[i'^\#] \wedge N = N \wedge k = k \rightarrow For2^\#(i'^\#, a[i'^\#], N, k)) \wedge k < N$$
$$\rightarrow v'^\# = a[k \leftarrow a[k]+1][i'^\#] \wedge N'^\# = N \wedge k'^\# = k+1 \rightarrow For2^\#(i'^\#, v'^\#, N'^\#, k'^\#) \quad (9)$$

where $v'^\#, i'^\#, N'^\#, k'^\#$ are new free variables of the clause.

Simplifying this clause for readability yields:

$$For2^{\#}(k, a[k], N, k) \wedge For2^{\#}(i'^{\#}, a[i'^{\#}], N, k) \wedge k < N$$
$$\rightarrow For2^{\#}(i'^{\#}, a[k \leftarrow a[k] + 1][i'^{\#}], N, k+1) \quad (10)$$

The call to *insts*, **which will be studied in Examples 8 and 10, was:**

$$insts(F_{\sigma_{Cell_1} \cdot \sigma_{id}^2}, (a, (N, k)), e_2 \rightarrow e'_{res})$$
$$= insts(F_{\sigma_{Cell_1} \cdot \sigma_{id}^2}, (a, (N, k)), k < N \rightarrow v'^{\#} = a[k \leftarrow a[k] + 1][i'^{\#}]$$
$$\wedge N'^{\#} = N \wedge k'^{\#} = k + 1 \rightarrow For2^{\#}((i'^{\#}, v'^{\#}), (N'^{\#}, k'^{\#}))) \quad (11)$$

Theorem 6 (*eliminate* **sound**). $\forall C, insts, \mathcal{M}, [\![eliminate(C, insts)]\!]_{\mathcal{M}} \Rightarrow [\![C]\!]_{\mathcal{M}}$

4.2   Constructing a Good Heuristic *insts*

To ensure relative completeness, and thus the predictability, of our overall abstraction (multiple calls to *dataabs* with different predicates followed by a call to *eliminate*), we need *eliminate* to be complete. The completeness of *eliminate* is highly tied to each call to *insts*, and we therefore define *completeness of a call to insts* such that whenever all calls are complete, *eliminate* is complete.

Definition 11 (Completeness of a call to *insts***).**
We say that a call $insts(F_\sigma, a, ctx)$ *is complete if and only if, for any* $\mathcal{M}$*, and any set* E *of elements of the types of* a*, 12 implies 13.*

$$\forall vars, (\forall (a^{\#}, q), F_\sigma[q](a^{\#}, a(vars)) \Rightarrow a^{\#} \in \alpha_\sigma(E)) \Rightarrow [\![ctx(vars)]\!]_{\mathcal{M}} \quad (12)$$

$$\forall vars, (\forall ((a^{\#}, q)) \in insts(F_\sigma, a, ctx)(vars),$$
$$F_\sigma[q](a^{\#}, a(vars)) \Rightarrow a^{\#} \in \alpha_\sigma(E)) \Rightarrow [\![ctx(vars)]\!]_{\mathcal{M}} \quad (13)$$

Remark 4. We always have 13 implies 12; soundness is based on this.

Remark 5. 12 should be understood as the clause before $(a^{\#}, q)$ is instantiated: $\alpha_\sigma(E)$ represents $\alpha(\mathcal{M})(P)$. Therefore, 12 is similar to $e_i \rightarrow ctx$ (of algorithm *eliminate*) which is the currified current state of the clause in the loop. 13 should be understood as $e_{res_i} \rightarrow ctx$

Theorem 7 (Completeness of *insts* **(implies that of** *eliminate*).**
For any $C, insts, \mathcal{M}$*, if during execution of* $eliminate(C, insts)$ *all calls to insts are complete, then* $[\![C]\!]_{\alpha_{\mathcal{G}}(\mathcal{M})} = [\![eliminate(C, insts)]\!]_{\alpha_{\mathcal{G}}(\mathcal{M})}$ *where* $\mathcal{G}$ *is such that* $\forall i, \gamma_{\mathcal{G}}(\mathcal{M}(P_i^{\#})) = \gamma_{\sigma_i}(P_i^{\#})$*, with* $i, P_i^{\#}, \sigma_i$ *as defined in eliminate.*

Remark 6. We only consider abstract models, that is, $\alpha_{\mathcal{G}}(\mathcal{M})$ where $\mathcal{G}$ represents the galois connection after multiple calls to *dataabs*. The result is then a consequence of Remark 5.

Although our previous completeness definition of *insts* correctly captures the necessary properties for our instantiation algorithm to keep equisatisfiability, it is too weak to reason on when using combinators (see Sect. 3.2). The desired property of the instantiation heuristic is what we call *strong completeness*.

Strong Completeness. The definition of *completeness* only applies in the context of boolean types, as required by the Algorithm *eliminate*. However, when handling the impact of the instantiation of a quantifier, one wishes to handle that impact with respect to an arbitrarily typed expression. For example, in the case of combinator $\sigma_1 \cdot \sigma_2$, the instantiation of the quantifiers generated by the abstraction σ_1 must be aware of its impact on the variables to be abstracted by σ_2. This leads to a definition of *strong completeness* that allows any expression type as context parameter of *insts*, and replaces the satisfiability requirement of the context by an equality requirement.

Definition 12 (Strong completeness of $insts(F_\sigma, a, ctx)$).
$insts(F_\sigma, a, ctx)$ *is said strongly complete if and only if, for any* $E, vars, \mathcal{M}$,
$$\forall((a^\#, q)) \in insts(F_\sigma, a, ctx)(vars), F_\sigma[q](a^\#, a(vars)) \Rightarrow a^\# \in \alpha_\sigma(E)$$
$$\Rightarrow \exists vars', (\forall(a^\#, q), F_\sigma[q](a^\#, a(vars'))) \Rightarrow a^\# \in \alpha_\sigma(E))$$
$$\wedge [\![ctx(vars)]\!]_\mathcal{M} = [\![ctx(vars')]\!]_\mathcal{M}$$

Remark 7. This definition is constructed by contraposing that of completeness.

Theorem 8 (Strong completeness implies completeness).
If ctx is of boolean type,
$insts(F_\sigma, a, ctx)$ *strongly complete* $\Rightarrow insts(F_\sigma, a, ctx)$ *complete*

We give now some results that enable to modularly design instantiation heuristics while remaining (strongly) complete.

Algorithm 3 (*insts* for finite abstractions). *When* $\sigma(a)$ *finite and* F_σ *has no existential quantifiers* $insts(F_\sigma, a, ctx) = \{(a^\#, ()), a^\# \in \sigma(a)\}$
    Thus $insts(F_{\sigma_{id}}, a, ctx) = \{(a, ())\}$ *and* $insts(F_{\sigma_\perp}, a, ctx) = \{(\perp, ())\}$

Algorithm 4 (*insts* for combinators). *We will use* @ *for tuple concatenation.*
$insts(F_{\sigma_1 \cdot \sigma_2}, (a_1, a_2), ctx) =$
  let $I_1 = insts(F_{\sigma_1}, a_1, (ctx, a_2))$ in   // *We want I_2 to keep the values of I_1 unchanged*
  let $I_2 = insts(F_{\sigma_2}, a_2, (ctx, a_1, I_1))$ in   // *We return $I_1 \times I_2$ with the right ordering*
  // *and the abstracted value at the top of the list.* .
  $\{((a_1^\#, a_2^\#), q_1 @ q_2) | (a_1^\#, q_1) \in I_1 \wedge (a_2^\#, q_2) \in I_2\}$

$inst s(F_{\sigma_1 \circ \sigma_2}, a, ctx) =$

> //We first instantiate σ_2
>
> let $I_2 = insts(F_{\sigma_2}, a, ctx)$ in $I_{tmp} := I_2;$ $I_f := \emptyset$
>
> //For each instantiation of σ_2 we instantiate with σ_1
>
> while $I_{tmp} \neq \emptyset$
>
>> //All orders for picking (q_0, q_2) are valid
>>
>> let $(q_0, q_2) \in I_{tmp}$ in $I_{tmp} := I_{tmp} - \{(q_0, q_2)\}$
>>
>> //We keep the other instantiation sets unchanged
>>
>> //We also keep "q_0 is an abstraction of a" and the global context unchanged
>>
>> let $I_{(q_0,q_2)} = insts(F_{\sigma_1}, q_0, (I_2 - \{(q_0, q_2)\}, I_f, F_{\sigma_2}[q_2](q_0, a), ctx))$ in
>>
>> //We combine $I_{(q_0,q_2)}$ with (q_0, q_2)
>>
>> $I_f := I_f \cup \{(a^\#, (q_0@q_1@q_2)) | ((a^\#, q_1)) \in I_{(q_0,q_2)}\}$
>
> return I_f

//Note : $(a^\#, (q_0@q_1@q_2)) \in I_f \equiv (q_0, q_2) \in I_2 \wedge (a^\#, q_1) \in I_{(q_0,q_2)}$
//Note : $I_{(q_0,q_2)}$ depends on I_f and thus on the picked order

Theorem 9 (Strong Completeness of *insts* of Algorithms 3 and 4). *If σ is finite, $insts(F_\sigma, a, ctx)$ is strongly complete. If its recursive calls are strongly complete, $insts(F_{\sigma_1 \cdot \sigma_2}, (a_1, a_2), ctx)$ is strongly complete. If σ_1, σ_2 are compatible: $\forall E \neq \emptyset, \alpha_{\sigma_2} \circ \gamma_{\sigma_2} \circ \gamma_{\sigma_1} \circ \alpha_{\sigma_1} \circ \alpha_{\sigma_2}(E) = \gamma_{\sigma_1} \circ \alpha_{\sigma_1} \circ \alpha_{\sigma_2}(E)$ and its recursive calls are strongly complete, then $insts(F_{\sigma_1 \circ \sigma_2}, a, ctx)$ is strongly complete.*

Remark 8. The compatibility condition is true for our abstractions (Theorem 10).

Example 8 (Using combinator instantiation).
In Example 7, we assumed the result of Call 11:

$$insts(F_{\sigma_{Cell_1} \cdot \sigma_{id}^2}, (a, (N, k)), k < N \rightarrow v'^\# = a[k \leftarrow a[k] + 1][i'^\#]$$
$$\wedge N'^\# = N \wedge k'^\# = k + 1 \rightarrow For2^\#((i'^\#, v'^\#), (N'^\#, k'^\#)))$$

Let us now expand this call further using our combinator construction for *insts*.

1. We enter the call $insts(F_{\sigma_1 \cdot \sigma_2}, (a_1, a_2), ctx)$ with $\sigma_1 = \sigma_{Cell_1}, \sigma_2 = \sigma_{id}^2, a_1 = a, a_2 = (N, k)$ and $ctx = k < N \rightarrow v'^\# = a[k \leftarrow a[k] + 1][i'^\#] \wedge N'^\# = N \wedge k'^\# = k + 1 \rightarrow For2^\#((i'^\#, v'^\#), (N'^\#, k'^\#))$

2. We compute $I_1 = insts(F_{\sigma_1}, a_1, (ctx, a_2))$ As we do not have yet an instantiation heuristic for σ_{Cell_1}, let us assume this call returns $I_1 = \{(k, a[k]), (i'^\#, a[i'^\#])\}$. This call is further expanded in Example 10.

3. We now compute $I_2 = insts(F_{\sigma_2}, a_2, (ctx, a_1, I_1))$ But $\sigma_2 = \sigma_{id}^2$ thus yielding an embedded call to the $\cdot$ combinator
   (a) We enter the call $insts(F_{\sigma_{id} \cdot \sigma_{id}}, (N, k), (ctx, a_1, I_1))$
   (b) We call $insts(F_{\sigma_{id}}, N, ((ctx, a_1, I_1), k))$, yielding $\{N\}$
   (c) We call $insts(F_{\sigma_{id}}, k, ((ctx, a_1, I_1), N, \{N\}))$, yielding $\{k\}$
   (d) We return $\{N, k\}$

4. We return the final result: $\{((k, a[k]), (N, k)), ((i'^\#, a[i'^\#]), (N, k + 1))\}$

Note that if the call to the instantiation using $Cell_1$ is strongly complete, then our final instantiation set is as well. The following call to the instantiation of $Cell_1$ is studied in Example 10.

$$insts(F_{\sigma_1}, a, (ctx, a_2)) = \left(insts(F_{\sigma_{Cell_1}}, a, (k < N \rightarrow v'^\# = a[k \leftarrow a[k] + 1][i'^\#]\right.$$
$$\left. \wedge N'^\# = N \wedge k'^\# = k + 1 \rightarrow For2^\#((i'^\#, v'^\#), (N'^\#, k'^\#)), (N, k)))\right) \quad (14)$$

5   Cell Abstraction: A Complete Data Abstraction

To illustrate our *data abstraction* technique, we show how to handle the cell abstractions of Monniaux and Gonnord [17].

5.1   Cell Abstractions

Cell abstractions consist in viewing arrays (maps from an index type to a value type) by a finite number of their cells. However, instead of using cells at specific fixed indices, such as the first or the last, we use parametric cells (*i.e.* cells with a non fixed index). $Cell_1$ of Example 5 corresponds to one parametric cell. In Definition 13, we extend $Cell_1$ to $Cell_n$.

Table 1. Properties specified by cell abstractions

Concrete	Abs	Abstract property
$a[0] = 0$	$Cell_1$	$i_1 = 0 \Rightarrow v_1 = 0$
$a[n] = 0$	$Cell_1$	$i_1 = n \Rightarrow v_1 = 0$
$a[0] = a[n]$	$Cell_2$	$(i_1 = 0 \wedge i_2 = n) \Rightarrow v_1 = v_2$
$\forall i, a[i] = 0$	$Cell_1$	$v_1 = 0$
$\forall i, a[i] = i^2$	$Cell_1$	$v_1 = i_1^2$
$\forall i, a[n] \geq a[i]$	$Cell_2$	$i_2 = n \Rightarrow v_2 \geq v_1$

Definition 13. *Cell abstractions $Cell_n$.*
$$\sigma_{Cell_n}(a) = \{(i_1, a[i_1]), \ldots, (i_n, a[i_n]))\} \ and$$
$$F_{\sigma_{Cell_n}}(((i_1, v_1), \ldots, (i_n, v_n)), a) \equiv v_1 = a[i_1] \wedge \ldots \wedge v_n = a[i_n].$$

Many interesting properties can be defined by cell abstractions (Table 1). Furthermore, our data abstraction framework allows formalizing other existing array abstractions by compositions of cell abstractions (Example 9).

Example 9. Array abstractions from cell abstractions.
Array smashing: $\sigma_{smash}(a) = \{a[i]\}$. This abstraction keeps the set of values reached but loses all information linking indices and values. It can be constructed using $Cell_1$ abstraction in the following way : $\sigma_{smash} \equiv (\sigma_\perp \cdot \sigma_{id}) \circ \sigma_{Cell_1}$[5]

---

[5] This is a semantic equivalence, not a strict equality: formally $(\sigma_\perp \cdot \sigma_{id}) \circ \sigma_{Cell_1}(a)$ returns $\{(\perp, a[i]\}$ instead of $\{a[i]\}$.

Array slicing: [6,8,11] There are several variations, and for readability we present the one that corresponds to "smashing each slice" and picking the slices $]-\infty, i[, [i,i],]i, \infty[$: $\sigma_{slice}(a) = \{(a[j_1], a[i], a[j_3]), j_1 < i \wedge j_3 > i\}$. It can be constructed using $Cell_1$ abstraction in the following way : $\sigma_{slice} \equiv (\sigma_{slice_1} \cdot \sigma_{slice_2} \cdot \sigma_{slice_3}) \circ \sigma_{Cell_3}{}^6$ with $\sigma_{s_k}(j,v) = ite(j \in slice_k, v, \perp)$

Theorem 10. *The abstractions of Example 9 have strongly complete instantiation heuristics when $Cell_n$ has.*

Remark 9. These abstractions are of the form $\sigma \circ \sigma_{Cell_n}$. Their strong completeness is proven because σ is finite and σ_{Cell_n} always verifies the compatibility condition of Theorem 9 when left-side composed.

5.2   Instantiating Cell Abstractions

The *data abstraction* framework requires an instantiation heuristic *insts* for $Cell_n$. To achieve the strong completeness property, we first compute all "relevant" indices of the abstracted array, that is, indices which when left unchanged ensure that *ctx* keeps its value.

Algorithm 5. *(relevant(a, expr)).* *We compute the set of relevant indices of the array a for expr. This set may contain $\top$ which signifies that there are relevant indices that the algorithm does not handle (and thus the final algorithm does not ensure strong completeness).*
In this algorithm $arrayStoreChain(b, I, V)$ denotes an array expression equal to $b[i_1 \leftarrow v_1][\ldots][i_n \leftarrow v_n]$ with $i_1, \ldots, i_n \in I$ and $v_1, \ldots, v_n \in V$. n may be 0.

$relevant(a, expr) =$

//For a a variable avar, return the indices that are "read"

let *read avar expr = match expr with*

$|arrayStoreChain(avar, I, V)[i] \rightarrow \{i\} \cup \bigcup\limits_{(j,v) \in (I,V)} read(avar, j) \cup read(avar, v)$

$|\forall q, e | \exists q, e \rightarrow map \ (fun \ x \rightarrow ite(q \in x, \top, x)) \ read(avar, e)$ **in**

$|Cons(exprs) \rightarrow \bigcup\limits_{expr \in exprs} read(avar, exprs) \qquad |avar \rightarrow \{\top\}$

//with Cons an expression constructor or predicate

//Reducing a to a variable avar

match a with

$|arrayStoreChain(avar, I, V) \ when \ is\_var(avar) \rightarrow I \cup read(avar, expr)$

$|\_ \rightarrow \{\top\}$

Remark 10. For readability, the algorithm is kept short, but may be improved to return $\top$ in fewer cases using techniques from [3]

---

[6] As for smashing, this is a semantic equivalence.

Theorem 11 (*relevant*($a, expr$) **is correct**). *If* $\top \notin relevant(a, expr)$ *then*
$\forall \mathcal{M}, vars, a', (\forall i \in relevant(a, expr), a'[i] = a(vars)[i]) \Rightarrow$
$$\exists vars', [\![expr(vars)]\!]_\mathcal{M} = [\![expr(vars')]\!]_\mathcal{M} \wedge a(vars') = a'$$

We use our relevant indices to construct an instantiation heuristic for $Cell_n$.

Algorithm 6 (Instantiation heuristic for $Cell_n$).

$insts(F_{\sigma Cell_n}, a, ctx) =$
  let $R = relevant(a, ctx)$ in   //Compute relevant set
  let $Ind = ite(R = \emptyset, \_, R - \{\top\})$ in   //Make it non empty and remove $\top$
  //$\_$ can be chosen as any value of the index type
  let $I = \{(i, a[i])|i \in Ind\}$ in$(I^n, ())$ // make it a pair index value, make n copies

Theorem 12 (Strong Completeness for cell Abstraction). *Any call to* $insts(F_{\sigma Cell_n}, a, ctx)$ *is strongly complete whenever* $\top \notin relevant(a, ctx)$.

Example 10 (Instantiation of $Cell_1$).
  In Example 8, we assumed the result of the Call 14:

$insts(F_{\sigma_1}, a, (ctx, a_2))$
$= insts(F_{\sigma Cell_1}, a, (k < N \rightarrow v'^{\#} = a[k \leftarrow a[k] + 1][i'^{\#}]$
$\wedge N'^{\#} = N \wedge k'^{\#} = k + 1 \rightarrow For2^{\#}((i'^{\#}, v'^{\#}), (N'^{\#}, k'^{\#})), (N, k)))$

Let us use our instantiation heuristic for $Cell_1$ to compute the result of that call.

1. We first compute the relevant set, we obtain $R = \{k, i'^{\#}\}$
2. It is already non empty and does not contain $\top$, so $Ind = R = \{k, i'^{\#}\}$
3. We add the value part, yielding $I = \{(k, a[k]), (i'^{\#}, a[i'^{\#}])\}$
4. $n = 1$, therefore the result is $I^1 = I = \{(k, a[k]), (i'^{\#}, a[i'^{\#}])\}$

And the call is complete as the relevant set did not contain $\top$.

6   Implementation and Experiments

In Sects. 3 and 4, we constructed the building blocks to verify programs using an abstraction technique that strives to ensure relative completeness and in Sect. 5, we gave a powerful abstraction for arrays. We now combine these sections to create a tool for the verification of programs with arrays. We benchmark this tool and compare it to other tools and then analyze the results.

6.1   The Full Algorithm

Our tool uses Algorithm 7 which has for only parameter n. The abstraction used consists in abstracting each array of each predicate by $Cell_n$.

Algorithm 7 (Full n-Cell Abstraction Algorithm $trs(\mathfrak{C}, n)$).
Input: A set of Horn clauses $\mathfrak{C}$, n the number of cells
Computation:

1. *Abstraction :* For each predicate P of C over types $t_1, \ldots, t_k$
   (a) Let $\sigma^P = \prod_{1 \leq i \leq k} ite(isArray(t_k), \sigma_{Cell_n}, \sigma_{id})$
   (b) Let $P^{\#}$ be an unused predicate.
   (c) $\mathfrak{C} := dataabs(\mathfrak{C}, F_\sigma^P, P, P^{\#})$
2. *Quantifier elimination :* For each clause $C \in \mathfrak{C}$
   $C := eliminate(C, insts)$ //*insts is the heuristic discussed in this article*
3. *Simplification (optional):* For each clause $C \in \mathfrak{C}$
   (a) $C := simplify(C, insts)$ //*we simplify as in Clause 10*
   (b) $C := Ackermannize(C)$ /**This step removes possible array writes by applying read over write axioms. Then if an array a is only used in read expressions, we eliminate it at quadratic cost [15, §3.3.1]. Note that this is not possible before abstraction because a is a parameter of predicates. */*

We implemented this algorithm, and used it on clauses generated by the Vaphor converter from mini-Java programs to Horn Clauses. The implementation is publicly available[7]. Overall the toolchain ensures soundness and relative completeness due to the strong completeness of our building blocks. To ensure that within the computation of $insts(F_{\sigma_{Cell_n}}, a, ctx)$, $relevant(a, ctx)$ does not contain $\top$, we rely on the form of clauses generated by the Vaphor converter, among which: 1. There are no array equalities. 2. There is at most one negative predicate per clause.

Table 2. Experimental results

	#prg	n	Noabs				VapHor				Dataabs				Dataabs acker			
			♠	○	?	≥1	♠	○	?	≥1	♠	○	?	≥1	♠	○	?	≥1
Buggy	4	1	4	0	0	4	4	0	0	4	4	0	0	4	4	0	0	4
Buggy	4	2	-	-	-	-	4	0	0	4	0	4	0	0	3	1	0	3
NotHinted	12	1	0	11.5	0.5	0	1	11	0	1	0	12	0	12	0	11.83	0.17	0
NotHinted	12	2	-	-	-	-	0	12	0	0	0	12	0	12	0	12	0	0
Hinted	12	1	0	11	1	0	4	8	0	7	8.99	2.84	0.17	11	8.83	3.17	0	**12**
Hinted	12	2	-	-	-	-	0	12	0	0	0	12	0	0	5.83	6.17	0	6

Columns: corresponds to the abstraction tool. 1. Noabs corresponds to no abstraction 2. Vaphor is the tool by Monniaux & Gonnord 3. Dataabs and Dataabs acker represent our implementation, with and without Ackermannisation.
Lines: files grouped by category and number of cells
Values: ♠(respectively ○, ?) correspond to the number of files that where correct (respectively timeout, unknown), averaged over the 3 naming options and the 2 random seeds. ≥ 1 represents the number of files for which at least one of the naming options and random seeds returned the correct result.

---

[7] https://github.com/vaphor.

6.2 Experimental Setting and Results

We modified the converter to take into account optional additional invariant information given by the programmer, in the form of "hints". These hints are additional assertion clauses so that the solver may converge more easily to the desired model. These additional clauses are also abstracted by our abstraction.

Our initial Horn clauses are generated by the converter from programs in three categories: 1. incorrect programs. 2. correct programs without hints. 3. correct programs with hints. We then compare our implementation of Algorithm 7 with no abstraction and the abstraction tool of Vaphor on the modified benchmarks of [17]. Note that the latter tool implements a variant of $Cell_n$ that always Ackermannizes in the process. We modified the benchmarks of [7,17] such that properties are checked using a loop instead of a random access, e.g., they take i random and assert $t[i] = 0$ to verify $\forall i\ t[i] = 0$, thus enforcing the use of quantified invariants. This is why Vaphor behaves much more poorly on our examples than in [17]. The modified benchmarks are available at https://github. com/vaphor/array-benchmarks.

We use as backend the state of the art solver Z3 version 4.8.8 - 64 bit with timeout 40s on a laptop computer. Because of issue https://github.com/ Z3Prover/z3/issues/909 that we have witnessed, we launch each benchmark with 3 different naming conventions for predicates in addition to using 2 random seeds. The results are presented in Table 2. We did not show columns for incorrect results or errors as there are none.

6.3 Analysis

Abstraction and Solving Timings. Our abstraction is fast: most of it is search & replace; most of the time is spent in the hand-written simplification algorithm, which is not the purpose of this paper. The solving time in Z3 is much higher. It seems that, for correct examples, Z3 either converges quickly (<5 s) or fails to converge regardless of timeout—only in 18 cases out of 1176 does it solve the problem between 5 s and the timeout.

Soundness and Relative Completeness. There are no incorrect results, confirming that all implementations are sound. There are cases where Z3 cannot conclude "correct" on its own but with enough help (*i.e.* hints and Ackermannization, different predicate names, and random seeds) all files are solved as shown by the hinted, $Cell_1$ line, column ≥ 1 of Dataabs acker. This confirms that our implementation is relatively complete, as proved in theory.

Tool Comparison. Z3 without abstraction is unable to solve any correct example, even with hints. We mostly behave better than Vaphor for $Cell_1$ on hinted examples, perhaps because we create smaller instantiation sets: Vaphor handles complex clauses greedily, using all indices read as instantiation set.

$Cell_1$ versus $Cell_2$. All our correct examples have invariants expressible by $Cell_1$, and thus also by $Cell_2$. However, the clauses generated using $Cell_2$ are bigger and the instantiation set sizes are squared, thus complexifying the clauses and

probably stopping Z3 from converging easily on an invariant. Vaphor, in contrast, generates fewer instantiations for $Cell2$ by using $\sigma_{Cell_2}(a) = \{(i, a[i], j, a[j]), i < j\}$, which explains its better performance on $Cell_2$ buggy examples.

Ackermannizing or not. Ackermannization completely removes arrays from the clauses, but changes neither the invariants nor the space in which invariants are sought. Z3 is supposed to handle the theory of arrays natively and should thus be more efficient than our eager Ackermannization; yet the latter improves results on non buggy examples.

Overall Results and Z3. Our tool transforms a Horn problem with arrays requiring quantified invariants which lie within the $Cell_n$ abstraction into an equivalently satisfiable Horn problem which needs neither quantifiers nor arrays. The non-hinted examples show that this is insufficient to make automatic proofs of programs with arrays practical, mainly because Z3 struggles to handle these array free Horn problems. In addition, Z3 sometimes succeeds or not, or even returns unknown, depending on details in the input (e.g., predicate naming, randon, Ackermannisation). Further work is needed on integer Horn solvers for better performance and reduced brittleness.

Benchmarks and Future Work. The current benchmarks are generated from a toy Java language and have invariants expressible in $Cell_1$. Future work includes (i) adding new challenging examples which require $Cell_2$ such as sortedness or even more complex invariants such as "the array content is preserved as a multistage" [17]; (ii) tackling challenging literature examples [1] in real langages, perhaps using a front end such as SeaHorn [9].

7 Related Work

Numerous abstractions for arrays have been proposed in the literature, among which array slicing [6,8,11]. In Example 9 we showed how they are expressible in our framework. Similarly to Monniaux and Alberti [16] we think that disconnecting the array abstraction from other abstractions and from solving enables using back-end solvers better. Like Monniaux and Gonnord [17] we use Horn Clauses to encode our program under verification, but we go a step further by using Horn Clauses as an intermediate representation to chain abstractions. Furthermore, our formalization is cleaner for multiple arrays and proves relative completeness.

Our instantiation method is inspired from previous work on solving quantified formulae [2,3,10]. [3] does not consider Horn clauses, that is, expressions with unknown predicates, but only expressions with quantifiers. [2] has an approach very similar to ours, but without casting it within the framework of *data abstractions*; they use trigger-based instantiation. Both instantiation methods of [2,3] lead to bigger instantiation sets than the one we suggest, yet, contrary to us, they do not prove completeness. Finally, the technique used in [10] creates instantiation sets not as pre-processing, but during analysis. Although more general, it is highly likely that the technique suffers from the same unpredictability that Horn solvers have. In our case, we believe that we can tailor the instantiation set to the abstraction and analyze its precision.

Finally, other recent approaches focus on more powerful invariants through proofs by induction [13]. However, as stated by their authors, their approach is complementary to ours: theirs is less specialized, and thus has trouble where our approach may easily succeed, but enables other invariants: our data abstraction framework may allow abstracting within their induction proofs.

8   Conclusion

We have proposed an approach for the definition, combination and solving of data abstractions for Horn Clauses. The framework also provides sufficient conditions for (relative) completeness, and prove the result for a large class of array abstractions. We propose an implementation and experimental evaluation on classical examples of the literature. Future work include extending the applicability of the framework for other data structures such that trees.

References

1. Beyer, D.: Automatic verification of C and Java programs: SV-COMP 2019. In: Beyer, D., Huisman, M., Kordon, F., Steffen, B. (eds.) TACAS 2019. LNCS, vol. 11429, pp. 133–155. Springer, Cham (2019). https://doi.org/10.1007/978-3-030-17502-3_9
2. Bjørner, N., McMillan, K., Rybalchenko, A.: On solving universally quantified horn clauses. In: Logozzo, F., Fähndrich, M. (eds.) SAS 2013. LNCS, vol. 7935, pp. 105–125. Springer, Heidelberg (2013). https://doi.org/10.1007/978-3-642-38856-9_8
3. Bradley, A.R., Manna, Z., Sipma, H.B.: What's decidable about arrays? In: Emerson, E.A., Namjoshi, K.S. (eds.) VMCAI 2006. LNCS, vol. 3855, pp. 427–442. Springer, Heidelberg (2005). https://doi.org/10.1007/11609773_28
4. Braine, J., Gonnord, L., Monniaux, D.: Data Abstraction: A General Framework to Handle Program Verification of Data Structures. Research Report RR-9408, Inria Grenoble Rhône-Alpes; VERIMAG UMR 5104, Université Grenoble Alpes, France; LIP - Laboratoire de l'Informatique du Parallélisme; Université Lyon 1 - Claude Bernard; ENS Lyon, May 2021. https://hal.inria.fr/hal-03214475
5. Cousot, P., Cousot, R.: Abstract interpretation: a unified lattice model for static analysis of programs by construction or approximation of fixpoints. In: POPL (1977)
6. Cousot, P., Cousot, R., Logozzo, F.: A parametric segmentation functor for fully automatic and scalable array content analysis. SIGPLAN Not. 46(1), 105–118 (2011)
7. Dillig, I., Dillig, T., Aiken, A.: Fluid updates: beyond strong vs. weak updates. In: Gordon, A.D. (ed.) ESOP 2010. LNCS, vol. 6012, pp. 246–266. Springer, Heidelberg (2010). https://doi.org/10.1007/978-3-642-11957-6_14
8. Gopan, D., Reps, T., Sagiv, M.: A framework for numeric analysis of array operations. In: PLDI (2005)
9. Gurfinkel, A., Kahsai, T., Komuravelli, A., Navas, J.: The SeaHorn verification framework. In: CAV (2015)
10. Gurfinkel, A., Shoham, S., Vizel, Y.: Quantifiers on demand. In: Lahiri, S.K., Wang, C. (eds.) ATVA 2018. LNCS, vol. 11138, pp. 248–266. Springer, Cham (2018). https://doi.org/10.1007/978-3-030-01090-4_15

11. Halbwachs, N., Péron, M.: Discovering properties about arrays in simple programs. In: Proceedings of the 29th ACM SIGPLAN Conference on Programming Language Design and Implementation (PLDI 2008). Association for Computing Machinery, New York, NY, USA (2008)

12. Hojjat, H., Rümmer, P.: The ELDARICA horn solver. In: FMCAD (2018)

13. Ish-Shalom, O., Itzhaky, S., Rinetzky, N., Shoham, S.: Putting the squeeze on array programs: loop verification via inductive rank reduction. In: Beyer, D., Zufferey, D. (eds.) VMCAI 2020. LNCS, vol. 11990, pp. 112–135. Springer, Cham (2020). https://doi.org/10.1007/978-3-030-39322-9_6

14. Kahsai, T., Rümmer, P., Schäf, M.: JayHorn: A Java Model Checker: (Competition Contribution) (2019)

15. Kroening, D., Strichman, O.: Decision Procedures. TTCS, Springer, Heidelberg (2008). https://doi.org/10.1007/978-3-540-74105-3

16. Monniaux, D., Alberti, F.: A simple abstraction of arrays and maps by program translation. In: Blazy, S., Jensen, T. (eds.) SAS 2015. LNCS, vol. 9291, pp. 217–234. Springer, Heidelberg (2015). https://doi.org/10.1007/978-3-662-48288-9_13

17. Monniaux, D., Gonnord, L.: Cell morphing: from array programs to array-free horn clauses. In: Rival, X. (ed.) SAS 2016. LNCS, vol. 9837, pp. 361–382. Springer, Heidelberg (2016). https://doi.org/10.1007/978-3-662-53413-7_18

18. de Moura, L., Bjørner, N.: Z3: an efficient SMT solver. In: Ramakrishnan, C.R., Rehof, J. (eds.) TACAS 2008. LNCS, vol. 4963, pp. 337–340. Springer, Heidelberg (2008). https://doi.org/10.1007/978-3-540-78800-3_24

Toward Neural-Network-Guided Program Synthesis and Verification

Naoki Kobayashi[1]($\boxtimes$) (iD), Taro Sekiyama[2] (iD), Issei Sato[1], and Hiroshi Unno[3,4] (iD)

[1] The University of Tokyo, Tokyo, Japan
{koba,issei.sato}@is.s.u-tokyo.ac.jp
[2] National Institute of Informatics and SOKENDAI, Tokyo, Japan
tsekiyama@acm.org
[3] University of Tsukuba, Ibaraki, Japan
[4] RIKEN AIP, Tokyo, Japan

Abstract. We propose a novel framework of program and invariant synthesis called neural network-guided synthesis. We first show that, by suitably designing and training neural networks, we can extract logical formulas over integers from the weights and biases of the trained neural networks. Based on the idea, we have implemented a tool to synthesize formulas from positive/negative examples and implication constraints, and obtained promising experimental results. We also discuss an application of our method for improving the qualifier discovery in the framework of ICE-learning-based CHC solving, which can in turn be applied to program verification and inductive invariant synthesis. Another potential application is to a neural-network-guided variation of Solar-Lezama's program synthesis by sketching.

1 Introduction

With the recent advance of machine learning techniques, there have been a lot of interests in applying them to program synthesis and verification. Garg et al. [6] have proposed the ICE-framework, where the classical supervised learning based on positive and negative examples been extended to deal with "implication constraints" to infer inductive invariants. Zhu et al. [32] proposed a novel approach to combining neural networks (NNs) and traditional software, where a NN controller is synthesized first, and then an ordinary program that imitates the NN's behavior; the latter is used as a *shield* for the neural net controller and the shield (instead of the NN) is verified by using traditional program verification techniques. There have also been various approaches to directly verifying NN components [1,8,16,21,30].

We propose yet another approach to using neural networks for program verification and synthesis. Unlike the previous approaches where neural networks are used either as black boxes [28,32] or white boxes [8,11], our approach treats neural networks as *gray* boxes. Given training data, which typically consist of input/output examples for a (quantifier-free) logical formula (as a part of a program component or a program invariant) to be synthesized, we first train a NN.

© Springer Nature Switzerland AG 2021
C. Drăgoi et al. (Eds.): SAS 2021, LNCS 12913, pp. 236–260, 2021.
https://doi.org/10.1007/978-3-030-88806-0_12

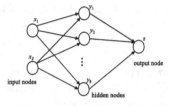

Fig. 1. A neural network with one hidden layer

We then synthesize a logical formula by using the weights and biases of the trained NN as hints. Extracting simple (or, "interpretable"), classical[1] program expressions from NNs has been considered difficult, especially for deep NNs; in fact, achieving "explainable AI" [2] has been a grand challenge in the field of machine learning. Our thesis here is, however, that if NNs are suitably designed with program or invariant synthesis in mind, and if the domain of the synthesis problems is suitably restricted to those which have reasonably simple program expressions as solutions, then it is actually often possible to extract program expressions (or logical formulas) by inspecting the weights of trained NNs.

To clarify our approach, we give an example of the extraction. Let us consider the three-layer neural network shown in Fig. 1. The NN is supposed to work as a binary classifier for two-dimensional data: it takes a pair of numbers (x_1, x_2) as an input, and outputs a single number z, which is expected to be a value close to either 1 or 0. The NN has eight hidden nodes, and the sigmoid function σ is used as activation functions for both the hidden and output nodes[2]. The lefthand side of Table 1 shows a training data set, where each row consists of inputs (x_1, x_2) ($-25 \leq x_1, x_2 \leq 25$), and their labels, which are 1 if $4x_1 + x_2 > 0 \wedge 2x_1 + 3x_2 + 9 < 0$. The righthand side of Table 1 shows the weights and biases of the trained NN. The i-th row shows information about each hidden node: $w_{1,i}$, $w_{2,i}$, and b_i ($i \in \{1, \ldots, 8\}$) are the weights and the bias for the links connecting the two input nodes and the i-th hidden node, and $w_{o,i}$ is the weight for the link connecting the hidden node and the output node. (Thus, the value y_i of the i-th hidden node for inputs (x_1, x_2) is $y_i = \sigma(b_i + w_{1,i}x_1 + w_{2,i}x_2)$, and the output of the whole network is $\sigma(b_o + \sum_{i=1}^{8} w_{o,i}y_i)$ for some bias b_o.) The rows are sorted according to the absolute value of $w_{o,i}$. We can observe that the ratios among w_1, w_2, b of the first four rows are roughly $2 : 3 : 9$, and those of the last four rows are roughly $4 : 1 : 0$. Thus, the value of each hidden node is close to $\sigma(\beta(2x_1 + 3x_2 + 9))$ or $\sigma(\beta(4x_1 + x_2))$ for some β. Due to the property that the value of the sigmoid function $\sigma(u)$ is close to 0 or 1 except near $u = 0$, we can guess that $2x_1 + 3x_2 + 9 \diamond 0$ and $4x_1 + x_2 \diamond 0$ (where $\diamond \in \{<, >, \leq, \geq\}$) are

---

[1] Since neural networks can also be expressed as programs, we call ordinary programs written without using neural networks *classical*, to distinguish them from programs containing NNs.

[2] These design details can affect the efficacy of our program expression extraction, as discussed later.

Table 1. Training data (left) and the Result of learning (right)

x_1	x_2	label
25	25	0
...		
25	−21	0
25	−20	1
25	−21	1
...		
25	−25	1
24	25	0
...		
−25	−25	0

$w_{1,i}$	$w_{2,i}$	b_i	$w_{o,i}$
4.037725448	6.056035518	18.18252372	−11.76355457
4.185569763	6.27788019	18.92045211	−11.36994552
3.775603055	5.662680149	16.86475944	−10.83486366
3.928676843	5.892404079	17.63601112	−10.78136634
−15.02299022	−3.758415699	1.357473373	−9.199707984
−13.6469354	−3.414942979	1.145593643	−8.159229278
−11.69845199	−2.927870512	0.8412334322	−7.779587745
−12.65479946	−3.168056249	0.9739738106	−6.938682556

relevant to the classification. Once the relevant atomic formulas are obtained, we can easily find the correct classifier $4x_1 + x_2 > 0 \land 2x_1 + 3x_2 + 9 < 0$ by solving the problem of Boolean function synthesis in a classical manner.

We envision two kinds of applications of our NN-guided predicate synthesis sketched above. One is to an ICE-based learning of inductive program invariants [4,6]. One of the main bottlenecks of the ICE-based learning method (as in many other verification methods) has been the discovery of appropriate qualifiers (i.e. atomic predicates that constitute invariants). Our NN-guided predicate synthesis can be used to find qualifiers, by which reducing the bottleneck. The other potential application is to a new program development framework called *oracle-based programming*. It is a neural-network-guided variation of Solar-Lezama's program synthesis by sketching [27]. As in the program sketch, a user gives a "sketch" of a program to be synthesized, and a synthesizer tries to find expressions to fill the holes (or *oracles* in our terminology) in the sketch. By using our method outlined above, we can first prepare a NN for each hole, and train the NN by using data collected from the program sketch and specification. We can then guess an expression for the hole from the weights of the trained NN.

The contributions of this paper are: (i) the NN-guided predicate synthesis method sketched above, (ii) experiments that confirm the effectiveness of the proposed method, and (iii) discussion and preliminary experiments on the potential applications to program verification and synthesis mentioned above.

Our idea of extracting useful information from NNs resembles that of symbolic regression and extrapolation [15,20,23], where domain-specific networks are designed and trained to learn mathematical expressions. Ryan et al. [22,29] recently proposed logical regression to learn SMT formulas and applied it to the discovery of loop invariants. The main differences from those studies are: (i) our approach is hybrid: we use NNs as gray boxes to learn relevant inequalities, and combine it with classical methods for Boolean function learning, and (ii) our learning framework is more general in that it takes into account positive/negative samples, and implication constraints; see Sect. 4 for more discussion.

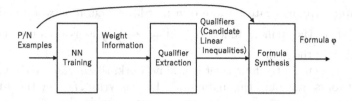

Fig. 2. An overall flow of our synthesis framework

The rest of this paper is structured as follows. Section 2 shows our basic method for synthesizing logical formulas from positive and negative examples, and reports experimental results. Section 3 extends the method to deal with *implication constraints* in the ICE-learning framework [6], and discusses an application to CHC (Constrained Horn Clauses) solving. Section 4 discusses related work and Sect. 5 concludes the paper. The application to the new framework of oracle-based programming is discussed in a longer version of this paper [13].

2 Predicate Synthesis from Positive/Negative Examples

In this section, we propose a method for synthesizing logical formulas on integers from positive and negative examples, and report experimental results. We will extend the method to deal with "implication constraints" [4,6] in Sect. 3.

2.1 The Problem Definition and Our Method

The goal of our synthesis is defined as follows.

Definition 1 (Predicate synthesis problem with P/N Examples). *The predicate synthesis problem with positive (P) and negative (N) examples (the PN synthesis problem, for short) is, given sets $P, N \subseteq \mathbf{Z}^k$ of positive and negative examples (where $\mathbf{Z}$ is the set of integers) such that $P \cap N = \emptyset$, to find a logical formula $\varphi(x_1, \ldots, x_k)$ such that $\models \varphi(v_1, \ldots, v_k)$ holds for every $(v_1, \ldots, v_k) \in P$ and $\models \neg\varphi(v_1, \ldots, v_k)$ for every $(v_1, \ldots, v_k) \in N$.*

For the moment, we assume that formulas are those of linear integer arithmetic (i.e. arbitrary Boolean combinations of linear integer inequalities); some extensions to deal with the modulo operations and polynomial constraints will be discussed later in Sect. 2.3.

The overall flow of our method is depicted in Fig. 2. We first (in the NN training phase) train a NN on a given set of P/N examples, and then (in the qualifier extraction phase) extract linear inequality constraints (which we call "qualifiers") by inspecting the weights and biases of the trained NN, as sketched in Sect. 1. Finally (in the formula synthesis phase), we construct a Boolean combination of the qualifiers that matches P/N examples. Note that the trained NN is used only for qualifier extraction; in the last phase, we use a classical algorithm for Boolean function learning.

Each phase is described in more detail below.

NN Training. We advocate the use of a four-layer neural network as depicted in Fig. 3, where the sigmoid function $\sigma(x) = \dfrac{1}{1 + e^{-x}}$ is used as the activation functions for all the nodes.

We briefly explain the four-layer neural network; those who are familiar with neural networks may skip this paragraph. Let us write $N_{i,j}$ for the j-th node in the i-th layer, and m_i for the number of the nodes in the i-th layer (hence, m_4, which is the number of output nodes, is 1). Each link connecting $N_{i-1,j}$ and $N_{i,k}$ ($i \in \{2, 3, 4\}$) has a real number called the *weight* $w_{i,j,k}$, and each node $N_{i,j}$ ($i \in \{2, 3, 4\}$) also has another real number $b_{i,j}$ called the *bias*. The value $o_{i,j}$ of each node $N_{i,j}$ ($i > 1$) is calculated from the input values $o_{0,j}$ by the equation:

$$o_{i,j} = f\left(b_{i,j} + \sum_{k=1}^{m_{i-1}} w_{i,k,j} \cdot o_{i-1,k}\right),$$

where the function f, called an activation function, is the sigmoid function σ here; other popular activation functions include $\mathrm{ReLU}(x) = max(0, x)$ and $\tanh = \dfrac{e^x - e^{-x}}{e^x + e^{-x}}$. The weights and biases are updated during the training phase. The training data are a set of pairs (d_i, ℓ_i) where $d_i = (o_{1,1}, \ldots, o_{1,m_1})$ is an input and ℓ_i is a label (which is 1 for a positive example and 0 for a negative one). The goal of training a NN is to adjust the weights and biases to (locally) minimize the discrepancy between the output $o_{4,1}$ of the NN and ℓ_i for each d_i. That is usually achieved by defining an appropriate *loss* function for the training data, and repeatedly updating the weights and biases in a direction to decrease the value of the loss function by using the gradient descent method.

Our intention in choosing the four-layer NN in Fig. 3 is to force the NN to recognize qualifiers (i.e., linear inequality constraints) in the second layer (i.e., the first hidden layer), and to recognize an appropriate Boolean combination of them in the third and fourth layers. The sigmoid function was chosen as the activation function of the second layer to make it difficult for the NN to propagate information on the inputs besides information about linear inequalities, so that we can extract linear inequalities only by looking at the weights and biases for the hidden nodes in the second layer. Note that the output of each hidden node in the second layer is of the form:

$$\sigma(b + w_1 x_1 + \cdots + w_k x_k).$$

Since the output of the sigmoid function is very close to 0 or 1 except around $b + w_1 x_1 + \cdots + w_k x_k = 0$ and input data $x_1, \ldots, x_k$ take discrete values, only information about $b + w_1 x_1 + \cdots + w_k x_k > c$ for small c's may be propagated to the second layer. In other words, the hidden nodes in the second layer can be expected to recognize "features" of the form $b + w_1 x_1 + \cdots + w_k x_k > c$, just like the initial layers of DNNs for image recognition tend to recognize basic features such as lines. The third and fourth layers are intended to recognize a (positive) Boolean combination of qualifiers. We expect the use of two layers (instead of only one layer) for this task makes it easier for NN to recognize Boolean formulas

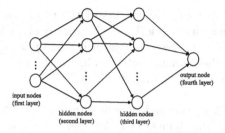

Fig. 3. A Four-Layer neural network

in DNF or CNF[3]. Notice that the conjunction $x_1 \wedge \cdots \wedge x_k$ and the disjunction $x_1 \vee \cdots \vee x_k$ can respectively be approximated by $\sigma(\beta(x_1 + \cdots + x_k - \frac{2k-1}{2}))$ and $\sigma(\beta(x_1 + \cdots + x_k - \frac{1}{2}))$ for a sufficiently large positive number β.

For the loss function of the NN, there are various candidates. In the experiments reported later, we tested the mean square error function (the average of $(o_i - \ell_i)^2$, where o_i is the output of NN for the i-th training data, and ℓ_i is the corresponding label) and the mean of a logarithmic error function (the average of $-\log(1 - |o_i - \ell_i|))^4$.

Qualifier Extraction. From the trained NN, for each hidden node $N_{2,i}$ in the second layer, we extract the bias $b_{2,i}$ (which we write $w_{2,0,i}$ below for technical convenience) and weights $w_{2,1,i}, \ldots, w_{2,k,i}$, and construct integer coefficients $c_0, c_1, \ldots, c_k$ such that the ratio c_n/c_m of each pair of coefficients is close to $w_{2,n,i}/w_{2,m,i}$. We then generate linear inequalities of the form $c_0 + c_1 x_1 + \cdots + c_k x_k > e$ where $e \in \{-1, 0, 1\}$ as qualifiers. The problem of obtaining the integer coefficients $c_0, \ldots, c_k$ is essentially a Diophantine approximation problem, which can be solved, for example, by using continued fraction expansion. The current implementation uses the following naive, ad hoc method[5]. We assume that the coefficients of relevant qualifiers are integers smaller than a certain value K ($K = 5$ in the experiments below). Given $w_0 + w_1 x_1 + \cdots + w_k x_k$, we pick $i > 0$ such that $|w_i|$ is the largest among $|w_1|, \ldots, |w_k|$, and normalize it to the form $w'_0 + w'_1 x_1 + \cdots + w'_k x_k$ where $w'_j = w_j/w_i$ (thus, $0 \le |w'_j| \le 1$ for $j > 0$). We then pick $-K < n_j, m_j < K$ such that n_j/m_j is closest to $|w'_j|$, and obtain $w'_0 + (n_1/m_1)x_1 + \cdots + (n_k/m_k)x_k$. Finally, by multiplying the expression with the least common multiple M of $m_1, \ldots, m_k$, and rounding Mw'_0 with an integer c_0, we obtain $c_0 + M(n_1/m_1)x_1 + \cdots + M(n_k/m_k)x_k$.

If too many qualifiers are extracted (typically when the number of hidden nodes is large; note that qualifiers are extracted from each hidden node), we

---

[3] According to the experimental results reported later, however, the three-layer NN as depicted in Fig. 1 also seems to be a good alternative. It is left for future work to test whether NNs with more than four layers are useful for our task.

[4] We actually used $-\log(\max(1 - |o_i - \ell_i|, \epsilon))$ for a small positive number ϵ, to avoid the overflow of floating point arithmetic.

[5] We plan to replace this with a more standard one based on continued fraction expansion.

prioritize them by inspecting the weights of the third and fourth layers, and possibly discard those with low priorities. The priority of qualifiers obtained from the i-th hidden node $N_{2,i}$ in the second layer is set to $p_i = \sum_j |w_{3,i,j} w_{4,j,1}|$, The priority p_i estimates the influence of the value of the i-th hidden node, hence the importance of the corresponding qualifiers.

Formula Synthesis. This phase no longer uses the trained NN and simply applies a classical method (e.g. the Quine-McCluskey method, if the number of candidate qualifiers is small) for synthesizing a Boolean formula from a truth table (with don't care inputs)[6]. Given qualifiers $Q_1, \dots, Q_m$ and P/N examples $d_1, \dots, d_n$ with their labels $\ell_1, \dots, \ell_n$, the goal is to construct a Boolean combination φ of $Q_1, \dots, Q_m$ such that $\varphi(d_i) = \ell_i$ for every i. To this end, we just need to construct a truth table where each row consists of $Q_1(d_i), \dots, Q_m(d_i), \ell_i$ ($i = 1, \dots, n$), and obtain a Boolean function $f(b_1, \dots, b_m)$ such that $f(Q_1(d_i), \dots, Q_m(d_i)) = \ell_i$ for every i, and let φ be $f(Q_1, \dots, Q_m)$. Table 2 gives an example, where $m = 2$, $Q_1 = x + 2y > 0$ and $Q_2 = x - y < 0$. In this case, $f(b_1, b_2) = b_1 \wedge b_2$, hence $\varphi = x + 2y > 0 \wedge x - y < 0$.

One may think that we can also use information on the weights of the third and fourth layers of the trained NN in the formula synthesis phase. Our rationale for not doing so is as follows.

- Classically (i.e. without using NNs) synthesizing a Boolean function is not so costly; it is relatively much cheaper than the task of finding relevant qualifiers in the previous phase.
- It is not so easy to determine from the weights what Boolean formula is represented by each node of a NN. For example, as discussed earlier, $x \wedge y$ and $x \vee y$ can be represented by $\sigma(\beta(x + y - \frac{3}{2}))$ and $\sigma(\beta(x + y - \frac{1}{2}))$, whose difference is subtle (only the additive constants differ).
- By only using partial information about the trained NN, we need not worry too much about the problem of overfitting. Indeed, as discussed later in Sect. 2.2 and Appendix A.1, a form of overfitting is observed also in our experiments, but even in such cases, we could extract useful qualifiers.
- As confirmed by the experiments reported later, not all necessary qualifiers may be extracted in the previous phase; in such a case, trying to extract a Boolean formula directly from the NN would fail. By using a classical approach to a Boolean function synthesis, we can easily take into account the qualifiers collected by other means (e.g., in the context of program invariant synthesis, we often collect relevant qualifiers from conditional expressions in a given program).

Nevertheless, it is reasonable to use the weights of the second and third layers of the trained NN as *hints* for the synthesis of φ, which is left for future work.

---

[6] The current implementation uses an ad hoc, greedy method, which will be replaced by a more standard one for Boolean decision tree construction.

Table 2. An example of truth tables constructed from qualifiers and examples

d_i	$x + 2y > 0$	$x - y < 0$	ℓ_i
(1,0)	1	1	1
(1,1)	1	0	0
...	...	...	...
$(-2, -1)$	0	1	0
$(-2, -2)$	0	0	0

2.2 Experiments

We have implemented a tool called NEUGUS based on the method described above using ocaml-torch[7], OCaml interface for the PyTorch library, and conducted experiments. The source code of our tool is available at https://github.com/naokikob/neugus. All the experiments were conducted on a laptop computer with Intel(R) Core(TM) i7-8650U CPU (1.90 GHz) and 16 GB memory; GPU was not utilized for training NNs.

Learning Conjunctive Formulas. As a warming-up, we have randomly generated a conjunctive formula $\varphi(x, y)$ of the form $A \wedge B$ where A and B are linear inequalities of the form $ax + by + c > 0$, and a, b and c are integers such that $-4 \leq a, b \leq 4$ and $-9 \leq c \leq 9$ with $ab \neq 0$. We set $P = \{(x, y) \in \mathbf{Z}^2 \cap ([-25, 25] \times [-25, 25]) \mid\models \varphi(x, y)\}$ and $N = \{(x, y) \in \mathbf{Z}^2 \cap ([-25, 25] \times [-25, 25]) \mid\models \neg\varphi(x, y)\}$ as the sets of positive and negative examples, respectively (thus, $|P \cup N| = 51 \times 51 = 2601$)[8]. The left-hand side of Fig. 4 plots positive examples for $A \equiv -2x - y + 4 > 0$ and $B \equiv 3x - 4y + 5 > 0$. We have randomly generated 20 such formula instances, and ran our tool three times for each instance to check whether the tool could find qualifiers A and B. In each run, the NN training was repeated either until the accuracy becomes 100% and the loss becomes small enough, or until the number of training steps (the number of forward and backward propagations) reaches 30,000. If the accuracy does not reach 100% within 30,000 steps or the loss does not become small enough (less than 10^{-4}), the tool retries the NN training from scratch, up to three times. (Even if the accuracy does not reach 100% after three retries, the tool proceeds to the next phase for qualifier discovery.) As the optimizer, we have used Adam [12] with the default setting of ocaml-torch ($\beta_1 = 0.9$, $\beta_2 = 0.999$, no weight decay), and the learning rate was 0.001. We did not use mini-batch training; all the training data were given at each training step.

Table 3 shows the result of experiments. The meaning of each column is as follows:

---

[7] https://github.com/LaurentMazare/ocaml-torch.
[8] We have excluded out instances where A or B is subsumed by the other, and those where the set of positive or negative examples is too small.

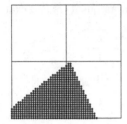 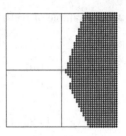

Fig. 4. Visualization of sample instances: $-2x - y + 4 > 0 \land 3x - 4y + 5 > 0$ (left) and $(2x + y + 1 > 0 \land x - y - 9 > 0) \lor (x + y > 0 \land 3x - y - 5 > 0)$ (right, Instance #10 for $(A \land B) \lor (C \land D)$). The small circles show positive examples, and the white area is filed with negative examples.

- "#hidden nodes": the number of hidden nodes. "$m_1 : m_2$" means that a four-layer NN was used, and that the numbers of hidden nodes in the second and third layers are respectively m_1 and m_2, while "m" means that a three-layer (instead of four-layer) NN was used, with the number of hidden nodes being m.

- "loss func.": the loss function used for training. "log" means $\frac{1}{n} \sum_{i=1}^{n} -\log(1 - |o_i - \ell_i|)$ (where o_i and ℓ_i are the prediction and label for the i-th example), and "mse" means the mean square error function.

- "#retry": the total number of retries. For each problem instance, up to 3 retries were performed. (Thus, there can be 20 (instances) × 3 (runs) × 3 (retries per run) = 180 retires in total at maximum.)

- "%success": the percentage of runs in which a logical formula that separates positive and negative examples was constructed. The formula may not be identical to the original formula used to generate the P/N examples (though, for this experiment of synthesizing $A \land B$, all the formulas synthesized were identical to the original formulas).

- "%qualifiers": the percentage of the original qualifiers (i.e., inequalities A and B in this experiment) found.

- "#candidates": the average number of qualifier candidates extracted from the NN. Recall that from each hidden node in the first layer, we extract three inequalities $(c_0 + c_1 x_1 + \cdots + c_k x_k > e$ for $e \in \{0, -1, 1\})$; thus, the maximum number of generated candidates is $3m$ for a NN with m hidden nodes in the second layer.

- "time": the average execution time per run. Note that the current implementation is naive and does not use GPU.

As shown in Table 3, our tool worked quite well; it could always find the original qualifiers, no matter whether the number of layers is three or four[9].

---

[9] We have actually tested our tool also with a larger number of nodes, but we omit those results since they were the same as the case for 4:4 and 4 shown in the table: 100% success rate and 100% qualifiers found.

Table 3. Experimental results for learning a conjunctive formula $A \wedge B$.

#hidden nodes	loss func.	#retry	%success	%qualifiers	#candidates	time (sec.)
4:4	log	0	100%	100%	6.8	27.7
4	log	0	100%	100%	6.7	25.2

Table 4. Experimental results for learning formulas of the form $(A \wedge B) \vee (C \wedge D)$.

#hidden nodes	loss func.	#retry	%success	%qualifiers	#candidates	time (sec.)
8:8	log	12	93.3%	96.7%	18.6	42.1
8:8	mse	17	86.7%	94.6%	18.1	40.6
16:16	log	0	91.7%	95.8%	26.2	32.9
16:16	mse	3	85.0%	92.5%	26.9	31.7
32:32	log	0	100%	97.9%	38.9	31.1
32:32	mse	15	85.0%	91.7%	40.4	39.9
8	log	156	36.7%	66.3%	21.6	92.4
16	log	54	95.0%	96.7%	37.1	55.8
32	log	2	100%	98.3%	58.5	36.3

Learning Formulas with Conjunction and Disjunction. We have also tested our tool for formulas with both conjunction and disjunction. We have randomly generated 20 formulas of the form $(A \wedge B) \vee (C \wedge D)$[10], where $A, B, C,$ and D are linear inequalities, and prepared the sets of positive and negative examples as in the previous experiment. The right-hand side of Fig. 4 plots positive examples for $(2x + y + 1 > 0 \wedge x - y - 9 > 0) \vee (x + y > 0 \wedge 3x - y - 5 > 0)$. As before, we ran our tool three times for each instance, with several variations of NNs.

The result of the experiment is summarized in Table 4, where the meaning of each column is the same as that in the previous experiment. Among four-layer NNs, 32:32 with the log loss function showed the best performance in terms of the columns %success and %qualifiers. However, 8:8 with the log function also performed very well, and is preferable in terms of the number of qualifier candidates generated (#candidates). As for the two loss functions, the log function generally performed better; therefore, we use the log function in the rest of the experiments. The running time does not vary among the variations of NNs; the number of retries was the main factor to determine the running time.

As for three-layer NNs, the NN with 8 hidden nodes performed quite badly. This matches the intuition that the third layer alone is not sufficient for recognizing the nested conjunctions and disjunctions. To our surprise, however, the NN with 32 hidden nodes actually showed the best performance in terms of %success and %qualifiers, although #candidates (smaller is better) is much larger than

---

[10] After the generation, we have manually excluded instances that have simpler equivalent formulas (e.g. $(x + y > 1 \wedge x + y > 0) \vee (x - y > 1 \wedge x - y > 0)$ is equivalent to $x + y > 1 \vee x - y > 1$, hence removed), and regenerated formulas.

those for four-layer NNs. We have inspected the reason for this, and found that the three-layer NN is not recognizing $(A \wedge B) \vee (C \wedge D)$, but classify positive and negative examples by doing a kind of patchwork, using a large number of (seemingly irrelevant) qualifiers which happened to include the correct qualifiers A, B, C, and D; for interested readers, we report our analysis in Appendix A.1. We believe, however, four-layer NNs are preferable in general, due to the smaller numbers of qualifier candidates generated. Three-layer NNs can still be a choice, if program or invariant synthesis tools (that use our tool as a backend for finding qualifiers) work well with a very large number of candidate qualifiers; for example, the ICE-learning-based CHC solver HoICE [4] seems to work well with 100 candidate qualifiers (but probably not for 1000 candidates).

As for the 32:32 four-layer NN (which performed best among four-layer NNs), only 5 correct qualifiers were missed in total and all of them came from Instance #10 shown on the right-hand side of Fig. 4. Among the four qualifiers, $x - y - 9 > 0$ was missed in all the three runs, and $x + y > 0$ was missed in two of the three runs; this is somewhat expected, as it is quite subtle to recognize the line $x - y - 9 = 0$ also for a human being. The NN instead found the qualifiers like $x > 6$ and $y < -5$ to separate the positive and negative examples.

Figure 5 shows the effect of the prioritization of qualifiers, as discussed in Sect. 2.1. We have sorted the hidden nodes in the second layer based on the weights of the third and fourth layers, and visualized, in the graph on the left-hand side, the average number of correct qualifiers (per run) extracted from top 50%, 75%, and 100% of the hidden nodes. The graph on the right-hand side shows the average number of candidate qualifiers (per run) extracted from top 50%, 75%, and 100% of the hidden nodes. As can be seen in the graphs, while the number of candidate qualifiers is almost linear in the number of hidden nodes considered, most of the correct qualifiers were found from top 75% of the hidden nodes. This justifies our strategy to prioritize qualifier candidates based on the weights of the third and fourth layers.

Appendix A.2 also reports experimental results to compare the sigmoid function with other activation functions.

To check whether our method scales to larger formulas, we have also tested our tool for formulas of the form $(A \wedge B \wedge C) \vee (D \wedge E \wedge F) \vee (G \wedge H \wedge I)$. where $A, \ldots, I$ are linear inequalities of the form $ax + by + c > 0$, and a and b are integers such that $-4 \leq a, b \leq 4$ and $-30 \leq c \leq 30$ with $ab \neq 0$. We set $P = \{(x, y) \in \mathbf{Z}^2 \cap ([-30, 30] \times [-30, 30]) \mid\models \varphi(x, y)\}$ and $N = \{(x, y) \in \mathbf{Z}^2 \cap ([-30, 30] \times [-30, 30]) \mid\models \neg\varphi(x, y)\}$ as the sets of positive and negative examples, respectively. We have collected 20 problem instances, by randomly generating formulas and then manually filtering out those that have a simpler representation than $(A \wedge B \wedge C) \vee (D \wedge E \wedge F) \vee (G \wedge H \wedge I)$. Table 5 summarizes the experimental results. We have used the log function as the loss function. For the qualifier extraction, we extracted five (as opposed to three, in the experiments above) inequalities of the form $(c_0 + c_1 x_1 + \cdots + c_k x_k > e$ for $e \in \{-2, -1, 0, 1, 2\})$ from each hidden node. The threshold for the loss was set to 10^{-5}, except that it was set to 10^{-4} for the three-layer NN with 32 nodes.

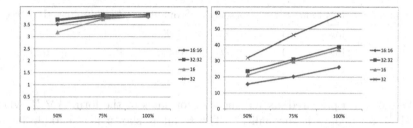

Fig. 5. The number of correct qualifiers discovered (left) and the number of qualifier candidates generated (right). Most of the correct qualifiers appear in top 50% of the candidates.

Table 5. Experimental results for learning formulas of the form $(A \wedge B \wedge C) \vee (D \wedge E \wedge F) \vee (G \wedge H \wedge I)$.

#hidden nodes	#retry	%success	%qualifiers	#candidates	time (sec.)
32	37	83.3%	86.5%	126.6	78.7
32:4	13	78.3%	84.6%	127.3	79.6
32:32	0	70.0%	79.6%	134.1	71.1
64	1	100%	90.2%	126.6	200.1
64:16	0	96.7%	86.7%	204.9	86.1
64:64	0	91.7%	84.1%	215.3	107.6

The result indicates that our method works reasonably well even for this case, if hyper-parameters (especially, the number of nodes) are chosen appropriately; how to adjust the hyper-parameters is left for future work. Interestingly, the result tends to be better for NNs with a smaller number of nodes in the third layer. Our rationale for this is that a smaller number of nodes in the third layer forces the nodes in the second layer more strongly to recognize appropriate features.

2.3 Extensions for Non-linear Constraints

We can easily extend our approach to synthesize formulas consisting of non-linear constraints such as polynomial constraints of a bounded degree and modulo operations. For that purpose, we just need to add auxiliary inputs like x^2, x mod 2 to a NN. We have tested our tool for quadratic inequalities of the form $ax^2 + bxy + cy^2 + dx + ey + f > 0$ (where $-4 \le a, b, c, d, e \le 4$ and $-9 \le f \le 9$; for ovals, we allowed f to range over $[-200, 199]$ because there are only few positive examples for small values of f), and their disjunctions. For a quadratic formula $\varphi(x, y)$, we set $P = \{(x, y, x^2, xy, y^2) \mid (x, y) \in \mathbf{Z}^2 \cap ([-20, 20] \times [-20, 20]), \models \varphi(x, y)\}$ and $N = \{(x, y, x^2, xy, y^2) \mid (x, y) \in \mathbf{Z}^2 \cap ([-20, 20] \times [-20, 20]), \models \neg\varphi(x, y)\}$ as the sets of positive and negative examples, respectively.

The table below shows the result for a single quadratic inequality. We have prepared four instances for each of ovals, parabolas, and hyperbolas. As can be seen in the table, the tool worked very well.

#hidden nodes	loss func.	#retry	%success	%qualifiers	#candidates	time (sec.)
4	log	0	100%	100%	7.4	22.2
8	log	0	100%	100%	10.7	18.3

We have also prepared six instances of formulas of the form $A \vee B$, where A and B are quadratic inequalities. The result is shown in the table below. The NN with 32 nodes performed reasonably well, considering the difficulty of the task. All the failures actually came from Instances #16 and #18, and the tool succeeded for the other instances. For #16, the tool struggled to correctly recognize the oval $-2x^2 - 2xy - 2y^2 - 3x - 4y + 199 > 0$ ($-2x^2 - 2xy - 2y^2 - 3x - 4y + 197 > 0$ was instead generated as a candidate; they differ at only two points $(0, 9)$ and $(0, -11)$), and for #18, it failed to recognize the hyperbola $-4x^2 - 4xy + y^2 + 2x - 2y - 2 > 0$.

#hidden nodes	loss func.	#retry	%success	%qualifiers	#candidates	time (sec.)
8	log	5	50%	52.8%	22.1	43.9
16	log	0	44.4%	55.6%	38.6	26.1
32	log	0	66.7%	80.6%	72.1	25.4

3   Predicate Synthesis from Implication Constraints and Its Application to CHC Solving

We have so far considered the synthesis of logical formulas in the classical setting of supervised learning of classification, where positive and negative examples are given. In the context of program verification, we are also given so called *implication constraints* [4,6], like $p(1) \Rightarrow p(2)$, which means "if $p(1)$ is a positive example, so is $p(2)$" (but we do not know whether $p(1)$ is a positive or negative example). As advocated by Garg et al. [6], implication constraints play an important role in the discovery of an *inductive* invariant (i.e. an invariant Inv that satisfies a certain condition of the form $\forall x, y.(\psi(Inv, x, y) \Rightarrow Inv(x))$; for a state transition system, $\psi(Inv, x, y)$ is of the form $Inv(y) \wedge R(y, x)$ where R is the transition relation). As discussed below, our framework of NN-guided synthesis can easily be adapted to deal with implication constraints. Implication constraints are also called *implication examples* below.

3.1   The Extended Synthesis Problem and Our Method

We first define the extended synthesis problem. A *predicate signature* is a map from a finite set $PVar = \{p_1, \ldots, p_m\}$ of predicate variables to the set **Nat** of natural numbers. For a predicate signature Ar, $\text{Ar}(p_i)$ denotes the arity of the predicate p_i. We call a tuple of the form $(p_i, n_1, \ldots, n_{\text{Ar}(p_i)})$ with $n_j \in \mathbf{Z}$ an *atom*, and often write $p_i(n_1, \ldots, n_{\text{Ar}(p_i)})$ for it; we also write $\tilde{n}$ for a sequence

$n_1, \ldots, n_{\mathrm{Ar}(p_i)}$ and write $p_i(\widetilde{n})$ for the atom $p_i(n_1, \ldots, n_{\mathrm{Ar}(p_i)})$. We write $\mathbf{Atoms_{Ar}}$ for the set of atoms consisting of the predicates given by the signature $\mathbf{Ar}$.

Definition 2 (Predicate synthesis problem with Implication Examples). *The goal of the predicate synthesis problem with positive/negative/implication examples (the PNI synthesis problem, for short) is, given:*

1. *a signature* $\mathbf{Ar} \in PVar \to \mathbf{Nat}$; *and*
2. *a set I of implication examples of the form $a_1 \wedge \cdots \wedge a_k \Rightarrow b_1 \vee \cdots \vee b_\ell$ where* $a_1, \ldots, a_k, b_1, \ldots, b_\ell \in \mathbf{Atoms_{Ar}}$, *and $k + \ell > 0$ (but k or ℓ may be 0)*

as an input, to find a map θ that assigns, to each $p_i \in PVar$, a logical formula $\varphi_i(x_1, \ldots, x_{\mathbf{Ar}(p_i)})$ such that $\models \theta a_1 \wedge \cdots \wedge \theta a_k \Rightarrow \theta b_1 \vee \cdots \vee \theta b_\ell$ holds for each implication example $a_1 \wedge \cdots \wedge a_k \Rightarrow b_1 \vee \cdots \vee b_\ell \in I$. Here, for an atom $a = p(n_1, \ldots, n_j)$, θa is defined as $(\theta p)[n_1/x_1, \ldots, n_j/x_j]$. We call an implication example of the form $\Rightarrow b$ ($a \Rightarrow$, resp.) as a positive (negative, resp.) example, and write $P \subseteq I$ and $N \subseteq I$ for the sets of positive and negative examples respectively.

Example 1. Let $\mathbf{Ar} = \{p \mapsto 1, q \mapsto 1\}$ and I be $P \cup N \cup I'$ where:

$$P = \{\Rightarrow p(0), \Rightarrow q(1)\} \qquad N = \{p(1) \Rightarrow, q(0) \Rightarrow\}$$
$$I' = \{p(2) \Rightarrow q(3), q(3) \Rightarrow p(4), p(2) \wedge q(2) \Rightarrow, p(3) \wedge q(3) \Rightarrow,$$
$$p(4) \wedge q(4) \Rightarrow, \Rightarrow p(2) \vee q(2), \Rightarrow p(3) \vee q(3), \Rightarrow p(4) \vee q(4)\}$$

Then $\theta = \{p \mapsto x_1 \mod 2 = 0, q \mapsto x_1 \mod 2 = 1\}$ is a valid solution for the synthesis problem $(\mathbf{Ar}, I)$. $\qquad\square$

We generalize the method described in Sect. 2.1 as follows.

1. Prepare a NN $\mathcal{N}_i$ for *each* predicate variable p_i. $\mathcal{N}_i$ has $\mathbf{Ar}(p_i)$ input nodes (plus additional inputs, if we aim to generate non-linear formulas, as discussed in Sect. 2.3). For an atom $a \equiv p_i(\widetilde{n})$, we write o_a for the output of $\mathcal{N}_i$ for $\widetilde{n}$ below (note that the value of o_a changes during the course of training).
2. Train all the NNs $\mathcal{N}_1, \ldots, \mathcal{N}_m$ together. For each atom $p_i(\widetilde{n})$ occurring in implication examples, $\widetilde{n}$ is used as a training datum for $\mathcal{N}_i$. For each implication example $e \equiv a_1 \wedge \cdots \wedge a_k \Rightarrow b_1 \vee \cdots \vee b_\ell \in I$, we define the loss $loss_e$ for the example by[11]:

$$loss_e = -\log(1 - \prod_{i=1}^{k} o_{a_i} \cdot \prod_{j=1}^{\ell} (1 - o_{b_j})).$$

The idea is to ensure that the value of $loss_e$ is 0 if one of o_{a_i}'s is 0 or one of o_{b_j}'s is 1, and that the value of $loss_e$ is positive otherwise. This reflects the

---

[11] In the implementation, we approximated $loss_e$ by $-\log \max(\epsilon, 1 - \prod_{i=1}^{k} o_{a_i} \cdot \prod_{j=1}^{\ell}(1 - o_{b_j}))$ for a small positive number ϵ in order to avoid an overflow of the floating point arithmetic.

fact that $a_1 \wedge \cdots \wedge a_k \Rightarrow b_1 \vee \cdots \vee b_\ell$ holds just if one of a_i's is false or one of b_j's is true. Note that the case where $k = 0$ and $\ell = 1$ ($k = 1$ and $\ell = 0$, resp.) coincides with the logarithmic loss function for positive (negative, resp.) examples in Sect. 2.1. Set the overall loss of the current NNs as the average of $loss_e$ among all the implication constraints, and use the gradient descent to update the weights and biases of NNs. Repeat the training until all the implication constraints are satisfied (by considering values greater than 0.5 as true, and those less than 0.5 as false).

3. Extract a set Q_i of qualifiers from each trained $\mathcal{N}_i$, as in Sect. 2.1.
4. Synthesize a formula for the predicate p_i as a Boolean combination of Q_i. This phase is also the same as Sect. 2.1, except that, as the label ℓ_a for each atom a, we use the prediction of the trained NNs. Note that unlike in the setting of the previous section where we had only positive and negative examples, we may not know the correct label of some atom due to the existence of implication examples. For example, given $p(0) \vee p(1) \Rightarrow$ and $\Rightarrow p(0) \vee p(1)$, we do not know which of $p(0)$ and $p(1)$ should hold. We trust the output of the trained NN in such a case. Since we have trained the NNs until all the implication constraints are satisfied, it is guaranteed that, for positive and negative examples, the outputs of NNs match the correct labels. Thus, the overall method strictly subsumes the one described in Sect. 2.1.

3.2 Preliminary Experiments

We have extended the tool based on the method described above, and tested it for several examples. We report some of them below.

As a stress test for implication constraints, we have prepared the following input, with no positive/negative examples (where $\mathtt{Ar} = \{p \mapsto 1\}$):

$$I = \{p(2n) \wedge p(2n + 1) \Rightarrow \mid n \in [-10, 10]\}$$
$$\cup \{\Rightarrow p(2n) \vee p(2n + 1) \mid n \in [-10, 10]\}$$

The implication examples mean that, for each integer $n \in [-10, 10]$, exactly one of $p(2n)$ and $p(2n + 1)$ is true. We ran our tool with an option to enable the "mod 2" operation, and obtained $\{p \mapsto x_1 \bmod 2 < 1\}$ as a solution (which is correct; another solution is $x_1 \bmod 2 > 0$).

We have also tested our tool for several instances of the CHC (Constrained Horn Clauses) solving problem [3]. A constrained Horn clause is a formula of the form $A_1 \wedge \cdots \wedge A_k \Rightarrow A_0$, where each A_i is a constraint (of linear arithmetic in this paper) or an atomic formula of the form $p(e_1, \ldots, e_k)$ where p is a predicate variable. The goal of CHC solving is, given a set of constrained Horn clauses, to check whether there is a substitution for predicate variables that makes all the clauses valid (and if so, output a substitution). Various program verification problems [3], as well as the problem of finding inductive invariants, can be reduced to the problem of CHC solving. Various CHC solvers [4,9,14,24] have been implemented so far, and HoICE [4] is one of the state-of-the-art solvers, which is based on the ICE-learning framework. As illustrated in Fig. 6, HoICE

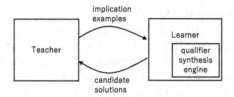

Fig. 6. Inside HoICE

consists of two main components: a teacher and a learner. The learner generates a candidate solution (a map from predicate variables to formulas) from implication examples, and the teacher checks whether the candidate solution is valid (i.e. satisfies all the clauses) by calling SMT solvers, and if not, generates a new implication example. The learner has a qualifier synthesis engine and combines it with a method for Boolean decision tree construction [7]. The main bottleneck of HoICE has been the qualifier synthesis engine, and the aim of our preliminary experiments reported below is thus to check whether our NN-guided synthesis method can be used to reduce the bottleneck.

To evaluate the usefulness of our NN-guided synthesis, we have implemented the following procedure, using HoICE and our NN-guided synthesis tool (called NeuGuS) as backends.

Step 1: Run HoICE for 10 s to collect implication examples.
Step 2: Run NeuGuS to learn qualifiers.
Step 3: Re-run HoICE with the qualifiers as hints (where the time limit is initially set to 10 s).
Step 4: If Step 3 fails, collect implication examples from the execution of Step 3, and go back to Step 2, with the time limit for HoICE increased by 5 s.

In Step 2, we used a four-layer NN, and set the numbers of hidden nodes in the second and third layers to 4. When NeuGuS returns a formula, the inequality constraints that constitute the formula as qualifiers are passed to Step 3; otherwise, all the qualifier candidates extracted from the trained NNs are passed to Step 3.

We have collected the following CHC problems that plain HoICE cannot solve.

- Two problems that arose during our prior analysis of the bottleneck HoICE (`plus`, `plusminus`). The problem `plusminus` consists of the following CHCs.

$$plus(m, n, r) \wedge minus(r, n, s) \Rightarrow m = s \qquad \text{true} \Rightarrow plus(m, 0, m)$$
$$n > 0 \wedge plus(m, n - 1, r) \Rightarrow plus(m, n, r + 2) \qquad \text{true} \Rightarrow minus(m, 0, m)$$
$$n > 0 \wedge minus(m, n - 1, r) \Rightarrow minus(m, n, r - 2)$$

The above CHC is satisfied for $plus(m, n, r) \equiv r = m + 2n$, $minus(m, n, r) \equiv r = m - 2n$. The ICE-based CHC solver HoICE [4], however, fails to solve the CHC (and runs forever), as HoICE is not very good at finding qualifiers involving more than two variables.

- The five problems from the Inv Track of SyGus 2018 Competition (https:// github.com/SyGuS-Org/benchmarks/tree/master/comp/2018/Inv_Track, cggmp2005_variant_true-unreach-call_true-termination, jmbl_cggmp-new, fib_17n, fib_32, and jmbl_hola.07, which are named cggmp, cggmp-new, fib17, fib32, and hola.07 respectively in Table 6); the other problems can be solved by plain HOICE, hence excluded out).
- The problem #93 from the code2inv benchmark set used in [22] (93; the other 123 problems can be solved by plain HOICE within 60 s).
- Two problems (pldi082_unbounded1.ml and xyz.ml) from the benchmark set (https://github.com/nyu-acsys/drift) of Drift [19][12], with a variant xyz_v.ml of xyz.ml, obtained by generalizing the initial values of some variables.

The implementation and the benchmark set described above are available at https://github.com/naokikob/neugus.

Table 6 summarizes the experimental results. The experiments were conducted on the same machine as those of Sect. 2.1. We used HOICE 1.8.3 as a backend. We used 4-layer NNs with 32 and 8 hidden nodes in the second and third layers respectively. The column '#pred' shows the number of predicates in the CHC problem, and columns '#P', '#N', and '#I' respectively show the numbers of positive, negative, and implication examples (the maximum numbers in the three runs). The column 'Cycle' shows the minimum and maximum numbers of Step 2 in the three runs. The column 'Time' shows the execution time in seconds (which is dominated by NEUGUS), where the time is the average for three runs, and '-' indicates a time-out (with the time limit of 600 s). The next column shows key qualifiers found by NEUGUS. For comparison with our combination of HOICE and NEUGUS, the last column shows the times (in seconds) spent by Z3 (as a CHC solver) for solving the problems[13].

The results reported above indicate that our tool can indeed be used to improve the qualifier discovery engine of ICE-learning-based CHC solver HOICE, which has been the main bottleneck of HOICE. With the default option, NEUGUS timed out for fib32 and xyz. For the problem fib32, the "mod 2" constraint is required. The row "fib32 -mod2" shows the result obtained by running NEUGUS with the "mod 2" constraint enabled. For the problem xyz, we discovered that the main obstacle was on the side of HOICE: HOICE (in the first step) finds no negative constraint for one of the two predicates, and no positive constraint for the other predicate; thus, NEUGUS returns "true" for the former predicate and "false" for the latter predicate. We have therefore prepared an option to eagerly collect learning data by applying unit-propagation to CHCs; the row "xyz -gen" shows the result for this option; see Appendix B for more detailed analysis of the problem xyz. Larger experiments on the application to CHC solvers are left for future work.

---

[12] The tool r_type was used to extract CHCs. The source programs have been slightly modified to remove Boolean arguments from predicates.

[13] Recall that our benchmark set collects only the problems that plain HOICE cannot solve: although many of those problems can be solved by Z3 [14] much more quickly, there are also problems that Z3 cannot solve but (plain) HOICE can.

Table 6. Experimental results on CHC solving

Problem	#pred	#P	#N	#I	Cycle	Time	Key qualifiers found	Z3
plus	1	29	48	35	1	23.8	$x_0 + 2x_1 + x_2 = 0$	-
plusminus	2	90	137	42	2	63.2	$x_0 + 2x_1 - x_1 = 0$	-
cggmp	1	25	95	11	1	20.0	$x_0 + 2x_1 - x_2 = 0$	0.05
cggmp-new	1	8	97	15	1	24.1	$x_0 + 2x_1 \geq 40, x_0 + 2x_1 \leq 42$	0.12
fib17n	1	44	139	35	7–10	349.7	$-x_0 + x_2 - x_3 \geq 0$	0.14
fib32	1	42	222	17	-	-	-	-
fib32 -mod2	1	42	222	17	1–3	53.7	$x_3 \mod 2 = 0$	-
hola.07	1	78	314	12	2 – 3	72.5	$x_0 + x_1 = 3x_2$	0.05
codeinv93	1	32	260	23	2 – 3	73.2	$-3x_0 + x_2 + x_3 = 0$	0.05
pldi082	2	15	42	34	1	24.6	$2x_0 - x_1 - x_2 \geq -2$	-
xyz	2	56	6	142	-	-	-	0.33
xyz -gen	2	251	139	0	3 – 5	185.9	$x_0 + 2x_1 \geq 0$	0.33
xyz_v	2	160	303	43	2 – 8	217.3	$x_0 - x_1 - 2x_2 + 2x_3 \geq 0$	-

4   Related Work

There have recently been a number of studies on verification of neural networks [1,8,16,21,30]: see [10] for an extensive survey. In contrast, the end goal of the present paper is to apply neural networks to verification and synthesis of *classical* programs. Closest to our use of NNs is the work of Ryan et al. [22,29] on Continuous Logic Network (CLN). CLN is a special neural network that imitates a logical formula (analogously like symbolic regressions discussed below), and it was applied to learn loop invariants. The main differences are: (i) The shape of a formula must be fixed in their original approach [22], while it need not in our method, thanks to our hybrid approach of extracting just qualifiers and using a classical method for constructing its Boolean combinations. Although their later approach [29] relaxes the shape restriction, it still seems less flexible than ours (in fact, the shape of invariants found by their tools seem limited, according to the code available at https://github.com/gryan11/cln2inv and https://github.com/jyao15/G-CLN). (ii) We consider a more general learning problem, using not only positive examples, but also negative and implication examples. This is important for applications to CHC solving discussed in Sect. 3 and oracle-based program synthesis discussed in the longer version [13].

Finding inductive invariants has been the main bottleneck of program verification, both for automated tools (where tools have to automatically find invariants) and semi-automated tools (where users have to provide invariants as hints for verification). In particular, finding appropriate qualifiers (sometimes called *features* [18], and also *predicates* in verification methods based on predicate abstraction), which are atomic formulas that constitute inductive invariants, has been a challenge. Various machine learning techniques have recently been applied to the discovery of invariants and/or qualifiers. As already mentioned,

Garg et al. [6,7] proposed a framework of semi-supervised learning called ICE learning, where implication constraints are provided to a learner in addition to positive and negative examples. The framework has later been generalized for CHC solving [4,5], but the discovery of qualifiers remained as a main bottleneck.

To address the issue of qualifier discovery, Zhu et al. [31] proposed a use of SVMs (support vector machines). Whilst SVMs are typically much faster than NNs, there are significant shortcomings: (i) SVMs are not good at finding a Boolean combination of linear inequalities (like $A \wedge B$) as a classifier. To address the issue, they combined SVMs (to find each qualifier A, B) with the Boolean decision tree construction [7], but it is in general unlikely that SVMs generate A and/or B as classifiers when $A \wedge B$ is a complete classifier (see Fig. 7). (ii) SVMs do not properly take implication constraints into account. Zhu et al. [31] label the data occurring only in implication constraints as positive or negative examples in an ad hoc manner, and pass the labeled data to SVMs. The problem with that approach is that the labeling of data is performed without considering the overall classification problem. Recall the example problem in Sect. 3.2 consisting of implication constraints of the form $p(2n) \wedge p(2n+1) \Rightarrow$ and $\Rightarrow p(2n) \vee p(2n+1)$ for $n \in [-10, 10]$. In this case, there are 2^{21} possible ways to classify data, of which only two classifications ($p(2n) = \texttt{true}$ and $p(2n+1) = \texttt{false}$ for all n, or $p(2n+1) = \texttt{true}$ and $p(2n) = \texttt{false}$ for all n) lead to a concise classification of $n \mod 2 = 0$ or $n \mod 2 = 1$. Sharma et al. [25] also applied SVMs to find interpolants. It would be interesting to investigate whether our approach is also useful for finding interpolants.

Padhi et al. [17,18] proposed a method for finding qualifiers (features, in their terminology) based on a technique of syntax-guided program synthesis and combined it with Boolean function learning. Since they enumerate possible features in the increasing order of the size of feature expressions ([18], Fig. 5), we think they are not good at finding a feature of large size (like quadratic constraints used in our experiment in Sect. 2.3). Anyway, since our technique has its own defects (in particular, for finding simple invariants, it is too much slower than the techniques above), our technique should be used as complementary to existing techniques. Si et al. [26] used neural reinforcement learning for learning loop invariants, but in a way quite different from ours. Rather than finding invariants in a data-driven manner, they let NNs to learn invariants from a graph representation of programs.

Although the goal is different, our technique is also related with the NN-based symbolic regression or extrapolation [15,20,23], where the goal is to learn a simple mathematical function expression (like $f(x) = \sin(x + x^2)$) from sample pairs of inputs and outputs. To this end, Martius and Lambert's method [15] prepares a NN whose activation functions are basic mathematical functions (like sin), trains it, and extracts the function from the trained NN. The main difference of our approach from theirs is to use NNs as a gray (rather than white) box, only for extracting qualifiers, rather than extracting the whole function computed by NN. Nevertheless, we expect that some of their techniques would be useful also in our context, especially for learning non-linear qualifiers.

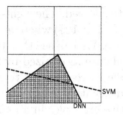

Fig. 7. SVM vs NN: Small circles denote positive examples, and the white space is filled with negative examples. The dashed line shows a linear classifier typically output by a SVM, while the thick line shows the (complete) classifier output by a NN.

5 Conclusion

We have proposed a novel method for synthesizing logical formulas using neural networks as *gray* boxes. The results of our preliminary experiments are quite promising. We have also discussed an application of our NN-guided synthesis to program verification through CHC solving. (Another application to program synthesis through the notion of oracle-based programming is also discussed in a longer version of this paper [13]). We plan to extend our NN-guided synthesis tool to enable the synthesis of (i) functions returning non-Boolean values (such as integers), (ii) predicates/functions on recursive data structures, and (iii) program expressions containing loops. For (ii) and (iii), we plan to deploy recurrent neural networks.

Acknowledgments. We would like to thank anonymous referees for useful comments. This work was supported by JSPS KAKENHI Grant Numbers JP20H05703, JP20H04162, and JP19K22842, and ERATO HASUO Metamathematics for Systems Design Project (No. JPMJER1603), JST.

Appendix

A   Additional Information for Sect. 2

A.1   On Three-Layer vs Four-Layer NNs

As reported in Sect. 2.2, three-layer NNs with a sufficient number of nodes performed well in the experiment on learning formulas $(A \wedge B) \vee (C \wedge D)$, contrary to our expectation. This section reports our analysis to find out the reason.

We used the instance shown on the left-hand side of Fig. 8, and compared the training results of three-layer and four-layer NNs. To make the analysis easier, we tried to train the NNs with a minimal number of hidden nodes in the second layer. For the four-layer-case, the training succeeded for only two hidden nodes in the second layer (plus eight hidden nodes in the third layer), and only relevant quantifiers of the form $x > c, x < c, y > c, y < c$ for $c \in \{-2, 1, 0, 1\}$ were generated. In contrast, for the three-layer case, 12 hidden nodes were required for the training to succeed. The right-hand side of Fig. 8 shows the lines $b_i+w_{i,x}x+w_{i,y}y = 0$ ($i \in \{1,\ldots,12\}$) where $w_{i,x}$, $w_{i,y}$ and b_i are the weights and bias for the i-th hidden node. We can see that the lines that are (seemingly) irrelevant to the original formula are recognized by the hidden nodes. Removing any hidden node (e.g., the node corresponding to line 1) makes the NN fail to properly separate positive and negative examples. Thus, the three-layer NN is recognizing positive and negative examples in a manner quite different from the original formula; it is performing a kind of patchwork to classify the examples. Nevertheless, even in that patchwork, there are lines close to the horizontal and vertical lines $y = 0$ and $x = 0$. Thus, if we use the trained NN only to extract qualifier candidates (rather than to recover the whole formula by inspecting also the weights of the third layer), three-layer NNs can be useful, as already observed in the experiments in Sect. 2.2.

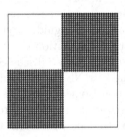 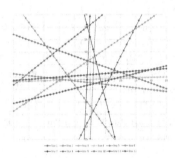

Fig. 8. Problem instance for learning $(x \geq 0 \wedge y \geq 0) \vee (x \leq 0 \wedge y \leq 0)$ (left) and lines recognized by Three-Layer NNs for problem instance $(x \geq 0 \wedge y \geq 0) \vee (x \leq 0 \wedge y \leq 0)$ (right).

A.2   On Activation Functions

To justify our choice of the sigmoid function as activation functions, we have replaced the activation functions with ReLU ($f(x) = x$ for $x \geq 0$ and $f(x) = 0$ for $x < 0$) and Leaky ReLU ($f(x) = x$ for $x \geq 0$ and $f(x) = -0.01x$ for $x < 0$) and conducted the experiments for synthesizing $(A \wedge B) \vee (C \wedge D)$ by using the same problem instances as those used in Sect. 2.2. Here are the results.

activation	#nodes	#retry	%success	%qualifiers	#candidates	time (sec.)
ReLU	32:32	15	18.3%	66.7%	72.4	55.9
Leaky ReLU	32:32	32	61.7%	88.8%	64.4	52.8
sigmoid	32:32	10	85.0%	91.7%	40.4	39.9

In this experiment, we have used the mean square error function as the loss function (since the log loss function assumes that the output belongs to $[0, 1]$, which is not the case here). For comparison, we have re-shown the result for the sigmoid function (with the mean square error loss function).

As clear from the table above, the sigmoid function performs significantly better than ReLU and Leaky ReLU, especially in %success (the larger is better) and #candidates (the smaller is better). This confirms our expectation that the use of the sigmoid function helps us to ensure that only information about $b + w_1 x_1 + \cdots + w_k x_k > c$ for small c's may be propagated to the output of the second layer, so that we can find suitable qualifiers by looking at only the weights and biases for the hidden nodes in the second layer. We do not report experimental results for the tanh function $(\tanh(x) = 2\sigma(x) - 1)$, but it should be as good as the sigmoid function, as it has similar characteristics.

A.3   On Biases

As for the biases in the second later, we have actually removed them and instead added a constant input 1, so that the weights for the constant input play the role of the biases (thus, for two-dimensional input (x, y), we actually gave three-dimensional input $(x, y, 1)$). This is because, for some qualifier that requires a large constant (like $x + y - 150 > 0$), adding additional constant inputs such as 100 (so that inputs are now of the form $(x, y, 1, 100)$) makes the NN training easier to succeed. Among the experiments reported in this paper, we added an additional constant input 10 for the experiments in Sect. 2.3.

Similarly, we also observed (in the experiments not reported here) that, when the scales of inputs vary extremely among different dimensions (like $(x, y) = (1, 100), (2, 200), ...$), then the normalization of the inputs helped the convergence of training.

B   Additional Information for Sect. 3

Here we provide more details about our experiments on the CHC problem xyz, which shows a general pitfall of the ICE-based CHC solving approach of HoICE (rather than that of our neural network-guided approach). Here is the source program of xyz written in OCaml (we have simplified the original program, by removing redundant arguments).

```
let rec loopa x z =
    if (x < 10) then loopa (x + 1) (z - 2) else z

let rec loopb x z =
    if (x > 0) then loopb (x-1) (z+2) else assert(z > (-1))

let main (mm:unit(*-:{v:Unit | unit}*)) =
    let x = 0 in let z = 0 in
    let r = loopa x z in
    let s = 10 in loopb s r
```

Here is (a simplified version of) the corresponding CHC generated by r_type.

$$x < 10 \wedge loopa(x+1, z-2, r) \Rightarrow loopa(x, z, r) \tag{1}$$

$$x \geq 10 \Rightarrow loopa(x, z, z) \tag{2}$$

$$x > 0 \wedge loopb(x, z) \Rightarrow loopb(x-1, z+2) \tag{3}$$

$$x \leq 0 \wedge loopb(x, z) \Rightarrow z > -1 \tag{4}$$

$$loopa(0, 0, r) \Rightarrow loopb(10, r) \tag{5}$$

When we ran HOICE for collecting learning data, we observed that *no* positive examples for *loopb* and *no* negative examples for *loopa* were collected. Thus NEUGUS returns a trivial solution such as $loopa(x, z, r) \equiv$ `true` and $loopb(x, z) \equiv$ `false`. The reason why HOICE generates no positive examples for *loopb* is as follows. A positive example of *loopb* can only be generated from the clause (5), only when a positive example of the form $loopa(0, 0, r)$ is already available. To generate a positive example of the form $loopa(0, 0, r)$, however, one needs to properly instantiate the clauses (2) and (1) repeatedly; since HOICE generates examples only lazily when a candidate model returned by the learner does not satisfy the clauses. In short, HOICE must follow a very narrow sequence of non-deterministic choices to generate the first positive example of *loopb*. Negative examples of *loopa* are rarely generated for the same reason.

Another obstacle is that even if HOICE can generate a negative counterexample through clause (5) with a luck, it is only of the form $loopa(0, 0, r)$. Although further negative examples can be generated through (1), the shape of the resulting negative examples are quite limited.

References

1. Anderson, G., Verma, A., Dillig, I., Chaudhuri, S.: Neurosymbolic reinforcement learning with formally verified exploration. In: Advances in Neural Information Processing Systems 33: Annual Conference on Neural Information Processing Systems 2020, NeurIPS 2020 (2020)
2. Arrieta, A.B., et al.: Explainable artificial intelligence (XAI): concepts, taxonomies, opportunities and challenges toward responsible AI. Inf. Fusion **58**, 82–115 (2020). https://doi.org/10.1016/j.inffus.2019.12.012
3. Bjørner, N., Gurfinkel, A., McMillan, K., Rybalchenko, A.: Horn clause solvers for program verification. In: Beklemishev, L.D., Blass, A., Dershowitz, N., Finkbeiner, B., Schulte, W. (eds.) Fields of Logic and Computation II. LNCS, vol. 9300, pp. 24–51. Springer, Cham (2015). https://doi.org/10.1007/978-3-319-23534-9_2
4. Champion, A., Chiba, T., Kobayashi, N., Sato, R.: ICE-based refinement type discovery for higher-order functional programs. J. Autom. Reason. **64**(7), 1393–1418 (2020). https://doi.org/10.1007/s10817-020-09571-y
5. Ezudheen, P., Neider, D., D'Souza, D., Garg, P., Madhusudan, P.: Horn-ICE learning for synthesizing invariants and contracts. In: Proceedings ACM Programming Language 2 (OOPSLA), pp. 131:1–131:25 (2018). https://doi.org/10.1145/3276501

6. Garg, P., Löding, C., Madhusudan, P., Neider, D.: ICE: a robust framework for learning invariants. In: Biere, A., Bloem, R. (eds.) CAV 2014. LNCS, vol. 8559, pp. 69–87. Springer, Cham (2014). https://doi.org/10.1007/978-3-319-08867-9_5

7. Garg, P., Neider, D., Madhusudan, P., Roth, D.: Learning invariants using decision trees and implication counterexamples. In: Proceedings of the 43rd Annual ACM SIGPLAN-SIGACT Symposium on Principles of Programming Languages, POPL 2016, pp. 499–512. ACM (2016). https://doi.org/10.1145/2837614.2837664

8. Gehr, T., Mirman, M., Drachsler-Cohen, D., Tsankov, P., Chaudhuri, S., Vechev, M.T.: AI2: safety and robustness certification of neural networks with abstract interpretation. In: 2018 IEEE Symposium on Security and Privacy. SP 2018, Proceedings, pp. 3–18. IEEE Computer Society (2018). https://doi.org/10.1109/SP.2018.00058

9. Hojjat, H., Rümmer, P.: The eldarica horn solver. In: 2018 Formal Methods in Computer Aided Design (FMCAD), pp. 1–7 (2018)

10. Huang, X., Kwiatkowska, M., Wang, S., Wu, M.: Safety verification of deep neural networks. In: Majumdar, R., Kunčak, V. (eds.) CAV 2017. LNCS, vol. 10426, pp. 3–29. Springer, Cham (2017). https://doi.org/10.1007/978-3-319-63387-9_1

11. Katz, G., Barrett, C., Dill, D.L., Julian, K., Kochenderfer, M.J.: Reluplex: an efficient SMT solver for verifying deep neural networks. In: Majumdar, R., Kunčak, V. (eds.) CAV 2017. LNCS, vol. 10426, pp. 97–117. Springer, Cham (2017). https://doi.org/10.1007/978-3-319-63387-9_5

12. Kingma, D.P., Ba, J.: Adam: a method for stochastic optimization. In: 3rd International Conference on Learning Representations, ICLR 2015, Conference Track Proceedings (2015). http://arxiv.org/abs/1412.6980

13. Kobayashi, N., Sekiyama, T., Sato, I., Unno, H.: Toward neural-network-guided program synthesis and verification. CoRR abs/2103.09414 (2021). https://arxiv.org/abs/2103.09414

14. Komuravelli, A., Gurfinkel, A., Chaki, S.: SMT-based model checking for recursive programs. Formal Methods Syst. Des. **48**(3), 175–205 (2016). https://doi.org/10.1007/s10703-016-0249-4

15. Martius, G., Lampert, C.H.: Extrapolation and learning equations. In: 5th International Conference on Learning Representations, ICLR 2017, Toulon, France, 24–26 April 2017, Workshop Track Proceedings. OpenReview.net (2017). https://openreview.net/forum?id=BkgRp0FYe

16. Narodytska, N., Kasiviswanathan, S.P., Ryzhyk, L., Sagiv, M., Walsh, T.: Verifying properties of binarized deep neural networks. In: Proceedings of the Thirty-Second AAAI Conference on Artificial Intelligence, (AAAI-18), the 30th innovative Applications of Artificial Intelligence (IAAI-18), and the 8th AAAI Symposium on Educational Advances in Artificial Intelligence (EAAI-18), pp. 6615–6624. AAAI Press (2018)

17. Padhi, S., Millstein, T., Nori, A., Sharma, R.: Overfitting in synthesis: theory and practice. In: Dillig, I., Tasiran, S. (eds.) CAV 2019. LNCS, vol. 11561, pp. 315–334. Springer, Cham (2019). https://doi.org/10.1007/978-3-030-25540-4_17

18. Padhi, S., Sharma, R., Millstein, T.D.: Data-driven precondition inference with learned features. In: Krintz, C., Berger, E. (eds.) Proceedings of the 37th ACM SIGPLAN Conference on Programming Language Design and Implementation, PLDI 2016, Santa Barbara, CA, USA, June 13–17, 2016. pp. 42–56. ACM (2016), https://doi.org/10.1145/2908080.2908099

19. Pavlinovic, Z., Su, Y., Wies, T.: Data flow refinement type inference. In: Proceedings ACM Programming Language 5(POPL), pp. 1–31 (2021). https://doi.org/10.1145/3434300

20. Petersen, B.K., Landajuela, M., Mundhenk, T.N., Santiago, C.P., Kim, S.K., Kim, J.T.: Deep symbolic regression: recovering mathematical expressions from data via risk-seeking policy gradients. In: Proceedings of the International Conference on Learning Representations (2021)

21. Pulina, L., Tacchella, A.: An abstraction-refinement approach to verification of artificial neural networks. In: Touili, T., Cook, B., Jackson, P. (eds.) CAV 2010. LNCS, vol. 6174, pp. 243–257. Springer, Heidelberg (2010). https://doi.org/10.1007/978-3-642-14295-6_24

22. Ryan, G., Wong, J., Yao, J., Gu, R., Jana, S.: CLN2INV: learning loop invariants with continuous logic networks. In: 8th International Conference on Learning Representations, ICLR 2020. OpenReview.net (2020)

23. Sahoo, S., Lampert, C., Martius, G.: Learning equations for extrapolation and control. In: Dy, J., Krause, A. (eds.) Proceedings of the 35th International Conference on Machine Learning. Proceedings of Machine Learning Research, vol. 80, pp. 4442–4450. PMLR, Stockholmsmässan, Stockholm Sweden, 10–15 July 2018. http://proceedings.mlr.press/v80/sahoo18a.html

24. Satake, Y., Unno, H., Yanagi, H.: Probabilistic inference for predicate constraint satisfaction. In: The Thirty-Fourth AAAI Conference on Artificial Intelligence, AAAI 2020, The Thirty-Second Innovative Applications of Artificial Intelligence Conference, IAAI 2020, The Tenth AAAI Symposium on Educational Advances in Artificial Intelligence. EAAI 2020, pp. 1644–1651. AAAI Press (2020)

25. Sharma, R., Nori, A.V., Aiken, A.: Interpolants as classifiers. In: Madhusudan, P., Seshia, S.A. (eds.) CAV 2012. LNCS, vol. 7358, pp. 71–87. Springer, Heidelberg (2012). https://doi.org/10.1007/978-3-642-31424-7_11

26. Si, X., Dai, H., Raghothaman, M., Naik, M., Song, L.: Learning loop invariants for program verification. In: Advances in Neural Information Processing Systems 31: Annual Conference on Neural Information Processing Systems 2018. NeurIPS 2018, pp. 7762–7773 (2018)

27. Solar-Lezama, A.: Program synthesis by sketching. Ph.D. thesis, University of California, Berkeley (2008)

28. Verma, A., Murali, V., Singh, R., Kohli, P., Chaudhuri, S.: Programmatically interpretable reinforcement learning. In: Proceedings of the 35th International Conference on Machine Learning, ICML 2018. Proceedings of Machine Learning Research, vol. 80, pp. 5052–5061. PMLR (2018)

29. Yao, J., Ryan, G., Wong, J., Jana, S., Gu, R.: Learning nonlinear loop invariants with gated continuous logic networks. In: Proceedings of the 41st ACM SIGPLAN International Conference on Programming Language Design and Implementation. PLDI 2020, pp. 106–120. ACM (2020). https://doi.org/10.1145/3385412.3385986

30. Zhao, H., Zeng, X., Chen, T., Liu, Z., Woodcock, J.: Learning safe neural network controllers with barrier certificates (2020)

31. Zhu, H., Magill, S., Jagannathan, S.: A data-driven CHC solver. In: Proceedings of the 39th ACM SIGPLAN Conference on Programming Language Design and Implementation. PLDI 2018, pp. 707–721. ACM (2018). https://doi.org/10.1145/3192366.3192416

32. Zhu, H., Xiong, Z., Magill, S., Jagannathan, S.: An inductive synthesis framework for verifiable reinforcement learning. In: Proceedings of the 40th ACM SIGPLAN Conference on Programming Language Design and Implementation. PLDI 2019, pp. 686–701. ACM (2019). https://doi.org/10.1145/3314221.3314638

Selective Context-Sensitivity for *k-CFA* with CFL-Reachability

Jingbo Lu[✉], Dongjie He, and Jingling Xue

Programming Languages and Compilers Group, School of Computer Science and
Engineering UNSW, Sydney, Australia
jlu@cse.unsw.edu

Abstract. *k-CFA* provides the most well-known context abstraction for
program analysis, especially pointer analysis, for a wide range of programming languages. However, its inherent context explosion problem
has hindered its applicability. To mitigate this problem, selective context-
sensitivity is promising as context-sensitivity is applied only selectively
to some parts of the program. This paper introduces a new approach to
selective context-sensitivity for supporting *k-CFA*-based pointer analysis,
based on CFL-reachability. Our approach can make *k-CFA*-based pointer
analysis run significantly faster while losing little precision, based on an
evaluation using a set of 11 popular Java benchmarks and applications.

Keywords: Pointer analysis · Context sensitivity · CFL reachability

1 Introduction

For the programs written in a wide range of programming languages, *k-CFA* [23]
represents the most well-known context abstraction for representing the calling
contexts of a method in program analysis, especially pointer analysis, where
one remembers only the last k callsites. However, this k-callsite-based context-
sensitive abstraction suffers from the combinatorial explosion of calling contexts.

For *k-CFA*-based pointer analysis, denoted *kcs*, different degrees of context-
sensitivity at different program points in a program can have vastly different impacts on its precision and efficiency. To mitigate its context explosion problem, selective context-sensitivity is promising, since context-sensitivity

Thanks to all the reviewers for their constructive comments. This work is supported
by Australian Research Council Grants (DP170103956 and DP180104069).

is applied only selectively to some parts of the program. However, existing attempts [10,12,16,25], while being applicable to other types of context-sensitivity, such as object-sensitivity [15] and type-sensitivity [24], are mostly heuristics-driven. For example, some heuristics used are related to the number of objects pointed to by some variables and certain pre-defined value-flow patterns found (according to the points-to information that is pre-computed by Andersen's (context-insensitve) analysis [3]).

In this paper, we introduce a new approach to selective context-sensitivity in order to enable kcs to run substantially faster while losing little precision. Our pre-analysis makes such selections systematically by reasoning about the effects of selective context-sensitivity on kcs, based on context-free language reachability, i.e., *CFL-reachability*. Our key insight is that the effects of analyzing a given variable/object context-sensitively on avoiding generating spurious points-to relations (elsewhere in the program) can be captured by CFL-reachability in terms of two CFLs, L_F for specifying field accesses and L_C for specifying context-sensitivity. This correlation is analytical rather than black-box-like as before. By regularizing L_F while keeping L_C unchanged, this correlation becomes efficiently verifiable (i.e., linear in terms of the number of edges in a pointer-assignment-graph representation of the program, in practice).

In summary, we make the following contributions:

- We introduce a CFL-reachability-based approach, SELECTX, for enabling selective context-sensitivity in kcs, by correlating the context-sensitivity of a variable/object selected at a program point and its effects on avoiding spurious points-to relations elsewhere (i.e., at other program points).
- We have implemented SELECTX in SOOT [33] with its source code being available at http://www.cse.unsw.edu.au/~corg/selectx.
- We have evaluated SELECTX using a set of 11 popular Java benchmarks and applications. SELECTX can boost the performance of kcs (baseline) substantially with little loss of precision. In addition, kcs also runs significantly faster for these programs overall under SELECTX than under ZIPPER [12] (an existing heuristics-based approach to selective context-sensitivity) while also being highly more precise.

The rest of this paper is organized as follows. Section 2 outlines our key insights and some challenges faced in developing SELECTX. Section 3 reviews an existing CFL-reachability formulation of kcs. Section 4 formulates SELECTX for supporting selective context-sensitivity. Section 5 evaluates SELECTX. Section 6 discusses the related work. Finally, Sect. 7 concludes the paper.

2   Challenges

We review briefly the classic *k-CFA*-based pointer analysis (kcs) and describe some challenges faced in enabling kcs to support selective context-sensitivity.

2.1 *k-CFA*

A context-insensitive pointer analysis, such as Andersen's analysis [3], uses a single abstraction for a variable/object. In contrast, a context-sensitive pointer analysis uses different abstractions for a variable/object for the different calling contexts of its containing method. Different flavors of context-sensitivity differ in how the calling contexts of a method (*method contexts*) and the "calling" (i.e., allocating) contexts of a heap object (*heap contexts*) are modeled. In *kcs*, a pointer analysis based on *k-CFA* [23], method and heap contexts are often represented by their k- and $(k-1)$-most-recent callsites, respectively [31].

Context-sensitively, if $pt(p)$ represents the points-to set of a variable/field p, the points-to relation between p and an object o that may be pointed to by p can be expressed as follows [15,24]:

$$(o, c') \quad \in \quad pt(p, c) \tag{1}$$

where c is the method context (i.e., calling context) of p's containing method and c' is the heap context of o (i.e., the calling context under which o is allocated). The precision of a context-sensitive pointer analysis is measured by the context-insensitive points-to information obtained (with all the contexts dropped):

$$o \quad \in \quad \overline{pt}(p) \tag{2}$$

which can be more precise than the points-to information obtained directly by applying a context-insensitive pointer analysis (as failing to analyze each method for each context separately will conflate the effects of all calls to the method).

```
1  Object m(Object n) {
2      return n;
3  }
4
5  Object w1 = new Object(); // o1
6  Object w2 = new Object(); // o2
7  Object v1 = m(w1); // c1
8  Object v2 = m(w2); // c2
```

Fig. 1. An example for illustrating context sensitivity.

Let us consider a simple program given in Fig. 1. A context-insensitive pointer analysis, such as Andersen's analysis [3], models a variable/object without distinguishing its contexts, leading to a single abstraction for variable n. As the analysis cannot filter out unrealizable paths, the parameters and return values of the two calls to m() are conflated, preventing the analysis from proving that the two calls can actually return two distinct objects. Thus, $\overline{pt}(\text{v1}) = \overline{pt}(\text{v2}) = \{\text{o1}, \text{o2}\}$, where o2 $\in \overline{pt}(\text{v1})$ and o1 $\in \overline{pt}(\text{v2})$ are spurious. On the other hand, $1cs$ will distinguish the two calling contexts of m() (by thus modeling n under contexts $c1$ and $c2$ with two different abstractions), yielding $pt(\text{v1}, []) = pt(\text{n}, [c1]) = pt(\text{w1}, []) = \{\text{o1}, []\}$ and $pt(\text{v2}, []) = pt(\text{n}, [c2]) = pt(\text{w2}, []) = \{\text{o2}, []\}$, and consequently, the following more precise points-to sets, $\overline{pt}(\text{v1}) = \{\text{o1}\}$ and $\overline{pt}(\text{v2}) = \{\text{o2}\}$ (without the spurious points-to relations $\text{o2} \in \overline{pt}(\text{v1})$ and $\text{o1} \in \overline{pt}(\text{v2})$).

In this paper, we focus on context-sensitivity, as some other dimensions of precision, e.g., flow sensitivity [7, 28] and path sensitivity [6, 29] are orthogonal.

2.2   Selective Context-Sensitivity

Even under k-limiting, kcs must take into account all the calling contexts for a method (and consequently, all its variables/objects) at all its call sites. As a result, kcs still suffers from the context explosion problem, making it difficult to increase its precision by increasing k. However, there are situations where adding more contexts does not add more precision to kcs. To improve its efficiency and scalability, some great progress on selective context-sensitivity [10, 12, 16, 25] has been made, with a particular focus on object-sensitivity [15] and type-sensitivity [24], two other types of context-sensitivity that are also used in analyzing object-oriented programs. However, these existing techniques (heuristics-based by nature) are not specifically tailored to kcs, often failing to deliver the full performance potentials or suffering from a great loss of precision, in practice.

Why is it hard to accelerate kcs with selective context-sensitivity efficiently without losing much precision? In Fig. 1, we can see that whether n is context-sensitive or not ultimately affects the precision of the points-to information computed for v1 and v2. However, n is neither v1 nor v2 and can be far away from both with complex field accesses on n via a long sequence of method calls in between. How do we know that making n context-sensitive can avoid some spurious points-to relations that would otherwise be generated for v1/v2?

We may attempt to resort to some heuristics-based rules regarding, e.g., the alias relations between n and v1/v2. However, such rules often do not admit a quantitative analysis of their sufficiency and necessity. In many cases, the effects of these rules on the efficiency and precision of kcs are unpredictable and often unsatisfactory. Can the correlation between context-sensitivity and the precision of a pointer analysis be captured to support selective context-sensitivity?

As discussed above, whether a variable/object is context-sensitive or not often does not affect its own points-to relations, but rather, the points-to relations of other variables/objects. What are then the conditions for a variable/object n to affect the points-to relation $o \in \overline{pt}(v)$, i.e., that a variable v points-to o? In general, if a points-to relation holds in a pointer analysis, then it will also hold in a less precise pointer analysis. Conversely, if a points-to relation does not hold in a pointer analysis, then it will also not hold in a more precise pointer analysis.

Let $\mathcal{A}$ be a (context-sensitive) k-CFA-based pointer analysis, say, kcs. Let $\mathcal{A}_{CI=\{n\}}$ be its version where only a particular variable/object n in the program is analyzed context-insensitively. A sufficient and necessary condition for requiring n to be analyzed context-sensitively (when examining n in isolation) is:

$$\exists \, o \in O, v \in V \; : \; \mathcal{A} \implies o \notin \overline{pt}(v) \quad \wedge \quad \mathcal{A}_{CI=\{n\}} \implies o \in \overline{pt}(v) \qquad (3)$$

where O is the set of objects and V is the set of variables in the program.

Consider again Fig. 1. Under $\mathcal{A}$, we have o1 $\notin \overline{pt}$(v2) (o2 $\notin \overline{pt}$(v1)), but under $\mathcal{A}_{CI=\{n\}}$, we have o1 $\in \overline{pt}$(v2) and o2 $\in \overline{pt}$(v1), as described in Sect. 2.1. According to Eq. (3), there exist o2 and v1 in the program such that

$$\mathcal{A} \implies \text{o2} \notin \overline{pt}(\text{v1}) \quad \wedge \quad \mathcal{A}_{CI=\{\mathtt{n}\}} \implies \text{o2} \in \overline{pt}(\text{v1}) \qquad (4)$$

For reasons of symmetry, there also exist o1 and v2 in the program such that

$$\mathcal{A} \implies \text{o1} \notin \overline{pt}(\text{v2}) \quad \wedge \quad \mathcal{A}_{CI=\{\mathtt{n}\}} \implies \text{o1} \in \overline{pt}(\text{v2}) \qquad (5)$$

Therefore, n affects the points-to information computed for v1 and v2. Thus, n should be analyzed context-sensitively in order to avoid the spurious points-to relations o1 $\in \overline{pt}$(v2) and o2 $\in \overline{pt}$(v1) that would otherwise be introduced. All the other variables/objects in the program can be context-insensitive as they do not affect any points-to relation computed in the entire program.

Let us modify this program by adding, v1 = w2, at its end (thus causing v1 to point to not only o1 but also o2). Now, if n is context-sensitive (under $\mathcal{A}$), we will obtain $\overline{pt}$(v1) = $\{$o1, o2$\}$ and $\overline{pt}$(v2) = $\{$o2$\}$. However, if n is context-insensitive, we will still obtain $\overline{pt}$(v1) = $\overline{pt}$(v2) = $\{$o1, o2$\}$ conservatively. In this case, there still exist v2 and o1 in the modified program such that Eq. (5) holds. According to Eq. (3), n must still be context-sensitive.

However, the condition stated in Eq. 3 is impractical to validate: (1) it is computationally expensive since we need to solve $\mathcal{A}$ and $\mathcal{A}_{CI=\{n\}}$ for every variable/object n in the program, and (2) it would have rendered the whole exercise meaningless since we would have already solved $\mathcal{A}$.

In this paper, we exploit CFL-reachability to develop a necessary condition that is efficiently verifiable (i.e., linear in terms of the number of edges in the pointer assignment graph of the program) in order to approximate conservatively the set of variables/objects that require context-sensitivity. This allows us to develop a fast pre-analysis to parameterize *kcs* with selective context-sensitivity so that the resulting pointer analysis runs substantially more efficiently than before while suffering only a small loss of precision.

3   Preliminary

3.1   CFL-Reachability Formulation of K-*CFA*-based Pointer Analysis

CFL-Reachability [19], which is an extension of standard graph reachability, can be used to formulate a pointer analysis that operates on a graph representation of the statements in the program. In addition, a context-sensitive pointer analysis is often expressed as the intersection of two separate CFLs [14,19,26,32], with one specifying field accesses and the other specifying method calls. We leverage such a dichotomy to develop a new approach to selective context-sensitivity.

With CFL-reachability, a pointer analysis operates the *Pointer Assignment Graph (PAG)*, $G = (N, E)$, of a program, where its nodes represent the variables/objects in the program and its edges represent the value flow through assignments. Figure 2 gives the rules for building the PAG for a Java program. For a method invocation at callsite c, $\widehat{c}$ and $\widecheck{c}$ represent the *entry context* and *exit context* for any callee invoked, respectively. Note that ret^m represents a unique return variable in any callee invoked. For a PAG edge, its label above indicates the kind of its associated statement and its label below indicates whether it is an *inter-context* (an edge spanning two different contexts) or *intra-context* edge (an edge spanning the same context). In particular, we shall speak of an (inter-context) *entry edge* $x \xrightarrow[\widehat{c}]{\text{assign}} y$, where $\widehat{c}$ is an entry context and an (inter-context) *exit edge* $x \xrightarrow[\widecheck{c}]{\text{assign}} y$, where $\widecheck{c}$ is an exit context. During the pointer analysis, we need to traverse the edges in G both forwards and backwards. For each edge $x \xrightarrow[c]{\ell} y$, its inverse edge is $y \xrightarrow[c]{\overline{\ell}} x$. For a below-edge label $\widehat{c}$ or $\widecheck{c}$, we have $\overline{\widehat{c}} = \widecheck{c}$ and $\overline{\widecheck{c}} = \widehat{c}$, implying that the concepts of entry and exit contexts for inter-context value-flows are swapped if their associated PAG edges are traversed inversely.

A CFL-reachability-based pointer analysis makes use of two CFLs, with one being defined in terms of only above-edge labels and the other in terms of only below-edge labels [32]. Let L be a CFL over Σ formed by the above-edge (below-edge) labels in G. Each path p in G has a string $L(p)$ in Σ^* formed by concatenating in order the above-edge (below-edge) labels in p. A node v in G is said to be *L-reachable* from a node u in G if there exists a path p from u to v, known as *L-path*, such that $L(p) \in L$.

Let L_F be the CFL defined (in terms of above-edge labels) below [22,26]:

$$
\begin{aligned}
\textit{flowsto} &\rightarrow \textbf{new flows}^* \\
\overline{\textit{flowsto}} &\rightarrow \overline{\textbf{flows}}^* \; \overline{\textbf{new}} \\
\textit{flows} &\rightarrow \textbf{assign} \;\mid\; \textbf{store}[f] \; \overline{\textit{flowsto}} \; \textit{flowsto} \; \textbf{load}[f] \\
\overline{\textit{flows}} &\rightarrow \overline{\textbf{assign}} \;\mid\; \overline{\textbf{load}[f]} \; \overline{\textit{flowsto}} \; \textit{flowsto} \; \overline{\textbf{store}[f]}
\end{aligned}
\tag{6}
$$

If o *flowsto* v, then v is L_F-reachable from o. In addition, o *flowsto* v iff v $\overline{\textit{flowsto}}$ o. This means that $\overline{\textit{flowsto}}$ actually represents the standard points-to relation. As a result, L_F allows us to perform a context-insensitive pointer analysis with CFL-reachability by solving a balanced parentheses problem for field accesses [19,27].

Let L_C be the CFL defined (in terms of below-edge labels) below [14,32]:

$$
\begin{aligned}
\textit{realizable} &\rightarrow \textit{exits entries} \\
\textit{exits} &\rightarrow \textit{exits balanced} \;\mid\; \widecheck{c} \; \textit{exits} \;\mid\; \epsilon \\
\textit{entries} &\rightarrow \textit{balanced entries} \;\mid\; \textit{entries} \; \widehat{c} \;\mid\; \epsilon \\
\textit{balanced} &\rightarrow \textit{balanced balanced} \;\mid\; \widehat{c} \; \textit{balanced} \; \widecheck{c} \;\mid\; \epsilon
\end{aligned}
\tag{7}
$$

A path p in G is said to be *realizable* in the traditional sense that "returns" must be matched with their corresponding "calls" iff it is an L_C-path.

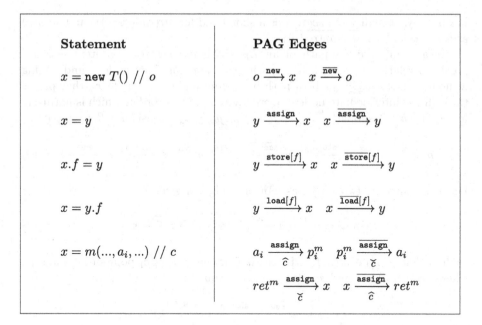

Fig. 2. Statements and their corresponding PAG edges.

Now, *kcs* can be expressed by reasoning about the intersection of these two CFLs, i.e., $L_{FC} = L_F \cap L_C$. A variable v points to an object o iff there exists a path p from o to v in G, such that $L_F(p) \in L_F$ (p is a *flowsto*-path) and $L_C(p) \in L_C$ (p is a realizable path). Such a path is referred to as an L_{FC}-*path*.

Note that this CFL-reachability-based formulation does not specify how the call graph is constructed. This can be either pre-computed by applying Andersen's analysis [3] or built on the fly. In Sect. 4, we discuss how this particular aspect of L_{FC} can cause SELECTX not to preserve the precision of *kcs*.

3.2 Transitivity of L_C-Path Concatenation

Given a realizable path p in G, where $L_C(p) \in L_C$, $L_C(p)$ is derived from the start symbol, *realizable*, starting with the production *realizable* $\to$ *exits entries*. Let us write $ex(p)$ for the prefix of $L_C(p)$ that is derived from *exits* and $en(p)$ for the suffix of $L_C(p)$ that is derived from *entries*. Let s be a string formed by some context labels, i.e., some below-edge labels in G. Let $can(s)$ be the canonical form of s with all balanced parentheses removed from s. For example, $can(\breve{c}_1\widehat{c}_2\breve{c}_2\widehat{c}_3) = \breve{c}_1\widehat{c}_3$. Let $str(s)$ return the same string s except that $\widehat{}$ or $\breve{}$ over each label in s has been removed. For example, $str(\breve{c}_1\widehat{c}_3) = c_1c_3$. Finally, $\overline{s}$ returns the same string s but reversed. For example, $\overline{c_1c_3} = c_3c_1$.

There exists an L_{FC}-path p from an object o to a variable v in G iff the following context-sensitive points-to relation is established:

$$(o, [str(can(ex(p)))]) \quad \in \quad pt(v, [\overline{str(can(en(p)))}]) \tag{8}$$

For brevity, we will write $scex(p)$ as a shorthand for $str(can(ex(p)))$ and $scen(p)$ as a shorthand for $str(can(en(p)))$.

As a result, any subpath of an L_{FC}-path induces some context-sensitive points-to relations. Let $p_{x,y}$ be a path in G, starting from node x and ending at node y. Let $p_{x_1,x_2,...,x_n}$ be a path in G from node x_1 to node x_n that passes through the intermediate nodes x_2, x_3, ..., x_{n-1} in that order, which is naturally formed by $n-1$ subpaths, $p_{x_1,x_2}, p_{x_2,x_3}, ..., p_{x_{n-1},x_n}$. Consider a flowsto-path:

$$p_{o,n,v} = o \xrightarrow{\text{new}} x \xrightarrow{\text{store}[f]} y \xrightarrow[\widehat{c_1}]{\overline{\text{assign}}} z \xrightarrow{\overline{\text{new}}} n \xrightarrow{\text{new}} z \xrightarrow[\check{c_2}]{\text{assign}} u \xrightarrow{\text{load}[f]} v \quad (9)$$

Let us examine its two subpaths. For one subpath given below:

$$p_{o,n} = o \xrightarrow{\text{new}} x \xrightarrow{\text{store}[f]} y \xrightarrow[\widehat{c_1}]{\overline{\text{assign}}} z \xrightarrow{\overline{\text{new}}} n \quad (10)$$

we find that $(o, [\,]) \in pt(n.f, [c_1])$, i.e., $n.f$ under context c_1 points to o under $[\,]$, where $scex(p_{o,n}) = \epsilon$ and $scen(p_{o,n}) = c_1$. From the other subpath:

$$p_{n,v} = n \xrightarrow{\text{new}} z \xrightarrow[\check{c_2}]{\text{assign}} u \xrightarrow{\text{load}[f]} v \quad (11)$$

we find that $pt(n.f, [c_2]) \subseteq pt(v, [\,])$, i.e., v under $[\,]$ points to whatever $n.f$ points to under context c_2, where $scex(p_{n,v}) = c_2$ and $scen(p_{n,v}) = \epsilon$.

In general, L_C-path concatenation is not transitive. In the following theorem. we give a sufficient and necessary condition to ensure its transitivity. Given two strings s_1 and s_2, we write $s_1 \simeq s_2$ to mean that one is the prefix of the other.

Theorem 1 (Transitive L_C-Path Concatenations). *Let $p_{x,z}$ be a path in G formed by concatenating two L_C-paths, $p_{x,y}$ and $p_{y,z}$. Then $p_{x,z}$ is an L_C-path iff $scen(p_{x,y}) \simeq scex(p_{y,z})$.*

Proof. As $L_C(p_{x,y}) \in L_C$, $L_C(p_{x,y}) = ex(p_{x,y})en(p_{x,y})$ holds. Similarly, as $L_C(p_{y,z}) \in L_C$, we also have $L_C(p_{y,z}) = ex(p_{y,z})en(p_{y,z})$. As $p_{x,z}$ is formed by concatenating $p_{x,y}$ and $p_{y,z}$, we have $L_C(p_{x,z}) = ex(p_{x,y})en(p_{x,y})ex(p_{y,z})en(p_{y,z})$. To show that $p_{x,z}$ is an L_C-path, it suffices to show that $L_C(p_{x,z}) \in L_C$. According to the grammar defining L_C, $L_C(p_{x,z}) \in L_C \iff en(p_{x,y})ex(p_{y,z}) \in L_C \iff can(en(p_{x,y}))can(ex(p_{y,z})) \in L_C$, where $can(en(p_{x,y}))$ is a sequence of entry contexts $\hat{c}$ and $can(ex(p_{y,x}))$ is a sequence of exit contexts $\check{c}$. By definition, $scen(p_{x,y}) = str(can(en(p_{x,y})))$ and $scex(p_{y,z}) = str(can(ex(p_{y,z})))$. Thus, $can(en(p_{x,y}))can(ex(p_{y,z})) \in L_C$ iff $scen(p_{x,y}) \simeq scex(p_{y,z})$.

Let us revisit the flowsto-path $p_{o,n,v}$ given in Eq. (9), which is a concatenation of two L_C-paths, $p_{o,n}$ and $p_{n,v}$, where $scen(p_{o,n}) = c_1$ and $scex(p_{n,v}) = c_2$. By Theorem 1, $p_{o,n,v}$ is an L_C-path iff $scen(p_{o,n}) \simeq scex(p_{n,v})$, i.e., iff $c_1 = c_2$.

4   CFL-Reachability-based Selective Context-Sensitivity

In this section, we introduce SELECTX, representing a new approach to selective context-sensitivity for accelerating *kcs*. Section 4.1 gives a necessary condition, which is efficiently verifiable, for making a node in G context-sensitive, based on L_{FC}. Section 4.2 describes the context-sensitivity-selection algorithm developed for SELECTX from this necessary condition for over-approximating the set of context-sensitive nodes selected. Section 4.3 explains why SELECTX may lose precision (due to the lack of provision for call graph construction in L_{FC}). Section 4.4 discusses its time and space complexities.

4.1   Necessity for Context-Sensitivity

For the *flowsto*-path $p_{o,n,v}$ given in Eq. (9) discussed in Sect. 3.2, we can see that whether $p_{o,n,v}$ is considered to be realizable depends on whether n is modeled context-sensitively or not. We can now approximate Eq. (3) in terms of CFL-reachability. Let $\mathcal{P}(G)$ be the set of paths in G. According to Theorem 1, we can conclude that a node (i.e., variable/object) n in G is context-sensitive only if the following condition holds:

$$\exists\, p_{o,n,v} \in \mathcal{P}(G) : L_F(p_{o,n,v}) \in L_F$$
$$\wedge\ L_C(p_{o,n}) \in L_C \wedge L_C(p_{n,v}) \in L_C \qquad (12)$$
$$\wedge\ scen(p_{o,n}) \neq scex(p_{n,v})$$

where o ranges over the set of objects and v over the set of variables in G.

To understand its necessity, we focus on one single fixed path $p_{o,n,v} \in \mathcal{P}(G)$, where $L_F(p_{o,n,v}) \in L_F \wedge L_C(p_{o,n}) \in L_C \wedge L_C(p_{n,v}) \in L_C$ holds. By Theorem 1, if $scen(p_{o,n}) \neq scex(p_{n,v})$, we will infer $o \in \overline{pt}(v)$ spuriously when n is context-insensitive ($\mathcal{A}_{CI=\{n\}} \implies o \in \overline{pt}(v)$) but $o \notin pt(v)$ when n is context-sensitive ($\mathcal{A} \implies o \notin \overline{pt}(v)$). To understand its non-sufficiency, we note that the same object may flow to a variable along several *flowsto*-paths.

Let us consider the program in Fig. 1, with its path $p_{o1,n,v2}$ given below:

$$o1 \xrightarrow{\text{new}} w1 \underset{\widehat{c1}}{\xrightarrow{\text{assign}}} n \underset{\widecheck{c2}}{\xrightarrow{\text{assign}}} v2 \qquad (13)$$

where $L_F(p_{o1,n,v2}) \in L_F$, $L_C(p_{o1,n}) \in L_C$, and $L_C(p_{n,v2}) \in L_C$. According to Eq. (12), n must be necessarily context-sensitive in order to avoid generating the spurious points-to relation $o1 \in \overline{pt}(v2)$ along this *flowsto*-path, since $scen(p_{o1,n}) = c1$ and $scex(p_{n,v2}) = c2$, where $c1 \neq c2$. All the other variables/objects in this program can be context-insensitive, as no such a path exists.

However, computing the CFL-reachability information according to $L_{FC} = L_F \cap L_C$ is undecidable [20]. Thus, verifying Equation (12), which is expressed in terms of L_{FC}, both efficiently and precisely for every node in G is not possible.

Below we over-approximate L_{FC} by regularizing L_F and maintaining L_C unchanged, so that the necessary condition stated in Eq. (12) for a node to be context-sensitive is weakened in the new language $L_{RC} = L_R \cap L_C$.

```
1   class A {
2       Object f;
3   }
4
5   Object id(Object n) {
6       A a = new A(); // o3
7       a.f = n;
8       return a;
9   }
10
11  Object w1 = new Object(); // o1
12  Object w2 = new Object(); // o2
13  Object v1 = id(w1); // c1
14  Object v2 = id(w2); // c2
```

Fig. 3. An example for illustrating an over-approximation of L_F with L_R.

By regularizing L_F, we obtain the regular language L_R defined below:

$$
\begin{aligned}
\textit{flowsto} &\rightarrow \text{new } \textit{flows}^* \\
\overline{\textit{flowsto}} &\rightarrow \overline{\textit{flows}}^* \; \overline{\text{new}} \\
\textit{flows} &\rightarrow \text{assign} \mid \text{store } \overline{\text{assign}}^* \; \overline{\text{new}} \text{ new} \\
\overline{\textit{flows}} &\rightarrow \overline{\text{assign}} \mid \overline{\text{new}} \text{ new assign}^* \text{store}
\end{aligned}
\tag{14}
$$

Here, the context-insensitive pointer analysis specified by L_R is field-insensitive. In addition, loads are treated equivalently as assignments, so that load [_] has been replaced by assign and $\overline{\text{load}}$[_] by $\overline{\text{assign}}$. Finally, store [_] and store[_] are no longer distinguished, so that both are now represented by store.

It is not difficult to see that L_R is a superset of L_F. Given $L_{RC} = L_R \cap L_C$, the necessary condition in Eq. (12) can now be weakened as follows:

$$
\begin{aligned}
\exists \, p_{o,n,v} \in \mathcal{P}(G) \; : \; &L_R(p_{o,n,v}) \in L_R \\
&\wedge L_C(p_{o,n}) \in L_C \wedge L_C(p_{n,v}) \in L_C \\
&\wedge scen(p_{o,n}) \neq scex(p_{n,v})
\end{aligned}
\tag{15}
$$

Let us illustrate this approximation by using the example given in Fig. 3, which is slightly modified from the example in Fig. 1. In this example, n can be context-insensitive by Eq. (12) but must be context-sensitive conservatively by Eq. (15). Consider the following path $p_{o1,n,v2}$ in G:

$$
\text{o1} \xrightarrow{\text{new}} \text{w1} \underset{\widehat{c1}}{\xrightarrow{\text{assign}}} \text{n} \xrightarrow{\text{store}[f]} \text{a} \xrightarrow{\overline{\text{new}}} \text{o3} \xrightarrow{\text{new}} \text{a} \underset{\check{c2}}{\xrightarrow{\text{assign}}} \text{v2}
\tag{16}
$$

where $L_C(p_{o1,n}) \in L_C$ and $L_C(p_{n,v2}) \in L_C$. As $scen(p_{o1,n}) = c_1$ and $scex(p_{n,v2}) = c_2$, we have $scen(p_{o1,n}) \neq scex(p_{n,v2})$. It is easy to see that $L_F(p_{o1,n,v2}) \notin L_F$ but

$L_R(p_{o1,n,v2}) \in L_R$ (with store[f] being treated as store). Thus, n should be context-sensitive according to Eq. (15) but context-insensitive according to Eq. (12), since $p_{o1,n,v2}$ is a flowsto-path in L_R but not in L_F.

4.2 SELECTX: A Context-Sensitivity Selection Algorithm

We describe our pre-analysis algorithm used in SELECTX for finding all context-sensitive nodes in G, by starting from the necessary condition stated in Eq. (15) and then weakening it further, so that the final necessary condition becomes efficiently verifiable. We will then use this final necessary condition as if it were sufficient to find all the context-sensitive nodes in G. As a result, SELECTX may classify conservatively some context-insensitive nodes as also being context-sensitive. When performing its pre-analysis on a program, SELECTX relies on the call graph built for the program by Andersen's analysis [3]. As is standard, all the variables in a method are assumed to be in SSA form.

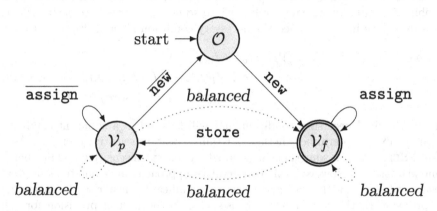

Fig. 4. A DFA for accepting L_R (with the summary edges shown in dotted lines). Note that in L_R loads are treated equivalently as assignments, so that load [-] is replaced by assign and $\overline{\text{load}}$[-] by $\overline{\text{assign}}$. In addition, store [-] and $\overline{\text{store}}$[-] are no longer distinguished, so that both are now represented by store.

As L_R is regular, Figure 4 gives a DFA (Deterministic Finite Automaton), A_R, for accepting this regular language over $G = (N, E)$ (the PAG of the program). There are three states: $S_R = \{\mathcal{O}, \mathcal{V}_f, \mathcal{V}_p\}$, where $\mathcal{O}$ is the start state and $\mathcal{V}_f$ is the accepting state. All the objects in N must stay only in state $\mathcal{O}$. However, a variable v in N can be in state $\mathcal{V}_f$ when it participates in the computation of flowsto into the variable and state $\mathcal{V}_p$ when it participates in the computation of $\overline{flowsto}$ from the variable. Therefore, $G = (N, E)$ leads naturally to a stateful version, $G_R = (N_R, E_R)$, where $N_R \subseteq N \times \{\mathcal{O}, \mathcal{V}_f, \mathcal{V}_p\}$ according to the state transitions given. For example, if $o \xrightarrow{\text{new}} v \in E$, then $(o, \mathcal{O}) \xrightarrow{\text{new}} (v, \mathcal{V}_f) \in E_R$, and if $x \xrightarrow{\text{store[-]}} y \in E$, then $(x, \mathcal{V}_f) \xrightarrow{\text{store[-]}} (y, \mathcal{V}_p) \in E_R$. For a pair of nodes

$n_1, n_2 \in N_R$, we write t_{n_1,n_2} if A_R can transit from n_1 to n_2 in a series of transitions and $p(t_{n_1,n_2})$ for the path traversed in G during these transitions. The four dotted summary edges (labeled *balanced*) will be discussed later.

We can now recast Eq. (15) in terms of A_R. A node $n \in N_R$ (with its state label dropped) is context-sensitive only if the following condition holds:

$$\exists\, o \in N \times \{\mathcal{O}\}, v \in N \times \{\mathcal{V}_f\} : t_{o,n} \wedge t_{n,v}$$
$$\wedge\, L_C(p(t_{o,n})) \in L_C \wedge L_C(p(t_{n,v})) \in L_C \quad (17)$$
$$\wedge\, scen(p(t_{o,n})) \neq scex(p(t_{n,v}))$$

where $t_{o,n} \wedge t_{n,v}$ holds iff the path consisting of $p(t_{o,n})$ and $p(t_{n,v})$ is a *flowsto*-path in L_R. This simplified condition can still be computationally costly (especially since SELECTX is developed as a pre-analysis), as there may be m_1 incoming paths and m_2 outgoing paths for n, resulting in $scen(p(t_{o,n})) \neq scex(p(t_{n,v}))$ to be verified in $m_1 m_2$ times unnecessarily.

Instead of verifying $scen(p(t_{o,n})) \neq scex(p(t_{n,v}))$ for each such possible path combination directly, we can simplify it into $scen(p(t_{o,n})) \neq \epsilon \wedge scex(p(t_{n,v})) \neq \epsilon$. As a result, we have weakened the necessary condition given in Eq. (17) to:

$$\exists\, o \in N \times \{\mathcal{O}\}, v \in N \times \{\mathcal{V}_f\} : t_{o,n} \wedge t_{n,v}$$
$$\wedge\, L_C(p(t_{o,n})) \in L_C \wedge L_C(p(t_{n,v})) \in L_C \quad (18)$$
$$\wedge\, scen(p(t_{o,n})) \neq \epsilon \wedge scex(p(t_{n,v})) \neq \epsilon$$

This is the final necessary condition that will be used as a sufficient condition in SELECTX to determine whether n requires context-sensitivity or not. As a result, SELECTX can sometimes mis-classify a context-insensitive node as being context-sensitive. However, this conservative approach turns out to be a good design choice: SELECTX can make *kcs* run significantly faster while preserving its precision (if the precision loss caused due to the lack of provision for call graph construction in L_{FC} is ignored as discussed in Sect. 4.3).

SELECTX makes use of the three rules given in Fig. 5 to determine that a node $n \in N_R$ (with its state label dropped) is context-sensitive if

$$n.enflow \neq \emptyset \quad \wedge \quad n.exflow \neq \emptyset \quad (19)$$

Each node $n \in N_R$ in a method m is associated with two attributes, *enflow* and *exflow*: (1) $n.enflow$ represents the set of sink nodes n_t of all the inter-context entry edges $n_s \xrightarrow{\hat{c}} n_t$ of m, such that n_t can reach n, and (2) $n.exflow$ represents the set of source nodes n_s of all the inter-context exit edges $n_s \xrightarrow{\check{c}} n_t$ of m, such that n can reach n_s. For reasons of symmetry, both attributes are computed in exactly the same way, except that the information flows in opposite directions.

Therefore, we explain only the parts of the three rules for computing *enflow*. In [INTER-CONTEXT], we handle an inter-context edge $n \xrightarrow{\hat{c}} n'$ by including n' in $n'.enflow$, i.e., initializing $n'.enflow$ to include also n'. In [INTRA-CONTEXT], we we handle an intra-context edge $n \to n'$ by simply propagating the data-flow

$$\frac{n \xrightarrow{\widehat{c}} n' \in E_R}{n' \in n'.\mathit{enflow}} \qquad \frac{n \xrightarrow{\widehat{c}} n' \in E_R}{n \in n.\mathit{exflow}} \qquad \text{[INTER-CONTEXT]}$$

$$\frac{n \to n' \in E_R}{n.\mathit{enflow} \subseteq n'.\mathit{enflow} \quad n'.\mathit{exflow} \subseteq n.\mathit{exflow}} \qquad \text{[INTRA-CONTEXT]}$$

$$\frac{n \xrightarrow{\widehat{c}} n' \in E_R \quad n'' \in n.\mathit{enflow} \vee n \in n''.\mathit{exflow} \quad n''' \xrightarrow{\widehat{c}} n'' \in E_R}{n''' \xrightarrow{\mathit{balanced}} n' \in E_R} \qquad \text{[CALLSITE-SUMMARY]}$$

Fig. 5. The rules used in SELECTX for realizing selective context-sensitivity for kcs. Note that all the above-edge labels in the PAG edges are irrelevant.

facts from the source node n to the sink node n'. In [CALLSITE-SUMMARY], we perform a standard context-sensitive summary for a callsite, as also done in the classic IFDS algorithm [21], by introducing a summary edge $n''' \xrightarrow{\mathit{balanced}} n'$ in $G_R = (N_R, E_R)$ to capture all possible forms of inter-procedural reachability, including, for example, a possible summary edge from an argument n''' to n' in $n' = foo(n''', ...)$, where foo is a callee method being analyzed.

To relate Eq. (18) with Eq. (19), we note that SELECTX ensures that

(1) n always lies on a *flowsto*-paths in L_R but the path may not necessarily have to start from an object as stated by $t_{o,n} \wedge t_{n,v}$ in Equation (18) ([INTER-CONTEXT] and [INTRA-CONTEXT]);
(2) $L_C(p(t_{o,n})) \in L_C \wedge L_C(p(t_{n,v})) \in L_C$ holds since SELECTX performs only context-sensitive summaries ([CALLSITE-SUMMARY]); and
(3) $scen(p(t_{o,n})) \neq \epsilon \wedge scex(p(t_{n,v})) \neq \epsilon$ are checked equivalently as $n.\mathit{enflow} \neq \emptyset \wedge n.\mathit{exflow} \neq \emptyset$.

Due to (1), Eq. (19) is slightly weaker than Eq. (18). As presented here, SELECTX becomes theoretically more conservative in the sense that it may identify potentially more context-insensitive nodes as being context-sensitive. In practice, however, the differences between the two conditions are negligible, as almost all the variables in a program are expected to be well initialized (i.e., non-null) and all the objects allocated in a (factory) method are supposed to be used outside (either as a receiver object or with its fields accessed). In our implementation, however, we have followed Eq. (18). Finally, global variables, which are encountered during the CFL-reachability analysis, can be handled simply by resetting its two attributes.

Let us apply these rules to the example in Fig. 1, as illustrated in Fig. 6. Given the two inter-context entry edges in G_R, $(\texttt{w1}, \mathcal{V}_f) \xrightarrow[\widehat{c1}]{\mathit{assign}} (\texttt{n}, \mathcal{V}_f)$ and $(\texttt{w2}, \mathcal{V}_f) \xrightarrow[\widehat{c2}]{\mathit{assign}} (\texttt{n}, \mathcal{V}_f)$, we have $(n, \mathcal{V}_f).\mathit{enflow} = \{(n, \mathcal{V}_f)\}$ by

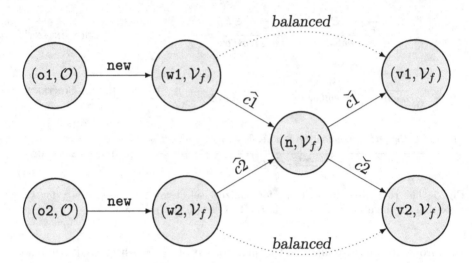

Fig. 6. Applying the rules given in Fig. 5 to the example program given in Fig. 1 (represented by its stateful PAG).

[INTER-CONTEXT]. Due to the two inter-context exit edges, $(n, \mathcal{V}_f) \xrightarrow[\breve{c1}]{\text{assign}}$ $(v1, \mathcal{V}_f)$ and $(n, \mathcal{V}_f) \xrightarrow[\breve{c2}]{\text{assign}} (v2, \mathcal{V}_f)$, we have $(w1, \mathcal{V}_f) \xrightarrow{\text{balanced}} (v1, \mathcal{V}_f)$ and $(w2, \mathcal{V}_f) \xrightarrow{\text{balanced}} (v2, \mathcal{V}_f)$ by [CALLSITE-SUMMARY]. Similarly, we obtain $(n, \mathcal{V}_f).exflow = \{(n, \mathcal{V}_f)\}$. Thus, n is context-sensitive by Eq. (19). For this example program, all the other nodes can be deduced to be context-insensitive.

4.3   Precision Loss

As SELECTX selects a node in G to be context-sensitive by using the necessary condition given in Eq. (18) as a sufficient condition, it is then expected to always over-approximate the set of context-sensitive nodes in G, and consequently, to always preserve the precision of any k-CFA-based pointer analysis algorithm like kcs being accelerated. However, this is not the case, as SELECTX may cause the pointer analysis to sometimes suffer from a small loss of precision due to the lack of provision in L_{FC} on how the call graph for the program being analyzed should be constructed *during the CFL-reachability-based pointer analysis*.

To illustrate this situation, let us consider an example given in Fig. 7. Class A defines two methods, foo() and bar(). Its subclass B inherits foo() from class A but overrides bar(). Note that foo() can be regarded as a wrapper method for bar(), as foo() simply invokes bar() on its "this" variable at line 4. If "this" is analyzed context-insensitively by kcs, then $pt(\text{this}, []) = \{(o1, []), (o3, [])\}$. This will cause the two bar() methods to be analyzed at line 4 whenever foo() is analyzed from each of its two callsites at lines 14 and 17, resulting in the conflation of o2 and o4 passed into the two bar() methods via their parameters

```
1   class A {
2       void bar(Object p) {}
3       void foo(Object s) {
4           this.bar(s); // c3
5       }
6   }
7
8   class B extends A {
9       void bar(Object q) {}
10  }
11
12  A a = new A(); // o1
13  Object v1 = new Object(); // o2
14  a.foo(v1); // c1
15  A b = new B(); // o3
16  Object v2 = new Object(); // o4
17  b.foo(v2); // c2
```

Fig. 7. An example for illustrating precision loss incurred when kcs is performed with selective context-sensitivity prescribed by SELECTX due to a lack of a call graph construction mechanism built-into L_{FC}.

at the two callsites. As a result, the two spurious points-to relations $o2 \in \overline{pt}(q)$ and $o4 \in \overline{pt}(p)$ will be generated. However, if the "this" variable is analyzed context-sensitively, then the two spurious points-to relations will be avoided.

If we apply Eq. (12) to "this" at line 4, we will conclude that "this" is context-insensitive due to the existence of only two paths passing through "this" in G: $o1 \xrightarrow{new} a \xrightarrow[\widehat{c1}]{assign} this$ and $o3 \xrightarrow{new} b \xrightarrow[\widehat{c2}]{assign} this$. Despite the value-flows that can continue from "this" along the two paths in the program, L_{FC} itself is "not aware" of such value-flows, as it does not have a call-graph-construction mechanism built into its underlying CFL reachability formulation. How to fill this gap in L_{FC} will be an interesting research topic. Currently, SELECTX may select some variables representing receivers (like "this" at line 4) to be analyzed context-insensitively, resulting in a small loss of precision (Sect. 5). Note that this problem does not exist in L_{FC}-based demand-driven pointer analysis algorithms [19,26], as they combine L_{FC} and a separate call-graph construction mechanism to compute the points-to information.

4.4 Time and Space Complexities

Time Complexity. Consider a program $\mathcal{P}$ with its PAG being $G = (N, E)$ and its corresponding stateful version being $G_R = (N_R, E_R)$, where $|N_R| < 2|N|$ and $|E_R| = |E|$. Let P be the maximum number of parameters (including "this" and the return variable) in a method in $\mathcal{P}$. For each node n, we have $|n.enflow| \leqslant P$ and $|n.exflow| \leqslant P$. Thus, the worst-case time complexity for handling all the intra-context edges in $\mathcal{P}$ is $O(P \times |E|)$. As for the inter-context edges, let M be the number of methods in $\mathcal{P}$ and I be the maximum number of inter-context entry edges per method in G (i.e., G_R). In [CALLSITE-SUMMARY]), $n'' \in n.enflow$ and $n \in n''.exflow$ can each be checked in $O(P)$, since $|n.enflow| = |n.exflow| = O(P)$. Thus, the worst-case time complexity for producing all the summary edges for $\mathcal{P}$ is $O(P \times M \times I)$. Finally, the worst-case time complexity for SELECTX is $O(P \times |E| + P \times M \times I)$, which should simplify to $O(|E|)$, since (1) $P \ll |E|$, and (2) $M \times I$ represents the number of inter-context entry edges in E.

For real-world programs, their PAGs are sparse. $|E|$ is usually just several times larger than $|N|$ rather than $O(|N|^2)$, making SELECTX rather lightweight.

Space Complexity. The space needed for representing G or G_R is $O(|N|+|E|)$. The space needed for storing the two attributes, *enflow* and *exflow*, at all the nodes in G_R is $O(|N| \times P)$. Thus, the worst-case space complexity for SELECTX is $O(|N| + |E| + |N| \times P)$, which simplifies to $O(|N| + |E|)$.

5 Evaluation

Our objective is to demonstrate that SELECTX can boost the performance of *kcs* (i.e., *k*-CFA-based pointer analysis) with only little loss of precision. To place this work in the context of existing research efforts to selective context-sensitivity [10,12,16,25], we also compare SELECTX with ZIPPER [12], a state-of-the-art pre-analysis that can also support selective context-sensitivity in *kcs*.

We conduct our evaluation using Java programs in SOOT [33], a program analysis and optimization framework for Java programs, as we expect our findings to carry over to the programs written in other languages. We have implemented *kcs* (the standard *k*-CFA-based pointer analysis) based on SPARK [11] (a context-insensitive Andersen's analysis [3]) provided in SOOT. We have also implemented SELECTX in SOOT, which performs its pre-analysis for a program based on the call graph pre-computed for the program by SPARK. For ZIPPER, we use its open-source implementation [12], which performs its pre-analysis for a program based on the points-to information pre-computed by SPARK.

We have used a set of 11 popular Java programs, including eight benchmarks from the DaCapo Benchmark suite (v.2006-10-MR2) [4] and three Java applications, checkstyle, findbugs and JPC, which are commonly used in evaluating pointer analysis algorithms for Java [9,10,14,25,30,31]. For DaCapo, lusearch is excluded as it is similar to luindex. We have also excluded bloat and jython, as 3*cs* fails to scale either by itself or when accelerated by any pre-analysis.

We follow a few common practices adopted in the recent pointer analysis literature [1,2,12,14,17,18,31]. We resolve Java reflection by using a dynamic reflection analysis tool, TAMIFLEX [5]. For native code, we make use of the method summaries provided in SOOT. String- and Exception-like objects are distinguished per dynamic type and analyzed context-insensitively. For the Java Standard Library, we have used JRE1.6.0_45 to analyze all the 11 programs.

We have carried out all our experiments on a Xeon E5-1660 3.2GHz machine with 256GB of RAM. The analysis time of a program is the average of 3 runs.

Table 1 presents our results, which will be analyzed in Sects. 5.1 and 5.2. For each $k \in \{2,3\}$ considered, kcs is the baseline, z-kcs is the version of kcs accelerated by ZIPPER, and s-kcs is the version of kcs accelerated by SELECTX. The results for SPARK (denoted ci) are also given for comparison purposes.

As is standard nowadays, kcs computes the points-to information for a program by constructing its call graph on the fly. As for exception analysis, we use SPARK's its built-in mechanism for handling Java exceptions during the pointer analysis. We wish to point out that how to handle exceptions does not affect the findings reported in our evaluation. We have also compared s-kcs with ci, kcs and z-kcs for all the 11 programs by ignoring their exception-handling statements (i.e., throw and catch statements). For each program, the precision and efficiency ratios obtained by all the four analyses are nearly the same

5.1 kcs vs. s-kcs

In this section, we discuss how SELECTX (developed based on CFL-reachability) can improve the efficiency of kcs with little loss of precision.

Efficiency. We measure the efficiency of a pointer analysis in terms of the analysis time elapsed in analyzing a program to completion. The time budget set for analyzing a program is 24 h. For all the metrics, smaller is better.

For k = 2, s-$2cs$ outperforms $2cs$ by 11.2x, on average. The highest speedup achieved is 23.5× for hsqldb, for which $2cs$ spends 244.2 s while s-$2cs$ has cut this down to only 10.4 s. The lowest speedup is 3.2x for findbugs, which is the second most time-consuming program to analyze by $2cs$. For this program, SELECTX has managed to reduce $2cs$'s analysis time from 1007.1 s to 286.2 s, representing an absolute reduction of 720.9 s.

For k = 3, $3cs$ is unscalable for all the 11 programs, but SELECTX has succeeded in enabling $3cs$ to analyze them scalably, in under 31 min each.

Precision. We measure the precision of a context-sensitive pointer analysis as in [25,26,31], in terms of three metrics, which are computed in terms of the final context-insensitive points-to information obtained ($\overline{pt}$). These are "#Call Edges" (number of call graph edges discovered), "#Poly Calls" (number of polymorphic calls discovered), and "#May-Fail Casts" (number of type casts that may fail).

For each precision metric m, let ci_m, $Baseline_m$ and P_m be the results obtained by SPARK, $Baseline$ and P, respectively, where $Baseline$ and P are

Table 1. Performance and precision of *kcs*, z-*kcs* (*kcs* accelerated by ZIPPER) and s-*kcs* (*kcs* accelerated by SELECTX). The results for *ci* (i.e., SPARK) are also included for comparison purposes. For all the metrics, smaller is better.

Program	Metrics	*ci*	2*cs*	z-2*cs*	s-2*cs*	3*cs*	z-3*cs*	s-3*cs*
antlr	Time (secs)	7.1	277.4	11.8	18.1	OoT	51.0	57.3
	#Call Edges	56595	54212	54366	54212	-	53768	53233
	#Poly Calls	1974	1861	1879	1861	-	1823	1792
	#May-Fail Casts	1140	841	862	847	-	794	665
chart	Time (secs)	10.7	712.4	94.4	113.7	OoM	2903.6	1832.9
	#Call Edges	75009	71080	71444	71080	-	70718	69579
	#Poly Calls	2462	2290	2314	2290	-	2213	2159
	#May-Fail Casts	2252	1819	1869	1825	-	1813	1693
eclipse	Time (secs)	7.0	442.5	45.1	51.1	OoM	748.2	621.8
	#Call Edges	55677	52069	52142	52071	-	51711	50878
	#Poly Calls	1723	1551	1563	1552	-	1507	1473
	#May-Fail Casts	1582	1237	1260	1250	-	1231	1135
fop	Time (secs)	5.4	321.1	16.2	20.1	OoM	84.7	96.8
	#Call Edges	39653	37264	37457	37264	-	36809	36416
	#Poly Calls	1206	1082	1106	1082	-	1038	1005
	#May-Fail Casts	919	637	658	643	-	620	573
hsqldb	Time (secs)	5.7	244.2	7.3	10.4	OoM	29.2	42.4
	#Call Edges	40714	37565	37751	37565	-	37087	36637
	#Poly Calls	1188	1065	1091	1065	-	1032	996
	#May-Fail Casts	902	635	657	641	-	616	566
luindex	Time (secs)	6.0	238.0	7.4	10.3	OoM	29.6	46.4
	#Call Edges	38832	36462	36649	36462	-	36051	35522
	#Poly Calls	1269	1144	1168	1144	-	1112	1075
	#May-Fail Casts	921	648	671	654	-	631	574
pmd	Time (secs)	9.2	980.3	266.6	286.8	OoM	3693.6	1374.3
	#Call Edges	69148	65877	66053	65877	-	65519	64402
	#Poly Calls	2965	2782	2798	2782	-	2729	2608
	#May-Fail Casts	2293	1941	1962	1948	-	1901	1778
xalan	Time (secs)	5.6	269.3	14.0	18.4	OoT	71.8	76.0
	#Call Edges	44061	40645	40800	40645	-	40189	39756
	#Poly Calls	1394	1260	1279	1260	-	1223	1192
	#May-Fail Casts	1063	742	763	748	-	724	664
checkstyle	Time (secs)	9.7	1103.0	354.7	317.2	OoT	6851.2	852.7
	#Call Edges	79808	74792	74962	74792	-	74367	73236
	#Poly Calls	2754	2564	2583	2564	-	2519	2492
	#May-Fail Casts	1943	1549	1573	1555	-	1519	1393
findbugs	Time (secs)	10.7	1007.1	286.2	317.0	OoT	5292.9	1806.7
	#Call Edges	82958	77133	77159	77133	-	76383	75421
	#Poly Calls	3378	3043	3047	3043	-	2952	2943
	#May-Fail Casts	2431	1972	2021	1988	-	1955	1821
JPC	Time (secs)	10.4	484.2	70.7	87.6	OoM	1085.5	677.9
	#Call Edges	71657	67989	68136	67999	-	67359	66060
	#Poly Calls	2889	2667	2693	2669	-	2617	2539
	#May-Fail Casts	2114	1658	1696	1666	-	1637	1543

Table 2. The analysis times of SELECTX (secs).

Program	antlr	chart	eclipse	fop	hsqldb	luindex	pmd	xalan	checkstyle	findbugs	JPC
SELECTX	10.6	33.1	12.7	9.1	7.5	8.4	28.7	10.2	31.0	34.7	12.0

two context-sensitive pointer analyses such that P is less precise than *Baseline*. We measure the precision loss of P with respect to *Baseline* for this metric by

$$\frac{((ci_m - Baseline_m) - (ci_m - P_m))}{(ci_m - Baseline_m)}.$$

Here, the precision improvement going from ci to *Baseline* is regarded as 100%. If $P_m = Baseline_m$, then P loses no precision at all. On the other hand, if $P_m = ci_m$, then P loses all the precision gained by *Baseline*.

Given the significant speedups obtained, SELECTX suffers from only small increases in all the three metrics measured across the 11 programs due to its exploitation of CFL-reachability for making its context-sensitivity selections. On average, the precision loss percentages for "#Call Edges", "#Poly Calls", and "#May-Fail Casts" are only 0.03%, 0.13%, and 2.21%, respectively.

Overhead. As a pre-analysis, SELECTX relies on SPARK (i.e., Andersen's pointer analysis [3]) to build the call graph for a program to facilitate its context-sensitivity selections. As shown in Tables 1 and 2, both SPARK (i.e., a context-insensitive pointer analysis (ci)) and SELECTX are fast. The pre-analysis times spent by SELECTX are roughly proportional to the pointer analysis times spent by SPARK across the 11 programs. SELECTX is slightly slower than SPARK but can analyze all the 11 programs in under 40 s each.

The overall overheads from both SPARK and SELECTX for all the 11 programs are negligible relative to the analysis times of *kcs*. In addition, these overheads can be amortized. The points-to information produced by SPARK is often reused for some other purposes (e.g., used by both ZIPPER and SELECTX here), and the same pre-analysis performed by SELECTX can often be used to accelerate a range of k-CFA-based pointer analysis algorithms (e.g., $k \in \{2,3\}$ here).

5.2   Z-kcs vs. s-kcs

We compare SELECTX with ZIPPER [12] in terms of the efficiency and precision achieved for supporting selective context-sensitivity in *kcs*. ZIPPER selects the set of methods in a program that should be analyzed context-sensitively and can thus be applied to not only *kcs* but also other types of context-sensitivity, such as object-sensitivity [15] and type-sensitivity [24]. SELECTX is, however, specifically designed for supporting *kcs* i.e., callsite-sensitivity.

Table 1 contains already the results obtained for z-*kcs* and s-*kcs*. Figure 8 compares and contrasts all the 5 analyses, 2*cs*, z-2*cs*, s-2*cs*, z-3*cs*, and s-3*cs*, in

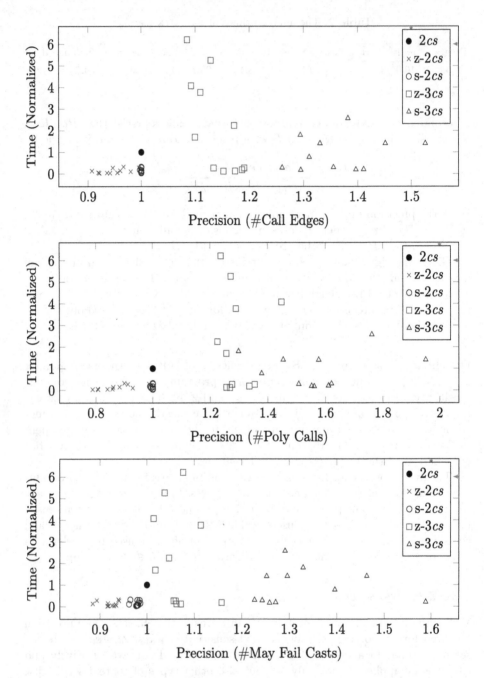

Fig. 8. Understanding the efficiency and precision of the five analyses by using the results obtained from Table 1 for all the 11 programs (normalized to 2*cs*). How these scatter graphs are plotted is explained precisely in Sect. 5.2. For each data point plotted, the lower and further to the right, the better.

terms of their efficiency and precision across all the 11 programs (normalized to $2cs$), in three scatter graphs, one per precision metric used. Note that $3cs$ is unscalable for all the 11 programs. For each metric m, let ci_m and A_m, where $A \in \{2cs, z-2cs, s-2cs, z-3cs, s-3cs\}$ be the results obtained by SPARK and A, respectively. If m is "analysis time", then A is plotted at $A_m/2cs_m$ along the y-axis. If $m \in \{$"#Call Edges", "#Poly Calls", "#May-Fail Casts"$\}$, then A is plotted at $(ci_m - A_m)/(ci_m - 2cs_m)$ along the x-axis. Hence, $2cs$ appears at $(1,1)$ (highlighted with a fat dot •) in all the three graphs. Here, $ci_m - A_m$ represents the absolute number of spurious call edges/poly calls/may-fail casts removed by A relative to ci. Therefore, when comparing z-kcs and s-kcs, for each $k \in \{2, 3\}$, the one that is lower is better (in terms of efficiency) and the one that is further to the right is better (in terms of a precision metric).

As discussed in Sect. 5.1, s-$2cs$ enables $2cs$ to achieve remarkable speedups (with ○'s appearing below •) at only small decreases in precision (with ○'s appearing very close to the left of •) with the percentage reductions being 0.03%, 0.13%, and 2.21% for "#Call Edges", "#Poly Calls", and "#May-Fail Casts", respectively, on average. On the other hand, z-$2cs$ is slightly faster than s-$2cs$ (by 1.2x, on average), but its percentage precision reductions over $2cs$ are much higher, reaching 5.22%, 12.94%, and 7.91% on average (with ×'s being further away from • to the left).

For $k = 3$, $3cs$ is not scalable for all the 11 programs. Both ZIPPER and SELECTX have succeeded in making it scalable with selective context-sensitivity for all the 11 programs. However, s-$3cs$ is not only faster than z-$3cs$ (by 2.0x on average) but also more precise (with z-$3cs$ exhibiting the percentage precision reductions of 16.38%, 16.96%, and 19.57% for "#Call Edges", "#Poly Calls", and "#May-Fail Casts", respectively, on average, relative to s-$3cs$). For five out of the 11 programs, z-$3cs$ is faster than s-$3cs$, but each of these five programs can be analyzed by each analysis in less than 2 min. However, s-$3cs$ is faster than z-$3cs$ for the remaining six programs, which take significantly longer to analyze each. In this case, s-$3cs$ outperforms z-$3cs$ by 3.0x, on average. A program worth mentioning is `checkstyle`, where s-$2cs$ spends 12% more analysis time than z-$2cs$, but s-$3cs$ is 8.0x faster than z-$3cs$ due to its better precision achieved.

6   Related Work

This paper is the first to leverage CFL reachability to accelerate kcs with selective context-sensitivity. There are some earlier general-purpose attempts [10,12,16,25] that can also be used for accelerating kcs with selective context-sensitivity.

Like SELECTX, "Introspective Analysis" [25] and ZIPPER [12] rely on performing a context-insensitive pointer analysis to guide their context-sensitivity selections. "Introspective Analysis" prevents some "bad" parts of a program from being analyzed context-sensitively based on some empirical threshold-based indicators. ZIPPER identifies so-called "precision-critical" methods by using classes as basic units to probe the flow of objects. In this paper, we have compared SELECTX with ZIPPER in terms of their effectiveness for improving kcs.

"Data-Driven Analysis" [10] is developed based on similar observations as in this paper: the effects of a node's context-sensitivity on the precision of a context-sensitive pointer analysis can be observed from its impact on the precision of a client analysis such as may-fail-casting. It applies machine learning to learn to make context-sensitivity selections. In contrast, SELECTX relies CFL-reachability instead without having to resort to an expensive machine learning process.

In [16], the authors also leverage a pre-analysis to decide whether certain callsites require context-sensitivity. However, unlike the three techniques [10,12, 25] discussed above and SELECTX, which rely on a context-insensitive pointer analysis to make their context-sensitivity selections, their paper achieves this by using a program analysis that is fully context-sensitive yet greatly simplified.

There are also other research efforts on accelerating *kcs*. MAHJONG [31] improves the efficiency of *kcs* by merging type-consistent allocation sites, targeting type-dependent clients, such as call graph construction, devirtualization and may-fail casting, but at the expense of alias relations. In [26], the authors accelerate a demand-driven *k-CFA*-based pointer analysis (formulated in terms of CFL-reachability) by adapting the precision of field aliases with a client's need.

EAGLE [13,14] represents a CFL-reachability-based pre-analysis specifically designed for supporting selective object-sensitivity [15] with no loss of precision. TURNER [8] goes further to exploit efficiency and precision trade-offs by exploiting also object containment. The pre-analyses discussed earlier [10,12,25] for parameterizing context-sensitive pointer analysis are also applicable to object-sensitivity.

7   Conclusion

We have introduced SELECTX, a new CFL-reachability-based approach that is specifically designed for supporting selective context-sensitivity in *k-CFA*-based pointer analysis (*kcs*). Our evaluation demonstrates that SELECTX can enable *kcs* to achieve substantial speedups while losing little precision. In addition, SELECTX also compares favorably with a state-of-the-art approach that also supports selective context-sensitivity. We hope that our investigation on CFL-reachability can provide some insights on developing new techniques for scaling *kcs* further to large codebases or pursuing some related interesting directions.

References

1. Ali, K., Lhoták, O.: Application-only call graph construction. In: Noble, J. (ed.) ECOOP 2012. LNCS, vol. 7313, pp. 688–712. Springer, Heidelberg (2012). https://doi.org/10.1007/978-3-642-31057-7_30
2. Ali, K., Lhoták, O.: AVERROES: whole-program analysis without the whole program. In: Castagna, G. (ed.) ECOOP 2013. LNCS, vol. 7920, pp. 378–400. Springer, Heidelberg (2013). https://doi.org/10.1007/978-3-642-39038-8_16
3. Andersen, L.O.: Program analysis and specialization for the C programming language. Ph.D. thesis, University of Copenhagen, Copenhagen (1994)

4. Blackburn, S.M., et al.: The DaCapo benchmarks: Java benchmarking development and analysis. In: Proceedings of the 21st annual ACM SIGPLAN Conference on Object-Oriented Programing, Systems, Languages, and Applications(OOPSLA 2006), pp. 169–190. ACM Press, New York, October 2006. http://doi.acm.org/10.1145/1167473.1167488

5. Bodden, E., Sewe, A., Sinschek, J., Oueslati, H., Mezini, M.: Taming reflection: aiding static analysis in the presence of reflection and custom class loaders. In: Proceedings of the 33rd International Conference on Software Engineering, pp. 241–250. ACM (2011)

6. Bodík, R., Anik, S.: Path-sensitive value-flow analysis. In: Proceedings of the 25th ACM SIGPLAN-SIGACT Symposium on Principles of Programming Languages (PoPL1998), pp. 237–251., Association for Computing Machinery, New York (1998). https://doi.org/10.1145/268946.268966

7. Hardekopf, B., Lin, C.: Flow-sensitive pointer analysis for millions of lines of code. In: Proceedings of the 9th Annual IEEE/ACM International Symposium on Code Generation and Optimization, pp. 289–298 (CGO2011), IEEE Computer Society (2011)

8. He, D., Lu, J., Gao, Y., Xue, J.: Accelerating object-sensitive pointer analysis by exploiting object containment and reachability. In: 35th European Conference on Object-Oriented Programming (ECOOP 2021). Schloss Dagstuhl-Leibniz-Zentrum für Informatik (2021)

9. Jeon, M., Jeong, S., Oh, H.: Precise and scalable points-to analysis via data-driven context tunneling. In: Proceedings of the ACM on Programming Languages 2 (OOPSLA), p. 140 (2018)

10. Jeong, S., Jeon, M., Cha, S., Oh, H.: Data-driven context-sensitivity for points-to analysis. In: Proceedings of the ACM on Programming Languages (OOPSLA), vol. 1 , p. 100 (2017)

11. Lhoták, O., Hendren, L.: Scaling java points-to analysis using SPARK. In: Hedin, G. (ed.) CC 2003. LNCS, vol. 2622, pp. 153–169. Springer, Heidelberg (2003). https://doi.org/10.1007/3-540-36579-6_12

12. Li, Y., Tan, T., Møller, A., Smaragdakis, Y.: A principled approach to selective context sensitivity for pointer analysis. ACM Trans. Program. Lang. Syst. **42**(2) (2020). https://doi.org/10.1145/3381915

13. Lu, J., He, D., Xue, J.: Eagle: CFL-reachability-based precision-preserving acceleration of object-sensitive pointer analysis with partial context sensitivity. ACM Transactions on Software Engineering and Methodology 30(4) (2021), to appear

14. Lu, J., Xue, J.: Precision-preserving yet fast object-sensitive pointer analysis with partial context sensitivity. In: Proceedings of the ACM on Programming Languages, vol. 3, Ocober 2019. https://doi.org/10.1145/3360574

15. Milanova, A., Rountev, A., Ryder, B.G.: Parameterized object sensitivity for points-to analysis for Java. ACM Trans. Softw. Eng. Methodol. (TOSEM) **14**(1), 1–41 (2005)

16. Oh, H., Lee, W., Heo, K., Yang, H., Yi, K.: Selective context-sensitivity guided by impact pre-analysis. SIGPLAN Not. **49**(6), 475–484 (2014). https://doi.org/10.1145/2666356.2594318

17. Raghothaman, M., Kulkarni, S., Heo, K., Naik, M.: User-guided program reasoning using Bayesian inference. In: Proceedings of the 39th ACM SIGPLAN Conference on Programming Language Design and Implementation, pp. 722–735. ACM (2018)

18. Rasthofer, S., Arzt, S., Miltenberger, M., Bodden, E.: Harvesting runtime values in Android applications that feature anti-analysis techniques. In: NDSS (2016)

19. Reps, T.: Program analysis via graph reachability. Inf. Softw. Technol. **40**(11–12), 701–726 (1998)
20. Reps, T.: Undecidability of context-sensitive data-dependence analysis. ACM Trans. Prog. Lang. Syst. (TOPLAS) **22**(1), 162–186 (2000)
21. Reps, T., Horwitz, S., Sagiv, M.: Precise interprocedural dataflow analysis via graph reachability. In: Proceedings of the 22nd ACM SIGPLAN-SIGACT Symposium on Principles of Programming Languages (POPL 1995), pp. 49–61. Association for Computing Machinery, New York (1995). https://doi.org/10.1145/199448.199462
22. Shang, L., Xie, X., Xue, J.: On-demand dynamic summary-based points-to analysis. In: Proceedings of the Tenth International Symposium on Code Generation and Optimization, pp. 264–274. ACM (2012)
23. Shivers, O.: Control-flow analysis of higher-order languages. Ph.D. thesis, Citeseer (1991)
24. Smaragdakis, Y., Bravenboer, M., Lhoták, O.: Pick your contexts well: understanding object-sensitivity. In: Proceedings of the 38th Annual ACM SIGPLAN-SIGACT Symposium on Principles of Programming Languages (POPL 2011), pp. 17–30. Association for Computing Machinery, New York (2011). https://doi.org/10.1145/1926385.1926390
25. Smaragdakis, Y., Kastrinis, G., Balatsouras, G.: Introspective analysis: context-sensitivity, across the board. In: Proceedings of the 35th ACM SIGPLAN Conference on Programming Language Design and Implementation (PLDI 2014), pp. 485–495. Association for Computing Machinery, New York (2014). https://doi.org/10.1145/2594291.2594320
26. Sridharan, M., Bodík, R.: Refinement-based context-sensitive points-to analysis for Java. In: Proceedings of the 27th ACM SIGPLAN Conference on Programming Language Design and Implementation (PLDI 2006), pp. 387–400. Association for Computing Machinery, New York (2006). https://doi.org/10.1145/1133981.1134027
27. Sridharan, M., Gopan, D., Shan, L., Bodík, R.: Demand-driven points-to analysis for Java. In: Proceedings of the 20th Annual ACM SIGPLAN Conference on Object-oriented Programming, Systems, Languages, and Applications (OOPSLA 2005), pp. 59–76. ACM, New York (2005). https://doi.org/10.1145/1094811.1094817
28. Sui, Y., Di, P., Xue, J.: Sparse flow-sensitive pointer analysis for multithreaded programs. In: Proceedings of the 2016 International Symposium on Code Generation and Optimization (CGO2016), pp. 160–170. Association for Computing Machinery, New York (2016). https://doi.org/10.1145/2854038.2854043
29. Sui, Y., Ye, S., Xue, J., Yew, P.: SPAS: scalable path-sensitive pointer analysis on full-sparse SSA. In: Yang, H. (ed.) Programming Languages and Systems - 9th Asian Symposium, APLAS 2011, Kenting, Taiwan, December 5–7, 2011. LNCS, vol. 7078, pp. 155–171. Springer (2011). https://doi.org/10.1007/978-3-642-25318-8_14
30. Tan, T., Li, Y., Xue, J.: Making k-object-sensitive pointer analysis more precise with still k-limiting. In: Rival, X. (ed.) SAS 2016. LNCS, vol. 9837, pp. 489–510. Springer, Heidelberg (2016). https://doi.org/10.1007/978-3-662-53413-7_24
31. Tan, T., Li, Y., Xue, J.: Efficient and precise points-to analysis: Modeling the heap by merging equivalent automata. In: Proceedings of the 38th ACM SIGPLAN Conference on Programming Language Design and Implementation. p. 278–291. PLDI 2017, Association for Computing Machinery, New York, NY, USA (2017). DOI: 10.1145/3062341.3062360

32. Thiessen, R., Lhoták, O.: Context transformations for pointer analysis. In: Proceedings of the 38th ACM SIGPLAN Conference on Programming Language Design and Implementation (PLDI 2017), pp. 263–277. Association for Computing Machinery, New York (2017). https://doi.org/10.1145/3062341.3062359

33. Vallée-Rai, R. Co, P., Gagnon, E., Hendren, L., Lam, P., Sundaresan, V.: Soot: a Java bytecode optimization framework. In: CASCON First Decade High Impact Papers, pp. 214–224. IBM Corp. (2010)

Selectively-Amortized Resource Bounding

Tianhan Lu[(✉)], Bor-Yuh Evan Chang[(✉)], and Ashutosh Trivedi[(✉)]

University of Colorado Boulder, Boulder, USA
{tianhan.lu,bec,ashutosh.trivedi}@colorado.edu

Abstract. We consider the problem of automatically proving resource bounds. That is, we study how to prove that an integer-valued resource variable is bounded by a given program expression. Automatic resource-bound analysis has recently received significant attention because of a number of important applications (e.g., detecting performance bugs, preventing algorithmic-complexity attacks, identifying side-channel vulnerabilities), where the focus has often been on developing precise amortized reasoning techniques to infer the most exact resource usage. While such innovations remain critical, we observe that fully precise amortization is not always necessary to prove a bound of interest. And in fact, by amortizing *selectively*, the needed supporting invariants can be simpler, making the invariant inference task more feasible and predictable. We present a framework for selectively-amortized analysis that mixes worst-case and amortized reasoning via a property decomposition and a program transformation. We show that proving bounds in any such decomposition yields a sound resource bound in the original program, and we give an algorithm for selecting a reasonable decomposition.

1 Introduction

In recent years, automatic resource-bound analysis has become an increasingly specialized area of automated reasoning because of a number of important and challenging applications, including statically detecting performance bugs, preventing algorithmic-complexity attacks, and identifying side-channel vulnerabilities. In this paper, we consider the specific problem of proving bounds on resource usage as follows: given an integer-valued resource variable r that models resource allocation and deallocation, prove that it is bounded by an expression e_{ub} at any program location—that is, prove assert $r \leq e_{ub}$ anywhere in the program. Resource allocations and deallocations can be modeled by (ghost) updates use $r\ e_{op}$ to the resource variable r (expressing that resource usage captured by r increments by e units), and we generically permit updates to be any expression e_{op}. For example, resource variables can model lengths of dynamically-sized

© Springer Nature Switzerland AG 2021
C. Drăgoi et al. (Eds.): SAS 2021, LNCS 12913, pp. 286–307, 2021.
https://doi.org/10.1007/978-3-030-88806-0_14

collections like lists and strings (e.g., `List.size()` or `StringBuilder.length()` in Java), and resource updates capture growing or shrinking such collections (e.g., `List.add(Object)`, `List.remove(Object)`, or `StringBuilder.append(String)`).

There are two natural ways to address this problem, by analogy to amortized computational complexity [36], for which we give intuition here. The first approach views the problem as an extension of the loop bounding problem, that is, inferring an upper bound on the number of times a loop executes [8,19,20,33–35,39]. Then to derive upper bounds on resource variables r, multiply the worst-case, or upper bound, of an update expression e_{op} by an upper bound on the number of times that update is executed, summed over each resource-use command `use` r e_{op}, thereby leveraging the existing machinery of loop bound analysis [8,9,35]. We call this approach *worst-case reasoning*, as it considers the worst-case cost of a given resource-use command for each loop iteration. This worst-case reasoning approach has two potential drawbacks. First, it presupposes the existence of loop bounds (i.e., assumes terminating programs), whereas we may wish to prove resource usage remains bounded in non-terminating, reactive programs (e.g., Lu et al. [28]) or simply where loop bounds are particularly challenging to derive. Second, as the terminology implies, it can be overly pessimistic because the value of the resource-use expression e_{op} may vary across loop iterations.

The second approach to resource bound verification is to directly adopt the well-established method of finding inductive invariants strong enough to prove assertions [31]. However, directly applying inductive invariant inference techniques (e.g., Chatterjee et al. [12], Colón et al. [13], Dillig et al. [16], Hrushovski et al. [24], Kincaid et al. [25–27], Sharma et al. [32]) to the resource bounding can be challenging, because the required inductive invariants are often particularly complex (e.g., polynomial) and are thus not always feasible or predictable to infer automatically [9,21]. We call this approach *fully-amortized reasoning*, as the strongest inductive invariant bounding the resource variable r may consider arbitrary relations to reason about how the resource-use expression e_{op} may vary across loop iterations, thereby reasoning about amortized costs across loop iterations.

The key insight of this paper is that the choice is not binary but rather the above two approaches are extremal instances on a spectrum of *selective amortization*. We can apply amortized reasoning within any sequence of resource updates and then reason about each sequence's contribution to the overall resource usage with worst-case reasoning. We show that the *decomposition* of the overall resource usage into *amortized segments* can be arbitrary, so it can be flexibly chosen to simplify inductive invariant inference for amortized reasoning of resources or to leverage loop bound inference where it is possible, easy, and precise. We then realize this insight through a program transformation that expresses a particular class of decompositions and enables using off-the-shelf amortized reasoning engines. In particular, we make the following contributions:

1. We define a space of amortized reasoning based on decomposing resource updates in different ways and then amortizing resource usage within the

resulting segments (Sect. 3). Different decompositions *select* different amortizations, and we prove that any decomposition yields a sound upper bound.

2. We instantiate selective amortization through a program transformation for a particular class of decompositions and define a notion of *non-interfering amortization segments* to suggest a segmentation strategy (Sect. 4).

3. We implemented a proof-of-concept of selective amortization in a tool BRBO (for *break*-and-*bo*und) that selects a decomposition and then delegates to an off-the-shelf invariant generator for amortized reasoning (Sect. 5). Our empirical evaluation provides evidence that selective amortization effectively leverages both worst-case and amortized reasoning.

Our approach is agnostic to the underlying amortized reasoning engine. Directly applying a relational inductive invariant generator on resource variables, as we do in our proof-of-concept (Sect. 5), corresponds to an aggregate amortized analysis, however this work opens opportunities to consider other engines based on alternative amortized reasoning (e.g., the potential method [22,23]).

2   Overview

Figure 1 shows the core of Java template engine class from the DARPA STAC [15] benchmarks. The `replaceTags` method applies a list of templates `ts` to the input `text` using an intermediate `StringBuilder` resource `sb` that we wish to bound globally. In this section, we aim to show that proving such a bound on `sb` motivates selective amortized reasoning.

At a high-level, the `replaceTags` method allocates a fresh `StringBuilder sb` to copy non-tag text or to replace tags using the input templates `ts` from the input `text`. The inner loop at program point 4 does this copy or tag replacement by walking through the ordered list of tag locations `tags` to copy the successive "chunks" of non-tag text `text.substring(p, l)` and a tag replacement `rep` at program points 6 and 11, respectively (the `assume` statement at program point 5 captures the ordered list of locations property). Then, the leftover text `text.substring(p, text.length())` after the last tag is copied at program point 11. The outer loop at program point 2 simply does this template-based tag replacement, and inserts a separator `sep` (at program point 12), for each template `t`. There are four program points where resources of interest are *used* (i.e., `sb` grows in length)—the `sb.append(...)` call sites mentioned here.

The `@Bound` assertion shown on line 1

$$\#sb \le \#ts \cdot (\#text + \#tags \cdot ts\#rep + \#sep)$$

follows the structure of the code sketched above. The template-based tag replacement is done `#ts` number of times where `#ts` models the size of the template list `ts`. Then, the length of the tag-replaced text is bounded by the length of `text` (i.e., `#text`) plus a bound on the length of all tag-replaced text `#tags · ts#rep` plus the length of the separator `sep` (i.e., `#sep`). A bound on each tag replacement `rep` is modeled with a variable `ts#rep` (which we name with `ts` to indicate its

```
    private String text;
    private List<Pair<Integer,Integer>> tags = ...text...;
    public String replaceTags(List<Templated> ts, String sep) {
 1    @Bound(#sb ≤ #ts·(#text + #tags·ts#rep + #sep)) StringBuilder
      sb = new StringBuilder();
 2    for (Templated t : ts) {
 3      int p = 0;
 4      for (Pair<Integer,Integer> lr : tags) {
 5        int l = lr.getLeft(); int r = lr.getRight();
            assume(p ≤ l ≤ r ≤ #text);
 6        sb.append(text.substring(p, l));
 7        String rep = ...t...lr...; assume(#rep ≤ ts#rep);
 8        sb.append(rep);
 9        p = r;
10      }
11      sb.append(text.substring(p, text.length()));
12      sb.append(sep);
13    }
      return sb.toString();
    }
```

Fig. 1. Motivating selective worst-case and amortized reasoning to analyze a Java template engine class (`com.cyberpointllc.stac.template.TemplateEngine`). An instance of this class stores some `text` that may have tags in it to replace with this engine. The tag locations are stored as an ordered list of pairs of start-end indexes in the `tags` field, which is computed from `text`. Suppose we want to globally bound the size of the `StringBulder sb` used by the `replaceTags` method to apply a list of templates `ts`. Let `#sb` be a resource variable modeling the length of `sb` (i.e., ghost state that should be equal to the run-time value of `sb.length()`). We express a global bound on `#sb` to prove with the `@Bound` annotation—here in terms of resource variables on the inputs `ts`, `text`, `tags`, and `sep`.

correspondence to a bound on all tag replacements described by input `ts`) and the `assume(#rep ≤ ts#rep)` statement at program point 7. Thus, a bound on the length of all tag-replaced text is `#tags · ts#rep`. Note that the coloring here is intended to ease tracking key variables but having color is not strictly necessary for following the discussion.

For explanatory purposes, the particular structure of this bound assertion also suggests a mix of worst-case and amortized reasoning that ultimately leads to our selectively-amortized reasoning approach that we describe further below. Starting from reasoning about the inner loop, to prove that the copying of successive "chunks" of `text` is bounded by `#text` requires amortized reasoning because the length of `text.substring(p, l)` at program point 6 varies on each loop iteration. In contrast, we bound the length of all tag-replaced text with `#tags · ts#rep` using worst-case reasoning: we assume a worst-case bound on the length of replacement text `rep` is `ts#rep`, so a worst-case bound with `#tags` number of tag replacements is `#tags · ts#rep`. Now thinking about the rest of the body of the outer loop at program point 11, the leftover text copy is amortized with the inner loop's copying of successive "chunks," so we just add the length of the separator #sep. Finally, considering the outer loop, we simply consider this resource usage bound for each loop iteration to bound #sb with #ts·(...).

The key observation here is that to prove this overall bound on #sb, even though we need to amortize the calls to sb.append(text.substring(p, 1)) at program point 6 over the iterations of the inner loop, we do not need to amortize the calls at this same site across iterations of the outer loop. Next, we translate this intuition into an approach for *selectively-amortized resource bounding*.

2.1   Decomposing Resource Updates to Selectively Amortize

The resource-bound reasoning from Fig. 1 may be similarly expressed in a numerical abstraction where all variables are of integer type as shown in Fig. 2a. There, we write use r e_{op} for tracking e_{op} units of resource use in r and $x := *$ for a havoc (i.e., a non-deterministic assignment). Note that text.substring(p, 1) translates to (1 - p). To express checking the global bound, we write assert(#sb $\leq e_{\mathrm{ub}}$) after each use update. We also note a pre-condition that simply says that all of the inputs sizes are non-negative. Crucially, observe to precisely reason about the resource usage #sb across all of these updates to #sb requires a polynomial loop invariant, as shown at program point 5 in braces {···}.

Yet, our informal reasoning above did not require this level of complexity. The key idea is that we can conceptually decompose the intermingled resource updates to #sb in any number of ways—and different decompositions select different amortizations. In Fig. 2b, we illustrate a particular decomposition of updates to #sb. We introduce three resource variables #sb1, #sb2, #sb3 that correspond to the three parts of the informal argument above (i.e., resource use for the non-tag text at program points 6 and 11, the tag-replaced text at program point 8, and the separator at program point 12, respectively). Let us first ignore the reset and ub commands (described further below), then we see that we are simply accumulating resource updates to #sb into separate variables or *amortization groups* such that #sb = #sb1 + #sb2 + #sb3. But we can now bound #sb1, #sb2, and #sb3 independently and have the sum of the bounds of these variables be a bound for the original resource variable #sb.

However, precisely reasoning about the resource usage in #sb1 still requires a polynomial loop invariant with the loop counters i, input #text, and internal variable p. Following the observation from above, we want to amortize updates to #sb1 across iterations of the inner loop but not between iterations of the outer loop. That is, we want to amortize updates to #sb1 in the sequence of resource uses within a single iteration of the outer loop and then apply worst-case reasoning to the resource bound amortized within this sequence. The *amortization reset* reset #sb1 after the initializer of the loop at program point 4 accomplishes this desired decoupling of the updates to #sb1 between outer-loop iterations by "resetting the amortization" at each outer-loop iteration. Conceptually,

global bound e_{ub}: $\#\mathtt{ts}\cdot(\#\mathtt{text}+\#\mathtt{tags}\cdot\mathtt{ts}\#\mathtt{rep}+\#\mathtt{sep})$
pre-condition: $\{0\le\#\mathtt{text}\wedge 0\le\#\mathtt{tags}\wedge 0\le\#\mathtt{ts}\wedge 0\le\mathtt{ts}\#\mathtt{rep}\wedge 0\le\#\mathtt{sep}\}$

```
1 #sb := 0;                              1
2 for (i := 0; i < #ts; i++) {           2 for (i := 0; i < #ts; i++) {
3   p := 0;                              3   p := 0;
4   for (j := 0                          4   for (j := 0,
          ; j < #tags; j++) {                    reset #sb1; j < #tags; j++) {

5     {#sb ≤ (i·#text+p)                  5     {#sb1♯ = i ∧ #sb1* ≤ #text ∧ #sb1 ≤ p ∧
            + ((i·#tags+j)·ts#rep)                 #sb2♯ = i·#tags+j-1 ∧
                                                   #sb2* ≤ ts#rep ∧ #sb2 ≤ ts#rep ∧
            + (i·#sep)}                            #sb3♯ = i-1 ∧
                                                   #sb3* ≤ #sep ∧ #sb3 ≤ #sep}

      l := *; r := *;                          l := *; r := *;
      assume(p ≤ l ≤ r ≤ #text);               assume(p ≤ l ≤ r ≤ #text);
6     use #sb (l - p);                    6     use #sb1 (l - p);
      assert(#sb ≤ e_ub);                        ub #sb1,#sb2,#sb3 e_ub
7     #rep := *;                          7     #rep := *;
      assume(0 ≤ #rep ≤ ts#rep);                 assume(0 ≤ #rep ≤ ts#rep);
8                                         8     reset #sb2;
      use #sb #rep;                              use #sb2 #rep;
      assert(#sb ≤ e_ub);                        ub #sb1,#sb2,#sb3 e_ub
9     p := r;                             9     p := r;
10  }                                     10  }
11  use #sb (#text - p);                  11  use #sb1 (#text - p);
    assert(#sb ≤ e_ub);                         ub #sb1,#sb2,#sb3 e_ub
12                                        12  reset #sb3;
    use #sb #sep;                               use #sb3 #sep;
    assert(#sb ≤ e_ub);                         ub #sb1,#sb2,#sb3 e_ub
13 }                                      13 }
```

(a) A numerical abstraction of the   (b) A resource usage decomposition and
replaceTags method from Fig. 1.   amortized segmentation of (a).

Fig. 2. Decomposing resource usage into amortized segments transforms the required supporting loop invariant at program point 5 needed to prove the global bound e_{ub} *from polynomial to linear.*

executions of the reset r mark the boundaries of the *amortization segments* of uses of resource r.

The result of this decomposition is the simpler invariant at program point 5 in the transformed program of Fig. 2b, which use some auxiliary summary variables like $\#\mathtt{sb1}^*$ and $\#\mathtt{sb1}^\sharp$. For every resource variable r, we consider two summary variables r^* and $r^\sharp$, corresponding, respectively, to the maximum of r in any segment and the number of "resetted" r segments so far. Concretely, the semantics of reset #sb1 is as follows: (1) increment the segment counter variable $\#\mathtt{sb1}^\sharp$ by 1, thus tracking the number of amortization segments of #sb1 uses; (2) bump up $\#\mathtt{sb1}^*$ if necessary (i.e., set $\#\mathtt{sb1}^*$ to max($\#\mathtt{sb1}^*$, #sb1)), tracking the maximum #sb1 in any segment so far; and finally, (3) resets #sb1 to 0 to start a new segment. As we see at program point 5 in the original and transformed programs of Fig. 2, we have decomposed the total non-tag text piece (i·#text+p) into $\text{\#sb1}^\sharp \cdot \text{\#sb1}^* + \text{\#sb1}$ where $\text{\#sb1}^\sharp = \text{i}$, $\text{\#sb1}^* \leq \text{\#text}$, and #sb1 $\leq \text{p}$. Intuitively, $\text{\#sb1}^\sharp \cdot \text{\#sb1}^*$ upper-bounds the cost of all *past* iterations of the outer loop, and the cost of the *current* iteration is precisely #sb1. Thus, $\text{\#sb1}^\sharp \cdot \text{\#sb1}^* + \text{\#sb1}$ is globally and inductively an upper bound for the total non-tag text piece of #sb. The same decomposition applies to #sb2 and #sb3 where note that $\text{\#sb3}^\sharp = \text{i-1}$, counts past segments separated from the current segment so that $\text{\#sb3}^\sharp \cdot \text{\#sb3}^* + \text{\#sb3}$ corresponds to (i·#sep) where both the past and current are summarized together. Overall, combining the amortization groups and segments, we have the following global invariant between the original program and the transformed one:

$$\text{\#sb} \leq (\text{\#sb1}^\sharp \cdot \text{\#sb1}^* + \text{\#sb1}) + (\text{\#sb2}^\sharp \cdot \text{\#sb2}^* + \text{\#sb2}) + (\text{\#sb3}^\sharp \cdot \text{\#sb3}^* + \text{\#sb3})$$

To verify a given bound in the transformed program, we simply check that this expression on the right in the above is bounded by the desired bound expression using any inferred invariants on $\text{\#sb1}^\sharp$, $\text{\#sb1}^*$, #sb1, etc. This is realized by the *upper-bound check* command at, for instance, program point 6 in Fig. 2b:

$$\text{ub \#sb1}, \text{\#sb2}, \text{\#sb3} \left(\text{\#ts} \cdot (\text{\#text} + \text{\#tags} \cdot \text{ts\#rep} + \text{\#sep}) \right) .$$

Here, ub $\bar{r}$ e asserts that the sum of amortization groups (internally decomposed into amortization segments) in the set $\bar{r}$ is bounded from above by e.

2.2   Finding a Selective-Amortization Decomposition

Figure 2b shows a decomposition of updates to #sb into groups (i.e., #sb1, #sb2, and #sb3) and segments (i.e., with resets) that realize a particular selective amortization. We show that any decomposition into groups and segments is sound in Sect. 3, but here, we discuss how we find such a decomposition.

Intuitively, we want to use worst-case reasoning whenever possible, maximizing decoupling of updates and simplifying invariant inference. But some updates should be considered together for amortization. Thus, any algorithm to select a decomposition must attempt to resolve the tension between two conflicting goals: partitioning use updates in the program into more groups and smaller segments, but also allowing amortizing costs inside larger segments to avoid precision loss. For example, it is important to use the same accumulation variable #sb1 for the two locations that contribute to the non-tag text (program points 6 and 11) to amortize over both use sites. In Sect. 4, we characterize the potential imprecision caused by worst-case reasoning over segments with a notion of *amortization segment non-interference*, which along with some basic restrictions motivates the approach we describe here.

In Fig. 3, we show the control-flow graph of the resource-decomposed program in Fig. 2b without the inserted `resets`. Node labels correspond to program points there, except for labels 2*, 4*, 13* that correspond to unlabeled program points in the initialization of the `for`-loops and the procedure exit. Edges are labeled by a single or a sequence of commands (where we omit keyword `assume` for brevity in the figure). Some nodes and edges are elided as ... that are not relevant for this discussion. Ignore node colors and the labels below the nodes for now.

Let us consider the class of *syntactic* selective-amortization transformations where we can rewrite resource use commands `use` r e to place `uses` into separate amortization groups, and we can insert a `reset` r' at a single program location to partition `uses` into amortization segments for each group r'. But otherwise, we make no other program transformation. We then use the notion of segment non-interference to select a group and segment decomposition under this syntactic restriction.

Now, the intuition behind amortization segment non-interference is that two segments for a resource r are non-interfering if under the same "low inputs," the resource usage of r is the same in both segments. In Fig. 3, the labels below the nodes show such low inputs to a particular `use` site from a particular program point. For example, under node 4, we show `p` as a low input for both the `use` sites at program points 6 and 11 (ignore the `:0`s for the moment).

So, an additional parameter in our search space is a partitioning of variables into "low" and "high" ones (which we note are not distinguished based on security relevance in the standard use of the non-interference term [1] but rather on relevance for amortized reasoning). We further fix the low variables in any segmentation we might use to be the internal variables on which the `uses` data-depend. This is based on the intuition that `uses` that share computation over internal variables are related for amortization. Because the `uses` for `#sb1` at program points 6 and 11 share `p` as an input at, for example, node 4, we place these `use` sites in the same group. Then, otherwise the other `use` sites at program points 8 and 12 are placed in other groups (namely, `#sb2` and `#sb3`, respectively).

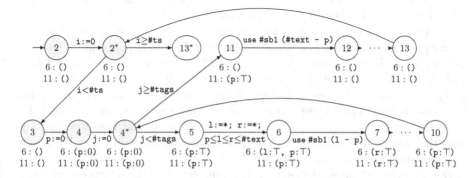

Fig. 3. Inserting a `reset` `#sb1` to select a segmentation for amortization group `#sb1`. We show the program from Fig. 2b here as a control-flow graph.

The set of variables on which use sites data-depend can be computed by a standard program slicing [37].

Finally, we insert a single reset for each group to define amortization segments. So that all use r e commands for a group r are always after some reset r, we consider program locations that control-dominate all use sites for r. In Fig. 3, any of the colored nodes control-dominate the two use sites for #sb1. To make the amortization segments as small as possible (while minimizing precision loss), we select the most immediate dominator where the low variables can be proven constant (i.e., the low inputs to the segments will always the same value). Node 4* (colored green) is this dominator for the two use sites for #sb1 because p is always 0 (shown as p:0) and where we insert reset #sb1. We can derive this constancy property with any numerical abstract domain (here, we show $\top$ for non-constant values from a standard constant propagation analysis for presentation), and we can pessimistically assume other variables to be low and also try to prove constancy for them to potentially recover some additional precision in segmentation.

Note that the analyses being applied here are classical ones. What is interesting here is not the analyses per se but their application to selecting amortization groups and segments to realize selectively-amortized resource bounding.

3   Decomposing Resource Usage

Our technique considers a resource-usage tracking program and splits a single resource variable into an arbitrary number of *resource decompositions*. By design, resource-usage tracking updates are generic in allowing updates with any integer-valued expression, enabling modeling non-monotonic resources like list additions and removals or memory allocation and deallocation. In this section, we define a core imperative language for resource-usage tracking, formalize selective-amortized analysis as a program transformation that inserts *amortization resets* into decomposed resource-usage tracking variables (Sect. 3.1), and show that any transformation is sound with respect to bound checks on resource usage (Sect. 3.2). While we focus on upper-bound checks, we will see that the approach can be easily adapted for lower-bound assertions.

In Fig. 4, we give the core resource-usage tracking language. We consider an unspecified expression language e, aside from including program variables x and its value forms v having integers n and booleans b. The command forms include standard imperative ones like the no-op unit skip, assignment $x := e$, and guard condition assume e. The remaining highlighted command forms work with resources r. In particular, use r e models a resource use where the usage of r is incremented by the value of e, and ub $\bar{r}$ e is an upper-bound assertion checking that the sum of the resources $\bar{r}$ is upper-bounded by the value of e. We abuse notation slightly by writing $\bar{r}$ both for a sequence $r_1 \dots r_n$ or a set $\{r_1, \dots, r_n\}$ of resources. Selective amortization is realized through resetting resources with the reset r command that we detail further below. Note that program expressions e do not contain resources variables r. Finally, programs p are given as control-flow graphs with edges $\ell -\!\![c]\!\!\rightarrow \ell'$ labeled by commands c between locations ℓ.

values $v ::= n \mid b \mid \cdots$ booleans $b ::= \mathtt{true} \mid \mathtt{false}$ expressions $e ::= x \mid v \mid \cdots$

commands $c ::= \mathtt{skip} \mid x := e \mid \mathtt{assume}\ e \mid \mathtt{use}\ r\ e \mid \mathtt{ub}\ \bar{r}\ e \mid \mathtt{reset}\ r$

programs $p ::= \cdot \mid p, \ell \dashv c \mapsto \ell'$

variables x resources r locations ℓ

stores $\rho ::= \cdot \mid \rho[x \mapsto v] \mid \rho[r \mapsto n] \mid \rho[r^* \mapsto n] \mid \rho[r^\sharp \mapsto n]$

$$\boxed{\langle \rho, e \rangle \Downarrow v \qquad \langle \rho, c \rangle \Downarrow \rho'}$$

E-UBCHECK

E-USE

$$\frac{\langle \rho, e \rangle \Downarrow n}{\langle \rho, \mathtt{use}\ r\ e \rangle \Downarrow \rho[r \mapsto \rho(r) + n]}$$

$$\frac{\langle \rho, e \rangle \Downarrow n \qquad \left(\sum_{r \in \bar{r}} \rho(r^\sharp) \cdot \rho(r^*) + \rho(r) \right) \leq n}{\langle \rho, \mathtt{ub}\ \bar{r}\ e \rangle \Downarrow \rho}$$

E-RESET

$$\frac{\rho' = \rho[r^\sharp \mapsto \rho(r^\sharp) + 1][r^* \mapsto \max(\rho(r^*), \rho(r))][r \mapsto 0]}{\langle \rho, \mathtt{reset}\ r \rangle \Downarrow \rho'}$$

Fig. 4. A core imperative language for resource-usage analysis. Resources r are modeled as integer-valued variables that may increase or decrease (via a use command) and bound-checked (via an ub assertion command). Selective amortization is realized through *resource* resets.

The states σ of a program are pairs $\langle \ell : \rho \rangle$ of locations ℓ and stores ρ. Stores are finite maps, mapping program variables to values $x \mapsto v$, as well as tracking resources in the remaining highlighted forms. A resource r is a integer-valued variable $r \mapsto n$. For any resource r, we consider two auxiliary resource-usage summary variables r^* and $r^\sharp$ used in resource resetting to be described later.

A judgment form for evaluating expressions $\langle \rho, e \rangle \Downarrow v$ stands for "In store ρ, expression e evaluates to value v." Similarly, a judgment form $\langle \rho, c \rangle \Downarrow \rho'$ stands for "In store ρ, command c updates the store to ρ'." In Fig. 4, we elide the standard rules for $\mathtt{skip}$, assignment $x := e$, and guard condition $\mathtt{assume}\ e$ and focus on the resource-manipulating commands.

The E-USE rule captures that the use $r\ e$ command says to increment r by the value of e. Note that we write $\rho(r)$ for looking up the mapping of r in store ρ and assume that any unmapped r maps to 0. That is, we consider all resources r initialized to 0. The E-UBCHECK describes an upper-bound check ub $\bar{r}\ e$ on a set of resources $\bar{r}$. Let us first consider a single resource r and assume that the auxiliary variable r^* is 0 in the store. Then, the rule simply checks that r is upper-bounded by the value of e (i.e., like $\mathtt{assert}\ r \leq e$). In the next subsection, we come back to the more general form of the upper-bound check shown in E-UBCHECK, which captures the essence of selectively-amortized resource bounding through an interaction with resource decomposition and amortization resets.

decompositions $D ::= \cdot \mid D, r \mathrel{-\!\!\in} \bar{r}$

$$\boxed{D \vdash c \mathrel{-\!\!\in} c'}$$

D-USE
$$\frac{r' \in \bar{r}}{D, r \mathrel{-\!\!\in} \bar{r} \vdash \text{use } r \ e \mathrel{-\!\!\in} \text{use } r' \ e}$$

D-UBCHECK
$$\frac{}{D, r \mathrel{-\!\!\in} \bar{r} \vdash \text{ub } r \ e \mathrel{-\!\!\in} \text{ub } \bar{r} \ e}$$

D-RESET
$$\frac{}{D \vdash \text{skip} \mathrel{-\!\!\in} \text{reset } r}$$

D-COMMAND
$$\frac{c \in \{\text{skip}, x := e, \text{assume } e\}}{D \vdash c \mathrel{-\!\!\in} c}$$

Fig. 5. Decomposing resource usage for selective-amortization analysis is described with a transformation that rewrites commands with a resource decomposition D. Decompositions D define the amortization groups, while inserted resets determine the amortization segments.

3.1   Selective Amortization by Decomposition

Recall from Sect. 2 that the essence of selectively-amortized resource bounding is we want to selectively choose the sequence of resource uses use $r \ e$ over which we apply amortized reasoning. To do this, we have two intertwined tools: resource decomposition $r \mathrel{-\!\!\in} \bar{r}$ into *amortization groups* and amortization resets reset r into *amortization segments*.

A resource decomposition $D ::= \cdot \mid D, r \mathrel{-\!\!\in} \bar{r}$ is a mapping from a resource r into a set of decomposed resource-usage tracking variables $\bar{r}$. The transformation takes use $r \ e$ and rewrites them to use $r' \ e$ for some $r' \in \bar{r}$, thus decomposing all uses of r into separate amortization groups given by $\bar{r}$. In Fig. 5, the judgment form $D \vdash c \mathrel{-\!\!\in} c'$ says, "Under resource decomposition D, command c can be resource-decomposed to command c'," stating valid decomposition transformations. The D-USE rule states exactly this transformation for use $r \ e$ commands.

Then, within separate amortization groups, resets reset r define the *segments* of execution over which to amortize resource uses while applying worst-case reasoning around them. To see this, consider the E-RESET rule in Fig. 4 where we can see reset r as corresponding to the following assignments (abusing notation slightly with assignments and expressions using resource variables):

$$r^{\sharp} := r^{\sharp} + 1; \quad r^{*} := \max(r^{*}, r); \quad r := 0;$$

That is, the reset r command increments the number of amortization segments for r seen so far in $r^{\sharp}$, saves the maximum value of r in any segment so far in r^{*}, and resets r to 0 ending the last amortization segment and starting the next one. So the r^{*} resource-usage summary captures the worst-case resource use of r over all segments, while the $r^{\sharp}$ summary saves the number of such amortization segments.

These summaries then enables amortized reasoning within segments and worst-case reasoning around them. To see this, let us consider a one-to-one resource decomposition $r_o \twoheadleftarrow r$. Without loss of generality, we assume the original program using r_o does not have any `resets` (but the transformed program with r may). Furthermore, we assume all amortization segments are paths of the form ρ `reset` $r \cdots \rho'$ `reset` r with no other `reset` r in the middle and that there are no resource uses `use` r e before an initial `reset` r (i.e., all executions of `use` r e are either in a segment bracketed by two `reset` rs or after the last `reset` r). Then the following selective-amortization assertion between r_o and r holds globally (in all reachable stores):

$$r_o \quad \leq \quad r^{\sharp} \cdot r^* + r$$

Intuitively, up to the last `reset` r, there have been $r^{\sharp}$ amortization segments and the worst-case use of r on all prior segments is r^*, so $r^{\sharp} \cdot r^*$ is an upper bound on the resource use up to the last `reset` r—thereby using worst-case reasoning on amortized segments. Then we just add r because the remaining uses `use` r e since the last reset have accumulated in r. Note that we thus consider all upper-bound summaries r^* initialized to 0 and all segment-counter summaries $r^{\sharp}$ initialized to -1.

Coming back to the E-UBCHECK rule describing the upper-bound check `ub` r e in Fig. 4 (for a single resource r), the assertion checks the bound e on exactly this amortized segments expression (i.e., like `assert` $r^{\sharp} \cdot r^* + r \leq e$). Then, with respect to amortization groups, a resource decomposition $r \twoheadleftarrow \bar{r}$ says that resource uses to r are distributed over uses to $\bar{r}$, so we simply sum over the amortization groups $\bar{r}$ (i.e., like `assert` $\left(\sum_{r \in \bar{r}} r^{\sharp} \cdot r^* + r\right) \leq e$).

Thus, the transformation from an upper-bound check `ub` r e on a resource r with decomposition $r \twoheadleftarrow \bar{r}$ yields `ub` $\bar{r}$ e as stated in rule D-UBCHECK from Fig. 5. As alluded to above, it is sound to insert `resets` arbitrarily into the transformed program corresponding to different amortization segments, which we state with rule D-RESET. Note that we consider programs p equivalent up to insertions of `skip` commands, so we can insert them into the original program as needed. The remaining non-resource manipulating commands are simply retained as-is with rule D-COMMAND. For simplicity in presentation, we assume the original program does not have `resets` and has only single-resource upper-bound checks `ub` r e. Overall, any choice of a resource decomposition D is sound corresponding to different amortization groups. Again for simplicity, we assume all resources r in the original program have a mapping in D (e.g., at least have $r \twoheadleftarrow r$ for no decomposition). We consider soundness in more detail further below.

3.2 Soundness of Group and Segment Decomposition

To consider the soundness of the resource decomposition transformation $D \vdash c \twoheadleftarrow c'$, we define program executions or paths π. In Fig. 6, we define paths π in a slightly non-standard way: they are sequences created by appending a state $\pi \sigma$ or appending a store-command pair $\pi \rho c$ and are well-formed if they consist of sequences corresponding to the stores from valid executions of the commands (as captured by the π ok judgment). Intentionally, we define paths

$$\text{states } \sigma ::= \langle \ell : \rho \rangle \qquad\qquad \text{paths } \pi \in \Pi ::= \cdot \mid \pi \sigma \mid \pi \rho c$$

$$\boxed{\pi \text{ ok} \qquad \sigma \rightarrow_p \sigma' \qquad [\![p]\!]\sigma = \Pi}$$

$$\text{Ok-Init} \over \sigma \text{ ok}$$

$$\text{Ok-Step} \\ \pi \langle \ell : \rho \rangle \text{ ok} \qquad \langle \rho, c \rangle \Downarrow \rho' \over \pi \rho c \langle \ell' : \rho' \rangle \text{ ok}$$

$$\text{Step} \\ \ell - \!\!\{c\}\!\!\rightarrow \ell' \in p \qquad \langle \rho, c \rangle \Downarrow \rho' \over \langle \ell : \rho \rangle \rightarrow_p \langle \ell' : \rho' \rangle$$

$$[\![p]\!]\sigma \overset{\text{def}}{=} \text{lfp } \lambda \Pi. \{\sigma\} \cup \bigcup_{\pi \langle \ell : \rho \rangle \in \Pi} \{\pi \rho c \sigma' \mid \langle \ell : \rho \rangle \rightarrow_p \sigma'\}$$

$$\boxed{D \vdash \pi \preceq \pi'}$$

$$\text{D-AppendCommand} \\ D \vdash \pi \langle \ell : \rho \rangle \preceq \pi' \langle \ell' : \rho' \rangle \quad D \vdash c \preceq c' \over D \vdash \pi \rho c \preceq \pi' \rho' c'$$

$$\text{D-Step} \\ D \vdash \pi \preceq \pi' \quad \pi' \sigma' \text{ ok} \quad \sigma \leqq_D \sigma' \over D \vdash \pi \sigma \preceq \pi' \sigma'$$

$$\text{D-Init} \over D \vdash \sigma \preceq \sigma$$

$$\boxed{\rho \leqq_D \rho' \qquad \sigma \leqq_D \sigma'}$$

$$\rho_o \leqq_D \rho \text{ iff } \rho_o(x) = \rho(x) \text{ for all } x \in \text{vars}(\rho_o) = \text{vars}(\rho) \text{ and}$$

$$\rho_o(r_o) \leq \sum_{r \in D(r_o)} \rho(r^\#) \cdot \rho(r^*) + \rho(r) \text{ for all } r_o \in \text{dom}(\rho_o)$$

$$\langle \ell : \rho \rangle \leqq_D \langle \ell' : \rho' \rangle \text{ iff } \rho \leqq_D \rho' \qquad\qquad \text{vars}(\rho) \overset{\text{def}}{=} \{x \mid x \in \text{dom}(\rho)\}$$

$$\boxed{D \vdash p \preceq p'}$$

$$\text{D-Transition} \\ D \vdash c \preceq c' \over D \vdash p, \ell - \!\!\{c\}\!\!\rightarrow \ell' \preceq p', \ell - \!\!\{c'\}\!\!\rightarrow \ell'$$

$$\text{D-EmptyProgram} \over D \vdash \cdot \preceq \cdot$$

Fig. 6. A semantic decomposition is captured with a path transformation $D \vdash \pi \preceq \pi'$ where paths π are sequences of command executions. The path transformation says we can rewrite according to the command transformation until reaching the same initial state. That is, choosing amortization groups with any decomposition D and amortization segments with any insertions of **resets** are sound. A syntactic decomposition is simply a lifting of the command transformation to programs $D \vdash p \preceq p'$ on the same control-flow structure.

mostly independent from programs, stripping out locations ℓ except for the last state $\langle \ell : \rho \rangle$. In most cases, we do not care about the program from which paths may come from. For example, the path well-formedness judgment π ok ignores program locations and simply checks that the triples of store ρ, command c, and store ρ' are valid executions $\langle \rho, c \rangle \Downarrow \rho'$ (rule Ok-Step). Unless otherwise stated, we assume all paths π are well formed (i.e., π ok holds for any path π).

The only reason paths mention locations is to define the path semantics $[\![p]\!]\sigma$ of a program p with initial state σ. The path semantics $[\![p]\!]\sigma$ is given as: (1) the judgment form $\sigma \rightarrow_p \sigma'$ defines a transition relation saying, "On program p, state σ steps to state σ'," and (2) the path semantics $[\![p]\!]\sigma$ collects all finite (but unbounded) prefixes of the transition system from the initial state σ.

The judgment form $D \vdash \pi \prec\!\!\epsilon\; \pi'$ states a selectively-amortized resource bounding on a path π' from an original path π. Divorcing paths from programs emphasizes that semantically, we can choose any amortization grouping with a choice of the resource decomposition D and select any amortization segmentation by inserting resets anywhere along the original path π. The D-APPENDCOMMAND rules says that a command along the original path can be rewritten according to the command transformation $D \vdash c \prec\!\!\epsilon\; c'$. Note that like with programs, we consider paths π equivalent up to insertions of skip commands, so we can insert them into the original path as needed.

To talk about resource-decomposed stores along paths, we define $\rho \leqq_D \rho'$ to be stores that are equal on program variables vars(ρ) (excluding resource variables r) and whose resource-usage tracking variables satisfy the selectively-amortized assertion from Sect. 3.1 (see Fig. 6 for a detailed definition). Then, the D-STEP rule says that the execution of the last command in π' must result in a state σ' consistent with the semantics of commands ($\pi'\,\sigma'$ ok) and with selective amortization ($\sigma \leqq_D \sigma'$). Finally, the D-INIT rule simply says that resource-decomposed paths should start with the same initial state.

We can then consider a more restricted, syntactic class of selectively-amortized resource-bounding transformations by simply transforming the commands of a program p (i.e., the judgment form $D \vdash p \prec\!\!\epsilon\; p'$ in Fig. 6). To achieve more semantic selective amortizations, one could, of course, first apply richer semantics-preserving program transformations to the original program (than inserting skips) before applying the resource-decomposition transformation.

We can now state the following soundness result.

Theorem 1 (Soundness of Selectively-Amortized Resource Bounding).

1. If $D \vdash c_0 \prec\!\!\epsilon\; c$, $\langle \rho, c \rangle \Downarrow \rho'$, and $\rho_0 \leqq_D \rho$, then $\langle \rho_0, c_0 \rangle \Downarrow \rho'_0$ with $\rho'_0 \leqq_D \rho'$.
2. If $D \vdash \pi_0 \prec\!\!\epsilon\; \pi$ and π ok, then π_0 ok.
3. If $D \vdash p_0 \prec\!\!\epsilon\; p$ and $\pi \in [\![p]\!]\sigma$, then there is a $\pi_0 \in [\![p_0]\!]\sigma$ s.t. $D \vdash \pi_0 \prec\!\!\epsilon\; \pi$.

The key lemma (part 1) states a preservation property that any command decomposition preserves the selectively-amortized resource-bounding invariant $\leqq_D$ (see the extended version [29] for details).

Verifying Bounds with Selective Amortization. Bound verification by selective amortization follows directly from the soundness theorem given above. In particular, given a particular resource composition D and a transformed program p from the original program p_0 such that $D \vdash p_0 \prec\!\!\epsilon\; p$, simply apply any off-the-shelf numerical verification or invariant generator to p to try to prove translated upper-bound assertions ub $\bar{r}\; e$ in p.

In Sect. 4, we describe an approach for selecting a resource decomposition and inserting amortization resets. However, we note that our key contribution described here is generically defining the space of selective amortizations.

Lower Bounds. While we focused on upper-bound checks in this section, we see that the approach can be adapted to lower-bound assertions in a straightforward manner by introducing a lower-bound resource-usage summary variable, say $r^{\dagger}$. This lower-bound summary is analogously updated on `reset` r with the minimum resource-usage so far (i.e., like $r^{\dagger} := \min(r^{\dagger}, r)$). We can then translate lower-bound assertions `lb` e r in the analogous manner and extend the selectively-amortized resource bounding invariant $\leq_D$ for lower bounds.

4   Selecting a Decomposition

In this section, we describe a way to select amortization groups (i.e., a resource decomposition D) and amortization segments (i.e., insertions of amortization `resets`) to algorithmically realize selectively-amortized resource bounding. As alluded to in Sect. 2, there is a tension between creating as many groups and as short segments as possible to focus amortized reasoning only where it is needed, simplifying the invariant inference needed to do so, versus not creating too many groups or too short segments that the needed amortization for precision is lost. More specifically, the built-in multiplication $r^{\sharp} \cdot r^{*}$ we apply for worst-case reasoning around segments simplifies the necessary invariants needed to prove bounds but only if r^{*} is sufficiently precise bound on resource usage per segment.

As hinted at in Sect. 3, the space of possible selective amortizations is huge. Even with some basic restrictions to make this search more feasible, the remaining space of selective amortizations is still large. In the remainder of this section, we first characterize when the resource-usage summary r^{*} is precise based on a notion of *non-interfering amortization segments*. Then, we describe the basic restrictions and their motivations to use segment non-interference to search within this restricted space.

Non-interfering Amortization Segments. Recall the selective-amortization assertion $r_{o} \leq r^{\sharp} \cdot r^{*} + r$ and the $r^{*} := \max(r^{*}, r)$ update for a `reset` r from Sect. 3.1. We can see that the difference between the sides of the inequality (i.e., $(r^{\sharp} \cdot r^{*} + r) - r_{o}$) comes from a difference between the current upper-bound summary r^{*} and the current resource accumulation in r (i.e., $r^{*} - r$) on a `reset` r. Thus intuitively, we want to insert amortization resets `reset` r at locations that would minimize this difference $r^{*} - r$ across all such amortization segments. This observation suggests a definition for segment non-interference:

Definition 1 (Amortization Segment Non-Interference). Consider two paths $\pi \colon (\rho_{\mathrm{lo}} \uplus \rho_{\mathrm{hi}})$ `reset` $r \cdots \rho$ `reset` r and $\pi' \colon (\rho_{\mathrm{lo}} \uplus \rho_{\mathrm{hi}}')$ `reset` $r \cdots \rho'$ `reset` r such that $\mathrm{dom}(\rho_{\mathrm{hi}}) = \mathrm{dom}(\rho_{\mathrm{hi}}')$. That is, we consider two amortization segments (i.e., paths that start and end in a `reset` r) and partition the input into low variables (i.e., $\mathrm{dom}(\rho_{\mathrm{lo}})$) and high variables (i.e., $\mathrm{dom}(\rho_{\mathrm{hi}})$). Then, we say segments π and π' are *non-interfering* iff for any (high) stores ρ_{hi} and ρ'_{hi}, and for any (low) store ρ_{lo}, we have that $\rho(r) = \rho'(r)$.

We see that if all pairs of amortization segments are non-interfering for a suitable partition of variables between high and low variables, then the selective amortization is as precise as the fully amortized solution. Then, we want to balance making amortization segments as small as possible (in order to simplify invariant inference and maximize worst-case reasoning) with the smallest set of low input variables (to maximize non-interference).

Computed Input-Independent Groups and Single Location-Based Segments. Definition 1 suggests an approach to selecting amortization groups and segments if we fix some basic restrictions: (1) First, we consider syntactic decomposition transformations $D \vdash p_{\mathrm{o}} \prec p$ from the original program p_{o}. (2) Second, we consider a single insertion of reset r into the transformed program p that control-dominates all uses use $r\ e$ for every resource r. Picking a control-dominating location ℓ ensures we do not have any use $r\ e$ before a reset r, and performing single insertion means we only need to consider segments that start and end at *single location* ℓ (where $\ell \dashv\!\{\text{reset } r\} \!\!\mapsto \ell' \in p$). (3) Third, we fix the low variables in any segmentation we consider to be the internal variables on which the uses data-depends, leaving any remaining variables at the segment start location ℓ to be high, including the inputs to the entry location of the original program p_{o}. Intuitively, we assume that uses that share computation over internal, low variables are related for amortization. However, there is still significant flexibility in choosing the resource decomposition D that defines the amortization groups and the uses-dominating location ℓ for each resource r in the transformed program p—it does not have to be the immediate dominator of the uses.

As we want to create more groups to simplify invariant inference, let us first consider the resource decomposition D such that each syntactic use $r\ e$ in p_{o} is translated to a unique resource variable and thus placed in a distinct group (i.e., such that $|D(r)| = |\{ (\ell, e, \ell') \mid \ell \dashv\!\{\text{use } r\ e\} \!\!\mapsto \ell' \in p_{\mathrm{o}} \}|$). However, to find cases where distinct groups are potentially insufficient, we consider possibly merging use sites pairwise (i.e., $\ell_1 \dashv\!\{\text{use } r_1\ e_1\} \!\!\mapsto \ell'_1$ and $\ell_2 \dashv\!\{\text{use } r_2\ e_2\} \!\!\mapsto \ell'_2$ in the transformed program p). Suppose we were to merge groups r_1 and r_2, then let us consider the immediate dominator ℓ of locations ℓ_1 and ℓ_2, which defines the possible amortization segments starting from and ending at location ℓ. Considering this potential segmentation and the shared low input variables that may affect the value of both r_1 and r_2 and if the values of these low input variables may change in the segment, then we want to merge these groups based on restriction (3) above (otherwise, they are *computed input independent*). We can then approximate this criteria with standard, backwards data-dependency slices [37] from the uses use $r_1\ e_1$ and use $r_2\ e_2$.

Once we have fixed a resource decomposition D defining amortization groups, selecting a location ℓ to insert each reset r for each r in the transformed program p is fairly straightforward. Following segment non-interference, for any use sites sharing the same resource r (i.e., $L = \{ \ell \mid \ell -\!\{use\ r\ e\}\!\!\mapsto \ell' \in p \}$), find the most immediate dominator of L where we can prove that the low input variables are constant (i.e., call this use-dominating location ℓ, then we have that $\rho(x_{lo}) = n$ for some n, for all low input variables x_{lo}, in all reachable states $\langle \ell : \rho \rangle$). If we can prove that the low input variables are constant in the program up to the amortization segment entry location ℓ, then we satisfy segment non-interference (up to non-determinism within segments).

Note that because of the tension between precision from simplifying invariant inference versus from amortization, selecting a decomposition is necessarily heuristic. Section 3 shows that picking any decomposition is sound, and Sect. 5 offers evidence that the principled heuristic described here provides a benefit.

5   Empirical Evaluation

Selective amortization represents a large space of possible approaches between worst-case and fully amortized reasoning. Here we attempt to provide evidence that selective amortization provides a benefit when compared with the two extremes, even with simply the heuristic decomposition strategy described in Sect. 4. It is this specific selective amortization strategy that we consider here in our experiments. We consider the following research question on *Effectiveness*: Can selective amortization improve the number of verified programs when compared with the worst-case and fully-amortized extremes?

Effectiveness. In Table 1, we summarize the comparison between selective amortization and the two extremes with the most precise configuration in each category **bolded**. For each category, we list the number of programs (num) and the total lines of code (loc). To test the effect of slightly weaker bound assertions, we consider two sets of assertions: for the most precise bounds and by

Table 1. Verifying with worst-case (Wor), fully-amortized (Ful), and selectively-amortized (Sel) with two sets of assertions: the most precise bounds and constant-weakened ones. For each configuration, we give the number of assertions proven (n) and the total verification time in seconds (s).

			Most precise bounds						Constant-weakened bounds					
			Wor		Ful		Sel		Wor		Ful		Sel	
Category	num	loc	(n)	(s)	(n)	(s)	(n)	(s)	(n)	(s)	(n)	(s)	(n)	(s)
lang3	20	667	**12**	175.7	8	44.2	**12**	249.5	**14**	302.7	**14**	89	**14**	252
stringutils	10	390	2	12.9	**4**	196.5	**4**	176.2	4	101.3	5	209	**6**	264.3
guava	3	90	0	0	1	7.6	0	0	2	18.3	**3**	30	**3**	73.3
stac	3	122	2	118.6	2	23	**3**	101.1	2	126.6	2	22.5	**3**	105.2
generated	200	3633	139	1510.2	43	198.3	**175**	1779.5	140	1567.8	69	325.3	**180**	1852.2
Total	236	4902	155	1817.4	58	469.6	**194**	2306.3	162	2116.7	93	675.8	**206**	2547

relaxing the constant coefficients from the most precise bounds. For each configuration, we applied the same verification tools after transformation with our tool BRBO [30] implemented in 6,000 lines of Scala, using Z3 [14] for SMT solving and ICRA [27] as an off-the-shelf invariant generator. For the two sets of bound assertions, 194 and 206 programs, respectively, were verified for the selective amortization configuration—more than the number with either extreme. The improvement over worst-case reasoning comes from amortizing the costs over multiple commands, while the improvement over fully-amortized reasoning comes from amortizing the costs over subprograms that are smaller than the whole program, so that inferring invariants becomes more manageable for ICRA.

The verification time in Table 1 consists of selecting amortizations, realizing amortizations via program transformations, and verifying bound assertions on the transformed programs, which include invariant generation. We observed that selecting amortizations and realizing them via program transformations consumed negligible amounts of time; invariant generation took up more than 95% of the total time. Selecting amortizations based on the approach described in Sect. 4 is fast because the selection only requires simple data- and control-dependency analysis.

As noted above, these experiments consider the specific decomposition strategy described in Sect. 4 *on the original benchmarks*, even though we show in Sect. 3 that picking any decomposition is sound. But as alluded to in Sect. 3, programs can be transformed in semantics-preserving ways that then expose different possible decompositions (to either the strategy described in Sect. 4 or even some other one). Others have made similar observations; for example, semantic program transformations that split a loop into multiple phases [32] may simplify the invariant generation by reducing the need for disjunctive invariants. Indeed, it may strike the best balance between scalability and precision if we can effectively perform different semantic transformations based on the precision we need for proving some desired bounds.

Benchmarks. We developed this benchmark suite specifically for the resource bounding problem (as it differs from, for example, the loop bounding problem). In particular, we collected code from 36 real-world programs (from 4 libraries or suites) that use `StringBuilder`. Furthermore, we created a suite of 200 synthetic programs generated by randomly nesting and sequencing two common loop idioms that are extracted from actual Java programs.

6   Related Work

Loop Bound Analysis and Worst-Case Reasoning. A large body of work has addressed bounding the number of loop iterations in imperative numeric programs [8,10,11,19–21,33,35,39]. These techniques rely on ranking functions to quantitatively track the changes in the rankings of states. The loop bounding problem can be seen as a special case of the resource bounding problem where the resource of interest is loop iteration, and the cost of each "use" (i.e., iteration) is a constant 1. Or in other words, the loop bounding problem can be extended to address the resource bounding problem, if one adopts what we call worst-case reasoning to fix a constant upper bound for each resource use. There are works that essentially take this perspective to apply loop bound analysis for invariant inference [8,9,35].

Worst-case execution time (WCET) analysis [38] is an area of study that attempts to automatically infer time bounds for machine code, considering precise models of hardware architectures. It can be seen as another instance of worst-case reasoning, focusing on defining precise worst-case bound models for instructions but generally assuming loop bounds are given or easy to derive.

Our approach is partly inspired by Gulwani et al. [21] that describes a loop bound analysis because we also rely on a program transformation to simplify the forms of the needed inductive invariants. At the same time, we improve on this work by first generalizing the reasoning of loop iterations to general resources, which can change in a non-trivial (i.e., non-monotonic and non-constant) way, and then introduce *selective amortization* that mixes in amortized reasoning from the next category of papers to address these challenges.

(Fully-)Amortized Reasoning. Several lines of work employ a number of different techniques to precisely reason about resource usage over *full* executions (i.e., attempt to perform fully-amortized reasoning). The COSTA project [2–6], which adopts the recurrence relation approach, reasons about resource usage by first abstracting program semantics into a set of recurrence relations and then finding closed-form solutions to these recurrence relations. The RAML project [22,23] analyzes the resource usage of functional programs with the potential method. This approach encodes the changes of a potential with linear programming constraints over the unknown coefficients of pre-determined bound templates. Carbonneaux et al. [10,11] adapts this approach to numerical imperative programs. Atkey [7] (and improvements [17,18]) develop expressive program logics that extend type-based amortized resource analysis with resource reasoning over heap data structures. The above approaches can be viewed as instances of fully-amortized reasoning, because it is in an amortized manner that they encode the sum of the resource usage into systems of constraints [2–6,10,11] or perform deductive proofs that amortize costs [7,17,18]. The key challenge in fully-amortized reasoning is to infer complex inductive invariants, which are the solutions of the constraint systems in, for example, COSTA and RAML. Instead, our approach may simplify the forms of the required invariants by decomposing the resource usage into groups and segments of amortized costs. Since our approach is agnostic to the underlying amortized reasoning engine, any fully-amortized reasoning approach, such as the above ones, can potentially be used in place of the relational inductive invariant generator applied in this paper.

7   Conclusion

In this paper we address the problem of automatically proving resource bounds, where resource usage is expressed via an integer-typed variable. We present a framework for selectively-amortized reasoning that mixes worst-case and fully amortized reasoning via a property decomposition and a program transformation. We show that proving bounds in any such decomposition yields a sound resource bound in the original program, and we give an algorithm for selecting an effective decomposition. Our empirical evaluation provides evidence that selective amortization effectively leverages both worst-case and amortized reasoning.

Acknowledgments. We thank Pavol Černý for his valuable contributions in the early stages of this research. We also thank the anonymous reviewers and members of the CUPLV lab for their helpful reviews and suggestions. This research was supported in part by the Defense Advanced Research Projects Agency under grant FA8750-15-2-0096, and also by the National Science Foundation under grant CCF-2008369.

References

1. Abadi, M., Banerjee, A., Heintze, N., Riecke, J.G.: A core calculus of dependency. In: Principles of Programming Languages (POPL), pp. 147–160 (1999). https://doi.org/10.1145/292540.292555

2. Albert, E., Arenas, P., Genaim, S., Puebla, G., Zanardini, D.: Cost analysis of Java bytecode. In: De Nicola, R. (ed.) ESOP 2007. LNCS, vol. 4421, pp. 157–172. Springer, Heidelberg (2007). https://doi.org/10.1007/978-3-540-71316-6_12

3. Albert, E., Genaim, S., Gómez-Zamalloa, M.: Heap space analysis for Java bytecode. In: International Symposium on Memory Management (ISMM), pp. 105–116 (2007). https://doi.org/10.1145/1296907.1296922

4. Albert, E., Genaim, S., Gómez-Zamalloa, M.: Live heap space analysis for languages with garbage collection. In: International Symposium on Memory Management (ISMM), pp. 129–138 (2009). https://doi.org/10.1145/1542431.1542450

5. Albert, E., Genaim, S., Masud, A.N.: More precise yet widely applicable cost analysis. In: Jhala, R., Schmidt, D. (eds.) VMCAI 2011. LNCS, vol. 6538, pp. 38–53. Springer, Heidelberg (2011). https://doi.org/10.1007/978-3-642-18275-4_5

6. Alonso-Blas, D.E., Genaim, S.: On the limits of the classical approach to cost analysis. In: Miné, A., Schmidt, D. (eds.) SAS 2012. LNCS, vol. 7460, pp. 405–421. Springer, Heidelberg (2012). https://doi.org/10.1007/978-3-642-33125-1_27

7. Atkey, R.: Amortised resource analysis with separation logic. In: Gordon, A.D. (ed.) ESOP 2010. LNCS, vol. 6012, pp. 85–103. Springer, Heidelberg (2010). https://doi.org/10.1007/978-3-642-11957-6_6

8. Brockschmidt, M., Emmes, F., Falke, S., Fuhs, C., Giesl, J.: Alternating runtime and size complexity analysis of integer programs. In: Ábrahám, E., Havelund, K. (eds.) TACAS 2014. LNCS, vol. 8413, pp. 140–155. Springer, Heidelberg (2014). https://doi.org/10.1007/978-3-642-54862-8_10

9. Cadek, P., Danninger, C., Sinn, M., Zuleger, F.: Using loop bound analysis for invariant generation. In: Formal Methods in Computer Aided Design (FMCAD), pp. 1–9 (2018). https://doi.org/10.23919/FMCAD.2018.8603005

10. Carbonneaux, Q., Hoffmann, J., Shao, Z.: Compositional certified resource bounds. In: Programming Language Design and Implementation (PLDI), pp. 467–478 (2015). https://doi.org/10.1145/2737924.2737955

11. Carbonneaux, Q., Hoffmann, J., Reps, T., Shao, Z.: Automated resource analysis with Coq proof objects. In: Majumdar, R., Kunčak, V. (eds.) CAV 2017. LNCS, vol. 10427, pp. 64–85. Springer, Cham (2017). https://doi.org/10.1007/978-3-319-63390-9_4

12. Chatterjee, K., Fu, H., Goharshady, A.K., Goharshady, E.K.: Polynomial invariant generation for non-deterministic recursive programs. In: Programming Language Design and Implementation (PLDI), pp. 672–687 (2020). https://doi.org/10.1145/3385412.3385969

13. Colón, M.A., Sankaranarayanan, S., Sipma, H.B.: Linear invariant generation using non-linear constraint solving. In: Hunt, W.A., Somenzi, F. (eds.) CAV 2003. LNCS, vol. 2725, pp. 420–432. Springer, Heidelberg (2003). https://doi.org/10.1007/978-3-540-45069-6_39

14. de Moura, L., Bjørner, N.: Z3: an efficient SMT solver. In: Ramakrishnan, C.R., Rehof, J. (eds.) TACAS 2008. LNCS, vol. 4963, pp. 337–340. Springer, Heidelberg (2008). https://doi.org/10.1007/978-3-540-78800-3_24

15. Defense Advanced Research Projects Agency (DARPA): Space/time analysis for cybersecurity (STAC) (2019). https://www.darpa.mil/program/space-time-analysis-for-cybersecurity

16. Dillig, I., Dillig, T., Li, B., McMillan, K.L.: Inductive invariant generation via abductive inference. In: Object-Oriented Programming Systems, Languages, and Applications (OOPSLA), pp. 443–456 (2013). https://doi.org/10.1145/2509136.2509511

17. Guéneau, A., Charguéraud, A., Pottier, F.: A fistful of dollars: formalizing asymptotic complexity claims via deductive program verification. In: Ahmed, A. (ed.) ESOP 2018. LNCS, vol. 10801, pp. 533–560. Springer, Cham (2018). https://doi.org/10.1007/978-3-319-89884-1_19

18. Guéneau, A., Jourdan, J.-H., Charguéraud, A., Pottier, F.: Formal proof and analysis of an incremental cycle detection algorithm. In: Interactive Theorem Proving (ITP), vol. 141, pp. 18:1–18:20 (2019). https://doi.org/10.4230/LIPIcs.ITP.2019.18

19. Gulwani, S., Zuleger, F.: The reachability-bound problem. In: Programming Language Design and Implementation (PLDI), pp. 292–304 (2010). https://doi.org/10.1145/1806596.1806630

20. Gulwani, S., Jain, S., Koskinen, E.: Control-flow refinement and progress invariants for bound analysis. In: Programming Language Design and Implementation (PLDI), pp. 375–385 (2009a). https://doi.org/10.1145/1542476.1542518

21. Gulwani, S., Mehra, K.K., Chilimbi, T.M.: SPEED: precise and efficient static estimation of program computational complexity. In: Principles of Programming Languages (POPL), pp. 127–139 (2009). https://doi.org/10.1145/1480881.1480898

22. Hoffmann, J., Aehlig, K., Hofmann, M.: Multivariate amortized resource analysis. In: Principles of Programming Languages (POPL), pp. 357–370 (2011). https://doi.org/10.1145/1926385.1926427

23. Hoffmann, J., Das, A., Weng, S.-C.: Towards automatic resource bound analysis for OCaml. In: Principles of Programming Languages (POPL), pp. 359–373 (2017). https://doi.org/10.1145/3009837.3009842

24. Hrushovski, E., Ouaknine, J., Pouly, A., Worrell, J.: Polynomial invariants for affine programs. In: Logic in Computer Science (LICS), pp. 530–539 (2018). https://doi.org/10.1145/3209108.3209142

25. Kincaid, Z., Breck, J., Boroujeni, A.F., Reps, T.W.: Compositional recurrence analysis revisited. In: Programming Language Design and Implementation (PLDI), pp. 248–262 (2017). https://doi.org/10.1145/3062341.3062373

26. Kincaid, Z., Cyphert, J., Breck, J., Reps, T.W.: Non-linear reasoning for invariant synthesis. Proc. ACM Program. Lang. 2(POPL), 54:1–54:33 (2018). https://doi.org/10.1145/3158142

27. Kincaid, Z., Breck, J., Cyphert, J., Reps, T.W.: Closed forms for numerical loops. Proc. ACM Program. Lang. **3**(POPL), 55:1–55:29 (2019). https://doi.org/10.1145/3290368

28. Lu, T., Černý, P., Chang, B.-Y.E., Trivedi, A.: Type-directed bounding of collections in reactive programs. In: Enea, C., Piskac, R. (eds.) VMCAI 2019. LNCS, vol. 11388, pp. 275–296. Springer, Cham (2019). https://doi.org/10.1007/978-3-030-11245-5_13

29. Lu, T., Chang, B.-Y.E., Trivedi, A.: Selectively-amortized resource bounding (extended version) (2021). https://arxiv.org/abs/2108.08263

30. Lu, T., Chang, B.-Y.E., Trivedi, A.: Selectively-amortized resource bounding (artifact) (2021). https://zenodo.org/record/5140586

31. Manna, Z., Pnueli, A.: Completing the temporal picture. Theor. Comput. Sci. **83**(1), 91–130 (1991). https://doi.org/10.1016/0304-3975(91)90041-Y

32. Sharma, R., Dillig, I., Dillig, T., Aiken, A.: Simplifying loop invariant generation using splitter predicates. In: Gopalakrishnan, G., Qadeer, S. (eds.) CAV 2011. LNCS, vol. 6806, pp. 703–719. Springer, Heidelberg (2011). https://doi.org/10.1007/978-3-642-22110-1_57

33. Sinn, M., Zuleger, F., Veith, H.: A simple and scalable static analysis for bound analysis and amortized complexity analysis. In: Biere, A., Bloem, R. (eds.) CAV 2014. LNCS, vol. 8559, pp. 745–761. Springer, Cham (2014). https://doi.org/10.1007/978-3-319-08867-9_50

34. Sinn, M., Zuleger, F., Veith, H.: Difference constraints: an adequate abstraction for complexity analysis of imperative programs. In: Formal Methods in Computer Aided Design (FMCAD), pp. 144–151 (2015)

35. Sinn, M., Zuleger, F., Veith, H.: Complexity and resource bound analysis of imperative programs using difference constraints. J. Autom. Reason. **59**(1), 3–45 (2017). https://doi.org/10.1007/s10817-016-9402-4

36. Tarjan, R.E.: Amortized computational complexity. SIAM J. Alg. Discrete Methods **6**(2), 306–318 (1985)

37. Weiser, M.: Program slicing. IEEE Trans. Software Eng. **10**(4), 352–357 (1984). https://doi.org/10.1109/TSE.1984.5010248

38. Wilhelm, R., et al.: The worst-case execution-time problem - overview of methods and survey of tools. ACM Trans. Embed. Comput. Syst. **7**(3):36:1–36:53 (2008). https://doi.org/10.1145/1347375.1347389

39. Zuleger, F., Gulwani, S., Sinn, M., Veith, H.: Bound analysis of imperative programs with the size-change abstraction. In: Yahav, E. (ed.) SAS 2011. LNCS, vol. 6887, pp. 280–297. Springer, Heidelberg (2011). https://doi.org/10.1007/978-3-642-23702-7_22

Reduced Products of Abstract Domains for Fairness Certification of Neural Networks

Denis Mazzucato$^{(\boxtimes)}$ and Caterina Urban

Inria & École Normale Supérieure | Université PSL, Paris, France
{denis.mazzucato,caterina.urban}@inria.fr

Abstract. We present LIBRA, an open-source abstract interpretation-based static analyzer for certifying fairness of ReLU neural network classifiers for tabular data. LIBRA combines a sound forward pre-analysis with an exact backward analysis that leverages the polyhedra abstract domain to provide definite fairness guarantees when possible, and to otherwise quantify and describe the biased input space regions. The analysis is configurable in terms of scalability and precision. We equipped LIBRA with new abstract domains to use in the pre-analysis, including a generic reduced product domain construction, as well as search heuristics to find the best analysis configuration. We additionally set up the backward analysis to allow further parallelization. Our experimental evaluation demonstrates the effectiveness of the approach on neural networks trained on a popular dataset in the fairness literature.

Keywords: Fairness · Neural networks · Reduced abstract domain products · Abstract interpretation · Static analysis

1 Introduction

Nowadays, machine learning software has an ever increasing societal impact by assisting or even automating decision making in fields such as social welfare, criminal justice, and even health care. At the same time, a number of recent cases have shown that such software may reproduce, or even reinforce, bias directly or indirectly present in the training data [3,16,17,23]. In April 2021, the European Commission proposed a first legal framework on machine learning software – the Artificial Intelligence Act [10]—which imposes strict requirements to minimize the risk of discriminatory outcomes. In this context, methods and tools for certifying fairness or otherwise detecting bias are extremely valuable.

C. Drăgoi et al. (Eds.): SAS 2021, LNCS 12913, pp. 308–322, 2021.
https://doi.org/10.1007/978-3-030-88806-0_15

In this paper we present LIBRA, an open-source static analyzer based on abstract interpretation [5] for certifying fairness of neural networks. LIBRA currently supports neural networks with ReLU activations [21], trained for classification of tabular data (e.g., stored in Excel files or relational databases). It is designed to certify that the classification is independent of the values of the inputs that are considered (directly or indirectly) sensitive to bias [12]. This fairness notion is *global*, relative to the entire input space (or a targeted subset of it), and our analysis is able to *quantify* the detected bias. The choice of the sensitive inputs is up to the user of the tool.

The static analysis run by LIBRA combines a cheap and sound forward pre-analysis with an expensive and exact backward analysis. The pre-analysis iteratively partitions the input space of the neural network into independent partitions that satisfy the configured resource requirements. Then, the backward analysis attempts to certify fairness for each of these partitions, and otherwise quantifies and reports their biased (sub)regions.

The pre-analysis can be configured to use any of the abstract domains implementations that LIBRA is equipped with. A preliminary version of LIBRA developed by Urban et al. [25] was equipped with the BOXES [4], SYMBOLIC [18], and the DEEPPOLY [24] abstract domains. In our tool, we additionally implemented the NEURIFY [26] abstract domain, and a generic reduced product domain construction [6] to combine any of these domains together. To the best of our knowledge, we are the first to explore and demonstrate the merits of reduced products of abstract domains for analyzing neural networks.

LIBRA can be further configured in terms of scalability and precision to adapt to the available resources (e.g., computation time or CPUs). We have additionally equipped LIBRA with a configuration auto-tuning mechanism to find the best analysis configuration according to a given search strategy. Finally, we set up the backward analysis to allow further parallelization and thus reduce idle times that were hindering the effective exploitation of multi-core architectures.

In our experimental evaluation we evaluate LIBRA on neural networks trained on a popular dataset and we demonstrate its effectiveness. In particular, we show that LIBRA (configured to use the product domain) outperforms its preliminary version [25] in terms of both precision and running time.

2   Tool Architecture

LIBRA is written in PYTHON. Its codebase is open-source on GitHub[1].

Figure 1 shows an overview of LIBRA's architecture. The tool takes as input a neural network and a specification of its input space and fairness requirements (cf. Sect. 2.1). The front-end (cf. Sect. 2.2) takes care of parsing the neural network and its specification, building an equivalent control flow graph structure, and passing it to the analysis engine (cf. Sect. 2.3). The analysis can be configured to use different (combinations of) abstract domains (cf. Sect. 2.4), and

---

[1] https://github.com/caterinaurban/Libra.git

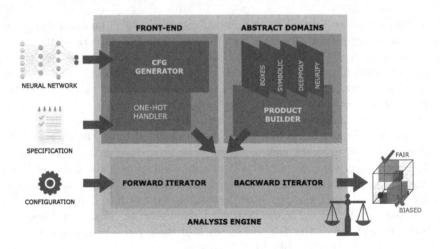

Fig. 1. Overview of LIBRA.

to be run incrementally to adapt to the available resources (e.g., computation time or CPUs). The tool outputs a partition of the neural network input space into regions that are certified to be fair, regions that are biased, and regions that could not be analyzed (if any) because the analysis exceeded the available resources (cf. Sect. 2.5). In the rest of the section, we provide more details on each tool component and configuration options.

2.1   Tool Input

LIBRA expects as input a feed-forward neural network with ReLU activation functions (i.e., $\text{ReLU(x)} = \max(0, \text{x})$ [21]) trained for classification of tabular data. The neural network should be written as a PYTHON program: affine layer transformations are modeled by variable assignments, and ReLU activations are modeled by calls to a ReLU function (i.e., a call ReLU(x) models the ReLU activation applied to the neuron represented by the variable x). Figure 2 depicts a toy network expressed in PYTHON syntax. Specifically, the network is composed by two input neurons $x_{0,1}$ and $x_{0,2}$, two output neurons $x_{3,1}$ and $x_{3,2}$ (one for each class in the output classification), and two hidden layers in between—each one with two hidden neurons. Lines $1, 2, 5, 6, 9,$ and 10 show affine computations, while $3, 4, 7,$ and 8 apply the activation functions. The output class of the network is determined by the output neuron with the maximum value. The codebase of LIBRA contains a script to automatically generate such input format from neural networks trained using the KERAS framework (https://keras.io).

In addition, LIBRA requires a specification of the neural network input space and fairness requirements. LIBRA supports both continuous input data features as well as one-hot encoded categorical data features. Thus, the input specification

```
1   x11 = −0.31*x01 + 0.99*x02 − 0.63
2   x12 = −1.25*x01 − 0.64*x02 + 1.88
3   ReLU(x11)
4   ReLU(x12)
5   x21 = 0.40*x11 + 1.21*x12 + 0.00
6   x22 = 0.64*x11 + 0.69*x12 − 0.39
7   ReLU(x21)
8   ReLU(x22)
9   x31 = 0.26*x21 + 0.33*x22 + 0.45
10  x32 = 1.42*x21 + 0.40*x22 − 0.45
```

Fig. 2. Toy neural network.

should define which input variables correspond to continuous and categorical data. Additionally, it should indicate which inputs should be considered sensitive to bias by the analysis. In our example in Fig. 2, we consider both inputs as continuous, i.e., $x_{0,1}, x_{0,2} \in [0, 1]$, and $x_{0,2}$ as sensitive to bias.

2.2 Front-End

The front-end of LIBRA parses the neural network and its specification and generates a control flow graph (CFG) structure to be given to the analysis engine. More specifically, the *CFG Generator* builds an acyclic graph which is essentially a sequence of nodes alternating between nodes of type affine and nodes of type ReLU, i.e., nodes grouping the affine transformations performed by a neural network layer, or nodes grouping the ReLU activations applied to a neural network layer. The entry node of the CFG is annotated with assumptions restricting the range of values of the input features (i.e., by default, features are assumed to be normalized in the range $[0, 1]$). For categorical features, the *One-Hot Handler* imposes additional constraints restricting the values of the corresponding individual inputs to be either 0 or 1, and their sum to be 1. Figure 3 shows the control flow graph corresponding to the toy network in Fig. 2. The caption of each node shows which line of code it represents.

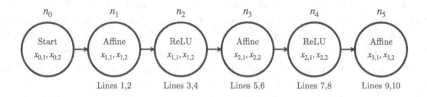

Fig. 3. Control flow graph for the toy network in Fig. 2.

2.3   Analysis Engine

LIBRA's analysis engine walks over the CFG in two phases: a forward pre-analysis, starting from the entry node of the CFG, followed by a backward analysis starting from the exit node of the CFG. Both analysis phases use a standard worklist algorithm [22] implemented using a FIFO queue. At each step, a CFG node is extracted from the worklist and its associated instructions are interpreted in an abstract domain (cf. Sect. 2.4) to update the current value of the analysis. All successor or predecessor nodes—depending on the analysis direction—are then put into the worklist. Each node is explored exactly once each iteration. The analysis terminates once the worklist is empty. In our example, cf. Fig. 2, the forward analysis visits the CFG nodes in the order from n_0, n_1, ..., up to n_5, while the backward analysis visits the node in the reverse order, i.e., from n_5, n_4, ..., down to n_0.

The forward pre-analysis is performed by the *Forward Iterator*. The pre-analysis begins with a value representing the entire neural network input space in a chosen **abstract domain**. This value is then propagated through the neural network. If the resulting output value implies that the network always produces a unique classification outcome, then fairness is trivially guaranteed as there is no way to discriminate between input data. Otherwise, there are two possibilities depending on how many ReLUs of the neural network are found to not have a fixed activation status (i.e., ReLU(x) is always active when x $\geq$ 0 and always inactive when x $<$ 0). If this number exceeds a chosen **upper bound** U, the pre-analysis bisects the input space along *any* of the non-sensitive dimensions (randomly chosen) and proceeds again on the resulting partitions. Instead, if the number of non-fixed ReLUs does not exceed U, the input space (partition) is deemed *feasible* and passed to the backward analysis along with its associated ReLU activation pattern. In our example, let the abstract domain be the boxes domain [4], which simply tracks the interval of possible values for each neuron in the neural network, and let U = 2. At first, the pre-analysis starts from the entire input space I, i.e., $x_{0,1}, x_{0,2} \in [0, 1]$. By propagating these interval values through the CFG, the analysis finds that the ReLUs at $x_{1,1}, x_{1,2}$, and $x_{2,2}$ are non-fixed while $x_{2,1}$ is always active. Since the number of non-fixed ReLUs exceed the upper bound U, the analysis bisects the input space along the only non-sensitive dimension $x_{0,1}$, yielding two partitions I_1 ($x_{0,1} \in [0, 0.5]$ and $x_{0,2} \in [0, 1]$) and I_2 ($x_{0,1} \in [0.5, 1]$ and $x_{0,2} \in [0, 1]$). By running the pre-analysis from I_1 and I_2, we find that I_1 is feasible since only the ReLU at $x_{1,1}$ is non-fixed (and all other activations are always active), while I_2 must be divided further.

To ensure termination, bisection may continue until the partition size becomes smaller than a chosen **lower bound** L. In such a case, the partition is *excluded* by the analysis as it exceeds the available resources. Continuing our example, let L = 0.25. The forward pre-analysis splits I_2 into $I_{2,1}$ ($x_{0,1} \in [0.5, 0.75]$ and $x_{0,2} \in [0, 1]$) and $I_{2,2}$ ($x_{0,1} \in [0.75, 1]$ and $x_{0,2} \in [0, 1]$). Now, the pre-analysis concludes that $I_{2,1}$ is feasible, with only the ReLUs at $x_{1,1}$ and $x_{2,2}$ being non-fixed. Instead $I_{2,2}$ is excluded, since only the ReLU at $x_{1,2}$ is fixed and the partition size (along the non-sensitive dimension $x_{0,1}$) has reached the lower bound L. Thus, only 75% of the input space is considered by the backward analysis.

The configuration of the pre-analysis (i.e., choices of an abstract domain, lower bound L, and upper bound U) allows trading-off between precision and scalability of the approach (cf. Table 2 in Sect. 3). Ultimately however, the optimal configuration largely depends on the analyzed neural network [25]. For this reason, we have equipped LIBRA with a *configuration auto-tuning mechanism*, which dynamically updates the lower bound and upper bound configuration according to a chosen **search heuristic**. By default, whenever an input partition exceeds the current configuration, the pre-analysis alternates between increasing the upper bound by one, up to a maximum upper bound U_{max}, and halving the lower bound, down to a minimum lower bound L_{min}. Other bound update patterns are configurable (e.g., by updating both bounds at the same time, or performing multiple increments to the upper bound before halving the lower bound, etc.). In our example, let $U_{max} = 3$, the pre-analysis can thus further increase the upper bound to $U = 3$. Therefore, also $I_{2,2}$ becomes feasible (with the ReLUs at $x_{1,1}, x_{1,2}$, and $x_{2,2}$ non-fixed).

The *Backward Iterator* takes care of performing the backward analysis independently for each feasible partition and associated ReLU activation pattern. Specifically, the backward analysis starts with different polyhedra abstract domain values [7], each representing a possible classification outcome of the neural network. In our example, the possible classification outcomes[2] are represented by the polyhedra $x_{32} < x_{31}$ and $x_{31} < x_{32}$. These values are then propagated backwards through the network, taking the current activation pattern into account to prune away unfeasible execution paths, and otherwise splitting polyhedra into two at each non-fixed ReLU in order to retain maximum precision (by analyzing their possible activations separately). Ultimately, for each partition, this yields a disjunction of polyhedra covering the inputs that lead to each possible output classification. We can then project away the value of the sensitive inputs and check for intersections between polyhedra leading to different classifications: any non-empty intersection is a region of the input space in which bias is definitely present, as all points in the region represent data that only differ in the values of the sensitive inputs and lead to different classification outcomes. Otherwise, if no intersection can be found, the input space partition is certified to be fair. In our example, the analysis concludes that the classification within I_1 is fair, while it is biased within $I_{2,1}$ and $I_{2,2}$. Inside the biased intersections, the neural network returns different output classes for inputs that only differ in the sensitive features (i.e., they have the same value for $x_{0,1}$ and different values for $x_{0,2}$).

In the preliminary version of LIBRA [25], feasible partitions are first grouped by activation pattern, i.e., activation patterns that fix more ReLUs are merged with those that fix fewer ReLUs. This way, in principle, the amount of work that the backward analysis has to do is reduced: it only needs to run once for each activation pattern, and can then perform all the checks for bias on each feasible

---

[2] For simplicity, we ignore ties as they can always be broken arbitrarily.

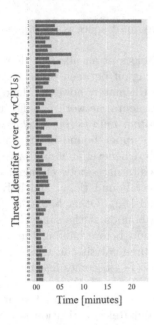
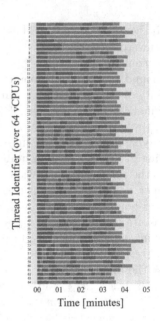
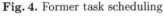

Fig. 4. Former task scheduling   **Fig. 5.** Current task scheduling

partition. In practice, the implementation prevents the parallelization of all bias checks[3], which are thus run sequentially. This hinders the preliminary version of LIBRA from exploiting multi-core architectures effectively. In the current version of LIBRA, we optimize the backward analysis in order to possibly repeat the analysis for the same activation pattern but allowing it to parallelize the bias checks. Figures 4 and 5 compare the previous and current backward analysis task scheduling on the same analysis instance. Each row in the Gantt diagrams shows computations of the same thread. Blue bars stand for activation pattern computations, while red bars indicate bias check computations. As shown in Fig. 4, the running time was determined almost completely by the task with the most associated bias checks, leaving all the other threads idle from the very beginning. The diagram in Fig. 5 is more compact, meaning that threads are always running jobs uniformly. Consequently, the backward analysis running time decreases from about 22 to only 5 min.

2.4   Abstract Domains

Different abstract domains can be used by LIBRA's forward pre-analysis. A preliminary version of LIBRA [25] was equipped with the BOXES [4], SYMBOLIC [18,27], and the DEEPPOLY [24] abstract domains. We additionally implemented

---

[3] This is solely for technical reasons as the serialization of abstract domain elements is not available for the polyhedra domain implementation that LIBRA relies on. We plan to address this shortcoming as part of our future work.

the NEURIFY [26] abstract domain, and a generic reduced product domain construction [6] to combine any of these domains together.

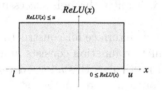

Fig. 6. Naive convex approximation of a ReLU activation.

The BOXES domain simply uses interval arithmetic [13] to compute concrete lower and upper bound estimations l and u for the value of each neuron x in the neural network. The SYMBOLIC domain combines BOXES with symbolic constant propagation [20]: in addition to being bounded by concrete lower and upper bounds, the value of each neuron x is represented symbolically as a linear combination of the input neurons and the value of the non-fixed ReLUs in previous layers. Specifically, given x bounded by $l < 0$ and $u > 0$, ReLU(x) is represented by a fresh symbolic variable bounded by 0 and u (cf. Fig. 6). By retaining variable dependencies, symbolic representations yield a tighter over-approximation of the value of each neuron in the network.

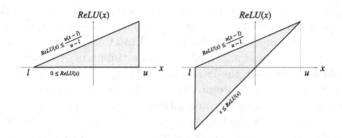

Fig. 7. DEEPOLY's convex approximations of a ReLU activation.

The DEEPPOLY domain associates to each neuron x of a neural network concrete lower and upper bounds l and u as well as symbolic bounds expressed as linear combinations of neurons in the preceding layer of the network. The concrete bounds are computed by back-substitution of the symbolic bounds up to the input layer. Non-fixed ReLUs are over-approximated by partially retaining dependencies with preceding neurons using the tighter convex approximation between those shown in Fig. 7 (i.e., the approximation shown on the left when $u \leq -l$, and the approximation shown on the right otherwise).

The NEURIFY domain similarly maintains symbolic lower and upper bounds *low* and *up* for each neuron x of neural network. Unlike DEEPPOLY, concrete lower and upper bounds are computed for *each* symbolic bound: l_{low} and u_{low} for the symbolic lower bound, and l_{up} and u_{up} for the symbolic upper bound. The over-approximation of non-fixed ReLUs is done *independently* for each symbolic bound,

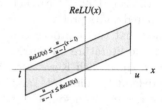

Fig. 8. Neurify's approximation of a ReLU activation.

i.e., for the *low* bound if $l_{low} < 0 < u_{low}$, and for the *up* bound if $l_{up} < 0 < u_{up}$. Figure 8 shows the approximation for $l = l_{low} = l_{up}$ and $u = u_{low} = u_{up}$. In general, the slope of the symbolic constraints will differ through successive approximation steps.

Finally, the *Product Builder* provides a parametric interface for constructing the product of any of the above domains. The reduction function consists in an exchange of concrete bounds between domains. In particular, this allows determining tighter lower and upper bound estimations for each neuron in the network and thus reducing the over-approximation error introduced by the ReLUs. New abstract domains only need to implement the interface to share bounds information to enable their combination with other domains by the Product Builder.

For the backward analysis, as mentioned, LIBRA uses the disjunctive polyhedra domain [7]. Its implementation relies on the APRON domain library [14].

2.5 Tool Output

LIBRA outputs which partitions of the input space could be analyzed and which were excluded because they exceeded the configuration of the pre-analysis. For all partitions that could be analyzed, it reports which (sub)regions could be certified to be fair and which were found to be biased. LIBRA also reports the percentage of the input space that was analyzed and (an estimate of) the percentage that was found biased. To obtain the latter, we simply use the size of a box wrapped around each biased region. More precise but also costlier solutions exist [1].

In our example, the analysis could analyze the entire input space, certifying partition I_1 to be fair and finding bias within $I_{2,1}$ and $I_{2,2}$. In particular, the analysis determines that bias occurs for $0.53 < x_{0,1} \leq 0.75$ within $I_{2,1}$ and for $0.75 \leq x_{0,1} < 1$ within $I_{2,2}$, which amounts to 45.76% of the entire input space.

3. Experimental Evaluation

To demonstrate the effectiveness of LIBRA, we evaluated it on neural networks trained on the Adult dataset[4] from the UCI Machine Learning Repository. The dataset assigns to individuals a yearly income greater or smaller than $50k based on personal attributes such as education and occupation but also gender, marital status, or race. We set LIBRA to use gender as sensitive input feature.

We show below the experimental results on the smaller neural networks used by Urban et al. [25], which better demonstrate the benefits of our implementation compared to its preliminary version. In practice, Urban et al. [25] have already shown that the approach can scale to much larger networks with sizes on par with the literature on fairness certification, e.g., [19,28]. The neural networks were trained with Keras for 50 iterations, using the RMSprop optimizer with the default learning rate, and categorical cross-entropy as the loss function. All networks are open source as part of LIBRA.

---

[4] https://archive.ics.uci.edu/ml/datasets/adult.

Table 1. Comparison of different neural networks

|M|	BOXES	SYMBOLIC	DEEPPOLY	NEURIFY	PRODUCT	
10	96.81%	98.72%	98.37%	98.51%	99.44%	INPUT
	6m 32s	4m 52s	3m 23s	4m 27s	4m 40s	TIME
12	69.10%	76.70%	66.39%	64.58%	77.29%	INPUT
	4m 53s	2m 27s	2m 0s	1m 31s	2m 30s	TIME
20	41.01%	56.11%	56.10%	53.06%	68.23%	INPUT
	4m 8s	9m 7s	3m 43s	3m 53s	8m 9s	TIME
40	0.35%	34.72%	38.69%	41.22%	51.18%	INPUT
	1m 3s	7m 2s	37m 16s	10m 33s	38m 27s	TIME
45	1.74%	43.78%	51.21%	50.59%	55.53%	INPUT
	50s	3m 42s	5m 14s	5m 10s	6m 22s	TIME

The experiments were conducted on the Inria Paris CLEPS infrastructure, on a machine with two 16-core Intel® Xeon® 5218 CPU @ 2.4 GHz, 192 GB of RAM, and running CentOS 7.7. with linux kernel 3.10.0. For each experiment, we report the average results of five executions to account for the effect of randomness in the input space partitioning done by the forward pre-analysis (cf. Sect. 2).

3.1 Effect of Neural Network Structure on Precision and Scalability

The precision and scalability of LIBRA's analysis depend on the analyzed neural network. Table 1 shows the result of running LIBRA on different neural networks with different choices for the abstract domain used by the pre-analysis. Column \|M\| refers to the analyzed neural network by the number of its ReLU activations. From top to bottom, the neural networks have the following number of hidden layers and nodes per layer: 2 and 5, 4 and 3, 4 and 5, 4 and 10, and 9 and 5. We configured the pre-analysis with lower bound L = 0.5 and upper bound U = 5. Each column shows the chosen abstract domain. We show here the results for BOXES, SYMBOLIC, DEEPPOLY, NEURIFY, and the reduced product DEEPPOLY+NEURIFY+SYMBOLIC (i.e., PRODUCT in the Table 1), which is the most precise of all possible reduced products. The INPUT rows show the average input-space coverage, that is, the average percentage of the input space that LIBRA was able to analyze with the chosen pre-analysis configuration. The TIME rows show the average running time.

For all neural networks, PRODUCT achieves the highest input-space coverage, an improvement of up to 12.49% over the best coverage obtained with only the abstract domains available in the preliminary version of LIBRA [25] (i.e., with respect to the DEEPPOLY domain for \|M\| = 40). Interestingly, such an improvement comes at the cost of a very modest increase in running time (i.e., just over 1 minute). Indeed, using a more precise abstract domain for the pre-analysis generally results in fewer input space partitions being passed to the backward analysis and, in turn, this reduces the overall running time.

Table 2. Comparison of different pre-analysis configurations

L	U	BOXES	SYMBOLIC	DEEPPOLY	NEURIFY	PRODUCT	
0.5	3	37.88%	48.78%	49.01%	46.49%	59.20%	INPUT
		36s	42s	1m 35s	32s	1m 58s	TIME
	5	41.01%	56.11%	56.15%	53.06%	68.23%	INPUT
		4m 8s	9m 10s	3m 47s	3m 57s	8m 16s	TIME
0.25	3	70.62%	83.63%	81.82%	81.40%	87.04%	INPUT
		5m 49s	5m 55s	5m 20s	5m 20s	7m 12s	TIME
	5	83.06%	91.67%	91.58%	92.33%	95.48%	INPUT
		26m 43s	21m 8s	22m 8s	25m 54s	21m 58s	TIME

For the smallest neural networks (i.e., $|M| \in \{10, 12, 20\}$), the SYMBOLIC abstract domain is the second best choice in terms of input-space coverage. This is likely due to the convex ReLU approximations of DEEPPOLY and NEURIFY which in some case produce a negative lower bound (cf. Fig. 7 and 8), while SYMBOLIC always sets the lower bound to zero (cf. Fig. 6).

Finally, for the largest neural networks (i.e., $|M| \in \{40, 45\}$), it is the structure of the network (rather than its number of ReLU activations) that impacts the precision and scalability of the analysis: for the deep but narrow network (i.e., $|M| = 45$), LIBRA achieves a higher input-space coverage in a shorter running time than for the shallow but wide network (i.e., $|M| = 40$).

3.2 Precision-vs-Scalability Tradeoff

The configuration of LIBRA's pre-analysis allows trading-off between precision and scalability. Table 2 shows the average results of running LIBRA on the neural network with 20 ReLUs with different lower and upper bound configurations, and different choices for the abstract domain used by the pre-analysis. Columns L and U show the configured lower and upper bounds. We tried $L \in \{0.5, 0.25\}$ and $U \in \{3, 5\}$. We again show the results for the BOXES, SYMBOLIC, DEEPPOLY, NEURIFY abstract domains, and the most precise reduced product domain DEEPPOLY+NEURIFY+SYMBOLIC (i.e., PRODUCT in Table 2).

As expected, decreasing the lower bound L or increasing the upper bound U improves the input-space coverage (INPUT rows) and increases the running time (TIME rows). We obtain an improvement of up to 12.44% by increasing U from 3 to 5 (with L = 0.25 and BOXES), and up to 42.05% by decreasing L from 0.5 to 0.25 (with U = 5 and BOXES). The smaller is L and the larger is U, the higher is the impact on the running time. Once again, for all lower and upper bound configurations, DEEPPOLY+NEURIFY+SYMBOLIC achieves the highest input-space coverage, improving up to 12.08% over the best coverage obtained with only the abstract domains available in the preliminary version of LIBRA (i.e., with respect to DEEPPOLY with L = 0.5 and U = 5). The improvement is more important for configurations with larger lower bounds.

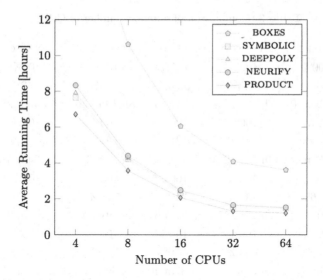

Fig. 9. Comparison of running times for different number of CPUs

Notably, Table 2 shows that *none among the* SYMBOLIC, DEEPPOLY, *and* NEURIFY *abstract domains is always more precise than the others.* There are cases where even SYMBOLIC (implemented by [27]) outperforms NEURIFY (implemented by [26] which is the successor of [27] and is believed to be strictly superior to its predecessor), e.g., configuration L = 0.5 and U = 5. We thus argue for using reduced products of abstract domains also in other contexts beyond fairness certification, e.g., verifying local robustness [18,24, etc.] or verifying functional properties of neural networks [15].

3.3   Leveraging Multiple CPUs

The optimal pre-analysis configuration in terms of precision or scalability depends on the analyzed neural network. In order to push LIBRA to its limits and obtain 100% input-space coverage on the neural network with 20 ReLUs, we used the new configuration auto-tuning mechanism starting with L = 1 and U = 0 (i.e., the most restrictive lower and upper bound configuration) and setting L_{min} = 0 and U_{max} = 20 (i.e., the most permissive configuration). For all choices of abstract domains, the pre-analysis eventually stabilizes with lower bound L = 0.015625 and upper bound U = 6.

Figure 9 compares the average running times for BOXES, SYMBOLIC, DEEPPOLY, NEURIFY, and the reduced product DEEPPOLY+NEURIFY+SYMBOLIC (i.e., PRODUCT) as a function of the number of available CPUs. With PRODUCT we obtained a running time improvement of 14.39% over SYMBOLIC, i.e., the fastest domain available in the preliminary version of LIBRA (a minimum improvement of 11.54% with 16 CPUs, and a maximum improvement of 18.24% with 64 vCPUs). As expected, adding more CPUs always improves LIBRA running time.

Table 3. Comparison of different number of CPUs

|CPU|	BOXES	SYMBOLIC	DEEPPOLY	NEURIFY	PRODUCT	
	100%	100%	100%	100%	100%	INPUT
4	4.55%	5.23%	5.20%	5.11%	5.42%	BIAS
	19h 20m 0s	7h 38m 43s	7h 54m 35s	8h 19m 36s	6h 43m 28s	TIME
	100%	100%	100%	100%	100%	INPUT
8	4.41%	5.16%	5.12%	5.18%	5.46%	BIAS
	10h 37m 28s	4h 13m 27s	4h 16m 13s	4h 24m 13s	3h 34m 38s	TIME
	100%	100%	100%	100%	100%	INPUT
16	4.56%	5.19%	5.12%	5.20%	5.34%	BIAS
	6h 3m 23s	2h 20m 37s	2h 27m 31s	2h 30m 4s	2h 4m 9s	TIME
	100%	100%	100%	100%	100%	INPUT
32	4.50%	5.11%	5.10%	5.10%	5.37%	BIAS
	4h 5m 16s	1h 33m 16s	1h 37m 40s	1h 39m 19s	1h 19m 23s	TIME
	100%	100%	100%	100%	100%	INPUT
64	4.51%	5.11%	5.20%	5.16%	5.37%	BIAS
	3h 37m 9s	1h 28m 38s	1h 29m 26s	1h 31m 28s	1h 12m 21s	TIME

The most limited improvement in running time that occurs between 32 CPUs and 64 vCPUs is likely due to the use of hyperthreading as context switches between processes running intense numeric computations produce more overhead.

Table 3 additionally shows the estimated percentage of bias detected with each abstract domain, i.e., LIBRA is able to certify fairness for about 95% of the neural network input space. Note that, the bias estimate depends on the partitioning of the input space computed by the pre-analysis, cf. Sect. 2. This explains the different percentages found even by runs with the same abstract domain. Within the same column, the difference is at most 0.14% on average.

Finally, we remark that *the new auto-tuning mechanisms is essential for scalability*. We tried repeating this experiment by directly running LIBRA with the configuration at which auto-tuning stabilizes, i.e., L = 0.015625 and U = 6. After six days it still had not completed and we had to interrupt it.

4   Conclusion and Future Work

In this paper, we presented our static analyzer LIBRA for certifying that ReLU-based neural network classifiers are independent of their input values that are sensitive to bias. In particular, we focused on the new release features of LIBRA: new abstract domains, including a generic reduced product domain construction, a configuration auto-tuning mechanism for finding the optimal configuration for LIBRA's forward pre-analysis, and a tasks scheduling optimization to leverage all the available CPUs for LIBRA's backward analysis. With our experimental evaluation, we showed that LIBRA outperforms its preliminary version [25] in precision as well as, for equal precision, in running time.

It remains for future work to implement support for other activation functions than ReLUs. It would also be straightforward to adapt LIBRA to support other fairness notions such as individual fairness [9]. Moreover, we plan to design and equip LIBRA with a smarter reduced product between domains, able to also exchange symbolic bounds along with the concrete bounds. Finally, we intend to extend our approach to other machine learning models, such as support vector machines [8] or decision tree ensembles [2,11].

Acknowledgement. The authors are grateful to the anonymous reviewers for their constructive comments and advice, and to the CLEPS infrastructure from the Inria of Paris for providing resources and support.

References

1. Barvinok, A.I.: A polynomial time algorithm for counting integral points in polyhedra when the dimension is fixed. Math. Oper. Res. **19**(4), 769–779 (1994). https://doi.org/10.1287/moor.19.4.769

2. Breiman, L.: Random forests. Mach. Learn. **45**(1), 5–32 (2001). https://doi.org/10.1023/A:1010933404324

3. Buolamwini, J., Gebru, T.: Gender shades: Intersectional accuracy disparities in commercial gender classification. In: FAT, vol. 81, pp. 77–91. PMLR (2018)

4. Cousot, P., Cousot, R.: Static determination of dynamic properties of programs. In: Second International Symposium on Programming, pp. 106–130 (1976)

5. Cousot, P., Cousot, R.: Abstract interpretation: a unified lattice model for static analysis of programs by construction or approximation of fixpoints. In: POPL, pp. 238–252 (1977). https://doi.org/10.1145/512950.512973

6. Cousot, P., Cousot, R.: Systematic design of program analysis frameworks. In: POPL, pp. 269–282 (1979). https://doi.org/10.1145/567752.567778

7. Cousot, P., Halbwachs, N.: Automatic discovery of linear restraints among variables of a program. In: POPL, pp. 84–96 (1978). https://doi.org/10.1145/512760.512770

8. Cristianini, N., Shawe-Taylor, J.: An Introduction to Support Vector Machines and Other Kernel-based Learning Methods. Cambridge University Press, Cambridge (2000). https://doi.org/10.1017/CBO9780511801389

9. Dwork, C., Hardt, M., Pitassi, T., Reingold, O., Zemel, R.S.: Fairness through awareness. In: ITCS, pp. 214–226. ACM (2012)

10. European commission: proposal for a regulation laying down harmonised rules on artificial intelligence (artificial intelligence act) (2021). https://digital-strategy.ec.europa.eu/en/library/proposal-regulation-laying-down-harmonised-rules-artificial-intelligence-artificial-intelligence

11. Friedman, J.H.: Greedy function approximation: a gradient boosting machine. Ann. Stat. **29**(5), 1189–1232 (2001). https://doi.org/10.1214/aos/1013203451

12. Galhotra, S., Brun, Y., Meliou, A.: Fairness testing: testing software for discrimination. In: FSE, pp. 498–510 (2017). https://doi.org/10.1145/3106237.3106277

13. Hickey, T.J., Ju, Q., van Emden, M.H.: Interval arithmetic: from principles to implementation. J. ACM **48**(5), 1038–1068 (2001)

14. Jeannet, B., Miné, A.: APRON: a library of numerical abstract domains for static analysis. In: CAV, pp. 661–667 (2009). https://doi.org/10.1007/978-3-642-02658-4_52

15. Katz, G., Barrett, C.W., Dill, D.L., Julian, K., Kochenderfer, M.J.: Reluplex: an efficient SMT solver for verifying deep neural networks. In: CAV, pp. 97–117 (2017). https://doi.org/10.1007/978-3-319-63387-9_5

16. Kay, M., Matuszek, C., Munson, S.A.: Unequal representation and gender stereotypes in image search results for occupations. In: CHI, pp. 3819–3828. ACM (2015)

17. Larson, J., Mattu, S., Kirchner, L., Angwin, J.: How we analyzed the COMPAS recidivism algorithm (2016). https://www.propublica.org/article/how-we-analyzed-the-compas-recidivism-algorithm

18. Li, J., Liu, J., Yang, P., Chen, L., Huang, X., Zhang, L.: Analyzing deep neural networks with symbolic propagation: towards higher precision and faster verification. In: SAS, pp. 296–319 (2019). https://doi.org/10.1007/978-3-030-32304-2_15

19. Manisha, P., Gujar, S.: FNNC: achieving fairness through neural networks. In: IJCAI, pp. 2277–2283 (2020)

20. Miné, A.: Symbolic methods to enhance the precision of numerical abstract domains. In: VMCAI, pp. 348–363 (2006). https://doi.org/10.1007/11609773_23

21. Nair, V., Hinton, G.E.: Rectified linear units improve restricted boltzmann machines. In: ICML, pp. 807–814 (2010)

22. Nielson, F., Nielson, H.R., Hankin, C.: Algorithms. In: Principles of Program Analysis, pp. 365–392. Springer, Heidelberg (1999). https://doi.org/10.1007/978-3-662-03811-6_6

23. Obermeyer, Z., Powers, B., Vogeli, C., Mullainathan, S.: Dissecting racial bias in an algorithm used to manage the health of populations. Science **366**, 447–453 (2019)

24. Singh, G., Gehr, T., Püschel, M., Vechev, M.T.: An abstract domain for certifying neural networks. Proc. ACM Prog. Lang. **3**(POPL), 41:1–41:30 (2019). https://doi.org/10.1145/3290354

25. Urban, C., Christakis, M., Wüstholz, V., Zhang, F.: Perfectly parallel fairness certification of neural networks. Proc. ACM Prog. Lang. **4**(OOPSLA), 185:1–185:30 (2020). https://doi.org/10.1145/3428253

26. Wang, S., Pei, K., Whitehouse, J., Yang, J., Jana, S.: Efficient formal safety analysis of neural networks. In: NeurIPS 2018, pp. 6369–6379 (2018)

27. Wang, S., Pei, K., Whitehouse, J., Yang, J., Jana, S.: Formal security analysis of neural networks using symbolic intervals. In: Security, pp. 1599–1614. USENIX (2018)

28. Yurochkin, M., Bower, A., Sun, Y.: Training individually fair ml models with sensitive subspace robustness. In: ICLR (2020)

A Multilanguage Static Analysis of Python Programs with Native C Extensions

Raphaël Monat[1]([✉]) , Abdelraouf Ouadjaout[1] , and Antoine Miné[1,2]

[1] Sorbonne Université, CNRS, LIP6, 75005 Paris, France
{raphael.monat,abdelraouf.ouadjaout,antoine.mine}@lip6.fr
[2] Institut Universitaire de France, 75005 Paris, France

Abstract. Modern programs are increasingly multilanguage, to benefit from each programming language's advantages and to reuse libraries. For example, developers may want to combine high-level Python code with low-level, performance-oriented C code. In fact, one in five of the 200 most downloaded Python libraries available on GitHub contains C code. Static analyzers tend to focus on a single language and may use stubs to model the behavior of foreign function calls. However, stubs are costly to implement and undermine the soundness of analyzers. In this work, we design a static analyzer by abstract interpretation that can handle Python programs calling C extensions. It analyses directly and fully automatically both the Python and the C source codes. It reports runtime errors that may happen in Python, in C, and at the interface. We implemented our analysis in a modular fashion: it reuses off-the-shelf C and Python analyses written in the same analyzer. This approach allows sharing between abstract domains of different languages. Our analyzer can tackle tests of real-world libraries a few thousand lines of C and Python long in a few minutes.

Keywords: Formal methods · Static analysis · Abstract interpretation · Dynamic programming language · Multilanguage analysis

1 Introduction

Modern programs are increasingly multilanguage. This allows developers to combine the strengths of different languages and reuse libraries written in other languages. A *host* language may call a *guest* language through an interface; this

This work is partially supported by the European Research Council under Consolidator Grant Agreement 681393—MOPSA.

interface is also called a *boundary*. The guest language is frequently C and is usually referred to as native code or native C. In this paper, the host language is Python, and the guest language is C. This work supports the Python API [40] as the interoperability mechanism between Python and C.[1] Using native C modules in Python is frequent as it allows writing high-level Python code, itself calling efficient C code. As a matter of fact, one in five of the 200 most downloaded Python libraries available on GitHub contains C code. Although useful, multilanguage programs generate additional sources of bugs. Indeed, developers need to take into account different safety mechanisms and memory representations. Python is safe to the extent that runtime errors in pure Python programs are encapsulated into exceptions, which can be caught later on. This safety property breaks when C modules are used since a runtime error in C may irremediably terminate the program or create an inconsistent state. Python and C also have different representations. For example, Python integer objects use at least 24 bytes of memory and have unlimited precision, while C integers have fixed lengths (generally ranging from 8 to 64 bits) and can suffer from overflows.

Static analysis aims at inferring program properties (e.g., the absence of runtime errors) by analyzing programs without executing them. Static analyzers tend to focus on analyzing one language at a time. They may use stubs to model the behavior of calls to other languages. These stubs may be time-consuming to implement if written by hand. They can undermine the soundness of the analyses since the actual code is not analyzed, and the stubs may be imprecise or wrong. For example, our previous work developing a type analysis for Python [33] uses official Python type annotations (defined by PEP 484 [39]) as stubs. While this analysis tracks uncaught Python exceptions, these type annotations do not declare which exceptions may be raised, thus adding an unchecked assumption to the soundness property [33, Section 6.2].

We aim at analyzing both the native C code and the Python code (including callbacks to Python code from the native side) within the same analyzer, called Mopsa [18]. We perform a precise, flow, and context-sensitive value analysis by abstract interpretation. Our analyzer works by induction on the syntax and switches from one language to the other just as the concrete program execution does. We present a multilanguage static analysis built upon pre-existing value static analyses by abstract interpretation [9] of C [37] and Python [33,34]. It detects runtime errors in the native C code (invalid pointer operations, invalid memory accesses, integer overflows), in the Python code (raised exceptions), and at the boundary between the languages. The underlying address allocation and numeric abstractions are shared. A few multilanguage static analyses exist, and focus mostly on analyzing Java and C ([12–14,22,43,45], cf. Sect. 6). They compute summaries of the effects of native code on the chosen abstract property in a bottom-up fashion. Those effects are then translated into the host language, where a standard analyzer for the host language can then be used. The use of

---

[1] Other interoperability mechanisms such as the `ctypes` from the standard library, the `cffi` library, the `cython` project, or the `swig` project all use code using this API or generate code targetting this API. We could thus analyze this generated code.

summaries to convey the abstract meaning of functions makes it easier to rely on independent analyzers for each language. However, the language and properties we target require precise context-sensitive value analyses that are difficult to perform bottom-up. Since Python is a dynamic programming language with a flexible semantics, it is not possible to analyze programs precisely in a context-insensitive fashion. Additionally, a precise description of the Python heap at a native call is mandatory to analyze the called C code, check for pointer errors, and infer effects. We believe the approach described in this paper is general and could be extended to other multilanguage settings, such as the analysis of Java and C through the JNI.

Contributions.

- We define a multilanguage semantics for Python programs with native C modules using the Python C API.
- We show how to lift analyses of Python and C into the multilanguage setting. The underlying address allocation and numeric abstractions are shared, paving the way for relational invariants between Python and C variables.
- We built an implementation on top of an existing static analysis platform called Mopsa that was previously used to design independent analyses for C and for Python. We added support for multilanguage C/Python programs by only adding domains modeling the boundary. We reuse the previous domains analyzing C and Python off-the-shelf. Thanks to this construction, we can detect runtime errors at the boundary, but also in the Python code and in the native C code.
- We evaluate our approach on six real-world libraries found on GitHub. We show that we can scale to libraries of 5,800 combined lines of Python and C code within five minutes.

Artifact. An artifact [35] is available alongside this article. The artifact makes Table 2 and the claim about the percentage of Python packages containing C code on Github (made in Sect. 1) reproducible. The example codes displayed in Fig. 1 and Fig. 12 are provided in the artifact, along with instructions to run our analyzer on them. The source code of the modified version of Mopsa is also included. We plan on merging our changes into the public version of Mopsa [19].

Limitations. Our concrete semantics is high-level and makes the assumption that builtin Python objects are only manipulated through the API in C (this assumption is verified by our analyzer). The garbage collection based on reference counting is not supported by our semantics. Thus, we cannot detect deallocations that are performed too soon or that are not performed at all. There is no formal soundness proof that our concrete semantics effectively models the behavior of the Python interpreter. Potential runtime errors in the API implementation modeled by our concrete semantics as builtins cannot be detected.[2]

---

[2] However, half of the API supported by our implementation uses the original C implementation, which is analyzed and where runtime errors would be detected.

Our implementation supports relational analyses, but those do not scale to real-world examples (thus, we use intervals for the numeric abstraction by default). These limitations could be removed in future work.

Outline. We start by showing a self-contained motivating example in Sect. 2, giving insights on how native C modules are defined and how they work with Python. We define the concrete semantics of these multilanguage programs in Sect. 3, and explain the abstractions performed in Sect. 4. Section 5 presents our implementation and the analysis results. We discuss related work in Sect. 6 and conclude in Sect. 7.

2   An Extension Module Example

This section provides an in-depth motivating example. We show how to define a native C extension module, and how it can be used by a Python client code. We end the section by discussing which errors may happen.

When developers want to run native C code in Python, they define native C extension modules using the Python API. These modules may contain attributes, methods, and classes, just as any other Python module. However, these methods and classes are now written in C. API functions are denoted by the Py prefix (and written in magenta in the listings). The semantics of some of these functions are described formally in Sect. 3.

Counter Module, Viewed from Python. Our example is a C module defining a Counter class, alongside some client code in Python. This example is self-contained and shown in Fig. 1. From a high-level point of view, the counter module defines a Counter class. Instances of Counter can be created (count.py, line 4); their internal counter can be incremented using the incr method, which takes an optional integer argument being the increment (lines 6–7); they also have a read-only attribute counter returning their current value (line 8).

Counter, Viewed from C. In C, instances of Counter will be stored using the CounterO struct. This **struct** starts with a PyObject ob_base field. All Python objects are represented as PyObjects in C. Putting the PyObject as the first field in the Counter structure allows casting to and from Python objects.[3] The PyObject definition is part of the API and shown in Fig. 2. Its fields are a reference counter for the garbage collector and a pointer to the class to which it belongs. PyTypeObject is Python's **type** object, from which all classes derive. The second field of CounterO is the instance's data: an integer count, not directly exposed to Python.

The Counter class' specification is defined lines 52–59. It has three methods stored in the Py_tp_new, Py_tp_init, and Py_tp_methods fields. It also defines

---

[3] According to the ISO C reference, "a pointer to a structure object, suitably converted, points to its initial member, and vice versa".

```
                    count.py                                          counter.c
1   import counter                            40   static PyMemberDef CounterMembers[] = {
2   import random                             41   {"counter", T_INT, offsetof(Counter0,
3                                             42      count), READONLY, ""}, {NULL}
4   c = counter.Counter()                      43   };
5   p = random.randrange(128)                  44
6   c.incr(2**p-1)                             45   static PyType_Slot CounterTSlots[] = {
7   c.incr()                                   46   {Py_tp_new, PyType_GenericNew},
8   r = c.counter                              47   {Py_tp_init, CounterInit},
                                              48   {Py_tp_methods, CounterMethods},
                    counter.c                  49   {Py_tp_members, CounterMembers}, {0, 0}
9   #include <Python.h>                        50   };
10  #include "structmember.h"                  51
11                                            52   static PyType_Spec CounterTSpec = {
12  typedef struct {                           53   .name = "counter.Counter",
13    PyObject ob_base;                        54   .basicsize = sizeof(Counter0),
14    int count;                               55   .itemsize = 0,
15  } Counter0;                                56   .flags = Py_TPFLAGS_DEFAULT
16                                            57        | Py_TPFLAGS_BASETYPE,
17  static PyObject*                           58   .slots = CounterTSlots
18  CounterIncr(Counter0 *self, PyObject *args) 59   };
19  {                                          60
20    int i = 1;                               61   static struct PyModuleDef countermod = {
21    if(!PyArg_ParseTuple(args, "|i", &i))    62   PyModuleDef_HEAD_INIT, .m_name = "counter",
22      return NULL;                           63   .m_methods = NULL, .m_size = -1
23    self->count += i;                        64   };
24    Py_RETURN_NONE;                          65
25  }                                          66   PyMODINIT_FUNC
26                                            67   PyInit_counter(void)
27  static int                                 68   {
28  CounterInit(Counter0 *self, PyObject *args, 69     PyObject *m = PyModule_Create(&countermod);
29              PyObject *kwds)                70     if(m == NULL) return NULL;
30  {                                          71     PyObject* CounterT =
31    self->count = 0;                         72        PyType_FromSpec(&CounterTSpec);
32    return 0;                                73     if(CounterT == NULL || PyModule_AddObject(
33  }                                          74        m, "Counter", CounterT) < 0) {
34                                            75        Py_DECREF(m);
35  static PyMethodDef CounterMethods[] = {     76        return NULL;
36  {"incr", (PyCFunction) CounterIncr,         77     }
37  METH_VARARGS, ""}, {NULL}                   78     return m;
38  };                                          79   }
```

Fig. 1. Example of a Python client program alongside a C counter module

```
1   typedef struct PyObject {             18    Py_ssize_t offset; int flags;
2     Py_ssize_t ob_refcnt;               19    const char *doc;
3     struct PyTypeObject *ob_type;       20   } PyMemberDef;
4   } PyObject;                           21
5                                         22   typedef struct PyTypeObject {
6   typedef PyObject *(*PyCFunction)      23     PyObject ob_base;
7     (PyObject *, PyObject *);           24     const char *tp_name;
8   typedef int (*initproc)               25     Py_ssize_t tp_basicsize;
9     (PyObject *, PyObject *, PyObject *); 26     Py_ssize_t tp_itemsize;
10                                        27     unsigned long tp_flags;
11  typedef struct PyMethodDef {          28     struct PyMethodDef *tp_methods;
12    const char *ml_name; PyCFunction ml_meth; 29   struct PyMemberDef *tp_members;
13    int ml_flags; const char *ml_doc;   30     struct PyTypeObject *tp_base;
14  } PyMethodDef;                        31     PyObject *tp_dict;
15                                        32     initproc tp_init;
16  typedef struct PyMemberDef {          33     newfunc tp_new;
17    const char *name; int type;         34   } PyTypeObject;
```

Fig. 2. Extract of Python's API header files

Table 1. Python `Counter` structure summary

Attribute	Encapsulating object	Underlying wrapper	Underlying C definition
`__new__`	`builtin_function`	`tp_new_wrapper`	`PyType_GenericNew`
`__init__`	`wrapper_descriptor`	`wrap_init`	`CounterInit`
`incr`	`method_descriptor`	$\emptyset$	`CounterIncr`
`counter`	`member_descriptor`	$\emptyset$	`CounterMembers[0]`

a special attribute member `counter` lines 41–42. The `PyTypeObject` structure is synthesized from the specification by `PyType_FromSpec` (line 72). These methods and members are lifted to become Python attributes and methods when the class is initialized (in `PyType_FromSpec`). Other fields are defined in the `PyTypeObject` structure. `tp_basicsize`, `tp_itemsize` define the size (in bytes) of instances. `tp_flags` is used to perform fast instance checks for builtin classes. `tp_base` points to the parent of the class. `tp_dict` is the class' dictionary used by Python to resolve attribute accesses (created during class initialization).

Module Import. When executing the `import counter` statement, the C function `PyInit_counter` is called. This function starts by creating a module whose name (line 62) is `counter` with no methods attached to it (line 63). Then, the `CounterT` class is created (lines 71–72), and the class is bound to the module (lines 73–74). Python uses a reference-counting-based garbage collector, which has to be manually handled using the `Py_INCREF` and `Py_DECREF` macros in C. If no errors have been encountered, the module object is returned at the end of the function, and `counter` will now point to this module in Python.

Class Initialization. The call to `PyType_FromSpec` creates the `Counter` class from its specification. The function `PyType_FromSpec` starts by creating the `PyTypeObject` and fills its fields according to the specification. This structure is then passed to `PyType_Ready` which populates the `tp_dict` field of the class. This field is the class' dictionary used by Python to resolve attribute accesses. Before this call, the attribute `counter` and the methods `__new__`, `__init__`, and `incr` do not exist on the Python side. We explain how these C functions are encapsulated into Python objects by `PyType_Ready`. The prototype of C functions for Python is `PyCFunction` (Fig. 2, line 6). Some signature adaptations may be needed for specific kinds of functions. For example, initialization methods (such as `CounterInit`) return a C `int` by convention. Thus, `CounterInit` will be wrapped into a function called `wrap_init`, which behaves as a `PyCFunction`. It is then encapsulated into a builtin Python descriptor object. Upon a call to this object, this descriptor performs pre- and post-call checks (described in Sect. 3). Continuing our example, `wrap_init` will be stored into an instance of the builtin `wrapper_descriptor` object. These descriptors are then added to the class dictionary. Table 1 describes the three other fields.

Counter Creation. When a new instance of Counter is created (line 4), Python starts by allocating it by calling Counter.__new__. This call will eventually be resolved into PyType_GenericNew (from tp_new), allocating the object and initializing the necessary fields (such as ob_refcnt and ob_type of PyObject). Then, Counter.__init__ is called and the C function CounterInit ends up being called. It initializes the count field of the Counter0 struct to 0.

Counter Increment. When the incr function is called, it is resolved through Python's attribute accesses into CounterIncr. CounterIncr uses the standard Python function prototype, corresponding to PyCFunction (Fig. 2). Its first argument is the object instance (here, the instance stored in variable c), and the second argument is a tuple of the arguments passed to the function (for the call at line 6 it is a tuple of length one containing 2**p-1, and an empty one for the second call at line 7). PyArg_ParseTuple is a helper C function from the Python API converting the Python arguments wrapped in the tuple into C values.[4] It uses a format string to describe the conversion. The | character separates mandatory arguments from the optional ones, while i signals a conversion from a Python integer to a C int. Internally, the conversion is done from a Python integer to a long (which may fail with an exception since Python integers are unbounded), which is then cast to an int if size permits (otherwise, another exception is set). In the first call to CounterIncr, i will be assigned 2**p-1 if the conversion is successful. In the second call, i will keep its default value, 1. The internal value of the counter is then incremented by i, and then Python's None value is returned.

Counter Access. Thanks to the complex semantics of Python, attribute accesses can actually hide calls to custom getter and setter functions through the descriptor protocol [33, Figure 6]. In our case, PyType_Ready takes the member declaration lines 40–43, and creates those custom getters and setters through a member_descriptor builtin object. The access to attribute counter at line 8 calls the getter of this member_descriptor object. This getter accesses the count field of the Counter0 struct and converts the C integer into a Python integer. The READONLY flag in the declaration ensures that any call to the setter function raises an exception. These member descriptors are supported by our analysis.

What Can Go Wrong? Depending on the chosen value of p the result r will range from (i) the expected value ($r = 2^p$ when $0 \leq p \leq 30$), (ii) conversion errors raised as OverflowError exceptions (with messages depending on whether $p \leq 62$), (iii) a silent integer overflow on the C side, causing a wrap-around which is an unexpected behavior for Python developers ($r = -2^{31}$ for $p = 31$). All these errors are due to different representations between the builtin values of the language. The C integer overflow does not interrupt the execution. This

---

[4] Py_BuildValue is the converse function translating C values to Python ones.

motivates the creation of our analysis targeting all kinds of runtime errors in both host and guest languages as well as at the boundary. Our analysis infers all reachable C and Python values, as well as raised exceptions in order to detect these runtime errors. In this example, our analyzer is able to detect all these cases. Our analyzer is also able to prove that the program is safe when p ranges between 0 and 30.

Common Bugs at the Boundary. We refer the reader to the work of Hu and Zhang [16] for an empirical evaluation of bugs at the boundary between Python and C. The most frequent bugs happening at the boundary are:

- mismatches between a returned NULL and the exception being set in C (NULL should be returned by Python C functions if and only if an exception has been set – cf. Fig. 8 in the next section),
- mismatches between the C and Python datatypes during conversion (in calls to PyArg_ParseTuple, PyLong_FromLong),
- integer overflows during conversions from arbitrary-precision Python integers to C,
- reference-counting errors (not supported by our analyzer).

3   Concrete Semantics

This section defines the semantics of the interface between Python and C. It is built upon the semantics of each language. Our goal is to delegate most of the work to the semantics of each language, each used in a black-box fashion. This delegation will also simplify our implementation as we will reuse the analyses of Python and C in a similar black-box fashion.

A key assumption of our semantics is that builtin Python objects (such as integers and dictionaries) can only be accessed from C through the API provided by the interpreter. As such, any access to the builtins through the C API can be encoded as a call back to the Python language. Thus, each language will have complementary representations of Python objects. Each language has a view of any Python object. Accesses to the other view are done by switching language. To illustrate this representation on our running example, the int count field from a Counter instance is only exposed from the C. It is possible to read the counter's value from Python. This can only be done by calling a C function performing the conversion of the C integer into a Python integer. This object is new and independent from the C integer. Hence, only C code directly dereferences the field value from the object memory. Conversely, an attribute that is dynamically added to a Python object is stored in the instance's dictionary. This dictionary is opaque from C. Accessing it through the C language using the API will ultimately be evaluated as a Python attribute access in our semantics. As illustrated in these examples, mutable parts of the objects are not *directly* available through both languages. There is thus no need to perform systematic state reductions when switching from one language to the other.

Our concrete semantics defines the operators working at the boundary. These operators allow switching from one language to another or converting the value of one language to the other. We define how Python may call C functions, and how C may perform callbacks to Python objects. We also define conversions between Python integers and C longs. API functions working on other builtin datatypes (such as floats, strings, lists, ...) exist and are supported by our analysis. They are similar to the integer case and are not described in this article. The definitions of these operators rely on calls to boundary functions between the two languages. These boundaries ensure that objects have the correct shape in the other language state. The boundary from C to Python also checks that only valid Python objects are passed back.

We define the state on which each semantics operates. In the following, Python-related states and expressions will be written in **green**. C-related states and expressions will be in orange. We reuse the states defined in the work of Monat et al. [33] for Python and Ouadjaout and Miné [37] for C. A set of heap addresses **Addr** (potentially infinite) is common to the states. Previous works [11,33,37] define the semantics of Python and C.

Python State (Fig. 3). Python objects are split into a nominal part and a structural part. The nominal part **ObjN** can be a builtin object such as an integer (we omit other builtins for the sake of concision), a function, a class, or an instance (defined by the address of the class from which it is instantiated). The structural part **ObjS** maps attribute names to their contents' addresses. A state Σ_p consists of an environment and a heap. The environment $\mathcal{E}_p$ maps variable identifiers **Id**$_p$ to addresses (or LocalUndef for local variables with an undefined value). The heap $\mathcal{H}_p$ maps addresses to objects. Given a state $\sigma_p \in \Sigma_p$, we write as $\sigma.\epsilon_p$ its environment and $\sigma.\eta_p$ its heap. Following Fromherz et al. [11], the state is additionally tagged by a flow token to handle non-local control-flow: *cur* represents the current flow on which all instructions that do not disrupt the control flow operate (e.g., assignments, but not raise); *exn* collects the states given by a raised exception. *exn* is indexed by the address of the exception object, so each exception will be kept separate. These continuation-tagged states are standard in abstract interpreters working by induction on the syntax to model non-local control-flow. Evaluating an expression e through $\mathbb{E}_p[\![\,e\,]\!]$ in a given state yields a Python value in a new state. This value may be $\perp$ if the evaluation fails. We use letb $v, \sigma = f(e)$ in body as syntactic sugar for let $r, \sigma = f(e)$ in if $r \neq \perp$ then body else $\perp, \sigma$.

C State (Fig. 4). The memory is decomposed into blocks **Base** which are either variables **Id**$_c$ or heap addresses **Addr**. Each block is decomposed into scalar elements (machine integers, floats, pointers). $\{b, o, \tau\}$ denotes the memory region in block b, starting at offset o and having type τ. C values Value$_c$ are either machine numbers $MNum$, or pointers Ptr defined by their block and offset. Additionally, pointers can be NULL or invalid. The state Σ_c consists of an environment and a heap. The environment $\mathcal{E}_c$ maps scalar elements to values.

$$\mathbf{ObjN} \stackrel{\text{def}}{=} \text{int}(i \in \mathbb{Z}) \cup \mathbf{Fun}(f)$$
$$\cup \, \mathbf{Class}(c) \cup \mathbf{Inst}(a \in \mathbf{Addr})$$
$$\mathbf{ObjS} \stackrel{\text{def}}{=} string \rightharpoonup \mathbf{Addr}$$
$$\mathbf{Value}_p \stackrel{\text{def}}{=} \mathbf{Addr}$$
$$\mathcal{F}_p \stackrel{\text{def}}{=} \{\, cur, exn\ a \in \mathbf{Addr} \,\}$$
$$\mathcal{E}_p \stackrel{\text{def}}{=} \mathbf{Id}_p \rightharpoonup \mathbf{Addr} \cup \texttt{LocalUndef}$$
$$\mathcal{H}_p \stackrel{\text{def}}{=} \mathbf{Addr} \rightharpoonup \mathbf{ObjN} \times \mathbf{ObjS}$$
$$\Sigma_p \stackrel{\text{def}}{=} \mathcal{F}_p \times \mathcal{E}_p \times \mathcal{H}_p$$
$$\mathbb{E}_p[\![\, expr \,]\!] : \Sigma_p \to \mathbf{Value}_p^{\perp} \times \Sigma_p$$
$$\mathbb{S}_p[\![\, stmt \,]\!] : \Sigma_p \to \Sigma_p$$

Fig. 3. Concrete Python State

$$\mathit{Cells} \stackrel{\text{def}}{=} \{\, \wp b, o, t \wp \mid b \in \mathbf{Base}, t : \text{scalar}$$
$$\text{type}, 0 \le o \le \text{sizeof}(b) - \text{sizeof}(t) \,\}$$
$$\mathit{Ptr} \stackrel{\text{def}}{=} (\mathbf{Base} \times \mathbb{Z}) \cup \{\, \texttt{NULL}, \texttt{invalid} \,\}$$
$$\mathbf{Base} \stackrel{\text{def}}{=} \mathbf{Id}_c \cup \mathbf{Addr}$$
$$\mathbf{Value}_c \stackrel{\text{def}}{=} \mathit{MNum} \cup \mathit{Ptr}$$
$$\mathcal{E}_c \stackrel{\text{def}}{=} \mathit{Cells} \rightharpoonup \mathbf{Value}_c$$
$$\mathcal{H}_c \stackrel{\text{def}}{=} \mathbf{Addr} \rightharpoonup \mathit{ident} \times \mathbb{N}$$
$$\Sigma_c \stackrel{\text{def}}{=} \mathcal{E}_c \times \mathcal{H}_c$$
$$\mathbb{E}_c[\![\, expr \,]\!] : \Sigma_c \to \mathbf{Value}_c^{\perp} \times \Sigma_c$$
$$\mathbb{S}_c[\![\, stmt \,]\!] : \Sigma_c \to \Sigma_c$$

Fig. 4. Concrete C State

$$\Sigma = \Sigma_p \times \Sigma_c$$
$${}^{p}\!\hookrightarrow_c : \mathbf{Value}_p \times \Sigma \to \mathbf{Value}_c \times \Sigma$$
$${}^{c}\!\hookrightarrow_p : \mathbf{Value}_c \times \Sigma \to \mathbf{Value}_p^{\perp} \times \Sigma$$
$$\mathbb{E}_{p \times c}[\![\, expr_p \,]\!] : \Sigma \to \mathbf{Value}_p^{\perp} \times \Sigma$$
$$\mathbb{E}_{p \times c}[\![\, expr_c \,]\!] : \Sigma \to \mathbf{Value}_c^{\perp} \times \Sigma$$

Fig. 5. Combined State

The heap $\mathcal{H}_c$ maps addresses to the type of allocated resource and their size. The type of allocated resource is `Malloc` when the standard C library `malloc` is used[5]. The Python allocator (called by `PyType_GenericNew`) will create resources of type `PyAlloc`, ensuring that: (i) Python objects are well constructed by the correct allocator (ii) the C code cannot access these "opaque" objects and needs to use the API.

Combined State (Fig. 5). Two new kinds of nominal objects are added to Python: **CFun** f for Python functions defined in C, **CClass** c for Python classes defined in C (where f and c denote the name of the underlying C function or class declaration). The combined state used for the multilanguage semantics is the product of the Python and C states, written Σ. Note that each state may reference addresses originally allocated by the other language (in the running example, the Python variable c points to the address of the Counter instance, which has been allocated on the C side by `PyType_GenericNew`). In the following, we define two boundary functions converting a Python value into a C value and conversely (written ${}^{p}\!\hookrightarrow_c$ and ${}^{c}\!\hookrightarrow_p$). The multilanguage semantics $\mathbb{E}_{p \times c}[\![\, \cdot \,]\!]$ is

---

[5] Other resources (such as file descriptors) can also be defined [37].

defined over Python and C expressions. It operates over the whole state Σ and its return value matches the language of the input expression. We define the semantics of some builtins working at the boundary between Python and C, which require the whole state. For expressions not working at the boundary, the multilanguage semantics defaults to the usual Python or C semantics:

$$\mathbb{E}_{p\times c}[\![\, expr_p \,]\!](\sigma_p, \sigma_c) = \mathbb{E}_p[\![\, expr_p \,]\!](\sigma_p), \sigma_c$$

$$\mathbb{E}_{p\times c}[\![\, expr_c \,]\!](\sigma_p, \sigma_c) = \sigma_p, \mathbb{E}_c[\![\, expr_c \,]\!](\sigma_c)$$

$${}^{p}\hookrightarrow_c(v_p, \sigma_p, \sigma_c) =$$
$$\quad \text{if } v_p \in \sigma.\eta_c \text{ then } (v_p, 0), \sigma_p, \sigma_c \text{ else}$$
$$\quad \text{letb } ty_p, \sigma_p = \mathbb{E}_p[\![\, type(v_p) \,]\!]\sigma_p \text{ in}$$
$$\quad \text{letb } (ty_c, 0), \sigma_p, \sigma_c = {}^{p}\hookrightarrow_c(ty_p, \sigma_p, \sigma_c) \text{ in}$$
$$\quad \text{let } \sigma_c = \mathbb{S}_c[\![\, v_p\text{->ob\_type} = ty_c \,]\!]\sigma_c \text{ in}$$
$$\quad \text{let } \sigma_p, \sigma_c =$$
$$\qquad \text{if } \sigma_p(v_p) = \textbf{Class}(c) \text{ then}$$
$$\qquad\quad \text{let } \sigma_c = \sigma.\epsilon_c, \sigma.\eta_c[v_p \mapsto \textbf{PyAlloc}, \text{sizeof}(\texttt{PyTypeObject})] \text{ in}$$
$$\qquad\quad \mathbb{E}_{p\times c}[\![\, \text{PyType\_Ready}(v_p) \,]\!](\sigma_p, \sigma_c)$$
$$\qquad \text{else } \sigma_p, (\sigma.\epsilon_c, \sigma.\eta_c[v_p \mapsto \textbf{PyAlloc}, \text{sizeof}(\texttt{PyObject})])$$
$$\quad \text{in } (v_p, 0), \sigma_p, \sigma_c$$

Fig. 6. Python to C value boundary

$${}^{c}\hookrightarrow_p(v_c, \sigma_p, \sigma_c) =$$
$$\text{if } v_c \notin \textbf{Addr} \times \{\, 0 \,\} \;||\; \sigma.\eta_c(\text{fst } v_c) \neq (\textbf{PyAlloc}, \_) \text{ then } \bot, \sigma_p, \sigma_c \text{ else}$$
$$\text{let } v = \text{fst } v_c \text{ in}$$
$$\text{if } v \in \sigma.\eta_p \text{ then } v, \sigma_p, \sigma_c \text{ else}$$
$$\text{letb } ty_c, \sigma_c = \mathbb{E}_c[\![\, ((\texttt{PyObject*})v)\text{->ob\_type} \,]\!]\sigma_c \text{ in}$$
$$\text{letb } ty_p, \sigma_p, \sigma_c = {}^{c}\hookrightarrow_p(ty_c, \sigma_p, \sigma_c) \text{ in}$$
$$\text{let } \sigma_p = \sigma.\epsilon_p, \sigma.\eta_p[v \mapsto \textbf{Inst}(ty_p), \emptyset] \text{ in } v, \sigma_p, \sigma_c$$

Fig. 7. C to Python value boundary

Boundary Functions. Boundary functions ensure that Python objects are correctly represented in the heap of each language. The C to Python boundary also ensures that only Python objects are passed back to Python. These functions do not convert values from one language to another. This kind of conversion is handled by builtin conversion functions such as `PyLong_AsLong`, `PyLong_FromLong` for Python integer to C long conversion. These boundary functions are lazy and shallow: (i) only objects switching languages are passed through those boundaries, (ii) an object that has already been converted does not need to be converted again (i.e., when its address is already in the other language's heap).

The boundary from Python to C is described in Fig. 6. The boundary is first applied recursively to the class of the object (using the `type` operator of Python). Then, the `ob_type` field of the object is initialized to point to its class. The last step performed is to update the heap: the object has been allocated by Python, and has the size of `PyObject` (if the object is a class, it has the size of `PyTypeObject`, and we call the class initializer afterward).

The converse boundary (Fig. 7) starts by checking that the value is a heap allocated Python object, allocated with resource type `PyAlloc`. It calls itself recursively on the class of the object (using the `ob_type` field in C). The Python heap is updated with the converted object.

C Call from Python (Fig. 8). The semantics of C function calls from Python is shown in Fig. 8. The function `in_check` enforces that e_1 should be an instance of the class to which f is bound. Otherwise, a `TypeError` exception is raised. C functions callable from Python can only have two arguments (cf. the type of `PyCFunction`, Fig. 2, line 6). Thus, the Python arguments are split into the first one e_1 and the other ones, bundled in a tuple. The boundary from Python to C is applied to e_1, and to the tuple containing the other arguments. Then, the C function is evaluated using the standard C semantics. Afterward, `out_check` ensures that the function returned `NULL` if and only if an exception has been set in the interpreter state. Otherwise, a `SystemError` exception is raised. Finally, the C value is passed through the boundary function.

$$\mathbb{E}_{p \times c} [\![(\mathbf{CFun}\, f)(e_1, e_2, \ldots, e_n)]\!](\sigma_p, \sigma_c) =$$
$$\text{letb } \sigma_p = \mathbf{in\_check}(\mathbf{CFun}\, f, e_1, \sigma_p) \text{ in}$$
$$\text{letb } c_1, \sigma_p, \sigma_c = {}^P\!\hookrightarrow_c (e_1, \sigma_p, \sigma_c) \text{ in}$$
$$\text{letb } p_2, \sigma_p = \mathbb{E}_p [\![tuple(e_2, \ldots, e_n)]\!]\sigma_p \text{ in}$$
$$\text{letb } c_2, \sigma_p, \sigma_c = {}^P\!\hookrightarrow_c (p_2, \sigma_p, \sigma_c) \text{ in}$$
$$\text{letb } c_f, \sigma_c = \mathbb{E}_c [\![f(c_1, c_2)]\!]\sigma_c \text{ in}$$
$$\text{letb } c_f, \sigma_c = \mathbf{out\_check}(c_f, \sigma_c) \text{ in}$$
$$ {}^c\!\hookrightarrow_p (c_f, \sigma_p, \sigma_c)$$

Fig. 8. C call from Python

$$\mathbb{E}_{p \times c} [\![\text{PyObject\_CallObject}(f, a)]\!] (\sigma_p, \sigma_c) =$$
$$\text{letb } f_p, \sigma_p, \sigma_c = {}^c \hookrightarrow_p (f, \sigma_p, \sigma_c) \text{ in}$$
$$\text{letb } a_p, \sigma_p, \sigma_c = {}^c \hookrightarrow_p (a, \sigma_p, \sigma_c) \text{ in}$$
$$\text{let } r_p, \sigma_p = \mathbb{E}_p [\![f_p(*a_p)]\!] \sigma_p \text{ in}$$
$$\text{if } \sigma_p = (cur, \_, \_) \text{ then } {}^p \hookrightarrow_c (r_p, \sigma_p, \sigma_c)$$
$$\text{else let } exn \ e, \epsilon_p, \eta_p = \sigma_p \text{ in}$$
$$\text{letb } e_c, \sigma_p, \sigma_c = {}^p \hookrightarrow_c (e, (cur, \epsilon_p, \eta_p), \sigma_c) \text{ in}$$
$$\text{NULL}, \sigma_p, \mathbb{S}_c [\![\text{PyErr\_SetNone}(e_c)]\!] \sigma_c$$

Fig. 9. Python call from C

Python Call from C (Fig. 9). Calls back to Python from the C code are possible using the `PyObject_CallObject` function. The first argument is the object being called. The second argument is a tuple containing all the parameters. These two arguments are first passed through the C to Python boundary. Then, we use the Python semantics to evaluate the call (the `*` operator in Python unpacks the tuple into the arguments of the variadic function). If the call is successful (i.e., the execution is normal, shown by flow token *cur*), the converse boundary function is applied. If an exception has been raised during the evaluation of the Python call, we revert to the *cur* flow token and pass the exception object e through the boundary. The result of the call will be `NULL`, and the exception will be set on the C side by calling `PyErr_SetNone`.

Python Exceptions in C. Python exceptions may be raised from the C code using the `PyErr_SetNone` builtin. In the Python interpreter, this sets a flag in a structure describing the interpreter's state. We model this by setting a global variable `exc` with the Python object passed as an argument. Additional functions such as `PyErr_Occurred` checking if an exception has been raised and `PyErr_Clear` removing raised exceptions are modeled by accessing and setting this same global variable.

Conversion Builtins of the API. We show conversion functions from C `long` to Python integers and back in Fig. 10. Converting a C `long` of value v_c to a Python integer is done by calling the integer constructor in the Python semantics, and applying the boundary afterwards. To perform the other conversion, we apply the boundary function to the C value. Then, we check if the corresponding Python value v_p is an integer by looking into the Python heap. If that is the case, we check that this integer fits in a C `long` (Python integers are unbounded). Otherwise we raise an `OverflowError` and the function returns -1. A `TypeError` exception is raised and the function returns -1 if the object is not an integer.

Thanks to the definition of builtins such as `PyLong_AsLong`, other builtins calling this function can be analyzed directly using their source code from the Python interpreter's implementation. For example, when `PyArg_ParseTuple`

$$\mathbb{E}_{p \times c}[\![\, \mathrm{PyLong\_FromLong}(v_c) \,]\!](\sigma_p, \sigma_c) = {}^{P}\hookrightarrow_c (\mathbb{E}_p[\![\, int(v_c) \,]\!](\sigma_p), \sigma_c)$$

$$\mathbb{E}_{p \times c}[\![\, \mathrm{PyLong\_AsLong}(v_c) \,]\!](\sigma_p, \sigma_c) =$$

$$\text{let } v_p, \sigma_p, \sigma_c = {}^{c}\hookrightarrow_p(v_c, \sigma_p, \sigma_c) \text{ in}$$

$$\text{if } \sigma.\eta_p = int(i) \text{ then}$$

$$\text{if } i \in [-2^{63}, 2^{63} - 1] \text{ then } i, \sigma_p, \sigma_c$$

$$\text{else } -1, \sigma_p, \mathbb{S}_c[\![\, \mathrm{PyErr\_SetNone}(\mathrm{PyExc\_OverflowError}) \,]\!]\sigma_c$$

$$\text{else } -1, \sigma_p, \mathbb{S}_c[\![\, \mathrm{PyErr\_SetNone}(\mathrm{PyExc\_TypeError}) \,]\!]\sigma_c$$

Fig. 10. Conversion from Python builtin integers to C long

```
1   long ival = PyLong_AsLong(obj);              10   else if (ival < INT_MIN) {
2   if(ival == -1 && PyErr_Occurred()) {         11     PyErr_SetString(PyExc_OverflowError,
3     return 0;                                   12       "signed integer is less than minimum");
4   } else if (ival > INT_MAX) {                  13     return 0;
5     PyErr_SetString(PyExc_OverflowError,        14   } else {
6       "signed integer is greater than maximum");15     *result = ival;
7     return 0;                                   16     return 1;
8   }                                             17   }
```

Fig. 11. Python integer to C int conversion as done by `PyArg_ParseTuple`

encounters an `'i'` `char` in its conversion string, it executes the code shown in Fig. 11.[6] As explained in our example from Sect. 2, it first calls `PyLong_AsLong` and converts the `long` to `int` checking for additional overflows. Our analyzer is able to analyze this piece of code directly. In our implementation, about half of the builtins use the original C implementation; their code is around 650 lines long.

Threats to Validity. Our goal is to analyze Python programs with native C modules and detect all runtime errors that may happen. Assuming that those C modules use Python's API rather than directly modify the internal representation of builtins seems reasonable when analyzing third-party modules. This is the recommended approach for developers, as it eases maintenance of the codebase since API changes are not frequent and documented. Our analysis is able to detect if a program does not use the Python API and tries to modify a builtin Python object directly.

This concrete semantics is already high-level. A lower-level semantics where implementation details of builtins are exposed would be much more complex. It would not benefit our analysis, which aims at detecting runtime errors in the user's codebase. We have established this semantics by reading the code of the reference Python interpreter. Proving that our semantics is a sound abstraction of such lower-level semantics is left as future work.

---

[6]   `PyArg_ParseTuple` is defined as stub (just as `PyLong_AsLong` is), but the case of integers is delegated to the interpreter's implementation shown in Fig. 11.

4   Abstract Semantics

Concrete states use numeric values in different places (e.g., the C state has machine numbers, pointer offsets and resource sizes). All these values will be centralized in a common numeric domain in the abstract state. This centralization allows expressing invariants between all those numeric variables, possibly improving the precision. We show a generic construction of the abstract multilanguage state. We assume the abstract semantics of Python and C are provided through $\mathbb{E}_p^\#[\![\cdot]\!], \mathbb{E}_c^\#[\![\cdot]\!]$. These can be instantiated in practice using previous works [34, 37]. We assume that each language's abstract state relies on an address allocation abstraction (such as the callsite abstraction or the recency abstraction [2]) and a numeric abstraction (such as intervals, octagons, ...). We write $\Sigma_u^\#$ the cartesian product of these two abstractions. The abstract Python (resp. C) state can then be decomposed as a product $\Sigma_p^\# = \tilde{\Sigma}_p^\# \times \Sigma_u^\#$ (resp. $\Sigma_c^\# = \tilde{\Sigma}_c^\# \times \Sigma_u^\#$). The multilanguage abstract state consists in the cartesian product of the Python and C abstract states, where the address allocation and numeric states are shared: $\Sigma_{p\times c}^\# = \tilde{\Sigma}_p^\# \times \tilde{\Sigma}_c^\# \times \Sigma_u^\#$.

Just as the concrete semantics builds upon the underlying C and Python semantics, so does our abstract semantics. The abstract semantics of the boundary operators is structurally similar to the concrete ones (each concrete operator is replaced with its abstract counterpart). We show this transformation on the abstract semantics of $\mathrm{PyLong\_FromLong}$ (to be compared with Fig. 10).

$$\mathbb{E}_{p\times c}^\#[\![\,\mathrm{PyLong\_FromLong}(v_c)\,]\!](\sigma_p^\#, \sigma_c^\#) = {}^{p}\hookrightarrow_c{}^\# \left(\mathbb{E}_p^\#[\![\,int(v_c)\,]\!](\sigma_p^\#), \sigma_c^\# \right)$$

Sharing the address allocation and numeric abstractions allows expressing relational invariants between the languages. In the example in Fig. 12, a nonrelational analysis would be able to infer that $0 \le i \le 99$, but it cannot infer that the number of calls to $incr$ is finite. It would thus infer that $-2^{31} \le r < 2^{31}$, report an overflow error and be unable to prove the assertion at the end. Note that the value of r originates from the C value of the $count$ field in the instance defined in c. With a relational analysis where C and Python variables are shared in the numeric domains, it is possible to infer that $num(@_{int}) + 1 = num(\langle\!\langle @_{Counter}, 16, \mathtt{s32}\rangle\!\rangle)$. $num(@_{int})$ is the numeric value of the integer bound to i. $num(\langle\!\langle @_{Counter}, 16, \mathtt{s32}\rangle\!\rangle)$ is the numeric value of the $\mathtt{Counter}$ instance (i.e., the value of $count$ in the $\mathtt{Counter}$ struct, here represented as the cell [31] referenced by the $\mathtt{Counter}$ instance, at offset 16 being a 32-bit integer). Our

```
─────── rel_count.py ───────
1 │ c = counter.Counter()
2 │ for i in range(randint(1, 100)):
3 │     c.incr()
4 │ r = c.counter
5 │ assert(r == i+1)
```

Fig. 12. Example code where relationality between C and Python improves precision

analyzer is able to prove that the assertion holds using the octagon abstract domain [32].

Soundness. Assuming the underlying abstract semantics of Python and C are sound, the only cases left in the soundness proof are those of the operators working at the boundary. Since the abstract semantics of those operators is in point-to-point correspondence with the concrete semantics, the soundness proof is straightforward.

5   Experimental Evaluation

Implementation. We have implemented our multilanguage analysis within the open-source, publicly-available static analysis framework called Mopsa [18,19]. A specific feature of Mopsa is to provide loosely-coupled abstract domains that the user combines through a configuration file to define the analysis. We were able to reuse off-the-shelf value analyses of C programs [37] and Python programs [34] already implemented into Mopsa. The only modification needed was to add a multilanguage domain, implementing the semantics of the operators at the boundary, just as our semantics (both concrete and abstract) do.

The configuration for the multilanguage analysis is shown in Fig. 13. A configuration is a directed acyclic graph, where nodes are either domains or

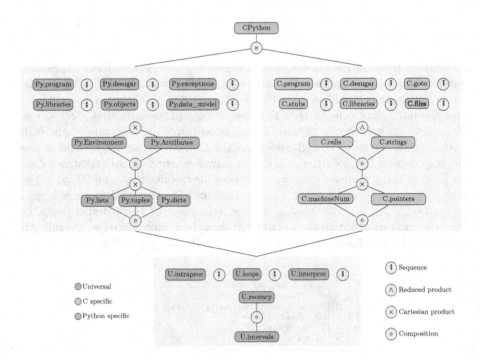

Fig. 13. Multilanguage configuration in Mopsa

domain combinators. Domains can have their own local abstract state. The global abstract state is the product of these local states. Domains can also be iterators over language constructions. Each analyzed expression (or statement) flows from the top domain of the configuration to the bottom until one domain handles it. The multilanguage domain is at the top. It dispatches statements not operating at the boundary to the underlying Python or C analysis. The Python and C analyses are in a cartesian product, ensuring that when a statement goes through them, it will be handled by only one of the two sub-configurations. An example of stateful domain is "C.pointers", which keeps points-to information. "Py.exceptions" is an example of iterator domain. It handles the `raise` and `try` operators of Python. Both Python and C analyses share an underlying "universal" analysis, to which they can delegate some statements. This "universal" part provides iterators for intra- and inter-procedural statements, as well as the address allocation and numeric abstractions. The numeric abstraction displayed here only uses intervals, but it can be changed to a reduced product between a relational domain and intervals, for example.

This multilanguage domain consists in 2,500 lines of OCaml code (measured using the `cloc` tool), implementing 64 builtin functions such as the ones presented in the concrete semantics. This is small compared to the 11,700 lines of OCaml for the C analysis and 12,600 lines of OCaml for the Python analysis. These domains rely on "universal" domains representing 5,600 lines of OCaml and a common framework of 13,200 lines of OCaml. We also reuse the C implementation of 60 CPython functions as-is.

Corpus Selection. In order to perform our experimental evaluation, we selected six popular Python libraries from GitHub (having in average 412 stars). These libraries are written in C and Python and do not have external dependencies. The `noise` library [10] aims at generating Perlin noise. Libraries `levenshtein, ahocorasick, cdistance` [15,30,36] implement various string-related algorithms. `llist` [17] defines linked-list objects (both single and double ones). `bitarray` [41] provides an implementation for efficient arrays of bits. Our analysis is context-sensitive in order to perform a precise value analysis. Thus, we needed some client code to analyze those libraries. We decided to analyze the tests defined by those libraries: they should cover most usecases of the library, and ensure that the transition between Python and C are frequent, which is ideal to stress-test our analysis. Some libraries (`noise, bitarray,` and `llist`) come with example programs with less than 50 lines of code that we analyze within 15 s. We have not been able to find applications with a well-defined entry point using those libraries (or they had big dependencies such as `numpy`). Our experimental evaluation thus focuses on the analysis of the libraries' tests.

Analysis Results. We show the results of our analysis in Table 2. The column |C| (resp. |Py|) shows the lines of code in C (resp. Python), measured using the `cloc` tool. The Python code corresponds mainly to the tests. It may also wrap C classes in custom classes. For example, `frozenbitarray` is defined in

Table 2. Analysis results of libraries using their unit tests

Library	|C|	|Py|	Tests	🕐	✅$_c$		✅$_p$		Assert.	Py⇝C
noise	722	675	15/15	19s	99.6%	(4952)	100.0%	(1738)	0/21	6.6
ahocorasick	3541	1336	46/92	59s	93.1%	(1785)	98.0%	(4937)	30/88	5.4
levenshtein	5441	357	17/17	1.6m	79.9%	(3106)	93.2%	(1719)	0/38	2.7
cdistance	1433	912	28/28	1.9m	95.3%	(1832)	98.3%	(11884)	88/207	8.6
llist	2829	1686	167/194	4.3m	99.0%	(5311)	98.8%	(30944)	235/691	51.7
bitarray	3244	2597	159/216	4.6m	96.3%	(4496)	94.6%	(21070)	97/374	14.9

Python, on top of the `bitarray` class. The "tests" column shows the number of tests we are able to analyze, compared to the total number of tests defined by the library. The ✅$_c$ column shows the time taken to analyze all the tests. Columns 🕐 (resp. ✅$_p$) show the selectivity of our analysis – the number of safe operations compared to the total number of runtime error checks, the latter being also displayed in parentheses – performed by the analyzer for C (resp. Python). The selectivity is computed by Mopsa during the analysis. The C analysis checks for runtime errors including integer overflows, divisions by zero, invalid memory accesses and invalid pointer operations. The Python analysis checks also for runtime errors, which include the `AttributeError, TypeError, ValueError` exceptions. Runtime errors happening at the boundary are considered as Python errors since they will be raised as Python `SystemError` exceptions. The second to last column shows the number of functional properties (expressed as assertions) defined by the tests that our analyzer is able to prove correct automatically. The last column shows the number of transitions between the analyzed Python code and the C code, averaged per test.

We observe that Mopsa is able to analyze these libraries in a few minutes with high selectivity for the detection of Python and C runtime errors. Our analysis is able to detect some bugs that were previously known. For example, the `ahocorasick` module forgets to initialize some of its iterator classes, and some functions of the `bitarray` module do not set an exception when they return an erroneous flag, raising a `SystemError` exception. We have not manually checked if unknown bugs were detected by our analysis. We have instrumented Mopsa to display the number of crossings (from Python to C, or C to Python). The average number of crossings per test is shown in the last column of Table 2. The minimal number of crossings is one per test. Thus these tests seem correct to benchmark our approach since they all alternate calls to native C code and Python code.

The multilanguage analysis is limited by the current precision level of the underlying C and Python analyses but would naturally benefit immediately from any improvements in these. However, we focused on the multilanguage domains only in this study. We leave as future work the improvements required independently on the C and Python analyses for our benchmarks. We now describe a few areas where the analysis could benefit from improvements. Mopsa is unable to support some tests for now, either because they use unsupported Python libraries or because the C analysis is too imprecise to resolve some pointers. The unsupported tests of the `ahocorasick` analysis are due to imprecisions in the C analysis, which is not able to handle a complex trie data structure being stored in a dynamic array and reallocated over and over again. In `llist`, some tests use the `getrefcount` method of the `sys` which is unsupported (and related to CPython's reference-based garbage collector, which we do not support). In addition, some tests make pure-Python classes inherit from C classes: this is currently not supported in our implementation, but it is an implementation detail that will be fixed. For the `bitarray` tests, tests are unsupported because they use the unsupported `pickle` module performing object serialization, or they use the unsupported `sys.getsizeof` method, or they perform some unsupported input-output operations in Python. In addition, the C analysis is too imprecise to resolve some pointers in 18 tests.

The selectivity is lower in the C analysis of `levenshtein`, where dynamic arrays of structures are accessed in loops: the first access at `tab[i].x` may raise an alarm and continue the analysis assuming that `i` is now a valid index access. However, subsequent accesses to `tab[i].y`, `tab[i].z` will also raise alarms as the non-relational numeric domain is unable to express that `i` is a valid index access. Proving the functional properties is more challenging, and not the main goal of our analysis, which aims detecting runtime errors. For example, the assertions of the `noise` library check that the result of complex, iterative non-linear arithmetic lies in the interval $[-1, 1]$. Some assertions in the `llist` or `bitarray` library aim at checking that converting their custom container class to a list preserves the elements. Due to the smashing abstraction [3] of the Python lists, we cannot prove these assertions.

6 Related Work

Native Code Analysis. Some works focus on analyzing native C code in the context of language interoperability, without analyzing the host language. Tan and Croft [42] perform an empirical study of native code use in Java and provide a classification by bug patterns; a similar study has been performed by Hu and Zhang [16] for the Python/C API. Kondoh and Onodera [20] check that native calls to Java methods should handle raised exceptions using a typestate analysis. Li and Tan [23] ensure that the native control-flow is correctly interrupted when a Java exception is raised. The work of Li and Tan [24,25] infers which Java exceptions may be raised by JNI code, allowing the exception type-safety property of Java programs to be extended to the JNI. CpyChecker [27] is a GCC plugin searching for common erroneous patterns in C code using the CPython API. Two works [26,28] aim at detecting reference counting errors in C code using the CPython API. Brown et al. [4] define specialized analyses for specific patterns of C++ interoperability that may jeopardize type or memory safety of JavaScript. Contrary to these works, we analyze both host and guest languages.

Multilanguage Semantics. The seminal work of Matthews and Findler [29] defines the first semantics of multilanguage systems, using the notion of boundaries to model conversion between languages. Buro and Mastroeni [7] generalize this construction using an algebraic framework. We use a similar notion of boundary in our concrete semantics.

Multilanguage Analyses. Buro et al. [6] define a theory based on abstract interpretation to combine analyses of different languages, and show how to lift the soundness property to the multilanguage setting. They provide an example of multilanguage setting where they combine a toy imperative language with a bit-level arithmetic language. The notion of boundary functions used in their work performs a full translation from the state of one language to the other. Our semantics works on the product of the states, although it can be seen as an abstraction of the semantics of C and Python, where the boundary performs a full state conversion (but the boundary from Python to C would be a concretization). From an implementation standpoint, our approach avoids costly state conversions at the boundary and allows sharing some abstract domains.

Chipounov et al. [8] perform symbolic execution of binaries, thus avoiding language considerations. Their approach is extended by the work of Bucur et al. [5], which supports any interpreted language by performing symbolic execution over the interpreter. Our approach is more costly to implement since we do not automatically lift the interpreter's code to obtain our analyzer. Thanks to its higher-level, we think our approach should be more precise and efficient.

The next works perform multilanguage analyses by translating specific effects of what native functions do (they usually generate a summary using a bottom-up analysis) to the host language. This allows removing the native code and use existing analyses of the host language. Tan and Morrisett [43] compile C code into an extended JVML syntax form, allowing the use of the bug-finding tool Jlint afterwards. Furr and Foster [12–14] perform inference of OCaml and Java types in C FFI code, which they crosscheck with the types used in the client OCaml/Java code. They assume there are no out-of-bounds accesses and no type casting in the C code. An inter-language, bottom-up taint analysis for Java and native binary code in the setting of Android applications is proposed by Wei et al. [45]. Lee et al. [22] aim at detecting wrong foreign function calls and mishandling of Java exceptions in Java/JNI code. They extract summaries of the Java callbacks and field accesses from the JNI code using Infer, transform these summaries into Java code, and call the FlowDroid analyzer on the whole. Contrary to these works, our analyzer supports both languages, and it switches between languages just as the real code does. The properties we target require precise context-sensitive value analyses that are difficult to perform bottom-up.

Library Analyses. Previous work aim at analyzing libraries with no access to their client code [1,38] using a "most-general client". The work of Kristensen and Møller [21] refines the notion of most-general client in the setting of dynamic programming languages. However, it focuses on libraries where functions are typed. Python libraries are not explicitly typed. Extending their work to our untyped, multilanguage setting is left as future work.

7 Conclusion

This article presents a multilanguage analysis able to infer runtime errors in Python code using native C extensions. Our analyzer is able to reuse value analyses of Python and C off-the-shelf. It shares the address allocation and numeric abstractions between the Python and C abstract domains. We are able to analyze within a few minutes real-world Python libraries written in C and having up to 5,800 lines of code. To the best of our knowledge, we have implemented the first static analyzer able to soundly detect runtime errors in multilanguage programs.

Future work includes extending our implementation to analyze the standard Python library and large Python applications. This will require handling more dependencies, having a relational analysis that scales, and addressing the precision limitations of the underlying C and Python analyses. We plan to instrument our implementation to verify (or infer) type annotations of the standard library provided in the typeshed [44] project. It would also be interesting to target multilanguage-specific safety properties (such as correct garbage collection counts). Another future work is to try our approach in other multilanguage settings (such as Java/C).

References

1. Allen, N., Krishnan, P., Scholz, B.: Combining type-analysis with points-to analysis for analyzing Java library source-code. In: SOAP@PLDI. ACM (2015)
2. Balakrishnan, G., Reps, T.: Recency-abstraction for heap-allocated storage. In: Yi, K. (ed.) SAS 2006. LNCS, vol. 4134, pp. 221–239. Springer, Heidelberg (2006). https://doi.org/10.1007/11823230_15
3. Blanchet, B., et al.: Design and implementation of a special-purpose static program analyzer for safety-critical real-time embedded software. In: Mogensen, T.Æ., Schmidt, D.A., Sudborough, I.H. (eds.) The Essence of Computation. LNCS, vol. 2566, pp. 85–108. Springer, Heidelberg (2002). https://doi.org/10.1007/3-540-36377-7_5
4. Brown, F., Narayan, S., Wahby, R.S., Engler, D.R., Jhala, R., Stefan, D.: Finding and preventing bugs in JavaScript bindings. In: SP. IEEE Computer Society (2017). https://doi.org/10.1109/SP.2017.68
5. Bucur, S., Kinder, J., Candea, G.: Prototyping symbolic execution engines for interpreted languages. In: ASPLOS, pp. 239–254. ACM (2014)
6. Buro, S., Crole, R.L., Mastroeni, I.: On multi-language abstraction. In: Pichardie, D., Sighireanu, M. (eds.) SAS 2020. LNCS, vol. 12389, pp. 310–332. Springer, Cham (2020). https://doi.org/10.1007/978-3-030-65474-0_14
7. Buro, S., Mastroeni, I.: On the multi-language construction. In: Caires, L. (ed.) ESOP 2019. LNCS, vol. 11423, pp. 293–321. Springer, Cham (2019). https://doi.org/10.1007/978-3-030-17184-1_11

8. Chipounov, V., Kuznetsov, V., Candea, G.: S2E: a platform for in-vivo multi-path analysis of software systems. In: ASPLOS, pp. 265–278. ACM (2011)
9. Cousot, P., Cousot, R.: Abstract interpretation: a unified lattice model for static analysis of programs by construction or approximation of fixpoints. In: POPL. ACM (1977)
10. Duncan, C.: Native-code and shader implementations of Perlin noise for Python (2021). https://github.com/caseman/noise. Accessed April 2021
11. Fromherz, A., Ouadjaout, A., Miné, A.: Static value analysis of python programs by abstract interpretation. In: Dutle, A., Muñoz, C., Narkawicz, A. (eds.) NFM 2018. LNCS, vol. 10811, pp. 185–202. Springer, Cham (2018). https://doi.org/10.1007/978-3-319-77935-5_14
12. Furr, M., Foster, J.S.: Checking type safety of foreign function calls. In: PLDI. ACM (2005). https://doi.org/10.1145/1065010.1065019
13. Furr, M., Foster, J.S.: Polymorphic type inference for the JNI. In: Sestoft, P. (ed.) ESOP 2006. LNCS, vol. 3924, pp. 309–324. Springer, Heidelberg (2006). https://doi.org/10.1007/11693024_21
14. Furr, M., Foster, J.S.: Checking type safety of foreign function calls. ACM Trans. Program. Lang. Syst. **30**(4), 1–63 (2008)
15. Haapala, A., Määttä, E., Jonatas, C.D., Ohtamaa, M., Necas, D.: Levenshtein Python C extension module (2021). https://github.com/ztane/python-Levenshtein/. Accessed April 2021
16. Hu, M., Zhang, Y.: The Python/C API: evolution, usage statistics, and bug patterns. In: SANER. IEEE (2020). https://doi.org/10.1109/SANER48275.2020.9054835
17. Jakubek, A., Gałczyński, R.: Linked lists for CPython (2021). https://github.com/ajakubek/python-llist. Accessed April 2021
18. Journault, M., Miné, A., Monat, R., Ouadjaout, A.: Combinations of reusable abstract domains for a multilingual static analyzer. In: Chakraborty, S., Navas, J.A. (eds.) VSTTE 2019. LNCS, vol. 12031, pp. 1–18. Springer, Cham (2020). https://doi.org/10.1007/978-3-030-41600-3_1
19. Journault, M., Miné, A., Monat, R., Ouadjaout, A.: MOPSA: modular open platform for static analysis (2021). https://gitlab.com/mopsa/mopsa-analyzer. Accessed April 2021
20. Kondoh, G., Onodera, T.: Finding bugs in Java native interface programs. In: ISSTA. ACM (2008). https://doi.org/10.1145/1390630.1390645
21. Kristensen, E.K., Møller, A.: Reasonably-most-general clients for JavaScript library analysis. In: ICSE. IEEE/ACM (2019). https://doi.org/10.1109/ICSE.2019.00026
22. Lee, S., Lee, H., Ryu, S.: Broadening horizons of multilingual static analysis: semantic summary extraction from C code for JNI program analysis. In: ASE. IEEE (2020). https://doi.org/10.1145/3324884.3416558
23. Li, S., Tan, G.: Finding bugs in exceptional situations of JNI programs. In: CCS. ACM (2009). https://doi.org/10.1145/1653662.1653716
24. Li, S., Tan, G.: JET: exception checking in the Java native interface. In: SPLASH. ACM (2011). https://doi.org/10.1145/2048066.2048095
25. Li, S., Tan, G.: Exception analysis in the Java native interface. Sci. Comput. Program. **89**, 273–297 (2014)
26. Li, S., Tan, G.: Finding reference-counting errors in Python/C programs with affine analysis. In: Jones, R. (ed.) ECOOP 2014. LNCS, vol. 8586, pp. 80–104. Springer, Heidelberg (2014). https://doi.org/10.1007/978-3-662-44202-9_4
27. Malcolm, D.: A static analysis tool for CPython extension code (2018). https://gcc-python-plugin.readthedocs.io/en/latest/cpychecker.html. Accessed April 2021

28. Mao, J., Chen, Y., Xiao, Q., Shi, Y.: RID: finding reference count bugs with inconsistent path pair checking. In: ASPLOS. ACM (2016). https://doi.org/10.1145/2872362.2872389
29. Matthews, J., Findler, R.B.: Operational semantics for multi-language programs. ACM Trans. Program. Lang. Syst. **31**(3), 1–44 (2009)
30. Meyer, M.: Distance library (2021). https://github.com/doukremt/distance. Accessed April 2021
31. Miné, A.: Field-sensitive value analysis of embedded C programs with union types and pointer arithmetics. In: LCTES. ACM (2006)
32. Miné, A.: The octagon abstract domain. High. Order Symb. Comput. **19**(1), 31–100 (2006)
33. Monat, R., Ouadjaout, A., Miné, A.: Static type analysis by abstract interpretation of Python programs. In: ECOOP, Schloss Dagstuhl - Leibniz-Zentrum für Informatik (2020). https://doi.org/10.4230/LIPIcs.ECOOP.2020.17
34. Monat, R., Ouadjaout, A., Miné, A.: Value and allocation sensitivity in static Python analyses. In: SOAP@PLDI. ACM (2020). https://doi.org/10.1145/3394451.3397205
35. Monat, R., Ouadjaout, A., Miné, A.: A multi-language static analysis of Python programs with native C extensions, July 2021. https://doi.org/10.5281/zenodo.5141314
36. Muła, W., Ombredanne, P.: Pyahocorasick library (2021). https://github.com/WojciechMula/pyahocorasick. Accessed April 2021
37. Ouadjaout, A., Miné, A.: A library modeling language for the static analysis of C programs. In: Pichardie, D., Sighireanu, M. (eds.) SAS 2020. LNCS, vol. 12389, pp. 223–247. Springer, Cham (2020). https://doi.org/10.1007/978-3-030-65474-0_11
38. Rinetzky, N., Poetzsch-Heffter, A., Ramalingam, G., Sagiv, M., Yahav, E.: Modular shape analysis for dynamically encapsulated programs. In: De Nicola, R. (ed.) ESOP 2007. LNCS, vol. 4421, pp. 220–236. Springer, Heidelberg (2007). https://doi.org/10.1007/978-3-540-71316-6_16
39. van Rossum, G., Lehtosalo, J., Langa, Ł.: Python Enhancement Proposal 484 (2021). https://www.python.org/dev/peps/pep-0484/. Accessed 03 Mar 2021
40. van Rossum, G.: The Python development team: Python/C API reference manual (2021). https://docs.python.org/3.8/c-api/index.html. Accessed April 2021
41. Schnell, I.: Bitarray library (2021). https://github.com/ilanschnell/bitarray. Accessed April 2021
42. Tan, G., Croft, J.: An empirical security study of the native code in the JDK. In: USENIX. USENIX Association (2008)
43. Tan, G., Morrisett, G.: ILEA: inter-language analysis across Java and C. In: OOPSLA. ACM (2007). https://doi.org/10.1145/1297027.1297031
44. Typeshed contributors: Typeshed (2021). https://github.com/python/typeshed/. Accessed April 2021
45. Wei, F., Lin, X., Ou, X., Chen, T., Zhang, X.: JN-SAF: precise and efficient NDK/JNI-aware inter-language static analysis framework for security vetting of Android applications with native code. In: SIGSAC. ACM (2018). https://doi.org/10.1145/3243734.3243835

Automated Verification of the Parallel Bellman–Ford Algorithm

Mohsen Safari[1], Wytse Oortwijn[2], and Marieke Huisman[1(✉)]

[1] Formal Methods and Tools, University of Twente, Enschede, The Netherlands
{m.safari,m.huisman}@utwente.nl
[2] ESI (TNO), Eindhoven, The Netherlands
wytse.oortwijn@tno.nl

Abstract. Many real-world problems such as internet routing are actually graph problems. To develop efficient solutions to such problems, more and more parallel graph algorithms are proposed. This paper discusses the mechanized verification of a commonly used parallel graph algorithm, namely the Bellman–Ford algorithm, which provides an inherently parallel solution to the Single-Source Shortest Path problem.

Concretely, we verify an unoptimized GPU version of the Bellman–Ford algorithm, using the VerCors verifier. The main challenge that we had to address was to find suitable global invariants of the graph-based properties for automated verification. This case study is the first deductive verification to prove functional correctness of the parallel Bellman–Ford algorithm. It provides the basis to verify other, optimized implementations of the algorithm. Moreover, it may also provide a good starting point to verify other parallel graph-based algorithms.

Keywords: Deductive verification · Graph algorithms · Parallel algorithms · GPU · Bellman–Ford · Case study

1 Introduction

Graph algorithms play an important role in computer science, as many real-world problems can be handled by defining suitable graph representations. This makes the correctness of such algorithms crucially important. As the real-world problems that we represent using graphs are growing exponentially in size—think for

The first and third author are supported by the NWO VICI 639.023.710 Mercedes project.

C. Drăgoi et al. (Eds.): SAS 2021, LNCS 12913, pp. 346–358, 2021.
https://doi.org/10.1007/978-3-030-88806-0_17

example about internet routing solutions—we need highly efficient, but still correct(!), graph algorithms. Massively parallel computing, as supported on GPUs for example, can help to obtain the required efficiency, but also introduces extra challenges to reason about the correctness of such parallel graph algorithms.

In the literature, several verification techniques to reason about the correctness of massively parallel algorithms have been proposed, see e.g. [5,7,11,25,26]. This paper uses such a verification technique to develop a mechanized proof of a parallel GPU-based graph algorithm. Our verification is based on deductive program verification, using a permission-based separation logic for GPU programs [7] as implemented in the VerCors program verifier [6]. In VerCors, the program to be verified is annotated with a specification, as well as intermediate (invariant) properties. From these annotations, suitable proof obligations are generated, which can then be discharged with Z3. Given the annotated program, the verification process is fully automatic.

The concrete graph algorithm that we study here is the Bellman–Ford algorithm [3,15], a solution for the Single-Source Shortest Path (SSSP) problem. This algorithm computes the shortest distance from a specific vertex to all other vertices in a graph, where the distance is measured in terms of arc weights. Other solutions exist for this problem, such as Dijkstra's shortest path algorithm [14]. However, the Bellman–Ford algorithm is inherently parallel, which makes it suitable to be used on massively parallel architectures, such as GPUs.

In this paper, we prove race freedom, memory safety and functional correctness of a standard parallel GPU-based Bellman–Ford algorithm. This correctness proof can be used as a starting point to also derive correctness of the various optimized implementations that have been proposed in the literature [1,9,18,20,32,34]. Moreover, this work and the experiences with automated reasoning about GPU-based graph algorithms will also provide a good starting point to verify other parallel GPU-based graph algorithms.

To the best of our knowledge, there is no similar work in the literature on the automated mechanized verification of parallel GPU-based graph algorithms— Bellman–Ford in particular. Previous works on graph algorithm verification either target sequential algorithms, or abstractions of concurrent non-GPU-based algorithms. Furthermore, most previous works on GPU program verification focus on proving memory safety/crash and race freedom, but not on functional correctness. In contrast, we prove functional correctness of the GPU-based Bellman–Ford algorithm.

The main challenge that we had to address in this work, was to find the suitable global invariants to reason about the graph-based algorithm, and in particular to make those amenable to mechanized verification. Therefore, we first outline the manual correctness proof, and then discuss how we formalized this proof in VerCors. As mentioned before, the Bellman–Ford algorithm is inherently parallel, and our proof indeed demonstrates this.

Organization. Section 2 discusses the Bellman–Ford algorithm, and also gives a brief introduction to the VerCors verifier. Section 3 discusses the manual proof of the algorithm, in particular introducing all the necessary invariants. Section 4

```
1  int[] Bellman–Ford(G, s) {
2     int[] cost = new int[|V|]; // declare cost array
3     cost[s] := 0; // initialize cost array
4     for every v ∈ V \ {s} do cost[v] := ∞;
5     for (i = 0 up to |V| − 1) { // start |V| − 1 rounds of cost relaxations
6        for every a ∈ A { // check every arc for potential cost relaxations
7           if (cost[src(a)] + w(a) < cost[dst(a)])
8              cost[dst(a)] := cost[src(a)] + w(a); // perform a cost relaxation
9        }
10    }
11    return cost;
12 }
```

Fig. 1. Pseudo-code implementation of the (sequential) Bellman–Ford algorithm.

continues with the formal proof by encoding the informal proof into the Ver-Cors verifier. Section 5 explains the evaluation and lessons learned from this case study. Section 6 discusses related work and Sect. 7 concludes the paper.

2   Background

This section describes the (parallel) Bellman–Ford algorithm (Sect. 2.1), and gives a brief introduction on deductive code verification with VerCors (Sect. 2.2).

2.1   The Bellman–Ford Algorithm

A directed weighted graph $G = (V, A, w)$ is a triple consisting of a finite set V of vertices, an binary arc relation $A \subseteq V \times V$, and a weight function $w : A \to \mathbb{N}$ over arcs. In the remainder of this paper we assume that A is irreflexive, since we do not consider graphs that contain self-loops. The *source* and *destination* of any arc $a = (u, v) \in A$ is defined $\mathsf{src}(a) \triangleq u$ and $\mathsf{dst}(a) \triangleq v$, respectively. Any finite arc sequence $P = (a_0, a_1, \ldots, a_n) \in A^*$ is a *path in G* if $\mathsf{dst}(a_i) = \mathsf{src}(a_{i+1})$ for every $0 \leq i < n$. We say that P is an (u, v)-*path* if $\mathsf{src}(a_0) = u$ and $\mathsf{dst}(a_n) = v$, under the condition that $0 < n$. The *length of P* is denoted $|P|$ and defined to be $n+1$. The *weight* of any path P is denoted $w(P)$, with w overloaded and lifted to sequences of arcs $A^* \to \mathbb{N}$ as follows: $w(a_0, a_1, \ldots, a_n) \triangleq \Sigma_{i=0}^n w(a_i)$. Any path P is *simple* if all its vertices are unique. Finally, any (u, v)-path P is a *shortest* (u, v)-*path in G* if for every (u, v)-path Q in G it holds that $w(P) \leq w(Q)$.

The Bellman–Ford algorithm [3,15] solves the *Single-Source Shortest Path (SSSP) problem*: given any input graph $G = (V, A, w)$ and vertex $s \in V$, find for any vertex $v \in V$ reachable from s the weight of the shortest (s, v)-path. Figure 1 shows the algorithm in pseudo-code. It takes as input a graph G and starting vertex s. The idea is to associate a cost to every vertex v, which amounts to the weight of the shortest (s, v)-path that has been found up to round i of the algorithm. Initially, s has cost 0 (line 3), while all other vertices start with cost

∞ (line 4). Then the algorithm operates in $|V| - 1$ rounds (line 5). In every round i, the cost of vertex v is *relaxed* on lines 7–8 in case a cheaper possibility of reaching v is found. After $|V| - 1$ such rounds of relaxations, the weights of the shortest paths to all reachable vertices have been found, intuitively because no simple path can contain more than $|V| - 1$ arcs.

The Bellman–Ford algorithm can straightforwardly be parallelized on a GPU, by executing the iterations of the for-loop on line 6 in parallel, thereby exploiting that arcs can be iterated over in arbitrary order. Such a parallelization requires lines 7–8 to be executed atomically, and all threads to synchronize (by a possibly implicit barrier) between every iteration of the round loop.

This paper demonstrates how VerCors is used to mechanically verify *soundness* and *completeness* of the parallelized version of the Bellman–Ford algorithm. Soundness in this context means that, after completion of the algorithm, for any $v \in V$ such that $\mathsf{cost}[v] < \infty$ it holds that there exists a shortest (s, v)-path P such that $\mathsf{cost}[v] = w(P)$. The property of completeness is that, for any v if there exists an (s, v)-path P after completion of the algorithm, it holds that $\mathsf{cost}[v] < \infty$. In addition to soundness and completeness we also use VerCors to verify memory safety and race-freedom of parallel Bellman–Ford.

2.2 The VerCors Verifier

VerCors [6] is an automated, SMT-based code verifier specialized in reasoning about parallel and concurrent software. VerCors takes programs as input that are annotated with logical specifications, and can automatically verify whether the code implementation adheres to these specifications. The specifications are formulated in a Concurrent Separation Logic (CSL) that supports permission accounting, and are annotated as pre/postconditions for functions and threads, and invariants for loops and locks [2,7]. However, to keep the paper accessible, this paper describes the formalization independent of specific knowledge of CSL, and explains any further necessary details whenever needed.

3 Approach

Our strategy for verifying parallel Bellman–Ford is to first construct an informal pen-and-paper proof of its correctness, and then to encode this proof in VerCors to mechanically check all proof steps. This section elaborates on the (informal) correctness argument of Bellman–Ford, after which Sect. 4 explains how this argument is encoded in, and then confirmed by, VerCors.

Postconditions. Proving correctness of parallel Bellman–Ford amounts to proving that the following three postconditions hold after termination of the algorithm, when given as input a graph $G = (V, A, w)$ and starting vertex $s \in V$:

$$\forall v.\, \mathsf{cost}[v] < \infty \implies \exists P.\, \mathsf{Path}(P, s, v) \land w(P) = \mathsf{cost}[v] \qquad \text{(PC1)}$$

$$\forall v.\, (\exists P.\, \mathsf{Path}(P, s, v)) \implies \mathsf{cost}[v] < \infty \qquad \text{(PC2)}$$

$$\forall v.\, \mathsf{cost}[v] < \infty \implies \forall P.\, \mathsf{Path}(P, s, v) \implies \mathsf{cost}[v] \leq w(P) \qquad \text{(PC3)}$$

The predicate $\mathsf{Path}(P, u, v)$ expresses that P is an (u, v)-path in G.

These three postconditions together express that cost characterizes reachable states as well as shortest paths. PC1 and PC2 imply soundness and completeness of reachability: $\mathsf{cost}[v] < \infty$ if and only if v is reachable from s. PC3 additionally ensures that cost contains the weights of all shortest paths in G.

Invariants. Our approach for proving the three postconditions above is to introduce *round invariants*: invariants for the loop on line 5 in Fig. 1 that should hold at the start and end of every round i for each thread. The proposed (round) invariants are:

$$\forall v \,.\, \mathsf{cost}[v] < \infty \implies \exists P \,.\, \mathsf{Path}(P, s, v) \land w(P) = \mathsf{cost}[v] \qquad (\text{INV1})$$

$$\forall v \,.\, (\exists P \,.\, \mathsf{Path}(P, s, v) \land |P| \le i) \implies \mathsf{cost}[v] < \infty \qquad (\text{INV2})$$

$$\forall v \,.\, \mathsf{cost}[v] < \infty \implies \forall P \,.\, \mathsf{Path}(P, s, v) \land |P| \le i \implies \mathsf{cost}[v] \le w(P) \qquad (\text{INV3})$$

One can prove that the round invariants imply the postconditions after termination of the round loop, as then $i = |V| - 1$. PC1 immediately follows from INV1 without additional proof. Proving that PC2 and PC3 follow from INV2 and INV3 resp. requires more work since these postconditions quantify over paths of unbounded length.

Therefore, we introduce an operation $\mathsf{simple}(P)$ that removes all cycles from any given (u, v)-path P, and gives a simple (u, v)-path, which makes it easy to establish the postconditions. The three main properties of simple that are needed for proving the postconditions are $|\mathsf{simple}(P)| \le |V| - 1$, $|\mathsf{simple}(P)| \le |P|$, and $w(\mathsf{simple}(P)) \le w(P)$ for any P. The latter two hold since $\mathsf{simple}(P)$ can only shorten P. Here we detail the proof for PC3; the proof for PC2 is similar.

Lemma 1. *If $i = |V| - 1$ then INV3 implies PC3.*

Proof. Let v be an arbitrary vertex such that $\mathsf{cost}[v] < \infty$, and P be an arbitrary (s, v)-path. Then $\mathsf{cost}[v] \le w(P)$ is shown by instantiating INV3 with v and $\mathsf{simple}(P)$, from which one can easily prove $\mathsf{cost}[v] \le w(\mathsf{simple}(P)) \le w(P)$. $\square$

Preservation of Invariants. However, proving that each round of the algorithm preserves the round invariants is significantly more challenging. It is non-trivial to show that validity of invariants INV1–INV3 at round $i + 1$ follows from their validity at round i combined with the contributions of all threads in round i. An additional difficulty is that cost relaxations are performed in arbitrary order.

Our approach was to first work out the proof details in pen-and-paper style, and to later encode all proof steps in VerCors. We highlight one interesting case:

Lemma 2. *Every iteration of the loop on lines 5–10 in Fig. 1 preserves INV3.*

Proof (outline). Suppose that INV1–INV3 hold on round i, that $i < |V| - 1$, and that all cost relaxations have happened for round i (i.e., lines 6–9 have been fully executed). We show that INV3 holds for $i + 1$. We write $\mathsf{old}(\mathsf{cost}[v])$ to refer to the "old" cost that any v had at the beginning of round i.

We create a proof by contradiction. Suppose that there exists a vertex v and an (s, v)-path P such that $\mathsf{cost}[v] < \infty$, $|P| \leq i + 1$, and $w(P) < \mathsf{cost}[v]$. It must be the case that $|P| = i + 1$, since otherwise, if $|P| < i + 1$, then INV1 and INV2 together would imply that $\mathsf{old}(\mathsf{cost}[v]) < w(P)$, which is impossible since vertex costs can only decrease. So P consists of at least one arc. Let a be the last arc on P so that $\mathsf{dst}(a) = v$, and let P' be the path P but without a, so that P' is an $(s, \mathsf{src}(a))$-path of length i. Let us abbreviate $\mathsf{src}(a)$ as v'. Instantiating INV2 and INV3 with v' and P' gives $\mathsf{old}(\mathsf{cost}[v']) < \infty$ and $\mathsf{old}(\mathsf{cost}[v']) < w(P')$.

Let us now consider what a's thread could have done in round i. When this thread got scheduled it must have observed that v' and v had some intermediate costs, which we refer to as $obs_{v'}$ and obs_v, respectively, for which it holds that $\mathsf{cost}[v'] \leq obs_{v'} \leq \mathsf{old}(\mathsf{cost}[v'])$ and $\mathsf{cost}[v] \leq obs_v \leq \mathsf{old}(\mathsf{cost}[v])$. And since

$$obs_{v'} + w(a) \leq \mathsf{old}(\mathsf{cost}[v']) + w(a) \leq w(P') + w(a) = w(P) < \mathsf{cost}[v] \leq obs_v$$

we know that a's thread must have updated the cost of v to be $obs_{v'} + w(a)$ in its turn. Since v's cost might have decreased further in round i by other threads, we have $\mathsf{cost}[v] \leq obs_{v'} + w(a) \leq w(P)$, which contradicts $w(P) < \mathsf{cost}[v]$. □

This proof outline emphasizes the non-triviality of verifying the Bellman–Ford algorithm using automated code verifiers. Interestingly, also all other invariant preservation proofs have been performed as a proof by contradiction.

4 Proof Mechanization

So far the correctness argument of parallel Bellman–Ford has been presented at the abstract level of mathematical definitions and pseudocode. This section discusses how this abstract reasoning translates to the GPU version of Bellman–Ford, by formalizing its correctness proof in VerCors. This required (i) encoding all specifications introduced in Sect. 3 into the VerCors specification language, (ii) adding additional permission specifications to guarantee memory safety, and (iii) using these specifications to formulate pre- and postconditions, as well as loop and lock invariants for the algorithm encoding. For step (i), the main challenge was to give these specifications in terms of concrete GPU data types, rather than mathematical structures (e.g., defining a graph representation in C arrays instead of mathematical sets). Furthermore, GPU memory (as a scarce resource) imposes more restrictions on how to represent large graphs in an efficient way (e.g., using a one-dimensional array instead of matrices, and assigning threads to arcs instead of vertices). For step (iii), the main challenge was to encode the lemmas and their proofs, as introduced in Sect. 3. We use *lemma functions* for this, which are pure functions whose function specification corresponds to the lemma property. The challenge was to encode the proofs of these lemmas in VerCors, as discussed in more detail below. The end result of our verification effort is the first machine-checked proof of a GPU version of parallel Bellman-Ford. The remainder of this section elaborates on the formalization of the informal specifications and proof outlines in VerCors, and on how these are used to verify the concrete GPU host and kernel code.

```
1  kernel_invariant \pointer((src, dst, w), A, read);
2  kernel_invariant \pointer(cost, V, write);
3  kernel_invariant ···; // encodings of INV1, INV2 and INV3
4  void Kernel-BF(int V, int A, int[] src, int[] dst, int[] w, int[] cost, int s) {
5      int tid = blockIdx.x × 512 + threadIdx.x;
6      atomicMin(&cost[dst[tid]], cost[src[tid]] + w[tid]);
7  }
8  context Graph(V, A, src, dst, w);
9  context \pointer((src, dst, w), A, read) ∧ \pointer(cost, V, write);
10 ensures ∀v. 0 ≤ v < V ∧ cost[v] < infty() ⇒ // encoding of PC1
11     ∃P. Path(V, A, src, dst, w, s, v, P) ∧ Weight(V, A, src, dst, w, P) = cost[v];
12 ensures ∀v. 0 ≤ v < V ⇒ // encoding of PC2
13     ∃P. Path(V, A, src, dst, w, s, v, P) ⇒ cost[v] < infty();
14 ensures ∀v. 0 ≤ v < V ∧ cost[v] < infty() ⇒ // encoding of PC3
15     ∀P. Path(V, A, src, dst, w, s, v, P) ⇒ cost[v] ≤ Weight(V, A, src, dst, w, P);
16 void Host-BF(int V, int A, int[] src, int[] dst, int[] w, int[] cost, int s) {
17     invariant Graph(V, A, src, dst, w);
18     invariant
         \pointer((src, dst, w), A, read) ∧ \pointer(cost, V, write);
19     invariant ∀v. 0 ≤ v < V ∧ cost[v] < infty() ⇒ // encoding of INV1
20         ∃P. Path(V, A, src, dst, w, s, v, P) ∧ Weight(V, A, src, dst, w, P) = cost[v];
21     invariant ∀v. (0 ≤ v < V ∧ ∃P. Path(V, A, src, dst, w, s, v, P) ∧ |P| ≤ i) ⇒
22         cost[v] < infty(); // encoding of INV2
23     invariant ∀v. 0 ≤ v < V ∧ cost[v] < infty() ⇒
24         ∀P. Path(V, A, src, dst, w, s, v, P) ∧ |P| ≤ i ⇒
25             cost[v] ≤ Weight(V, A, src, dst, w, P); // encoding of INV3
26     for (i = 0 up to V − 1) {
27         Kernel-BF(V, A, src, dst, w, cost, s);
28         lemma_inv_pres(...); // apply invariant preservation lemma functions
29     }
30     lemma_post_establ(...); // apply postcond. establishment lemma functions
31 }
```

Fig. 2. The simplified GPU version of Bellman-Ford, annotated with VerCors specifications. The total number of threads (*tid*) is the same as the number of arcs (*A*).

Proof Outline and Specification Encoding. Figure 2 presents a simplified[1] overview of our specification of parallel Bellman–Ford. Lines 1–7 and lines 8–31 show the annotated CPU host code and GPU kernel code, respectively. Observe that the algorithm uses a representation of directed weighted graphs that is typical for GPU implementations: using three C arrays, src, dst and w.

On line 8 in the specification we require (and ensure)[2] that these three arrays indeed form a graph, by means of the predicate Graph(V, A, src, dst, w),

---

[1] Various details have been omitted for presentational clarity. We highlight only the most interesting aspects of the specification. The full specification is available at [31].

[2] The keyword context is an abbreviation for both requires and ensures.

```
1 pure bool Graph(int V, int A, int[] src, int[] dst, int[] w) =
2   0 < V ∧ 0 < A ∧ |src| = A ∧ |dst| = A ∧ |w| = A ∧
3   (∀i . 0 ≤ i < A ⇒ 0 ≤ src[i] < V ∧ 0 ≤ dst[i] < V ∧ src[i] ≠ dst[i] ∧ 0 < w[i]) ∧
4   (∀i,j . 0 ≤ i < A ∧ 0 ≤ j < A ∧ i ≠ j ∧ src[i] = src[j] ⇒ dst[i] ≠ dst[j]);
```

Fig. 3. The Graph predicate, that determines whether src, dst and w form a graph.

as defined in Fig. 3. The integer V represents the total number of vertices, and A the total number of arcs. Then any index $a \in [0, A)$ represents an arc from src[a] to dst[a] with weight w[a]. Similarly, any index $v \in [0, V)$ represents a vertex in the graph such that cost[v] is the current cost assigned to v by the algorithm. The integer s, with $0 \leq s < V$, is the starting vertex. This representation can handle large graphs on GPU memory, and by assigning threads to arcs more parallelism and hence more performance can be obtained.

Lines 10–15 and 19–25 contain the VerCors encoding of the postconditions and round invariants introduced in Sect. 3, respectively. These encodings are defined over various other predicates such as Path and Weight, whose definitions are the same in spirit as the one of Graph.

Verifying Memory Safety. Verifying data-race freedom requires explicitly specifying ownership over heap locations using *fractional permissions*, in the style of Boyland [8]. Fractional permissions capture which heap locations may be accessed by which threads. We use the predicate \pointer$((S_0, \ldots, S_n), \ell, \pi)$ to indicate that all array references $S_0, \ldots, S_n$ have length ℓ, and that the current thread has permission $\pi \in (0, 1]$ for them[3]. We often use the keywords **read** and **write** instead of concrete fractional values to indicate read or write access.

Lines 9 and 18 indicate that initially and in each iteration of the algorithm we have read permission over all locations in src, dst and w. Moreover, we also have write permission over all locations in cost. Within the kernel, threads execute in parallel, meaning that the updates to cost have to be done atomically (line 6)[4]. The kernel invariants specify shared resources and properties that may be used by a thread while in the critical section. After leaving the critical section, the thread should ensure all the kernel invariants are re-established (see [2] for more details).

The kernel invariants on lines 1 and 2 specify that each thread within the critical section has read permission over all locations in src, dst and w (line 1) and write permission in cost (line 2). Note that the atomic operations execute in an arbitrary order, but as there always is at most one thread within the critical section, this is sufficient to guarantee data-race freedom.

Lemma Functions. As mentioned above, to show the preservation of INV1, INV2 and INV3 we apply the corresponding lemmas at the end of the loop (line 28).

---

[3] To specify permissions over a specific location *idx* of an array S we use \pointer_index(S, idx, π), where *idx* is a proper index in S.

[4] atomicMin() is a built-in GPU function that compares its two arguments and assigns the minimum one to the first argument.

```
1  requires Graph(...) ∧ 0 ≤ i < V − 1 ∧ |P| ≤ i + 1;
2  requires cost[v] ≤ oldcost[v] < infty();
3  requires Weight(V, A, src, dst, w, P) < cost[v];
4  requires ∀a . 0 ≤ a < A ∧ oldcost[src[a]]+w[a] < oldcost[dst[a]] ⇒
5     cost[dst[a]] ≤ oldcost[src[a]] + w[a];
6  requires ∀v . 0 ≤ v < V ∧ cost[v] < infty() ⇒
7     ∃P . Path(V, A, src, dst, w, s, v, P)∧
8        Weight(V, A, src, dst, w, P) = oldcost[v]; // encoding of INV1
9  requires ∀v . (0 ≤ v < V ∧ ∃P . Path(V, A, src, dst, w, s, v, P) ∧ |P| ≤ i) ⇒
10    oldcost[v] < infty(); // encoding of INV2
11 requires ∀v . 0 ≤ v < V ∧ oldcost[v] < infty() ⇒
12    ∀P . Path(V, A, src, dst, w, s, v, P) ∧ |P| ≤ i ⇒
13       oldcost[v] ≤ Weight(V, A, src, dst, w, P); // encoding of INV3
14 ensures false;
15 pure bool lemma_2(int i, int v, int[] P, ...) {
16    assert 0 < |P| ∧ |P| = i + 1; a := P[|P| − 1]; P' := P[0 .. |P| − 2];
17    assert |P'| ≤ i; v' := src(a);
18    assert oldcost[v'] ≤ Weight(V, A, src, dst, w, P'); // from INV2 and INV3
19    assert cost[v'] ≤ oldcost[v'] ∧ cost[v'] ≤ Weight(V, A, src, dst, w, P');
20    assert lemma-transitivity(V, A, src, dst, w, s, v', v, P', a);
21    assert cost[v] ≤ Weight(V, A, src, dst, w, P); // contradiction
22 }
```

Fig. 4. The (simplified) VerCors encoding of Lemma 2.

Note that these invariants must hold in the kernel as well (line 3). Similarly, to establish PC1, PC2 and PC3 we apply the corresponding lemmas after termination of the loop when $i = |V| - 1$ (line 30).

All the proofs of the lemmas mentioned in Sect. 3 that show the preservation of the round invariants and establishment of postconditions are encoded in VerCors as *lemma functions* [16, 35]. Lemma functions have specifications that capture the desired property, while the proof is encoded as a side effect-free imperative program. Most of our lemmas (e.g., the proof of Lemma 2) were proven by contradiction. Proving a property ϕ by contradiction amounts to proving $\neg \phi \Rightarrow$ false. Therefore, to show preservation of, e.g., INV3 (Lemma 2), we proved that $(\text{INV1}(i) \land \text{INV2}(i) \land \text{INV3}(i) \land \phi(i) \land \neg \text{INV3}(i + 1)) \Rightarrow$ false, with $\phi(i)$ describing the contributions of all threads in round i.

Lemma 4 shows how the VerCors encoding of Lemma 2 looks, where the lemma is implicitly quantified over the function parameters: iteration round i, vertex v, and path P. The function body encodes all proof steps. The main challenge was finding the precise assertions that explicitly describe all the steps from the informal proof. In particular, we had to prove various auxiliary lemmas such as lemma-transitivity (line 20), which models the transitivity property of paths along with its weight, and which required an induction over paths in its proof.

5   Evaluation and Discussion

Evaluation. The algorithm encoding and its specification consists of 541 lines of code. Of these 541 lines, 30 are for the encoding of the algorithm (5.5%) and the remaining 511 are specification (94.5%). The specification part can be subdivided further: of the 511 lines, 6.1% is related to permissions, 30.7% to invariant preservation proofs, 45.1% to proofs for establishing the postconditions, and 18.1% to definitions (e.g., of graphs and paths) and proving basic properties.

The total verification effort was about six weeks. Most of this time was spent on the mechanization aspects: spelling out all the details that were left implicit in the the pen-and-paper proof. The fully annotated Bellman–Ford implementation takes about 12 min to verify using VerCors on a Macbook Pro (early 2017) with 16 GB RAM, and an Intel Core i5 3.1 GHz CPU.

Discussion. In order to understand what verification techniques are suitable and effective for verifying parallel algorithms, we need the experience from different non-trivial case studies such as the one in this paper. Therefore, the value of this case study is more than just the verification of Bellman–Ford.

This case study confirms the importance of lemma functions in verifying non-trivial case studies, and in particular for encoding proofs by contradiction, which are common in the context of graphs. This paper also gives a representation of graphs that is suitable for GPU architectures, and can form the foundation of other verifications. Finally, we learned that deductive code verifiers are powerful enough to reason about non-trivial parallel algorithms—but they cannot do this yet without the human expertize to guide the prover.

6   Related Work

The work that is closest to ours is by Wimmer et al. [39], who prove correctness of a sequential version of the Bellman–Ford algorithm using Isabelle. Their proof strategy is different from ours: they use a framework from Kleinberg and Tardos [21] to refine a correct recursive function into an efficient imperative implementation. They first define Bellman–Ford as a recursive function that computes the shortest distances between all vertices using dynamic programming, and then use Isabelle to prove that it returns the shortest path. Then this recursive function is refined into an efficient imperative implementation (see the proof in [36]). However, this imperative implementation cannot be naturally parallelized. Moreover, because of the refinement approach, their correctness arguments are different from ours and do not depend on property preservation, which makes them unsuitable for standard deductive code verification.

In the literature there is ample work on the verification of other sequential graph algorithms. Some of these verifications are fully automatic, while others are semi-automatically done by interactive provers. Lammich et al. [23,24] propose a framework for verifying sequential DFS in Isabelle [19]. Chen et al. [10] provide a formal correctness proof of Tarjan's sequential SCC algorithm using three (both automated and interactive) proof systems: Why3 [38], Coq [12] and Isabelle. There is also a collection of verified sequential graph algorithms in Why3 [37]. Van de Pol [29] verified the sequential Nested DFS algorithm in Dafny [13]. Guéneau et al. [17] improved Bender et al.'s [4] incremental cycle detection algorithm to turn it into an online algorithm. They implemented it in OCaml and proved its functional correctness and worst-case amortized asymptotic complexity (using Separation logic combined with Time Credits).

In contrast, there is only limited work on the verification of concurrent graph algorithms. Raad et al. [30] verified four concurrent graph algorithms using a logic without abstraction (CoLoSL), but their proofs have not been automated. Sergey et al. [33] verified a concurrent spanning tree algorithm using Coq.

As far as we are aware, there is no work on automated code verification of massively parallel GPU-based graph algorithms. Most similar to our approach is the work by Oortwijn et al. [27,28], who discuss the automated verification of the parallel Nested Depth First Search (NDFS) algorithm of Laarman et al. [22]. Although they are the first to provide a mechanical proof of a parallel graph algorithm, their target is not massively parallel programs on GPUs.

7   Conclusion

Graph algorithms play an important role in solving many real-world problems. This paper shows how to mechanically prove correctness of the parallel Bellman–Ford GPU algorithm, with VerCors. To the best of our knowledge, this is the first work on automatic code verification of this algorithm.

Since we prove the general classic Bellman–Ford algorithm without applying GPU optimization techniques, we plan to investigate how to reuse the current proof for the optimized implementations. Moreover, we also would like to investigate how we can generate part of the annotations automatically.

References

1. Agarwal, P., Dutta, M.: New approach of Bellman Ford algorithm on GPU using compute unified design architecture (CUDA). Int. J. Comput. Appl. **110**(13) (2015)
2. Amighi, A., Darabi, S., Blom, S., Huisman, M.: Specification and verification of atomic operations in GPGPU programs. In: SEFM, vol. 9276 (2015)
3. Bellman, R.: On a routing problem. Q. Appl. Math. **16**, 87–90 (1958)
4. Bender, M.A., Fineman, J.T., Gilbert, S., Tarjan, R.E.: A new approach to incremental cycle detection and related problems. ACM Trans. Algorith. (TALG) **12**(2), 1–22 (2015)
5. Betts, A., Chong, N., Donaldson, A., Qadeer, S., Thomson, P.: GPUVerify: a verifier for GPU kernels. In: OOPSLA, pp. 113–132. ACM (2012)
6. Blom, S., Darabi, S., Huisman, M., Oortwijn, W.: The VerCors tool set: verification of parallel and concurrent software. In: Polikarpova, N., Schneider, S. (eds.) IFM 2017. LNCS, vol. 10510, pp. 102–110. Springer, Cham (2017). https://doi.org/10.1007/978-3-319-66845-1_7

7. Blom, S., Huisman, M., Mihelčić, M.: Specification and verification of GPGPU programs. Sci. Comput. Prog. **95**, 376–388 (2014)
8. Boyland, J.: Checking interference with fractional permissions. In: Cousot, R. (ed.) SAS 2003. LNCS, vol. 2694, pp. 55–72. Springer, Heidelberg (2003). https://doi.org/10.1007/3-540-44898-5_4
9. Busato, F., Bombieri, N.: An efficient implementation of the Bellman-Ford algorithm for Kepler GPU architectures. IEEE Trans. Parall. Distrib. Syst. **27**(8), 2222–2233 (2016)
10. Chen, R., Cohen, C., Lévy, J.J., Merz, S., Théry, L.: Formal proofs of Tarjan's algorithm in Why3, Coq, and Isabelle. arXiv preprint arXiv:1810.11979 (2018)
11. Collingbourne, P., Cadar, C., Kelly, P.H.J.: Symbolic testing of openCL code. In: Eder, K., Lourenço, J., Shehory, O. (eds.) HVC 2011. LNCS, vol. 7261, pp. 203–218. Springer, Heidelberg (2012). https://doi.org/10.1007/978-3-642-34188-5_18
12. The Coq proof assistant. https://coq.inria.fr/
13. Dafny program verifier, https://www.microsoft.com/en-us/research/project/dafny-a-language-and-program-verifier-for-functional-correctness/
14. Dijkstra, E.W.: A note on two problems in connexion with graphs. Numerische mathematik **1**(1), 269–271 (1959)
15. Ford, L.R., Jr.: Network flow theory. Tech. rep, DTIC Document (1956)
16. Grov, G., Tumas, V.: Tactics for the Dafny program verifier. In: Chechik, M., Raskin, J.-F. (eds.) TACAS 2016. LNCS, vol. 9636, pp. 36–53. Springer, Heidelberg (2016). https://doi.org/10.1007/978-3-662-49674-9_3
17. Guéneau, A., Jourdan, J.H., Charguéraud, A., Pottier, F.: Formal proof and analysis of an incremental cycle detection algorithm. In: Interactive Theorem Proving. No. 141, Schloss Dagstuhl-Leibniz-Zentrum fuer Informatik (2019)
18. Hajela, G., Pandey, M.: Parallel implementations for solving shortest path problem using Bellman-Ford. Int. J. Comput. Appl. **95**(15) (2014)
19. Isabelle interactive theorem prover. http://isabelle.in.tum.de/index.html
20. Jeong, I.K., Uddin, J., Kang, M., Kim, C.H., Kim, J.M.: Accelerating a Bellman-Ford routing algorithm using GPU. In: Frontier and Innovation in Future Computing and Communications, pp. 153–160. Springer (2014)
21. Kleinberg, J., Tardos, E.: Algorithm design. Pearson Education India, New Delh (2006)
22. Laarman, A., Langerak, R., van de Pol, J., Weber, M., Wijs, A.: Multi-core nested depth-first search. In: Bultan, T., Hsiung, P.-A. (eds.) ATVA 2011. LNCS, vol. 6996, pp. 321–335. Springer, Heidelberg (2011). https://doi.org/10.1007/978-3-642-24372-1_23
23. Lammich, P., Neumann, R.: A Framework for Verifying Depth-First Search Algorithms. In: CPP, pp. 137–146. ACM (2015)
24. Lammich, P., Wimmer, S.: IMP2-simple program verification in Isabelle/HOL. Archive of Formal Proofs (2019)
25. Li, G., Gopalakrishnan, G.: Scalable SMT-based verification of GPU kernel functions. In: SIGSOFT FSE 2010, Santa Fe, pp. 187–196. ACM (2010)
26. Li, G., Li, P., Sawaya, G., Gopalakrishnan, G., Ghosh, I., Rajan, S.P.: GKLEE: concolic verification and test generation for GPUs. In: ACM SIGPLAN Notices. vol. 47, pp. 215–224. ACM (2012)
27. Oortwijn, W.: Deductive techniques for model-based concurrency verification. Ph.D. thesis, University of Twente, Netherlands (2019). https://doi.org/10.3990/1.9789036548984

28. Oortwijn, W., Huisman, M., Joosten, S.J.C., van de Pol, J.: Automated verification of parallel nested DFS. In: TACAS 2020. LNCS, vol. 12078, pp. 247–265. Springer, Cham (2020). https://doi.org/10.1007/978-3-030-45190-5_14

29. van de Pol, J.C.: Automated verification of nested DFS. In: Núñez, M., Güdemann, M. (eds.) FMICS 2015. LNCS, vol. 9128, pp. 181–197. Springer, Cham (2015). https://doi.org/10.1007/978-3-319-19458-5_12

30. Raad, A., Hobor, A., Villard, J., Gardner, P.: Verifying concurrent graph algorithms. In: Igarashi, A. (ed.) APLAS 2016. LNCS, vol. 10017, pp. 314–334. Springer, Cham (2016). https://doi.org/10.1007/978-3-319-47958-3_17

31. Safari, M., Oortwijn, W., Huisman, M.: Artifact for automated verification of the parallel bellman-ford algorithm. In: SAS (2021). https://github.com/Safari1991/SSSP-Verification

32. Safari, M., Ebnenasir, A.: Locality-based relaxation: an efficient method for GPU-based computation of shortest paths. In: Mousavi, M.R., Sgall, J. (eds.) TTCS 2017. LNCS, vol. 10608, pp. 43–58. Springer, Cham (2017). https://doi.org/10.1007/978-3-319-68953-1_5

33. Sergey, I., Nanevski, A., Banerjee, A.: Mechanized verification of fine-grained concurrent programs. In: PLDI, pp. 77–87 (2015)

34. Surve, G.G., Shah, M.A.: Parallel implementation of bellman-ford algorithm using CUDA architecture. In: 2017 International conference of Electronics, Communication and Aerospace Technology (ICECA), vol. 2, pp. 16–22. IEEE (2017)

35. Volkov, G., Mandrykin, M., Efremov, D.: Lemma functions for Frama-c: C programs as proofs. In: 2018 Ivannikov Ispras Open Conference (ISPRAS), pp. 31–38. IEEE (2018)

36. A Theory of Bellman-Ford, in Isabelle. https://www.isa-afp.org/browser_info/current/AFP/Monad_Memo_DP/Bellman_Ford.html. Accessed Jan 2021

37. Why3 gallery of formally verified programs. http://toccata.lri.fr/gallery/graph.en.html

38. Why3 program verifier. http://why3.lri.fr/

39. Wimmer, S., Hu, S., Nipkow, T.: Verified memoization and dynamic programming. In: Avigad, J., Mahboubi, A. (eds.) ITP 2018. LNCS, vol. 10895, pp. 579–596. Springer, Cham (2018). https://doi.org/10.1007/978-3-319-94821-8_34

Improving Thread-Modular Abstract Interpretation

Michael Schwarz[1]($\boxtimes$), Simmo Saan[2], Helmut Seidl[1], Kalmer Apinis[2], Julian Erhard[1], and Vesal Vojdani[2]

[1] Technische Universität München, Garching, Germany
{m.schwarz,helmut.seidl,julian.erhard}@tum.de
[2] University of Tartu, Tartu, Estonia
{simmo.saan,kalmer.apinis,vesal.vojdani}@ut.ee

Abstract. We give thread-modular non-relational value analyses as abstractions of a local trace semantics. The semantics as well as the analyses are formulated by means of global invariants and side-effecting constraint systems. We show that a generalization of the analysis provided by the static analyzer GOBLINT as well as a natural improvement of Antoine Miné's approach can be obtained as instances of this general scheme. We show that these two analyses are incomparable w.r.t. precision and provide a refinement which improves on both precision-wise. We also report on a preliminary experimental comparison of the given analyses on a meaningful suite of benchmarks.

Keywords: Concurrent systems · Thread-modular abstract interpretation · Collecting trace semantics · Global invariants · Side-effects

1 Introduction

In a series of papers starting around 2012, Antoine Miné and his co-authors developed methods for abstract interpretation of concurrent systems [10–12,20,21], which can be considered the *gold standard* for thread-modular static analysis of these systems. The core analysis from [10] consists of a refinement of data flow which takes schedulability into account by propagating values written before unlock operations to corresponding lock operations—provided that appropriate side-conditions are met. Due to these side-conditions, more flows are generally excluded than in approaches as, e.g., [4,13]. An alternative approach, suggested by Vojdani [22,23], is realized in the static analyzer GOBLINT. This analysis

C. Drăgoi et al. (Eds.): SAS 2021, LNCS 12913, pp. 359–383, 2021.
https://doi.org/10.1007/978-3-030-88806-0_18

is not based on data flows. Instead, for each global g, a set of mutexes that definitely protect accesses to g is determined. Then *side-effects* during the analysis of the threads' local states are used to accumulate an abstraction of the set of all possibly written values. This base approach then is enhanced by means of *privatization* to account for exclusive manipulations by individual threads. This approach is similar to the thread-local shape analysis of Gotsman et al. [6], which infers lock-invariants [16] by privatizing carved-out sections of the heap owned by a thread. Despite its conceptual simplicity and perhaps to our surprise, it turns out the Vojdani style analysis is *not* subsumed by Miné's approach but is incomparable. Since Miné's analysis is more precise on many examples, we highlight only non-subsumption in the other direction here.

Example 1. We use sets of integers for abstracting int values. Consider the following concurrent program with global variable g and local variables x and y, and assume here that g is initialized to 0:

```
main :                      t1 :
    y = create(t1);             lock(a);
    lock(a);                    lock(b);
    lock(b);                    g = 42;
    x = g;                      unlock(a);
    ...                         g = 17;
                                unlock(b);
```

Program execution starts at program point main where, after creation of another thread t1 and locking of the mutexes a and b, the value of the global g is read. The created thread, on the other hand, also locks the mutexes a and b. Then, it writes to g the two values 42 and 17 where mutex a is unlocked in-between the two writes, and mutex b is unlocked only in the very end.

According to Miné's analysis, the value $\{42\}$ is merged into the local state at the operation lock(a), while the value $\{17\}$ is merged at the operation lock(b). Thus, the local x receives the value $\{0, 17, 42\}$.

Vojdani's analysis, on the other hand, finds out that all accesses to g are protected by the mutex b. Unlocking of a, therefore, does not publish the intermediately written value $\{42\}$, but only the final value $\{17\}$ at unlock(b) is published. Therefore, the local x only receives the value $\{0, 17\}$.   □

The goal of this paper is to better understand this intriguing incomparability and develop precision improvements to refine these analyses. We concentrate only on the basic setting of *non-relational* analysis and a concurrent setting without precise thread *ids*. We also ignore add-ons such as thread priorities or effects of weak memory, which are of major concern in [1,5,20,21]. As a common framework for the comparison, we use *side-effecting* constraint systems [2]. Constraint systems with side-effects extend ordinary constraint systems in that during the evaluation of the right-hand side of one unknown, contributions to other unknowns may also be triggered. This kind of formalism allows combining flow- and context-sensitive analysis of the local state with flow- and context-insensitive analysis of globals. Within the analyzer GOBLINT, this has been applied to the analysis of multi-threaded systems [22,23]. While in GOBLINT a single unknown is introduced per global, we show how to express Miné's analysis in this formalism using multiple unknowns per global.

To prove the given thread-modular analyses correct, we rely on a trace semantics of the concurrent system. Here, we insist on maintaining the *local views* of executing threads (*ego threads*) only. The idea of tracking the events possibly affecting a particular local thread configuration goes back to [9] (see also [19]), and is also used extensively for the verification of concurrent systems via separation logic [3,14,15,18]. Accordingly, we collect all attained local configurations of threads affecting a thread-local configuration $\bar{u}$ of an ego thread into the *local trace* reaching $\bar{u}$. A *thread-local* concrete semantics was also used in Mukherjee et al. [13] for proving the correctness of thread-modular analyses. The semantics there, however, is based on *interleaving* and permits *stale* values for unread globals. In contrast, we consider a *partial order* of past events and explicitly exclude the *values* of globals from local traces. These are instead recovered from the local trace by searching for the *last preceding write* at the point when the value of the global is accessed. We show that the set of all local traces can conveniently be described by the least solution of a side-effecting constraint system which is of a form quite similar to the ones used by the analyses and thus well-suited for proving their correctness.

Having formulated both the analyses of Miné [10] and Vojdani [22,23] by means of side-effecting constraint systems, our contributions thus can be summarized as follows:

- we provide enhancements of each of these analyses which significantly increase their precision—but still are incomparable;
- since both analyses are expressed within the same framework, these improved versions can be integrated into one combined analysis;
- we prove the new analyses correct relative to a concrete local trace semantics of concurrent programs;
- we provide implementations of the new analyses to compare their precision and efficiency.

The paper is organized as follows. After a brief introduction into side-effecting constraint systems in Sect. 2, we introduce our toy language for which the concrete local trace semantics as well as the analyses are formalized and indicate its operational semantics (Sect. 3). Our analyses then are provided in Sect. 4, while their correctness proofs are deferred to an extended version [17]. The experimental evaluation is provided in Sect. 5. Section 6 finally concludes.

2   Side-Effecting Systems of Constraints

In [2], side-effecting systems of constraints are advocated as a convenient framework for formalizing the accumulation of flow- (and possibly also context-) sensitive information together with flow- (as well as context-) insensitive information. Assume that X is a set of unknowns where for each $x \in X$, $\mathcal{D}_x$ is a complete lattice of possible (abstract or concrete) values of x. Let $\mathcal{D}$ denote the disjoint union of all sets $\mathcal{D}_x$. Let $X{\Rightarrow}\mathcal{D}$ denote the set of all mappings $\eta : X \to \mathcal{D}$ where $\eta\, x \in \mathcal{D}_x$. Technically, a (side-effecting) constraint takes the form $x \sqsupseteq f_x$ where $x \in X$ is the left-hand side and the right-hand side $f_x : (X{\Rightarrow}\mathcal{D}) \to ((X{\Rightarrow}\mathcal{D}) \times \mathcal{D}_x)$ takes a mapping $\eta : X{\Rightarrow}\mathcal{D}$, while returning a collection of side-effects to other unknowns in X together with the contribution to the left-hand side.

Let $\mathcal{C}$ denote a set of such constraints. A mapping $\eta : X{\Rightarrow}\mathcal{D}$ is called *solution* of $\mathcal{C}$ if for all constraints $x \sqsupseteq f_x$ of $\mathcal{C}$, it holds for $(\eta', d) = f_x\, \eta$ that $\eta \sqsupseteq \eta'$ and $\eta\, x \sqsupseteq d$; that is, all side-effects of the right-hand side and its contribution to the left-hand side are accounted for by η. Assuming that all right-hand sides are monotonic, the system $\mathcal{C}$ is known to have a *least* solution.

3 A Local Trace Semantics

Let us assume that there are disjoint sets $\mathcal{X}, \mathcal{G}$ of local and global variables which take values from some set $\mathcal{V}$ of values. Values may be of built-in types to compute with, e.g., of type **int**, or a thread *id* from a subset $\mathcal{I} \subseteq \mathcal{V}$. The latter values are assumed to be *abstract*, i.e., can only be compared with other thread *ids* for equality. We implicitly assume that all programs are well-typed; i.e., a variable either always holds thread *ids* or **int** values. Moreover, there is one particular local variable self $\in \mathcal{X}$ holding the thread *id* of the current thread which is only implicitly assigned at program start or when creating the thread. Before program execution, global variables are assumed to be uninitialized and will receive initial values via assignments from the main thread, while local variables (except for self) may initially have any value. Finally, we assume that there is a set M of mutexes. A *local program state* thus is a mapping $\sigma : \mathcal{X} \to \mathcal{V}$ where $\sigma\, \text{self} \in \mathcal{I}$. Let Σ denote the set of all local program states.

Let $\mathcal{A}$ denote the set of actions. Each thread is assumed to be represented by some control-flow graph where each edge e is of the form (u, A, u') for program points u, u' and action A. Let $\mathcal{N}$ and $\mathcal{E}$ denote the sets of all program points and control-flow edges. Let $\mathcal{T}$ denote a set of *local traces*. A local trace should be understood as the *view* of a particular thread, the *ego* thread, on the global execution of the system. Each $t \in \mathcal{T}$ ends at some program point u with local state σ where the ego thread *id* is given by $\sigma\, \text{self}$. This pair (u, σ) can be extracted from t via the mapping sink : $\mathcal{T} \to \mathcal{N} \times \Sigma$. For a local trace t and local variable x, we also write $t(x)$ for the result of $\sigma(x)$ if sink $t = (u, \sigma)$. Likewise, the functions id : $\mathcal{T} \to \mathcal{I}$ and loc : $\mathcal{T} \to \mathcal{N}$ return the thread *id* and the program point of the unique sink node, respectively.

We assume that there is a set init of initial local traces $\mathbf{0}_\sigma$ with sink $\mathbf{0}_\sigma = (u_0, \sigma)$ where u_0 and σ are the start point and initial assignment to the local variables of the initial thread, respectively. In particular, $\sigma\, \text{self} = 0$ for the initial thread *id* 0. For every local trace that is not in init and where the ego thread has not just been started, there should be a last action in $\mathcal{A}$ executed by the ego thread. It can be extracted by means of the function last : $\mathcal{T} \to \mathcal{A} \cup \{\perp\}$. For local traces in init or local traces where the ego thread has just been started, last returns $\perp$. For realizing thread creation, we make the assumption that starting from (u, σ), there is at most one outgoing edge at which a thread is created. For convenience, we also assume that each thread execution provides a unique program point u_1 at which the new thread is meant to start where the local state of the created thread agrees with the local state before thread creation – only that the variable self receives a fresh value. Accordingly, we require a function new : $\mathcal{N} \to \mathcal{T} \to 2^{\mathcal{T}}$ so that new $u_1 \, t$ either returns the empty set, namely, when creation of a thread starting at point u_1 is not possible for t, or a set $\{t_1\}$ for a single trace t_1 if such thread creation is possible. In the latter case,

$$\mathsf{last}(t_1) = \bot, \mathsf{sink}(t_1) = (u_1, \sigma_1)$$

where for $\mathsf{sink}(t) = (u, \sigma)$, $\sigma_1 = \sigma \oplus \{\mathsf{self} \mapsto \nu(t)\}$ for some function $\nu : \mathcal{T} \to \mathcal{I}$ providing us with a fresh thread id. As thread ids are unique for a given creation history in $\mathcal{T}$, we may identify the set $\mathcal{I}$ with $\mathcal{T}$ and let ν be the identity function.

For each edge $e = (u, A, u')$, we also require an operation $[\![e]\!] : \mathcal{T}^k \to 2^{\mathcal{T}}$ where the arity k for different actions may vary between 1 and 2 according to the arity of operations A at the edges and where the returned set either is empty (i.e., the operation is undefined), singleton (the operation is defined and deterministic), or a larger set (the operation is non-deterministic, e.g., when reading unknown input). This function takes a local trace and extends it by executing the action corresponding to edge e, thereby incorporating the matching trace from the second argument set (if necessary and possible). In particular for $t \in [\![e]\!](t_0, \ldots, t_{k-1})$, necessarily,

$$\mathsf{loc}(t_0) = u, \quad \mathsf{last}(t) = A \quad \text{and} \quad \mathsf{loc}(t) = u' \tag{1}$$

The set $\mathcal{T}$ of all local traces is the least solution of the constraints

$$\begin{aligned}
\mathcal{T} &\supseteq \mathbf{fun} \_ \to (\emptyset, \mathsf{init}) \\
\mathcal{T} &\supseteq \mathbf{fun}\, \mathcal{T} \to (\emptyset, \mathsf{new}\, u_1\, \mathcal{T}), & (u_1 \in \mathcal{N}) \\
\mathcal{T} &\supseteq \mathbf{fun}\, \mathcal{T} \to (\emptyset, [\![e]\!](\mathcal{T}, \ldots, \mathcal{T})), & (e \in \mathcal{E})
\end{aligned} \tag{2}$$

where sets of side-effects are empty. Here (and subsequently), we abbreviate for functions $f : \mathcal{T}^k \to 2^{\mathcal{T}}$ and subsets $T_0, \ldots, T_{k-1} \subseteq \mathcal{T}$, the longish formula $\bigcup \{ f(t_0, \ldots, t_{k-1}) \mid t_0 \in T_0, \ldots, t_{k-1} \in T_{k-1} \}$ to $f(T_0, \ldots, T_{k-1})$.

The constraint system (2) globally collects all local traces into one set $\mathcal{T}$. It serves as the definition of all (valid) local traces (relative to the definitions of the functions $[\![e]\!]$ and new) and thus, as our reference trace semantics. Subsequently, we provide a *local* constraint system for these traces. Instead of collecting one big set, the local constraint system introduces unknowns $[u]$, $u \in \mathcal{N}$, together with individual constraints for each control-flow edge $e \in \mathcal{E}$. The value for unknown $[u]$ is meant to collect the set of those local traces t that reach program point u (i.e., $\mathsf{loc}(t) = u$), while the constraints for edges describe the possible relationships between these sets—quite as for the trace semantics of a sequential programming language. In order to deal with concurrency appropriately, we additionally introduce unknowns $[m], m \in \mathsf{M}$ for mutexes. These unknowns will not have right-hand sides on their own but receive their values via side-effects. In general, we will have the following constraints

$$[u_0] \supseteq \mathbf{fun}_- \to (\emptyset, \mathsf{init})$$
$$[u'] \supseteq [\![u, A]\!], \qquad\qquad ((u, A, u') \in \mathcal{E}) \qquad (3)$$

where the concrete form of the right-hand side $[\![u, A]\!]$ depends on the action A of the corresponding edge $e = (u, A, u')$. In the following, we detail how the constraints corresponding to the various actions are constructed.

3.1   Thread Creation

Recall that we assume that within the set $\mathcal{X}$ of local variables, we have one dedicated variable self holding the thread id of the ego thread. In order to deal with thread creation the set $\mathcal{A}$ of actions provides the $x = \mathsf{create}(u_1);$ operation where u_1 is a program point where thread execution should start, and x is a local variable which is meant to receive the thread id of the created thread. The effect of create is modeled as a side-effect to the program point u_1. This means for a program point u:

$$[\![u, x = \mathsf{create}(u_1)]\!]\,\eta = \mathbf{let}\ T = [\![e]\!](\eta\,[u])\ \mathbf{in}$$
$$(\{[u_1] \mapsto \mathsf{new}\,u_1\,(\eta\,[u])\}, T)$$

3.2   Locking and Unlocking

For simplicity, we only consider a fixed finite set M of mutexes. If instead a semantics with dynamically created mutexes were to be formalized, we could identify mutexes, e.g., via the local trace of the creating thread (as we did for threads). For a fixed set M of mutexes, the set $\mathcal{A}$ of actions provides operations $\mathsf{lock}(a)$ and $\mathsf{unlock}(a)$, $a \in \mathsf{M}$, where these operations are assumed to return no value, i.e., do always succeed. Additionally, we assume that $\mathsf{unlock}(a)$ for $a \in \mathsf{M}$ is only called by a thread currently holding the lock of a, and that mutexes are not re-entrant; i.e., trying to lock a mutex already held is undefined. For convenience, we initialize the unknowns $[a]$ for $a \in \mathsf{M}$ to init. Then we set

$$[\![u, \mathsf{lock}(a)]\!]\,\eta \quad = (\emptyset, [\![e]\!](\eta\,[u], \eta\,[a]))$$

$$[\![u, \mathsf{unlock}(a)]\!]\,\eta = \mathbf{let}\ T = [\![e]\!](\eta\,[u])\ \mathbf{in}$$
$$(\{[a] \mapsto T\}, T)$$

3.3   Local and Global Variables

Expressions r occurring as guards as well as non-variable right-hand sides of assignments may refer to local variables only. For these, we assume an evaluation function $[\![\,.\,]\!]$ so that for each $\sigma : \mathcal{X} \to \mathcal{V}$, $[\![r]\!]\,\sigma$ returns a value in $\mathcal{V}$. For convenience, we here encode boolean values as integers where 0 denotes *false* and every non-zero value *true*. This evaluation function $[\![\,.\,]\!]$ allows defining the semantics $[\![e]\!]$ of a control-flow edge e whose action A is either a guard or an assignment to a local variable. Since no side-effect is triggered, we have

$$[\![u, A]\!]\,\eta = (\emptyset, [\![e]\!](\eta\,[u]))$$

For reading from and writing to globals, we consider the actions $g = x$; (copy value of the local x into the global g) and $x = g$; (copy value of the global g into the local x) only. Thus, $g = g + 1$; for global g is not directly supported by our language but must be simulated by reading from g into a local, followed by incrementing the local whose result is eventually written back into g.

We assume for the concrete semantics that program execution is always *sequentially consistent*, and that both reads and writes to globals are *atomic*. The latter is enforced by introducing a dedicated mutex $m_g \in \mathsf{M}$ for each global g which is acquired before g is accessed and subsequently released. This means that each access A to g occurs as $\mathtt{lock(m_g)}$; $\mathtt{A}$; $\mathtt{unlock(m_g)}$;..

Under this proviso, the current value of each global g read by some thread can be determined just by inspection of the current local trace. We have

$$[\![u, x = g]\!] \, \eta = (\emptyset, [\![e]\!](\eta\,[u]))$$
$$[\![u, g = x]\!] \, \eta = (\emptyset, [\![e]\!](\eta\,[u]))$$

i.e., both reading from and writing to global g is a transformation of individual local traces only.

3.4   Completeness of the Local Constraint System

With the following assumption on $[\![e]\!]$ in addition to Eq. (1),

– The binary operation $[\![(u, \mathsf{lock}(a), u')]\!](t_0, t_1)$ only returns a non-empty set if $t_1 \in \mathsf{init} \vee \mathsf{last}(t_1) = (\mathsf{unlock}(a))$, i.e., locking only incorporates local traces from the set init or local traces ending in a corresponding $\mathsf{unlock}(a)$

We obtain:

Theorem 1. *Let $\mathcal{T}$ denote the least solution of the global constraint system* (2), *and η denote the least solution of the local constraint system* (3). *Then*

1. $\eta\,[u] = \{t \in \mathcal{T} \mid \mathsf{loc}(t) = u\}$ *for all $u \in \mathcal{N}$;*
2. $\eta\,[a] = \mathsf{init} \cup \{t \in \mathcal{T} \mid \mathsf{last}(t) = (\mathsf{unlock}(a))\}$ *for all $a \in \mathsf{M}$.*

In fact, Theorem 1 holds for any formalism for traces matching these assumptions. Before detailing an example trace formalism in Sect. 3.5, we proceed with an intuitive example.

Example 2. Consider the following program and assume that execution starts at program point u_0.

u0 :	*u6* :
`    x = create(u6);`	`    y = 1;`
`    lock(m_g);`	`    lock(m_g);`
`    g = 1;`	`    g = 2;`
`    unlock(m_g);`	`    unlock(m_g);`

In this example, one of the traces in the set init of initial local traces is the trace 0_σ with $\mathsf{sink}\, 0_\sigma = (u_0, \sigma_{u_0}) = (u_0, \{x \mapsto 0, \mathsf{self} \mapsto 0\})$; i.e., local variable x has value 0, y has value 0, and the initial thread has thread id 0. One of the traces reaching program point u_1 is t which is obtained by prolonging 0_σ where $\mathsf{sink}\, t = (u_1, \sigma_{u_1}) = (u_1, \{x \mapsto 1, \mathsf{self} \mapsto 0\})$. We abbreviate $\bar{u}_k$ for (u_k, σ_{u_k}) and show traces as graphs (Fig. 1). Since $[\![\mathsf{lock}(m_g)]\!]$ is a binary operation, to compute the set of local traces reaching u_2, not only the local traces reaching its predecessor u_1 but also those traces stored at the constraint system unknown $[m_g]$ need to be considered.

Figure 1 shows all local traces starting with $\bar{u}_0$ stored at $[m_g]$, i.e., all local traces in which the last action of the ego thread is $\mathsf{unlock}(m_g)$ (that start with $\bar{u}_0$). Out of these, traces (a) and (c) are compatible with t. Prolonging the resulting traces for the following assignment and unlock operations leads to traces (b) and (d) reaching the program point after the $\mathsf{unlock}(m_g)$ in this thread. Therefore, (b) and (d) are among those traces that are side-effected to $[m_g]$.

3.5   Example Formalism for Local Traces

The concrete concurrency semantics imposes *restrictions* onto when binary actions are defined. In particular, binary operations $[\![e]\!]$ may only be defined for a pair (t_0, t_1) if certain parts of t_0 and t_1 represent the same computation. In order to make such restrictions explicit, we introduce a concrete representation of local traces.

A *raw* (finite) trace of single thread $i \in \mathcal{I}$ is a sequence $\lambda = \bar{u}_0 a_1 \ldots \bar{u}_{n-1} a_n \bar{u}_n$ for states $\bar{u}_j = (u_j, \sigma_j)$ with $\sigma_j\, \mathsf{self} = i$, and actions $a_j \in \mathcal{A}$ corresponding to the local state transitions of the thread i starting in configuration $\bar{u}_0$ and executing actions a_j. In that sequence, every action $\mathsf{lock}(m)$ is assumed to succeed, and when accessing a global g, any value may be read. We may view λ as an acyclic graph whose nodes are the 3-tuples $(j, u_j, \sigma_j), j = 0, \ldots, n$, and whose edges are $((j-1, u_{j-1}, \sigma_{j-1}), a_j, (j, u_j, \sigma_j)), j = 1, \ldots, n$. Let $V(\lambda)$ and $E(\lambda)$ denote the set of nodes and edges of this graph, respectively.

Let $\Lambda(i)$ denote the set of all individual traces for thread i, and Λ the union of all these sets.

A *raw global trace* of threads is an acyclic graph $\tau = (\mathcal{V}, \mathcal{E})$ where $\mathcal{V} = \bigcup\{V(\lambda_i) \mid i \in I\}$ and $\mathcal{E} = \bigcup\{E(\lambda_i) \mid i \in I\}$ for a set I of thread *ids* and raw local traces $\lambda_i \in \Lambda(i)$. On the set $\mathcal{V}$, we define the *(immediate) program order* as the set of all pairs $\bar{u} \to_p \bar{u}'$ for which there is an edge $(\bar{u}, a, \bar{u}')$ in $\mathcal{E}$. In order to formalize our notion of local traces, we extend the program order to a *causality order* which additionally takes the order into account in which threads are created as well as the order in which mutex locks are acquired and released.

For $a \in \mathsf{M}$, let $a^+ \subseteq \mathcal{V}$ denote the set of nodes $\bar{u}$ where an incoming edge is labeled $\mathsf{lock}(a)$, i.e., $\exists x\, (x, \mathsf{lock}(a), \bar{u}) \in \mathcal{E}$, and a^- analogously for $\mathsf{unlock}(a)$. On the other hand, let C denote the set of nodes with an *outgoing* edge labeled $x' = \mathsf{create}(u_1)$ (for any local variable x' and program point u_1). Let S denote the set of minimal nodes w.r.t. to $\to_p$, i.e., the points at which threads start and let $\mathbf{0}$ the node $(0, u_0, \sigma_0)$ where $\sigma_0\, \mathsf{self} = 0$.

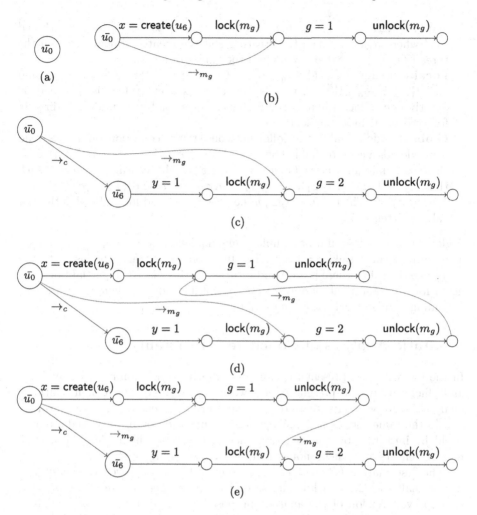

Fig. 1. Local traces of Example 2 starting with $\bar{u}_0$ stored at $[m_g]$.

A *global trace* t then is represented by a tuple $(\tau, \to_c, (\to_a)_{a\in\mathsf{M}})$ where τ is a raw global trace and the relations $\to_c$ and $\to_a$ $(a \in \mathsf{M})$ are the create and locking orders for the respective mutexes. The *causality order* $\le$ of t then is obtained as the reflexive and transitive closure of the union $\to_p \cup \to_c \cup \bigcup_{a\in\mathsf{M}} \to_a$. These orders should satisfy the following properties.

– **Causality order** $\le$ should be a partial order with unique least element $(0, u_0, \sigma_0)$ where $\sigma_0\,\mathsf{self} = 0$;
– **Create order:** $\to_c \subseteq C \times (S \setminus \{\mathbf{0}\})$: $\forall s \in (S \setminus \{\mathbf{0}\}) : |\{z \mid z \to_c s\}| = 1$, i.e., every thread except the initial thread is created by exactly one $\mathsf{create}(...)$ action and $\forall x : |\{z \mid x \to_c z\}| \le 1$, i.e., each $\mathsf{create}(...)$ action creates at most one thread. Additionally, for $((j-1, u_{j-1}, \sigma_{j-1}), x = \mathsf{create}(v), (j, u_j, \sigma_j)) \in \mathcal{E}$

and $(j-1, u_{j-1}, \sigma_{j-1}) \rightarrow_c (0, v, \sigma_0')$: $\sigma_0' = \sigma_{j-1} \oplus \{\mathsf{self} \mapsto i'\}$ for some thread id i' where $\sigma_j\, x = i'$, i.e., the creating and the created thread agree on the thread id of the created thread and the values of locals.

- **Locking order:** $\forall a \in \mathsf{M} :\rightarrow_a \subseteq (a^- \cup \mathbf{0}) \times a^+$: $\forall x : |\{z \mid x \rightarrow_a z\}| \le 1$ and $\forall y : |\{z \mid z \rightarrow_a y\}| = 1$, that is, for a mutex a every lock is preceded by exactly one unlock (or it is the first lock) of a, and each unlock is directly followed by at most one lock.

- **Globals:** Additionally, the following consistency condition on values read from globals needs to hold: For $((j-1, u_{j-1}, \sigma_{j-1}), x = g, (j, u_j, \sigma_j)) \in \mathcal{E}$, there is a maximal node $(j', u_{j'}, \sigma_{j'})$ w.r.t. to the causality order $\le$ such that $((j'-1, u_{j'-1}, \sigma_{j'-1}), g = y, (j', u_{j'}, \sigma_{j'})) \in \mathcal{E}$ and $(j', u_{j'}, \sigma_{j'}) \le (j-1, u_{j-1}, \sigma_{j-1})$. Then $\sigma_j\, x = \sigma_{j'-1}\, y$, i.e., the value read for a global is the last value written to it.

A global trace t is *local* if it has a unique maximal element $\bar{u} = (j, u, \sigma)$ (w.r.t $\le$). Then in particular, $\mathsf{sink}(t) = (u, \sigma)$. The function last extracts the last action A of the ego thread (if there is any) and returns $\bot$ otherwise. The partial functions $\mathsf{new}\, u$ for program points u and $[\![e]\!]$ for control-flow edges e then are defined by extending a given local trace appropriately.

4 Static Analysis of Concurrent Programs

In the following, we present four analyses which we will compare for precision and efficiency. In the present paper, we are only interested in non-relational analyses. Also, we concentrate on mutexes only and hence do not track thread ids. In the same way as in Miné's paper, the precision of all presented analyses could be improved by tracking (abstract or concrete) thread ids. Also, weak memory effects at asynchronous memory accesses are ignored.

The first analysis (*Protection-Based Reading*) is an improved version of Vojdani's analysis [22,23], while the second analysis (*Lock-Centered Reading*) is an improved version of the analysis proposed by Miné [10]. The first analysis assumes that for each global g, some set $\mathcal{M}[g]$ of mutexes exists which is held at each write operation to g and maintains a private copy of the global as long as one of the mutexes from $\mathcal{M}[g]$ is known to be held. Since the assumption of non-empty program-wide protecting locksets is rather restrictive, we present a third analysis (*Write-Centered Reading*) which lifts this extra assumption and thus strictly subsumes *Protection-Based Reading*. Interestingly, *Write-Centered Reading* and *Lock-Centered Reading* are still incomparable. We therefore sketch a fourth analysis which is more precise than either of them.

Throughout this section, we assume that $\mathcal{D}$ is a complete lattice abstracting sets of values of program variables.

4.1 Protection-Based Reading

The original analysis proposed by Vojdani [22,23] and implemented in the GOB-LINT system assumes that for each global g, there is a set of mutexes definitely held whenever g is accessed. The best information about the values of g visible after acquiring a protecting lock is maintained in a separate unknown $[g]$. The value of the unknown $[g]$ for the global g is eagerly privatized: It is incorporated into the local state for a program point and currently held lockset whenever g first becomes protected, i.e., a mutex protecting g is acquired while none was held before. As long as one of these protecting mutexes is held, all reads and writes refer to this local copy of the global and this copy can be destructively updated. It is only when no mutex protecting g is held anymore that the value of the local copy is published to the unknown $[g]$. This base analysis setting is enhanced in three ways:

- Instead of assuming a set of mutexes protecting both reading and writing of g, we now just assume a set of mutexes definitely held at each write. While this does not necessarily lead to an improvement in precision, it allows for analyzing interesting patterns where, e.g., only a subset of mutexes is acquired for reading from a global, while a superset is held when writing to it.
- Besides the unknown $[g]$ for describing the possible values of the global g for protected accesses, another unknown $[g]'$ is introduced for the results of unprotected read accesses to g.
- Instead of incorporating the value of the global g stored at $[g]$ into the local state at each lock operation of a mutex from the protecting set, the local state for a program point and currently held lockset only keeps track of the values written by the ego thread. At a read operation $x = g$, the value of global g is assigned to the local variable x. For that the analysis relies on the value stored at unknown $[g]$ together with the value of g stored in the local state, unless the ego thread has definitely written to g since acquiring a protecting mutex and not yet released all protecting mutexes since then.

Recall that $\mathcal{M} : \mathcal{G} \to 2^{\mathbb{M}}$ maps each global g to the set of mutexes definitely held when g is *written to*. Due to our atomicity assumption, the set $\mathcal{M}[g]$ is non-empty, since $m_g \in \mathcal{M}[g]$ always holds. For the moment, we assume this mapping to be given. The unknown $[g]'$ stores an abstraction of all values ever written to g, while the unknown $[g]$ stores an abstraction of all values that were written *last* before releasing a protecting mutex of g other than m_g. For each pair (u, S) of program point u and currently held lockset S, on the other hand, the analysis maintains (1) a set P of definitely written globals g since a protecting mutex of g has been acquired and not all protecting mutexes have been released, together with (2) a variable assignment $\sigma : \mathcal{X} \cup \mathcal{G} \to \mathcal{D}$ of potential descriptions of values for local or global variables.

In case one of the mutexes in $\mathcal{M}[g]$ is definitely held, after a write to variable g, all processing on g is performed destructively on the local copy. Immediately after the write to g (at the unlock(m_g)) the value of the updated local copy is merged into $[g]'$ via a side-effect. On the other hand, the value of that copy must be merged into the value of $[g]$ only when it no longer can be guaranteed that all other protecting mutexes $(\mathcal{M}[g] \setminus m_g)$ are held.

We start by giving the right-hand-side function for the start state at program point $u_0 \in \mathcal{N}$ with the empty lockset $\emptyset$, i.e., $[u_0, \emptyset] \sqsupseteq \mathsf{init}^\sharp$ where

$$\mathsf{init}^\sharp \_ = \mathbf{let}\ \sigma = \{x \mapsto \top \mid x \in \mathcal{X}\} \cup \{g \mapsto \bot \mid g \in \mathcal{G}\}\ \mathbf{in}$$
$$(\emptyset, (\emptyset, \sigma))$$

Now, consider the right-hand side $[v, S'] \sqsupseteq [\![[u, S], A]\!]^\sharp$ for the edge $e = (u, A, v)$ of the control-flow graph and appropriate locksets S, S'. Consider the right-hand side for a thread creation edge. For this, we require a function $\nu^\sharp\, u\, (P, \sigma)\, u_1$ that returns the (abstract) thread *id* of a thread started at an edge originating from u in local state (P, σ), where the new thread starts execution at program point u_1. Since we do not track thread *ids*, $\nu^\sharp$ may return $\top$ whereby all variables holding thread *ids* are also set to $\top$.

$$[\![[u, S], x = \mathsf{create}(u_1)]\!]^\sharp \eta = \mathbf{let}\ (P, \sigma) = \eta\,[u, S]\ \mathbf{in}$$
$$\mathbf{let}\ i = \nu^\sharp\, u\, (P, \sigma)\, u_1\ \mathbf{in}$$
$$\mathbf{let}\ \sigma' = \sigma \oplus (\{\mathsf{self} \mapsto i\} \cup \{g \mapsto \bot \mid g \in \mathcal{G}\})\ \mathbf{in}$$
$$\mathbf{let}\ \rho = \{[u_1, \emptyset] \mapsto (\emptyset, \sigma')\}\ \mathbf{in}$$
$$(\rho, (P, \sigma \oplus \{x \mapsto i\}))$$

This function has no effect on the local state apart from setting x to the abstract thread *id* of the newly created thread, while providing an appropriate initial state to the startpoint of the newly created thread. For guards and computations on locals, the right-hand-side functions are defined in the intuitive manner—they operate on σ only, leaving P unchanged.

Concerning locking and unlocking of mutexes a, the lock operation does not affect the local state, while at each unlock, all local copies of globals g for which not all protecting mutexes are held anymore, are published via a side-effect to the respective unknowns $[g]$ or $[g]'$. Moreover, globals for which none of the protecting mutexes are held anymore, are removed from P:

$$[\![[u, S], \mathsf{lock}(a)]\!]^\sharp \eta\ \ = (\emptyset, \eta\,[u, S])$$
$$[\![[u, S], \mathsf{lock}(m_g)]\!]^\sharp \eta\ \ = (\emptyset, \eta\,[u, S])$$
$$[\![[u, S], \mathsf{unlock}(m_g)]\!]^\sharp \eta = \mathbf{let}\ (P, \sigma) = \eta\,[u, S]\ \mathbf{in}$$
$$\mathbf{let}\ P' = \{h \in P \mid ((S \setminus \{m_g\}) \cap \mathcal{M}[h]) \neq \emptyset\}\ \mathbf{in}$$
$$\mathbf{let}\ \rho = \{[g]' \mapsto \sigma\, g\} \cup \{[g] \mapsto \sigma\, g \mid \mathcal{M}[g] = \{m_g\}\}\ \mathbf{in}$$
$$(\rho, (P', \sigma))$$
$$[\![[u, S], \mathsf{unlock}(a)]\!]^\sharp \eta\ \ = \mathbf{let}\ (P, \sigma) = \eta\,[u, S]\ \mathbf{in}$$
$$\mathbf{let}\ P' = \{g \in P \mid ((S \setminus \{a\}) \cap \mathcal{M}[g]) \neq \emptyset\}\ \mathbf{in}$$
$$\mathbf{let}\ \rho = \{[g] \mapsto \sigma\, g \mid a \in \mathcal{M}[g]\}\ \mathbf{in}$$
$$(\rho, (P', \sigma))$$

for $a \notin \{m_g \mid g \in \mathcal{G}\}$. We remark that the locksets S' of the corresponding left-hand unknowns now take the forms of $S' = S \cup \{a\}$, $S' = S \cup \{m_g\}$, $S' = S \setminus \{m_g\}$ and $S' = S \setminus \{a\}$, respectively. Recall that the dedicated mutex m_g for each global g has been introduced for guaranteeing atomicity. It is always acquired immediately before and always released immediately after each access to g. The special treatment of this dedicated mutex implies that all values written to g are side-effected to the unknown $[g]'$, while values written to g are side-effected to the unknown $[g]$ only when unlock is called for a mutex *different* from m_g.

For global g and local x, we define for writing to and reading from g,

$$[\![[u,S],g = x]\!]^\sharp \eta = \textbf{let } (P,\sigma) = \eta\,[u,S] \textbf{ in}$$
$$(\emptyset, (P \cup \{g\}, \sigma \oplus \{g \mapsto (\sigma\,x)\}))$$
$$[\![[u,S],x = g]\!]^\sharp \eta = \textbf{let } (P,\sigma) = \eta\,[u,S] \textbf{ in}$$
$$\textbf{if } (g \in P) \textbf{ then}$$
$$(\emptyset, (P, \sigma \oplus \{x \mapsto (\sigma\,g)\}))$$
$$\textbf{else if } (S \cap \mathcal{M}[g] = \{m_g\}) \textbf{ then}$$
$$(\emptyset, (P, \sigma \oplus \{x \mapsto \sigma\,g \sqcup \eta\,[g]'\})$$
$$\textbf{else } (\emptyset, (P, \sigma \oplus \{x \mapsto \sigma\,g \sqcup \eta\,[g]\}))$$

Altogether, the resulting system of constraints $\mathcal{C}_1$ is monotonic (given that the right-hand-side functions for local computations as well as for guards are monotonic)—implying that the system has a unique least solution, which we denote by η_1. We remark that for this unique least solution η_1, $\eta_1\,[g] \sqsubseteq \eta_1\,[g]'$ holds.

Example 3. Consider, e.g., the following program fragment and assume that $\mathcal{M}[g] = \{a, m_g\}$ and that that we use value sets for abstracting int values.

```
lock(a);
lock(m_g);   g = 5;      unlock(m_g);
lock(b);
unlock(b);
lock(m_g);   x = g;      unlock(m_g);
lock(m_g);   g = x+1;    unlock(m_g);
unlock(a);
```

Then after unlock(b), the state attained by the program (where variable self is omitted for clarity of presentation) is

$$s_1 = (\{g\}, \{g \mapsto \{5\}, x \mapsto \top\})$$

where $[g]'$ has received the contribution $\{5\}$ but no side-effect to $[g]$ has been triggered. The read of g in the subsequent assignment refers to the local copy. Accordingly, the second write to g and the succeeding $unlock(m_g)$ result in the local state

$$s_2 = (\{g\}, \{g \mapsto \{6\}, x \mapsto \{5\}\})$$

with side-effect $\{6\}$ to $[g]'$ and no side-effect to $[g]$. Accordingly, after unlock(a), the attained state is

$$s_3 = (\emptyset, \{g \mapsto \{6\}, x \mapsto \{5\}\})$$

and the value of $[g]$ is just $\{6\}$ – even though g has been written to twice. We remark that without separate treatment of m_g, the value of $\{5\}$ would immediately be side-effected to $[g]$. □

Theorem 2. Protection-Based Reading *is sound w.r.t. the trace semantics.*

Proof. In the extended version of this paper [17, Section 5.3] we show that this analysis computes an abstraction of the result of the analysis presented in Sect. 4.3, which we then prove to be sound with respect to the trace semantics in [17, Section 5.2] .   □

Thus, we never remove any values from the variable assignment for a local state. An implementation may, however, in order to keep the representation of local states small, additionally track for each program point and currently held lockset, a set W of all globals which possibly have been written (and not yet published) while holding protecting mutexes. A local copy of a global g may then safely be removed from σ if $g \notin P \cup W$. This is possible because for each $g \notin P \cup W$, σg has already been side-effected and hence already is included in $\eta[g]$ and $\eta[g]'$, and thus σg need not be consulted on the next read of g.

As presented thus far, this analysis requires the map $\mathcal{M} : \mathcal{G} \to 2^{\mathsf{M}}$ to be given beforehand. This map can, e.g., be provided by some pre-analysis onto which the given analysis builds. Alternatively, our analysis can be modified to infer $\mathcal{M}$ on the fly. For that, we consider the $\mathcal{M}[g]$ to be separate unknowns of the constraint system. They take values in the complete lattice 2^{M} (ordered by superset) and are initialized to the full set of all mutexes M. The right-hand-side function for writes to global g then is extended to provide the current lockset as a contribution to $\mathcal{M}[g]$. This means that we now have:

$$[\![[u, S], g = x]\!]^{\sharp}\eta = \mathbf{let}\ (P, \sigma) = \eta\,[u, S]\ \mathbf{in}$$
$$(\{\mathcal{M}[g] \mapsto S\}, (P \cup \{g\}, \sigma \oplus \{g \mapsto (\sigma\,x)\}))$$

There is one (minor) obstacle, though: the right-hand-side function for control-flow edges with unlock(a) is no longer monotonic in the unknowns $\mathcal{M}[g], g \in \mathcal{G}$: If $\mathcal{M}[g]$ shrinks to no longer contain a, unlock(a) will no longer produce a side-effect to the unknown $[g]$, whereas it previously did.

Another practical consideration is that, in order to further improve efficiency, it is also possible to abandon state-splitting according to held locksets—at the cost of losing some precision. To this end, it suffices to additionally track for each program point a set $\bar{S}$ of must-held mutexes as part of the local state from the lattice 2^{M} (ordered by superset), and replace S with $\bar{S}$ in all right-hand sides.

4.2   Lock-Centered Reading

The analysis by Miné from [10], when stripped of thread *ids* and other features specific to real-time systems such as ARINC653 and reformulated by means of side-effecting constraint systems, works as follows: It maintains for each pair (u, S) of program point u and currently held lockset S, copies of globals g whose values are weakly updated whenever the lock for some mutex a is acquired. In order to restrict the set of possibly read values, the global g is split into unknowns $[g, a, S']$ where S' is a *background* lockset held by another thread immediately after executing $\mathsf{unlock}(a)$. Then only the values of those unknowns $[g, a, S']$ are taken into account where $S \cap S' = \emptyset$.

For a more detailed discussion and our side-effecting formulation of Miné's analysis see [17, Appendix A]. We identify two sources of imprecision in this analysis. One source is *eager reading*, i.e., reading in values of g at every $\mathsf{lock}(a)$ operation. This may import the values of *too many* unknowns $[g, a, S']$ into the local state. Instead, it suffices for each mutex a, to read values at the *last* $\mathsf{lock}(a)$ before actually accessing the global.

Let $\mathcal{U}_{\mathcal{M}}$ denote the set of all upward-closed subsets of M, ordered by subset inclusion. For convenience, we represent each non-empty value in $\mathcal{U}_{\mathcal{M}}$ by the set of its minimal elements. Thus, the *least* element of $\mathcal{U}_{\mathcal{M}}$ is $\emptyset$, while the *greatest* element is given by the *full* power set of mutexes (represented by $\{\emptyset\}$).

We now maintain a map $L : \mathsf{M} \to \mathcal{U}_{\mathcal{M}}$ in the local state that tracks for each mutex a all minimal background locksets that were held when a was acquired last. This abstraction of acquisition histories [7,8] allows us to delay the reading of globals until the point where the program actually accesses their values. We call this behavior *lazy reading*.

The other source of imprecision is that each thread may publish values it has not written itself. In order to address this issue, we let $\sigma\,g$ only maintain values the ego thread itself has written.

A consequence of *lazy reading* is that values for globals are now read from the global invariant at each read. In case the ego thread has definitely written to a variable and no additional locks have occurred since, only the local copy needs to be read. To achieve that, we introduce an additional map $V : \mathsf{M} \to 2^{\mathcal{G}}$. For mutex a, $V\,a$ is the set of global variables that were definitely written since a was last acquired. In case that a has never been acquired by the ego thread, we set $V\,a$ to the set of all global variables that have definitely been written since the start of the thread.

We start by giving the right-hand-side function for the start state at program point $u_0 \in \mathcal{N}$ with the empty lockset $\emptyset$, i.e., $[u_0, \emptyset] \sqsupseteq \mathsf{init}^{\sharp}$ where

$$
\begin{aligned}
\mathsf{init}^{\sharp}\_ = \ &\mathbf{let}\ V = \{a \mapsto \emptyset \mid a \in \mathsf{M}\}\ \mathbf{in} \\
&\mathbf{let}\ L = \{a \mapsto \emptyset \mid a \in \mathsf{M}\}\ \mathbf{in} \\
&\mathbf{let}\ \sigma = \{x \mapsto \top \mid x \in \mathcal{X}\} \cup \{g \mapsto \bot \mid g \in \mathcal{G}\}\ \mathbf{in} \\
&(\emptyset, (V, L, \sigma))
\end{aligned}
$$

Next, we sketch the right-hand-side function for a thread creation edge.

$$
\begin{aligned}
[\![[u, S], x = \mathsf{create}(u_1)]\!]^{\sharp}\eta = \ &\mathbf{let}\ (V, L, \sigma) = \eta\,[u, S]\ \mathbf{in} \\
&\mathbf{let}\ V' = \{a \mapsto \emptyset \mid a \in \mathsf{M}\}\ \mathbf{in} \\
&\mathbf{let}\ L' = \{a \mapsto \emptyset \mid a \in \mathsf{M}\}\ \mathbf{in} \\
&\mathbf{let}\ i = \nu^{\sharp}\,u\,(V, L, \sigma)\,u_1\ \mathbf{in} \\
&\mathbf{let}\ \sigma' = \sigma \oplus (\{\mathsf{self} \mapsto i\} \cup \{g \mapsto \bot \mid g \in \mathcal{G}\})\ \mathbf{in} \\
&\mathbf{let}\ \rho = \{[u_1, \emptyset] \mapsto (V', L', \sigma')\}\ \mathbf{in} \\
&(\rho, (V, L, \sigma \oplus \{x \mapsto i\}))
\end{aligned}
$$

This function has no effect on the local state apart from setting x to the abstract thread *id* of the newly created thread, while providing an appropriate initial state to the startpoint of the newly created thread. For guards and computations on locals, the right-hand-side functions are once more defined in the obvious way.

Locking a mutex a resets $V a$ to $\emptyset$ and updates L, whereas unlock side-effects the value of globals to the appropriate unknowns.

$$
\begin{aligned}
[\![u, S], \mathsf{lock}(a)]\!]^\sharp \eta \ &= \mathbf{let} \ (V, L, \sigma) = \eta \, [u, S] \ \mathbf{in} \\
&\quad \mathbf{let} \ V' = V \oplus \{a \mapsto \emptyset\} \ \mathbf{in} \\
&\quad \mathbf{let} \ L' = L \oplus \{a \mapsto \{S\}\} \ \mathbf{in} \\
&\quad (\emptyset, (V', L', \sigma)) \\
[\![u, S], \mathsf{unlock}(a)]\!]^\sharp \eta &= \mathbf{let} \ (V, L, \sigma) = \eta \, [u, S] \ \mathbf{in} \\
&\quad \mathbf{let} \ \rho = \{[g, a, S \setminus \{a\}] \mapsto \sigma \, g \mid g \in \mathcal{G}\} \ \mathbf{in} \\
&\quad (\rho, (V, L, \sigma))
\end{aligned}
$$

The right-hand-side function for an edge writing to a global g then consists of a strong update to the local copy and addition of g to $V a$ for all mutexes a. For reading from a global g, those values $[g, a, S']$ need to be taken into account where a is one of the mutexes acquired in the past and the intersection of some set in $L a$ with the set of mutexes S' held while publishing is empty.

$$
\begin{aligned}
[\![u, S], g = x]\!]^\sharp \eta &= \mathbf{let} \ (V, L, \sigma) = \eta \, [u, S] \ \mathbf{in} \\
&\quad \mathbf{let} \ V' = \{a \mapsto (V a \cup \{g\}) \mid a \in \mathsf{M}\} \ \mathbf{in} \\
&\quad (\emptyset, (V', L, \sigma \oplus \{g \mapsto (\sigma x)\})) \\
[\![u, S], x = g]\!]^\sharp \eta &= \mathbf{let} \ (V, L, \sigma) = \eta \, [u, S] \ \mathbf{in} \\
&\quad \mathbf{let} \ d = \bigsqcup \{\eta[g, a, S'] \mid a \in \mathsf{M}, g \notin V a, B \in L a, B \cap S' = \emptyset\} \ \mathbf{in} \\
&\quad (\emptyset, (V, L, \sigma \oplus \{x \mapsto \sigma \, g \sqcup d\}))
\end{aligned}
$$

In case that $L a = \emptyset$, i.e., if according to the analysis no thread reaching u with lockset S has ever locked mutex a, then no values from $[g, a, S']$ will be read.

Theorem 3. Lock-Centered Reading *is sound w.r.t. to the trace semantics.*

Proof. The proof is deferred to the extended version [17, Section 5.1]. The central issue is to prove that when reading a global g, the restriction to the values of unknowns $[g, a, S']$ as indicated by the right-hand-side function is sound (see [17, Proposition 2]). □

4.3 Write-Centered Reading

In this section, we provide a refinement of *Protection-Based Reading* which abandons the assumption that each global g is write-protected by some fixed set of mutexes $\mathcal{M}[g]$. In order to lift the assumption, we introduce the additional data-structures $W, P : \mathcal{G} \to \mathcal{U}_\mathcal{M}$ to be maintained by the analysis for each unknown $[u, S]$ for program point u and currently held lockset S. The map W tracks for each global g the set of minimal locksets held when g was last written by the ego thread. At the start of a thread, no global has been written by it yet; hence, we set $W g = \emptyset$ for all globals g. The map P on the other hand, tracks for each global g all minimal locksets the ego thread has held since its last write to g. A global g not yet written to by the ego thread is mapped to the *full* power set of mutexes (represented by $\{\emptyset\}$). The unknowns for a global g now are of the form $[g, a, S, w]$ for mutexes a, background locksets S at $\mathsf{unlock}(a)$ and minimal lockset w when g was last written.

We start by giving the right-hand-side function for the start state at program point $u_0 \in \mathcal{N}$ with the empty lockset $\emptyset$, i.e., $[u_0, \emptyset] \sqsupseteq \mathsf{init}^\sharp$ where

$$\mathsf{init}^\sharp \_ = \mathbf{let}\ W = \{g \mapsto \emptyset \mid g \in \mathcal{G}\}\ \mathbf{in}$$
$$\mathbf{let}\ P = \{g \mapsto \{\emptyset\} \mid g \in \mathcal{G}\}\ \mathbf{in}$$
$$\mathbf{let}\ \sigma = \{x \mapsto \top \mid x \in \mathcal{X}\} \cup \{g \mapsto \bot \mid g \in \mathcal{G}\}\ \mathbf{in}$$
$$(\emptyset, (W, P, \sigma))$$

Next comes the right-hand-side function for a thread creating edge.

$$[\![[u, S], x = \mathsf{create}(u_1)]\!]^\sharp \eta = \mathbf{let}\ (W, P, \sigma) = \eta\,[u, S]\ \mathbf{in}$$
$$\mathbf{let}\ W' = \{g \mapsto \emptyset \mid g \in \mathcal{G}\}\ \mathbf{in}$$
$$\mathbf{let}\ P' = \{g \mapsto \{\emptyset\} \mid g \in \mathcal{G}\}\ \mathbf{in}$$
$$\mathbf{let}\ i = \nu^\sharp u\,(W, P, \sigma)\,u_1\ \mathbf{in}$$
$$\mathbf{let}\ \sigma' = \sigma \oplus (\{\mathsf{self} \mapsto i\} \cup \{g \mapsto \bot \mid g \in \mathcal{G}\})\ \mathbf{in}$$
$$\mathbf{let}\ \rho = \{[u_1, \emptyset] \mapsto (W', P', \sigma')\}\ \mathbf{in}$$
$$(\rho, (W, P, \sigma \oplus \{x \mapsto i\}))$$

This function has no effect on the local state apart from setting x to the abstract thread id of the newly created thread while providing an appropriate initial state to the startpoint of the newly created thread. For guards and computations on locals, the right-hand-side functions are once more defined intuitively—they operate on σ only, leaving W and P unchanged. While nothing happens at locking, unlocking now updates the data-structure P and additionally side-effects the current local values for each global g to the corresponding unknowns.

$$[\![[u, S], \mathsf{lock}(a)]\!]^\sharp \eta\ \ = (\emptyset, \eta\,[u, S])$$
$$[\![[u, S], \mathsf{unlock}(a)]\!]^\sharp \eta = \mathbf{let}\ (W, P, \sigma) = \eta\,[u, S]\ \mathbf{in}$$
$$\mathbf{let}\ P' = \{g \mapsto P\,g \sqcup \{S \setminus \{a\}\} \mid g \in \mathcal{G}\}\ \mathbf{in}$$
$$\mathbf{let}\ \rho = \{[g, a, S \setminus \{a\}, w] \mapsto \sigma\,g \mid g \in \mathcal{G}, w \in W\,g\}\ \mathbf{in}$$
$$(\rho, (W, P', \sigma))$$

When writing to a global g, on top of recording the written value in σ, $W\,g$ and $P\,g$ are set to the set $\{S\}$ for the current lockset S. When reading from a global g, now only values stored at $\eta\,[g, a, S', w]$ are taken into account, provided

- $a \in S$, i.e., a is one of the currently held locks;
- $S \cap S' = \emptyset$; i.e., the intersection of the current lockset S with the background lockset at the corresponding operation $\mathsf{unlock}(a)$ after the write producing the value stored at this unknown is empty;
- $w \cap S'' = \emptyset$ for some $S'' \in P\,g$, i.e., the background lockset at the write producing the value stored at this unknown is disjoint with one of the locksets in $P\,g$. This excludes writes where the ego thread has since its last thread-local write always held at least one of the locks in w. In this case, that write can not have happened between the last thread-local write of the reading ego thread and its read;

– $a \notin S'''$ for some $S''' \in P\,g$, i.e., a has not been continuously held by the thread since its last write to g.

Accordingly, we define

$$
\begin{aligned}
[\![[u,S],g = x]\!]^\sharp \eta = \ &\mathbf{let}\ (W,P,\sigma) = \eta\,[u,S]\ \mathbf{in}\\
&\mathbf{let}\ W' = W \oplus \{g \mapsto \{S\}\}\ \mathbf{in}\\
&\mathbf{let}\ P' = P \oplus \{g \mapsto \{S\}\}\ \mathbf{in}\\
&(\emptyset, (W', P', \sigma \oplus \{g \mapsto (\sigma\,x)\}))\\
[\![[u,S],x = g]\!]^\sharp \eta = \ &\mathbf{let}\ (W,P,\sigma) = \eta\,[u,S]\ \mathbf{in}\\
&\mathbf{let}\ d = \sigma\,g \sqcup \bigsqcup \{\eta[g,a,S',w] \mid a \in S, S \cap S' = \emptyset,\\
&\qquad \exists S'' \in P\,g : S'' \cap w = \emptyset,\\
&\qquad \exists S''' \in P\,g : a \notin S'''\}\ \mathbf{in}\\
&(\emptyset, (W, P, \sigma \oplus \{x \mapsto d\}))
\end{aligned}
$$

Example 4. We use integer sets for abstracting int values. Consider the following concurrent program with global variable g and local variables x, y, and z:

```
main :                                   t1 :
  y = create(t1);                          lock(a);
  z = create(t2);                          lock(b);
  lock(c);                                 lock(m_g); g = 42; unlock(m_g);
  lock(m_g); g = 31; unlock(m_g);          unlock(a);
  lock(a);                                 lock(m_g); g = 17; unlock(m_g);
  lock(b);                                 unlock(b);
  lock(m_g); x = g; unlock(m_g);
  ...                                    t2 :
                                           lock(c);
                                           lock(m_g); g = 59; unlock(m_g);
                                           unlock(c);
```

At the read $x = g$, the current lockset is $\{a,b,c,m_g\}$ and in the local state $P\,g = \{\{c\}\}$. The only unknown where all conditions above are fulfilled is the unknown $[g,b,\emptyset,\{b,m_g\}]$ which has value $\{17\}$. Hence this is the only value read from the unknowns for g and together with the value $\{31\}$ from $\sigma\,g$ the final value for x is $\{17,31\}$. This is more precise than either of the analyses presented thus far: *Protection-Based Reading* cannot exclude any values of x as $\mathcal{M}[g] = \{m_g\}$, and thus has $\{17,31,42,59\}$ for x. *Lock-Centered Reading* has $V\,c = \{g\}$ at the read. This excludes the write by $t2$ and thus results in $\{17,31,42\}$ for x.   □

Theorem 4. Write-Centered Reading *is sound w.r.t. the local trace semantics.*

The complete proof is deferred to the extended version [17, Section 5.3], we only outline some key steps here. The first step is to ensure that the concrete and the abstract constraint system share the same set of unknowns and that their side-effects are comparable.

Let the constraint system for the analysis be called $\mathcal{C}_3$. We construct from the constraint system $\mathcal{C}$ for the concrete semantics a system $\mathcal{C}'$ such that its set of unknowns matches the set of unknowns of $\mathcal{C}_3$: Each unknown $[u]$ for program point u is replaced with the set of unknowns $[u, S]$, $S \subseteq \mathsf{M}$, while the unknown $[a]$ for a mutex a is replaced with the set of unknowns $[g, a, S, w]$, $g \in \mathcal{G}, S \subseteq \mathsf{M}, w \subseteq \mathsf{M}$. Accordingly, the constraint system $\mathcal{C}'$ consists of these constraints:

$$
\begin{aligned}
&[u_0, \emptyset] && \supseteq \mathbf{fun} \_ \to (\emptyset, \mathsf{init}) \\
&[u', S \cup \{a\}] && \supseteq [\![[u, S], \mathsf{lock}(a)]\!]' && (u, \mathsf{lock}(a), u') \in \mathcal{E}, a \in \mathsf{M} \\
&[u', S \setminus \{a\}] && \supseteq [\![[u, S], \mathsf{unlock}(a)]\!]' && (u, \mathsf{unlock}(a), u') \in \mathcal{E}, a \in \mathsf{M} \\
&[u', S] && \supseteq [\![[u, S], A]\!]' && (u, A, u') \in \mathcal{E}, \forall a \in \mathsf{M} : \\
& && && A \neq \mathsf{lock}(a), A \neq \mathsf{unlock}(a)
\end{aligned}
$$

where the right-hand-side functions for reading and writing remain unmodified and the other right-hand-side functions (relative to the semantics $[\![e]\!]$ of control-flow edges e) are given by

$$
\begin{aligned}
[\![[u, S], x = \mathsf{create}(u_1)]\!]' \, \eta' &= \mathbf{let}\ T = [\![e]\!](\eta'\,[u, S])\ \mathbf{in} \\
&\quad (\{[u_1, \emptyset] \mapsto \mathsf{new}\ u_1\ (\eta'\,[u, S])\}, T) \\
[\![[u, S], \mathsf{lock}(a)]\!]' \, \eta' &= \mathbf{let}\ T' = \bigcup\{\eta'\,[g, a, S', w] \mid g \in \mathcal{G}, S' \subseteq \mathsf{M}, w \subseteq \mathsf{M}\}\ \mathbf{in} \\
&\quad (\emptyset, [\![e]\!](\eta'\,[u, S], T')) \\
[\![[u, S], \mathsf{unlock}(a)]\!]' \, \eta' &= \mathbf{let}\ T = [\![e]\!](\eta'\,[u, S])\ \mathbf{in} \\
&\quad \mathbf{let}\ \rho = \{[g, a, S \setminus \{a\}, w] \mapsto \{t\} \mid t \in T, g \in \mathcal{G}, w \subseteq \mathsf{M}, \\
&\qquad ((\mathsf{last\_tl\_write}_g\, t = (\bar{u}, g = x, \bar{u}') \wedge L_t[\bar{u}'] \subseteq w) \\
&\qquad \vee(\mathsf{last\_tl\_write}_g\, t = \bot))\}\ \mathbf{in} \\
&\quad (\rho, T)
\end{aligned}
$$

where $\mathsf{last\_tl\_write}_g$ extracts the last *thread-local* write to g, or returns $\bot$ if none exists and $L_t[\bar{u}]$ denotes the lockset held by the *ego* thread at program point $\bar{u}$. In contrast to the right-hand-side functions of $\mathcal{C}$, the new right-hand sides now also re-direct side-effects to appropriate more specific unknowns $[g, a, S', w], g \in \mathcal{G}, a \in \mathsf{M}, S' \subseteq \mathsf{M}, w \subseteq \mathsf{M}$. For a mapping η from the unknowns of $\mathcal{C}$ to $2^{\mathcal{T}}$, we construct a mapping $\mathsf{split}[\eta]$ from the unknowns of $\mathcal{C}'$ to $2^{\mathcal{T}}$ by

$$
\begin{aligned}
\mathsf{split}[\eta][u, S] &= \eta[u] \cap \mathcal{T}_S && \text{for } u \in \mathcal{N}, S \subseteq \mathsf{M} \\
\mathsf{split}[\eta][g, a, S, w] &= \eta[a] \cap \{t \in \mathcal{T}_S \mid && \text{for } g \in \mathcal{G}, a \in \mathsf{M}, S \subseteq \mathsf{M}, w \subseteq \mathsf{M} \\
&\quad (\mathsf{last\_tl\_write}_g\, t = (\bar{u}, g = x, \bar{u}') \wedge L_t[\bar{u}'] \subseteq w) \\
&\quad \vee (\mathsf{last\_tl\_write}_g\, t = \bot)\}
\end{aligned}
$$

where $\mathcal{T}_S$ denotes the set of local traces in which the *ego* thread holds lockset S at the sink. Thus,

$$
\begin{aligned}
\eta[u] &= \bigcup\{\mathsf{split}[\eta][u, S] \mid S \subseteq \mathsf{M}\} && \text{for } u \in \mathcal{N} \\
\eta[a] &= \bigcup\{\mathsf{split}[\eta][g, a, S, w] \mid g \in \mathcal{G}, S \subseteq \mathsf{M}, w \subseteq \mathsf{M}\} && \text{for } a \in \mathsf{M}
\end{aligned}
$$

Proposition 1. *The following two statements are equivalent:*

- η *is the least solution of* $\mathcal{C}$
- $\mathsf{split}[\eta]$ *is the least solution of* $\mathcal{C}'$.

Proof. The proof of Proposition 1 is by fixpoint induction.   □

Our goal is to relate post-solutions of $\mathcal{C}'$ and $\mathcal{C}_3$ to each other. While the sets of unknowns of these systems are the same, the side-effects to unknowns are still not fully comparable. Therefore, we modify the side-effects produced by $\mathcal{C}_3$ for unlock operations to obtain yet another constraint system $\mathcal{C}_3'$. All right-hand-side functions remain the same except for $\mathsf{unlock}(a)$ which is now given by:

$$[[u, S], \mathsf{unlock}(a)]_{3'}^{\sharp} \eta_3' = \mathbf{let}\ (W, P, \sigma) = \eta\,[u, S]\ \mathbf{in}$$
$$\mathbf{let}\ P' = \{g \mapsto P\,g \sqcup \{S \setminus \{a\}\} \mid g \in \mathcal{G}\}\ \mathbf{in}$$
$$\mathbf{let}\ \rho = \{[g, a, S \setminus \{a\}, w] \mapsto \sigma\,g \mid$$
$$g \in \mathcal{G}, w' \in W\,g, w' \subseteq w\}\ \mathbf{in}$$
$$(\rho, (W, P', \sigma))$$

Instead of only side-effecting to *minimal* sets w' of locks held on a write to g, the value now is side-effected to *all* supersets w of such minimal elements. This modification of the constraint system only changes the values computed for globals, but not those for program points and currently held locksets: Upon reading, all $[g, a, S, w]$ are consulted where there is an empty intersection of w and some $P\,g$. If this is the case for w, it also holds for $w' \subseteq w$. Accordingly, the values additionally published to $[g, a, S, w]$, are already read from $[g, a, S, w']$ directly in $\mathcal{C}_3$. More formally, let η_3 be a post-solution of $\mathcal{C}_3$, define η_3' by

$$\eta_3'\,[u, S] \quad = \eta_3\,[u, S] \qquad\qquad \text{for } u \in \mathcal{N}, S \subseteq \mathsf{M}$$
$$\eta_3'\,[g, a, S, w] = \bigsqcup\{\eta_3\,[g, a, S, w'] \mid w' \subseteq w\} \ \text{ for } g \in \mathcal{G}, a \in \mathsf{M}, S \subseteq \mathsf{M}, w \subseteq \mathsf{M}$$

Proposition 2. *η_3' as constructed above is a post-solution of $\mathcal{C}_3'$.*

Proof. The proof of Proposition 2 is by verifying for each edge (u, A, v) of the control-flow graph, each possible lockset S, and η_3' as constructed above, that $[[u, S], A]_{3'}^{\sharp} \eta_3' \sqsubseteq (\eta_3', \eta_3'\,[v, S'])$ holds.   □

It thus remains to relate post-solution of $\mathcal{C}'$ and $\mathcal{C}_3'$ to each other. As a first step, we define a function β that extracts from a local trace t for each global g the minimal lockset $W\,g$ held at the last *thread-local* write to g, as well as all minimal locksets $P\,g$ since the last *thread-local* write to g. Additionally, it extracts a map σ that contains the values of the locals at the sink of t as well as the last-written *thread-local* values of globals. Thus, we define

$$\beta\,t = (W, P, \sigma) \qquad \text{where}$$
$$W = \{g \mapsto \{L_t[\bar{u}']\} \mid g \in \mathcal{G}, (\_, g = x, \bar{u}') = \mathsf{last\_tl\_write}_g\,t\}$$
$$\quad \cup \{g \mapsto \emptyset \mid g \in \mathcal{G}, \bot = \mathsf{last\_tl\_write}_g\,t\ \}$$
$$P = \{g \mapsto \mathsf{min\_lockset\_since}\,t\,\bar{u}' \mid g \in \mathcal{G}, (\_, g = x, \bar{u}') = \mathsf{last\_tl\_write}_g\,t\}$$
$$\quad \cup \{g \mapsto \{\emptyset\} \mid g \in \mathcal{G}, \bot = \mathsf{last\_tl\_write}_g\,t\ \}$$
$$\sigma = \{x \mapsto \{t(x)\} \mid x \in \mathcal{X}\} \cup \{g \mapsto \emptyset \mid g \in \mathcal{G}, \bot = \mathsf{last\_tl\_write}_g\,t\}$$
$$\quad \cup \{g \mapsto \{\sigma_{j-1}\,x\} \mid g \in \mathcal{G}, ((j-1, u_{j-1}, \sigma_{j-1}), g = x, \_) = \mathsf{last\_tl\_write}_g\,t\}$$

where min_lockset_since extracts the upwards-closed set of minimal locksets the ego thread has held since a given node. The abstraction function β is used to specify concretization functions for the values of unknowns $[u, S]$ for program points and currently held locksets as well as for unknowns $[g, a, S, w]$.

$$\gamma_{u,S}(P^\sharp, W^\sharp, \sigma^\sharp) = \{t \in \mathcal{T}_S \mid \mathsf{loc}\, t = u, \beta\, t = (W, P, \sigma),$$
$$\sigma \subseteq \gamma_\mathcal{D} \circ \sigma^\sharp, W \sqsubseteq W^\sharp, P \sqsubseteq P^\sharp\}$$

where $\subseteq, \sqsubseteq$ are extended point-wise from domains to maps into domains. Moreover,

$$\gamma_{g,a,S,w}(v) = \{t \in \mathcal{T}_S \mid \mathsf{last}\, t = \mathsf{unlock}(a),$$
$$((\_, \_, \sigma_{j-1}), g = x, \bar{u}') = \mathsf{last\_tl\_write}_g\, t,$$
$$\sigma_{j-1}\, x \in \gamma_\mathcal{D}(v), w \subseteq L_t[\bar{u}']\}$$
$$\cup \{t \in \mathcal{T}_S \mid \mathsf{last}\, t = \mathsf{unlock}(a), \mathsf{last\_tl\_write}_g\, t = \bot\}$$

where $\gamma_\mathcal{D} : \mathcal{D} \to 2^\mathcal{V}$ is the concretization function for abstract values in $\mathcal{D}$. Let η'_3 be a post-solution of $\mathcal{C}'_3$. We then construct from it a mapping η' by:

$$\eta'[u, S] \quad = \gamma_{u,S}(\eta'_3[u, S]) \qquad \text{for } u \in \mathcal{N}, S \subseteq \mathsf{M}$$
$$\eta'[g, a, S, w] = \gamma_{g,a,S,w}(\eta'_3[g, a, S, w]) \quad \text{for } g \in \mathcal{G}, a \in \mathsf{M}, S \subseteq \mathsf{M}, w \subseteq \mathsf{M}$$

Altogether, the correctness of the constraint system $\mathcal{C}_3$ follows from:

Theorem 5. *Every post-solution of $\mathcal{C}_3$ is sound w.r.t. the local trace semantics.*

Proof. Recall from Proposition 1, that the least solution of $\mathcal{C}'$ is sound w.r.t. the local trace semantics as specified by constraint system $\mathcal{C}$. By Proposition 2, it thus suffices to prove that the mapping η' as constructed above, is a post-solution of the constraint system $\mathcal{C}'$. For that, the central issue is to prove that when reading a global g, the restriction to the values of unknowns $[g, a, S', w]$ as indicated by the right-hand-side function is sound (see [17, Proposition 4]).

Having shown that, we verify by fixpoint induction that for the i-th approximation η^i to the least solution split$[\eta]$ of $\mathcal{C}'$, $\eta^i \subseteq \eta'$ holds. To this end, we verify for the start point u_0 and the empty lockset, that

$$(\emptyset, \mathsf{init}) \subseteq (\eta', \eta'[u_0, \emptyset])$$

holds and for each edge (u, A, v) of the control-flow graph and each possible lockset S, that

$$[\![[u, S], A]\!]'\, \eta^{i-1} \subseteq (\eta', \eta'[v, S'])$$

holds.   □

Protection-Based Reading from Sect. 4.1 is shown to be an abstraction of this analysis in [17, Section 5.1].

The analyses described in this section and in Sect. 4.2 are both sound, yet incomparable. This is evidenced by Example 4, in which *Write-Centered* is more precise than *Lock-Centered Reading*, and [17, Example 5] where the opposite is the case. To obtain an analysis that is sound and more precise than *Write-Centered* and *Lock-Centered Reading*, both can be combined. For the combination, we do not rely on a reduced product construction, but instead directly exploit the information of the simultaneously tracked data-structures V, W, P, and L together for improving the sets of writes read at read operations. A detailed description of this analysis is deferred to [17, Section 4.4].

5   Experimental Evaluation

We have implemented the analyses described in the previous sections as well as the side-effecting formulation of Miné's analysis (see [17, Appendix A]) within the static analyzer framework GOBLINT, which analyzes C programs. For *Protection-Based Reading*, we implemented the variant that does not require prior information on the locksets $\mathcal{M}[g]$ protecting globals g, but instead discovers this information during the analysis. The solvers in GOBLINT can handle the non-monotonicity in the side-effects this entails.

For experimental evaluation, we use six multi-threaded POSIX programs from the GOBLINT benchmark suite[1] and seven large SV-COMP benchmarks in c/ldv-linux-3.14-races/ from the CONCURRENCYSAFETY-MAIN category[2]. The programs range from 1280 to 12778 physical LoC, with logical LoC[3] being between 600 and 3102. The analyses are performed context-sensitively with a standard points-to analysis for addresses and inclusion/exclusion sets as the domain for integer values. The evaluation was carried out on Ubuntu 20.04.1 and OCAML 4.11.1, running on a standard AMD EPYC processor.

We analyzed each of the programs with each of the analyses where the required analysis times are presented in Fig. 2. On smaller programs, *Protection-Based Reading* is almost twice as fast as the others, which have very similar running times. On larger programs, the differences are much larger: *Protection-Based Reading* there is up to an order of magnitude faster, while the running times of the remaining analyses grow with their sophistication.

Since the analyses use different local and global domains, their precision cannot be compared directly via the constraint system solutions. Instead, we record and compare the observable behavior in the form of abstract values of global variables read at program locations. Our comparison reveals that, for 11 out of 13 programs, all analyses are equally precise. For the remaining two programs, pfscan and ypbind, all but Miné's analysis are equally precise, while Miné's was less precise at 6% and 16% of global reads, respectively.

Thus our experiments indicate that *Protection-Based Reading* offers sufficient precision at a significantly shorter analysis time, while the more involved *Lock-* and *Write-Centered Reading* do not offer additional precision. Moreover, the incomparability identified in the introduction can in fact be observed on at least some real-world programs. Still, more experimentation is required as the selection

---

[1] https://github.com/goblint/bench.

[2] https://github.com/sosy-lab/sv-benchmarks.

[3] Only lines with executable code, excluding struct and extern function declarations.

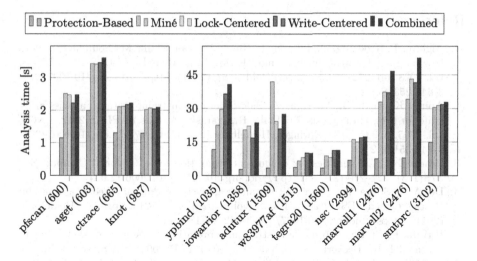

Fig. 2. Analysis times per benchmark program (logical LoC in parentheses).

of benchmarks may be biased towards programs using quite simple protection patterns. Also, only one particular value domain for globals was considered.

6   Conclusion

We have provided enhanced versions of the analyses by Miné [10] as well as by Vojdani [22,23]. To Miné's original analysis, we added lazy reading of globals and restricting local copies of globals to the values written by the ego thread. Vojdani's approach was purged of the assumption of common protecting mutexes, while additionally, background locksets are taken into account to exclude certain written values from being read. For a better comparison, we relied on side-effecting constraint systems as a convenient framework within which all analyses could be formalized. That framework also enabled us to specify a concrete semantics of *local traces* w.r.t. which all analyses could be proven correct. We also provided an implementation of all these analyses and practically compared them for precision and efficiency. Interestingly, the simplest of all analyses still provided decent precision while out-performing the others.

The given comparison and enhancements refer just to the first and most fundamental analysis introduced by Miné. We would therefore like to address possible extensions to *relational* analyses in future work. Also, we would like to explore how the framework can be extended so that *weak memory* effects can conveniently be taken into account.

Acknowledgements. This work was supported by Deutsche Forschungsgemeinschaft (DFG) – 378803395/2428 CONVEY and the Estonian Research Council grant PSG61.

References

1. Alglave, J., Kroening, D., Lugton, J., Nimal, V., Tautschnig, M.: Soundness of data flow analyses for weak memory models. In: Yang, H. (ed.) APLAS 2011. LNCS, vol. 7078, pp. 272–288. Springer, Heidelberg (2011). https://doi.org/10.1007/978-3-642-25318-8_21

2. Apinis, K., Seidl, H., Vojdani, V.: Side-effecting constraint systems: a swiss army knife for program analysis. In: Jhala, R., Igarashi, A. (eds.) APLAS 2012. LNCS, vol. 7705, pp. 157–172. Springer, Heidelberg (2012). https://doi.org/10.1007/978-3-642-35182-2_12

3. Brookes, S.: A semantics for concurrent separation logic. Theoret. Comput. Sci. **375**(1–3), 227–270 (2007). https://doi.org/10.1016/j.tcs.2006.12.034

4. De, A., D'Souza, D., Nasre, R.: Dataflow analysis for datarace-free programs. In: Barthe, G. (ed.) ESOP 2011. LNCS, vol. 6602, pp. 196–215. Springer, Heidelberg (2011). https://doi.org/10.1007/978-3-642-19718-5_11

5. Ferrara, P.: Static analysis via abstract interpretation of the happens-before memory model. In: Beckert, B., Hähnle, R. (eds.) TAP 2008. LNCS, vol. 4966, pp. 116–133. Springer, Heidelberg (2008). https://doi.org/10.1007/978-3-540-79124-9_9

6. Gotsman, A., Berdine, J., Cook, B., Sagiv, M.: Thread-modular shape analysis. In: PLDI 2007, pp. 266–277. ACM (2007). https://doi.org/10.1145/1250734.1250765

7. Kahlon, V., Ivančić, F., Gupta, A.: Reasoning about threads communicating via locks. In: Etessami, K., Rajamani, S.K. (eds.) CAV 2005. LNCS, vol. 3576, pp. 505–518. Springer, Heidelberg (2005). https://doi.org/10.1007/11513988_49

8. Kahlon, V., Yang, Yu., Sankaranarayanan, S., Gupta, A.: Fast and accurate static data-race detection for concurrent programs. In: Damm, W., Hermanns, H. (eds.) CAV 2007. LNCS, vol. 4590, pp. 226–239. Springer, Heidelberg (2007). https://doi.org/10.1007/978-3-540-73368-3_26

9. Lamport, L.: Time, clocks, and the ordering of events in a distributed system. Commun. ACM **21**(7), 558–565 (1978)

10. Miné, A.: Static analysis of run-time errors in embedded real-time parallel C programs. Log. Meth. Comput. Sci. **8**(1), 1–63 (2012). https://doi.org/10.2168/LMCS-8(1:26)2012

11. Miné, A.: Relational thread-modular static value analysis by abstract interpretation. In: McMillan, K.L., Rival, X. (eds.) VMCAI 2014. LNCS, vol. 8318, pp. 39–58. Springer, Heidelberg (2014). https://doi.org/10.1007/978-3-642-54013-4_3

12. Monat, R., Miné, A.: Precise thread-modular abstract interpretation of concurrent programs using relational interference abstractions. In: Bouajjani, A., Monniaux, D. (eds.) VMCAI 2017. LNCS, vol. 10145, pp. 386–404. Springer, Cham (2017). https://doi.org/10.1007/978-3-319-52234-0_21

13. Mukherjee, S., Padon, O., Shoham, S., D'Souza, D., Rinetzky, N.: Thread-local semantics and its efficient sequential abstractions for race-free programs. In: Ranzato, F. (ed.) SAS 2017. LNCS, vol. 10422, pp. 253–276. Springer, Cham (2017). https://doi.org/10.1007/978-3-319-66706-5_13

14. Nanevski, A., Banerjee, A., Delbianco, G.A., Fábregas, I.: Specifying concurrent programs in separation logic: morphisms and simulations. PACMPL **3**(OOPSLA), 1–30 (2019). https://doi.org/10.1145/3360587

15. Nanevski, A., Ley-Wild, R., Sergey, I., Delbianco, G.A.: Communicating state transition systems for fine-grained concurrent resources. In: Shao, Z. (ed.) ESOP 2014. LNCS, vol. 8410, pp. 290–310. Springer, Heidelberg (2014). https://doi.org/10.1007/978-3-642-54833-8_16

16. O'Hearn, P.W.: Resources, concurrency, and local reasoning. Theoret. Comput. Sci. **375**(1), 271–307 (2007). https://doi.org/10.1016/j.tcs.2006.12.035
17. Schwarz, M., Saan, S., Seidl, H., Apinis, K., Erhard, J., Vojdani, V.: Improving thread-modular abstract interpretation (2021). arXiv:2108.07613
18. Sergey, I., Nanevski, A., Banerjee, A.: Mechanized verification of fine-grained concurrent programs. In: PLDI 2015, pp. 77–87. ACM, June 2015. https://doi.org/10.1145/2737924.2737964
19. van Steen, M., Tanenbaum, A.S.: Distributed Systems. Distributed-systems.net, 3rd edn. (2017)
20. Suzanne, T., Miné, A.: From array domains to abstract interpretation under store-buffer-based memory models. In: Rival, X. (ed.) SAS 2016. LNCS, vol. 9837, pp. 469–488. Springer, Heidelberg (2016). https://doi.org/10.1007/978-3-662-53413-7_23
21. Suzanne, T., Miné, A.: Relational thread-modular abstract interpretation under relaxed memory models. In: Ryu, S. (ed.) APLAS 2018. LNCS, vol. 11275, pp. 109–128. Springer, Cham (2018). https://doi.org/10.1007/978-3-030-02768-1_6
22. Vojdani, V.: Static data race analysis of heap-manipulating C programs. Ph.D. thesis, University of Tartu, December 2010
23. Vojdani, V., Apinis, K., Rõtov, V., Seidl, H., Vene, V., Vogler, R.: Static race detection for device drivers: the Goblint approach. In: ASE 2016, pp. 391–402. ACM (2016). https://doi.org/10.1145/2970276.2970337

Thread-Modular Analysis
of Release-Acquire Concurrency

Divyanjali Sharma$^{(\boxtimes)}$ and Subodh Sharma$^{(\boxtimes)}$

Indian Institute of Technology Delhi, Delhi, India
{divyanjali,svs}@cse.iitd.ac.in

Abstract. We present a thread-modular abstract interpretation (TMAI) technique to verify programs under the *release-acquire* (RA) memory model for safety property violations. The main contributions of our work are: we capture the execution order of program statements as an abstract domain, and propose a sound *upper approximation* over this domain to efficiently reason over RA concurrency. The proposed domain is general in its application and captures the ordering relations as a first-class feature in the abstract interpretation theory. In particular, the domain represents a set of sequences of *modifications* of a global variable in concurrent programs as a *partially ordered* set. Under the upper approximation, older *sequenced-before* stores of a global variable are forgotten and only the latest stores per variable are preserved. We establish the soundness of our proposed abstractions and implement them in a prototype abstract interpreter called PRIORI. The evaluations of PRIORI on existing and challenging RA benchmarks demonstrate that the proposed technique is not only competitive in refutation, but also in verification. PRIORI shows significantly fast analysis runtimes with higher precision compared to recent state-of-the-art tools for RA concurrency.

1 Introduction

We investigate the problem of verifying programs with assertions executing under the *release-acquire* (RA) fragment of the C11 standard [15] where every store is a *release* write and every load is an *acquire* read. The reachability problem under the RA model (with *compare-and-swap*) has been recently shown to be undecidable [1]. The model is described *axiomatically* and correctness of programs under the model is defined by acyclicity axioms, which can appear obscure.

Notwithstanding the undecidability result, RA model is still one of the cleaner subsets of the C11 standard with relatively well-behaved semantics and has been a subject of active study in recent times [1,4,18,19,23,34]. An incomplete but intuitive understanding of RA concurrency is usually provided through reorderings – the redordering of an acquire load (or release store) with any access that follow (or precede) it in program order is disallowed. The RA model indeed provides weaker guarantees than SC, which allows for the construction of high performance implementations (*e.g.*, read-copy-update synchronisation [34]) without making programmability overly complex.

© Springer Nature Switzerland AG 2021
C. Drăgoi et al. (Eds.): SAS 2021, LNCS 12913, pp. 384–404, 2021.
https://doi.org/10.1007/978-3-030-88806-0_19

However, as noted in [23], RA programs can produce counter-intuitive outcomes that are unexplainable via interleaving of instructions. Consider the example *execution graph* (or just execution) of a 4-threaded program (IRIW) in Fig. 1. It shows through appropriate *reads-from* (rf), *sequence-before* (sb) and data/control *dependency* (dep) edges that the property P can evaluate to false under RA model (*i.e.*, $r1 = r3 = 1$, $r2 = r4 = 0$). However, when the execution is interpreted under interleaving execution semantics (such as in SC, TSO, and PSO),

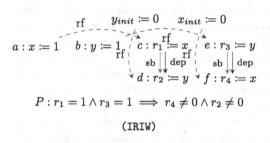

$$P : r_1 = 1 \wedge r_3 = 1 \implies r_4 \neq 0 \wedge r_2 \neq 0$$

(IRIW)

Fig. 1. IRIW execution graph with *reads-from* (rf) and *sequence-before* (sb) edges

the property is evidently valid because of a total ordering between a and b (*i.e.*, a before b or vice-versa). Nonetheless, there are some fascinating aspects of RA semantics – (i) a total order on the stores of each global memory location (called the *modification order*) that restricts loads reading from overwritten stores, and (ii) when a load instruction of a thread t observes (or *synchronizes* with) a store from another thread t', then all the prior stores observed by t' up to the synchronizing store also become observable to t. It is worth noting that this lack of immediate global visibility of updates, as mentioned in (ii) above, makes programs under RA semantics naturally amenable to *localized* or *thread-modular* reasoning, which is a well-considered area of research.

Thread-modular approaches are known to be sound for safety properties [13]. The basic idea behind thread-modular reasoning is to verify each thread separately with an environment assumption to model the effects of the execution of other threads. The environment assumption of each thread is usually specified by a relation (referred to as *interference relation* in this paper), which includes all the stores to global memory of other threads that may affect the loads of the thread. The analysis proceeds iteratively until for each thread the effects of its environment assumption on its operations reach a fix-point. As a model checking approach, they were first introduced for programs under SC semantics [10]. In the recent past, several thread-modular contributions [21,22,26,32,33] have been presented in the context of verifying programs under weak memory models such as TSO, PSO and RMO. However, in our observation, prior proposals run into fundamental limitations when applying them to RA or other *non-multicopy-atomic* memory models such as ARMv7 and POWER.

Techniques presented in [32,33] model store buffers to analyze TSO and PSO programs. Evidently, RA program behaviors cannot be simulated using store buffers [23]. Thus, extending these contributions is not feasible without re-modeling for the operational semantics of RA [18]. Contributions such as WATTS [21] and FRUITTREE [22] extend TMAI with lightweight flow- and context-sensitivity. However, they do not capture inter-thread ordering dependencies beyond two threads. Finally, the abstract interpretation technique used in DUET [9] is neither thread-modular nor geared for RA programs. While DUET performs analysis with an unbounded number of threads, it may infer gross over-approximations on some simple programs. Consider the following program where initially $x = 0 : a : x + +\|b : x + +$. DUET will infer the value $x = \infty$ at termination. FRUITTREE [22] also suffers from the same imprecision, though it does not terminate.

Contributions and Outline: In this paper, (C1) as our first contribution, we propose a TMAI technique (see Sect. 7) for RA programs using a novel abstract domain which is based on partial orders (PO). The proposed domain succinctly captures abstract ordering dependencies among instructions in a program (see Sect. 6). While the use of partial orders to analyze concurrency is well-known, to the best of our knowledge this is the first work that formulates the ordering information as an abstract domain. In particular, we model the concrete program semantics as a set of total orders on stores per global variable, also known as *modification order* (mo)(see Sect. 5). A collection of mos are then represented as a PO domain. Notably, the use of PO domain has the following merits: (M1) PO domain is general in its scope and is applicable beyond RA concurrency (see Sect. 6.1 and Sect. 6.4). (M2) Introduction of ordering information as a first-class object in abstract interpretation theory permits further abstractions or refinements on the object, an instance of which is presented in contribution (C2).

(C2) We present an *abstract upper approximation* of PO domain (see Sect. 6.3) where only the *latest stores* per thread per variable are preserved and all the older *sb*-ordered stores are forgotten.

(C3) Furthermore, to establish that our analysis preserves soundness and is terminating, we show that (i) the lattice corresponding to the abstract semantics is *complete*, (ii) establish a *Galois connection* between the concrete and PO domains, (iii) prove that the *abstract upper approximation* is sound, and (iv) provide a widening operator to ensure termination of the analysis

(C4) Finally, we implement our proposal in a prototype tool called PRIORI, and demonstrate its effectiveness in refutation and verification of RA programs by comparison with recent state-of-the-art tools in the RA domain (see Sect. 8).

We present related work in Sect. 2 followed by an intuitive account of our contributions with the help of examples in Sect. 3.

2   Related Work

Weak memory models, in particular C11 model, have been topics of active research in recent years. Many studies have provided proof and logic frameworks [8,24,35,36] and recommended strengthening the C11 models [18,23]. Many existing contributions have proposed stateless model checking algorithms for RA programs using state-reduction techniques such as dynamic partial order reduction or event structures [2,19,20,25,28,38].

In contrast, there have been relatively fewer investigations of RA concurrency using symbolic analysis. While some works have explored using TMAI (which have already been discussed in Sect. 1), others have proposed BMC as solutions to verify programs under models such as TSO, PSO and RMO.

Bounded Model Checking. BMC contributions in [1,3,12] operate by placing a bound on the number of loop unrollings or on the number of contexts or both. *Dartagnan* [12] is a BMC framework that offers support for parameterized reasoning over memory models. While, in principle, Dartagnan can perform bounded reasoning of RA programs, it currently does not support RA semantics.

VBMC [1], a recent BMC solution for RA concurrency, works with an additional bound on the number of *views* in a RA program – a *view* of a thread is a collection of timestamps of the latest stores it has observed for each variable. A *view-switch* takes place when a load operation in a thread, say t_2, reads from a store in a thread, t_1, with a timestamp higher than that of any variable in the view of t_2. While efficient in refutation, VBMC fails to discover property violations in programs which are parametric in the number of readers where the number of view-switches required is beyond the default bound of two (see [30] for a detailed discussion).

PO Encodings and Unfoldings. The use of partial order encodings is diverse and rich in areas of concurrent program verification and testing. The works in [11,14,37] use partial order encodings in dynamic verification tools to predictively reason about multithreaded and message-passing programs. Partial order encoding presented in [3] relies on the axiomatic semantics of memory models such as SC, Intel X86 and IBM POWER and is implemented in a BMC tool. The contributions in [29] and [17] use unfolding semantics to verify and test SC programs, respectively.

A recent study (POET [31]) combines unfolding semantics with abstract interpretation. The solution they have proposed is elegant and close to our proposal, but with several fundamental differences: (D1) POET defines the unfolding under a variant of the *independence* relation used in the partial order reduction theory [5]. Evidently, the independence relation assumes an interleaving model of computation. While unfoldings can capture *true concurrency*, the independence relation fundamentally limits their general applicability and restricts POET 's application to only those memory models that can be explained with interleavings. As a result, we have found POET 's technique to be unsound for RA programs. (D2) POET uses unfoldings as an auxiliary object which is external to the abstract interpretation theory. Thus, it is not straightforward to define further abstractions on the unfolding object once created. On the contrary, in our proposal, the PO domain is treated as a first-class object of the abstract interpretation theory, which is open to further abstractions as is witnessed in our contribution (C2). (D3) POET is not thread-modular and navigates an unfolding object of an entire program which is much larger than the PO domains maintained per location per variable in our technique.

3   Overview

We provide an overview of thread-modular analysis using PO domain with the help of small examples.

Let a and b be load and store operations, respectively from different threads to a global memory location. The store b is then called an *interference* for load a (denoted by $a \to^{rf} b$, since b can potentially read from a).

3.1   Thread Modular Analysis with Partial Order Domain

Consider the message passing program (MP) shown below on the left. Under RA semantics if $r_1 = 1$, then $r_2 = 0$ is infeasible. Thus, property P is known to be valid.

$$x_{init} := 0 \qquad y_{init} := 0$$

$$
\begin{array}{ll}
\text{(MP)} \\
a : x := 1 & c : r_1 := y \\
b : y := 1 & d : r_2 := x \\
P : r_1 = 1 \implies r_2 = 1
\end{array}
$$

$$
\begin{array}{l}
(\boxed{a\bullet},\boxed{})\ a : x := 1 \ \overset{rf}{\nearrow}\ c : r_1 := y\ (\boxed{a\bullet},\boxed{b\bullet}) \\
\qquad\qquad\qquad sb\downarrow \qquad\qquad \downarrow sb \\
(\boxed{a\bullet},\boxed{b\bullet})\ b : y := 1 \ \overset{hb}{\longrightarrow}\ d : r_2 := x\ (\boxed{a\bullet},\boxed{b\bullet})
\end{array}
$$

Program State. Let poset PO_x and V_x represent the partial order on the observed stores and the abstract value of variable $x \in \mathcal{V}$ where $\mathcal{V}$ is the set of all shared variables in a program. We present the program state (or just state) at each program location (or just location) as a tuple $(\Pi_{x \in \mathcal{V}} PO_x, \Pi_{x \in \mathcal{V}} V_x)$, where Π is a cartesian product operator defined over indexed family of sets. Consider an execution of (MP) shown above on the right. At location a, the state in components is: $PO_x = (\{a\}, \emptyset), PO_y = (\emptyset, \emptyset), V_x = \{1\}, V_y = \emptyset$ (Note that the second argument of a poset is the ordering relation). For brevity, we only show the posets of variables (as location-labeled Hasse diagram in a box) and suppress the abstract value in the above and future illustrations.

Interferences. Consider the above MP example again. Thread 1 has no loads; therefore, has no computable interferences. In thread 2, the set of interferences at locations c and d are $\{b \to^{rf} c, \texttt{ctx} \to^{rf} c\}$ and $\{a \to^{rf} d, \texttt{ctx} \to^{rf} d\}$, respectively. Note that $\texttt{ctx}$ refers to a special label representing *context* – *i.e.*, in the absence of any interfering stores, a load instruction will either read from the latest preceding po (program order) store or from the store values that have traveled embedded in the program states up to that load instruction.

TMAI. In the first iteration, the states of thread 1 are computed as shown in the above illustration for locations a and b. In thread 2, in the absence of any interefering store, the states are computed with the information from $\texttt{ctx}$, where PO_x and PO_y are empty. Therefore, both at c and d we have: $PO_x = (\emptyset, \emptyset), PO_y = (\emptyset, \emptyset)$.

In the second iteration, the interference $b \to^{rf} c$ is applied, and the effects of *all* the instructions prior to b from thread 1 are carried to c and d. Thus, at c, we have: $PO_x = (\{a\}, \emptyset), PO_y = (\{b\}, \emptyset)$. As a result, the effect of a, which is available at c is now also available at d (since it is now part of $\texttt{ctx}$ of thread 2). Thus, the application of interference $a \rightarrow^{rf} d$ becomes redundant. As a matter of fact, the interference $a \rightarrow^{rf} d$ turns out to be infeasible at d. This is because *extending* the PO_x at d with the PO_x at a (by taking the *meet* of the two orders, see Sect. 6.1) breaks the acyclicity of PO_x at d – one can visualise this by adding an edge from a to itself in the Hasse diagram of the resulting order). In general, to address this issue of invalid application of effects at a state, we introduce the *valid extensionality* check (see Sect. 6.1). Thus, maintaining states this way avoids the need to perform expensive *interference infeasibility* checks. Notably, such expensive checks are used by other techniques for precision, such as FruitTree [22].

After two iterations, a fix-point is reached. We can now observe that at d there is only a single state reachable when $r1 = 1$, which is: $(PO_x, V_x) = ((\{a\}, \emptyset), 1), (PO_y, V_y) = ((\{b\}, \emptyset), 1)$. Thus the property P is shown to be valid by our analysis.

3.2 Over-Approximating PO Domain

Posets are *history-preserving* and their use lends precision to our analysis, however, at the expense of possibly maintaining many posets. We show through a simple example that with further abstraction of forgetting older sb-ordered stores in the posets (see C2) one can obtain succinct posets, thereby resulting in fewer abstract states, in many scenarios. Consider the two example posets (leftmost and center) on variable x denoting two distinct states at a location in a program as shown in Fig. 2. Assume that stores a and b are *sb*-ordered and store d is from a different thread. By forgetting the older *sb*-ordered store a, a smaller abstract PO_x is obtained, which is shown as the rightmost poset in the figure. Notice that for two distinct states with differing posets at a location, the same abstract poset is obtained; consequently a single abstract state. This results in a smaller abstract state graph. However, if the value of store at a was read in a variable that affected an assertion, then the over-approximated abstract state could result in a loss of precision leading to a possible false positive. A detailed example program corresponding the illustrated example posets can be found in extended version of the paper in [30].

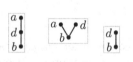

Fig. 2. Two posets and an abstract poset

4   Preliminaries

RA Semantics. Given a multithreaded program $P := \|_{i \in \text{Tid}} P_i$, where $\text{Tid} = \{1, \ldots, n\}$ is the set of thread ids and $\|$ is a parallel composition operator. Let $\mathcal{V}$, and $\mathcal{L}$ be the set of shared variables and set of program locations, respectively. We use (ℓ, i) to denote the event corresponding to the ith occurrence of program instruction labeled ℓ. Let St, Ld and RMW be the set of all store, load and rmw (read-modify-write) events from P, respectively. We denote relations sequenced-before and reads-from of RA model [4,24] by $\rightarrow^{sb}$ and $\rightarrow^{rf}$, respectively. The notation $a \rightarrow^{sb} b$ and $s \rightarrow^{rf} l$ represents $(a, b) \in \rightarrow^{sb}$ and $(s, l) \in \rightarrow^{rf}$, respectively.

The *happens-before* (hb) relation for RA concurrency is defined as a transitive closure $(\rightarrow^{rf} \cup \rightarrow^{sb})^+$. Let $(M_x, \leqslant_{M_x})$ denote the *modification order* (mo) over a set of store and rmw events $M_x \subseteq \mathsf{St} \cup \mathsf{RMW}$ to a memory location x in a program execution. As defined in [4,24], every valid RA program execution must have a mo that is consistent with hb.

Loset. The total ordering relation $\leqslant_{M_x}$ is a relation between every pair of stores $w_1, w_2 \in M_x$ in a program execution (alternatively represented as $w_1 \leqslant_{M_x} w_2$). We alternatively refer to a modification order as a *loset* (linearly ordered set). Let M^S be the the the set of all possible linear orderings over the set $S \subseteq \mathsf{St} \cup \mathsf{RMW}$. Let $L(S, \preccurlyeq)$ be a function that gives all possible linearizations of elements in $S \subseteq \mathsf{St} \cup \mathsf{RMW}$ that respect the set of ordering constraints $\preccurlyeq$ (note the difference with $\leqslant$). For example $L(\{a, b\}, \emptyset)$ will result in $\{\{(a, b)\}, \{(b, a)\}\}$. Similarly, $L(\{a, b, c\}, \{(a, b), (a, c)\})$ will produce: $\{(a, b), (a, c), (b, c)\}$ and $\{(a, b), (a, c), (c, b)\}$.

Interference. Following the description of interferences in Sect. 3, we define interference as a relation $\mathcal{I} \subseteq \mathsf{Tid} \times \mathsf{Ld} \times (\mathsf{St} \cup \mathsf{RMW})$ such that $\mathcal{I}(t)(\mathtt{ld}) \overset{\text{def}}{=} \mathtt{ctx} \cup \mathsf{St} \cup \mathsf{RMW}$, $\mathtt{ctx}$ is the store in the program state at some label in $pre(\mathtt{ld})$ for thread t. We define $pre(\mathtt{ld})$ as the set of labels immediately preceding $\mathtt{ld}$ in sb order.

5 Concrete Semantics

We consider the set of mo losets per global variable as concrete semantics of a program. Evidently, the set of mo losets is already a sound over-approximation of the set of concrete executions (see Definition 5 in [24]). Thus, considering the set of mo losets as concrete program semantics does not break the soundness of our analysis framework [7]; in fact, it serves the purpose of keeping the concrete semantics expressible enough while maintaining the ease of further abstractions.

5.1 Modification Orders as Posets

We define the concrete/collecting semantics by the set $\mathcal{T}$ such that each element $t \in \mathcal{T}$ is a subset of M^S where $S \subseteq \mathsf{St} \cup \mathsf{RMW}$. Let $t_1 \overset{\text{def}}{=} (S_1, \{\!\!\{\leqslant\}\!\!\}_{S_1})$ and $t_2 \overset{\text{def}}{=} (S_2, \{\!\!\{\leqslant\}\!\!\}_{S_2})$ be two elements of $\mathcal{T}$, where $\{\!\!\{\leqslant\}\!\!\}_S$ denotes a set of losets over S i.e. $\{\!\!\{\leqslant\}\!\!\}_S = \{\leqslant_1, \leqslant_2, \ldots\}$. Two elements $t_1, t_2 \in \mathcal{T}$ are related by an ordering relation $\sqsubseteq$, denoted by $t_1 \sqsubseteq t_2$. The definition of the ordering relation is as follows.

Definition 1. $t_1 \sqsubseteq t_2 \iff (S_1 \supseteq S_2 \wedge \forall \leqslant_i \in \{\!\!\{\leqslant\}\!\!\}_{S_1} \exists \leqslant_j \in \{\!\!\{\leqslant\}\!\!\}_{S_2} . \forall a, b \in S_2 \; a \leqslant_i b \implies a \leqslant_j b)$.

We extend the set $\mathcal{T}$ with a special element $\bot_{\mathcal{T}}$ such that $\forall t \in \mathcal{T} . \bot_{\mathcal{T}} \sqsubseteq t$. Each element in $\mathcal{T}$ is a set of mo losets that represents a set of (possibly partial) executions. For instance, t_1 in Fig. 3a is an over-approximation of all the executions whose mos satisfy either m_{11} or m_{12}. Note $t_1 \sqsubseteq t_2$, which means that the set of executions corresponding to t_2 is larger than the set of executions corresponding

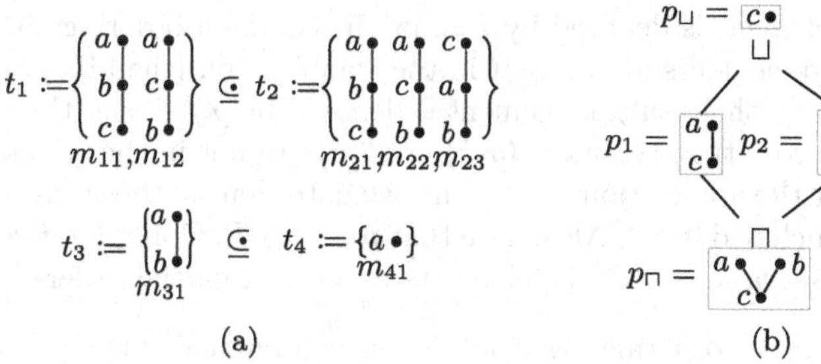

Fig. 3. Orderings over $\mathcal{T}, \mathcal{P}$

to t_1. We infer that t_1 gives us more precise information on execution possibilities than t_2 for the same program. Similarly, in Fig. 3a element t_3 is ordered below t_4. The set of executions having m_{41} as a part of their mo is larger than set of executions having m_{31} as part of their mo.

The element $\bot_{\mathcal{T}}$ represents a set in which all modification orders are inconsistent, and hence represents an invalid execution. Likewise, we introduce element $\top_{\mathcal{T}} = (\emptyset, \emptyset)$ in the $\mathcal{T}$ representing an empty set of constraints, which is equivalent to the set of all valid executions. By definition, $\top_{\mathcal{T}}$ is ordered above all the elements $\mathcal{T}$ in the $\subseteq$. We establish that $\mathcal{T}$ is a poset under the relation $\subseteq$.

Lemma 1. $(\mathcal{T}, \subseteq)$, *is a poset.*[1]

6 Abstract Semantics

We present a two-layered abstraction to arrive at final abstract RA program semantics. In particular, (i) the set of mo losets of a program is abstracted in to PO domains, and (ii) the PO domains are further over-approximated, where for each variable all stores older than the latest store under sb ordering in its poset are forgotten. Further, we demonstrate that abstract semantics produced in step (i) from above forms a *complete lattice* and establish a *Galois connection* between the concrete and abstract domains.

6.1 Mo Posets as Lattices

In this section we define a lattice over $\mathcal{P}$ which is the set of all partial orders. We use the terms mo poset and PO domain interchangeably for this lattice.

We combine two or more mo losets and respresent them as a collection of partial orders. For instance, consider mo losets p_1 and p_2 (shown in Fig. 3b) in $\mathcal{P}$. These can be combined in the following two ways: (i) the orderings in p_1 and p_2 are both present in the combination (the binary operator is denoted by $\sqcap$ and

---

[1] Proofs of all lemmas and theorems in this article are available in the extended version at [30].

the resulting element is denoted by $p_\sqcap$), or (ii) common orderings in p_1 and p_2 on the common elements are present in the combination (the binary operator is denoted by $\sqcup$ and the resulting element is denoted by $p_\sqcup$). After the application of step (i), we note that the pairs (a, b) or (b, a) are not in the relation $p_1 \sqcap p_2$. Similarly, after the application of step (ii), we note that all those executions that contain c are included in $p_\sqcup$. Also, note that $p_\sqcap, p_\sqcup \in \mathcal{P}$. Going forward we define the following operations over the elements in a set of partial orders:

Less ($p_1 \sqsubseteq p_2$): An ordering relation among two partial orders $p_1 = (M_x, \preccurlyeq_1)$ and $p_2 = (N_x, \preccurlyeq_2)$, $p_1, p_2 \neq \perp$ is defined as following: $p_1 \sqsubseteq p_2 \iff M_x \supseteq N_x \wedge a \preccurlyeq_2 b \implies a \preccurlyeq_1 b)$ and $\forall p \in \mathcal{P}, \perp \sqsubseteq p$

Is Consistent ($p_1 \uparrow p_2$): Two partial orders are consistent with each other if they do not contain any *conflicting* pair and $\perp$ is not consistent with any element. Formally, $\perp \uparrow p_2 \overset{\text{def}}{=} false$, $p_1 \uparrow \perp \overset{\text{def}}{=} false$ and $\forall p_1, p_2 \neq \perp, p_1 \uparrow p_2 \overset{\text{def}}{=} \forall a, b \in M_x \cup N_x . a \neq b, (a, b) \in \preccurlyeq_1 \implies (b, a) \notin \preccurlyeq_2$. We denote inconsistent partial orders using the notation $p_1 \not\uparrow p_2$.

Is Valid Extension ($p \lhd st$): A store event st is a valid extension of the partial order $p = (M_x, \preccurlyeq)$ *iff* there is no instruction ordered after st in the ordering relation $\preccurlyeq$. Formally, $p \lhd st \overset{\text{def}}{=} \forall a \in M_x, (st, a) \notin \preccurlyeq$. A invalid extension of a partial order p by a store st is denoted by $p \not\lhd st$).

Append ($p \lozenge st$): Appends the store operation st at the end of modification order $p = (M_x, \preccurlyeq)$ if st is a valid extension of p i.e. $p \lozenge st \overset{\text{def}}{=}$ if $p \lhd st$ then $(M_x \cup \{st\}, \preccurlyeq \cup \{(a, st) \mid a \in M_x\})$ else $\perp$.

Meet ($p_1 \sqcap p_2$): The meet of two partial orders $p_1 = (M_x, \preccurlyeq_1)$ and $p_2 = (N_x, \preccurlyeq_2)$ is defined as: $p_1 \sqcap p_2 \overset{\text{def}}{=}$ if $p_1 \uparrow p_2$ then $(M_x \cup N_x, \preccurlyeq_1 \cup \preccurlyeq_2)$ else $\perp$.

Join ($p_1 \sqcup p_2$): The join of two partial order $p_1 = (M_x, \preccurlyeq_1)$ and $p_2 = (N_x, \preccurlyeq_2)$, $p_1, p_2 \neq \perp$ is defined as the intersection of common ordered pairs in the partial orders, i.e., $p_1 \sqcup p_2 \overset{\text{def}}{=} (M_x \cap N_x, \preccurlyeq_1 \cap \preccurlyeq_2)$. We define $\perp \sqcup p_2 \overset{\text{def}}{=} p_2$ and $p_1 \sqcup \perp \overset{\text{def}}{=} p_1$.

Widening ($p_1 \nabla p_2$): The widening operator over two partial orders $p_1 = (M_x, \preccurlyeq_1)$ and $p_2 = (N_x, \preccurlyeq_2)$, $p_1, p_2 \neq \perp$ is defined as $p_1 \nabla p_2 \overset{\text{def}}{=} (Q_x, \preccurlyeq)$, where $Q_x = \{a \mid a = (\ell, i) \in M_x \cap N_x \wedge \nexists b = (\ell, j) \in M_x \cap N_x . j < i\}$ and $\preccurlyeq = \{(a, b) \mid (a, b) \in \preccurlyeq_1 \cap \preccurlyeq_2 \wedge a, b \in Q_x\}$. We define $\perp \nabla p_2 \overset{\text{def}}{=} p_2$ and $p_1 \nabla \perp \overset{\text{def}}{=} p_1$.

Lemma 2. *The operators $\sqcup$ and $\sqcap$ define the lub and glb of any two elements of $\mathcal{P}$, respectively.(See footnote 1)*

Lemma 3. *$(\mathcal{P}, \sqsubseteq, \sqcup, \sqcap, \perp, \top)$ is a complete lattice, where $\mathcal{P}$ is set of all possible partial orders over elements of set $\mathsf{St} \cup \mathsf{RMW}$, $\top$ is defined as empty poset, and $\perp$ is a special element that is ordered below all the elements of $\mathcal{P}$ in $\sqsubseteq$.(See footnote 1)*

The proof of Lemma 3 follows from Lemma 2, the definition of $\sqcup$ and $\sqcap$ operations of $\mathcal{P}$, and standard properties of operators.

Lemma 4. *The binary operation ∇ defines a widening operator over the elements of the lattice $(\mathcal{P}, \sqsubseteq, \sqcup, \sqcap, \bot, \top)$.(See footnote 1)*

We explain the widening operator ∇ using an example. Recall that each element of lattice $\mathcal{P}$ is a partial order over program events. Let $p = (Q_x, \preccurlyeq) = p_1 \nabla p_2$, then the set of events in p maintains the earliest occurrence of common events in M_x and N_x corresponding to p_1 and p_2, respectively. Consider the events $e_2 = (\ell, 2)$ and $e_3 = (\ell, 3)$, which are generated by the same program instruction labeled ℓ. If both p_1 and p_2 contain the ordering e_2 and e_3, then the result of widening will contain the earliest occurrence of an event from ℓ, i.e., e_2 so long as $e_1 = (\ell, 1) \notin M_x \cap N_x$. The set of orderings $\preccurlyeq$ is defined over the elements of Q_x. Hence no ordering involving e_3 in this example will be in $\preccurlyeq$.

Given a monotone function $f : \mathcal{P} \to \mathcal{P}$, consider the chain $f_\nabla^0, f_\nabla^1, f_\nabla^2 \ldots$ with $f_\nabla^0 = \bot$ and $f_\nabla^i = f_\nabla^{i-1} \nabla f(f_\nabla^{i-1})$ for some $i > 0$. An essential requirement on ∇ for it to be a widening operator is that the above chain must stabilize, i.e., $f(f_\nabla^n) \sqsubseteq f_\nabla^n$ for some $n > 0$. It means that the function f is *reductive* at f_∇^n. We show in the proof of Lemma 4 that our defined operator ∇ is indeed a widening operator. Using Tarski's fixpoint theorem, it follows that $\mathrm{lfp}(f) \sqsubseteq f_\nabla^n$, where $\mathrm{lfp}(f)$ is the least fixed point of f. As a result, f_∇^n is a sound over-approximation of f, which guarantees termination of analysis with infinite lattices having infinite ascending chains.

Definition 2. *The abstraction function $\alpha : \mathcal{T} \to \mathcal{P}$ is defined as $\alpha(\bot_{\mathcal{T}}) \overset{def}{=} \bot$ and $\forall t \neq \bot_{\mathcal{T}}$, $\alpha(t) \overset{def}{=} (M_x, \preccurlyeq)$ for some $t = (S, \{\!\{\leqslant\}\!\})$ given $M_x = S$, and $\preccurlyeq = \bigcap \leqslant_i$.*

Definition 3. *The concretization function $\gamma : \mathcal{P} \to \mathcal{T}$ is defined as $\gamma(\bot) \overset{def}{=} \bot_{\mathcal{T}}$ and $\forall p \neq \bot$, $\forall p \neq \bot$, $\gamma(p) \overset{def}{=} (S, \{\!\{\leqslant\}\!\})$ for some $p = (M_x, \preccurlyeq)$ given $S = M_x$ and $\{\!\{\leqslant\}\!\}$ is set of all possible linearizations of $\preccurlyeq$ i.e. $\{\!\{\leqslant\}\!\} = L(S, \preccurlyeq)..$*

Having defined the abstraction and concretization operators, we can now establish the Galois connection between the poset $\mathcal{T}$ and the lattice $\mathcal{P}$.

Theorem 1. $(\mathcal{T}, \subseteq) \xleftrightarrow[\alpha]{\gamma} (\mathcal{P}, \sqsubseteq, \sqcup, \sqcap, \bot, \top)$.*(See footnote 1)*

We lift the result from Theorem 1 to the product lattices of all the program variables. Theorem 2 articulates that the Galois connection between concrete and abstract product lattices is preserved.

Theorem 2. *The correspondence between $\prod_{x \in \mathcal{V}} \mathcal{P}_x$ and $\prod_{x \in \mathcal{V}} \mathcal{T}_x$ is a Galois connection.(See footnote 1)*

It is worthwhile to note that lattice $\mathcal{P}$ is not tied to the RA semantics. As such, the PO domain is not specific to any memory model. We present a discussion in Sect. 6.4, on the applicability of PO domain beyond RA semantics. Below, we give a description of transfer functions for the operations in RA programs.

$$\frac{\begin{array}{c}(pre(\ell), mo, m) \in \mathcal{S} \quad m' = m[x \to v] \\ mo' = mo[x \to mo(x) \lozenge \ell]\end{array}}{\mathcal{S} \xrightarrow{\ell: \text{st } x \ v} \mathcal{S} \uplus (\ell, mo', m')} \text{STORE}$$

$$\frac{\begin{array}{c}(pre(\ell), mo, m) \in \mathcal{S} \\ (pre(\ell), mo, m) \xrightarrow{\ell: \text{ld } x} (\ell, mo'', m'') \\ m''(x) = v \\ (pre(\ell), mo'', m'') \xrightarrow{\ell: \text{st } x \ v'} (\ell, mo', m')\end{array}}{\mathcal{S} \xrightarrow{\ell: \text{rmw } x \ v \ v'} \mathcal{S} \uplus (\ell, mo', m')} \text{RMW}$$

$$\frac{\begin{array}{c}(pre(\ell), mo_l, m_l) \in \mathcal{S} \quad \text{st} \in \mathcal{I}(t)(\ell) \\ (\text{st}, mo_s, m_s) \in \mathcal{S} \\ (pre(\ell), mo', m'') = \text{AI}((pre(\ell), mo_l, m_l), (\text{st}, mo_s, m_s)) \\ m' = m''[x \to m_s(x)]\end{array}}{\mathcal{S} \xrightarrow{\ell: \text{ld } x} \mathcal{S} \uplus (\ell, mo', m')} \text{LOAD}$$

Fig. 4. Transfer functions for RA programs. $\text{AI}((\ell_1, mo_1, mo_2), (\ell_2, mo_2, m_2)) \overset{\text{def}}{=} (\ell_1, (mo_1 \lozenge \ell_2) \sqcap mo_2, m_1 \sqcup m_2)$; AI applies the interference from (ℓ_2, mo_2, m_2) to the memory and mo poset state of (ℓ_1, mo_1, mo_2).

6.2 Abstract Semantics of RA Programs

The values of shared variables in the program can be abstracted to any known numeric abstract domain such as interval, octagon, or polyhedra. Let $\mathbb{V}^\sharp$ represents the set of values in the chosen abstract domain. Let $\mathcal{M} : \mathcal{V} \to \mathbb{V}^\sharp$ define the memory state of a program. Let $\mathbb{M} : \mathcal{V} \to \mathcal{P}$ represent a map from shared variables to corresponding elements in the abstract mo poset lattice $\mathcal{P}$. We abuse notations $\lozenge, \sqcup, \sqcap, \nabla, \uparrow$, and $\lhd$ to represent the corresponding pointwise-lifted operators for $\mathbb{M}$. For instance, the pointwise lifting of $\lozenge$ appends the stores of variable v only to its modification order (*i.e.*, $\mathbb{M}(v)$); the modification orders $\mathbb{M}(v')$ for variables $v' \neq v$ remain unchanged. The pointwise lifting for other operators is straighforward. From Theorem 2, it follows that $\mathbb{M}$ along with the pointwise lifted operators constitute the sought abstract domain.

Let $\Sigma \subseteq \mathcal{L} \times (\mathbb{M} \times \mathcal{M})$ represents the set of all reachable program states. The transfer functions for operations ld, st and rmw are defined in Fig. 4. The transfer functions of lock and unlock operations have been omitted for the brevity. Since we assume the SSA representation of programs, arithmetic operations only modify the thread local variables. As a result, $\mathbb{M}$ remains unchanged. The effects of arithmetic operations on shared variables is captured via numeric abstract domains. Thus, the transfer functions for such operations are excluded from our presentation. The semantic definitions in Fig. 4 are parameterized in terms of the set of currently explored reachable program states, $\mathcal{S} \subseteq \Sigma$, at a some point during the analysis.

Consider the LOAD rule which, defines the semantics of a load operation. A load of a shared variable x at ℓ is performed at program state(s) $\mathcal{S}$ using the following steps. Let st be an interfering instruction for ℓ. Each explored program state

$(\mathtt{st}, mo_s, m_s)$ at instruction label $\mathtt{st}$ is considered as an interference and analyzed with the set of program states at label $pre(\ell)$ using the function $\mathtt{AI}$ (defined in the caption of Fig. 4). When the interference from program state (ℓ_2, mo_2, m_2) is successfully applied to the program state (ℓ_1, mo_1, mo_2) by function $\mathtt{AI}$ (the load at ℓ_1 reads from the store at ℓ_2), then as a result ℓ_2 is appended in the partial order at ℓ_1, i.e., mo_1. For all other events prior to ℓ_1 and ℓ_2 , the precise ordering information among them is computed by taking the *meet* of mo_1 and mo_2, i.e., $mo_1 \sqcap mo_2$ (because the ordering of such events must be consistent with both mo_1 and mo_2).

In the state at ℓ_1, the value of variables other than interfering variable x can come from either m_1 or m_2. The function $\mathtt{AI}$ *joins* the maps m_1 and m_2 to obtain all feasible values for such variables. To compute $\sqcup$ on memory values, one can choose abstract domains such as intervals or octagons. Let $\mathtt{AI}$ return $(pre(\ell), mo', m'')$ when the interference is applied from $(\mathtt{st}, mo_s, m_s)$ to $(pre(\ell), mo_l, m_l)$. The value of variable x read by the load operation ℓ in the program state $(pre(\ell), mo', m'')$ will be the same as the value of variable x in the interfering program state $m_s(x)$. Thus, we substitute $m''(x)$ with $m_s(x)$ to construct the reachable program state (ℓ, mo', m').

Finally, the resulting state at ℓ is combined with the currently existing states by the $\uplus$ operator. The operator $\uplus$ performs instruction-wise join of states, i.e., it joins the memory state of two states if their instruction labels and $\mathtt{mo}$ posets are the same. It also joins the $\mathtt{mo}$ poses if the instruction label and the memory states are the same, otherwise, it leaves the two states as is. Formally, the operation $\uplus$ replaces any two program states (say (ℓ_1, mo_1, m_1) and (ℓ_2, mo_2, m_2)), with a single program state (ℓ_1, mo_1, m), where $m = m_1 \sqcup m_2$, if $mo_1 = mo_2 \wedge \ell_1 = \ell_2$, and with (ℓ_1, mo, m_1), where $mo = mo_1 \sqcup mo_2$, if $m_1 = m_2 \wedge \ell_1 = \ell_2$.

Transfer functions for RMW and STORE can be interpreted in a similar way. Readers may note that, in general, two successful RMW operations will never read from the same store as is assumed in our rule. However, our definition is sound (and simple to understand); we provide a more precise definition in Sect. 7.2, which is also implemented in PRIORI.

6.3   Abstracting the Abstraction: Approximating Mo Posets

We leverage the ordering rules of the RA memory model to further abstract the modification orders. Let $p \stackrel{\text{def}}{=} (Q_x, \preccurlyeq), p_1 \stackrel{\text{def}}{=} (M_x, \preccurlyeq_1), p_2 \stackrel{\text{def}}{=} (N_x, \preccurlyeq_2), p_a \stackrel{\text{def}}{=} (A_x, \preccurlyeq_a)$ be some elements in $\mathcal{P}$. We shall use these definitions whenever p, p_1, p_2 and p_a appear in definitions and predicates below.

Our abstraction function $\alpha^{\sharp} : \mathcal{P} \to \mathcal{P}$ can be defined as follows: $\alpha^{\sharp}(\bot) = \bot$ and $\forall p \neq \bot, \alpha^{\sharp}(p) \stackrel{\text{def}}{=} (A_x, \preccurlyeq_a)$, where $A_x = Q_x \setminus \{a \mid \exists b \in Q_x . a \to^{sb} b \wedge a \neq b\}$ and $\preccurlyeq_a = \preccurlyeq \setminus \{(a, b) \mid (a, b) \in \preccurlyeq \wedge (a \notin A_x \vee b \notin A_x)\}$.

Soundness of $\alpha^{\sharp}$ Abstraction: Let relation $\beta \in \wp(\mathcal{P} \times \mathcal{P})$, where $\wp$ denotes power set, be defined as $\exists p_1, p_2 \in \mathcal{P}, (p_1, p_2) \in \beta \iff p_1 = \bot \vee (N_x \subseteq M_x \setminus \{a \mid \exists b \in M_x . a \to^{sb} b \wedge a \neq b\} \wedge \preccurlyeq_2 \subseteq \preccurlyeq_1)$. Through Lemma 5 we establish that our definition of β indeed provides a soundness relation.

Lemma 5. $(p_1, p_2) \in \beta \implies p_1 \sqsubseteq p_2$. *(See footnote 1)*

Lemma 6. *Abstract soundness assumption holds under* β, *i.e.,* $\forall p, p_1, p_2 \in \mathcal{P}$.
$(p, p_1) \in \beta \wedge p_1 \sqsubseteq p_2 \implies (p, p_2) \in \beta$. *(See footnote 1)*

In other words, Lemma 6 allows us to conclude that if p_1 is a sound over-approximation of p, then every element ordered above p_1 in lattice $\mathcal{P}$ is also a sound over-approximation of p under β. We shall use Lemmas 5–6 to establish the soundness of $\alpha^\sharp$ in the theorem below.

Theorem 3. *Abstraction relation* $\alpha^\sharp$ *is minimal sound abstraction under sound-ness relation* β, *i.e.,* $(p_1, p_2) \in \beta \iff \alpha^\sharp(p_1) \sqsubseteq p_2$. *(See footnote 1)*

The proof of Theorem 3 is obtained by a straightforward application of the definitions of $\alpha^\sharp$, β and Lemma 6.

We redefine some of the operations described in Sect. 6.1 in order to assist with the computation of transfer functions under the $\alpha^\sharp$ abstraction:

Is Consistent $(p_1 \uparrow p_2)$: $\perp \uparrow p_2 \overset{\text{def}}{=} false$, $p_1 \uparrow \perp \overset{\text{def}}{=} false$ and $\forall p_1, p_2 \neq \perp$
$p_1 \uparrow p_2 \overset{\text{def}}{=} \forall a, b\ ((a,b) \in \preccurlyeq_1 \implies \forall b{\rightarrow}^{sb}c\ .\ (c, a) \notin \preccurlyeq_2) \wedge ((a, b) \in \preccurlyeq_2$
$\implies \forall b{\rightarrow}^{sb}c\ .\ (c, a) \notin \preccurlyeq_1)$. Note that $\rightarrow^{sb}$ is reflexive. As before, we use the notation $p_1 \not\uparrow p_2$ when p_1 and p_2 are inconsistent.

Is Valid Extension $(p \lhd \mathtt{st})$: $p \lhd \mathtt{st} \overset{\text{def}}{=} \forall a(\mathtt{st}, a) \notin \preccurlyeq \wedge \nexists b \in Q_x\ .\ \mathtt{st}{\rightarrow}^{sb}b$. We use the notation $p \not\lhd \mathtt{st}$ to indicate that $\mathtt{st}$ is not a valid extension of p.

Append $(\,p \lozenge \mathtt{st})$: If $\mathtt{st}$ is a valid extension of p, then append the store operation $\mathtt{st}$ at the end of partial order p and delete the older instructions, if any, i.e.
$p \lozenge \mathtt{st} \overset{\text{def}}{=}$ if $p \lhd \mathtt{st}$ then $(Q_x \cup \mathtt{st} \backslash \{a \mid a {\rightarrow}^{sb} \mathtt{st}\}, \preccurlyeq \cup \{(a, \mathtt{st}) \mid a \in Q_x\} \backslash \{(a, b) \mid (a {\rightarrow}^{sb} \mathtt{st} \wedge a \neq \mathtt{st}) \vee (b {\rightarrow}^{sb} \mathtt{st} \wedge b \neq \mathtt{st})\})$ else $\perp$.

Over-Approximating the Semantics of RA Programs
We use the modified definitions of $\lozenge, \uparrow, \not\uparrow, \lhd$ and $\not\lhd$ operators to perform analysis under $\alpha^\sharp$ abstraction. The semantics of $\mathtt{st}, \mathtt{ld}$ and $\mathtt{rmw}$ operations and the set of all program states Σ remain the same as under $\alpha^\sharp$, as defined in Sect. 6.2.

6.4 Posets as a Generic Abstraction

In this section, we discuss the possibility of using the lattice $(\mathcal{P}, \sqsubseteq, \sqcup, \sqcap, \perp, \top)$ as a generic abstraction, and using it for reasoning memory models other than RA. As a first step, we reinvestigate how we define the collecting semantics for programs under non-RA memory models. The mo losets may not be best suited collecting semantics to reason over programs under other memory models.

Consider, for instance, the TSO model. The collecting semantics for TSO model require an ordering over all the events of shared variables in the program, except among the store-load pairs of different variables from the same thread. Thus, using losets as concrete semantics over loads and stores of all the shared variables in which the store-load pair of different variables in a thread can appear in any order will suffice. This allows us to capture rfe (reads-from-external,

---

Algorithm 1: TMAI

Data: Tid is the set of threads in the program
1 **Function** ThreadModularAnalysis(Tid):
   | // Initialization
2 | $\sigma \leftarrow \phi$;
3 | $\mathcal{I} \leftarrow$ GetInterfs(Tid) ;
4 | **repeat**
5 | | $\mathcal{S} \leftarrow \sigma$;
6 | | **foreach** $t \in$ Tid **do**
7 | | | $\sigma \leftarrow \sigma \uplus$ SeqAI$(t, \mathcal{S}, \mathcal{I}(t))$
8 | **until** $\mathcal{S} = \sigma$;

---

rfe=rf \ po) in the loset. Similarly, considering the PSO model the concrete semantics containing one loset per variable containing all the load and store events of that variable will suffice.

Note that once the collecting semantics is suitably fixed, then formal objects such as $(\mathcal{T}, \sqsubseteq)$, $(\mathcal{P}, \sqsubseteq, \sqcup, \sqcap, \perp, \top)$, and functions α and γ can be used in the analysis without requiring any change. However, designing $\alpha^\sharp$ for other memory models may require careful analysis, and is left as future work.

7   Thread-Modular Abstract Interpretation

7.1   Analysis Algorithms

We present Algorithm 1 in which procedure **ThreadModularAnalysis** analyzes the entire program by considering one thread at a time. The analysis begins with the initialization of the set of explored program states (line 2). For each thread $t \in$ Tid, relation $\mathcal{I}(t)$ is computed (line 3) according to the definition in Sect. 4. Each thread is analyzed under all possible interferences in $\mathcal{I}$ until a fixed point is reached (lines 4–8). The function SeqAI$(t, \mathcal{S}, \mathcal{I}(t))$ is a standard work-list based sequential abstract interpretation over a single thread [27]. Our work adapts this analysis by replacing the transfer functions with the ones given in Sect. 6.2. The function returns a set of states for all the locations in the thread t. The operator $\uplus$ performs instruction-wise join (explained in Sect. 6.2) of environments in the existing (σ, line 5) and the newly computed program states (SeqAI$(t, \mathcal{S}, \mathcal{I}(t))$). The details of RA memory model, interferences, abstractions and semantics of transfer functions are all embedded in line 7 of the algorithm.

7.2   A Note on Precision

When the older sb-ordered stores are forgotten in a mo poset and those program states having the same mo poset are combined, it results in the merging of multiple program executions into a single over-approximation. In theory, it is possible that one or more forgotten (older) stores were critical to prove the property. We can achieve higher precision if we can discern such critical stores and preserve the ordering constraints over such stores in the mo posets.

In our study, we found that many benchmarks that model mutual exclusion under the RA memory model use rmw instructions as synchronization fences. These rmw events are instances of critical stores, and we flag them as such and preserve all the older rmw instructions in $\preccurlyeq_x$.

Updated Semantics of RMW The semantics of RMW given in Fig. 4 (for a shared variable x), while sound, are not precise according to RA semantics. We update the semantics in the following way: the consistency check of two elements $p_1 = (M_x, \preccurlyeq_{M_x})$ and $p_2 = (N_x, \preccurlyeq_{N_x})$ will return true iff $p_1 \uparrow p_2 \land \forall \text{rmw}_1 \in p_1, \text{rmw}_2 \in p_2, ((\text{rmw}_1, \text{rmw}_2) \in \preccurlyeq_{M_x} \lor (\text{rmw}_1, \text{rmw}_2) \in \preccurlyeq_{N_x} \lor (\text{rmw}_2, \text{rmw}_1) \in \preccurlyeq_{M_x} \lor (\text{rmw}_2, \text{rmw}_1) \in \preccurlyeq_{N_x})$. The mentioned update prohibits the combination of those two partial orders such that if they were to be combined then the rmw events no longer remain in a total order.

7.3 Loops and Termination

Widening [6] is generally used to handle non-terminating loops or to accelerate fix-point computation in programs. Consider a loop that contains store operations. The value to be stored can be over-approximated using widening. Since mo posets contain abstracted execution histories, adding a store event in posets at least once for each store instruction within the loop will suffice to inform that the store has occurred at least once in the execution. However, one can always choose to add different events corresponding to the same store instruction depending on the precision requirement and then widen using ∇, as necessary.

Note that one can use widening after analyzing some fixed n iterations of a program loop. In particular, widening is applied in the transfer function for store and rmw in function SeqAI.

8   Implementation and Evaluation

In this section, we discuss the details of PRIORI's implementation and evaluation. In the absence of TMAI tools for RA programs, we have shown the comparison of PRIORI with the existing tools designed for the RA memory model. VBMC [1] is the most recent BMC technique among these tools. Other static tools such as CPPMEM and HERD are not designed as verification tools. CPPMEM is designed to help investigate possible ordering relations in programs under the C/C++11 memory model. It computes all the relations of all possible executions. HERD is designed to generate litmus tests for different memory models or to simulate a memory model. Both of these tools are relatively very slow compared to existing verification or bug-finding tools. We have also compared PRIORI with dynamic tools such as CDSCHECKER [28], TRACER [2], and RCMC [19] to evaluate how well PRIORI performs as a refutation tool; although the input coverage guarantee of PRIORI and dynamic checkers is quite different.

8.1   Implementation

PRIORI is implemented as an LLVM Compiler analysis pass written in C++ (code size ∼5.4KLOC). PRIORI uses the APRON library [16] for manipulating the variable values in octagon and interval numerical abstract domains. PRIORI takes as input an LLVM IR of an RA program compiled with -O1 flag, and analyzes user assertions in programs; if assertions are not provided, then it can generate the set of reachable program states at load operations for further reasoning. In addition to the transfer functions in Fig. 4, PRIORI supports lock and unlock operations. PRIORI currently does not support dynamic thread creation and non-integer variables. Function calls in the program are inlined.

Handling Loops: PRIORI provides support for loops in three ways: (i) by using the assume clause, (ii) by unrolling the loops, and (iii) by a combination of assume clause and loop unrolling. The assume clause is useful in modeling spin-wait loops in programs. The option of unrolling loops is used when either the assume clause is inadequate (such as in non-terminating loops), or when we have a fixed number of iterations in the loop (such as counting loops).

Experimental Setup: We have used Ubuntu 16.04 machine with Intel(R) Xeon(R) 3.60 GHz CPU and 32 GB of RAM. The listed analysis time for each benchmark is an average of four runs. The analysis times reported are in seconds.

8.2   Summary of Benchmarks

Benchmarks from Tracer: The benchmarks from TRACER [2] are known to have no assertion violations. We craft an unfenced version of the dijkstra benchmark to introduce assertion-violating behaviors in it. CO-2+2W benchmark has no interferences; we use this benchmark to distinguish the performance of interference-based PRIORI and non-interference-based VBMC and POET. The benchmark fibonacci has a high number of load and store operations, and is used to stress-test interference-based techniques.

Benchmarks from VBMC: The benchmarks from VBMC [1] are divided into two categories: (i) the first category has benchmarks with assertion violations with respect to the RA memory model, and (ii) the second category consists the same benchmarks with appropriate fences inserted to ensure mutual exclusion under RA semantics.

Driver Benchmarks: The benchmarks ib700wdt and keybISR are Linux device drivers taken from [9,21,22]. We have modified these benchmarks to use C11 constructs. The program ib700wdt simulates multiple writers accessing a buffer and one *closer* that closes the buffer. The benchmark keybISR is an interrupt service routine for the keyboard.

8.3   Observations

Comparison of PRIORI with VBMC: Tables 1 and 2 show the performance comparison of PRIORI and VBMC for discovering assertion violations and proving programs correct, respectively. VBMC with the view-bound of two, which is

Table 1. Comparison for bug hunting

Name	PRIORI		VBMC		CDS	TRACER	RCMC
	T	#It	T	VS			
peterson3	0.12	3	0.55	3	0.01	0.01	0.05
10R1W	0.02	2	3.99	10	0.01	0.01	0.03
15R1W	0.03	2	24.45	15	0.02	0.01	0.03
szymanski(7)	0.06	1	6.58	2	TO	TO	TO
fmax(2,7)	1.00	2	×	-	0.15	0.05	TO

TO: Timeout (10 min), ×: Did not run

Table 2. Comparison for proof of correctness.

Name	PRIORI		VBMC	CDS	TRACER	RCMC
	T	#It	T			
CO-2+2W(5)	0.01	3	0.32	0.01	0.01	17.26
CO-2+2W(15)	0.02	3	1.29	0.02	0.01	TO
dijkstra_fen	0.10	5	206.70†	0.01	0.01	0.03
burns_fen	0.02	4	37.37†	0.02	0.01	0.02
peterson_fen	0.10	6	44.12†	0.02	0.01	0.03
tbar	0.04	6	18.58	0.02	0.01	0.14
hehner_c11	0.03	6	107.16†	0.07	0.02	0.04
red_co_20	0.04	3	31.47	23.32	0.13	TO
exp_bug_6	0.45	6	×	97.13	0.96	37.82
exp_bug_9	0.57	6	×	TO	2.98	437.47
stack_true(12)	0.06	4	×	TO	589.81	TO
ib700wdt (1)	0.01	3	31.73	0.01	0.01	0.02
ib700wdt (20)	0.05	3	TO	0.01	0.01	TO
ib700wdt (40)	0.07	3	TO	0.01	0.01	TO
keybISR	0.01	4	0.01	0.01	0.01	0.03
fibonacci	0.11†	5	310.75	TO	56.4	20.61
lamport_fen	0.17†	4	431.40	0.09	0.03	0.04

†: False positive, TO: Timeout (10 min), ×: Did not run

the same bound used in [1], is insufficient to prove the properties in the program correct. We increase the view bound one at a time and report the cumulative time. PRIORI found the assertion violations in benchmarks of Table 1 in better time than VBMC. It is worth noting that in peterson3, 10R1W, and 15R1W, VBMC could not find the violation with the tool's default bound of two.

The results of VBMC can be considered proof only if view bounding is relaxed and the *unwiding assertions* (in CBMC) hold. However, we could not find an option in VBMC to disable view bounding. Thus, we made a decision to run

VBMC with a view-bound of 500 (assuming it to be sufficiently large) for the benchmarks in Table 2. The results in Table 2 illustrate that the runtimes of PRIORI are consistently better than that of VBMC. VBMC was unable to analyze benchmarks marked with ×, since they have mutex lock/unlock operations.

Many of the mutual exclusion benchmarks have fences, which are implemented with rmw operations. These rmw operations are critical in order to prove the property. As a matter of fact, PRIORI produces false positives without the improvements discussed in Sect. 7.2. Identifying rmw operations as critical operations and not deleting older sb-ordered rmw operations enables PRIORI to attain the sought precision.

False Positives in PRIORI. The last two rows in Table 2 shows the false positive results produced by PRIORI. Our technique combines the states of different executions (having the same abstract modification order) into a single abstracted program state. This results in an over-approximation of values leading to the observed false positives in fibonacci and lamport_fen benchmarks. For instance, the false positive in lamport_fen is caused by two different branch conditions (which cannot be true simultaneously in any concrete state) evaluating to true under the abstracted program states.

Comparison of PRIORI with Dynamic Tools: The results in Table 1 indicate that PRIORI performs competitively or faster than dynamic tools on these benchmarks. Evidently, most of the executions of these benchmarks are buggy. Hence, the probability of dynamic analyses finding the first explored execution to be buggy is very high, leading to their considerably fast analysis times. The results in Table 2 show the analysis time over non-buggy benchmarks.

Comparison of PRIORI with Poet: POET is unsound under the RA model and reports false negatives in most of the benchmarks from Table 1. The elapsed time when POET produced sound results is as follows: (i) TO for POET on on 10R1W and 15R1W while PRIORI analyzes them in ∼0.03 s, and (ii) POET takes 80.43 s seconds on fmax(2,7), while PRIORI analyzes the benchmark in ∼1 s.

9   Conclusions

We have presented a thread modular analysis technique for RA programs that uses partial orders over the set of totally ordered stores as abstract domains. We showed that the abstract domain forms a complete lattice and further established a *Galois* correspondence between the set of modification orders and the abstract domain. By forgetting the sb-ordered older stores, we provided a sound overapproximation on the abstract domain, which is shown to be sound for RA programs. We implemented our proposal in a tool called PRIORI, and demonstrated its effectiveness in not only finding bugs, but also for proving program properties. Our experimental results revealed that PRIORI attains a high degree of precision with significantly low analysis runtimes in comparison to other tools for RA concurrency.

Acknowledgment. We thank Sanjana Singh for her help during initial discussions. This work is partially supported by the Department of Science and Technology under the grant number DST ECR/2017/003427.

References

1. Abdulla, P.A., Arora, J., Atig, M.F., Krishna, S.: Verification of programs under the release-acquire semantics. In: Proceedings of the 40th ACM SIGPLAN Conference on Programming Language Design and Implementation (PLDI 2019), pp. 1117–1132. ACM, New York (2019). https://doi.org/10.1145/3314221.3314649, http://doi.acm.org/10.1145/3314221.3314649

2. Abdulla, P.A., Atig, M.F., Jonsson, B., Ngo, T.P.: Optimal stateless model checking under the release-acquire semantics. In: Proceedings of the ACM on Programming Languages 2 (OOPSLA), p. 135 (2018)

3. Alglave, J., Kroening, D., Tautschnig, M.: Partial orders for efficient bounded model checking of concurrent software. In: Sharygina, N., Veith, H. (eds.) . Proceedings of the Computer Aided Verification - 25th International Conference (CAV 2013), Saint Petersburg, Russia, July 13–19, 2013, LNCS, vol. 8044, pp. 141–157. Springer (2013). https://doi.org/10.1007/978-3-642-39799-8_9

4. Batty, M., Owens, S., Sarkar, S., Sewell, P., Weber, T.: Mathematizing C++ concurrency. In: Proceedings of the 38th Annual ACM SIGPLAN-SIGACT Symposium on Principles of Programming Languages (POPL2011), ACM (2011). https://doi.org/10.1145/1926385.1926394

5. Clarke, E.M., Grumberg, O., Kroening, D., Peled, D.A., Veith, H.: Model Checking. MIT Press, Cambridge (2018)

6. Cousot, P., Cousot, R.: Comparing the Galois connection and widening/narrowing approaches to abstract interpretation. In: Bruynooghe, M., Wirsing, M. (eds.) PLILP 1992. LNCS, vol. 631, pp. 269–295. Springer, Heidelberg (1992). https://doi.org/10.1007/3-540-55844-6_142

7. Cousot, P., Cousot, R.: Abstract interpretation: Past, present and future. In: Proceedings of the Joint Meeting of the Twenty-Third EACSL Annual Conference on Computer Science Logic (CSL) and the Twenty-Ninth Annual ACM/IEEE Symposium on Logic in Computer Science (LICS) (CSL-LICS'2014), Association for Computing Machinery, New York (2014). https://doi.org/10.1145/2603088.2603165

8. Doko, M., Vafeiadis, V.: A program logic for C11 memory fences. In: Jobstmann, B., Leino, K.R.M. (eds.) VMCAI 2016. LNCS, vol. 9583, pp. 413–430. Springer, Heidelberg (2016). https://doi.org/10.1007/978-3-662-49122-5_20

9. Farzan, A., Kincaid, Z.: DUET: static analysis for unbounded parallelism. In: Sharygina, N., Veith, H. (eds.) CAV 2013. LNCS, vol. 8044, pp. 191–196. Springer, Heidelberg (2013). https://doi.org/10.1007/978-3-642-39799-8_12

10. Flanagan, C., Qadeer, S.: Thread-modular model checking. In: Ball, T., Rajamani, S.K. (eds.) Model Checking Software, pp. 213–224. Springer, Berlin (2003)

11. Forejt, V., Joshi, S., Kroening, D., Narayanaswamy, G., Sharma, S.: Precise predictive analysis for discovering communication deadlocks in MPI programs. ACM Trans. Program. Lang. Syst. **39**(4), 15:1–15:27 (2017). https://doi.org/10.1145/3095075

12. Gavrilenko, N., Ponce-de-León, H., Furbach, F., Heljanko, K., Meyer, R.: BMC for weak memory models: relation analysis for compact SMT encodings. In: Dillig, I., Tasiran, S. (eds.) CAV 2019. LNCS, vol. 11561, pp. 355–365. Springer, Cham (2019). https://doi.org/10.1007/978-3-030-25540-4_19

13. Henzinger, T.A., Jhala, R., Majumdar, R., Qadeer, S.: Thread-modular abstraction refinement. In: Hunt, W.A., Somenzi, F. (eds.) CAV 2003. LNCS, vol. 2725, pp. 262–274. Springer, Heidelberg (2003). https://doi.org/10.1007/978-3-540-45069-6_27

14. Huang, S., Huang, J.: Maximal causality reduction for TSO and PSO. In: Visser, E., Smaragdakis, Y. (eds.) Proceedings of the 2016 ACM SIGPLAN International Conference on Object-Oriented Programming, Systems, Languages, and Applications (OOPSLA 2016), Part of SPLASH 2016, Amsterdam October 30 - November 4, 2016, pp. 447–461. ACM (2016). https://doi.org/10.1145/2983990.2984025

15. ISO/IEC-JTC1/SC22/WG21: Programming languages - C++ (2013). http://www.open-std.org/jtc1/sc22/wg21/docs/papers/2013/n3690.pdf

16. Jeannet, B., Miné, A.: APRON: a library of numerical abstract domains for static analysis. In: Bouajjani, A., Maler, O. (eds.) CAV 2009. LNCS, vol. 5643, pp. 661–667. Springer, Heidelberg (2009). https://doi.org/10.1007/978-3-642-02658-4_52

17. Kähkönen, K., Saarikivi, O., Heljanko, K.: Unfolding based automated testing of multithreaded programs. Autom. Softw. Eng. 22(4), 475–515 (2015). https://doi.org/10.1007/s10515-014-0150-6

18. Kang, J., Hur, C.K., Lahav, O., Vafeiadis, V., Dreyer, D.: A promising semantics for relaxed-memory concurrency. In: Proceedings of the 44th ACM SIGPLAN Symposium on Principles of Programming Languages (POPL 2017) (2017). https://doi.org/10.1145/3009837.3009850

19. Kokologiannakis, M., Lahav, O., Sagonas, K., Vafeiadis, V.: Effective stateless model checking for C/C++ concurrency. In: Proceedings of the ACM Programming Language 2(POPL), pp. 17:1–17:32 (2017). https://doi.org/10.1145/3158105

20. Kokologiannakis, M., Raad, A., Vafeiadis, V.: Model checking for weakly consistent libraries. In: McKinley, K.S., Fisher, K. (eds.) Proceedings of the 40th ACM SIGPLAN Conference on Programming Language Design and Implementation (PLDI 2019), Phoenix, AZ, USA, June 22–26, 2019. pp. 96–110. ACM (2019). https://doi.org/10.1145/3314221.3314609

21. Kusano, M., Wang, C.: Flow-sensitive composition of thread-modular abstract interpretation. In: Proceedings of the 2016 24th ACM SIGSOFT International Symposium on Foundations of Software Engineering (FSE 2016) ACM (2016). http://doi.acm.org/10.1145/2950290.2950291

22. Kusano, M., Wang, C.: Thread-modular static analysis for relaxed memory models. In: Proceedings of the 2017 11th Joint Meeting on Foundations of Software Engineering (ESEC/FSE 2017), pp. 337–348. ACM, New York (2017). https://doi.org/10.1145/3106237.3106243

23. Lahav, O., Giannarakis, N., Vafeiadis, V.: Taming release-acquire consistency. In: Proceedings of the 43rd Annual ACM SIGPLAN-SIGACT Symposium on Principles of Programming Languages (POPL 2016), pp. 649–662. ACM, New York (2016). https://doi.org/10.1145/2837614.2837643

24. Lahav, O., Vafeiadis, V.: Owicki-gries reasoning for weak memory models. In: Automata, Languages, and Programming. Springer, Berlin Heidelberg (2015)

25. Lahav, O., Vafeiadis, V., Kang, J., Hur, C.K., Dreyer, D.: Repairing sequential consistency in C/C++11. In: Proceedings of the 38th ACM SIGPLAN Conference on Programming Language Design and Implementation (PLDI 2017) (2017). http://doi.acm.org/10.1145/3062341.3062352

26. Monat, R., Miné, A.: Precise thread-modular abstract interpretation of concurrent programs using relational interference abstractions. In: Bouajjani, A., Monniaux, D. (eds.) VMCAI 2017. LNCS, vol. 10145, pp. 386–404. Springer, Cham (2017). https://doi.org/10.1007/978-3-319-52234-0_21

27. Nielson, F., Nielson, H.R., Hankin, C.: Principles of Program Analysis, Springer, Berlin (2010)
28. Norris, B., Demsky, B.: A practical approach for model checking C/C++11 code. ACM Trans. Program. Lang. Syst. **38**(3), 10:1–10:51 (2016)
29. Rodríguez, C., Sousa, M., Sharma, S., Kroening, D.: Unfolding-based partial order reduction. In: Aceto, L., de Frutos-Escrig, D. (eds.) 26th International Conference on Concurrency Theory (CONCUR 2015) Madrid, September 1.4, 2015. LIPIcs, vol. 42, pp. 456–469. Schloss Dagstuhl - Leibniz-Zentrum für Informatik (2015). https://doi.org/10.4230/LIPIcs.CONCUR.2015.456
30. Sharma, D., Sharma, S.: Thread-modular analysis of release-acquire concurrency. CoRR abs/2107.02346 (2021). https://arxiv.org/abs/2107.02346
31. Sousa, M., Rodríguez, C., D'Silva, V., Kroening, D.: Abstract interpretation with unfoldings. In: Majumdar, R., Kuncak, V. (eds.) Proceedings of the Computer Aided Verification - 29th International Conference (CAV 2017), Heidelberg, Germany, July 24–28, 2017, Part II. LNCS, vol. 10427, pp. 197–216. Springer (2017). https://doi.org/10.1007/978-3-319-63390-9_11
32. Suzanne, T., Miné, A.: From array domains to abstract interpretation under store-buffer-based memory models. In: Static Analysis. Springer, Berlin (2016)
33. Suzanne, T., Miné, A.: Relational thread-modular abstract interpretation under relaxed memory models. In: Ryu, S. (ed.) APLAS 2018. LNCS, vol. 11275, pp. 109–128. Springer, Cham (2018). https://doi.org/10.1007/978-3-030-02768-1_6
34. Tassarotti, J., Dreyer, D., Vafeiadis, V.: Verifying read-copy-update in a logic for weak memory. In: Proceedings of the 36th ACM SIGPLAN Conference on Programming Language Design and Implementation. (PLDI 2015), pp. 110–120. Association for Computing Machinery, New York (2015). https://doi.org/10.1145/2737924.2737992
35. Turon, A., Vafeiadis, V., Dreyer, D.: Gps: Navigating weak memory with ghosts, protocols, and separation. In: Proceedings of the 2014 ACM International Conference on Object Oriented Programming Systems Languages & Applications (OOPSLA 2014), pp. 691–707. ACM, New York, NY, USA (2014). http://doi.acm.org/10.1145/2660193.2660243
36. Vafeiadis, V., Narayan, C.: Relaxed separation logic: a program logic for c11 concurrency. In: Proceedings of the 2013 ACM SIGPLAN International Conference on Object Oriented Programming Systems Languages & Applications (OOPSLA 2013), pp. 867–884. ACM, New York (2013). http://doi.acm.org/10.1145/2509136.2509532
37. Wang, C., Kundu, S., Ganai, M.K., Gupta, A.: Symbolic predictive analysis for concurrent programs. In: Cavalcanti, A., Dams, D. (eds.) of the Computer Science, LNCS, vol. 5850, pp. 256–272. Springer (2009). https://doi.org/10.1007/978-3-642-05089-3_17
38. Zhang, N., Kusano, M., Wang, C.: Dynamic partial order reduction for relaxed memory models. In: Grove, D., Blackburn, S. (eds.) Proceedings of the 36th ACM SIGPLAN Conference on Programming Language Design and Implementation, June 15–17, 2015, pp. 250–259. Portland, ACM (2015). https://doi.org/10.1145/2737924.2737956

Symbolic Automatic Relations and Their Applications to SMT and CHC Solving

Takumi Shimoda, Naoki Kobayashi🆔, Ken Sakayori(✉)🆔, and Ryosuke Sato🆔

The University of Tokyo, Tokyo, Japan
`sakayroi@kb.is.s.u-tokyo.ac.jp`

Abstract. Despite the recent advance of automated program verification, reasoning about recursive data structures remains as a challenge for verification tools and their backends such as SMT and CHC solvers. To address the challenge, we introduce the notion of symbolic automatic relations (SARs), which combines symbolic automata and automatic relations, and inherits their good properties such as the closure under Boolean operations. We consider the satisfiability problem for SARs, and show that it is undecidable in general, but that we can construct a sound (but incomplete) and automated satisfiability checker by a reduction to CHC solving. We discuss applications to SMT and CHC solving on data structures, and show the effectiveness of our approach through experiments.

1 Introduction

The recent advance of automated or semi-automated program verification tools owes much to the improvement of SMT (Satisfiability Modulo Theory) and CHC (Constrained Horn Clauses) solvers. The former [1,23] can automatically check the satisfiability of quantifier-free formulas modulo background theories (such as linear integer arithmetic), and the latter [6,17,20] can automatically reason about recursively defined predicates (which can be used to model loops and recursive functions). Various program verification problems can be reduced to CHC solving [3]. The current SMT and CHC solvers are, however, not very good at reasoning about recursive data structures (such as lists and trees), compared with the capability of reasoning about basic data such as integers and real numbers. Indeed, improving the treatment of recursive data structures has recently been an active research topic, especially for CHC solvers [6,9,13,28].

In the present paper, we propose an automata-based approach for checking the satisfiability of formulas over recursive data structures. (For the sake of simplicity, we focus on lists of integers; our approach can, in principle, be extended

C. Drăgoi et al. (Eds.): SAS 2021, LNCS 12913, pp. 405–428, 2021.
https://doi.org/10.1007/978-3-030-88806-0_20

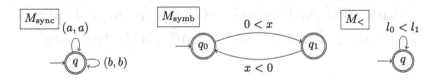

Fig. 1. Examples of synchronous, symbolic and symbolic synchronous automaton.

for more general data structures). More precisely, we introduce the notion of *symbolic automatic relations*, which is obtained by combining *automatic relations* [4] and *symbolic automata* [8,29,30].

A k-ary automatic relation is a relation on k words[1] that can be recognized by a finite state automaton that reads k words in a synchronous manner (so, given k words, $x_{01} \cdots x_{0m}, \ldots, x_{(k-1)1} \cdots x_{(k-1)m}$, the automaton reads a tuple $(x_{0i}, \ldots, x_{(k-1)i})$ at each transition; if the input words have different lengths, the special padding symbol $\square$ is filled at the end). For example, the equality relation on two words over the alphabet $\{a, b\}$ is an automatic relation, since it is recognized by the automaton with a single state q (which is both initial and accepting) with the transition $\delta(q, (a, a)) = q$ and $\delta(q, (b, b)) = q$. By using automatic relations, we can express and manipulate relations on data structures.

Since data structures typically contain elements from an infinite set, we extend automatic relations by using symbolic automata. Here, a symbolic automaton is a variation of finite state automaton whose alphabet is possibly infinite, and whose transition is described by a formula over elements of the alphabet. For example, M_{symb} on Fig. 1 is a symbolic automaton that accepts the sequences of integers in which positive and negative integers occur alternately, and the first element is a positive integer. The *symbolic automatic relations* introduced in this paper are relations recognized by symbolic automata that read input words (over a possibly infinite alphabet) in a synchronous manner. For example, consider the binary relation:

$$\mathcal{R}_< = \{(l_{01} \cdots l_{0n}, l_{11} \cdots l_{1n}) \in \mathbb{Z}^* \times \mathbb{Z}^* \mid l_{0i} < l_{1i} \text{ for every } i \in \{1, \ldots, n\}\}.$$

It is a symbolic automatic relation, as it is recognized by the symbolic synchronous automaton $M_<$ on Fig. 1 (where l_0 and l_1 are bound to l_{0i} and l_{1i} at the i-th transition step).

Symbolic automatic relations (SARs) inherit good properties of automatic relations and symbolic automata: SARs are closed under Boolean operations, and the emptiness problem of SAR (the problem of deciding whether $\mathcal{R} = \emptyset$, given the representation of a SAR $\mathcal{R}$) is decidable if the underlying theory (e.g. linear integer arithmetic) used for representing transitions is decidable.

We are interested in the satisfiability problem for SARs, i.e., the problem of checking whether a given existentially-quantified formula (obtained by extending the signature of linear integer arithmetic with SARs and list constructors/destructors) is satisfiable. For example, whether $\mathcal{R}_<(X, Y) \wedge \mathcal{R}_<(Y, X)$

---

[1] We use "lists", "words", and "sequences" interchangeably.

is satisfiable (the answer is "No") is an instance of the problem. The class of existentially-quantified formulas considered in the satisfiability problem is reasonably expressive. For example, although the sortedness predicate $sorted(X)$ and the predicate $nth(X, i, x)$ (the i-th element of X is x) are themselves not automatic relations, we can allow those predicates to occur in the formulas, as explained later. (Unfortunately, however, we cannot express the "append" relation.)

We first show that the satisfiability problem for SARs is undecidable, unfortunately. The proof is based on a reduction from the undecidability of the halting problem for Minsky machines (or, two-counter machines). Next, we show that the satisfiability problem for SARs can be reduced to the satisfiability problem for Constrained Horn Clauses (CHCs) over integers (*without* lists). Thanks to the recent development of efficient CHC solvers [6,17,20], we can thus obtain a sound, automated (but incomplete) procedure for solving the satisfiability problem for SARs. We show, through experiments, that our reduction is effective, in that the combination of our reduction with off-the-shelf CHC solvers can solve the satisfiability problem for various formulas over lists that cannot be solved by state-of-the-art SMT solvers such as Z3 and CVC4.

Besides the above-mentioned improvement of SMT solvers on recursive data structures, we also have in mind an application to CHC solving (indeed, improving CHC solvers was the original motivation of our work). The goal of CHC solving is to check whether a given set of CHCs has a model (interpretations for predicate variables that make all the clauses valid). Many of the CHC solvers prove the satisfiability of given CHCs by constructing an actual model. The main problem on such CHC solvers in dealing with recursive data structures is that the language for describing models is too restrictive: especially, it cannot express recursively defined predicates on recursive data structures (apart from some built-in predicates such as the "length" predicate). Our symbolic automatic relations can be used to enhance the expressive power of the language. The above-mentioned procedure for the SAR satisfiability problem can be directly applied to an ICE-based CHC solver like HoIce [6]. HoIce consists of a learner, which constructs a candidate model, and a teacher, which checks whether the candidate is indeed a model. Our procedure can be used by the teacher, when a given candidate is described by using symbolic automatic relations. Later in the paper, we give examples of CHCs whose models can only be expressed by using symbolic automatic relations, and show through experiments that our procedure can indeed be used for checking the validity of models described by using symbolic automatic relations.

Our contributions are: (i) introduction of symbolic automatic relations and discussions of applications to SMT and CHC solving; (ii) a proof of the undecidability of the satisfiability problem on SARs; (iii) a sound (but incomplete) decision procedure for the satisfiability problem on SARs, via a reduction to CHC solving on integers (iv) an implementation and experiments to confirm the effectiveness of the above decision procedure.

The rest of this paper is structured as follows. Section 2 briefly reviews the notions used in many-sorted first-order logic. Section 3 defines symbolic automatic relations and demonstrates how they can be used to express predicates over lists. Section 4 shows that the satisfiability problem for SARs is undecidable. Section 5 shows a reduction from the satisfiability problem for SARs to CHC solving, and Sect. 6 reports experimental results. Section 7 discusses related work and Sect. 8 concludes the paper. Omitted proofs and the details of the experiment are found in an extended version [26].

2   Preliminaries

This section introduces basic notions and notations used in the sequel.

Notations. Given a set S, we write S^* for the set of all finite sequences over S. A word $w \in S^*$ is either written as $w = a_1 \cdots a_n$ or $w = [a_1, \ldots, a_n]$, where $a_i \in S$; the empty word is denoted as ϵ or $[\,]$. The set of integers is written as $\mathbb{Z}$.

2.1   FOL with List

Syntax. A (multi-sorted) *signature* is a triple $(\mathbf{Ty}, \mathbf{Fn}, \mathbf{Pd})$, where $\mathbf{Ty}$ is a set of sorts (aka types), $\mathbf{Fn}$ is a set of (typed) function symbols, and $\mathbf{Pd}$ is a set of (typed) predicate symbols. There are two signatures that play important roles in this paper: the signature of integer arithmetic and the signature for integer lists. We define the signature of integer arithmetic τ_{int} as $(\{Int\}, \mathbf{Fn}_{\mathrm{int}}, \mathbf{Pd}_{\mathrm{int}})$. The set $\mathbf{Fn}_{\mathrm{int}}$ contains the function symbols for integer arithmetic such as $0, s, +$ and $\mathbf{Pd}_{\mathrm{int}}$ contains the predicates for integer arithmetic such as $=_{\mathrm{int}}, <, \leq$; the precise definition is not important. The signature of integer lists is defined by $\tau_{\mathrm{list}} \overset{\mathrm{def}}{=} (\{Int, List\ Int\}, \mathbf{Fn}_{\mathrm{int}} \cup \mathbf{Fn}_{\mathrm{list}}, \mathbf{Pd}_{\mathrm{int}} \cup \{=_{\mathrm{list}}\})$, where $\mathbf{Fn}_{\mathrm{list}} \overset{\mathrm{def}}{=} \{nil, cons, head, tail\}$. Here, *nil* and *cons* have type *List Int* and $(Int, List\ Int) \rightarrow List\ Int$ and their intended meanings are the empty list and the "cons function", respectively. As the name suggests, *head* : *List Int* $\rightarrow$ *Int* and *tail* : *List Int* $\rightarrow$ *List Int* will be interpreted as head and tail functions.

The set of *terms* and the set of *formulas* over a signature $\tau = (\mathbf{Ty}, \mathbf{Fn}, \mathbf{Pd})$ is defined as follows:

$$t ::= x \mid f(t_1, \ldots, t_n)$$
$$\varphi ::= \top \mid \bot \mid P(t_1, \ldots, t_n) \mid \neg\varphi \mid \varphi_1 \wedge \varphi_2 \mid \varphi_1 \vee \varphi_2 \mid \forall x \varphi \mid \exists x \varphi$$

where x ranges over the denumerable set of variables, f ranges over $\mathbf{Fn}$ and P ranges over $\mathbf{Pd}$. In what follows, we only consider well-typed formulas; we omit the definition of typing rules as they are standard.

Let us set some notational conventions for terms and formulas over the signature τ_{list} (or τ_{int}). We use $X, Y, Z, \ldots$ to range over the set of variables of type *List Int* and $x, y, z, \ldots$ to range over the set of variables of type *Int*. A term is called an *integer term* if it has type *Int* and is called a *list term* if it has type

List Int. We use T and t to range over the set of list terms and integer terms, respectively. We write $\widetilde{x}$ (resp. $\widetilde{X}$) to represent a possibly empty sequence of integer variables (resp. list variables); $\widetilde{t}$ and $\widetilde{T}$ are defined similarly.

Semantics. A *model* $\mathcal{M}$ (or *structure*) over a signature $\tau = (\mathbf{Ty}, \mathbf{Fn}, \mathbf{Pd})$ is a triple $((U_\iota)_{\iota \in \mathbf{Ty}}, (f^{\mathcal{M}})_{f \in \mathbf{Fn}}, (P^{\mathcal{M}})_{P \in \mathbf{Pd}})$, where each U_ι is a non-empty set called a *universe*, $f^{\mathcal{M}}$ is a function over the universes, $P^{\mathcal{M}}$ is a relation over the universes. If f has type $(\iota_1, \ldots, \iota_n) \to \iota_{n+1}$ then $f^{\mathcal{M}}$ is a function from $U_{\iota_1} \times \cdots \times U_{\iota_n}$ to $U_{\iota_{n+1}}$; the same applies to $R^{\mathcal{M}}$. We write $(\mathbb{Z}, (f^{\mathbb{Z}})_{f \in \mathbf{Fn}_{\mathrm{int}}}, (P^{\mathbb{Z}})_{P \in \mathbf{Pd}_{\mathrm{int}}})$ or simply $\mathbb{Z}$ for the standard model of integer arithmetic. The *standard model for integer lists* $\mathcal{M}_{list}$ is a model over τ_{list} such that $U_{Int} \stackrel{\mathrm{def}}{=} \mathbb{Z}$ and $U_{List\ Int} \stackrel{\mathrm{def}}{=} \mathbb{Z}^*$; $f^{\mathcal{M}_{\mathrm{list}}} \stackrel{\mathrm{def}}{=} f^{\mathbb{Z}}$ for $f \in \mathbf{Fn}_{\mathrm{int}}$; $P^{\mathcal{M}_{\mathrm{list}}} \stackrel{\mathrm{def}}{=} P^{\mathbb{Z}}$ for $P \in \mathbf{Pd}_{\mathrm{int}}$; $=^{\mathcal{M}_{\mathrm{list}}}_{\mathrm{list}}$ is the diagonal relation on $\mathbb{Z}^*$; and the interpretations for symbols in $\mathbf{Fn}_{\mathrm{list}}$ are defined in a natural way. Formally, interpretations for symbols in $\mathbf{Fn}_{\mathrm{list}}$ is defined by $nil^{\mathcal{M}_{\mathrm{list}}} \stackrel{\mathrm{def}}{=} \epsilon$; $cons^{\mathcal{M}_{\mathrm{list}}}(i, w) = iw$; $head^{\mathcal{M}_{\mathrm{list}}}(iw) \stackrel{\mathrm{def}}{=} i$ and $head^{\mathcal{M}_{\mathrm{list}}}(\epsilon) \stackrel{\mathrm{def}}{=} 0$; and $tail^{\mathcal{M}_{\mathrm{list}}}(iw) \stackrel{\mathrm{def}}{=} w$ and $tail^{\mathcal{M}_{\mathrm{list}}}(\epsilon) \stackrel{\mathrm{def}}{=} \epsilon$, where $i \in \mathbb{Z}$ and $w \in \mathbb{Z}^*$.[2]

The semantics of terms and formulas are defined in the standard way. Let τ be a signature and $\mathcal{M}$ be a model over τ. An *assignment* α in $\mathcal{M}$ maps variables of type ι to elements of the universe associated with ι. A triple $(t, \mathcal{M}, \alpha)$ of a term with type ι, a model and an assignment determines an element of the universe associated with ι, which we write as $[\![t]\!]_{\mathcal{M}, \alpha}$. Similarly, a triple $(\varphi, \mathcal{M}, \alpha)$, where φ is a formula, determines whether the satisfaction relation $\mathcal{M}, \alpha \models \varphi$ holds. We omit the precise definitions of $[\![t]\!]_{\mathcal{M}, \alpha}$ and the satisfaction relation as they are defined as usual. Since the truth or falsity of $\mathcal{M}, \alpha \models \varphi$ depends only on the values of α for free variables of φ, we may write $\mathcal{M}, [\widetilde{x} \mapsto \widetilde{a}] \models \varphi$ if the free variables of φ are among $\widetilde{x} = x_1, \ldots, x_n$ and $\widetilde{a} = \alpha(x_1), \ldots, \alpha(x_n)$. We say that a formula φ is *satisfiable in* $\mathcal{M}$ if there is an assignment α such that $\mathcal{M}, \alpha \models \varphi$ and φ is *satisfiable* if there is a model $\mathcal{M}$ in which φ is satisfiable. A formula φ is *valid in* $\mathcal{M}$ if $\mathcal{M}, \alpha \models \varphi$ holds for all assignments α; φ is *valid* if it is valid in all the models. Two formulas φ_1 and φ_2 are $\mathcal{M}$-*equivalent* if, for all assignments α, $\mathcal{M}, \alpha \models \varphi_1$ if and only if $\mathcal{M}, \alpha \models \varphi_2$.

3   Symbolic Automatic Relations

In this section, we introduce the notion of *symbolic automatic relations*. We first introduce the notion of a *symbolic synchronous automaton* in Sect. 3.1, which is a special kind of symbolic automaton [8], which serves as the representation of a symbolic automatic relation. We then define symbolic automatic relations in Sect. 3.2. For the sake of simplicity we consider symbolic automatic relations on integer sequences (or, lists of integers). It would not be difficult to extend them to deal with tree-structured data, by using (symbolic, synchronous) tree automata; see also Remark 3.

---

[2] Note that $head^{\mathcal{M}_{\mathrm{list}}}$ and $tail^{\mathcal{M}_{\mathrm{list}}}$ are defined as total functions. This matches the behaviors of the existing SMT solvers such as Z3 or CVC4.

3.1 Symbolic Synchronous Automata

We first extend the model $\mathbb{Z}$ by adding the special padding symbol $\square$, which will be used in the definition of symbolic synchronous automata.

Definition 1 (Partial model for integer arithmetic). *A partial model for integer arithmetic* $(\mathbb{Z}_\square, (f^{\mathbb{Z}_\square})_{f \in \mathbf{Fn}_{\mathrm{int}}}, (P^{\mathbb{Z}_\square})_{P \in \mathbf{Pd}_{\mathrm{int}}})$ *is a model over the signature* $\tau_{\mathrm{int} \cup \{\square\}} \stackrel{\mathrm{def}}{=} (\{Int\}, \mathbf{Fn}_{\mathrm{int}}, \mathbf{Pd}_{\mathrm{int}} \cup \{pad\})$, *where*

- *the universe* $\mathbb{Z}_\square$ *is* $\mathbb{Z} \cup \{\square\}$, *where* $\square \notin \mathbb{Z}$ *is called a padding symbol,*
- *for every k-ary function symbol f,* $f^{\mathbb{Z}_\square}(a_1, \ldots, a_k) \stackrel{\mathrm{def}}{=} f^{\mathbb{Z}}(a_1, \ldots, a_k)$ *if* $a_i \in \mathbb{Z}$ *for all* $1 \le i \le k$ *and* $f^{\mathbb{Z}_\square}(a_1, \ldots, a_k) \stackrel{\mathrm{def}}{=} \square$ *otherwise, and*
- *for every* $P \in \mathbf{Pd}_{\mathrm{int}}$, $P^{\mathbb{Z}_\square} \stackrel{\mathrm{def}}{=} P^{\mathbb{Z}}$ *and* $pad^{\mathbb{Z}_\square} \stackrel{\mathrm{def}}{=} \{\square\}$.

By abuse of notation, we may write $\mathbb{Z}_\square$ *to denote the partial model for integers.*

Remark 1. The semantics of the negation $\neg$ is a little tricky for the partial model. For example, the interpretation of $x < y$ is different from $\neg(x \ge y)$: "$1 < \square$" is false but "$\neg(1 \ge \square)$" is true.

Definition 2 (Symbolic synchronous automaton). *A k-ary symbolic synchronous nondeterministic finite automaton with n parameters[3] $\widetilde{x} = x_0, \ldots, x_{n-1}$ ((k,n)-ary ss-NFA for short) is a quadruple* $M(\widetilde{x}) = (Q, I, F, \Delta)$ *where*

- Q *is a finite set of* states,
- $I \subseteq Q$ *is the set of* initial states,
- $F \subseteq Q$ *is the set of* final states,
- $\Delta \subseteq Q \times \Psi_k^{\widetilde{x}} \times Q$ *is a finite set of* transitions. *Here $\Psi_k^{\widetilde{x}}$ is a subset of formulas over the signature $\tau_{\mathrm{int} \cup \{\square\}}$ containing only formulas, whose free variables are among $l_0, \ldots, l_{k-1}, x_0, \ldots, x_{n-1}$.*

Intuitively, the free variables l_i are bound to the i-th input at each transition step and x_i are bound to integer values that do not change at each step. Formally, for $\widetilde{j} = (j_0, \ldots, j_{n-1}) \in \mathbb{Z}^n$ and $a = (i_0, \ldots, i_{k-1}) \in \mathbb{Z}_\square^k$, an a-transition of $M(\widetilde{j})$ is a transition $q \stackrel{\varphi}{\to} q'$ such that $\mathbb{Z}_\square, [\widetilde{x} \mapsto \widetilde{j}, l_0 \mapsto i_0, \ldots, l_{k-1} \mapsto i_{k-1}] \models \varphi$. This a-transition is denoted as $q \stackrel{a}{\to}_{M(\widetilde{j})} q'$ (or $q \stackrel{a}{\to} q'$ when $M(\widetilde{j})$ is clear from the context).

A (k,n)-ary ss-NFA $M(\widetilde{x}) = (Q, I, F, \Delta)$ is effective *if*

$$\{(i_0, \ldots, i_{k-1}, j_0, \ldots, j_{n-1}) \in \mathbb{Z}_\square^k \times \mathbb{Z}^n \mid \mathbb{Z}_\square, [\widetilde{l} \mapsto \widetilde{i}, \widetilde{x} \mapsto \widetilde{j}] \models \varphi\}$$

is a decidable set for all $q \stackrel{\varphi}{\to} q' \in \Delta$. We sometimes call a $(k,0)$-ary ss-NFA just a k-ary ss-NFA.

The existence of parameters allows us to use ss-NFAs as representations of relations that take not only words but also integers as arguments.

---

[3] The parameters $\widetilde{x}$ are "bound variables" and we identify "α-equivalent" automata.

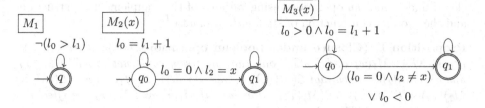

Fig. 2. Examples of ss-NFAs.

Definition 3 (Language of ss-NFA). *Let $M(\widetilde{x}) = (Q, I, F, \Delta)$ be a (k,n)-ary ss-NFA and $\widetilde{j} \in \mathbb{Z}^n$. A word $w \in (\mathbb{Z}_\square^k)^*$ is accepted by $M(\widetilde{j})$ if*

- *$w = \epsilon$ and $I \cap F \neq \emptyset$, or*
- *$w = a_1 \cdots a_m$ and for all $1 \leq i \leq m$, there exist transitions $q_i \xrightarrow{a_i}_{M(\widetilde{j})} q_{i+1}$ such that $q_1 \in I$ and $q_{m+1} \in F$.*

A word accepted by $M(\widetilde{j})$ is called an accepting run *of $M(\widetilde{j})$. The* language *accepted by $M(\widetilde{j})$, denoted $\mathcal{L}(M(\widetilde{j}))$, is the set of words accepted by $M(\widetilde{j})$. We also write $\mathcal{L}(M(\widetilde{x}))$ for the relation $\{(w, \widetilde{j}) \mid w \in \mathcal{L}(M(\widetilde{j}))\}$.*

Example 1. Consider the ss-NFAs in Fig. 2. The automaton M_1 is formally defined as a 2-ary ss-NFA without parameter $M_1 \overset{\text{def}}{=} (\{q\}, \{q\}, \{q\}, \{(q, \neg(l_0 > l_1), q)\})$. The automaton $M_2(x)$ is a 3-ary ss-NFA, with one parameter x, defined by $M_2(x) \overset{\text{def}}{=} (\{q_0, q_1\}, \{q_0\}, \{q_1\}, \Delta)$, where $\Delta \overset{\text{def}}{=} \{(q_0, l_0 = l_1 + 1, q_0), (q_0, l_0 = 0 \wedge l_2 = x, q_1), (q_1, \top, q_1)\}$; the automaton $M_3(x)$ can be formally described in a similar manner. These automata will be used to define predicates $sorted(X)$ and $nth(i, x, X)$ later in this section.

The acceptance language of $M_2(x)$, i.e. $\mathcal{L}(M_2(x)) \subseteq \mathbb{Z}_\square^3 \times \mathbb{Z}$, is given as

$$\left\{ \left(\begin{bmatrix} a_{01} \\ a_{11} \\ a_{21} \end{bmatrix} \cdots \begin{bmatrix} a_{0n} \\ a_{1n} \\ a_{2n} \end{bmatrix}, j \right) \middle| \begin{array}{l} \exists m.\ 1 \leq m \leq n \wedge a_{0m} = 0 \wedge a_{2m} = j \\ \wedge\ (\forall i.\ 1 \leq i < m \implies a_{0i} = a_{1i} + 1) \end{array} \right\}.$$

$\square$

We introduce some terminology on ss-NFAs. A (k,n)-ary ss-NFA $M(\widetilde{x}) = (Q, I, F, \Delta)$ is *deterministic* if $|I| = 1$ and for all transitions $q \xrightarrow{\varphi_1} q_1$ and $q \xrightarrow{\varphi_2} q_2$, if $\varphi_1 \wedge \varphi_2$ is satisfiable in $\mathbb{Z}_\square$ then $q_1 = q_2$. A state q of $M(\widetilde{x})$ is called *complete* if for all $a \in \mathbb{Z}_\square^k$ and $\widetilde{j} \in \mathbb{Z}^n$ there exists an a-transition $q \xrightarrow{a}_{M(\widetilde{j})} q'$ for some q'. A ss-NFA $M(\widetilde{x})$ is *complete* if all states of $M(\widetilde{x})$ are complete.

Since ss-NFA are just a special kind of symbolic automata and symbolic automata can be determinized and completed, it can be shown that ss-NFAs are closed under Boolean operations using variants of the complement construction and the product construction of standard automata.[4]

Proposition 1. (Closure under boolean operations *[30])*. *Given (k, n)-ary ss-NFAs $M_1(\widetilde{x})$ and $M_2(\widetilde{x})$, one can effectively construct ss-NFAs $M_1^c(\widetilde{x})$ and $(M_1 \times M_2)(\widetilde{x})$ such that $\mathcal{L}(M_1^c(\widetilde{x})) = ((\mathbb{Z}_\square^k)^* \times \mathbb{Z}^n) \setminus \mathcal{L}(M_1(\widetilde{x}))$ and $\mathcal{L}((M_1 \times M_2)(\widetilde{x})) = \mathcal{L}(M_1(\widetilde{x})) \cap \mathcal{L}(M_2(\widetilde{x}))$. Moreover, if $M_1(\widetilde{x})$ and $M_2(\widetilde{x})$ are effective, so are $M_1^c(\widetilde{x})$ and $(M_1 \times M_2)(\widetilde{x})$.* $\square$

3.2   Symbolic Automatic Relations

A symbolic automatic relation (SAR) is basically an acceptance language of a ss-NFA, but not every acceptance language of a ss-NFA is a SAR. Recall that a run of a k-ary ss-NFA is a word $w \in (\mathbb{Z}_\square^k)^*$ and thus it does not necessarily correspond to tuples of words over $\mathbb{Z}$ since the "padding symbol" can appear at any position of w. In order to exclude such "invalid inputs", we first define the convolution operation, which converts a tuple of words to a word of tuples.

Definition 4 (Convolution). *Given k words $w_0, ..., w_{k-1} \in \mathbb{Z}^*$, with $w_i = a_{i1} \cdots a_{il_i}$ and $l = \max(l_0, ..., l_{k-1})$, the convolution of words $w_0, ..., w_{k-1}$, denoted as $c(w_0, ..., w_{k-1})$, is defined by*

$$c(w_0, ..., w_{k-1}) \stackrel{\text{def}}{=} \begin{bmatrix} a'_{01} \\ \vdots \\ a'_{(k-1)1} \end{bmatrix} \cdots \begin{bmatrix} a'_{0l} \\ \vdots \\ a'_{(k-1)l} \end{bmatrix} \in (\mathbb{Z}_\square^k)^* \quad and \quad c() \stackrel{\text{def}}{=} \epsilon$$

where $a'_{ij} = a_{ij}$ if $j \le l_i$ and $a'_{ij} = \square$ otherwise. The padding symbol is appended to the end of some words w_i to make sure that all words have the same length.

We write $\mathbb{Z}^{\otimes k}$ for the set of convoluted words, i.e. $\mathbb{Z}^{\otimes k} \stackrel{\text{def}}{=} \{c(w_0, \ldots, w_{k-1}) \mid (w_0, \ldots, w_{k-1}) \in (\mathbb{Z}^*)^k\}$. This set can be recognized by a ss-NFA.

Proposition 2. *Let k and n be natural numbers. Then there is a (k, n)-ary ss-NFA $M(\widetilde{x})$ such that $\mathcal{L}(M(\widetilde{x})) = \mathbb{Z}^{\otimes k} \times \mathbb{Z}^n$.* $\square$

Because of this proposition, there is not much difference between ss-NFAs that only take convoluted words as inputs and ss-NFAs that take any word $w \in (\mathbb{Z}_\square^k)^*$ as inputs. Given a ss-NFA $M(\widetilde{x})$, we can always restrict the form of inputs by taking the product with the automaton that recognizes $\mathbb{Z}^{\otimes k} \times \mathbb{Z}^n$.

Definition 5 (Symbolic automatic relation). *A relation $\mathcal{R} \subseteq (\mathbb{Z}^*)^k \times \mathbb{Z}^n$ is called a (k, n)-ary symbolic automatic relation (SAR) if $\{(c(w_0, \ldots, w_{k-1}), \widetilde{j}) \mid (w_0, \ldots, w_{k-1}, \widetilde{j}) \in \mathcal{R}\} = \mathcal{L}(M(\widetilde{x}))$ for some (k, n)-ary ss-NFA $M(\widetilde{x})$; in this case, we say that $\mathcal{R}$ is recognized by $M(\widetilde{x})$.*

---

[4] The fact that determinization is possible and that symbolic automata are closed under boolean operations were originally shown for symbolic automata without parameters [30], but the existence of parameters does not affect the proof.

Given a (k,n)-ary ss-NFA $M(\widetilde{x})$, the (k,n)-ary SAR represented by $M(\widetilde{x})$, denoted as $\mathcal{R}(M(\widetilde{x}))$, is defined as $\{(w_0,\ldots,w_{k-1},\widetilde{j}) \mid (c(w_0,\ldots,w_{k-1}),\widetilde{j}) \in \mathcal{L}(M(\widetilde{x}))\}$. Note that $\mathcal{R}(M(\widetilde{x}))$ is indeed a SAR because $\mathcal{R}(M(\widetilde{x}))$ is recognized by the product of $M(\widetilde{x})$ and the automaton that recognizes $\mathbb{Z}^{\otimes k} \times \mathbb{Z}^n$.

3.3 Expressing Predicates on Lists

We demonstrate that various predicates over lists can be expressed as logical formulas obtained by extending the signature τ_{list} with SARs. Moreover, we show that those predicates belong to a class of formulas called Σ_1^{sar}-*formulas*. We are interested in Σ_1^{sar}-formulas because, as we shall see in Sect. 6, checking whether a simple Σ_1^{sar}-formula is satisfiable can often be done automatically.

Henceforth, we allow SARs to appear in the syntax of formulas. Formally, we consider formulas over τ_{sar}, where τ_{sar} is defined as the signature obtained by adding predicate symbols of the form $R_{M(\widetilde{x})}$, which we also call SAR, to the signature τ_{list}. Here the subscript $M(\widetilde{x})$ represents ss-NFAs. In what follows, the term "formula" means a formula over the signature τ_{sar}, unless the signature is explicitly specified. The predicate symbols $R_{M(\widetilde{x})}$ are interpreted symbols. We consider a fixed model $\mathcal{M}$ in which every predicate symbol of the form $R_{M(\widetilde{x})}$ is interpreted as the symbolic automatic relation represented by $M(\widetilde{x})$ and other symbols are interpreted as in $\mathcal{M}_{\text{list}}$.

Definition 6. *A formula φ is a Δ_0^{sar}-formula if one can effectively construct a formula $R_{M(\widetilde{x})}(\widetilde{T},\widetilde{t})$ (where $R_{M(\widetilde{x})}$ is a SAR) that is $\mathcal{M}$-equivalent to φ. A formula φ is a Σ_1^{sar}-formula if one can effectively construct a formula of the form $\exists\widetilde{x}\exists\widetilde{X}\varphi_0$ that is $\mathcal{M}$-equivalent to φ and φ_0 is a Δ_0^{sar}-formula. We say that a formula φ is a Δ_1^{sar}-formula if both φ and $\neg\varphi$ are Σ_1^{sar}-formulas.*

Example 2. Let us consider the predicate $sorted(X)$, which holds just if X is sorted in ascending order. The predicate $sorted$ can be defined as a Δ_0^{sar}-formula, by $sorted(X) \overset{\text{def}}{=} R_{M_1}(X, tail(X))$, where M_1 is the ss-NFA used in Example 1.

The predicate $nth(i,x,X)$, meaning that "the i-th element of X is x", can be defined as a Δ_1^{sar}-formula. To show this, we use the automata M_2 and M_3 used in Example 1. We can define nth by $nth(i,x,X) \overset{\text{def}}{=} \exists Y. R_{M_2(x)}(cons(i,Y),Y,X,x)$. In this definition, the list represented by Y works as a "counter". Suppose that $cons(i,Y)$ is interpreted as w_0 and assume that the first n transitions were all $q_0 \xrightarrow{l_0=l_1+1} q_0$. Then we know that the list w_0 must be of the form $[i,(i-1),\ldots(i-n),\ldots]$, which can be seen as a decrementing counter starting from i. The transition from q_0 to q_1 is only possible when the counter is 0 and this allows us to "access to the i-th element" of the list represented by X. The negation of $nth(i,x,X)$ can be defined as $\exists Y. R_{M_3(x)}(cons(i,Y),Y,X,x)$. Using the same technique, we can define the predicate $length(X,i)$ ("the length of X is i") as a Δ_1^{sar}-formula.

$\square$

The following proposition and example are useful for constructing new examples of Σ_1^{sar}-formulas.

Proposition 3. *The class of Δ_0^{sar}-formulas and Δ_1^{sar}-formulas are closed under boolean operations.*

Proof. The fact that Δ_0^{sar}-formulas are closed under boolean operations follows from the fact that ss-NFAs are closed under boolean operations (Proposition 1) and that the set of convoluted words is a language accepted by a ss-NFA (Proposition 2).

By the definition of Δ_1^{sar}-formulas, Δ_1^{sar}-formulas are clearly closed under negation. Given formulas $\exists \widetilde{x} \exists \widetilde{X} \varphi_1$ and $\exists \widetilde{y} \exists \widetilde{Y} \varphi_2$, where φ_1 and φ_2 are Δ_0^{sar}-formulas, $(\exists \widetilde{x} \exists \widetilde{X} \varphi_1) \wedge (\exists \widetilde{y} \exists \widetilde{Y} \varphi_2)$ is equivalent to $\exists \widetilde{x} \widetilde{y} \exists \widetilde{X} \widetilde{Y} (\varphi_1 \wedge \varphi_2)$. Since $\varphi_1 \wedge \varphi_2$ is a Δ_0^{sar}-formula, it follows that Δ_1^{sar}-formulas are closed under conjunction. $\square$

Example 3. Every arithmetic formula, i.e. a formula over the signature τ_{int}, is a Δ_0^{sar}-formula. Given an arithmetic formula φ whose free variables are $x_0, \ldots, x_{k-1}$, we can construct a $\mathcal{M}$-equivalent formula $R_{M_\varphi}([x_0], \ldots, [x_{k-1}])$, where $[x_i] \overset{\text{def}}{=} cons(x_i, nil)$ and $M_\varphi \overset{\text{def}}{=} (\{q_0, q_1\}, \{q_0\}, \{q_1\}, \{(q_0, \varphi[l_0/x_0, \ldots, l_{k-1}/x_{k-1}], q_1)\})$. Similar transformation works even if a formula of the form $head(X)$ appears inside a formula φ of type *Int*.

Equality relation on two lists is also a Δ_0^{sar}-formula because it can be described by a ss-NFA. $\square$

Thanks to Proposition 3 and Example 3, we can now write various specification over lists as (negations of) closed Σ_1^{sar}-formulas. For example, consider the following formula that informally means "if the head element of a list sorted in ascending order is greater or equal to 0, then all the elements of that list is greater or equal to 0":

$$\varphi \overset{\text{def}}{=} \forall x. \forall i. \forall X. \; X \neq nil \wedge sorted(X) \wedge head(X) \geq 0 \wedge nth(i, x, X) \implies x \geq 0$$

The negation of φ is a Σ_1^{sar}-formula because $sorted(X)$ and $nth(i, x, X)$ are Δ_1^{sar}-formulas as we saw in Example 2. Note that the validity of φ can be checked by checking that $\neg \varphi$ is unsatisfiable, which can be done by a satisfiability solver for Σ_1^{sar}-formulas.

3.4   An Application to ICE-Learning-Based CHC Solving with Lists

We now briefly discuss how a satisfiability solver for Σ_1^{sar}-formulas may be used in the teacher part of ICE-learning-based CHC solvers for lists. As mentioned in Sect. 1, ICE-learning-based CHC solvers [6,12] consist of a learner, which constructs a candidate model, and a teacher, which checks whether the candidate is indeed a model, i.e., whether the candidate model satisfies every clause. Each clause is of the form

$$\forall \widetilde{x}. \forall \widetilde{X}. A_1 \wedge \cdots \wedge A_n \implies B$$

where $A_1, \ldots, A_n$ and B are either primitive constraints or atoms of the form $P(t_1, \ldots, t_k)$ where P is a predicate variable. Assuming that the learner returns an assignment θ of Δ_1^{sar}-formulas to predicate variables, the task of the teacher is to check that

$$\varphi := \forall \widetilde{x}.\forall \widetilde{X}.\theta A_1 \wedge \cdots \wedge \theta A_n \implies \theta B$$

is a valid formula for each clause $\forall \widetilde{x}.\forall \widetilde{X}.\theta A_1 \wedge \cdots \wedge \theta A_n \implies \theta B$. The negation of φ can be expressed as a closed Σ_1^{sar}-formula $\exists \widetilde{x}.\exists \widetilde{X}.R_{M(\widetilde{y})}(\widetilde{T}, \widetilde{t})$. By invoking a satisfiability solver for a Σ_1^{sar}-formulas we can check whether $R_{M(\widetilde{y})}(\widetilde{T}, \widetilde{t})$ is unsatisfiable, which is equivalent to checking if φ is valid. If $R_{M(\widetilde{y})}(\widetilde{T}, \widetilde{t})$ is satisfiable, then φ is invalid. In this case, the teacher should generate a counterexample against φ.

Example 4. Let us consider the following set of constrained horn clauses:

$$P(X) \Leftarrow X = nil \vee X = cons(x, nil)$$
$$P(cons(x, cons(y, X))) \Leftarrow x \leq y \wedge P(cons(y, X))$$
$$Q(cons(0, X)) \Leftarrow \top \quad Q(cons(x, X)) \Leftarrow Q(X) \quad \bot \Leftarrow P(cons(1, X)) \wedge Q(X)$$

A model of this set of CHCs is $P(X) \mapsto sorted(X), Q(X) \mapsto hasZero(X)$, where *sorted* is the predicate we have seen in Example 2 and $hasZero(X)$ is a predicate that holds if 0 appears in the list X. It is easy to check that *hasZero* is a Δ_0^{sar}-formula. Hence, if there is a learner part, which is yet to be implemented, that provides *sorted* and *hasZero* as a candidate model, then a satisfiability solver for Σ_1^{sar}-formulas can check that this candidate model is a valid model. □

Remark 2. As discussed later in Sect. 5, the satisfiability problem for SARs is solved by a reduction to CHC solving without data structures. Thus, combined with the translation above, we translate a part of the problem of solving CHCs with data structures to the problem of solving CHCs without data structures. This makes sense because solving CHCs without data structures is easier *in practice* (although the problem is undecidable in general, even without data structures). One may wonder why we do not directly translate CHCs with data structures to those without data structures, as in [9,10]. The detour through SARs has the following advantages. First, it provides a uniform, streamlined approach thanks to the closure of SARs under Boolean operations. Second, SARs serve as certificates of the satisfiability of CHCs.

4   Undecidability Result

This section shows that the satisfiability problem for SARs is undecidable in general. The *satisfiability problem for SARs* is the problem of deciding whether there is an assignment α such that $\mathcal{M}, \alpha \models \varphi$, given a τ_{sar}-formula φ. We prove that the satisfiability problem is undecidable even for the class of Δ_0^{sar}-formulas, by reduction from the halting problem for two-counter machines.

Definition 7. (Minsky's two-counter machine [22]). Minsky's two-counter machine *consists of (i) two integer registers* r_0 *and* r_1, *(ii) a set of instructions, and (iii) a program counter that holds a non-negative integer. Intuitively, the value of the program counter corresponds to the line number of the program currently being executed.*

A program *is a pair* $P = (\mathbf{Line}, \mathbf{Code})$, *where* $\mathbf{Line}$ *is a finite set of non-negative integers such that* $0 \in \mathbf{Line}$ *and* $\mathbf{Code}$ *is a map from a finite set of non-negative integers to* $\mathbf{Inst}$, *the set of* instructions. *The set* $\mathbf{Inst}$ *consists of:*

- $\mathbf{inc}(i,j)$: *Increment the value of register* r_i *and set the program counter to* $j \in \mathbf{Line}$.
- $\mathbf{jzdec}(i,j,k)$: *If the value of register* r_i *is positive, decrement it and set the program counter to* $j \in \mathbf{Line}$. *Otherwise, set the program counter to* $k \in \mathbf{Line}$.
- $\mathbf{halt}$: *Stop operating.*

Initially, r_0, r_1 *and the program counter are all set to* 0. *Given a program* $P = (\mathbf{Line}, \mathbf{Code})$ *the machine executes* $\mathbf{Code}(i)$, *where* i *is the value of the program counter until it executes the instruction* $\mathbf{halt}$.

Given a program P we simulate its execution using a formula of the form $R_M(X_0, X_1, tail(X_0), tail(X_1))$. The states and edges of M are used to model the control structure of the program, and the list variables X_0 and X_1 are used to model the "execution log" of registers r_0 and r_1, respectively.

Theorem 1 (Undecidability of satisfiability of SARs). *Given a* k-*ary symbolic automatic relation* R_M *represented by an effective* $(k, 0)$-*ary ss-NFA* M *and list terms* $T_1, \ldots, T_k$, *it is undecidable whether* $R_M(T_1, \ldots, T_k)$ *is satisfiable in* $\mathcal{M}$.

Proof. We show that for a given program $P = (\mathbf{Line}, \mathbf{Code})$, we can effectively construct a SAR R_{M_P} that satisfies "P halts iff there are assignments for X_0 and X_1 that satisfy $R_{M_P}(X_0, X_1, tail(X_0), tail(X_1))$". Intuitively, X_i denotes the "execution log of r_i", i.e., the sequence of values taken by r_i in a terminating execution sequence of P, and R_{M_P} takes as arguments both X_i and $tail(X_i)$ to check that X_i represents a valid sequence. The ss-NFA M_P is defined as (Q, I, F, Δ), where $Q \overset{\text{def}}{=} \{q_i \mid i \in \mathbf{Line}\} \cup \{q_{\text{accept}}\}$, $I \overset{\text{def}}{=} \{q_0\}$, and $F \overset{\text{def}}{=} \{q_{\text{accept}}\}$. We define the set of transitions so that M_P has a transition $q_i \xrightarrow{(c_0, c_1, c'_0, c'_1)} q_j$ iff the two-counter machine has a transition from the configuration (i, c_0, c_1) (where i is the current program pointer and c_i is the value of r_i) to (j, c'_0, c'_1). We also add transition from q_i to the final state q_{accept} if $\mathbf{Code}(i) = \mathbf{halt}$. Formally, Δ is defined as the smallest set that satisfies the following conditions:

- $(q_i, l'_r = l_r + 1 \wedge l_{1-r} = l_{1-r}, q_j) \in \Delta$ if $\mathbf{Code}(i) = \mathbf{inc}(r,j)$.
- $(q_i, l_r > 0 \wedge l'_r = l_r - 1 \wedge l'_{1-r} = l_{1-r}, q_j), (q_i, l_r = 0 \wedge l'_0 = l_0 \wedge l'_1 = l_1, q_k) \in \Delta$ if $\mathbf{Code}(i) = \mathbf{jzdec}(r,j,k)$.
- $(q_i, pad(l'_0) \wedge pad(l'_1), q_{\text{accept}}) \in \Delta$ if $\mathbf{Code}(i) = \mathbf{halt}$.

Here, we have written l'_0 and l'_1 for l_2 and l_3.

Based on the intuitions above, it should be clear that P halts and the execution log of r_i obtained by running P is w_i, if and only if M_P accepts $c(w_0, w_1, w'_0, w'_1)$, where w'_i is the tail of w_i. Thus, P halts if and only if R_{M_P} is satisfiable. Since the halting problem for two-counter machines is undecidable, so is the satisfiability of R_M.

$\square$

5   Reduction to CHC Solving

This section describes the reduction from the satisfiability problem of SARs to CHC solving, whose constraint theory is mere integer arithmetic. Precisely speaking, the reduction works for a fragment of τ_{sar}-formulas, namely the Σ_1^{sar}-formulas. This section starts with a brief overview of the reduction. We then give the formal definition and prove the correctness of the reduction.

5.1   Overview

Let us first present intuitions behind our reduction using an example. Consider the predicate nth we defined in Example 2. Let i be a non-negative integer constant, and suppose that we wish to check whether $nth(i, x, X)$ is satisfiable, i.e., whether $\exists x \exists X. nth(i, x, X)$ holds. We construct a set of CHCs Π such that $\mathcal{M} \models \exists x \exists X. nth(i, x, X)$ iff Π is unsatisfiable. That is, we translate Δ_0^{sar}-formula $R_{M_2(x)}(cons(i, Y), Y, X, x)$ preserving its satisfiability. The following CHCs are obtained by translating $R_{M_2(x)}(cons(i, Y), Y, X, x)$.

$$\underline{q_0}(v_0, v_1, v_2, x) \Leftarrow v_0 = i \tag{1}$$

$$\underline{q_0}(v_0, v_1, v_2, x) \Leftarrow \underline{q_0}(u_0, u_1, u_2, x) \wedge u_0 = u_1 + 1 \wedge v_0 = u_1 \wedge \neg\varphi_{\text{end}} \tag{2}$$

$$\underline{q_1}(v_0, v_1, v_2, x) \Leftarrow \underline{q_0}(u_0, u_1, u_2, x) \wedge u_0 = 0 \wedge u_2 = x \wedge v_0 = u_1 \wedge \neg\varphi_{\text{end}} \tag{3}$$

$$\underline{q_1}(v_0, v_1, v_2, x) \Leftarrow \underline{q_1}(u_0, u_1, u_2, x) \wedge v_0 = u_1 \wedge \neg\varphi_{\text{end}} \tag{4}$$

$$\bot \Leftarrow \underline{q_1}(u_0, u_1, u_2, x) \wedge \varphi_{\text{end}} \tag{5}$$

Here $\varphi_{\text{end}} \stackrel{\text{def}}{=} \bigwedge_{j \in \{0,1,2\}} pad(u_j)$. The predicate $\underline{q}$ corresponds to the state q and $\underline{q}(v_0, v_1, v_2, x)$ intuitively means "there exists an assignment α for X, Y and x such that given $(cons(i, \alpha(Y)), \alpha(Y), \alpha(X))$ as input, $M_2(\alpha(x))$ visits state q, with the next input letters being (v_0, v_1, v_2)". The clause (1) captures the fact that $M_2(\alpha(x))$ is initially at state q_0, with the first element v_0 of the initial input is i. The clauses (2), (3), and (4) correspond to transitions $q_0 \xrightarrow{l_0 = l_1 + 1} q_0$, $q_0 \xrightarrow{l_1 = 0 \wedge l_2 = x} q_1$, and $q_1 \xrightarrow{\top} q_1$ respectively. The constraints in the bodies of those clauses consist of: (i) the labels of the transitions (e.g., $u_0 = u_1 + 1$ in (2)), (ii) the equation $u_1 = v_0$, which captures the co-relation between the arguments $cons(i, Y)$ and Y of $R_{M_2}(x)$, (iii) $\neg\varphi_{\text{end}}$ indicating that there is still an input to read. The last clause (5) captures the acceptance condition: a contradiction is derived if $M_2(x)$ reaches the final state q_1, having read all the inputs. It follows from the intuitions above that the set of CHCs above is unsatisfiable, if and only if, $R_{M_2(x)}(cons(i, Y), Y, X, x)$ is satisfiable.

5.2 Translation

We now formalize the translation briefly discussed in the previous subsection. To simplify the definition of the translation, we first define the translation for terms in a special form. Then we will show that every term of the form $R_M(T_1, \ldots, T_k, t_1, \ldots, t_n)$ can be translated into the special form, preserving the satisfiability (or the unsatisfiability).

Definition 8. *Let $\mathcal{L}$ be a set of list terms. Then $\mathcal{L}$ is*

- *cons-free if for all $T \in \mathcal{L}$, T is of the form nil or $tail^n(X)$.*
- *gap-free if $tail^n(X) \in \mathcal{L}$ implies $tail^m(X) \in \mathcal{L}$ for all $0 \leq m \leq n$.*

Here $tail^m(X)$ is defined by $tail^0(X) \stackrel{\text{def}}{=} X$ and $tail^{m+1}(X) \stackrel{\text{def}}{=} tail(tail^m(X))$.
  We say that a formula of the form $R_{M(\widetilde{x})}(T_1, \ldots, T_k, t_1, \ldots, t_n)$ is normal if $\{T_1, \ldots, T_k\}$ is cons-free and gap-free, and every t_i is an integer variable.

Definition 9. *Let $R_{M(\widetilde{x})}$ be a (k, n)-ary SAR, where $M(\widetilde{x}) = (Q, I, F, \Delta)$, $\widetilde{T} \stackrel{\text{def}}{=} T_0, \ldots, T_{k-1}$ be list terms and $\widetilde{y} \stackrel{\text{def}}{=} y_0, \ldots, y_{n-1}$ be integer variables. Suppose that $R_{M(\widetilde{x})}(\widetilde{T}, \widetilde{y})$ is normal. Then the set of CHCs translated from $R_{M(\widetilde{x})}(\widetilde{T}, \widetilde{y})$, written $(\!|R_{M(\widetilde{x})}(\widetilde{T}, \widetilde{y})|\!)$, consists of the following clauses:*

1. *The clause (written $(\!|p \xrightarrow{\varphi} q|\!)$):*

$$\underline{q}(v_0, \ldots, v_{k-1}, \widetilde{x}) \Leftarrow \frac{p(u_0, \ldots, u_{k-1}, \widetilde{x}) \wedge \varphi[u_0/l_0, \ldots, u_{k-1}/l_{k-1}]}{\wedge \varphi_{\text{shift}} \wedge \varphi_{\text{pad}} \wedge \neg\varphi_{\text{end}}}$$

   for each $p \xrightarrow{\varphi} q \in \Delta$.
2. *The clause*

$$\underline{q}(v_0, \ldots, v_{k-1}, \widetilde{x}) \Leftarrow \varphi_{\text{nil}} \wedge \varphi_{\text{tail(nil)}} \wedge \widetilde{x} = \widetilde{y}$$

   for each $q \in I$.
3. *The clause:*

$$\bot \Leftarrow \underline{q}(u_0, \ldots, u_{k-1}, \widetilde{x}) \wedge \varphi_{\text{end}}$$

   for each $q \in F$.

Here the definitions and the informal meanings of φ_{end}, φ_{shift}, φ_{pad}, φ_{nil} and $\varphi_{\text{tail(nil)}}$ are given as follows:

$$\varphi_{\text{end}} \stackrel{\text{def}}{=} \bigwedge_{i \in \{0, \ldots, k-1\}} pad(u_i) \qquad \text{``there is no letter to read''}$$

$$\varphi_{\text{shift}} \stackrel{\text{def}}{=} \bigwedge \{v_i = u_j \vee (pad(v_i) \wedge pad(u_j)) \mid T_i = tail^m(X), T_j = tail^{m+1}(X)\}$$

"the l-th element of the list represented by $tail^{m+1}(X)$ is

the $(l+1)$-th element of the list represented by $tail^m(X)$"

$$\varphi_{\text{pad}} \stackrel{\text{def}}{=} \bigwedge_{i \in \{0, \ldots, k-1\}} pad(u_i) \Rightarrow pad(v_i)$$

"if a padding symbol $\square$ is read, then the next input is also $\square$"

$$\varphi_{\text{nil}} \stackrel{\text{def}}{=} \bigwedge \{pad(v_i) \mid T_i = nil\}$$

"there is no letter to read from an empty list"

$$\varphi_{\text{tail(nil)}} \stackrel{\text{def}}{=} \bigwedge \{pad(v_i) \Rightarrow pad(v_j) \mid T_i = tail^m(X), T_j = tail^{m+1}(X)\}$$

"if there is no letter to read from the input represented by $tail^m(X)$

then there is nothing to read from the input represented by $tail^{m+1}(X)$"

We next show that we can assume that $R_{M(\widetilde{x})}(\widetilde{T}, \widetilde{t})$ is normal without loss of generality. First, observe that ensuring that $\widetilde{T}$ is gap-free is easy. If $\widetilde{T}$ is not gap-free then we just have to add additional inputs, corresponding to the list represented by $tail^n(X)$, to the automaton $M(\widetilde{x})$ and ignore those inputs. Ensuring that $\widetilde{t}$ is a sequence of integer variables is also easy. If t is not an integer variable, then we can embed t to the transitions of the automaton and add the free variables of t to the parameter or as inputs of the automaton. Therefore, the only nontrivial condition is the cons-freeness:

Lemma 1. *Let $R_{M(\widetilde{x})}$ be a (k, n)-ary SAR, $\widetilde{T} \stackrel{\text{def}}{=} T_1, \ldots, T_k$ be list terms and $\widetilde{t} \stackrel{\text{def}}{=} t_1, \ldots, t_n$ be integer terms. Then we can effectively construct a $(k, n + m)$-ary ss-NFA $M'(\widetilde{x}, \widetilde{x}')$, list terms $\widetilde{T'} \stackrel{\text{def}}{=} T'_1, \ldots, T'_k$ and integer terms $\widetilde{t'} \stackrel{\text{def}}{=} t'_1, \ldots, t'_{n+m}$ such that (1) $R_{M(\widetilde{x})}(\widetilde{T}, \widetilde{t})$ is satisfiable in $\mathcal{M}$ iff $R_{M'(\widetilde{x}, \widetilde{x}')}(\widetilde{T'}, \widetilde{t'})$ is satisfiable in $\mathcal{M}$ and (2) $\{T'_1, \ldots, T'_k\}$ is cons-free.* $\square$

Instead of giving a proof, we look at an example. Consider the formula $\varphi \stackrel{\text{def}}{=} R_{M_2(x)}(cons(1, cons(t, Y)), cons(0, Y), X, x)$, where $M_2(x)$ is the automaton given in Example 1. We explain how to remove $cons(t, \cdot)$ from the first argument; by repeating this argument we can remove all the "cons". Let φ' be a formula defined as $R_{M'_2(x,y)}(cons(1, Y), cons(0, tail(Y)), X, x, t)$, where $M'_2(x, y)$ is the ss-NFA in Fig. 3. Then it is easy to see that φ is satisfiable in $\mathcal{M}$ iff φ' is satisfiable in $\mathcal{M}$. If $\mathcal{M}, \alpha \models \varphi$ with $\alpha(Y) = w$ and $[\![t]\!]_{\mathcal{M}, \alpha} = i$ then $\mathcal{M}, \alpha[Y \mapsto iw] \models \varphi'$; the opposite direction can be checked in a similar manner. The idea is to embed the information that "the second element is t" into the ss-NFA by replacing l_0 with y in the edges that corresponds to the "second step"

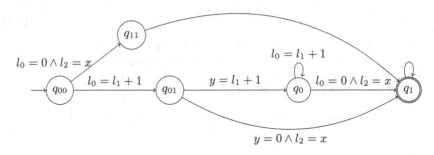

Fig. 3. The ss-NFA used to explain the idea behind Lemma 1.

and passing t as the actual argument. Note that we had to "unroll the ss-NFA $M_2(x)$" to ensure that the transition that contains y is used at most once.

Remark 3. We have so far considered symbolic automatic relations on lists. We expect that the reduction above can be extended to deal with symbolic automatic relations on tree structures, as follows. Let us consider a (symbolic, synchronous) bottom-up tree automaton, with transitions of the form

$$\langle l_1, \ldots, l_k, x_1, \ldots, x_n \rangle (q_1, \ldots, q_m), \varphi \to q,$$

which means "when the current node is labeled with $\langle l_1, \ldots, l_k, x_1, \ldots, x_n \rangle$ and the i-th child has been visited with state q_i, then the current node is visited with state q if $l_1, \ldots, l_k, x_1, \ldots, x_n$ satisfy φ". To reduce the satisfiability problem to CHCs on integers, it suffices to prepare a predicate $\underline{q}$ for each state q, so that $\underline{q}(l_1, \ldots, l_k, x_1, \ldots, x_n)$ holds just if there exists an input that allows the automaton to visit state q after reading $\langle l_1, \ldots, l_k, x_1, \ldots, x_n \rangle$. As for the definition of "normal form", it suffices to replace $tail(T)$ with $child_i(T)$ (which denotes the i-th child of tree T), and define the cons-freeness and gap-freeness conditions accordingly. The formalization of the extension is left for future work.

5.3   Correctness

The correctness of the translation is proved by associating a derivation of $\perp$ to an accepting run and vice versa.

We first define the notion of *derivations* for CHCs, as a special case of the SLD resolution derivation [21]. Since the system of CHCs obtained by translating a Δ_0^{sar}-formula is *linear*, which means that each clause contains at most one predicate in the body, we specialize the notion of derivations for linear CHCs.

Definition 10 (Derivation). *A derivation state (or simply a state) is a pair $\langle A \mid \psi \rangle$, where A is either $\top$ or $P(\tilde{t})$, i.e. an uninterpreted predicate symbol P applied to terms $\tilde{t}$, and ψ is a constraint. Let C be a linear constrained horn* clause of the form $P(\widetilde{t_1}) \Leftarrow A \wedge \psi'$, where A is either $\top$ or formula of the form $Q(\widetilde{t_2})$ and ψ' is a constraint. Then we write $\langle P(\widetilde{t}) \mid \psi \rangle \overset{(C,\theta)}{\rightsquigarrow} \langle \theta A \mid \theta(\psi \wedge \psi') \rangle$, if $P(\widetilde{t})$ and $P(\widetilde{t_1})$ are unifiable by a unifier θ.

Let Π be a system of linear CHCs, i.e. a finite set of linear constrained horn clauses. A derivation from state S_0 with respect to Π is a finite sequence of the form $S_0 \overset{(C_1,\theta_1)}{\rightsquigarrow} S_1 \overset{(C_2,\theta_2)}{\rightsquigarrow} \ldots \overset{(C_n,\theta_n)}{\rightsquigarrow} S_n$ such that (i) $C_i \in \Pi$ for all i and (ii) S_n is of the form $\langle \top \mid \psi \rangle$ such that ψ is a constraint that is satisfiable in $\mathbb{Z}_\square$.

Now we are ready to prove the correctness of the translation. Due to the lack of space we only sketch the proof; a detailed version is in [26].

Theorem 2. Let $R_{M(\widetilde{x})}$ be a (k,n)-ary SAR, and suppose that $R_{M(\widetilde{x})}(\widetilde{T},\widetilde{y})$ is normal. Then $R_{M(\widetilde{x})}(\widetilde{T},\widetilde{y})$ is satisfiable in $\mathcal{M}$ iff $(\!|R_{M(\widetilde{x})}(\widetilde{T},\widetilde{y})|\!)$ is unsatisfiable modulo $\mathbb{Z}_\square$.

Proof (Sketch). Suppose that $M(\widetilde{x}) = (Q,I,F,\Delta)$, $\widetilde{T} = T_0,\ldots,T_{k-1}$, $\widetilde{y} = y_0,\ldots,y_{n-1}$ and let $\Pi \overset{\text{def}}{=} (\!|R_{M(\widetilde{x})}(\widetilde{T},\widetilde{y})|\!)$. By the completeness of the SLD resolution, it suffices to show that $R_{M(\widetilde{x})}(\widetilde{T},\widetilde{y})$ is satisfiable if and only if there is a derivation starting from $\langle \underline{q}(\widetilde{u},\widetilde{x}) \mid \varphi_{\text{end}} \rangle$ with respect to Π for some $q \in F$. We separately sketch the proof for each direction.

(Only if) Since $R_{M(\widetilde{x})}(\widetilde{T},\widetilde{y})$ is satisfiable, there exists an assignment α such that $\mathcal{M}, \alpha \models R_{M(\widetilde{x})}(\widetilde{T},\widetilde{y})$. Let $w_i \overset{\text{def}}{=} [\![T_i]\!]_{\mathcal{M},\alpha}$ for each $i \in \{0,\ldots,k-1\}$, $j_i \overset{\text{def}}{=} \alpha(y_i)$ for $i \in \{0,\ldots,n-1\}$ and $\widetilde{j} \overset{\text{def}}{=} j_0,\ldots,j_{n-1}$. Because $\mathcal{M}, \alpha \models R_{M(\widetilde{x})}(\widetilde{T},\widetilde{y})$, we have an accepting run of $M(\widetilde{j})$, $q_0 \overset{a_0}{\longrightarrow} q_1 \overset{a_2}{\longrightarrow} \cdots \overset{a_{m-1}}{\longrightarrow} q_m$, where the run $a_0 a_2 \cdots a_{m-1}$ is $c(w_0,\ldots,w_{k-1})$. From this run, we can construct a derivation

$$\langle \underline{q_m}(\widetilde{u},\widetilde{x}) \mid \varphi_{\text{end}} \rangle \overset{\xi_{m-1}}{\rightsquigarrow} \langle \underline{q_{m-1}}(a_{m-1},\widetilde{j}) \mid \psi_{m-1} \rangle \overset{\xi_{m-2}}{\rightsquigarrow} \cdots \overset{\xi_0}{\rightsquigarrow} \langle \underline{q_0}(a_0,\widetilde{j}) \mid \psi_0 \rangle \overset{(C,\theta)}{\rightsquigarrow} \langle \top \mid \psi \rangle$$

where $\xi_i = (C_i, \theta_i)$. Here, $\underline{q_i}(a_i,\widetilde{j})$ means the predicate symbol $\underline{q_i}$ applied to constants that represent the elements of a_i and $\widetilde{j}$. In particular, the derivation can be constructed by taking the clause that corresponds to the transition $q_i \overset{a_i}{\longrightarrow} q_{i+1}$ for the clause C_i.

(If) By assumption, there is a derivation

$$\langle \underline{q_m}(\widetilde{u},\widetilde{x}) \mid \psi_m \rangle \overset{(C_m,\theta_m)}{\rightsquigarrow} \cdots \overset{(C_1,\theta_1)}{\rightsquigarrow} \langle \underline{q_0}(\widetilde{u},\widetilde{x}) \mid \psi_0 \rangle \overset{(C_0,\theta_0)}{\rightsquigarrow} \langle \top \mid \psi \rangle$$

where $\psi_m = \varphi_{\text{end}}$. We construct an accepting run of $M(\widetilde{x})$ using an assignment in $\mathbb{Z}_\square$ and the unifiers. Take an assignment α such that $\mathbb{Z}_\square, \alpha \models \psi$, which exists because ψ is satisfiable in $\mathbb{Z}_\square$. Let $\theta_{\leq i} \overset{\text{def}}{=} \theta_0 \circ \theta_1 \circ \cdots \circ \theta_i$. We define $a_{ij} \in \mathbb{Z}_\square$, where $0 \leq i \leq m$ and $0 \leq j \leq k-1$, by $a_{ij} \overset{\text{def}}{=} [\![\theta_{\leq i}(u_j)]\!]_{\mathbb{Z}_\square,\alpha}$ and set $a_i \overset{\text{def}}{=} (a_{i0},\ldots,a_{ik-1})$. We also define $j_i \overset{\text{def}}{=} [\![\theta_0(x_i)]\!]_{\mathcal{M},\alpha}$ and write $\widetilde{j}$ for $j_0,\ldots,j_n$. Then we can show that $a_0 a_1 \cdots a_{m-1}$ is an accepting run of $M(\widetilde{j})$. Moreover, we can show that $a_0 a_1 \cdots a_{m-1}$ can be given as a convolution of words $c(w_0,\ldots,w_{k-1})$

by using the constraint $\neg\varphi_{\text{end}}$ that appears in clauses corresponding to transition relations. Finally, we can show that there is an assignment β in $\mathcal{M}$ such that $[\![T_i]\!]_{\mathcal{M},\beta} = w_i$ for every $i \in \{0, \ldots, k-1\}$ by using the cons-freeness and gap-freeness, and the constraints φ_{shift}, φ_{nil} and $\varphi_{\text{tail(nil)}}$.   □

The correspondence between resolution proofs and accepting runs should allow us to generate a witness of the satisfiability of $R_{M(\widetilde{x})}(\widetilde{T}, \widetilde{y})$. A witness of the satisfiability is important because it serves as a counterexample that the teacher part of an ICE-based CHC solver provides (cf. Sect. 3.4). Since some CHC solvers like ELDARICA [17] outputs a resolution proof as a certificate of the unsatisfiability, it should be able to generate counterexamples by using these solvers as a backend of the teacher part. The formalization and the implementation of this counterexample generation process are left for future work.

6   Experiments

We have implemented a satisfiability checker for Δ_1^{sar}-formulas. An input of the tool consists of (i) definitions of Δ_1^{sar}-predicates (expressed using ss-NFA), and (ii) a Δ_1^{sar}-formula consisting of the defined predicates, list constructors and destructors, and integer arithmetic. For (i), if a predicate is defined using existential quantifiers, both the definitions of a predicate and its negation should be provided (recall nth in Example 1); we do not need to provide the predicates in normal forms because our tool automatically translates the inputs into normal forms. The current version of our tool only outputs SAT, UNSAT, or TIMEOUT and does not provide any witness of the satisfiability. We used Spacer [20], HoIce [6], and ELDARICA [17] as the backend CHC solver (to solve the CHC problems obtained by the reduction in Sect. 5). The experiments were conducted on a machine with AMD Ryzen 9 5900X 3.7 GHz and 32 GB of memory, with a timeout of 60 s. The implementation and all the benchmark programs are available in the artifact [25]. Detailed experimental results are also shown in [26].

We have tested our tool for three benchmarks. All the ss-NFAs used in the benchmarks are effective; in fact, all the formulas appearing as the labels of transitions are formulas in quantifier-free linear integer arithmetic. The first benchmark "IsaPlanner" is obtained from the benchmark [18] of IsaPlanner [11], which is a proof planner for the interactive theorem prover Isabelle [24]. We manually converted the recursively defined functions used in the original benchmark into SARs. The second benchmark "SAR_SMT" consists of valid/invalid formulas that represent properties of lists.

Each instance of the third benchmark "CHC" consists of (i) CHCs on data structures and (ii) a candidate model (given as a map from predicate variables to Δ_1^{sar}-formulas); the goal is to check that the candidate is a valid model for the CHCs (which is the task of the "teacher" part of ICE-based CHC solving [6]). This benchmark includes CHCs obtained by a reduction from the refinement type-checking problem for functional programs [15,27,28,31]. For many of the instances in the benchmark set, symbolic automatic relations are required to

Table 1. Summary of the experimental results

Benchmark	IsaPlanner	SAR_SMT	CHC	All
#Instances	15 (15/0)	60 (47/13)	12 (12/0)	87 (74/13)
Ours-Spacer				
#Solved	8 (8/0/0)	43 (30/13/0)	8 (8/0/0)	59 (46/13/0)
Average time	0.995	0.739	1.981	0.942
Ours-HoIce				
#Solved	14 (14/0/1)	55 (42/13/0)	11 (11/0/0)	80 (67/13/1)
Average time	7.296	4.498	6.584	5.275
Ours-Eldarica				
#Solved	14 (14/0/0)	59 (46/13/2)	12 (12/0/0)	85 (72/13/2)
Average time	4.539	2.441	11.078	4.006
Z3 (rec)				
#Solved	5 (5/0/0)	32 (19/13/0)	1 (1/0/0)	38 (25/13/0)
Average time	0.023	0.022	0.017	0.022
CVC4 (rec)				
#Solved	5 (5/0/0)	32 (19/13/0)	3 (3/0/0)	40 (27/13/0)
Average time	0.014	0.015	0.050	0.017
Z3 (assert)				
#Solved	7 (7/0/0)	20 (20/0/0)	3 (3/0/0)	30 (30/0/0)
Average time	0.018	0.018	0.022	0.019
CVC4 (assert)				
#Solved	6 (6/0/0)	19 (19/0/0)	3 (3/0/0)	28 (28/0/0)
Average time	0.057	0.008	0.015	0.019

express models. For example, the set of CHCs given in Example 4 is included in the benchmark.

To compare our tool with the state-of-the-art SMT solvers, Z3 (4.8.11) [23] and CVC4 (1.8) [1], which support user-defined data types and recursive function definition, we manually translated the instances to SMT problems that use recursive functions on lists. We tested two different translations. One is to translate the Δ_1^{sar}-predicates (such as nth) directly into recursive functions by using `define-fun-rec`, and the other is to translate the predicates into assertions, like `(assert (forall ...))`, that describe the definition of functions.

Table 1 summarizes the experimental results. In the first column, "Ours-XXX" means our tool with the underlying CHC solver XXX, "(rec)" means the translation to recursive functions, and "(assert)" means the translation to assertions. The row "Benchmark" shows the names of the benchmarks. The column "All" show the summary of the all benchmarks. The row "#Instances" shows the number of instances in the benchmark, and the first two numbers in the parentheses show the numbers of valid and invalid instances respectively, and the last number in the parentheses shows the number of solved instances that were not solved by the other tools. The row "#Solved" shows the number of solved instances, and the numbers in the parentheses are the same as ones in "#Instances". The row "Average time" shows the average running time of the solved instances in seconds.

Ours-ELDARICA successfully verified all the instances except two. Since one of them needs non-linear properties on integers such as $x \geq y \times z$, the reduced CHC problem cannot be proved by the underlying CHC solvers used in the experiments. The other one is proved by Ours-HoIce. As shown in the rows "Z3" and "CVC4", many of the problems were not verified by the SMT solvers regardless of the way of translation. Especially, they did not verify most of the instances that require inductions over lists. Moreover, all the invalid instances translated by using assertions were not verified by Z3 nor CVC4, while those translated by using recursive functions were verified by Z3 and CVC4.

We explain some benchmark instances below. The instance "prop_77" in IsaPlanner benchmark is the correctness property of *insert* function of insertion sort. That is, if a list X is sorted and a list Y is X with some integer inserted by *insert*, then Y is sorted. As stated above, we manually converted the recursively defined functions into SARs. As an example, we now describe how to translate *insert* function into a SAR. The original *insert* function is defined as follows (written in OCaml-like language):

```
let rec insert(x, y) = match y with
  | [] -> x :: []
  | z::xs -> if x <= z then x::y else z::insert(x, xs)
```

We first translate it into the following recursively defined predicate.

```
let rec insert'(x, ys, rs) = match ys, rs with
  | [],      r::rs'              -> x = r && ys = rs'
  | y::ys', r::rs' when x <= y -> x = r && ys = rs'
  | y::ys', r::rs' when x > y  -> y = r && insert'(x, ys', rs')
  | _                           -> false
```

The predicate insert'(x,ys,rs) means that insert(x,ys) returns rs. We can now translate it into a SAR. To express this predicate, we need two states—one for insert' and one for equality of lists (ys = rs'). In addition, to check the equality of ys and the tail of rs, we need a one-shifted list of ys that has a dummy integer 0 in its head, i.e., $cons(0, ys)$. Hence, predicate $insert(x, X, Y)$ (which means Y is X with x inserted) can be expressed as $R_{M_{ins}(x)}(cons(0, X), X, Y)$ where $M_{ins}(x)$ is shown in Fig. 4. The transition from q_0 to q_0 corresponds to the third case of the pattern matching of insert', and the transition from q_0 to q_1 corresponds to the first two cases.

The instance "prefix_trans" in SAR_SMT benchmark is the transitivity property of predicate *prefix*. The predicate *prefix* takes two lists, and it holds if the first argument is the prefix of the second argument. The transitivity of *prefix*

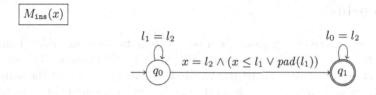

Fig. 4. The ss-NFA for function *insert*.

is that, if *prefix*(X, Y) and *prefix*(Y, Z), then *prefix*(X, Z) holds. The instance "sorted" in CHC benchmark is the problem explained in Example 4. All the instances explained here were solved by our tool, while neither Z3 nor CVC4 verified them.

7   Related Work

Although both automatic relations/structures [4,14,19] and symbolic automata [8,29,30] and their applications to verification have been well studied, the combination of them is new to our knowledge, at least in the context of program verification. D'Antoni and Veanes [7] studied the notion of extended symbolic finite automata (ESFA) which take a single word as an input, but read multiple consecutive symbols simultaneously. ESFA is related to our symbolic automatic relations in that the language accepted by ESFA can be expressed as $\{w \mid \mathcal{R}(w, tail(w), \dots, tail^{k-1}(w))\}$ using a symbolic automatic relation $\mathcal{R}$.

Haudebourg [16, Chapter 6] recently applied tree automatic relations to CHC solving. Since he uses ordinary (i.e. non-symbolic) automata, his method can only deal with lists and trees consisting of elements from a finite set.

As mentioned in Sect. 1, the current SMT solvers do not work well for recursive data structures. In the case of lists, one may use decidable theories on arrays or inductive data types [2,5]. The decidable fragments of those theories are limited. Our procedure is necessarily incomplete (due to the undecidability of the satisfiability problem), but can be used as complementary to the procedures implemented in the current SMT solvers, as confirmed by the experiments. We have focused on lists in this paper, but our approach can be extended to deal with more general recursive data structures, by replacing automatic relations with *tree* automatic ones.

There are other approaches to solving CHCs on recursive data structures. Unno et al. [28] proposed a method for automatically applying induction on data structures, and De Angelis et al. [9,10] proposed a method based on fold/unfold transformation. An advantage of our approach is that we can generate a symbolic automatic relation as a certificate of the satisfiability of CHCs. To make a proper comparison, however, we have to devise and implement a missing component – a procedure for automatically generating a candidate model (recall that we have given only a procedure for checking the validity of a candidate model).

8   Conclusion

We have introduced the notion of symbolic automatic relations (SARs) and considered the satisfiability problem for SARs, with applications to SMT and CHC solving on recursive data structures in mind. We have shown that the satisfiability problem is undecidable in general, but developed a sound (but incomplete) procedure to solve the satisfiability problem by a reduction to CHC solving on integers. We have confirmed the effectiveness of the proposed approach through experiments. We plan to implement an ICE-based CHC solver based on the proposed approach. To that end, we need to implement a learner's algorithm to automatically discover appropriate SARs, following the approach of Haudebourg [16].

Acknowledgments. We would like to thank anonymous referees for useful comments. This work was supported by JSPS KAKENHI Grant Number JP20H05703.

References

1. Barrett, C., et al.: CVC4. In: Gopalakrishnan, G., Qadeer, S. (eds.) CAV 2011. LNCS, vol. 6806, pp. 171–177. Springer, Heidelberg (2011). https://doi.org/10.1007/978-3-642-22110-1_14

2. Barrett, C.W., Shikanian, I., Tinelli, C.: An abstract decision procedure for a theory of inductive data types. J. Satisf. Boolean Model. Comput. **3**(1–2), 21–46 (2007). https://doi.org/10.3233/sat190028

3. Bjørner, N., Gurfinkel, A., McMillan, K., Rybalchenko, A.: Horn clause solvers for program verification. In: Beklemishev, L.D., Blass, A., Dershowitz, N., Finkbeiner, B., Schulte, W. (eds.) Fields of Logic and Computation II. LNCS, vol. 9300, pp. 24–51. Springer, Cham (2015). https://doi.org/10.1007/978-3-319-23534-9_2

4. Blumensath, A., Grädel, E.: Automatic structures. In: 15th Annual IEEE Symposium on Logic in Computer Science, Santa Barbara, California, USA, 26–29 June 2000, pp. 51–62. IEEE Computer Society (2000). https://doi.org/10.1109/LICS.2000.855755

5. Bradley, A.R., Manna, Z., Sipma, H.B.: What's decidable about arrays? In: Emerson, E.A., Namjoshi, K.S. (eds.) VMCAI 2006. LNCS, vol. 3855, pp. 427–442. Springer, Heidelberg (2005). https://doi.org/10.1007/11609773_28

6. Champion, A., Chiba, T., Kobayashi, N., Sato, R.: ICE-based refinement type discovery for higher-order functional programs. J. Autom. Reason. **64**(7), 1393–1418 (2020). https://doi.org/10.1007/s10817-020-09571-y

7. D'Antoni, L., Veanes, M.: Extended symbolic finite automata and transducers. Formal Methods Syst. Des. **47**(1), 93–119 (2015). https://doi.org/10.1007/s10703-015-0233-4

8. D'Antoni, L., Veanes, M.: The power of symbolic automata and transducers. In: Majumdar, R., Kunčak, V. (eds.) CAV 2017. LNCS, vol. 10426, pp. 47–67. Springer, Cham (2017). https://doi.org/10.1007/978-3-319-63387-9_3

9. De Angelis, E., Fioravanti, F., Pettorossi, A., Proietti, M.: Solving horn clauses on inductive data types without induction. TPLP **18**(3–4), 452–469 (2018). https://doi.org/10.1017/S1471068418000157

10. De Angelis, E., Fioravanti, F., Pettorossi, A., Proietti, M.: Removing algebraic data types from constrained horn clauses using difference predicates. In: Peltier, N., Sofronie-Stokkermans, V. (eds.) IJCAR 2020. LNCS (LNAI), vol. 12166, pp. 83–102. Springer, Cham (2020). https://doi.org/10.1007/978-3-030-51074-9_6

11. Dixon, L., Fleuriot, J.: IsaPlanner: a prototype proof planner in Isabelle. In: Baader, F. (ed.) CADE 2003. LNCS (LNAI), vol. 2741, pp. 279–283. Springer, Heidelberg (2003). https://doi.org/10.1007/978-3-540-45085-6_22

12. Ezudheen, P., Neider, D., D'Souza, D., Garg, P., Madhusudan, P.: Horn-ICE learning for synthesizing invariants and contracts. Proc. ACM Program. Lang. 2(OOPSLA), 131:1–131:25 (2018). https://doi.org/10.1145/3276501

13. Fedyukovich, G., Ernst, G.: Bridging arrays and ADTs in recursive proofs. In: Groote, J.F., Larsen, K.G. (eds.) TACAS 2021. LNCS, vol. 12652, pp. 24–42. Springer, Cham (2021). https://doi.org/10.1007/978-3-030-72013-1_2

14. Grädel, E.: Automatic structures: twenty years later. In: Hermanns, H., Zhang, L., Kobayashi, N., Miller, D. (eds.) LICS 2020: 35th Annual ACM/IEEE Symposium on Logic in Computer Science, Saarbrücken, Germany, 8–11 July 2020, pp. 21–34. ACM (2020). https://doi.org/10.1145/3373718.3394734

15. Hashimoto, K., Unno, H.: Refinement type inference via horn constraint optimization. In: Blazy, S., Jensen, T. (eds.) SAS 2015. LNCS, vol. 9291, pp. 199–216. Springer, Heidelberg (2015). https://doi.org/10.1007/978-3-662-48288-9_12

16. Haudebourg, T.: Automatic verification of higher-order functional programs using regular tree languages. Ph.D. thesis, Universitéx Rennes (2020)

17. Hojjat, H., Rümmer, P.: The ELDARICA horn solver. In: Bjørner, N., Gurfinkel, A. (eds.) 2018 Formal Methods in Computer Aided Design, FMCAD 2018, Austin, TX, USA, 30 October–2 November 2018, pp. 1–7. IEEE (2018). https://doi.org/10.23919/FMCAD.2018.8603013

18. Johansson, M., Dixon, L., Bundy, A.: Case-analysis for rippling and inductive proof. In: Kaufmann, M., Paulson, L.C. (eds.) ITP 2010. LNCS, vol. 6172, pp. 291–306. Springer, Heidelberg (2010). https://doi.org/10.1007/978-3-642-14052-5_21

19. Khoussainov, B., Nerode, A.: Automatic presentations of structures. In: Leivant, D. (ed.) LCC 1994. LNCS, vol. 960, pp. 367–392. Springer, Heidelberg (1995). https://doi.org/10.1007/3-540-60178-3_93

20. Komuravelli, A., Gurfinkel, A., Chaki, S.: SMT-based model checking for recursive programs. Formal Methods Syst. Des. 48(3), 175–205 (2016). https://doi.org/10.1007/s10703-016-0249-4

21. Kowalski, R.A.: Predicate logic as programming language. In: Rosenfeld, J.L. (ed.) Information Processing, Proceedings of the 6th IFIP Congress 1974, Stockholm, Sweden, 5–10 August 1974, pp. 569–574. North-Holland (1974)

22. Minsky, M.L.: Recursive unsolvability of post's problem of "tag" and other topics in theory of turing machines. Ann. Math. 74(3), 437–455 (1961)

23. de Moura, L., Bjørner, N.: Z3: an efficient SMT solver. In: Ramakrishnan, C.R., Rehof, J. (eds.) TACAS 2008. LNCS, vol. 4963, pp. 337–340. Springer, Heidelberg (2008). https://doi.org/10.1007/978-3-540-78800-3_24

24. Paulson, L.C. (ed.): Isabelle. LNCS, vol. 828. Springer, Heidelberg (1994). https://doi.org/10.1007/BFb0030541

25. Shimoda, T., Kobayashi, N., Sakayori, K., Sato, R.: Symbolic automatic relations and their applications to SMT and CHC solving [data set] (2021). https://doi.org/10.5281/zenodo.5140576

26. Shimoda, T., Kobayashi, N., Sakayori, K., Sato, R.: Symbolic automatic relations and their applications to SMT and CHC solving [extended version] (2021). https://arxiv.org/abs/2108.07642
27. Unno, H., Kobayashi, N.: Dependent type inference with interpolants. In: Porto, A., López-Fraguas, F.J. (eds.) Proceedings of the 11th International ACM SIGPLAN Conference on Principles and Practice of Declarative Programming, Coimbra, Portugal, 7–9 September 2009, pp. 277–288. ACM (2009). https://doi.org/10.1145/1599410.1599445
28. Unno, H., Torii, S., Sakamoto, H.: Automating induction for solving horn clauses. In: Majumdar, R., Kunčak, V. (eds.) CAV 2017. LNCS, vol. 10427, pp. 571–591. Springer, Cham (2017). https://doi.org/10.1007/978-3-319-63390-9_30
29. Veanes, M., Bjørner, N., de Moura, L.: Symbolic automata constraint solving. In: Fermüller, C.G., Voronkov, A. (eds.) LPAR 2010. LNCS, vol. 6397, pp. 640–654. Springer, Heidelberg (2010). https://doi.org/10.1007/978-3-642-16242-8_45
30. Veanes, M., de Halleux, P., Tillmann, N.: Rex: symbolic regular expression explorer. In: Third International Conference on Software Testing, Verification and Validation, ICST 2010, Paris, France, 7–9 April 2010, pp. 498–507. IEEE Computer Society (2010). https://doi.org/10.1109/ICST.2010.15
31. Zhu, H., Jagannathan, S.: Compositional and lightweight dependent type inference for ML. In: Giacobazzi, R., Berdine, J., Mastroeni, I. (eds.) VMCAI 2013. LNCS, vol. 7737, pp. 295–314. Springer, Heidelberg (2013). https://doi.org/10.1007/978-3-642-35873-9_19

Compositional Verification of Smart Contracts Through Communication Abstraction

Scott Wesley[1]($\boxtimes$) (iD), Maria Christakis[2], Jorge A. Navas[3] (iD), Richard Trefler[1],
Valentin Wüstholz[4], and Arie Gurfinkel[1] (iD)

[1] University of Waterloo, Waterloo, Canada
aswesley@uwaterloo.ca
[2] MPI-SWS, Kaiserslautern, Saarbrücken, Germany
[3] SRI International, Menlo Park, USA
[4] ConsenSys, Kaiserslautern, Germany

Abstract. Solidity smart contracts are programs that manage up to 2^{160} users on a blockchain. Verifying a smart contract relative to all users is intractable due to state explosion. Existing solutions either restrict the number of users to under-approximate behaviour, or rely on manual proofs. In this paper, we present *local bundles* that reduce contracts with arbitrarily many users to sequential programs with a few *representative* users. Each representative user abstracts concrete users that are locally symmetric to each other relative to the contract and the property. Our abstraction is semi-automated. The representatives depend on communication patterns, and are computed via static analysis. A summary for the behaviour of each representative is provided manually, but a default summary is often sufficient. Once obtained, a local bundle is amenable to sequential static analysis. We show that local bundles are relatively complete for parameterized safety verification, under moderate assumptions. We implement local bundle abstraction in SMARTACE, and show order-of-magnitude speedups compared to a state-of-the-art verifier.

1 Introduction

Solidity smart contracts are distributed programs that facilitate information flow between users. Users alternate and execute predefined transactions, that each terminate within a predetermined number of steps. Each user (and contract) is assigned a unique, 160-bit address, that is used by the smart contract to map the user to that user's data. In theory, smart contracts are finite-state systems with 2^{160} users. However, in practice, the state space of a smart contract is huge—with at least $2^{2^{160}}$ states to accommodate all users and their data (conservatively counting one bit per user). In this paper, we consider the challenge of automatically verifying Solidity smart contracts that rely on user data.

This work was supported, in part, by Individual Discovery Grants from the Natural Sciences and Engineering Research Council of Canada, and Ripple Fellowship. Jorge A. Navas was supported by NSF grant 1816936.

© Springer Nature Switzerland AG 2021
C. Drăgoi et al. (Eds.): SAS 2021, LNCS 12913, pp. 429–452, 2021.
https://doi.org/10.1007/978-3-030-88806-0_21

```
 1  contract Auction {                                16
 2    mapping(address => uint) bids;                  17    function withdraw() public {
 3    address manager; uint leadingBid; bool stopped; 18      require(msg.sender != manager);
 4    uint _sum;                                       19      require(bids[msg.sender] != leadingBid);
 5                                                     20      require(!stopped);
 6    constructor(address mgr) public { manager = mgr; } 21     _sum = _sum + 0 - bids[msg.sender];
 7                                                     22      bids[msg.sender] = 0;
 8    function bid(uint amount) public {               23    }
 9      require(msg.sender != manager);                24
10      require(amount > leadingBid);                  25    function stop() public {
11      require(!stopped);                             26      require(msg.sender == manager);
12      _sum = _sum + amount - bids[msg.sender];       27      stopped = true;
13      bids[msg.sender] = amount;                     28    }
14      leadingBid = amount;                           29  }
15    }
```

Fig. 1. A smart contract that implements a simple auction.

```
 1  Auction _a = new Auction(address(2));             11    // Selects a sender.
 2  _a.address = address(1);                           12    msg.sender = *;
 3                                                     13    require(msg.sender > address(1));
 4  while (true) {                                      14    require(msg.sender < address(5));
 5    // Applies an interference invariant.            15    require(msg.sender < address(4));
 6    uint bid = *;                                     16    // Selects a call.
 7    uint maxBid = _a.leadingBid;                      17    if      (*) _a.bid(*);
 8    require(bid <= maxBid);                           18    else if (*) _a.withdraw();
 9    require(bid == maxBid || bid + maxBid <= _a.sum); 19    else if (*) _a.stop();
10    _a.bids[address(3)] = bid;                        20  }
```

Fig. 2. A harness to verify **Prop. 1** (ignore the highlighted lines) and **Prop. 2**.

A naive solution for smart contract verification is to verify the finite-state system directly. However, verifying systems with at least $2^{2^{160}}$ states is intractable. The naive solution fails because the state space is exponential in the number of users. Instead, we infer correctness from a small number of representative users to ameliorate state explosion. To restrict a contract to fewer users, we first generalize to a *family* of finite-state systems parameterized by the number of users. In this way, smart contract verification is reduced to parameterized verification.

For example, consider `Auction` in Fig. 1 (for now, ignore the highlighted lines). In `Auction`, each user starts with a bid of 0. Users alternate, and submit increasingly larger bids, until a designated manager stops the auction. While the auction is not stopped, a non-leading user may withdraw their bid[1]. `Auction` satisfies **Prop. 1**: *"Once stop() is called, all bids are immutable."* **Prop. 1** is satisfied since `stop()` sets `stopped` to true, no function sets `stopped` to false, and while `stopped` is true neither `bid()` nor `withdraw()` is enabled. Formally, **Prop. 1** is initially true, and remains true due to **Prop. 1b**: *"Once stop() is called, stopped remains true."* **Prop. 1** is said to be inductive relative to its *inductive strengthening* **Prop. 1b**. A *Software Model Checker (SMC)* can establish **Prop. 1** by an exhaustive search for its inductive strengthening. However, this requires a bound on the number of addresses, since a search with all 2^{160} addresses is intractable.

A bound of at least four addresses is necessary to represent the zero-account (i.e., a null user that cannot send transactions), the smart contract account, the manager, and an arbitrary sender. However, once the arbitrary sender submits a bid, the sender is now the leading bidder, and cannot withdraw its bid. To enable `withdraw()`, a fifth user is required. It follows by applying the results of [20], that a bound of five addresses is also sufficient, since users do not read

---

[1] For simplicity of presentation, we do not use Ether, Ethereum's native currency.

each other's bids, and adding a sixth user does not enable additional changes to leadingBid [20]. The bounded system, known as a harness, in Fig. 2 assigns the zero-account to address 0, the smart contract account to address 1, the manager to address 2, the arbitrary senders to addresses 3 and 4, and then executes an unbounded sequence of arbitrary function calls. Establishing **Prop. 1** on the harness requires finding its inductive strengthening. A strengthening such as **Prop. 1b** (or, in general, a counterexample violating **Prop. 1**) can be found by an SMC, directly on the harness code.

The above bound for **Prop. 1** also works for checking all control-reachability properties of Auction. This, for example, follows by applying the results of [20]. That is, Auction has a *Small Model Property (SMP)* (e.g., [1,20]) for such properties. However, not all contracts enjoy an SMP. Consider **Prop. 2**: *"The sum of all active bids is at least* leadingBid." Auction satisfies **Prop. 2** since the leading bid is never withdrawn. To prove Auction satisfies **Prop. 2**, we instrument the code to track the current sum, through the highlighted lines in Fig. 1. With the addition of _sum, Auction no longer enjoys an SMP. Intuitively, each user enables new combinations of _sum and leadingBid. As a proof, assume that there are N users (other than the zero-account, the smart contract account, and the manager) and let $S_N = 1 + 2 + \cdots + N$. In every execution with N users, if leadingBid is $N + 1$, then _sum is less than S_{N+1}, since active bids are unique and S_{N+1} is the sum of $N + 1$ bids from 1 to $N + 1$. However, in an execution with $N + 1$ users, if the i-th user has a bid of i, then leadingBid is $N + 1$ and _sum is S_{N+1}. Therefore, increasing N extends the reachable combinations of _sum and leadingBid. For example, if $N = 2$, then $S_3 = 1 + 2 + 3 = 6$. If the leading bid is 3, then the second highest bid is at most 2, and, therefore, _sum $\leq 5 < S_3$. However, when $N = 3$, if the three active bids are $\{1, 2, 3\}$, then _sum is S_3. Therefore, instrumenting Auction with _sum violates the SMP of the original Auction.

Despite the absence of such an SMP, each function of Auction interacts with at most one user per transaction. Each user is classified as either the zero-account, the smart contract, the manager, or an arbitrary sender. In fact, all arbitrary senders are indistinguishable with respect to **Prop. 2**. For example, if there are exactly three active bids, $\{2, 4, 8\}$, it does not matter which user placed which bid. The leading bid is 8 and the sum of all bids is 14. On the other hand, if the leading bid is 8, then each participant of Auction must have a bid in the range of 0 to 8. To take advantage of these classes, rather than analyze Auction relative to all 2^{160} users, it is sufficient to analyze Auction relative to a representative user from each class. In our running example, there must be representatives for the zero-account, the smart contract account, the manager, and an (arbitrary) sender. The key idea is that each representative user can correspond to one or *many* concrete users.

Intuitively, each representative user summarizes the concrete users in its class. If a representative's class contains a single concrete user, then there is no difference between the concrete user and the representative user. For example, the zero-account, the smart contract account, and the manager each correspond to single concrete users. The addresses of these users, and in turn, their bids, are known with absolute certainty. On the other hand, there are many arbitrary senders. Since senders are indistinguishable from each other, the precise address of the representative sender is unimportant. What matters is that the representative sender does not share an address with the zero-account, the smart contract account, nor the manager. However, this means that at the start of each transaction the location of the representative sender is not absolute, and, therefore, the sender has a range of possible bids. To account for this, we introduce a predicate that is true of all initial bids, and holds inductively across all transactions. We provide this predicate manually, and use it to over-approximate all possible bids. An obvious predicate for Auction is that all bids are at most leadingBid, but this predicate is not strong enough to prove **Prop. 2**. For example, the representative sender could first place a bid of 10, and then (spuriously) withdraw a bid of 5, resulting in a sum of 5 but a leading bid of 10. A stronger predicate, that is adequate to prove **Prop. 2**, is given by θ_U: "*Each bid is at most* leadingBid. If a bid is not leadingBid, then its sum with leadingBid is at most _sum.*"

Given θ_U, **Prop. 2** can be verified by an SMC. This requires a new harness, with representative, rather than concrete, users. The new harness, Fig. 2 (now including the highlighted lines), is similar to the SMP harness in that the zero-account, the smart contract account, and the manager account are assigned to addresses 0, 1, and 2, respectively, followed by an unbounded sequence of arbitrary calls. However, there is now a single sender that is assigned to address 3 (line 15). That is, the harness uses a fixed configuration of representatives in which the fourth representative is the sender. Before each function call, the sender's bid is set to a non-deterministic value that satisfies θ_U (lines 6–10). If the new harness and **Prop. 2** are provided to an SMC, the SMC will find an inductive strengthening such as, "*The leading bid is at most the sum of all bids.*"

The harness in Fig. 2 differs from existing smart contract verification techniques in two ways. First, each address in Fig. 2 is an abstraction of one or more concrete users. Second, msg.sender is restricted to a finite address space by lines 13 to 15. If these lines are removed, then an inductive invariant must constrain all cells of bids, to accommodate bids[msg.sender]. This requires quantified invariants over arrays that is challenging to automate. By introducing lines 13 to 15, a quantifier-free predicate, such as our θ_U, can directly constrain cell bids[msg.sender] instead. Adding lines 13–15 makes the contract finite state. Thus, its verification problem is decidable and can be handled by existing SMCs. However, as illustrated by **Prop. 2**, the restriction on each user must not exclude feasible counterexamples. Finding such a restriction is the focus of this paper.

In this paper, we present a new approach to smart contract verification. We construct finite-state abstractions of parameterized smart contracts, known as *local bundles*. A local bundle generalizes the harness in Fig. 2, and is constructed from a set of representatives and their predicates. When a local bundle and a property are provided to an SMC, there are three possible outcomes. First, if a predicate does not over-approximate its representative, a counterexample to the predicate is returned. Second, if the predicates do not entail the property, then a counterexample to verification is returned (this counterexample refutes the proof, rather than the property itself). Finally, if the predicates do entail the property, then an inductive invariant is returned. As opposed to deductive smart contract solutions, our approach finds inductive strengthenings automatically [17,44]. As opposed to other model checking solutions for smart contracts, our approach is not limited to pre- and post-conditions [21], and can scale to 2^{160} users [24].

Key theoretical contributions of this paper are to show that verification with local bundle abstraction is an instance of Parameterized Compositional Model Checking (PCMC) [31] and the automation of the side-conditions for its applicability. Specifically, Theorem 3 shows that the local bundle abstraction is a sound proof rule, and a static analysis algorithm (PTGBuilder in Sect. 4) computes representatives so that the rule is applicable. Key practical contributions are the implementation and the evaluation of the method in a new smart contract verification tool SMARTACE, using SEAHORN [15] for SMC. SMARTACE takes as input a contract and a predicate. Representatives are inferred automatically from the contract, by analyzing the communication in each transaction. The predicate is then validated by SEAHORN, relative to the representatives. If the predicate is correct, then a local bundle, as in Fig. 2, is returned.

The rest of the paper is structured as follows. Section 2 reviews parameterized verification. Section 3 presents MicroSol, a subset of Solidity with network semantics. Section 4 relates user interactions to representatives. We formalize user interactions as *Participation Topologies (PTs)*, and define *PT Graphs (PTGs)* to over-approximate PTs for arbitrarily many users. Intuitively, each PTG over-approximates the set of representatives. We show that a PTG is computable for every MicroSol program. Section 5 defines local bundles and proves that our approach is sound. Section 6 evaluates SMARTACE and shows that it can outperform VERX, a state-of-the-art verification tool, on all but one VERX benchmark.

2 Background

In this section, we briefly recall *Parameterized Compositional Model Checking (PCMC)* [31]. We write $\mathbf{u} = (u_0, \ldots, u_{n-1})$ for a vector of n elements, and $\mathbf{u}_i$ for the i-th element of $\mathbf{u}$. For a natural number $n \in \mathbb{N}$, we write $[n]$ for $\{0, \ldots, n-1\}$.

Labeled Transition Systems. A *labeled transition system (LTS)*, M, is a tuple (S, P, T, s_0), where S is a set of states, P is a set of actions, $T : S \times P \to 2^S$ is a transition relation, and $s_0 \in S$ is an initial state. M is *deterministic* if T is a function, $T : S \times P \to S$. A (finite) *trace* of M is an alternating sequence of states and actions, $(s_0, p_1, s_1, \ldots, p_k, s_k)$, such that $\forall i \in [k] \cdot s_{i+1} \in T(s_i, p_{i+1})$. A state s is *reachable* in M if s is in some trace $(s_0, p_1, \ldots, s_k)$ of M; that is, $\exists i \in [k+1] \cdot s_i = s$. A *safety property* for M is a subset of states (or a predicate[2]) $\varphi \subseteq S$. M satisfies φ, written $M \models \varphi$, if every reachable state of M is in φ.

Many transition systems are parameterized. For instance, a client-server application is parameterized by the number of clients, and an array-manipulating program is parameterized by the number of cells. In both cases, there is a single

---

[2] Abusing notation, we refer to a subset of states φ as a *predicate* and do not distinguish between the syntactic form of φ and the set of states that satisfy it.

control process that interacts with many *user processes*. Such systems are called *synchronized control-user networks (SCUNs)* [31]. We let N be the number of processes, and $[N]$ be the process identifiers. We consider SCUNs in which users only synchronize with the control process and do not execute code on their own.

An SCUN $\mathcal{N}$ is a tuple $(S_C, S_U, P_I, P_S, T_I, T_S, c_0, u_0)$, where S_C is a set of control states, S_U a set of user states, P_I a set of internal actions, P_S a set of synchronized actions, $T_I : S_C \times P_I \to S_C$ an internal transition function, $T_S : S_C \times S_U \times P_S \to S_C \times S_U$ a synchronized transition function, $c_0 \in S_C$ is the initial control state, and $u_0 \in S_U$ is the initial user state. The semantics of $\mathcal{N}$ are given by a parameterized LTS, $M(N) := (S, P, T, s_0)$, where $S := S_C \times (S_U)^N$, $P := P_I \cup (P_S \times [N])$, $s_0 := (c_0, u_0, \dots, u_0)$, and $T : S \times P \to S$ such that: (1) if $p \in P_I$, then $T((c, \mathbf{u}), p) = (T_I(c, p), \mathbf{u})$, and (2) if $(p, i) \in P_S \times [N]$, then $T((c, \mathbf{u}), (p, i)) = (c', \mathbf{u'})$ where $(c', \mathbf{u'_i}) = T_S(c, \mathbf{u}_i, p)$, and $\forall j \in [N] \setminus \{i\} \cdot \mathbf{u'_j} = \mathbf{u}_j$.

Parameterized Compositional Model Checking (PCMC). Parameterized systems have parameterized properties [16,31]. A k-*universal safety property* [16] is a predicate $\varphi \subseteq S_C \times (S_U)^k$. A state $(c, \mathbf{u})$ satisfies predicate φ if $\forall \{i_1, \dots, i_k\} \subseteq [N] \cdot \varphi(c, \mathbf{u}_{i_1}, \dots, \mathbf{u}_{i_k})$. A parameterized system $M(N)$ satisfies predicate φ if $\forall N \in \mathbb{N} \cdot M(N) \models \varphi$. For example, **Prop. 1** (Sect. 1) of `SimpleAuction` (Fig. 1) is 1-universal: *"For every user u, if* `stop()` *has been called, then u is immutable."*

Proofs of k-universal safety employ compositional reasoning, e.g., [2,16,31,33]. Here, we use PCMC [31]. The keys to PCMC are *uniformity*—the property that finitely many neighbourhoods are distinguishable—and a *compositional invariant*—a summary of the reachable states for each equivalence class, that is closed under the actions of every other equivalence class. For an SCUN, the compositional invariant is given by two predicates $\theta_C \subseteq S_C$ and $\theta_U \subseteq S_C \times S_U$ satisfying:

Initialization. $c_0 \in \theta_C$ and $(c_0, u_0) \in \theta_U$;
Consecution 1. If $c \in \theta_C$, $(c, u) \in \theta_U$, $p \in P_S$, and $(c', u') \in T_S(c, u, p)$, then $c' \in \theta_C$ and $(c', u') \in \theta_U$;
Consecution 2. If $c \in \theta_C$, $(c, u) \in \theta_U$, $p \in P_C$, and $c' = T_I(c, p)$, then $c' \in \theta_C$ and $(c', u) \in \theta_U$;
Non-Interference. If $c \in \theta_C$, $(c, u) \in \theta_U$, $(c, v) \in \theta_U$, $u \neq v$, $p \in P_S$, and $(c', u') = T_S(c, u, p)$, then $(c', v) \in \theta_C$.

By PCMC [31], if $\forall c \in \theta_C \cdot \forall \{(c, u_1), \dots, (c, u_k)\} \subseteq \theta_U \cdot \varphi(c, u_1, \dots, u_k)$, then $M \models \varphi$. This is as an extension of Owicki-Gries [33], where θ_C summarizes the acting process and θ_U summarizes the interfering process. For this reason, we call θ_C the *inductive invariant* and θ_U the *interference invariant*.

3   MicroSol: Syntax and Semantics

This section provides network semantics for MicroSol, a subset of Solidity[3]. Like Solidity, MicroSol is an imperative object-oriented language with built-in communication operations. The syntax of MicroSol is in Fig. 3. MicroSol restricts Solidity to a core subset of communication features. For example, MicroSol does not

---

[3] https://docs.soliditylang.org/

⟨FName⟩ ::= *a valid function name*
⟨VName⟩ ::= *a valid variable name*
⟨CName⟩ ::= *a valid contract name*
⟨Literal⟩ ::= *an integer, Boolean, or address literal*
⟨Types⟩ ::= uint | bool | address | mapping(address => uint) | ⟨CName⟩
⟨Operator⟩ ::= == | != | < | > | + | - | * | / | && | || | !
    ⟨Expr⟩ ::= ⟨Literal⟩ | ⟨VName⟩ | this | msg.sender | ⟨Expr⟩ ⟨Operator⟩ ⟨Expr⟩
            | address(⟨VName⟩) | ⟨Expr⟩.⟨FName⟩ (⟨Expr⟩, ...)
            | ⟨FName⟩ (⟨Expr⟩, ...) | ⟨Expr⟩ [⟨Expr⟩] ... [⟨Expr⟩]
    ⟨Assign⟩ ::= ⟨VName⟩ = ⟨Expr⟩ | ⟨Expr⟩ = new ⟨CName⟩(⟨Expr⟩, ...)
            | ⟨Expr⟩ [⟨Expr⟩] ... [⟨Expr⟩] = ⟨Expr⟩
    ⟨Decl⟩ ::= ⟨Types⟩ ⟨VName⟩
    ⟨Stmt⟩ ::= ⟨Decl⟩ | ⟨Assign⟩ | require(⟨Expr⟩) | assert(⟨Expr⟩) | return
            | if(⟨Expr⟩) { ⟨Stmt⟩ } | while(⟨Expr⟩) { ⟨Stmt⟩ } | ⟨Stmt⟩; ⟨Stmt⟩
    ⟨Ctor⟩ ::= constructor (⟨Decl⟩, ...) public { ⟨Stmt⟩ }
    ⟨Func⟩ ::= function ⟨FName⟩ (⟨Decl⟩, ...) public { ⟨Stmt⟩ }
⟨Contract⟩ ::= contract ⟨CName⟩ { ⟨Decl⟩; ...; ⟨Ctor⟩ ⟨Func⟩ ... }
    ⟨Bundle⟩ ::= ⟨Contract⟩ ⟨Contract⟩ ...

Fig. 3. The formal grammar of the MicroSol language.

include inheritance, cryptographic operations, or mappings between addresses. In our evaluation (Sect. 6), we use a superset of MicroSol, called MiniSol (see the extended version [42]), that extends our semantics to a wider set of smart contracts. Throughout this section, we illustrate MicroSol using Auction in Fig. 1.

A MicroSol *smart contract* is similar to a class in object-oriented programming, and consists of variables, and transactions (i.e., functions) for users to call. A transaction is a deterministic sequence of operations. Each smart contract user has a globally unique identifier, known as an *address*. We view a smart contract as operating in an SCUN: the control process executes each transaction sequentially, and the user processes are contract users that communicate with the control process. Users in the SCUN enter into a transaction through a synchronized action, then the control process executes the transaction as an internal action, and finally, the users are updated through synchronized actions. For simplicity of presentation, each transaction is given as a global transition.

A constructor is a special transaction that is executed once after contract creation. Calls to new (i.e., creating new smart contracts) are restricted to constructors. Auction in Fig. 1 is a smart contract that defines a constructor (line 6), three other functions (lines 8, 17, and 25), and four state variables (lines 2–3).

MicroSol has four types: *address, numeric* (including bool), *mapping*, and *contract reference*. Address variables prevent arithmetic operations, and numeric variables cannot cast to address variables. Mapping and contract-reference variables correspond to dictionaries and object pointers in other object-oriented languages. Each typed variable is further classified as either *state, input,* or *local*. We use *role* and *data* to refer to state variables of address and numeric types, respectively. Similarly, we use *client* and *argument* to refer to inputs of address and numeric types, respectively. In Auction of Fig. 1, there is 1 role (manager), 2 contract data (leadingBid and stopped), 1 mapping (bids), 1 client common to all transactions (msg.sender), and at most 1 argument in any transaction (amount).

Note that in MicroSol, *user* denotes any user process within a SCUN. A *client* is defined relative to a transaction, and denotes a user passed as an input.

Semantics of MicroSol. Let $\mathcal{C}$ be a MicroSol program with a single transaction tr (see the extended version [42] for multiple transactions). An N-user *bundle* is an N-user network of several (possibly identical) MicroSol programs. The semantics of a bundle is an LTS, $\mathsf{lts}(\mathcal{C}, N) := (S, P, f, s_0)$, where $S_C := \mathsf{control}(\mathcal{C}, [N])$ is the set of control states, $S_U := \mathsf{user}(\mathcal{C}, [N])$, is the set of user states, $s_\perp$ is the error state, $S \subseteq (S_C \cup \{s_\perp\}) \times (S_U)^N$ is the set of LTS states, $P := \mathsf{action}(\mathcal{C}, [N])$ is the set of actions, $f : S \times P \to S$ is the *transition function*, and s_0 is the initial state. We assume, without loss of generality, that there is a single control process[4].

Let $\mathbb{D}$ be the set of 256-bit unsigned integers. The state space of a smart contract is determined by the address space, $\mathcal{A}$, and the state variables of $\mathcal{C}$. In the case of $\mathsf{lts}(\mathcal{C}, N)$, the address space is fixed to $\mathcal{A} = [N]$. Assume that n, m, and k are the number of roles, data, and mappings in $\mathcal{C}$, respectively. State variables are stored by their numeric indices (i.e., variable 0, 1, etc.). Then, $\mathsf{control}(\mathcal{C}, \mathcal{A}) \subseteq \mathcal{A}^n \times \mathbb{D}^m$ and $\mathsf{user}(\mathcal{C}, \mathcal{A}) \subseteq \mathcal{A} \times \mathbb{D}^k$. For $c = (\mathbf{x}, \mathbf{y}) \in \mathsf{control}(\mathcal{C}, \mathcal{A})$, $\mathsf{role}(c, i) = \mathbf{x}_i$ is the i-th role and $\mathsf{data}(c, i) = \mathbf{y}_i$ is the i-th datum. For $u = (z, \mathbf{y}) \in \mathsf{user}(\mathcal{C}, \mathcal{A})$, z is the address of u, and $\mathsf{map}(u) = \mathbf{y}$ are the mapping values of u.

Similarly, actions are determined by the address space, $\mathcal{A}$, and the input variables of tr. Assume that q and r are the number of clients and arguments of tr, respectively. Then $\mathsf{action}(\mathcal{C}, \mathcal{A}) \subseteq \mathcal{A}^q \times \mathbb{D}^r$. For $p = (\mathbf{x}, \mathbf{y}) \in \mathsf{action}(\mathcal{C}, \mathcal{A})$, $\mathsf{client}(p, i) = \mathbf{x}_i$ is the i-th client in p and $\mathsf{arg}(p, i) = \mathbf{y}_i$ is the i-th argument in p. For a fixed p, we write $f_p(s, \mathbf{u})$ to denote $f((s, \mathbf{u}), p)$.

The initial state of $\mathsf{lts}(\mathcal{C}, N)$ is $s_0 := (c, \mathbf{u}) \in \mathsf{control}(\mathcal{C}, [n]) \times \mathsf{user}(\mathcal{C}, [n])^N$, where $c = (\mathbf{0}, \mathbf{0})$, $\forall i \in [N] \cdot \mathsf{map}(\mathbf{u}_i) = \mathbf{0}$, and $\forall i \in [N] \cdot \mathsf{id}(\mathbf{u}_i) = i$. That is, all variables are zero-initialized and each user has a unique address.

An N-user transition function is determined by the (usual) semantics of tr, and a *bijection* from addresses to user indices, $\mathcal{M} : \mathcal{A} \to [N]$. If $\mathcal{M}(a) = i$, then address a belongs to user $\mathbf{u}_i$. In the case of $\mathsf{lts}(\mathcal{C}, N)$, the i-th user has address i, so $\mathcal{M}(i) = i$. We write $f := [\![\mathcal{C}]\!]_{\mathcal{M}}$, and given an action p, f_p updates the state variables according to the source code of tr with respect to $\mathcal{M}$. If an assert fails or an address is outside of $\mathcal{A}$, then the error state $s_\perp$ is returned. If a require fails, then the state is unchanged. Note that f preserves the address of each user.

For example, $\mathsf{lts}(\mathsf{Auction}, 4) = (S, P, f, s_0)$ is the 4-user bundle of Auction. Assume that $(c, \mathbf{u})$ is the state reached after evaluating the constructor. Then $\mathsf{role}(c, 0) = 2$, $\mathsf{data}(c, 0) = 0$, $\mathsf{data}(c, 1) = 0$, and $\forall i \in [4] \cdot \mathsf{map}(\mathbf{u}_i)_0 = 0$. That is, the manager is at address 2, the leading bid is 0, the auction is not stopped, and there are no active bids. This is because variables are zero-indexed, and stopped

---

[4] Restrictions place on new ensure that the number of MicroSol smart contracts in a bundle is a static fact. Therefore, all control states are synchronized, and can be combined into a product machine.

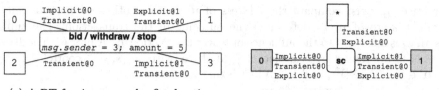

(a) A PT for 4 users and a fixed action.　　(b) The PTG from PTGBuilder.

Fig. 4. A PT of Auction contrasted with a PTG for Auction.

is the second numeric variable (i.e., at index 1). If the user at address 3 placed a bid of 10, this corresponds to $p \in P$ such that $\mathsf{client}(p, 0) = 3$ and $\mathsf{arg}(p, 0) = 10$. A complete LTS for this example is in the extended version [42].

Limitations of MicroSol. MicroSol places two restrictions on Solidity. First, addresses are not numeric. We argue that this restriction is reasonable, as address manipulation is a form of pointer manipulation. Second, new must only appear in constructors. In our evaluation (Sect. 6), all calls to new could be moved into a constructor with minimal effort. We emphasize that the second restriction does not preclude the use of abstract interfaces for arbitrary contracts.

4　Participation Topology

The core functionality of any smart contract is communication between users. Usually, users communicate by reading from and writing to designated mapping entries. That is, the communication paradigm is shared memory. However, it is convenient in interaction analysis to re-imagine smart contracts as having rendezvous synchronization in which users explicitly participate in message passing. In this section, we formally re-frame smart contracts with explicit communication by defining a (semantic) participation topology and its abstractions.

A user u participates in communication during a transaction f whenever the state of u affects execution of f or f affects a state of u. We call this *influence*. For example, in Fig. 1, the sender influences withdraw on line 19. Similarly, withdraw influences the sender on line 22. In all cases, the influence is *witnessed* by the state of the contract and the configuration of users that exhibit the influence.

Let $\mathcal{C}$ be a contract, $N \in \mathbb{N}$ be the network size, $(S, P, f, s_0) = \mathsf{lts}(\mathcal{C}, N)$, and $p \in P$. A user with address $a \in \mathbb{N}$ *influences* transaction f_p if there exists an $s, r, r' \in \mathsf{control}(\mathcal{C}, [N])$, $\mathbf{u}, \mathbf{u}', \mathbf{v}, \mathbf{v}' \in \mathsf{user}(\mathcal{C}, [N])^N$, and $i \in [N]$ such that:

1. $\mathsf{id}(\mathbf{u}_i) = a$;
2. $\forall j \in [N] \cdot (\mathbf{u}_j = \mathbf{v}_j) \iff (i \neq j)$;
3. $(r, \mathbf{u}') = f_p(s, \mathbf{u})$ and $(r', \mathbf{v}') = f_p(s, \mathbf{v})$;
4. $(r = r') \Rightarrow (\exists j \in [N] \setminus \{i\} \cdot \mathbf{u}'_j \neq \mathbf{v}'_j)$.

That is, there exists two network configurations that differ only in the state of the user $\mathbf{u}_i$, and result in different network configurations after applying f_p. In practice, f_p must compare the address of $\mathbf{u}_i$ to some other address, or must use the state of $\mathbf{u}_i$ to determine the outcome of the transaction. The tuple $(s, \mathbf{u}, \mathbf{v})$ is a *witness* to the influence of a over transaction f_p. A user with address $a \in \mathbb{N}$ is *influenced* by transaction f_p if there exists an $s, s' \in \text{control}(\mathcal{C}, [N])$, $\mathbf{u}, \mathbf{u}' \in \text{user}(\mathcal{C}, [N])^N$, and $i \in [N]$ such that:

1. $\text{id}(\mathbf{u}_i) = a$;
2. $(s', \mathbf{u}') = f_p(s, \mathbf{u})$;
3. $\mathbf{u}'_i \neq \mathbf{u}_i$.

That is, f_p must write into the state of $\mathbf{u}_i$, and the changes must persist after the transaction terminates. The tuple $(s, \mathbf{u})$ is a *witness* to the influence of transaction f_p over user a.

Definition 1 (Participation). *A user with address $a \in \mathbb{N}$ participates in a transaction f_p if either a influences f_p, witnessed by some $(s, \mathbf{u}, \mathbf{v})$, or f_p influences a, witnessed by some $(s, \mathbf{u})$. In either case, s is a* witness state.

Smart contracts facilitate communication between many users across many transactions. We need to know every possible participant, and the cause of their participation—we call this the *participation topology (PT)*. A PT associates each communication (sending or receiving) with one or more participation classes, called *explicit*, *transient*, and *implicit*. The participation is *explicit* if the participant is a client of the transaction; *transient* if the participant has a role during the transaction; *implicit* if there is a state such that the participant is neither a client nor holds any roles. In the case of MiniSol, all implicit participation is due to literal address values, as users designated by literal addresses must participate regardless of clients and roles. An example of implicit participation is when a client is compared to the address of the zero-account (i.e., address(0)) in Fig. 1.

Definition 2 (Participation Topology). *A Participation Topology of a transaction f_p is a tuple $pt(\mathcal{C}, N, p) := (\text{Explicit}, \text{Transient}, \text{Implicit})$, where:*

1. *Explicit $\subseteq \mathbb{N} \times [N]$ where $(i, a) \in$ Explicit iff a participates during f_p, with client$(p, i) = a$;*
2. *Transient $\subseteq \mathbb{N} \times [N]$ where $(i, a) \in$ Transient iff a participates during f_p, as witnessed by a state $s \in$ control$(\mathcal{C}, [N])$, where role$(s, i) = a$;*
3. *Implicit $\subseteq [N]$ where $a \in$ Implicit iff a participates during f_p, as witnessed by a state $s \in$ control$(\mathcal{C}, [N])$, where $\forall i \in \mathbb{N}$, role$(s, i) \neq a$ and client$(p, i) \neq a$.*

For example, Fig. 4a shows a PT for any function of Fig. 1 with 4 users. From Sect. 1, it is clear that each function can have an affect. The zero-account and smart contract account are both implicit participants, since changing either account's address to 3 would block the affect of the transaction. The manager is a transient participant and the sender is an explicit participant, since the (dis)equality of their addresses is asserted at lines 9, 18, and 26.

Definition 2 is semantic and dependent on actions. A syntactic summary of all PTs for all actions is required to reason about communication. This summary is analogous to over-approximating control-flow with a "control-flow graph" [3]. This motivates the *Participation Topology Graph (PTG)* that is a syntactic over-approximation of all possible PTs, independent of network size. A PTG has a vertex for each user and each action, such that edges between vertices represent participation classes. In general, a single vertex can map to many users or actions.

PTG edges are labeled by participation classes. For any contract C, there are at most m explicit classes and n transient classes, where n is the number of roles, and m is the maximum number of clients taken by any function of C. On the other hand, the number of implicit classes is determined by the PTG itself. In general, there is no bound on the number of implicit participants, and it is up to a PTG to provide an appropriate abstraction (i.e., L in Definition 3). The label set common to all PTGs is $AP(C) := \{explicit@i \mid i \in [n]\} \cup \{transient@i \mid i \in [m]\}$.

Definition 3 (Participation Topology Graph). *Let L be a finite set of implicit classes, $V \subsetneq \mathbb{N}$ be finite, $E \subseteq V \times V$, and $\delta \subseteq E \times (AP(C) \cup L)$. A PT Graph for a contract C is a tuple $((V, E, \delta), \rho, \tau)$, where (V, E, δ) is a graph labeled by δ, $\rho \subseteq action(C, \mathbb{N}) \times V$, and $\tau \subseteq action(C, \mathbb{N}) \times \mathbb{N} \times V$, such that for all $N \in \mathbb{N}$ and for all $p \in action(C, [N])$, with $pt(C, N, p) = (Explicit, Transient, Implicit)$:*

1. *If $(i, a) \in Explicit$, then there exists a $(p, u) \in \rho$ and $(p, a, v) \in \tau$ such that $(u, v) \in E$ and $\delta((u, v), explicit@i)$;*
2. *If $(i, a) \in Transient$, then there exists a $(p, u) \in \rho$ and $(p, a, v) \in \tau$ such that $(u, v) \in E$ and $\delta((u, v), transient@i)$;*
3. *If $a \in Implicit$, then there exists a $(p, u) \in \rho$, $(p, a, v) \in \tau$, and $l \in L$ such that $(u, v) \in E$ and $\delta((u, v), l)$.*

In Definition 3, τ and ρ map actions and users to vertices, respectively. An edge between an action and a user indicates the potential for participation. The labels describe the potential participation classes. As an example, Fig. 4b is a PTG for Fig. 1, where all actions map to sc, the zero-account maps to vertex 0, the smart contract account maps to vertex 1, and all other users map to $\star$. The two implicit classes have the label $implicit@0$ and $implicit@1$, respectively.

Theorem 1. *Let C be a contract with a PTG (G, ρ, τ), $G = (V, E, \delta)$, and $\delta \subseteq E \times (AP(C) \cup L)$. Then, for all $N \in \mathbb{N}$ and all $p \in action(C, [N])$, $pt(C, N, p) = (Explicit, Transient, Implicit)$ is over-approximated by (G, ρ, τ) as follows:*

1. *If $Explicit(i, a)$, then $\exists (u, v) \in E \cdot \rho(p, u) \wedge \tau(p, a, v) \wedge \delta((u, v), explicit@i)$;*
2. *If $Transient(i, a)$, then $\exists (u, v) \in E \cdot \rho(p, u) \wedge \tau(p, a, v) \wedge \delta((u, v), transient@i)$;*
3. *If $Implicit(a)$, then $\exists (u, v) \in E \cdot \exists l \in L \cdot \rho(p, u) \wedge \tau(p, a, v) \wedge \delta((u, v), l)$.*

For any PT, there are many over-approximating PTGs. The weakest PTG joins every user to every action using all possible labels and a single implicit class. Figure 4b, shows a simple, yet stronger, PTG for Fig. 1. First, note that there are two implicit participants, identified by addresses 0 and 1, with labels $implicit@0$ and $implicit@1$, respectively. Next, observe that any arbitrary user can become the manager. Finally, the distinctions between actions are ignored. Thus, there are three user vertices, two which are mapped to the zero-account and smart contract account, and another mapped to all other users. Such a PTG is constructed automatically using an algorithm named `PTGBuilder`.

`PTGBuilder` takes a contract $\mathcal{C}$ and returns a PTG. The implicit classes are $L := \{implicit@a \mid a \in \mathbb{N}\}$, where $implicit@a$ signifies implicit communication with address a. PTG construction is reduced to taint analysis [23]. Input address variables, state address variables, and literal addresses are tainted sources. Sinks are memory writes, comparison expressions, and mapping accesses. `PTGBuilder` computes $(Args, Roles, Lits)$, where (1) $Args$ is the set of indices of input variables that propagate to a sink; (2) $Roles$ is the set of indices of state variables that propagate to a sink; (3) $Lits$ is the set of literal addresses that propagate to a sink. Finally, a PTG is constructed as (G, ρ, τ), where $G = (V, E, \delta)$, $\rho \subseteq \mathsf{action}(\mathcal{C}, \mathbb{N}) \times V$, $\tau \subseteq \mathsf{action}(\mathcal{C}, \mathbb{N}) \times \mathbb{N} \times V$, sc, and $\star$ are unique vertices:

1. $V := Lits \cup \{sc, \star\}$ and $E := \{(sc, v) \mid v \in V \backslash \{sc\}\}$;
2. $\delta := \{(e, explicit@i) \mid e \in E, i \in Args\} \cup \{(e, transient@i) \mid e \in E, i \in Roles\} \cup \{((sc, a), transient@a) \mid a \in Lits\}$;
3. $\rho := \{(p, sc) \mid p \in \mathsf{action}(\mathcal{C}, \mathbb{N})\}$;
4. $\tau := \{(p, a, \star) \mid p \in \mathsf{action}(\mathcal{C}, \mathbb{N}), a \in \mathbb{N} \backslash Lits\} \cup \{(p, a, a) \mid p \in \mathsf{action}(\mathcal{C}, \mathbb{N}), a \in Lits\}$.

`PTGBuilder` formalizes the intuition of Fig. 4b. Rule 1 ensures that every literal address has a vertex, and that all user vertices connect to sc. Rule 2 over-approximates explicit, transient, and implicit labels. The first set states that if an input address is never used, then the client is not an explicit participant. This statement is self-evident, and over-approximates explicit participation. The second and third set make similar claims for roles and literal addresses Rules 3 and 4 define ρ and τ as expected. Note that in MicroSol, implicit participation stems from literal addresses, since addresses do not support arithmetic operations, and since numeric expressions cannot be cast to addresses.

By re-framing smart contracts with rendezvous synchronization, each transaction is re-imagined as a communication between several users. Their communication patterns are captured by the corresponding PT. A PTG over-approximates PTs of all transactions, and is automatically constructed using `PTGBuilder`. This is crucial for PCMC as it provides an upper bound on the number of equivalence classes, and the users in each equivalence class (see the extended version [42]).

5   Local Reasoning in Smart Contracts

In this section, we present a proof rule for the parameterized safety of MicroSol programs. Our proof rule extends the existing theory of PCMC. The section is structured as follows. Section 5.1 introduces syntactic restrictions, for properties and interference invariants, that expose address dependencies. Section 5.2, defines local bundle reductions, that reduce parameterized smart contract models to finite-state models. We show that for the correct choice of local bundle reduction, the safety of the finite-state model implies the safety of the parameterized model.

5.1   Guarded Properties and Split Invariants

Universal properties and interference invariants might depend on user addresses. However, PCMC requires explicit address dependencies. This is because address dependencies allow predicates to distinguish subsets of users. To resolve this, we introduce two syntactic forms that make address dependencies explicit: guarded universal safety properties and split interference invariants. We build both forms from so called *address-oblivious* predicates that do not depend on user addresses.

For any smart contract $\mathcal{C}$ and any address space $\mathcal{A}$, a pair of user configurations, $\mathbf{u}, \mathbf{v} \in \text{user}(\mathcal{C}, \mathcal{A})^k$, are k-*address similar* if $\forall i \in [k] \cdot \text{map}(\mathbf{u}_i) = \text{map}(\mathbf{v}_i)$. A predicate $\xi \subseteq \text{control}(\mathcal{C}, \mathcal{A}) \times \text{user}(\mathcal{C}, \mathcal{A})^k$ is address-oblivious if, for every choice of $s \in \text{control}(\mathcal{C}, \mathcal{A})$, and every pair of k-address similar configurations, $\mathbf{u}$ and $\mathbf{v}$, $\xi(s, \mathbf{u}) \iff \xi(s, \mathbf{v})$. **Prop. 1** and **Prop. 2** in Sect. 1 are address-oblivious.

A *guarded k-universal safety property* is built from a single k-user address-oblivious predicate. The predicate is guarded by constraints over its k user addresses. Each constraint compares a single user's address to either a literal address or a role. This notion is formalized by Definition 4, and illustrated in Example 1.

Definition 4 (Guarded Universal Safety). *For $k \in \mathbb{N}$, a guarded k-universal safety property is a k-universal safety property φ, given by a tuple (L, R, ξ), where $L \subsetneq \mathbb{N} \times [k]$ is finite, $R \subsetneq \mathbb{N} \times [k]$ is finite, and ξ is an address-oblivious k-user predicate, such that:*

$$\varphi(s, \mathbf{u}) := \left(\left(\bigwedge_{(a,i) \in L} a = id(\mathbf{u}_i) \right) \wedge \left(\bigwedge_{(i,j) \in R} role(s, i) = id(\mathbf{u}_j) \right) \right) \Rightarrow \xi(s, \mathbf{u})$$

Note that $\mathcal{A}_L := \{a \mid (a, i) \in L\}$ and $\mathcal{A}_R := \{i \mid (i, j) \in R\}$ and define the literal *and* role *guards for φ.*

Example 1. Consider the claim that in `Auction` of Fig. 1, the zero-account cannot have an active bid. This claim is stated as **Prop. 3**: *For each user process $\mathbf{u}$, if $id(\mathbf{u}_0) = 0$, then $\text{map}(\mathbf{u}_0)_0 = 0$.* That is, **Prop. 3** is a guarded 1-universal safety property $\varphi_1(s, \mathbf{u}) := (0 = id(\mathbf{u}_0)) \Rightarrow (\text{map}(\mathbf{u}_0)_0 = 0)$. Following Definition 4, φ_1 is determined by $(L_1, \varnothing, \xi_1)$, where $L_1 = \{(0, 0)\}$ and $\xi_1(s, \mathbf{u}) := \text{map}(\mathbf{u}_0)_0 = 0$. The second set is $\varnothing$ as there are no role constraints in **Prop. 3**. If a state $(s, \mathbf{u})$ satisfies φ_1, then $\forall \{i\} \subseteq [N] \cdot \varphi_1(s, (\mathbf{u}_i))$. Note that $\mathbf{u}$ is a singleton vector, and that φ_1 has 1 literal guard, given by $\{0\}$. □

The syntax of a *split interference invariant* is similar to a guarded safety property. The invariant is constructed from a list of address-oblivious predicates, each guarded by a single constraint. The final predicate is guarded by the negation of all other constraints. Intuitively, each address-oblivious predicate summarizes the class of users that satisfy its guard. The split interference invariant is the conjunction of all (guarded predicate) clauses. We proceed with the formal definition in Definition 5 and a practical illustration in Example 2.

Definition 5 (Split Interference Invariant). *A split interference invariant is an interference invariant θ, given by a tuple $(\mathcal{A}_L, \mathcal{A}_R, \zeta, \mu, \xi)$, where $\mathcal{A}_L = \{l_0, \ldots, l_{m-1}\} \subsetneq \mathbb{N}$ is finite, $\mathcal{A}_R = \{r_0, \ldots, r_{n-1}\} \subsetneq \mathbb{N}$ is finite, ζ is a list of* *m address-oblivious 1-user predicates, μ is a list of n address-oblivious 1-user predicates, and ξ is an address-oblivious 1-user predicate, such that:*

$$\psi_{\text{Lits}}(s, \mathbf{u}) := \left(\bigwedge_{i=0}^{m-1} id(\mathbf{u}_0) = l_i \right) \Rightarrow \zeta_i(s, \mathbf{u})$$

$$\psi_{\text{Roles}}(s, \mathbf{u}) := \left(\bigwedge_{i=0}^{n-1} id(\mathbf{u}_0) = role(s, r_i) \right) \Rightarrow \mu_i(s, \mathbf{u})$$

$$\psi_{\text{Else}}(s, \mathbf{u}) := \left(\left(\bigwedge_{i=0}^{m-1} id(\mathbf{u}_0) \neq l_i \right) \wedge \left(\bigwedge_{i=0}^{n-1} id(\mathbf{u}_0) \neq role(s, r_i) \right) \right) \Rightarrow \xi(s, \mathbf{u})$$

$$\theta(s, \mathbf{u}) := \psi_{\text{Roles}}(s, \mathbf{u}) \wedge \psi_{\text{Lits}}(s, \mathbf{u}) \wedge \psi_{\text{Else}}(s, \mathbf{u})$$

Note that $\mathcal{A}_L$ and $\mathcal{A}_R$ define literal *and* role *guards of θ, and that $|\mathbf{u}| = 1$.*

Example 2. To establish φ_1 from Example 1, we require an adequate interference invariant such as **Prop. 4**: *The zero-account never has an active bid, while all other users can have active bids.* That is, **Prop. 4** is a split interference invariant:

$$\theta_1(s, \mathbf{u}) := (id(\mathbf{u}_0) = 0 \Rightarrow (map(\mathbf{u}_0))_0 = 0) \wedge (id(\mathbf{u}_0) \neq 0 \Rightarrow (map(\mathbf{u}_0))_0 \geq 0)$$

Following Definition 5, θ_1 is determined by $Inv = (\mathcal{A}_L, \varnothing, (\xi_1), \varnothing, \xi_2)$, where $\mathcal{A}_L = \{0\}$, ξ_1 is defined in Example 1, and $\xi_2(s, \mathbf{u}) := map(\mathbf{u}_0)_0 \geq 0$. The two instances of $\varnothing$ in Inv correspond to the lack of role constraints in θ_1. If Inv is related back to Definition 5, then $\psi_{\text{Roles}}(s, \mathbf{u}) := \top$, $\psi_{\text{Lits}}(s, \mathbf{u}) := (id(\mathbf{u}_0) = 0) \Rightarrow (map(\mathbf{u}_0)_0 = 0)$, and $\psi_{\text{Else}}(s, \mathbf{u}) := (id(\mathbf{u}_0) \neq 0) \Rightarrow (map(\mathbf{u}_0)_0 \geq 0)$. $\square$

5.2   Localizing a Smart Contract Bundle

A local bundle is a finite-state abstraction of a smart contract bundle. This abstraction reduces smart contract PCMC to software model checking. At a high level, each local bundle is a non-deterministic LTS and is constructed from three components: a smart contract, a candidate interference invariant, and a neighbourhood. The term *candidate interference invariant* describes any predicate with the syntax of an interference invariant, regardless of its semantic interpretation. Sets of addresses are used to identify representatives in a neighbourhood.

Let $\mathcal{A}$ be an N-user neighbourhood and θ_U be a candidate interference invariant. The local bundle corresponding to $\mathcal{A}$ and θ_U is defined using a special relation called an N-*user interference relation*. The N-user interference relation (for θ_U) sends an N-user smart contract state to the set of all N-user smart contract states that are reachable under the interference of θ_U. A state is reachable under the interference of θ_U if the control state is unchanged, each address is unchanged, and all user data satisfies θ_U. For example, lines 6–10 in Fig. 2 apply a 4-user interference relation to the states of Auction. Note that if the interference relation for θ_U fails to relate $(s, \mathbf{u})$ to itself, then $(s, \mathbf{u})$ violates θ_U.

Definition 6 (Interference Relation). *Let $N \in \mathbb{N}$, $\mathcal{C}$ be a contract, $S = control(\mathcal{C}, \mathbb{N}) \times user(\mathcal{C}, \mathbb{N})^N$, and θ_U be a split candidate interference invariant. The N-user interference relation for θ_U is the relation $g : S \to 2^S$ such that $g(c, \mathbf{u}) := \{(c, \mathbf{v}) \in S \mid \forall i \in [N] \cdot id(\mathbf{u}_i) = id(\mathbf{v}_i) \wedge \theta_U(s, \mathbf{v}_i)\}$.*

Each state of the *local bundle* for $\mathcal{A}$ and θ_U is a tuple $(s, \mathbf{u})$, where s is a control state and $\mathbf{u}$ is an N-user configuration. The N users in the local bundle correspond to the N representatives in $\mathcal{A}$, and therefore, the address space of the local bundle can be non-consecutive. The transition relation of the local bundle is defined in terms of the (global) transaction function f. First, the transition relation applies f. If the application of f is closed under θ_U, then the interference relation is applied. Intuitively, θ_U defines a safe envelop under which the interference relation is compositional.

Definition 7 (Local Bundle). *Let $\mathcal{C}$ be a contract, $\mathcal{A} = \{a_0, \ldots, a_{N-1}\} \subseteq \mathbb{N}$ be an N-user neighbourhood, θ_U be a candidate split interference invariant, and g be the N-user interference relation for θ_U. A local bundle is an LTS $local(\mathcal{C}, \mathcal{A}, \theta_U) := (S, P, \hat{f}, s_0)$, such that $S := control(\mathcal{C}, \mathcal{A}) \times user(\mathcal{C}, \mathcal{A})^N$, $P := action(\mathcal{C}, \mathcal{A})$, $s_0 := (c_0, \mathbf{u})$, $c_0 := (\mathbf{0}, \mathbf{0})$, $\forall i \in [N] \cdot id(\mathbf{u}_i) = a_i \wedge map(\mathbf{u}_i) = \mathbf{0}$, and $\hat{f}$ is defined with respect to $\mathcal{M} : \mathcal{A} \to [N]$, $\mathcal{M}(a_i) = i$, such that:*

$$\hat{f}((s, \mathbf{u}), p) := \begin{cases} g(s', \mathbf{u}') & \text{if } (s', \mathbf{u}') = [\![\mathcal{C}]\!]_{\mathcal{M}}((s, \mathbf{u}), p) \wedge (s', \mathbf{u}') \in g(s', \mathbf{u}') \\ [\![\mathcal{C}]\!]_{\mathcal{M}}((s, \mathbf{u}), p) & \text{otherwise} \end{cases}$$

Example 3. We briefly illustrate the transition relation of Definition 7 using Auction of Fig. 1. Let $\mathcal{A}_1 = \{0, 1, 2, 3\}$ be a neighbourhood, θ_1 be as in Example 2, g be the 4-user interference relation for θ_1, and $(S, P, \hat{f}, s_0) = local(\mathcal{C}, \mathcal{A}_1, \theta_1)$. Consider applying $\hat{f}$ to $(s, \mathbf{u}) \in S$ with action $p \in P$, such that $s = \{\text{manager} \mapsto 2; \text{leadingBid} \mapsto 0\}$, $\forall i \in [4] \cdot map(\mathbf{u}_i) = 0$, and p is a bid of 10 from a sender at address 3.

By definition, if $(s', \mathbf{v}) = f(s, \mathbf{u}, p)$, then the leading bid is now 10, and the bid of the sender is also 10, since the sender of p was not the manager and the leading bid was less than 10. Clearly $(s', \mathbf{v}) \in g(s', \mathbf{v})$, and therefore, $g(s', \mathbf{v}) = \hat{f}((s, \mathbf{u}), p)$. A successor state is then selected, as depicted in Fig. 5a. This is done by first assigning an arbitrary bid to each representative, and then requiring that each bid satisfies θ_1 relative to s'. In Fig. 5a, a network is selected in which $\forall i \in [4] \cdot id(\mathbf{v}_i) = i$. As depicted in Fig. 5a, θ_1 stipulates that the zero-account must satisfy ξ_1 and that all other users must satisfy ξ_2.

In Fig. 5b, a satisfying bid is assigned to each user. The choice for d_0 was fixed since $\xi_1(s, \mathbf{v}_0)$ entails $d_0 = 0$. For d_1 to d_3, any non-negative value could have been selected. After the transaction is executed, $map(\mathbf{u}'_0)_0 = 0$, $map(\mathbf{u}'_1)_0 = 1$, $map(\mathbf{u}'_2)_0 = 2$, $map(\mathbf{u}'_3)_0 = 3$, and $s' = \{\text{manager} \mapsto 2; \text{leadingBid} \mapsto 10\}$. Then $(s', \mathbf{u}') \in \hat{f}(s, \mathbf{u})$, as desired. Note that $(s', \mathbf{u}')$ is not reachable in $lts(\mathcal{C}, 4)$. $\square$

Example 3 motivates an important result for local bundles. Observe that $(s', \mathbf{u}') \models \theta_1$. This is not by chance. First, by the compositionality of θ_1, all user configurations reached by $local(\mathcal{C}, \mathcal{A}_1, \theta_1)$ must satisfy θ_U. Second, and far less

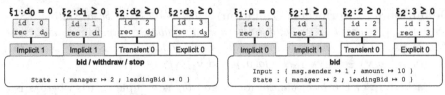

(a) A local 4-user configuration.   (b) The saturating property of $\mathcal{A}_1$.

Fig. 5. The local bundle for Auction in Fig. 1, as defined by $\mathcal{A}_1$ and θ_1 in Example 3.

obviously, by choice of $\mathcal{A}_1$, if all reachable user configurations satisfy θ_1, then θ_1 must be compositional. The proof of this result relies on a saturating property of $\mathcal{A}_1$.

A neighbourhood $\mathcal{A}$ is *saturating* if it contains representatives from each participation class of a PTG, and for all role guards ($\mathcal{A}_R \subsetneq \mathbb{N}$) and literal guards ($\mathcal{A}_L \subseteq \mathbb{N}$) of interest. Intuitively, each participation class over-approximates an equivalence class of $\mathcal{C}$. The number of representatives is determined by the equivalence class. In the case of PTGBuilder, a saturating neighbourhood contains one address for each participation class. For an implicit class, such as *implicit@x*, x is literal and must appear in the neighbourhood. All other addresses are selected arbitrarily. The saturating property of $\mathcal{A}_1$ is depicted in Fig. 5b by the correspondence between users and participation classes ($\mathcal{A}_R = \varnothing$, $\mathcal{A}_L = \{0\}$).

Definition 8 (Saturating Neighbourhood). *Let* $\mathcal{A}_R, \mathcal{A}_L \subseteq \mathbb{N}$, $\mathcal{C}$ *be a contract,* (G, ρ, τ) *be the PTGBuilder PTG of* $\mathcal{C}$, *and* $G = (V, E, \delta)$ *such that* $\mathcal{A}_R$ *and* $\mathcal{A}_L$ *are finite. A saturating neighbourhood for* $(\mathcal{A}_R, \mathcal{A}_L, (G, \rho, \tau))$ *is a set* $\mathcal{A}_{\mathrm{Exp}} \cup \mathcal{A}_{\mathrm{Trans}} \cup \mathcal{A}_{\mathrm{Impl}}$ *s.t.* $\mathcal{A}_{\mathrm{Exp}}, \mathcal{A}_{\mathrm{Trans}}, \mathcal{A}_{\mathrm{Impl}} \subseteq \mathbb{N}$ *are pairwise disjoint and:*

1. $|\mathcal{A}_{\mathrm{Exp}}| = |\{i \in \mathbb{N} \mid \exists e \in E \cdot \delta(e, \mathit{explicit@i})\}|$,
2. $|\mathcal{A}_{\mathrm{Trans}}| = |\{i \in \mathbb{N} \mid \exists e \in E \cdot \delta(e, \mathit{transient@i})\} \cup \mathcal{A}_R|$,
3. $\mathcal{A}_{\mathrm{Impl}} = \{x \in \mathbb{N} \mid \exists e \in E \cdot \delta(e, \mathit{implicit@x})\} \cup \mathcal{A}_L$.

A saturating neighbourhood can be used to reduce compositionality and k-safety proofs to the safety of local bundles. We start with compositionality. Consider a local bundle with a neighbourhood $\mathcal{A}^+$, where $\mathcal{A}^+$ contains a saturating neighbourhood, the guards of θ_U, and some other address a. The neighbourhood $\mathcal{A}^+$ contains a representative for: each participation class; each role and literal user distinguished by θ_U; an arbitrary user under interference (i.e., a). We first claim that if θ_U is compositional, then a local bundle constructed from θ_U must be safe with respect to θ_U (as in Example 3). The first claim follows by induction. By **Initialization** (Sect. 2), the initial users satisfy θ_U. For the inductive step, assume that all users satisfy θ_U and apply $\hat{f}_p$. The users that participate in $\hat{f}_p$ maintain θ_U by **Consecution** (Sect. 2). The users that do not participate also maintain θ_U by **Non-Interference** (Sect. 2). By induction, the first claim is true. We also claim that for a sufficiently large neighbourhood—say $\mathcal{A}^+$—the converse is also true. Intuitively, $\mathcal{A}^+$ is large enough to represent each equivalence class imposed by both the smart contract and θ_U, along with an arbitrary user under interference. Our key insight is that the reachable control states of the local bundle form an inductive invariant θ_C. If the local bundle is safe, then the interference relation is applied after each transition, and, therefore, the local bundle considers every pair of control and user states (c, u) such that $c \in \theta_C$ and $(c, u) \in \theta_U$. Therefore, the safety of the local bundle implies **Initialization**, **Consecution**, and **Non-Interference**. This discussion justifies Theorem 2.

Theorem 2. *Let C be a contract, G be a PTG for C, θ_U be a candidate split interference invariant with role guards $\mathcal{A}_R$ and literal guards $\mathcal{A}_L$, $\mathcal{A}$ be a saturating neighbourhood for $(\mathcal{A}_R, \mathcal{A}_L, G)$, $a \in \mathbb{N} \backslash \mathcal{A}$, and $\mathcal{A}^+ = \{a\} \cup \mathcal{A}$. Then, $\mathsf{local}(C, \mathcal{A}^+, \theta_U) \models \theta_U$ if and only if θ_U is an interference invariant for C.*

Next, we present our main result: a sound proof rule for k-universal safety. As in Theorem 2, 3 uses a saturating neighbourhood $\mathcal{A}^+$. This proof rule proves inductiveness, rather than compositionality, so $\mathcal{A}^+$ does not require an arbitrary user under interference. However, a k-universal property can distinguish between k users at once. Thus, $\mathcal{A}^+$ must have at least k arbitrary representatives.

Theorem 3. *Let φ be a k-universal safety property with role guards $\mathcal{A}_R$ and literal guards $\mathcal{A}_L$, C be a contract, θ_U be an interference invariant for C, G be a PTG for C, $\mathcal{A} = \mathcal{A}_{\mathrm{Exp}} \cup \mathcal{A}_{\mathrm{Trans}} \cup \mathcal{A}_{\mathrm{Impl}}$ be a saturating neighbourhood for $(\mathcal{A}_R, \mathcal{A}_L, G)$. Define $\mathcal{A}^+ \subseteq \mathbb{N}$ such that $\mathcal{A} \subseteq \mathcal{A}^+$ and $|\mathcal{A}^+| = |\mathcal{A}| + \max(0, k - |\mathcal{A}_{\mathrm{Exp}}|)$. If $\mathsf{local}(C, \mathcal{A}^+, \theta_U) \models \varphi$, then $\forall N \in \mathbb{N} \cdot \mathsf{lts}(C, N) \models \varphi$.*

Theorem 3 completes Example 2. Recall $(\varphi_1, \theta_1, \mathcal{A}_1)$ from Example 3. Since φ_1 is 1-universal and $\mathcal{A}_1$ has one explicit representative, it follows that $\mathcal{A}^+ = \mathcal{A}_1 \cup \varnothing$. Using an SMC, $\mathsf{local}(C, \mathcal{A}_1^+, \theta_1) \models \varphi_1$ is certified by an inductive strengthening θ_1^*. Then by Theorem 3, C is also safe for 2^{160} users. Both the local and global bundle have states exponential in the number of users. However, the local bundle has 4 users (a constant fixed by C), whereas the global bundle is defined for any number of users. This achieves an exponential state reduction with respect to the network size. Even more remarkably, θ_1^* must be the inductive invariant from Sect. 2, as it summarizes the safe control states that are closed under the interference of θ_1. Therefore, we have achieved an exponential speedup in verification and have automated the discovery of an inductive invariant.

6   Implementation and Evaluation

We implement smart contract PCMC as an open-source tool called SMARTACE, that is built upon the Solidity compiler. It works in the following automated steps: (1) consume a Solidity smart contract and its interference invariants; (2) validate the contract's conformance to MiniSol; (3) perform source-code analysis and transformation (i.e., inheritance inlining, devirtualization, PTGBuilder); (4) generate a local bundle in LLVM IR; (5) verify the bundle using SEAHORN [15]. In this section, we report on the effectiveness of SMARTACE in verifying real-world smart contracts. A full description of the SMARTACE architecture and of

Table 1. Experimental results for SMARTACE. All reported times are in seconds.

Contracts			SMARTACE			VERX
Name	Prop.	LOC	Time	Inv. Size	Users	Time
Alchemist	3	401	7	0	7	29
ERC20	9	599	12	1	5	158
Melon	16	462	30	0	7	408
MRV	5	868	2	0	7	887
Overview	4	66	4	0	8	211
PolicyPal	4	815	26	0	8	20,773
Zebi	5	1,209	8	0	7	77
Zilliqa	5	377	8	0	7	94
Brickblock	6	549	13	0	10	191
Crowdsale	9	1,198	223	0	8	261
ICO	8	650	371	0	16	6,817
VUToken	5	1,120	19	0	10	715
Mana	4	885	—	—	—	41,409
Fund	2	38	1	0	6	—
Auction	1	42	1	1	5	—
QSPStaking	4	1,550	3	7	8	—

each case study is beyond the scope of this paper. Both SMARTACE and the case studies are available[5]. Our evaluation answers the following research questions:

RQ1: Compliance. Can MiniSol represent real-world smart contracts?
RQ2: Effectiveness. Is SMARTACE effective for MiniSol smart contracts?
RQ3: Performance. Is SMARTACE competitive with other techniques?

Benchmarks and Setup. To answer the above research questions, we used a benchmark of 89 properties across 15 smart contracts (see Table 1). Contracts `Alchemist` to `Mana` are from VERX [34]. Contracts `Fund` and `Auction` were added to offset the lack of parameterized properties in existing benchmarks. The `QSPStaking` contract comprises the Quantstamp Assurance Protocol[6] for which we checked real-world properties provided by Quantstamp. Some properties require additional instrumentation techniques (i.e., temporal [34] and aggregate [17] properties). Aggregate properties allow SMARTACE to reason about the sum of all records within a mapping. In Table 1, *Inv. Size* is the clause size of an interference invariant manually provided to SMARTACE and *Users* is the maximum number of users requested by `PTGBuilder`. All experiments were run on an Intel® Core i7® CPU @ 2.8 GHz 4-core machine with 16 GB of RAM on Ubuntu 18.04.

---

[5] https://github.com/contract-ace
[6] https://github.com/quantstamp/qsp-staking-protocol

RQ1: Compliance. To assess if the restrictions of MiniSol are reasonable, we find the number of *compliant* VERX benchmarks. We found that 8 out of 13 benchmarks are compliant after removing dead code. With manual abstraction, 4 more benchmarks complied. `Brickblock` uses inline assembly to revert transactions with smart contract senders. We remove the assembly as an over-approximation. To support `Crowdsale`, we manually resolve dynamic calls not supported by SMARTACE. In `ICO`, calls are made to arbitrary contracts (by address). However, these calls adhere to *effectively external callback freedom* [12,34] and can be omitted. Also, `ICO` uses dynamic allocation, but the allocation is performed once. We inline the first allocation, and assert that all other allocations are unreachable. To support `VUToken`, we replace a dynamic array of bounded size with variables corresponding to each element of the array. The function `_calcTokenAmount` iterates over the array, so we specialize each call (i.e.,`_calcTokenAmount_{1,2,3,4}`) to eliminate recursion. Two other functions displayed unbounded behaviour (i.e., `massTransfer` and `addManyToWhitelist`), but are used to sequence calls to other functions, and do not impact reachability. We conclude that the restrictions of MiniSol are reasonable.

RQ2: Effectiveness. To assess the effectiveness of SMARTACE, we determined the number of properties verified from compliant VERX contracts. We found that all properties could be verified, but also discovered that most properties were not parameterized. To validate SMARTACE with parameterized properties, we conducted a second study using `Auction`, as described on our development blog[7]. To validate SMARTACE in the context of large-scale contract development, we performed a third study using `QSPStaking`. In this study, 4 properties were selected at random, from a specification provided by Quantstamp, and validated. It required 2 person days to model the environment, and 1 person day to discover an interference invariant. The major overhead in modeling the environment came from manual abstraction of unbounded arrays. The discovery of an interference invariant and array abstractions were semi-automatic, and aided by counterexamples from SEAHORN. For example, one invariant used in our abstraction says that all elements in the array `powersOf100` must be non-zero. This invariant was derived from a counterexample in which 0 was read spuriously from `powersOf100`, resulting in a division-by-zero error. We conclude that SMARTACE is suitable for high-assurance contracts, and with proper automation, can be integrated into contract development.

RQ3: Performance. To evaluate the performance of SMARTACE, we compared its verification time to the reported time of VERX, a state-of-the-art, semi-automated verification tool. Note that in VERX, predicate abstractions must be provided manually, whereas SMARTACE automates this step. VERX was evaluated on a faster processor (3.4GHz) with more RAM (64GB)[8]. In each case, SMARTACE significantly outperformed VERX, achieving a speedup of at least

---

[7] http://seahorn.github.io/blog/

[8] We have requested access to VERX and are awaiting a response.

10x for all but 2 contracts[9]. One advantage of SMARTACE is that it benefits from state-of-the art software model checkers, whereas the design of VERX requires implementing a new verification tool. In addition, we suspect that local bundle abstractions obtained through smart contract PCMC are easier to reason about than the global arrays that VERX must quantify over. However, a complete explanation for the performance improvements of SMARTACE is challenging without access to the source code of VERX. We observe that one bottleneck for SMARTACE is the number of users (which extends the state space). A more precise `PTGBuilder` would reduce the number of users. Upon manual inspection of `Melon` and `Alchemist` (in a single bundle), we found that user state could be reduced by 28%. We conclude that SMARTACE can scale.

7   Related Work

In recent years, the program analysis community has developed many tools for smart contract analysis. These tool range from dynamic analysis [19,43] to static analysis [5,13,25–27,30,32,39,40] and verification [17,21,29,34,38,41]. The latter are most related to SMARTACE since their focus is on functional correctness, as opposed to generic rules (e.g., the absence of reentrancy [14] and integer overflows). Existing techniques for functional correctness are either deductive, and require that most invariants be provided manually (i.e., [17,41]), or are automated but neglect the parameterized nature of smart contracts (i.e., [28,29,34,38]). The tools that do acknowledge parameterization employ static analysis [5,25]. In contrast, SMARTACE uses a novel local reasoning technique that verifies parameterized safety properties with less human guidance than deductive techniques.

More generally, parameterized systems form a rich field of research, as outlined in [4]. The use of SCUNs was first proposed in [11], and many other models exist for both synchronous and asynchronous systems (e.g., [9,36,37]). The approach of PCMC is not the only compositional solution for parameterized verification. For instance, environmental abstraction [6] considers a process and its environment, similar to the inductive and interference invariants of SMARTACE. Other approaches [10,35] generalize from small instances through the use of ranking functions. The combination of abstract domains and SMPs has also proven useful in finding parameterized invariants [2]. The addresses used in our analysis are similar to the scalarsets of [18]. Most compositional techniques require cutoff analysis—considering network instances up to a given size [7,20,22]. Local bundles avoid explicit cutoff analysis by simulating all smaller instances, and is similar to existing work on bounded parameterized model checking [8]. SMARTACE is the first application of PCMC in the context of smart contracts.

8   Conclusions

In this paper, we present a new verification approach for Solidity smart contracts. Unlike many of the existing approaches, we automatically reason about smart

---

[9] We compare the average time for VERX to the total evaluation time for SMARTACE.

contracts relative to all of their clients and across multiple transaction. Our approach is based on treating smart contracts as a parameterized system and using Parameterized Compositional Model Checking (PCMC).

Our main theoretical contribution is to show that PCMC offers an exponential reduction for k-universal safety verification of smart contracts. That is, verification of safety properties with k arbitrary clients.

The theoretical results of this paper are implemented in an automated Solidity verification tool SMARTACE. SMARTACE is built upon a novel model for smart contracts, in which users are processes and communication is explicit. In this model, communication is over-approximated by static analysis, and the results are sufficient to find all local neighbourhoods, as required by PCMC. The underlying parameterized verification task is reduced to sequential Software Model Checking. In SMARTACE, we use the SEAHORN verification framework for the underlying analysis. However, other Software Model Checkers can potentially be used as well.

Our approach is almost completely automated – SMARTACE automatically infers the necessary predicates, inductive invariants, and transaction summaries. The only requirement from the user is to provide an occasional interference invariant (that is validated by SMARTACE). However, we believe that this step can be automated as well through reduction to satisfiability of Constrained Horn Clauses. We leave exploring this to future work.

References

1. Abdulla, P.A., Haziza, F., Holík, L.: All for the price of few. In: Giacobazzi, R., Berdine, J., Mastroeni, I. (eds.) VMCAI 2013. LNCS, vol. 7737, pp. 476–495. Springer, Heidelberg (2013). https://doi.org/10.1007/978-3-642-35873-9_28
2. Abdulla, P.A., Haziza, F., Holík, L.: Parameterized verification through view abstraction. Int. J. Softw. Tools Technol. Transf. **18**(5), 495–516 (2016). https://doi.org/10.1007/s10009-015-0406-x
3. Allen, F.E.: Control flow analysis. In: Proceedings of a Symposium on Compiler Optimization, pp. 1–19. Association for Computing Machinery, New York, NY, USA (1970). https://doi.org/10.1145/800028.808479
4. Bloem, R., et al.: Decidability in parameterized verification. SIGACT News **47**(2), 53–64 (2016). https://doi.org/10.1145/2951860.2951873
5. Brent, L., Grech, N., Lagouvardos, S., Scholz, B., Smaragdakis, Y.: Ethainter: a smart contract security analyzer for composite vulnerabilities. In: Donaldson, A.F., Torlak, E. (eds.) Proceedings of the 41st ACM SIGPLAN International Conference on Programming Language Design and Implementation, PLDI 2020, London, UK, 15–20 June 2020, pp. 454–469. ACM (2020). https://doi.org/10.1145/3385412.3385990
6. Clarke, E., Talupur, M., Veith, H.: Environment abstraction for parameterized verification. In: Emerson, E.A., Namjoshi, K.S. (eds.) VMCAI 2006. LNCS, vol. 3855, pp. 126–141. Springer, Heidelberg (2005). https://doi.org/10.1007/11609773_9
7. Emerson, E.A., Namjoshi, K.S.: On reasoning about rings. Int. J. Found. Comput. Sci. **14**(4), 527–550 (2003). https://doi.org/10.1142/S0129054103001881

8. Emerson, E.A., Trefler, R.J., Wahl, T.: Reducing model checking of the few to the one. In: Liu, Z., He, J. (eds.) ICFEM 2006. LNCS, vol. 4260, pp. 94–113. Springer, Heidelberg (2006). https://doi.org/10.1007/11901433_6

9. Esparza, J., Ganty, P., Majumdar, R.: Parameterized verification of asynchronous shared-memory systems. In: Sharygina, N., Veith, H. (eds.) CAV 2013. LNCS, vol. 8044, pp. 124–140. Springer, Heidelberg (2013). https://doi.org/10.1007/978-3-642-39799-8_8

10. Fang, Y., Piterman, N., Pnueli, A., Zuck, L.: Liveness with invisible ranking. In: Steffen, B., Levi, G. (eds.) VMCAI 2004. LNCS, vol. 2937, pp. 223–238. Springer, Heidelberg (2004). https://doi.org/10.1007/978-3-540-24622-0_19

11. German, S.M., Sistla, A.P.: Reasoning about systems with many processes. J. ACM 39(3), 675–735 (1992). https://doi.org/10.1145/146637.146681

12. Gershuni, E., et al.: Simple and precise static analysis of untrusted linux kernel extensions. In: McKinley, K.S., Fisher, K. (eds.) Proceedings of the 40th ACM SIGPLAN Conference on Programming Language Design and Implementation, PLDI 2019, Phoenix, AZ, USA, 22–26 June 2019, pp. 1069–1084. ACM (2019). https://doi.org/10.1145/3314221.3314590

13. Grech, N., Kong, M., Jurisevic, A., Brent, L., Scholz, B., Smaragdakis, Y.: Madmax: surviving out-of-gas conditions in ethereum smart contracts. In: Proceedings ACM Programming Language 2(OOPSLA), pp. 116:1–116:27 (2018). https://doi.org/10.1145/3276486

14. Grossman, S., et al.: Online detection of effectively callback free objects with applications to smart contracts. In: Proceedings ACM Programming Language 2(POPL), pp. 48:1–48:28 (2018). https://doi.org/10.1145/3158136

15. Gurfinkel, A., Kahsai, T., Komuravelli, A., Navas, J.A.: The SeaHorn verification framework. In: Kroening, D., Păsăreanu, C.S. (eds.) CAV 2015. LNCS, vol. 9206, pp. 343–361. Springer, Cham (2015). https://doi.org/10.1007/978-3-319-21690-4_20

16. Gurfinkel, A., Shoham, S., Meshman, Y.: SMT-based verification of parameterized systems. In: Zimmermann, T., Cleland-Huang, J., Su, Z. (eds.) Proceedings of the 24th ACM SIGSOFT International Symposium on Foundations of Software Engineering, FSE 2016, Seattle, WA, USA, 13–18 November 2016, pp. 338–348. ACM (2016). https://doi.org/10.1145/2950290.2950330

17. Hajdu, Á., Jovanović, D.: SOLC-VERIFY: a modular verifier for solidity smart contracts. In: Chakraborty, S., Navas, J.A. (eds.) VSTTE 2019. LNCS, vol. 12031, pp. 161–179. Springer, Cham (2020). https://doi.org/10.1007/978-3-030-41600-3_11

18. Ip, C.N., Dill, D.L.: Better verification through symmetry. In: Agnew, D., Claesen, L.J.M., Camposano, R. (eds.) Computer Hardware Description Languages and their Applications, Proceedings of the 11th IFIP WG10.2 International Conference on Computer Hardware Description Languages and their Applications - CHDL 1993, sponsored by IFIP WG10.2 and in cooperation with IEEE COMPSOC, Ottawa, Ontario, Canada, 26–28 April 1993. IFIP Transactions, vol. A-32, pp. 97–111. North-Holland (1993)

19. Jiang, B., Liu, Y., Chan, W.K.: Contractfuzzer: fuzzing smart contracts for vulnerability detection. In: Huchard, M., Kästner, C., Fraser, G. (eds.) Proceedings of the 33rd ACM/IEEE International Conference on Automated Software Engineering, ASE 2018, Montpellier, France, 3–7 September 2018, pp. 259–269. ACM (2018). https://doi.org/10.1145/3238147.3238177

20. Kaiser, A., Kroening, D., Wahl, T.: Dynamic cutoff detection in parameterized concurrent programs. In: Touili, T., Cook, B., Jackson, P. (eds.) CAV 2010. LNCS, vol. 6174, pp. 645–659. Springer, Heidelberg (2010). https://doi.org/10.1007/978-3-642-14295-6_55

21. Kalra, S., Goel, S., Dhawan, M., Sharma, S.: ZEUS: analyzing safety of smart contracts. In: 25th Annual Network and Distributed System Security Symposium, NDSS 2018, San Diego, California, USA, 18–21 February 2018. The Internet Society (2018)

22. Khalimov, A., Jacobs, S., Bloem, R.: Towards efficient parameterized synthesis. In: Giacobazzi, R., Berdine, J., Mastroeni, I. (eds.) VMCAI 2013. LNCS, vol. 7737, pp. 108–127. Springer, Heidelberg (2013). https://doi.org/10.1007/978-3-642-35873-9_9

23. Kildall, G.A.: A unified approach to global program optimization. In: Fischer, P.C., Ullman, J.D. (eds.) Conference Record of the ACM Symposium on Principles of Programming Languages, Boston, Massachusetts, USA, pp. 194–206. ACM Press, October 1973. https://doi.org/10.1145/512927.512945

24. Kolb, J.: A Languge-Based Approach to Smart Contract Engineering. Ph.D. thesis, University of California at Berkeley, USA (2020)

25. Kolluri, A., Nikolic, I., Sergey, I., Hobor, A., Saxena, P.: Exploiting the laws of order in smart contracts. In: Zhang, D., Møller, A. (eds.) Proceedings of the 28th ACM SIGSOFT International Symposium on Software Testing and Analysis, ISSTA 2019, Beijing, China, 15–19 July 2019, pp. 363–373. ACM (2019). https://doi.org/10.1145/3293882.3330560

26. Krupp, J., Rossow, C.: teether: Gnawing at ethereum to automatically exploit smart contracts. In: Enck, W., Felt, A.P. (eds.) 27th USENIX Security Symposium, USENIX Security 2018, Baltimore, MD, USA, 15–17 August 2018, pp. 1317–1333. USENIX Association (2018)

27. Luu, L., Chu, D., Olickel, H., Saxena, P., Hobor, A.: Making smart contracts smarter. In: Weippl, E.R., Katzenbeisser, S., Kruegel, C., Myers, A.C., Halevi, S. (eds.) Proceedings of the 2016 ACM SIGSAC Conference on Computer and Communications Security, Vienna, Austria, 24–28 October 2016, pp. 254–269. ACM (2016). https://doi.org/10.1145/2976749.2978309

28. Marescotti, M., Otoni, R., Alt, L., Eugster, P., Hyvärinen, A.E.J., Sharygina, N.: Accurate smart contract verification through direct modelling. In: Margaria, T., Steffen, B. (eds.) ISoLA 2020. LNCS, vol. 12478, pp. 178–194. Springer, Cham (2020). https://doi.org/10.1007/978-3-030-61467-6_12

29. Mavridou, A., Laszka, A., Stachtiari, E., Dubey, A.: VeriSolid: correct-by-design smart contracts for ethereum. In: Goldberg, I., Moore, T. (eds.) FC 2019. LNCS, vol. 11598, pp. 446–465. Springer, Cham (2019). https://doi.org/10.1007/978-3-030-32101-7_27

30. Mossberg, M., et al.: Manticore: a user-friendly symbolic execution framework for binaries and smart contracts. In: 34th IEEE/ACM International Conference on Automated Software Engineering, ASE 2019, San Diego, CA, USA, 11–15 November 2019, pp. 1186–1189. IEEE (2019). https://doi.org/10.1109/ASE.2019.00133

31. Namjoshi, K.S., Trefler, R.J.: Parameterized compositional model checking. In: Chechik, M., Raskin, J.-F. (eds.) TACAS 2016. LNCS, vol. 9636, pp. 589–606. Springer, Heidelberg (2016). https://doi.org/10.1007/978-3-662-49674-9_39

32. Nikolic, I., Kolluri, A., Sergey, I., Saxena, P., Hobor, A.: Finding the greedy, prodigal, and suicidal contracts at scale. In: Proceedings of the 34th Annual Computer Security Applications Conference, ACSAC 2018, San Juan, PR, USA, 03–07 December 2018, pp. 653–663. ACM (2018). https://doi.org/10.1145/3274694.3274743

33. Owicki, S.S., Gries, D.: An axiomatic proof technique for parallel programs I. Acta Informatica 6, 319–340 (1976). https://doi.org/10.1007/BF00268134

34. Permenev, A., Dimitrov, D., Tsankov, P., Drachsler-Cohen, D., Vechev, M.T.: Verx: Safety verification of smart contracts. In: 2020 IEEE Symposium on Security and Privacy, SP 2020, San Francisco, CA, USA, May 18–21, 2020. pp. 1661–1677. IEEE (2020). DOI: https://doi.org/10.1109/SP40000.2020.00024

35. Pnueli, A., Ruah, S., Zuck, L.: Automatic deductive verification with invisible invariants. In: Margaria, T., Yi, W. (eds.) TACAS 2001. LNCS, vol. 2031, pp. 82–97. Springer, Heidelberg (2001). https://doi.org/10.1007/3-540-45319-9_7

36. Siegel, S.F., Avrunin, G.S.: Verification of MPI-Based software for scientific computation. In: Graf, S., Mounier, L. (eds.) SPIN 2004. LNCS, vol. 2989, pp. 286–303. Springer, Heidelberg (2004). https://doi.org/10.1007/978-3-540-24732-6_20

37. Siegel, S.F., Gopalakrishnan, G.: Formal analysis of message passing. In: Jhala, R., Schmidt, D. (eds.) VMCAI 2011. LNCS, vol. 6538, pp. 2–18. Springer, Heidelberg (2011). https://doi.org/10.1007/978-3-642-18275-4_2

38. So, S., Lee, M., Park, J., Lee, H., Oh, H.: VERISMART: a highly precise safety verifier for ethereum smart contracts. In: 2020 IEEE Symposium on Security and Privacy, SP 2020, San Francisco, CA, USA, 18–21 May 2020, pp. 1678–1694. IEEE (2020). https://doi.org/10.1109/SP40000.2020.00032

39. Tsankov, P., Dan, A.M., Drachsler-Cohen, D., Gervais, A., Bünzli, F., Vechev, M.T.: Securify: Practical security analysis of smart contracts. In: Lie, D., Mannan, M., Backes, M., Wang, X. (eds.) Proceedings of the 2018 ACM SIGSAC Conference on Computer and Communications Security, CCS 2018, Toronto, ON, Canada, 15–19 October 2018, pp. 67–82. ACM (2018). https://doi.org/10.1145/3243734.3243780

40. Wang, S., Zhang, C., Su, Z.: Detecting nondeterministic payment bugs in ethereum smart contracts. In: Proceedings ACM Programming Language 3(OOPSLA), pp. 189:1–189:29 (2019). https://doi.org/10.1145/3360615

41. Wang, Y., et al.: Formal verification of workflow policies for smart contracts in azure blockchain. In: Chakraborty, S., Navas, J.A. (eds.) VSTTE 2019. LNCS, vol. 12031, pp. 87–106. Springer, Cham (2020). https://doi.org/10.1007/978-3-030-41600-3_7

42. Wesley, S., Christakis, M., Navas, J.A., Trefler, R.J., Wüstholz, V., Gurfinkel, A.: Compositional verification of smart contracts through communication abstraction (extended). CoRR abs/2107.08583 (2021). https://arxiv.org/abs/2107.08583

43. Wüstholz, V., Christakis, M.: Harvey: a greybox fuzzer for smart contracts. In: Devanbu, P., Cohen, M.B., Zimmermann, T. (eds.) ESEC/FSE '20: 28th ACM Joint European Software Engineering Conference and Symposium on the Foundations of Software Engineering, Virtual Event, USA, 8–13 November 2020, pp. 1398–1409. ACM (2020). https://doi.org/10.1145/3368089.3417064

44. Zhong, J.E., et al.: The move prover. In: Lahiri, S.K., Wang, C. (eds.) CAV 2020. LNCS, vol. 12224, pp. 137–150. Springer, Cham (2020). https://doi.org/10.1007/978-3-030-53288-8_7

Automatic Synthesis of Data-Flow Analyzers

Xuezheng Xu$^{(\boxtimes)}$, Xudong Wang, and Jingling Xue

Programming Languages and Compilers Group, School of Computer Science
and Engineering, UNSW Sydney, Sydney, Australia

Abstract. Data-flow analyzers (DFAs) are widely deployed in many
stages of software development, such as compiler optimization, bug detection, and program verification. Automating their synthesis is non-trivial
but will be practically beneficial. In this paper, we propose DFASY,
a framework for the automatic synthesis of DFAs. Given a specification consisting of a control flow graph and the expected data-flow facts
before and after each of its nodes, DFASY automatically synthesizes a
DFA that satisfies the specification, including its flow direction, meet
operator, and transfer function. DFASY synthesizes transfer functions
by working with a domain-specific language that supports rich data-flow
fact extraction operations, set operations, and logic operations. To avoid
exploding the search space, we introduce an abstraction-guided pruning
technique to assess the satisfiability of partially instantiated candidates
and drop unsatisfiable ones from further consideration as early as possible. In addition, we also introduce a brevity-guided pruning technique to
improve the readability and simplicity of synthesized DFAs and further
accelerate the search. We have built a benchmark suite, which consists
of seven classic (e.g., live variable analysis and null pointer detection)
and seven custom data-flow problems. DFASY has successfully solved
all the 14 data-flow problems in 21.8 s on average, outperforming significantly the three baselines compared. Both DFASY and its associated
benchmark suite have been open-sourced.

Keywords: Program synthesis · Data flow analysis · DSL

1 Introduction

Data-flow analysis has many applications, including compiler optimization [2,
10,52], bug detection [4,20,47,50] and program verification [13,27]. However,

Thanks to all the reviewers for their constructive comments. This work is supported
by Australian Research Council Grants (DP170103956 and DP180104069).

© Springer Nature Switzerland AG 2021
C. Drăgoi et al. (Eds.): SAS 2021, LNCS 12913, pp. 453–478, 2021.
https://doi.org/10.1007/978-3-030-88806-0_22

creating data-flow analyzers (DFAs) can be non-trivial, as it requires DFA-related expertise, domain-specific knowledge, and handling of corner cases. Without an automated tool to assist, manually-designed DFAs may be suboptimal, hindering their wide adoption [9]. Program synthesis [18], which aims at automatically finding programs that satisfy user intent, has made much progress in many areas, including program suggestion [19,53], program repair [28,39,51] and data wrangling [17]. Despite this, automatic synthesis of DFAs is relatively unexplored.

Problem Statement. Given an input-output specification consisting of a control flow graph (CFG) as input and the data-flow facts expected before and after its nodes as output (obtained manually or by code instrumentation [9]), we aim to automatically synthesize a DFA (including its flow direction, meet operator and transfer function) that satisfies the specification. We consider a family of widely used data-flow problems, known as the *gen-kill* problems. We focus on synthesizing intra-procedural and path-insensitive DFAs. However, our synthesized DFAs can also be deployed in an inter-procedural and/or path-sensitive setting, once they are integrated with an IFDS/IDE framework [36,37] and an SMT solver [8]. To the best of our knowledge, this is the first study on synthesizing general-purpose DFAs (from input-output examples). Previously, attempts have beem made to synthesize static analysis rules but pre-defined client-specific rule templates [9] or relations [38] are required.

Automatic synthesis of DFAs can be practically beneficial. For the DFAs used in, say, compilers, where correctness is required, automated DFA-creating tools can help uncover tricky corner-case bugs in state-of-the-art hand-crafted DFAs, such as Facebook's Flow [9], and produce quickly a reference implementation with several input-output examples. In the cases where some correctness can be sacrificed (including bug detection), we envisage that automated tools can be used to generate customized DFAs that can tolerate a certain degree of false negatives and false positives (prescribed by the input-output examples given).

Challenges. There are three challenges in synthesizing DFAs. First, existing program synthesis tasks usually handle common data types such as integers and strings while our DFA synthesis task focuses mainly on program elements (e.g., variables, constants, and expressions). A simple-minded approach that synthesizes a DFA from fully-fledged languages like C and Java would explode the search space. Second, a DFA synthesizer is expected to have balanced expressivity [18] in order to generate a variety of DFAs efficiently. Finally, a DFA synthesizer should generate simple DFAs to facilitate readability and maintainability, making it necessary to consider not only its correctness but also its brevity.

Our Solution. We propose DFASY, a framework for the automatic synthesis of DFAs. Given a CFG and the expected data-flow facts for its nodes, DFASY iteratively generates and validates DFA candidates and outputs the simplest satisfying DFA. Specifically, DFASY aims at finding the three components for a specification-satisfying DFA: its flow direction, meet operator, and transfer function. To generate a transfer function, we use a domain-specific language (DSL)

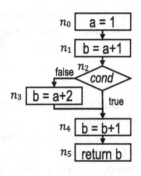

(a) Input CFG.

Node	Value Sets	
	Before	After
n_0	$\emptyset$	$\{n_0\}$
n_1	$\{n_0\}$	$\{n_0, n_1\}$
n_2	$\{n_0, n_1\}$	$\{n_0, n_1\}$
n_3	$\{n_0, n_1\}$	$\{n_0, n_3\}$
n_4	$\{n_0, n_1, n_3\}$	$\{n_0, n_4\}$
n_5	$\{n_0, n_4\}$	$\{n_0, n_4\}$

(b) Output data-flow facts.

Flow Direction:	*forward*
Meet Operator:	*union*
Transfer Function: $s_{out} = \mathsf{gen}(n, \mathsf{kill}(n, s_{in}))$	

$$\mathsf{kill}(n, s) = s - \{x \mid x \in s \wedge \mathsf{def}(x) = \mathsf{def}(n)\}$$
$$\mathsf{gen}(n, s) = \begin{cases} s \cup \{n\} & \text{if } \mathsf{def}(n) \neq \emptyset \\ s & \text{otherwise} \end{cases}$$

(c) The synthesized DFA.

Fig. 1. A motivating example: reaching definitions.

that supports a set of common data-flow fact extraction operations, set operations, and logic operations. To accelerate the search, we propose two pruning techniques: (1) *abstraction-guided pruning* that first evaluates partially instantiated DFA candidates from their abstract semantics and then removes unsatisfiable candidates as early as possible, and (2) *brevity-guided pruning* that evaluates the brevity of each DFA candidate with a cost function and keeps only the simplest among the semantically-equivalent DFA candidates.

We have built a benchmark suite consisting of 7 classic (e.g., live variable analysis and null pointer detection) and 7 custom data-flow problems. Our evaluation shows that DFASY can successfully solve all the 14 DFA problems in 21.8 s, on average, with abstraction- and brevity-guided pruning techniques, outperforming significantly the three baselines.

Contributions. Our main contributions are: (1) a framework, DFASY, for synthesizing DFAs by examples, (2) A DSL for describing transfer functions, supporting data-flow fact extractions, set operations, and logic operations, (3) The abstraction- and brevity-guided pruning techniques for accelerating the search for the simplest satisfying DFAs, and (4) an evaluation of DFASY with a benchmark suite consisting of 7 classic and 7 custom DFA synthesis problems and an open-source implementation (http://www.cse.unsw.edu.au/~corg/dfasy/).

2 Motivation

We illustrate DFASY's key design choices in synthesizing a classic DFA, "reaching definitions", which statically determines the definitions that may reach a given statement. Figure 1(a) gives a CFG as an input. Figure 1(b) gives the expected data-flow facts for each node as an output, expressed in terms of the sets of reaching statements before and after the node. We use a *value set* to represent the data-flow facts at a program point. For example, the value sets before and after node n_3 are expressed as $\{n_0, n_1\}$ and $\{n_0, n_3\}$, respectively. As b is re-defined in n_3, its previous definition in n_1 is removed on entry of n_3 and the new definition in n_3 is added on exit of n_3.

Figure 1(c) gives the DFA synthesized by DFASY, including a *forward* flow direction, a *union* meet operator, and a transfer function that takes an input value set s_{in} and a node n, and gives an output value set s_{out}. We represent a transfer function in the gen-kill form [2] in terms of two sub-functions, $\mathsf{gen}(n, s)$ and $\mathsf{kill}(n, s)$. When propagating the reaching definitions from s_{in} to s_{out}, $\mathsf{kill}(n, s)$ filters out the statements that define the same variable that is re-defined in node n and $\mathsf{gen}(n, s)$ generates a new reaching definition in n (if any). We use $\mathsf{def}(n)$ to represent the variable defined in node n. To synthesize such a transfer function, DFASY works with a DSL that supports the following three kinds of operations:

- **Data-Flow Fact Extractions.** Different DFAs operate on different data-flow facts, e.g., whether a variable is defined in a statement in "reaching definitions". We will handle this by making use of rich *attention functions*, i.e., functions that extract facts from program elements. In "reaching definitions", for example, $\mathsf{def}(n)$ extracts the defined variable from node n.
- **Set Operations.** Transfer functions mostly operate on value sets, e.g., kill and gen work with the set difference and union, respectively.
- **Logic Operations.** To handle branching, we need logic operators (e.g., *or* and *not*) and relation operators (e.g., set *equal* and *subset*).

DFASY works with a common generate-and-validate workflow, which first generates fully instantiated DFA candidates and then validates them with respect to the given specification. However, a DSL that supports the set of rich operations required as discussed above will inevitably explode the search space. To overcome this problem, we introduce the following two pruning techniques:

- **Abstraction-Guided Pruning.** Before producing a fully instantiated DFA, we validate each partially instantiated DFA by checking if an over-approximation of its data-flow facts (based on abstract semantics) will potentially yield the data-flow facts expected at every CFG node, and discard it, and consequently, prune all the concrete DFAs it may induce later during the search

$$
\begin{array}{lll}
node & := & cond \mid stmt \\
cond & := & if \; a_1 \; \bigwedge a_2 \\
stmt & := & v = a \mid v_1 = v_2.f \mid v.f = a \\
     &   & \mid v = \mathbf{new} \; o \mid v = expr \mid \mathbf{return} \; a \\
expr & := & a_1 \oplus a_2 \mid a_1 \bigwedge a_2 \\
a   & := & v \mid const \mid \bot \\
const & := & null \mid integer-literal \mid true \mid false
\end{array}
$$

$$node \in \mathbf{Node} \qquad cond \in \mathbf{Cond} \qquad stmt \in \mathbf{Stmt}$$
$$v \in \mathbf{Var} \qquad o \in \mathbf{Obj} \qquad new \in \mathbf{New}$$
$$const \in \mathbf{Const} \qquad expr \in \mathbf{Expr} \qquad f \in \mathbf{Field}$$
$$v.f \in \mathbf{FieldRef} = (\mathbf{Var} \cup \mathbf{Obj}) \times \mathbf{Field}$$
$$\bigwedge \in \mathbf{RelOp} = \{\&\&, \|, !, ==, >, <, ...\}$$
$$\oplus \in \mathbf{ArithOp} = \{+, -, *, /, \%, \&, |, ...\}$$

$$\mathbf{Value} = \mathbf{Node} \cup \mathbf{Var} \cup \mathbf{Obj} \cup \mathbf{FieldRef} \cup \mathbf{Const} \cup \mathbf{Expr} \cup \mathbf{New}$$
$$\mathbf{ValueSet} = \wp(\mathbf{Value})$$

Fig. 2. A simple Java-like language for describing the nodes in a CFG. $\wp(s)$ is the power set of a set s and o is the abstract object created at an allocation-site.

if this is not the case. For example, we will discard a DFA candidate with an uninstantiated gen but a fully instantiated kill: $\mathrm{kill}(n_3, \{n_0, n_1\}) = \{n_0, n_1\}$. In this case, we will build an abstract gen by assuming that a gen function can only generate new facts but cannot remove any old facts. We can then infer that $\mathrm{gen}(n_3, \{n_0, n_1\})$ must contain at least n_0 and n_1, causing the expected set of facts $\{n_0, n_3\}$ at node n_3 to be unsatisfiable.

- **Brevity-Guided Pruning.** We propose a cost function to estimate the brevity of a DFA candidate and keep only the one with the lowest cost among all the semantically equivalent candidates. For example, we discard gen′, which is the same as gen, except that gen′ uses $\mathrm{def}(n) \cap \mathrm{def}(n) \neq \emptyset$ as the guarding condition for $s \cup \{n\}$ but gen uses a simpler one, $\mathrm{def}(n) \neq \emptyset$, instead.

With our abstraction- and brevity-guided pruning techniques, DFASY has successfully synthesized the DFA in Fig. 1(c) in 12 s by pruning over 99% of the candidates before validation.

3 Approach

We formalize our synthesis task (Sect. 3.1) and introduce a DSL with syntactic templates for building gen-kill transfer functions (Sect. 3.2). We then describe our abstraction-guided (Sect. 3.3) and brevity-guided (Sect. 3.4) pruning techniques. Finally, we give a synthesis algorithm (Sect. 3.5).

3.1 Problem Definition

Synthesis of DFAs. Given a specification (G, R), where $G = (N, E)$ is a CFG as input and R gives the expected data-flow facts at its nodes as output, our synthesis task aims to find a DFA D that satisfies the specification on G, i.e., $D(G) = R$. For each node n in G, the expected data-flow facts are expressed as a pair, (r_n^B, r_n^A), where r_n^B is a value set containing the facts available just before n and r_n^A is a value set containing the facts just after n.

Figure 2 gives a simple Java-like language for describing the nodes in G. A node represents a conditional expression (*cond*) or a statement (*stmt*). Both relational and arithmetic expressions are supported (*expr*). Standard constants (*const*), null, integer literals and Boolean values, are allowed. For an allocation-site abstraction at line i, o_i denotes the abstract object created. All program elements, including the keyword **new**, belong to the **Value** type.

We define a DFA as a triple, $D = (\Gamma, \Delta, \Theta)$ [2], consisting of a flow direction Γ ($\Downarrow$ (*forward*) or $\Uparrow$ (*backward*)), a meet operator Δ ($\cup$ (*union*) or $\cap$ (*intersection*)), and a transfer function Θ that transforms a value set at a node into another.

Iterative Algorithm. We use the standard iterative algorithm from a standard textbook [2] to run a DFA at each CFG node $n \in N$ as follows:

$$s_n^{I,\Gamma} = \underset{n' \in \mathsf{Src}_\Gamma(n)}{\Delta} s_{n'}^{O,\Gamma}, \qquad s_n^{O,\Gamma} = \Theta(n, s_n^{I,\Gamma}) \tag{1}$$

where $s_n^{I,\Gamma}$ and $s_n^{O,\Gamma}$ denote the input and output value sets of n along the flow direction Γ, respectively. The signature of Δ is $\wp(\textbf{ValueSet}) \to \textbf{ValueSet}$. Src_Γ returns a set of predecessors (successors) of n in G if Γ is forward (backward):

$$\mathsf{Src}_\Gamma(n) = \begin{cases} \{n' \mid (n', n) \in E\} & \text{if } \Gamma = \ \Downarrow \\ \{n' \mid (n, n') \in E\} & \text{if } \Gamma = \ \Uparrow \end{cases} \tag{2}$$

Once a fixpoint has been reached, we check whether the synthesized DFA generates the data-flow facts as expected as follows:

$$D(G) = R \quad \Leftrightarrow \quad \forall n \in N, \ s_n^{I,\Gamma} = r_n^{I,\Gamma} \land s_n^{O,\Gamma} = r_n^{O,\Gamma} \tag{3}$$

where $r_n^{I,\Gamma}$ and $r_n^{O,\Gamma}$ are mapped from r_n^B and r_n^A by:

$$r_n^{I,\Downarrow} = r_n^B, \ r_n^{O,\Downarrow} = r_n^A, \ r_n^{I,\Uparrow} = r_n^A, \ r_n^{O,\Uparrow} = r_n^B \tag{4}$$

3.2 Syntax-Guided Synthesis

Domain Specific Language. Figure 3 introduces a DSL for synthesizing transfer functions and Fig. 4 gives its semantics.

A transfer function Θ takes a node n and a value set s as input and operates on s in terms of a set expression S. It also supports compound functions so that

$$\Theta := \lambda n \ s.S \quad | \quad \lambda n \ s.\Theta_1(n, \Theta_2(n, s))$$

$$S := if(B, S) \quad | \quad filter(\lambda x.B, S) \quad | \quad A(x) \quad | \quad s \quad | \quad S_1 - S_2 \quad | \quad S_1 \cup S_2$$

$$B := S_1 \bowtie S_2 \quad | \quad \triangleright S \quad | \quad true \quad | \quad false \quad | \quad B_1 \wedge B_2 \quad | \quad B_1 \vee B_2 \quad | \quad \neg B$$

$$A := R \sqcap T \quad | \quad R \quad | \quad T \quad | \quad id$$

$$R := (R_1 + R_2) \quad | \quad right \quad | \quad base \quad | \quad def \quad | \quad use$$

$$T := (T_1 + T_2) \quad | \quad var \quad | \quad fldref \quad | \quad const \quad | \quad expr$$

$$\bowtie := eq \quad | \quad sub \quad | \quad sup \quad | \quad ovlp$$

$$\triangleright := mty \quad | \quad isnul \quad | \quad isnew$$

$S \in$ **SetExpr**	$B \in$ **BoolExpr**
$\Theta \in$ **TranferFunc**	: **Node** $\times$ **ValueSet** $\to$ **ValueSet**
$\bowtie \in$ **BinRelFunc**	: **ValueSet** $\times$ **ValueSet** $\to$ **Boolean**
$\triangleright \in$ **UnaRelFunc**	: **ValueSet** $\to$ **Boolean**
A, R, T $\in$ **AttnFunc**	: **Value** $\to$ **ValueSet**
if	: **Boolean** $\times$ **ValueSet** $\to$ **ValueSet**
filter	: (**Value** $\to$ **Boolean**) $\times$ **ValueSet** $\to$ **ValueSet**

Fig. 3. A DSL for synthesizing transfer functions (where **Node**, **Value** and **ValueSet** are defined in Fig. 2).

we can turn it into a gen-kill form. Common set operations on S are supported, such as union ($\cup$), difference ($-$), guarded, i.e., conditional set operation (if), element filtering operation (filter) and feature extraction function (A).

A Boolean expression B can be built in terms of binary ($\bowtie$) and unary ($\triangleright$) relational functions (operators) on sets and logic functions $\wedge$, $\vee$ and $\neg$. There are four binary functions for describing relations between sets: equality (eq), subset (sub), superset (sup), and non-disjointness (ovlp). Three unary functions can be used to check if a set is empty (mty), or contains only *null* (isnul) or **new** (isnew).

An attention function A allows us to extract data-flow facts from a program element. The simplest one is id, which returns a singleton containing only the input fact. The other three functions are used for extracting facts based on roles (R), types (T), and both (R $\sqcap$ T). A role-based attention function extracts facts according to their roles, including the right-hand value of an assignment (right), the base object of a field reference (base), the defined variable of an assignment (def), and the used values of an assignment or conditional expression (use). A type-based attention function T works similarly but focuses on fact types, such as variables (var), field references (fldref), constants (const), and expressions (expr).

Example 1. Given a node $n : v_1 = v_2 + 3$, the sets of facts extracted from n with several attention function are given below:

$$var(n) = \{v_1, v_2\} \qquad def(n) = \{v_1\} \qquad\qquad use(n) = \{v_2, 3, v_2 + 3\}$$

$$expr(n) = \{v_2 + 3\} \quad const(n) = \{3\} \quad (var + const) \sqcap use(n) = \{v_2, 3\}$$

Syntactic Templates. If we use the DSL in Fig. 3 directly, the search space for all possible DFA candidates will be infinite. To work with a finite search space,

$$x, y \in \textbf{Value}$$
$$n \in \textbf{Node}$$
$$s \in \textbf{ValueSet}$$

$$\mathcal{B}[\![true]\!] = \text{True}$$
$$\mathcal{B}[\![false]\!] = \text{False}$$
$$\mathcal{B}[\![S_1 \text{ eq } S_2]\!] = \mathcal{S}[\![S_1]\!] == \mathcal{S}[\![S_2]\!]$$
$$\mathcal{B}[\![S_1 \text{ sub } S_2]\!] = \mathcal{S}[\![S_1]\!] \subseteq \mathcal{S}[\![S_2]\!]$$
$$\mathcal{B}[\![S_1 \text{ sup } S_2]\!] = \mathcal{S}[\![S_1]\!] \supseteq \mathcal{S}[\![S_2]\!]$$
$$\mathcal{B}[\![S_1 \text{ ovlp } S_2]\!] = \mathcal{S}[\![S_1]\!] \cap \mathcal{S}[\![S_2]\!] \neq \emptyset$$
$$\mathcal{B}[\![\text{mty } S]\!] = \mathcal{S}[\![S]\!] == \emptyset$$
$$\mathcal{B}[\![\text{isnew } S]\!] = \mathcal{S}[\![S]\!] == \{new\}$$
$$\mathcal{B}[\![\text{isnul } S]\!] = \mathcal{S}[\![S]\!] == \{null\}$$
$$\mathcal{B}[\![B_1 \wedge B_2]\!] = \mathcal{B}[\![B_1]\!] \wedge \mathcal{B}[\![B_2]\!]$$
$$\mathcal{B}[\![B_1 \vee B_2]\!] = \mathcal{B}[\![B_1]\!] \vee \mathcal{B}[\![B_2]\!]$$
$$\mathcal{B}[\![\neg B]\!] = \neg \mathcal{B}[\![B]\!]$$
$$\mathcal{A}[\![R \sqcap T]\!] = \lambda x. \mathcal{A}[\![R]\!](x) \cap \mathcal{A}[\![T]\!](x)$$
$$\mathcal{A}[\![(R_1 + R_2)]\!] = \lambda x. \mathcal{A}[\![R_1]\!](x) \cup \mathcal{A}[\![R_2]\!](x)$$
$$\mathcal{A}[\![(T_1 + T_2)]\!] = \lambda x. \mathcal{A}[\![T_1]\!](x) \cup \mathcal{A}[\![T_2]\!](x)$$
$$\mathcal{A}[\![\text{id}]\!] = \lambda x. \mathcal{S}[\![\text{id}(x)]\!]$$
$$\mathcal{A}[\![\text{var}]\!] = \lambda x. \mathcal{S}[\![\text{var}(x)]\!]$$
$$\mathcal{A}[\![\text{fldref}]\!] = \lambda x. \mathcal{S}[\![\text{fldref}(x)]\!]$$
$$\mathcal{A}[\![\text{const}]\!] = \lambda x. \mathcal{S}[\![\text{const}(x)]\!]$$
$$\mathcal{A}[\![\text{expr}]\!] = \lambda x. \mathcal{S}[\![\text{expr}(x)]\!]$$
$$\mathcal{A}[\![\text{def}]\!] = \lambda x. \mathcal{S}[\![\text{def}(x)]\!]$$
$$\mathcal{A}[\![\text{use}]\!] = \lambda x. \mathcal{S}[\![\text{use}(x)]\!]$$
$$\mathcal{A}[\![\text{right}]\!] = \lambda x. \mathcal{S}[\![\text{right}(x)]\!]$$
$$\mathcal{A}[\![\text{base}]\!] = \lambda x. \mathcal{S}[\![\text{base}(x)]\!]$$

$$\mathcal{F}[\![\lambda n \ s.S]\!] = \lambda n \ s.\mathcal{S}[\![S]\!]$$
$$\mathcal{F}[\![\lambda n \ s.\Theta_1(n, \Theta_2(n, s))]\!] = \lambda n \ s.\mathcal{F}[\![\Theta_1]\!](n, \mathcal{F}[\![\Theta_2]\!](n, s))$$
$$\mathcal{S}[\![s]\!] = s$$
$$\mathcal{S}[\![A(x)]\!] = \mathcal{A}[\![A]\!](x)$$
$$\mathcal{S}[\![S_1 - S_2]\!] = \{x \mid x \in \mathcal{S}[\![S_1]\!] \wedge x \notin \mathcal{S}[\![S_2]\!]\}$$
$$\mathcal{S}[\![S_1 \cup S_2]\!] = \{x \mid x \in \mathcal{S}[\![S_1]\!] \vee x \in \mathcal{S}[\![S_2]\!]\}$$
$$\mathcal{S}[\![\text{if}(B, S)]\!] = \begin{cases} \mathcal{S}[\![S]\!] & \text{if } \mathcal{B}[\![B]\!] \text{ is "True"} \\ \emptyset & \text{if } \mathcal{B}[\![B]\!] \text{ is "False"} \end{cases}$$
$$\mathcal{S}[\![\text{filter}(\lambda x.B, S)]\!] = \{x \mid x \in \mathcal{S}[\![S]\!] \wedge \mathcal{B}[\![B]\!]\}$$
$$\mathcal{S}[\![\text{id}(x)]\!] = \begin{cases} \{o.f \mid o \in pts(v)\} & \text{if } x \text{ is "}v.f\text{"} \\ \{x\} & \text{otherwise} \end{cases}$$
$$\mathcal{S}[\![\text{right}(x)]\!] = \begin{cases} \mathcal{S}[\![\text{id}(x_2)]\!] & \text{if } x \text{ is "}x_1 = x_2\text{"} \\ \emptyset & \text{otherwise} \end{cases}$$
$$\mathcal{S}[\![\text{base}(x)]\!] = \begin{cases} \{o\} & \text{if } x \text{ is "}o.f\text{"} \\ \{o \mid o \in pts(v)\} & \text{if } x \text{ is "}v.f\text{"} \\ \mathcal{S}[\![\text{base}(x_1)]\!] \cup \mathcal{S}[\![\text{base}(x_2)]\!] & \text{if } x \text{ is "}x_1 = x_2\text{"} \\ \emptyset & \text{otherwise} \end{cases}$$
$$\mathcal{S}[\![\text{def}(x)]\!] = \begin{cases} \mathcal{S}[\![\text{id}(x_1)]\!] & \text{if } x \text{ is "}x_1 = x_2\text{"} \\ \emptyset & \text{otherwise} \end{cases}$$
$$\mathcal{S}[\![\text{use}(x)]\!] = \begin{cases} \{v\} & \text{if } x \text{ is "}v.f\text{"} \\ \{a_1, a_2\} & \text{if } x \text{ is "}a_1 \oplus a_2\text{"} \\ \{a_1, a_2\} & \text{if } x \text{ is "}a_1 \oslash a_2\text{"} \\ \{a\} & \text{if } x \text{ is "return } a\text{"} \\ \{a_1 \oslash a_2, a_1, a_2\} & \text{if } x \text{ is "}if \ a_1 \oslash a_2\text{"} \\ \mathcal{S}[\![\text{use}(x_1)]\!] \cup \mathcal{S}[\![\text{id}(x_2)]\!] \cup \mathcal{S}[\![\text{use}(x_2)]\!] & \text{if } x \text{ is "}x_1 = x_2\text{"} \\ \emptyset & \text{otherwise} \end{cases}$$
$$\mathcal{S}[\![\text{var}(x)]\!] = \{y \mid y \in \mathcal{S}[\![\text{def}(x)]\!] \cup \mathcal{S}[\![\text{use}(x)]\!] \wedge y \in \textbf{Var}\}$$
$$\mathcal{S}[\![\text{fldref}(x)]\!] = \{y \mid y \in \mathcal{S}[\![\text{def}(x)]\!] \cup \mathcal{S}[\![\text{use}(x)]\!] \wedge y \in \textbf{FieldRef}\}$$
$$\mathcal{S}[\![\text{expr}(x)]\!] = \{y \mid y \in \mathcal{S}[\![\text{use}(x)]\!] \wedge y \in \textbf{Expr}\}$$
$$\mathcal{S}[\![\text{const}(x)]\!] = \{y \mid y \in \mathcal{S}[\![\text{use}(x)]\!] \wedge y \in \textbf{Const}\}$$

Fig. 4. Semantics of the DSL given in Fig. 3. $\mathcal{F}$, $\mathcal{S}$, $\mathcal{B}$, and $\mathcal{A}$ denote the semantics of transfer functions, set expressions, Boolean expressions, and attention functions, respectively. $pts(v)$ represents the points-to set of variable v.

we will adopt the syntactic templates in Fig. 5 to formulate Θ in the gen-kill form in terms of two auxiliary transfer functions, kill and gen. A non-terminal with a wary line (e.g., $\widetilde{\Theta}$) is constrained to be expanded by using only the productions, i.e., syntactic templates in Fig. 5. However, a free non-terminal (e.g., A, which represents an attention function) can be expanded according to the productions in Fig. 3. In particular, $\widetilde{\Theta}$ constrains Θ to be in the gen-kill form, where kill filters out some old data-flow facts from s based on a Boolean expression $\widetilde{B}^k$ and gen adds some new data-flow facts extracted in $A(n)$ to s subject to $\widetilde{B}^g$. Note that the right operands of $\bowtie$ in $\widetilde{B}^{k_1}$ and $\widetilde{B}^{g_1}$ are different, since kill is responsible for filtering out some data-flow facts in s but gen is not.

These syntactic templates, which serve to drive the automatic synthesis of gen-kill transfer functions, require no task-specific knowledge. Despite the constraints imposed, the search space, which contains over 2.08×10^{19} DFA candidates is still huge. This estimate is obtained based on the productions in Figs. 3

$$\widetilde{\Theta} \;\rightsquigarrow\; \lambda n \; s.\mathsf{kill}(n, \mathsf{gen}(n, s)) \quad | \quad \lambda n \; s.\mathsf{gen}(n, \mathsf{kill}(n, s))$$

$$\mathsf{kill} \;\rightsquigarrow\; \lambda n \; s.s - \mathsf{filter}(\lambda x.\widetilde{\mathsf{B}}^k, s)$$

$$\mathsf{gen} \;\rightsquigarrow\; \lambda n \; s.s \cup \mathsf{if}(\widetilde{\mathsf{B}}^g, \mathsf{A}(n))$$

$$\widetilde{\mathsf{B}}^k \;\rightsquigarrow\; true \quad | \quad false \quad | \quad \widetilde{\mathsf{B}}^{k_1} \quad | \quad \widetilde{\mathsf{B}}^{k_2} \quad | \quad \widetilde{\mathsf{B}}^{k_1} \wedge \widetilde{\mathsf{B}}^{k_2} \quad | \quad \widetilde{\mathsf{B}}^{k_1} \vee \widetilde{\mathsf{B}}^{k_2}$$

$$\widetilde{\mathsf{B}}^g \;\rightsquigarrow\; true \quad | \quad false \quad | \quad \widetilde{\mathsf{B}}^{g_1} \quad | \quad \widetilde{\mathsf{B}}^{g_2} \quad | \quad \widetilde{\mathsf{B}}^{g_1} \wedge \widetilde{\mathsf{B}}^{g_2} \quad | \quad \widetilde{\mathsf{B}}^{g_1} \vee \widetilde{\mathsf{B}}^{g_2}$$

$$\widetilde{\mathsf{B}}^{k_1} \;\rightsquigarrow\; \mathsf{A}_1(n) \bowtie \mathsf{A}_2(x) \quad | \quad \neg \, \mathsf{A}_1(n) \bowtie \mathsf{A}_2(x)$$

$$\widetilde{\mathsf{B}}^{k_2} \;\rightsquigarrow\; \triangleright \mathsf{A}(n) \quad | \quad \neg \, \triangleright \mathsf{A}(n)$$

$$\widetilde{\mathsf{B}}^{g_1} \;\rightsquigarrow\; \mathsf{A}(n) \bowtie s \quad | \quad \neg \, \mathsf{A}(n) \bowtie s$$

$$\widetilde{\mathsf{B}}^{g_2} \;\rightsquigarrow\; \triangleright \mathsf{A}(n) \quad | \quad \neg \, \triangleright \mathsf{A}(n)$$

Fig. 5. Syntactic templates for transfer functions.

and 5 with the understanding that, when deriving an attention function by applying $\mathsf{T} := \mathsf{T}_1 + \mathsf{T}_2$ and $\mathsf{R} := \mathsf{R}_1 + \mathsf{R}_2$ recursively, each terminal attention function (e.g., var and def) needs to appear at most once.

3.3   Abstraction-Guided Search Space Pruning

Our first pruning technique works by dropping partially instantiated DFA candidates from further consideration if their fully instantiated DFAs will never satisfy the specification given. This is achieved by checking, across all the CFG nodes individually, if an over-approximation of their data-flow facts (based on abstract semantics) may potentially yield the expected data-flow facts. We write $\mathsf{Pn}(D)$ to mean that a DFA candidate, D, is unsatisfiable and thus pruned. Specifically, the three components of a DFA can be individually pruned, as discussed separately below. For example, $\mathsf{Pn}(\Downarrow, \cup)$ indicates that all the DFA candidates with the forward flow direction and the union meet operator can be ignored.

Pruning Flow Directions. To drop an unsatisfiable flow direction during the search, we define two abstract DFAs, $\widehat{D}_\Downarrow$ with the forward flow direction and $\widehat{D}_\Uparrow$ with the backward direction:

$$\widehat{D}_\Downarrow = (\Downarrow, \widehat{\Delta}, \widehat{\Theta}), \quad \widehat{D}_\Uparrow = (\Uparrow, \widehat{\Delta}, \widehat{\Theta}) \tag{5}$$

where $\widehat{\Delta}$ denotes an abstract meet operator and $\widehat{\Theta}$ denotes an abstract transfer function, with both being defined as follows:

$$\widehat{\Delta} : \lambda S.\{\bigcup_{s \in S} s, \; \bigcap_{s \in S} s\}$$

$$\widehat{\Theta} : \lambda n \; s.\wp(s \cup (\mathsf{id} + \mathsf{def} + \mathsf{use} + \mathsf{base})(n)) \tag{6}$$

where their signatures are $\wp(\mathbf{ValueSet}) \rightarrow \wp(\mathbf{ValueSet})$ and $\mathbf{Node} \times \mathbf{ValueSet} \rightarrow \wp(\mathbf{ValueSet})$, respectively. $\widehat{\Delta}$ includes both the union and intersection of all the sets in s and $\widehat{\Theta}$ returns all the possible value sets that can be produced from s at node n.

Instead of running the iterative algorithm given in Eq. 1, we run $\widehat{D_\Gamma}$, where $\Gamma \in \{\Downarrow, \Uparrow\}$, at each node $n \in N$ individually:

$$\widehat{s}_n^{I,\Gamma} = \underset{n' \in \mathsf{Src}_\Gamma(n)}{\widehat{\Delta}} r_{n'}^{O,\Gamma}, \qquad \widehat{s}_n^{O,\Gamma} = \widehat{\Theta}(n, r_n^{I,\Gamma}) \tag{7}$$

where $r_n^{I,\Gamma}$ and $r_n^{O,\Gamma}$ are obtained from Eq. 4.

Then we use the following rule, [Ab-Γ], to prune an unsatisfiable flow direction if the above over-approximate analysis along this direction fails to produce some data-flow fact(s) expected.

Rule [Ab-Γ]. For a flow direction $\Gamma \in \{\Uparrow, \Downarrow\}$, we have:

$$\exists\, n \in N, r_n^{I,\Gamma} \notin \widehat{s}_n^{I,\Gamma} \vee r_n^{O,\Gamma} \notin \widehat{s}_n^{O,\Gamma} \implies \mathsf{Pn}(\Gamma)$$

Example 2. When synthesizing the reaching definitions in Fig. 1, the backward flow direction $\Uparrow$ can be pruned. We find that

$$r_{n_4}^{I,\Uparrow} = r_{n_4}^A = \{n_0, n_4\}, \quad r_{n_4}^{O,\Uparrow} = r_{n_4}^B = \{n_0, n_1, n_3\}$$
$$\widehat{s}_{n_4}^{I,\Uparrow} = \underset{n' \in \mathsf{Src}_\Uparrow(n_4)}{\widehat{\Delta}} r_{n'}^{O,\Uparrow} = \{r_{n_5}^{O,\Uparrow}\} = \{r_{n_5}^B\} = \{\{n_0, n_4\}\}$$
$$\widehat{s}_{n_4}^{O,\Uparrow} = \widehat{\Theta}(n_4, \{n_0, n_4\}) = \wp(\{n_0, n_4, b, b+1, 1\})$$

According to [Ab-Γ], we have $r_{n_4}^{O,\Uparrow} \notin \widehat{s}_{n_4}^{O,\Uparrow} \implies \mathsf{Pn}(\Uparrow)$.

Pruning Meet Operators. Given a plausible flow direction Γ, we apply the following rule to prune a meet operator Δ.

Rule [Ab-Δ]. For a meet operator $\Delta \in \{\cup, \cap\}$, we have:

$$\exists\, n \in N, \; r_n^{I,\Gamma} \neq s_n^{I,\Gamma} \implies \mathsf{Pn}(\Gamma, \Delta)$$

where $s_n^{I,\Gamma} = \underset{n' \in \mathsf{Src}_\Gamma(n)}{\Delta} r_{n'}^{O,\Gamma}$. As before, the expected data-flow facts given in $r_n^{I,\Gamma}$ and $r_{n'}^{O,\Gamma}$ are obtained from Eq. 4.

Example 3. Consider the example in Fig. 1. If $\Downarrow$ is considered, the intersection meet operator $\cap$ can be pruned. We find that

$$r_{n_4}^{I,\Downarrow} = r_{n_4}^B = \{n_0, n_1, n_3\}, \quad \mathsf{Src}_\Downarrow(n_4) = \{n_2, n_3\}$$
$$s_{n_4}^{I,\Downarrow} = \underset{n \in \mathsf{Src}_\Downarrow(n_4)}{\cap} r_n^{O,\Downarrow} = r_{n_2}^{O,\Downarrow} \cap r_{n_3}^{O,\Downarrow} = r_{n_2}^A \cap r_{n_3}^A = \{n_0\}$$

According to [Ab-Δ], we have $r_{n_4}^{I,\Downarrow} \neq s_{n_4}^{I,\Downarrow} \implies \mathsf{Pn}(\Downarrow, \cap)$.

Pruning Transfer Functions. We consider the following two forms of partially instantiated transfer functions:

$$\Theta^g : \lambda n \; s.\mathsf{kill}(n, \mathsf{gen}(n, s)) \qquad \Theta^k : \lambda n \; s.\mathsf{gen}(n, \mathsf{kill}(n, s)) \qquad (8)$$

In the *gen-before-kill* (*kill-before-gen*) form above, when its sub-function gen (kill) is instantiated, we will build an abstract transfer function $\widehat{\Theta}^g$ ($\widehat{\Theta}^k$) given below by replacing its other sub-function kill (gen) with an abstract version $\widehat{\mathsf{kill}}$ ($\widehat{\mathsf{gen}}$):

$$\widehat{\Theta}^g : \lambda n \; s.\widehat{\mathsf{kill}}(n, \mathsf{gen}(n, s)) \qquad \widehat{\Theta}^k : \lambda n \; s.\widehat{\mathsf{gen}}(n, \mathsf{kill}(n, s)) \qquad (9)$$

With $\widehat{\Theta}$ given in Eq. 6, $\widehat{\mathsf{kill}}$ and $\widehat{\mathsf{gen}}$ are defined as:

$$\widehat{\mathsf{kill}} : \lambda n \; s.\wp(s) \qquad \widehat{\mathsf{gen}} : \lambda n \; s.\{s \cup s' \mid s' \in \widehat{\Theta}(n, \emptyset)\} \qquad (10)$$

In Eqs. 9 and 10, each of the four abstract functions has the same signature: **Node** $\times$ **ValueSet** $\to \wp(\textbf{ValueSet})$. Thus, for each node n, $\widehat{\mathsf{kill}}$ ($\widehat{\mathsf{gen}}$) returns the set of all possible value sets that can be obtained from a given value set s due to a kill (gen) operation.

Rule [Ab-Θ]. For $\Theta^i \in \{\Theta^k, \Theta^g\}$ defined in Eq. 8, we have:

$$\exists \; n \in N, \; r_n^{O,\Gamma} \notin \widehat{\Theta}^i(n, r_n^{I,\Gamma}) \implies \mathsf{Pn}(\Gamma, \Theta^i)$$

Example 4. When synthesizing the reaching definitions in Fig. 1, we will prune a partially instantiated gen-before-kill DFA candidate with the forward direction and a transfer function Θ^g, in which $\mathsf{gen}(n_4, r_{n_4}^{I,\Downarrow}) = \{n_0, n_1, n_3\}$, where $r_{n_4}^{I,\Downarrow} = r_{n_4}^B = \{n_0, n_1, n_3\}$, but kill is uninstantiated and thus abstracted as $\widehat{\mathsf{kill}}$. Since

$$r_{n_4}^{O,\Downarrow} = r_{n_4}^A = \{n_0, n_4\}, \quad \widehat{\Theta}^g(n_4, r_{n_4}^{I,\Downarrow}) = \widehat{\mathsf{kill}}(n_4, \{n_0, n_1, n_3\}) = \wp(\{n_0, n_1, n_3\})$$

we have $r_{n_4}^{O,\Downarrow} \notin \widehat{\Theta}^g(n_4, r_{n_4}^{I,\Downarrow}) \implies$ *beenconsideredyet.Pruning*$\mathsf{Pn}(\Downarrow, \Theta^g)$ according to [Ab-Θ].

Example 5. Similarly, a DFA candidate that has a kill-before-gen transfer function Θ^k, in which $\mathsf{kill}(n_4, r_{n_4}^{I,\Downarrow}) = \{n_3\}$ but gen is uninstantiated and thus abstracted as $\widehat{\mathsf{gen}}$ will be pruned by [Ab-Θ]:

$$r_{n_4}^{O,\Downarrow} = r_{n_4}^A = \{n_0, n_4\}, \quad \widehat{\Theta}(n_4, \emptyset) = \wp(\{n_4, b, b + 1, 1\})$$

$$\widehat{\Theta}^k(n_4, r_{n_4}^{I,\Downarrow}) = \widehat{\mathsf{gen}}(n_4, \{n_3\}) = \{r_{n_4}^{I,\Downarrow} \cup s \mid s \in \widehat{\Theta}(n_4, \emptyset)\}$$

$$= \{\{n_0, n_4\} \cup s \mid s \in \wp(\{n_4, b, b + 1, 1\})\}$$

$$r_{n_4}^{O,\Downarrow} \notin \widehat{\Theta}^k(n_4, r_{n_4}^{I,\Downarrow}) \implies \mathsf{Pn}(\Downarrow, \Theta^k)$$

3.4 Brevity-Guided Search Space Pruning

Our second pruning technique works with a cost function (Sect. 3.4), which estimates the cost (brevity) of each DFA candidate, to select the simplest satisfying solution, i.e., the satisfying DFA with the smallest cost, and accelerate the search (Sect. 3.4).

Cost Estimation. We assume reasonably that a DFA spends nearly all its analysis time on evaluating its transfer function. The cost Cst of a transfer function Θ depends mainly on the number of its constituent relational functions (e.g., $\bowtie$ and $\triangleright$) and attention functions (e.g., def and use). Formally, Cst is defined as:

$$\mathsf{Cst}(\Theta) = \sum_{A_i \in f_A(\Theta)} \mathsf{Cst}(A_i) + \sum_{\bowtie_i \in f_\bowtie(\Theta)} \mathsf{Cst}(\bowtie_i) + \sum_{\triangleright_i \in f_\triangleright(\Theta)} \mathsf{Cst}(\triangleright_i)$$

where f_A, $f_\bowtie$ and $f_\triangleright$ return a set of attention functions A, binary operators $\bowtie$, and unary operators $\triangleright$ appearing in Θ, respectively.

We set the cost of an atomic attention function A to 1 (e.g., $\mathsf{Cst}(\mathsf{id}) = 1$) and compute the cost of a compound one A by:

$$\mathsf{Cst}(R \times T) = \mathsf{Cst}(R) + \mathsf{Cst}(T)$$
$$\mathsf{Cst}(R_1 + R_2) = \mathsf{Cst}(R_1) + \mathsf{Cst}(R_2)$$
$$\mathsf{Cst}(T_1 + T_2) = \mathsf{Cst}(T_1) + \mathsf{Cst}(T_2)$$

In principle, the simpler an attention function, the lower its cost. We treat four different binary relational operators $\bowtie$ in Fig. 3 differently since they have different amounts of information entropy. For example, if two sets are equal, they are also subsets (supersets) of each other. Thus, their costs are estimated to be:

$$\mathsf{Cst}(\mathsf{sub}) = \mathsf{Cst}(\mathsf{sup}) = 1, \quad \mathsf{Cst}(\mathsf{ovlp}) = 1^+, \quad \mathsf{Cst}(\mathsf{eq}) = 1^-$$

where we use 1.01 and 0.99 to implement 1^+ and 1^-, respectively.

We set the cost of every unary relational operator $\triangleright$ in Fig. 3 to 1^- (e.g., $\mathsf{Cst}(\mathsf{mty}) = 1^-$), which is also implemented as 0.99.

Example 6. The cost of Θ in Fig. 1(c) is estimated as:

$\Theta : \lambda n\ s.\mathsf{gen}(n, \mathsf{kill}(n, s))$

$\mathsf{kill} : \lambda n\ s.s - \mathsf{filter}(\lambda x.\mathsf{def}(x)\ \mathsf{eq}\ \mathsf{def}(n), s)$

$\mathsf{gen} : \lambda n\ s.s \cup \mathsf{if}(\neg\mathsf{mty}\ \mathsf{def}(n), \mathsf{id}(n))$

$\mathsf{Cst}(\Theta) = 3 \cdot \mathsf{Cst}(\mathsf{def}) + \mathsf{Cst}(\mathsf{eq}) + \mathsf{Cst}(\mathsf{mty}) + \mathsf{Cst}(\mathsf{id}) = 3 + 1^- + 1^- + 1 = 5.98$

Search Acceleration. For a partially instantiated transfer function Θ, we use Cst to calculate the cost of its already instantiated components, which represents the lower bound for the cost of Θ once its fully instantiated. Such lower bound cost estimation can be used to accelerate the search with *branch-and-cut* [30].

Rule [Br-Θ]. Let Θ_p be a fully instantiated transfer function satisfying the specification given. A (fully or partially instantiated) transfer function Θ will be ignored if it does not cost less than Θ_p:

$$\mathsf{Cst}(\Theta) \geqslant \mathsf{Cst}(\Theta_p) \implies \mathsf{Pn}(\Theta)$$

However, this rule is used only after a satisfying Θ has been found. Therefore, we also rely on two additional rules, [Br-A] and [Br-gk], on attention functions and gen/kill functions, respectively, to prune those DFA candidates that are functionally equivalent to some others but are not computationally cheaper.

Rule [Br-A]. For a given attention function A, we have:

$$\exists\, \mathtt{A}' \in \mathbf{AttnFunc} - \{\mathtt{A}\}, (\forall x \in \mathbf{Value}, \mathtt{A}(x) = \mathtt{A}'(x))$$
$$\wedge\, \mathsf{Cst}(\mathtt{A}) \geq \mathsf{Cst}(\mathtt{A}') \Longrightarrow \mathsf{Pn}(\mathtt{A}) \tag{11}$$

For a given synthesis problem (specified by a CFG as input and the expected data-flow facts at its nodes as output), the domain of x, **Value**, will be determined by the actual specification given.

Example 7. A : var ⋒ (def + use) will be pruned by [Br-A] since

$$(\forall x \in \mathbf{Value}, \mathsf{A}(x) = \mathsf{var}(x)) \wedge \mathsf{Cst}(\mathsf{A}) > \mathsf{Cst}(\mathsf{var})$$

Rule [Br-gk]. Let **F** be the set of fully instantiated gen/kill functions of the form defined in Fig. 5. For a given gen/kill function f ∈ **F**, we have:

$$\exists\, \mathsf{f}' \in \mathbf{F} - \{\mathsf{f}\}, (\forall\, n \times s \in \mathbf{Node} \times \mathbf{ValueSet}, \mathsf{f}(n,s) = \mathsf{f}'(n,s))$$
$$\wedge\, \mathsf{Cst}(\mathsf{f}) \geq \mathsf{Cst}(\mathsf{f}') \Longrightarrow \mathsf{Pn}(\mathsf{f}) \tag{12}$$

Example 8. Let gen and gen' be the two gen functions given below. According to [Br-gk], gen can be pruned, since gen' is functionally equivalent but computationally cheaper (to evaluate):

$$\mathsf{gen} : \lambda n\ s.s \cup \mathsf{if}(\neg\mathsf{mty}\ \mathsf{def}(n) \wedge \neg\mathsf{mty}\ \mathsf{use}(n), \mathsf{id}(n))$$
$$\mathsf{gen}' : \lambda n\ s.s \cup \mathsf{if}(\neg\mathsf{mty}\ \mathsf{def}(n), \mathsf{id}(n))$$

Pruning gen (when it is fully instantiated) can significantly reduce the search space for a gen-before-kill transfer function since kill hasn't been considered yet. Pruning gen even earlier will be ineffective due to the lack of information available about a partially instantiated gen. The reasoning applies to the kill pruning.

3.5   The DFASy Synthesis Algorithm

As shown in Algorithm 1, DFASy takes a specification consisting of a CFG G and the expected data-flow facts in R at its nodes as input and returns a DFA D_{best} that satisfies this specification as output. Its main search loop appears in lines 6–14, processing each DFA candidate D in the worklist in turn. D is pruned if it satisfies any pruning rule introduced in Sects. 3.3 and 3.4 (line 8). If D is fully instantiated, we run the iterative algorithm given in Eq. 1 to validate it and update D_{best}, if necessary (lines 9–11). Otherwise, we call Derive() to continue instantiating D (lines 13–14).

Derive() takes a partially instantiated DFA $D = (\Gamma, \Delta, \Theta)$ and returns a set of DFAs that are further instantiated from it. We handle its flow direction Γ and its meet operator Δ in lines 18–20 and lines 21–23, respectively. To handle

Algorithm 1: DFASY
Input: G (CFG) and R (Expected Data-Flow Facts)
Output: D_{best} (DFA)
1   **Function** DFASy(G, R)
2      $workList \leftarrow \emptyset$ // an empty stack;
3      $D \leftarrow$ an uninstantiated DFA; $c_{min} \leftarrow +\infty$; $workList$.push(D);
4   **while** $workList \neq \emptyset$ **do**
5          $D \leftarrow workList$.pop();
6   **if** D satisfies any pruning rule **then** continue;
7   **if** D is fully instantiated **then**
8   **if** D $(G) = R$ and $\mathsf{Cst}(D) < c_{min}$ **then**
9                  $c_{min} \leftarrow \mathsf{Cst}(D)$; $D_{best} \leftarrow D$;
10   **else**
11   **foreach** D' in Derive (D) **do**
12                  $workList$.push(D')
13   **return** D_{best};
14 **Function** Derive(D) // $D = (\Gamma, \Delta, \Theta)$
15      $s_D \leftarrow \emptyset$;
16   **if** Γ is not initialized **then**
17          $D_{\Downarrow} \leftarrow (\Downarrow, \Delta, \Theta)$; $D_{\Uparrow} \leftarrow (\Uparrow, \Delta, \Theta)$; Add $D_{\Downarrow}$ and $D_{\Uparrow}$ to s_D;
18   **else if** Δ is not initialized **then**
19          $D_{\cup} \leftarrow (\Gamma, \cup, \Theta)$; $D_{\cap} \leftarrow (\Gamma, \cap, \Theta)$; Add $D_{\cup}$ and $D_{\cap}$ to s_D;
20   **else**
21   Let N be the first non-terminal symbol in Θ;
22   **foreach** production $\mathsf{N} := X_1...X_n$ **do**
23              $D_{\Theta} \leftarrow (\Gamma, \Delta, \Theta)$; Substitute $X_1...X_n$ for N in Θ; Add D_{Θ} to s_D;
24   **return** s_D;

its transfer function Θ (lines 24–29), we instantiate it further by adopting a leftmost derivation according the productions given in Figs. 3 and 5, with the understanding that, in the gen-before-kill (kill-before-gen) form, gen (kill) will be applied first and thus considered to appear conceptually on the left of kill (gen). As a result, the instantiation process of each DFA can be represented by a so-called derivation tree, showing how its non-terminals are expanded in a top-down, left-to-right fashion.

Example 9. Figure 6 gives a simplified derivation tree for the transfer function in Fig. 1(c) (by continuing from Example 6). Such a depth-first search allows us to apply pruning rules as early as possible. As discussed in Example 5, we may make a pruning attempt after kill has been fully instantiated, i.e., after the 7-th non-terminal symbol A_2 has been fully derived.

4   Evaluation

We show that DFASY, assisted with its pruning techniques, is highly effective in synthesizing a range of DFAs satisfying their given specifications. We have

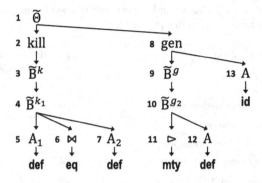

Fig. 6. The simplified derivation tree of the transfer function in Fig. 1(c). The number i in blue indicates that the corresponding non-terminal is the i-th one derived. (Color figure online)

verified manually the correctness of the DFAs generated for the DFA problems considered. Thus, our evaluation aims to answer the following research questions:

- **RQ1:** Is DFASY effective in synthesizing DFAs?
- **RQ2:** Is DFASY's abstraction-guided pruning effective?
- **RQ3:** Is DFASY's brevity-guided pruning effective?

We also include a case study on the null pointer detection problem.

4.1 Implementation

We have implemented DFASY and the DSL given in Fig. 3 for specifying transfer functions in Java. We use SOOT [48] to construct a CFG in its built-in Jimple IR and run the iterative algorithm given in Eq. 1 on the CFG for validation purposes. The points-to information required by some DFA problems is obtained by a flow-sensitive intra-procedural algorithm. Different pointer analysis algorithms [21, 23, 40, 44–46] may be applied since it is orthogonal to the DFA synthesis problem considered in this paper.

DFASY is multi-threaded. There is one thread dedicated for handling every possible combination of flow directions ($\{\Uparrow, \Downarrow\}$), meet operators ($\{\cup, \cap\}$) and transfer function templates ($\{$gen-before-kill, kill-before-gen$\}$). Thus, the maximum number of threads used is 8.

Our experiments are done on a machine with 4 Intel® Xeon® Gold E5-2637 CPUs equipped with 8GB memory, running Ubuntu 16.04. The time budget for solving each DFA problem is 1 h. We repeat each experiment 5 times and report the average.

4.2 Dataset

Table 1 gives our dataset consisting of 14 DFA problems, with three requiring the points-to information (as indicated). We have collected seven classic DFA

Table 1. A dataset with 7 classic and 7 custom DFA synthesis problems. For each CFG, #Node is the number of nodes in the CFG.

Problem	Description	#Node	Pointer analysis needed beforehand?
Classic DFA problems			
ReachDef	Reaching definitions	9	
LiveVar	Live variables	9	
AvailExpr	Available expressions	12	
BusyExpr	Very busy expressions	14	
NullCheck	Null pointer detection	20	✓
NonnullCheck	Non-null pointer verification	18	✓
InitVar	Variable initialization	8	
Custom DFA problems			
DerefObj	Detecting dereferenced objects	12	✓
AE-Const	Detecting available expressions with some constant operands	13	
AE-NoConst	Detecting available expressions without constant operands	14	
BE-Const	Detecting very busy expressions with some constant operands	14	
BE-NoConst	Detecting very busy expressions without constant operands	14	
RF-Expr	Detecting reaching definitions with each's RHS being an *expr* (Fig. 2)	9	
RF-Const	Detecting reaching definitions with each's RHS being a *const* (Fig. 2)	9	

problems from different application domains, including compiler optimization, bug detection, and program verification. The other seven custom DFA problems are variations of these classic problems. For each DFA problem, we obtain its specification (G, R) for synthesizing an satisfying DFA as follows. We first manually implement an oracle DFA D_o to solve the problem. We then create G (with its nodes described in the Java-like language in Fig. 2), based on a number of representative CFGs given in standard text [2] and real code, by adding nodes, if necessary, to cover corner cases. Finally, we run D_o over G to obtain R. In Table 1, the number of CFG nodes for each problem is given.

There are two caveats about how input-output examples are interpreted in the DFA synthesis problem. First, we use one CFG for each DFA problem. Even if several CFGs are used, they can be conceptually regarded as just one CFG, since all the CFGs can be merged into one by adding a pseudo entry (exit) node and connecting it with the existing entry (exit) nodes. Second, a specification

Table 2. Comparing DFASy with the three baselines on 14 DFA problems (in seconds). "#Validated" gives the number of fully-instantiated candidates validated, i.e., that have survived pruning. "#Plausible" gives the number of satisfying DFA candidates. "Best?" represents whether the simplest satisfying DFA has been found. If a synthesizer runs out of 1-h time budget, its synthesis time is marked as "OOB". For DFASy-BR, its average synthesis time does not include the two OOB cases.

Problem	DFASy-NAIVE			DFASy-AB				DFASy-BR				DFASy			
	Time	#Validated	#Plausible	Time	#Validated	#Plausible	Best?	Time	#Validated	#Plausible	Best?	Time	#Validated	#Plausible	Best?
ReachDef	OOB	4.1×10^8	0	OOB	4.0×10^8	19632	✗	146.4	3.4×10^7	9	✓	12.0	751241	9	✓
LiveVar	OOB	6.8×10^8	0	OOB	8.1×10^8	0	✗	1151.1	6.0×10^8	23	✓	17.3	3283330	23	✓
AvailExpr	OOB	5.3×10^8	0	OOB	4.8×10^8	501120	✗	82.1	2.1×10^7	6	✓	4.7	794176	6	✓
BusyExpr	OOB	5.2×10^8	0	OOB	4.5×10^8	2637126	✗	608.4	2.7×10^8	17	✓	3.4	4651	17	✓
NullCheck	OOB	3.3×10^8	0	OOB	2.9×10^8	0	✗	OOB	5.9×10^8	0	✗	111.6	1.5×10^7	10	✓
NonullCheck	OOB	4.0×10^8	0	OOB	3.2×10^8	0	✗	OOB	8.3×10^8	0	✗	86.2	1563236	9	✓
InitVar	OOB	6.7×10^8	0	OOB	2.8×10^8	2.2×10^7	✗	7.8	1514901	20	✓	4.0	6099	20	✓
DerefObj	OOB	7.8×10^8	0	OOB	4.8×10^8	1.5×10^7	✗	59.4	1.28×10^7	37	✓	19.3	24784	37	✓
AE-Const	OOB	4.0×10^8	0	OOB	2.5×10^8	0	✗	256.0	5.4×10^7	6	✓	9.5	988016	6	✓
AE-Noconst	OOB	1.1×10^8	0	OOB	9.2×10^7	0	✗	144.3	7420965	11	✓	16.5	1040017	11	✓
BE-Const	OOB	5.1×10^8	0	OOB	5.9×10^8	117288	✗	1867.3	7.67×10^8	7	✓	3.6	46775	7	✓
BE-Noconst	OOB	3.2×10^8	0	OOB	3.5×10^8	216504	✗	612.9	1.26×10^8	10	✓	5.2	54695	10	✓
RF-Expr	OOB	4.7×10^8	0	OOB	4.8×10^8	3188	✗	109.7	1.9×10^7	9	✓	6.9	344042	9	✓
RF-Const	OOB	5.5×10^8	0	OOB	5.5×10^8	8015	✗	63.9	9598712	6	✓	4.9	77918	6	✓
Average		4.8×10^8	0		4.1×10^8	2944504		425.8^*	2.4×10^8	11.5		21.8	1736232	12.9	

(G, R) can also be understood as consisting of as many input-output examples as the number of nodes in G (in the form of (r_n^B, r_n^A) for each node n).

Our implementation for DFASY and the dataset used are publicly available (http://www.cse.unsw.edu.au/~corg/dfasy/).

4.3   Baselines

Since DFASY is the first tool to synthesize general-purpose DFAs, we have designed three baselines to evaluate the effectiveness of its abstraction- and brevity-guided pruning techniques as follows: (1) DFASY-NAIVE: a version of DFASY without applying either abstraction- or brevity-guided pruning technique, (2) DFASY-AB: a version of DFASY with abstraction-guided pruning only, and (3) DFASY-BR: a version of DFASY with brevity-guided pruning only.

4.4   Results and Analysis

RQ1. DFASy's Overall Effectiveness. Table 2 compares DFASY with the three baselines on solving the 14 DFA synthesis problems. DFASY has successfully found the simplest DFA solution for each DFA problem in 21.8 s, on average. Due to the abstraction- and brevity-guided pruning techniques used, its search space has been reduced from 2.08×10^{19} (Sect. 3.2) to 1736232, on average. For the most time-consuming problem, NullCheck, DFASY spends 111.6 s only and has validated 1.5×10^7 (fully instantiated) candidates.

DFASY-NAIVE fails to synthesize any DFA due to the search space explosion problem. Under one-hour time budget, DFASY-NAIVE has explored only 4.8×10^8 candidates, on average, for each DFA problem, which is still more than 10 orders of magnitude away from the number of candidates (2.08×10^{19}) to be explored.

By applying abstraction-guided pruning alone, DFASY-AB has found some plausible, i.e., satisfying DFAs in 9 out of the 14 DFA problems, but not the simplest solution in any case. By applying brevity-guided pruning only, DFASY-BR has successfully found the simplest solutions in 12 out of the 14 DFA problems, but significantly more costly than DFASY (with an average slowdown of 81.8x on each of these 12 problems and time outs on NullCheck and NonnullCheck). We analyze both pruning techniques below.

RQ2. Effectiveness of Abstraction-Guided Pruning. As shown in Table 2, DFASY-AB has found plausible solutions in 9 DFA problems by validating 4.1×10^8 DFA candidates per problem, on average. On the other hand, DFASY-NAIVE cannot find any plausible solution but has validated even more DFA candidates per problem, on average. This suggests that many partially instantiated but unsatisfiable candidates have been pruned by the three rules introduced in Sect. 3.3, [Ab-Γ], [Ab-Δ] and [Ab-Θ].

To analyze quantitatively the contribution by each of these three pruning rules, we run DFASY and report the number of times each rule is applied during

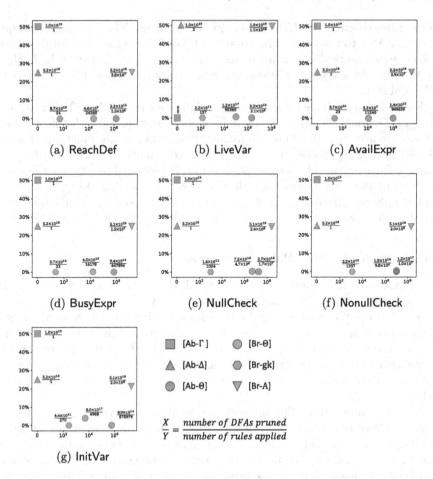

Fig. 7. Analyzing 3 abstraction-guided and 3 brevity-guided pruning rules in the 7 classic DFA problems. The x axis represents how many times a rule is used. The y axis represents the percentage of DFA candidates pruned over the total (2.08×10^{19}).

the search and the number/percentage of DFAs pruned for the 7 classic DFA problems in Fig. 7. Rule [Ab-Γ], which aims to prune an unsatisfiable flow direction, can eliminate half of the DFA candidates by acting only once, for all the 7 DFA problems except for LiveVar. [Ab-Γ] is inapplicable to LiveVar, since every live (i.e., used) variable in a backward analysis can also be treated as a defined variable in a forward analysis. Fortunately, [Ab-Δ] comes into play in pruning both the forward direction and the meet operator for LiveVar. In addition, [Ab-Δ] has also eliminated one-quarter of the candidates in each of the other 6 DFA problems by acting only once. Finally, [Ab-Θ] is the most frequently used among the three pruning rules, as it is applied to uninstantiated transfer functions. For each DFA problem, the number of candidates pruned is in the order of at least 10^{14}.

RQ3. Effectiveness of Brevity-Guided Pruning. This pruning technique allows DFASY to work with branch-and-cut [30] by selecting the simplest DFA among the semantically equivalent candidates (Sect. 3.4). As shown in Table 2, DFASY-BR can accelerate the search dramatically by solving 12 out of the 14 DFA problems.

Figure 7 also analyzes the effectiveness of its three rules, [Br-Θ], [Br-A] and [Br-gk]. Overall, [Br-A] is the most frequently used, pruning the most candidates, since attention functions are frequently used in transfer functions (Fig. 5). [Br-Θ] and [Br-gk] also make considerable contributions to the search space pruning. Once a plausible solution Θ_p is found, [Br-Θ] will be used continuously to filter out the transfer functions that cost no less than Θ_p. [Br-gk], which is applied only to fully instantiated gen and kill, is the least frequently used, but has also effectively pruned more than 10^{10} candidates for each DFA problem.

4.5   Case Study: Null Pointer Detection

We discuss NullCheck illustrated in Fig. 8, All the other synthesized DFAs can be reproduced (https://sites.google.com/view/dfasy).

This DFA problem aims to find a DFA for detecting the null pointers at each CFG node in Fig. 8(a), e.g., the null pointer x after n_1 and the four null pointers, x, y, $o_1.f$ and z, after n_9, as expected in Fig. 8(b). DFASY has successfully synthesized a DFA as a forward analysis shown in Fig. 8(c), by making use of the points-to information already computed (to handle also aliases), as formalized in Fig. 4.

Let us examine this DFA in more detail. When analyzing a node, its kill function filters out whatever is defined at the node (even in terms of null) but its gen function will discover any new null pointer found at the node. For example, when node n_1 is analyzed, x is detected by gen as a new null pointer at its exit, since isnul right(n_1) is true, i.e., right(n_1) = {*null*}. Later, when n_4 is encountered, the null pointer x is filtered out by kill, and at the same time, cannot be possibly re-generated by gen, since q is neither null itself nor appears as a null pointer already at its entry.

4.6   Discussions

As evaluated earlier, DFASY is quite efficient due to its abstraction- and brevity-guided pruning techniques used. However, DFASY currently adopts a naive depth-first search strategy (Fig. 6), which can be further optimized by incorporating some advanced search techniques like genetic programming [6]. One possible heuristic (fitness) function for guiding the search is to rely on the number of expected data-fact facts satisfied by each DFA candidate.

In DFASY, we have implemented a number of attention functions or operators for synthesizing general-purpose DFAs. However, we can extend DFASY easily by adding client-specific functions or operators, including, for example, a unary operator issrc to define the *sources* of taints to facilitate taint analysis.

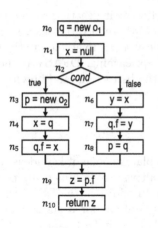

| Node | Value Sets | |
	Before	After
n_0	$\emptyset$	$\emptyset$
n_1	$\emptyset$	$\{x\}$
n_2	$\{x\}$	$\{x\}$
n_3	$\{x\}$	$\{x\}$
n_4	$\{x\}$	$\emptyset$
n_5	$\emptyset$	$\emptyset$
n_6	$\{x\}$	$\{x, y\}$
n_7	$\{x, y\}$	$\{x, y, o_1.f\}$
n_8	$\{x, y, o_1.f\}$	$\{x, y, o_1.f\}$
n_9	$\{x, y, o_1.f\}$	$\{x, y, o_1.f, z\}$
n_{10}	$\{x, y, o_1.f, z\}$	$\{x, y, o_1.f, z\}$

(a) Input CFG   (b) Output data-flow facts

Flow Direction:	$forward\ (\Gamma = \ \Downarrow)$
Meet Operator:	$union\ (\Delta = \cup)$
Transfer Function:	$\Theta : \lambda n\ s.\mathsf{gen}(n, \mathsf{kill}(n, s))$

kill : $\lambda n\ s.\mathsf{filter}(\lambda x.\mathsf{def}(n)\ \mathsf{eq}\ \mathsf{id}(x), s)$

gen : $\lambda n\ s.\mathsf{if}(\mathsf{isnul}\ \mathsf{right}(n)\ \vee\ \mathsf{right}(n)\ \mathsf{ovlp}\ s, \mathsf{def}(n))$

Corresponding Semantics:

$\mathsf{kill}(n, s) = s - \{x \mid x \in s \wedge x == \mathsf{def}(n)\}$

$\mathsf{gen}(n, s) = \begin{cases} s \cup \mathsf{def}(n) & \text{if } \mathsf{right}(n) == \{null\} \text{ or } \mathsf{right}(n) \cap s \neq \emptyset \\ s & \text{otherwise} \end{cases}$

(c) The synthesized DFA

Fig. 8. A case study: null pointer detection (NullCheck).

5   Related Work

5.1   Synthesis by Examples

Program synthesis has a wide range of applications, including data wrangling [16,17], code suggestion [19,32,35,53], program repair [28,39,51], and concurrent programming [11,25,49]. In this paper, DFASy aims at synthesizing general-purpose data-flow analyzers automatically. Since the intent specifications are usually unavailable or expressed in a natural language, most synthesis systems work with programming-by-example (PBE), thereby defining synthesis problems by input-output examples [18,29,33,34]. Several advanced techniques have been proposed to guide the search. In [14,15,29,33], type systems are proposed to prune ill-typed programs. Katz and Peled [24] exploit genetic programming to guide their synthesis. Smith and Albarghouthi [41] reduce the search space by equivalence reduction. So and Oh [42] use static analysis to accelerate the search. Balog et al. [5] guide their synthesis with deep learning. DFASY proposed in this paper is also a PBE system, equipped with abstraction- and brevity-guided pruning techniques to guide the search.

5.2 Synthesis by Templates

Restricting the search space by syntactic templates is one of key ideas in modern program synthesis [3,18]. SKETCH [43] allows programmers to provide a high-level structure for an intended program. In addition, the DSLs, which are designed to reason about code patterns or templates for a specific task, can also be effective to restrict the search space. For example, FLASHFILL DSL [16] focuses on string operations in spreadsheets, FLASHEXTRACT DSL [26] is proposed to synthesize programs that can return an instance of an expected data structure from a large string, and FLASHRELATE DSL [7] include programs that can extract a relational table from a spreadsheet. QBS [12] synthesizes optimized database-backed applications with a subset of the SQL DSL. Panchekha and Torlak [31] synthesize spreadsheet styles from layout constraints with a CSS-specific DSL. In this paper, we have introduced a DSL for synthesizing transfer functions for data-flow analyzers. In addition, we use syntactic templates to guide their synthesis in the gen-kill form.

5.3 Data-Flow Analysis

A range of data-flow analysis algorithms have been proposed for supporting compiler optimization [2,10,52], bug detection [20,22,47,50], and program verification [13,27]. Reps et al. [36] introduce an efficient framework for solving the IFDS data-flow problem and generalize it into the IDE framework [37]. The IFDS/IDE algorithm has been implemented in a number of program analysis frameworks, such as WALA [1], SOOT [48] and FLOWDROID [4]. In this paper, DFASY aims at automatically synthesizing DFAs, including its three components, which can be directly integrated into these existing data-flow analysis frameworks.

5.4 Synthesis of Static Analysis Rules

Recently, several approaches have been proposed to synthesize rules for static analysis. Bielik et al. [9] use the ID3 algorithm to synthesize rules for pointer analysis and allocation site analysis for JavaScript. Si et al. [38] use syntactic templates to guide the synthesis of rules in Datalog programs. These approaches require pre-defined templates or relations for specific tasks. In this paper, DFASY is equipped with different data-flow fact extraction functions to synthesize general-purpose DFAs.

6   Conclusion

In this paper, we have introduced DFASY, a framework for synthesizing general-purpose DFAs by examples. To facilitate its automatic synthesis, we have also proposed a DSL that focuses main on data-flow fact extractions, set operations, and logic operations. To accelerate the search and find the simplest DFAs, we have designed abstraction- and brevity-guided pruning techniques. We have developed a benchmark suite consisting of 14 DFA synthesis problems for evaluation purposes. DFASY has successfully solved all the problems in 21.8 s, on average, outperforming significantly the three baselines compared.

References

1. T.j. watson libraries for analysis (wala). http://wala.sourceforge.net/wiki, http://wala.sourceforge.net/wiki
2. Aho, A.V., Lam, M.S., Sethi, R., Ullman, J.D.: Compilers: Principles, Techniques, and Tools, 2nd edn. Addison-Wesley Longman Publishing Co. Inc., Boston (2006)
3. Alur, R., et al.: Syntax-guided synthesis. IEEE (2013)
4. Arzt, S., et al.: FlowDroid: precise context, flow, field, object-sensitive and lifecycle-aware taint analysis for android apps. Acm Sigplan Not. **49**(6), 259–269 (2014)
5. Balog, M., Gaunt, A.L., Brockschmidt, M., Nowozin, S., Tarlow, D.: DeepCoder: learning to write programs. arXiv preprint arXiv:1611.01989 (2016)
6. Banzhaf, W., Nordin, P., Keller, R.E., Francone, F.D.: Genetic Programming. Springer, Heidelberg (1998). https://doi.org/10.1007/BFb0055923
7. Barowy, D.W., Gulwani, S., Hart, T., Zorn, B.: FlashRelate: extracting relational data from semi-structured spreadsheets using examples. ACM SIGPLAN Not. **50**(6), 218–228 (2015)
8. Barrett, C., Tinelli, C.: Satisfiability modulo theories. In: Handbook of Model Checking, pp. 305–343. Springer, Cham (2018). https://doi.org/10.1007/978-3-319-10575-8_11
9. Bielik, P., Raychev, V., Vechev, M.: Learning a static analyzer from data. In: Majumdar, R., Kunčak, V. (eds.) CAV 2017. LNCS, vol. 10426, pp. 233–253. Springer, Cham (2017). https://doi.org/10.1007/978-3-319-63387-9_12
10. Cai, Q., Xue, J.: Optimal and efficient speculation-based partial redundancy elimination. In: 2003 International Symposium on Code Generation and Optimization, CGO 2003, pp. 91–102 (2003). https://doi.org/10.1109/CGO.2003.1191536
11. Černý, P., Chatterjee, K., Henzinger, T.A., Radhakrishna, A., Singh, R.: Quantitative synthesis for concurrent programs. In: Gopalakrishnan, G., Qadeer, S. (eds.) CAV 2011. LNCS, vol. 6806, pp. 243–259. Springer, Heidelberg (2011). https://doi.org/10.1007/978-3-642-22110-1_20
12. Cheung, A., Solar-Lezama, A., Madden, S.: Optimizing database-backed applications with query synthesis. ACM SIGPLAN Not. **48**(6), 3–14 (2013)
13. Das, M., Lerner, S., Seigle, M.: ESP: path-sensitive program verification in polynomial time. In: Proceedings of the ACM SIGPLAN 2002 Conference on Programming Language Design and Implementation, pp. 57–68 (2002)
14. Feser, J.K., Chaudhuri, S., Dillig, I.: Synthesizing data structure transformations from input-output examples. ACM SIGPLAN Not. **50**(6), 229–239 (2015)
15. Frankle, J., Osera, P.M., Walker, D., Zdancewic, S.: Example-directed synthesis: a type-theoretic interpretation. ACM SIGPLAN Not. **51**(1), 802–815 (2016)

16. Gulwani, S.: Automating string processing in spreadsheets using input-output examples. ACM SIGPLAN Not. **46**(1), 317–330 (2011)
17. Gulwani, S.: Programming by examples. Dependable Softw. Syst. Eng. **45**(137), 3–15 (2016)
18. Gulwani, S., Polozov, A., Singh, R.: Program Synthesis, vol. 4, August 2017. https://www.microsoft.com/en-us/research/publication/program-synthesis/
19. Gvero, T., Kuncak, V., Kuraj, I., Piskac, R.: Complete completion using types and weights. In: Proceedings of the 34th ACM SIGPLAN Conference on Programming Language Design and Implementation, pp. 27–38 (2013)
20. Hallem, S., Chelf, B., Xie, Y., Engler, D.: A system and language for building system-specific, static analyses. In: Proceedings of the ACM SIGPLAN 2002 Conference on Programming Language Design and Implementation, pp. 69–82 (2002)
21. Hardekopf, B., Lin, C.: Flow-sensitive pointer analysis for millions of lines of code. In: CGO 2011, pp. 289–298 (2011)
22. He, D., et al.: Performance-boosting sparsification of the IFDS algorithm with applications to taint analysis. In: 2019 34th IEEE/ACM International Conference on Automated Software Engineering (ASE), pp. 267–279. IEEE (2019)
23. He, D., Lu, J., Gao, Y., Xue, J.: Accelerating object-sensitive pointer analysis by exploiting object containment and reachability. In: Møller, A., Sridharan, M. (eds.) 35th European Conference on Object-Oriented Programming (ECOOP 2021). Leibniz International Proceedings in Informatics (LIPIcs), vol. 194, pp. 16:1–16:31. Schloss Dagstuhl - Leibniz-Zentrum für Informatik, Dagstuhl (2021). https://doi.org/10.4230/LIPIcs.ECOOP.2021.16. https://drops.dagstuhl.de/opus/volltexte/2021/14059
24. Katz, G., Peled, D.: Genetic programming and model checking: synthesizing new mutual exclusion algorithms. In: Cha, S.S., Choi, J.-Y., Kim, M., Lee, I., Viswanathan, M. (eds.) ATVA 2008. LNCS, vol. 5311, pp. 33–47. Springer, Heidelberg (2008). https://doi.org/10.1007/978-3-540-88387-6_5
25. Kuperstein, M., Vechev, M., Yahav, E.: Automatic inference of memory fences. ACM SIGACT News **43**(2), 108–123 (2012)
26. Le, V., Gulwani, S.: FlashExtract: a framework for data extraction by examples. In: Proceedings of the 35th ACM SIGPLAN Conference on Programming Language Design and Implementation, pp. 542–553 (2014)
27. Madhavan, R., Komondoor, R.: Null dereference verification via over-approximated weakest pre-conditions analysis. ACM SIGPLAN Not. **46**(10), 1033–1052 (2011)
28. Nguyen, H.D.T., Qi, D., Roychoudhury, A., Chandra, S.: SemFix: program repair via semantic analysis. In: 2013 35th International Conference on Software Engineering (ICSE), pp. 772–781. IEEE (2013)
29. Osera, P.M., Zdancewic, S.: Type-and-example-directed program synthesis. ACM SIGPLAN Not. **50**(6), 619–630 (2015)
30. Padberg, M., Rinaldi, G.: A branch-and-cut algorithm for the resolution of large-scale symmetric traveling salesman problems. SIAM Rev. **33**(1), 60–100 (1991)
31. Panchekha, P., Torlak, E.: Automated reasoning for web page layout. In: Proceedings of the 2016 ACM SIGPLAN International Conference on Object-Oriented Programming, Systems, Languages, and Applications, pp. 181–194 (2016)
32. Perelman, D., Gulwani, S., Ball, T., Grossman, D.: Type-directed completion of partial expressions. In: Proceedings of the 33rd ACM SIGPLAN Conference on Programming Language Design and Implementation, pp. 275–286 (2012)
33. Polikarpova, N., Kuraj, I., Solar-Lezama, A.: Program synthesis from polymorphic refinement types. ACM SIGPLAN Not. **51**(6), 522–538 (2016)

34. Polozov, O., Gulwani, S.: FlashMeta: a framework for inductive program synthesis. In: Proceedings of the 2015 ACM SIGPLAN International Conference on Object-Oriented Programming, Systems, Languages, and Applications, pp. 107–126 (2015)

35. Raychev, V., Vechev, M., Yahav, E.: Code completion with statistical language models. In: Proceedings of the 35th ACM SIGPLAN Conference on Programming Language Design and Implementation, pp. 419–428 (2014)

36. Reps, T., Horwitz, S., Sagiv, M.: Precise interprocedural dataflow analysis via graph reachability. In: Proceedings of the 22nd ACM SIGPLAN-SIGACT Symposium on Principles of Programming Languages, pp. 49–61 (1995)

37. Sagiv, M., Reps, T., Horwitz, S.: Precise interprocedural dataflow analysis with applications to constant propagation. Theor. Comput. Sci. **167**(1–2), 131–170 (1996)

38. Si, X., Lee, W., Zhang, R., Albarghouthi, A., Koutris, P., Naik, M.: Syntax-guided synthesis of datalog programs. In: Proceedings of the 2018 26th ACM Joint Meeting on European Software Engineering Conference and Symposium on the Foundations of Software Engineering, pp. 515–527 (2018)

39. Singh, R., Gulwani, S., Solar-Lezama, A.: Automated feedback generation for introductory programming assignments. In: Proceedings of the 34th ACM SIG-PLAN Conference on Programming Language Design and Implementation, pp. 15–26 (2013)

40. Smaragdakis, Y., Bravenboer, M., Lhoták, O.: Pick your contexts well: understanding object-sensitivity. In: Proceedings of the 38th Annual ACM SIGPLAN-SIGACT Symposium on Principles of Programming Languages, POPL 2011, pp. 17–30. Association for Computing Machinery, New York (2011). https://doi.org/10.1145/1926385.1926390

41. Smith, C., Albarghouthi, A.: Program synthesis with equivalence reduction. In: Enea, C., Piskac, R. (eds.) VMCAI 2019. LNCS, vol. 11388, pp. 24–47. Springer, Cham (2019). https://doi.org/10.1007/978-3-030-11245-5_2

42. So, S., Oh, H.: Synthesizing imperative programs from examples guided by static analysis. In: Ranzato, F. (ed.) SAS 2017. LNCS, vol. 10422, pp. 364–381. Springer, Cham (2017). https://doi.org/10.1007/978-3-319-66706-5_18

43. Solar-Lezama, A., Bodik, R.: Program synthesis by sketching. Citeseer (2008)

44. Sui, Y., Xue, J.: SVF: interprocedural static value-flow analysis in LLVM. In: Proceedings of the 25th International Conference on Compiler Construction, pp. 265–266. ACM, New York (2016)

45. Tan, T., Li, Y., Xue, J.: Efficient and precise points-to analysis: modeling the heap by merging equivalent automata. In: Proceedings of the 38th ACM SIGPLAN Conference on Programming Language Design and Implementation, pp. 278–291. Association for Computing Machinery, New York (2017). https://doi.org/10.1145/3140587.3062360

46. Thiessen, R., Lhoták, O.: Context transformations for pointer analysis. In: Proceedings of the 38th ACM SIGPLAN Conference on Programming Language Design and Implementation, PLDI 2017, pp. 263–277. Association for Computing Machinery, New York (2017). https://doi.org/10.1145/3062341.3062359

47. Tripp, O., Pistoia, M., Fink, S.J., Sridharan, M., Weisman, O.: Taj: effective taint analysis of web applications. ACM SIGPLAN Not. **44**(6), 87–97 (2009)

48. Vallée-Rai, R. Co, P., Gagnon, E., Hendren, L., Lam, P., Sundaresan, V.: Soot: a Java bytecode optimization framework. In: CASCON 2010, p. 13 (2010)

49. Vechev, M., Yahav, E., Yorsh, G.: Abstraction-guided synthesis of synchronization. In: Proceedings of the 37th Annual ACM SIGPLAN-SIGACT Symposium on Principles of Programming Languages, pp. 327–338 (2010)

50. Wassermann, G., Su, Z.: Static detection of cross-site scripting vulnerabilities. In: 2008 ACM/IEEE 30th International Conference on Software Engineering, pp. 171–180. IEEE (2008)
51. Xu, X., Sui, Y., Yan, H., Xue, J.: VFix: value-flow-guided precise program repair for null pointer dereferences. In: 2019 IEEE/ACM 41st International Conference on Software Engineering (ICSE), pp. 512–523 (2019). https://doi.org/10.1109/ICSE.2019.00063
52. Xue, J., Cai, Q.: A lifetime optimal algorithm for speculative PRE. ACM Trans. Arch. Code Optim. 3(2), 115–155 (2006). https://doi.org/10.1145/1138035.1138036
53. Zhang, H., Jain, A., Khandelwal, G., Kaushik, C., Ge, S., Hu, W.: Bing developer assistant: improving developer productivity by recommending sample code. In: Proceedings of the 2016 24th ACM SIGSOFT International Symposium on Foundations of Software Engineering, pp. 956–961 (2016)

Author Index

Printed in the United States
by Baker & Taylor Publisher Services